The
Dark
Side
of the
Left

American Political Thought

EDITED BY

Wilson Carey McWilliams & Lance Banning

The Dark Side of the Left

Illiberal Egalitarianism in America

Richard J. Ellis

University Press of Kansas

© 1998 by the University Press of Kansas

Published by the University Press of Kansas (Lawrence, Kansas 66049), which was organized by the Kansas Board of Regents and is operated and funded by Emporia State University, Fort Hays State University, Kansas State University, Pittsburg State University, the University of Kansas, and Wichita State University.

A version of chapter 5 first appeared in *Review of Politics* 58 (Winter 1996), 109–54, and is reprinted here by permission of the publisher.

Library of Congress Cataloging-in-Publication Data

Ellis, Richard (Richard J.)
    The dark side of the Left: illiberal Egalitarianism in America / Richard J. Ellis.
      p.   cm.—(American political thought)
    Includes bibliographical references and index.
    ISBN 0-7006-0875-3 (alk. paper)
    1. Radicalism — United States.   2. Authoritarianism—United States.
    3. Authoritarianism (Personality trait)—United States.   4. Fanaticism—United States.
    I. Title. II. Series.
    HN90.R3E55   1998
    303.48′4—dc21   97-27340

British Library Cataloguing in Publication Data is available.

Printed in the United States of America

10 9 8 7 6 5 4 3 2 1

The paper used in this publication meets the minimum requirements of the American National Standard for Permanence of Paper for Printed Library Materials z39.48-1984.

For Juli, Eleanor, and Nicholas

CONTENTS

Preface *ix*

Introduction *1*

I The Nineteenth and Early Twentieth Centuries

1 Radical Abolitionism: Purity and Violence *17*

2 Illiberal Utopianism in the Age of Reform *44*

3 The Revolting Masses: From Walt Whitman to Mike Gold *73*

II SDS, The New Left, and the 1960s

4 The Illiberal Turn: Tom Hayden, SDS, and the New Left *115*

5 Romancing the Oppressed: The New Left and the Left Out *147*

6 When More (Democracy) Is Less *174*

III Egalitarianism Today

7 Radical Feminism: The Personal is Political *193*

8 Earth First! and the Misanthropy of Radical Egalitarianism *228*

9 Apocalypse and Authoritarianism in the Radical
   Environmental Movement *252*

Conclusion *271*

Notes *287*

Index *407*

PREFACE

"Allan Bloom would have hated this book. So will Lynne Cheney, William Bennett, Gertrude Himmelfarb, George Will and Dinesh D'Souza. . . . Here are grounds enough, surely . . . for rejoicing." So begins an appreciative review in the *Nation* of Lawrence Levine's newest book, *The Opening of the American Mind*.[1] I came across this judgment as I was putting the finishing touches on my own book, and I could not help but hear faint echoes of that favorite question from the late 1960s: "Which side are you on?"[2] I also could not help wondering whether my book, too, would be sucked up into the politicized vortex of the "culture wars" and reduced to one of two political sides: conservative or liberal, right or left? Better that than ignored, I suppose.

Well, which side *am* I on? Given my focus on "the dark side of the left" it may surprise some to learn that I am a lifelong Democrat who voted for Jimmy Carter in 1980, Walter Mondale in 1984, Michael Dukakis in 1988, and Bill Clinton in 1992 and 1996. I am a card-carrying member of the American Civil Liberties Union and an avid supporter of public broadcasting and Big Bird. I consider myself an environmentalist, although not so green that I am unable to appreciate the humor and truth in Harvey Mansfield's wicked putdown of environmentalism as "school prayer for liberals."[3] I am not sure that I would describe myself as a feminist, but I have no doubts that the women's movement has helped to open doors for women in ways that have immeasurably improved the lives and expanded the autonomy of women, and that have made America a more just society than it was thirty years ago. And the final straw: I believe that politicians, bureaucrats, and the federal government generally make this country a better place. Such confessions are perhaps ill-advised and they are certainly unseemly, but it just goes to show the lengths a liberal will go to avoid being called a conservative.

How did someone who considers himself a liberal come to write a book so strongly critical of the left? Indeed, why write such a book? Doesn't it just play into the hands of conservatives who wish contemporary liberalism only ill?[4] A book that might make William Bennett or Dinesh D'Souza happy must be reason enough for regret if not condemnation. Many years ago, George Orwell confronted this same argument: "Whenever A and B are in opposition to one another, anyone who attacks or criticizes A is accused of aiding and abetting B. And it is often true, objectively and on a short-term analysis, that he *is* making things easier for B. Therefore, say the supporters of A, shut up and don't criticize: or at least criticize 'constructively,' which in practice always means favorably." This mode of thinking, as Orwell points out, presupposes a binary opposition in which "A represents progress and B reaction."[5] But in the vast majority of American policy debates, from affirmative action to abortion, there is precious little agreement on what counts as "progressive" or "reactionary." More to the point, no political position is strengthened by suppressing or slighting inconvenient facts or covering up weakness. Protected from criticism, any argument becomes lazy and prone to excess. Vigorous criticism, as John Stuart Mill emphasized, helps toughen a position, making it stronger by identifying its weaknesses or vulnerabilities. Ultimately, the left's best friends are its most penetrating critics, not its loudest boosters. In criticizing the illiberal side of the left, my aim is to toughen the liberal reform tradition, not to discredit or reject it.[6]

To highlight the dark side of the left is not to say that only the left has a dark side. I could as easily have written a book on the dark side of the right. The illiberalism of the radical right is only too obvious in the wake of the Oklahoma City bombing and the conspiratorial fantasies spawned by the Waco debacle. Anti-Semitism, nativism, and especially intolerance of homosexuals remain unlovely features of right-wing politics in this country. Nor is this particularly surprising:[7] it is consistent with some of the best social science of the postwar decades, which has taught us to expect intolerance and prejudice, even paranoia and authoritarianism, to come from the right.[8] Students of American political history have long been accustomed to finding illiberalism on the right: the Alien and Sedition Acts, the Red Scare after World War I, McCarthyism, and the Moral Majority, to mention a few of the more notable instances. Illiberalism coming from the egalitarian left, however, appears to me less well understood and more paradoxical.

It is paradoxical because liberalism is unimaginable without a belief in equality. The Declaration of Independence, the seminal document of American liberalism, teaches us that it is a self-evident truth "that all men are created equal." From its earliest roots in the seventeenth century, liberalism meant recognizing the equal worth of people's capacities and preferences. The belief that each individual, regardless of station or wealth, deserves to be treated equally is at the very heart of liberalism. Equality before the law, "equal rights," and even equal opportunity are all ideals that are inseparable from liberalism. Liberalism needs equality, but equality, pursued to the exclusion of other ideals, can have illiberal consequences as well.

By "illiberal" I mean, as Webster's dictionary defines it, "intolerant; bigoted; narrow-minded," but I also have in mind a broader collection of related attitudes and behaviors, including disregard for civil liberties or individual autonomy, an authoritarian, antipolitical, or antidemocratic ethos, a Manichaean view of the world as a battleground between absolute good and absolute evil, demonization of the enemy or moral absolutism, a conspiratorial, apocalyptic, or millennial outlook, and glorification of violence. The core doctrinal and institutional elements of "liberalism," as I understand that famously slippery term, are constitutional government, equality before the law, free and competitive elections, personal security, private property, boundaries between public and private life, and freedom of expression, assembly, conscience, travel, and so on.[9] The overriding aim of liberalism, as Judith Shklar explains, is "to secure the political conditions that are necessary for the exercise of political freedom."[10]

I am particularly attracted to Shklar's "liberalism of fear," a liberalism chastened by the horrors of the twentieth century.[11] It is a liberalism that affirms the rule of law, constitutionalism, toleration, and personal freedom, but jettisons naive and untenable assumptions about ineluctable progress and natural human goodness, preferring "a strongly developed historical memory" to abstract or formalistic efforts to deduce universally shared liberal principles. It is a liberalism that fears the state, believing that although "the sources of social oppression are indeed numerous, none has the deadly effect of those who, as the agents of the modern state, have unique resources of physical might and persuasion at their disposal."[12] To some, this may sound more like conservatism than liberalism, but "putting cruelty first," as Shklar insists, takes one well beyond the minimal state envisioned by libertarians and laissez-faire conservatives. The liberalism of fear, Shklar makes clear, cannot ignore the power of large corporations. Those who put cruelty first worry that large disparities in economic wealth may lead to unrestrained political power for the few and vulnerability for the many.[13] Insisting on limited government (that is, government limited by law) is not the same thing as calling for less or minimal government. Indeed, putting cruelty first often means calling on the government to do more to protect those who are the most vulnerable to cruelty, the poor and the weak. Avoiding cruelty or humiliation may be not be sufficiently inspiring or heroic for some, but it is far from complacency or status quo conservatism.[14]

If I imagine Shklar whispering in one ear, perched on my other shoulder is Isaiah Berlin. Like Shklar, Berlin is a skeptical, antiutopian liberal with an acute sense of historical memory and human irrationality. What appeals to me about Berlin in particular is his unwavering insistence that we inevitably face trade-offs between rival goods and rival visions of the good life. "We are doomed to choose," writes Berlin, "and every choice may entail an irreparable loss." Not all good things go together, not now, not ever. To be sure, a tragic view of life — that "one cannot have everything," as Berlin puts it — may not be what many people would associate with what we today tend to call liberalism, yet it is a sensibility that is properly a foundation stone of liberal democracy. The desire to achieve a unity that would transcend the messy conflict of values and interests has been the moving force behind virtually all the illiberal and antidemocratic movements and regimes of the twentieth century.[15] One of the great virtues of the modern liberal welfare state is that it does not pretend to have discovered the ultimate solution that will dissolve all contradictions; rather the welfare state explicitly "muddles through," institutionalizing the understanding that no single value, not equality, not liberty, not individualism, not community, not order, can be the polestar of public policy. The liberal welfare state recognizes that all institutional structures and arrangements, capitalist markets as well as governmental control, have weaknesses that must be compensated for if we are to achieve a decent and humane society.

The illiberalism of the left may be inadequately understood, but it has hardly gone unnoticed. Throughout the writing of this book I have been aided by those who have thought deeply and profoundly about the questions I have asked. Raymond Aron, Richard Hofstadter, Stephen Holmes, Irving Howe, Leszek Kolakowski, George Orwell, Michael Walzer, and Bernard Yack, among others, have brilliantly illuminated my path along the way. Many of the most acute analyses of the illiberalism that has periodically scarred or hampered left-wing movements in America come from those who would to a greater or lesser extent situate themselves on the left. I have learned a tremendous amount from Jo Freeman and Alice

Echols on radical feminism, Todd Gitlin and James Miller on the New Left, Arthur Lipow and John Thomas on Edward Bellamy, Casey Blake and Paul Gorman on the Young Americans, Lawrence Friedman and Lewis Perry on radical abolitionism, and Martin Lewis on radical environmentalism. Their willingness to criticize a side they identify with is a tribute to their scholarship and an inspiration to my own.

More material assistance came my way from a generous fellowship from the George A. and Eliza Gardner Howard Foundation, which enabled me to take a leave in the 1993–1994 academic year to begin this project in earnest. Supplementary grants from the Earhart and Carthage Foundations also helped make that crucial year possible. Completion of the book was expedited by course release in the spring semester of 1997, courtesy of Willamette University's new Faculty Study Time Program, one of the many things that Dean Larry Cress has done to facilitate scholarship at Willamette. Preliminary work on the project began with the assistance of a Willamette University Atkinson grant in the summer of 1992.

I was fortunate to have the help of some exceptionally talented undergraduate research assistants. Morgan Allen helped out on environmentalism and abolitionism, and Brian Shipley assisted on Catherine MacKinnon. Matthew Hindman's assistance on chapter 3 was invaluable, particularly what he taught me about Walt Whitman. Kara Ritzheimer helped check the accuracy of the notes, and Stacy Hereau helped create the index. Thanks are also due to the many students in my "Liberalism and Its Critics" course who helped to enrich my understanding of the strengths and weaknesses of liberalism.

Among those who commented helpfully on parts of the book are Suresht Bald, Sammy Basu, Joe Bowersox, John Ellis, Dave Ericson, Richard Flacks, Todd Gitlin, Dean Hammer, Jenny Jopp, Martin Lewis, Charles Lockhart, and Laura Scalia. Particularly deserving of my thanks are Booth Fowler, Eldon Eisenach, Donald Lutz, Lewis Perry, and John Thomas, each of whom read the entire manuscript and offered frank criticism and valuable encouragement. Here the usual disclaimers are more than usually necessary, since several of these people disagreed strongly with my arguments. Still, their objections helped me sharpen those arguments and make them, I hope, somewhat less objectionable.

INTRODUCTION

We have in mind many people who begin with more-or-less socialist and democratic premises yet, by a curious route, end with authoritarian conclusions.

    Lewis Coser and Irving Howe[1]

A little over forty years ago the great American historian Richard Hofstadter published his most important and influential work, *The Age of Reform*.[2] In that book, Hofstadter drew attention to the "coexistence of illiberalism and [liberal] reform." "One of the most interesting and least studied aspects of American life," Hofstadter observed, "has been the frequent recurrence of the demand for reforms, many of them aimed at the remedy of genuine ills, combined with strong moral convictions and with the choice of hatred as a kind of creed." Surveying the Populist and Progressive reform movements between 1890 and 1917, Hofstadter found abundant and troubling evidence of intolerance and moral absolutism.[3] Hofstadter's thesis was an arresting challenge to those who had uncritically portrayed the progressive or liberal reform tradition as a liberating battle against the backward and retrograde forces in American political culture.[4]

The Age of Reform helped spur historians and social scientists to take a more critical view of American reform movements. The Populists, in particular, came under heavy criticism for their alleged anti-Semitism, nativism, isolationism, Manichaeanism, conspiratorial theories, and hostility to modernity. Hofstadter and others traced the parallels and connections between the Populist reformers of the late nineteenth century and the "radical right" of the post–World War II period. Both leftist radicals and the radical right were alleged to be backward-looking, intolerant, anti-intellectual, and suffering from what Hofstadter termed "the paranoid style." Reform and reaction seemed less opposites than soul mates.

Many of the hypotheses put forward by Hofstadter in *The Age of Reform* and in a subsequent book, *The Paranoid Style in American Politics* (1965), were met with vigorous and often devastating criticisms. Hofstadter's explanation of Progressive reform in terms of an elite's "status anxiety" was found sorely wanting.[5] Other critics zeroed in on the supposed genealogical link between Populism and McCarthyism, showing that the two movements in fact had quite distinct constituencies.[6] Still other scholars showed that if Populists were anti-Semitic and nativist they were no more so and perhaps quite a bit less so than non-Populists of the same period.[7]

Hofstadter, of course, never expected *The Age of Reform* to be accepted as a flawless final judgment. Indeed, Hofstadter explicitly cautioned that his ideas were intended "as a prelude and a spur to further studies of American reform movements."[8] That *The Age of Reform* has spurred further studies of American reform movements is beyond question, but unfortunately much of that research agenda was chased down a blind alley. In part, this wrong turn can be attributed to scholars who pursued Hofstadter's ideas without the subtlety and nuance that characterized Hofstadter's own work.[9] But Hofstadter, too, was responsible for the unhappy evolution of his original ideas. For it was Hofstadter himself, particularly in *The Paranoid Style*, who allowed contemporary concerns with the radical right—McCarthy, the John Birch Society, and the Goldwater candidacy—to distract from his original objective of understanding the relationship between progressive reform and illiberalism.

Rather than probe the complex relationship between illiberalism and liberal reform movements he had sketched out in *The Age of Reform*, Hofstadter now largely focused on the illiberalism of the radical right. Part I of *The Paranoid Style*, which included the lead essay, "The Paranoid Style" (1963), as well as "The Pseudo-Conservative Revolt" (1954), "Pseudo-Conservatism Revisited" (1965), and "Goldwater and Pseudo-Conservative Politics" (1965), was titled "Studies in the American Right."[10] These papers, Hofstadter explained, were designed to explore the "conditions that have given rise to the extreme right of the 1950's and 1960's."[11] An important topic, even or especially today, but it constituted a clear departure from the research agenda he had so promisingly mapped out in *The Age of Reform*.

Such an evolution was certainly understandable as liberals like Hofstadter focused their attention in the early 1960s on the evils of segregation, the reactionary and often brutally violent resistance to civil rights for blacks, the conspiratorial fantasies of the John Birch Society, and the Goldwater candidacy that seemed to legitimize these and other illiberal forces. By the time of Hofstadter's death in 1970, however, the political tides had shifted in ways that seemed to make Hofstadter's original interest in the relationship between illiberalism and liberal reform relevant again. The youthful optimism of Students for a Democratic Society (SDS) had degenerated into sectarianism and the fanatacism of the Weathermen. Within the Student Nonviolent Coordinating Committee, a vision of nonviolence and integration was supplanted by the separatism and violence of Black Power. The desire to reform American society evolved into the desire to repudiate and destroy it. The illiberalism of the New Left that flourished in the late 1960s and early 1970s beckons us to look anew at Hofstadter's paradox of illiberal reform.

More recently, the controversies over "political correctness" provide further reason to revisit Hofstadter's observations about the puzzling coexistence of progressive reform and illiberalism. Of course, some will insist that the phenomenon of "political correctness" is little more than an invention of right-wing ideologues, politicians, and foundations intent on discrediting the left. This defensive reaction is understandable but lamentable, for it closes off inquiry into a real and puzzling phenomenon that those on the left have the greatest need to understand. It is the leftist Mark E. Kann, not the conservative Dinesh D'Souza, who observes that American radicals "have advocated dissent against bourgeois norms, political practices, and economic institutions" while also advocating "virtually unqualified consent to their own organizations and leaders, treating dissidents more as traitors than as friendly critics."[12] Moreover, some antipornography ordinances and restrictions on "hate speech" stand as monuments to the left's ambivalent relationship toward central liberal ideals. In the wake of the "political correctness" controversy, it seems that understanding the sociocultural logic by which progressive reform movements spawn illiberal policies has never been more important than today.

Hofstadter's *Age of Reform* helps to sensitize us to the paradoxical coexistence of illiberalism and reform, and to remind us that this coexistence has historical precedent. But in thinking about the illiberalism of the New Left or Earth First! or radical feminism or "political correctness," I found that many of the concepts that Hofstadter had used to make sense of reform at the turn of the century were not particularly helpful. The New Left could hardly be seen as an agrarian revolt against modernity, nor was it characterized by the nativism and anti-Semitism that Hofstadter found among the Populists. Nor did I find the nebulous idea of "status anxiety," which Hofstadter employed to understand the Progressives (and David Donald used to understand the abolitionists),[13] any help in explaining the radical social and political movements of the 1960s. And while the later New Left certainly propagated a Manichaean and conspiratorial view of the world, Hofstadter's concept of the "paranoid style" condemned without explaining.[14]

In *The Age of Reform*, and even more explicitly in *The Paranoid Style*, Hofstadter advanced a strict dichotomy between a rational, interest-based politics on the one hand and a nonrational, emotional, and symbolic politics on the other. Hofstadter's focus on the emotional and symbolic side of political life enabled him to insist that historians address not just "Who gets what, when, how?" but "Who perceives what public issues, in what way, and why?"[15] At his best, Hofstadter was the keenest student of American political culture in his or any other generation. But, especially in *The Paranoid Style*, Hofstadter was sometimes too quick to reduce political preferences to the projection of irrational or even abnormal feelings and impulses. Psychopathology threatened to drive out culture.[16]

My aim is to examine the phenomenon of illiberalism through a cultural lens rather than a narrowly psychological one. Some of the individuals discussed in this book, from William Lloyd Garrison to Tom Hayden, may very well have had personal demons to exorcise, but to reduce their political actions and beliefs to the projection of personal anxieties and phobias is unsatisfactory. It begs the question of why other quite different personalities adopted the same pattern of beliefs and behaviors, as well as the further question of why many other individuals with similar personalities adopted totally different patterns of belief and behavior. By focusing on how culture shapes preferences, we can avoid having to choose between rationally calculated self-interest on the one side and irrational psychological projection on the other.

The Illiberalism of Egalitarianism

All of us, every day, make choices about how we wish to live with each other. Some of us prefer social relationships that preserve formality and accent differences in station, rank, or office; others prefer more informal, egalitarian relationships. Authority is anathema to some of us, indispensable for others. Some abhor the constraints imposed by rules and regulations; others find predictable structures or rigid timetables to be immensely comforting or helpful. A solitary life is attractive to some, while others seek out human fellowship on every possible occasion. Some prefer to go through life uncommitted; others long to commit body and soul to a tightly knit group. Taking culture seriously means recognizing the multiplicity of ways that individuals wish to live their lives, even within a single society. Each of these choices, moreover, has something to recommend it. A cultural perspective should not, however, be limited to affirming the value of every cultural choice. For every cultural choice, as anthropologist Mary Douglas points out, has its "miseries" as well as its "compensations." "When one chooses how one wants to be dealt with and how to deal with others," Douglas continues, "it is just as well to be clear as to what else may be unintentionally chosen."[17] In choosing a way of life, people do not intentionally seek out the miseries, but they often get them nonetheless.

My subject is the inadvertent miseries — the illiberalism — that come with egalitarian choices, particularly radical egalitarian choices.[18] Egalitarians choose, most obviously, equality. But equality for the egalitarian typically goes beyond a belief in "mere" equality before the law. The egalitarian often echoes Anatole France's biting criticism, "The law, in its majestic equality, forbids the rich as well as the poor to sleep under bridges, to beg in the streets, and to steal bread."[19] Egalitarians generally wish to equalize resources or conditions rather than just processes.[20] They are committed to reducing differences between people, not creating opportunities for people to become more unequal.[21]

In its pure form, egalitarianism entails rejecting hierarchical authority as a violation of individual autonomy and equality, and repudiating self-seeking, competitive market relations for disregarding or degrading human fellowship and cooperation. The preferred way of life becomes a fellowship of equals: "the beloved community." This is not the only egalitarian choice, however. A few egalitarians show little or no interest in collective solidarity. C. Wright Mills, for instance, is supposed to have confided once that "of the three great goals of the French Revolution, he could appreciate liberty and equality — but not fraternity."[22] Here egalitarianism joins with individualism to create what Max Eastman called "libertarian socialism."[23] Other egalitarians opt for either state socialism or social democracy, joining a commitment to equalizing outcomes with support for strong central authority.

The politics of pure or radical egalitarianism are oppositional in character. Although not without influence on the center, radical egalitarians situate themselves and their movements at the margins of society and define themselves in opposition to "the system." The causes they espouse may become popular, but popular success is a threat to the radical egalitarian identity and the coherence of the egalitarian collectivity. What keeps radical egalitarian groups together is the knowledge that the outside world is hopelessly corrupt or inequitable. Popularity and effectiveness bring compromise and co-optation, but radical purity has its costs as well: isolation and futility.

This book traces radical egalitarianism in America in an episodic rather than exhaustive fashion,[24] from the radical abolitionism of the 1830s to the radical environmentalism of Earth First! today. In taking the story back to before the Civil War, I do not mean to convey that there is no difference between Wendell Phillips and Catharine MacKinnon or William Lloyd Garrison and Tom Hayden, nor that these diverse individuals are linked by an unbroken intellectual tradition.[25] But the obvious differences in historical circumstances, as well as the striking intellectual and institutional discontinuities between radical movements in this country, make it even more notable that one can indeed discern patterns across time in beliefs and behaviors. I am aware, as Hofstadter was, too, of the dangers of becoming too present-minded, of losing "respect for the integrity, the independence, the pastness, of the past."[26] But with Hofstadter I believe that those risks must be weighed against the benefits of identifying regularities that transcend time and place.

My aim, then, is to identify the recurrent organizational and ideological dilemmas that have periodically thrown radical egalitarian political thinkers and movements down illiberal tracks. What is it about radical egalitarian commitments that make adherents of that way of life susceptible to illiberalism? Why do well-intentioned people committed to reforming society in a more egalitarian direction sometimes end up embracing intolerance, welcoming authoritarianism, or even preaching violence?

Beginning with the abolitionists may seem strange, even perverse, given that they were attacking slavery, the most egregiously illiberal institution in American history. Yet the abolitionists' crusade against slavery sometimes took strikingly illiberal forms. Many abolitionists vigorously supported the most high-handed Civil War leaders, such as General Benjamin Butler, because they believed that only such leaders followed the dictates of justice and conscience rather than law or political expediency. What mattered was less the cruelty or arbitrariness of a particular act than whether the actor was on the side of the righteous. Thus while the violence of the slave system was rightly condemned, the "righteous violence" of John Brown and others who took the law into their own hands was often extravagantly praised. In rejecting the arbitrary and cruel power of the slaveholder, the abolitionists were quintessentially liberal; in constructing a Manichaean battle between righteous crusaders and a corrupting "slave power," abolitionists justified the sorts of arbitrary acts, all the more dangerous for being clothed in the mantle of righteousness, that are antithetical to a liberal regime's commitment to democratic politics and the rule of law.

Radical egalitarians typically desire not only to ameliorate current wrongs but also to transform human beings as we know them. The perfectionist faith is a source of immense hope, but it can also be a route to authoritarianism and even totalitarianism. In chapter 2, I explore the connection between egalitarian utopianism and illiberalism by examining two of the most important and widely read utopian novels of the late nineteenth century: Edward Bellamy's *Looking Backward* (1888) and Ignatius Donnelly's *Caesar's Column* (1890). The imagined future in which conflict has been banished and coercion eliminated rests upon the assumption of a transformation in human nature or, at least, a recovering of humanity's natural goodness. Absent that change, the dream remains a dream or, worse, becomes a nightmare, as differences of opinion and interests are seen as evidence of deviancy or a vestigial selfishness that needs to be stamped out by the authorities. The undemocratic utopia celebrated in *Looking Backward* underscores the dark side of egalitaran efforts to privilege collective solidarity, harmony of interests, and equality of condition, while the apocalyptic *Caesar's Column* illustrates how utopian hopes of what is possible can fuel indiscriminate hatred for what actually exists.

The phenomenon of illiberal utopianism is not merely a matter of imagined communities. Throughout the late 1880s and especially the 1890s, utopian colonies attempting to realize the new cooperative commonwealth sprang up across the United States, just as they had during the antebellum era. Despite the best efforts of the colonists, these utopian colonies never came close to eliminating conflict; what they did succeed in doing was to drive conflict underground, where it would periodically erupt, with devastating consequences for the colony. Where conflict was not recognized as legitimate, the way was paved for authoritarian leaders who claimed to speak for the good of the whole and regarded dissent as evidence of maliciousness and even treason. Hoping to do away with authority, colonists created a microclimate in which unaccountable authoritarian leaders frequently flourished.

Enamored with people as they might be, radical egalitarians can be disdainful of people as they are. Radical egalitarians identify with and celebrate the common people, but paradoxically they often express contempt for the mundane lives of ordinary people. This egalitarian ambivalence toward everyday life is the subject of chapter 3, which critically examines the political thought of "America's Poet," Walt Whitman, the Young American writers at the *Seven Arts*, and the most talented Communist writer of the 1920s, Mike Gold. These writers aspired to express the latent authentic American life, but that often meant denigrating the manifest lives of actual Americans as shallow and inauthentic, materialistic and selfish. Hatred of the meanness and spiritual barrenness of capitalism spilled over into either a patronizing pity for passive victims or utter contempt for mindless dupes. Either way, disdain for the shallowness of the people crippled the radicals' commitment to democracy, leaving them waiting instead for a literary or political genius who could almost single-handedly bring about the latent American promise.

Disenchanted with the acquisitiveness and selfishness of actually existing Americans, these literary radicals sought out other peoples in whom they could safely invest their hopes for an egalitarian future. Before World War I the "lyrical left" of Waldo Frank, Randolph Bourne, and Van Wyck Brooks looked to France and Germany, Mexicans and Native Americans, in a desperate, often aburdly uncritical search for repositories of egalitarian community and virtue. After the war, radical intellectuals often looked to revolutionary Russia for the fulfillment of their egalitarian hopes, overlooking or denying the authoritarian character of Soviet politics. Mike Gold's crude apologies for Stalinist repression and his championing of politicized art represent a nadir in the history of radical egalitarianism.

If Gold's defense of the Stalinist party line represents radical egalitarianism at its most myopic, Bourne's biting antiwar essays in the *Seven Arts* represent radical egalitarianism at its most skeptical and indispensable. Against the smug certainties of established power, Bourne was the marginalized voice of radical skepticism, speaking truth to power, puncturing official pomposity, and exposing elite hypocrisy. Against the liberals' utopian efforts to invest World War I with redemptive promise ("the war to end all wars"), Bourne offered sober reminders of the irrationality of war and the tremendous powers that accrue to the state during war. Contrasting Gold and Bourne reminds us that liberal democracy has far less to fear from the harsh barbs and stinging reprimands of the egalitarian critic than it does from the egalitarian's uncritical embrace of state power to remake human society.

In an effort to compensate for the episodic coverage of the early chapters, Part II focuses in a more sustained manner on a single egalitarian movement in a single decade. By focusing on the 1960s New Left, and particularly SDS, I hope to unpack in detail the organizational and ideological dynamics of a radical egalitarian movement. Looking particularly closely at the 1960s is also warranted by the important role social movements of that decade have had in shaping the egalitarian movements of today, from environmentalism to feminism to multiculturalism.

How did SDS move from the nonviolence of the *Port Huron Statement* to the violent fantasies of the Days of Rage? The pathologies of the New Left in the late 1960s, I argue in chapter 4, were embedded in important ways in the early New Left's decision to distance and detach themselves from established institutions. The impulse to effect social change was increasingly preempted and distorted by a desire to retain an uncorrupted honesty or purity. The SDS worldview increasingly became one of "us" versus "them," the good inside versus the evil outside. The less SDS was willing to work with established groups to effect change, the more political institutions seemed unchangeable and the more violent confrontation in the streets seemed the only viable alternative.

Although those in the New Left increasingly walled themselves off from "the system," they did not abandon the search for allies in their struggle. Rather, as chapter 5 shows, they sought to reach out to those whom they perceived to be most oppressed — blacks, the poor, unemployed youths. The New Left, like virtually all radical egalitarian movements, looked to the oppressed for an indictment of the system as well as for an affirmation of their own preference for a noncoercive, egalitarian community outside of the mainstream. Accompanying this turn to the oppressed, even among the most intellectual of New Left students, was a growing anti-intellectualism and denigration of university life. Efforts to organize these oppressed groups, moreover, consistently failed; the poor, especially in the northern ghettos, were more passive, distrustful, and diverse than the radicals' romanticized view of the oppressed had led them to expect. As efforts to mobilize the poor and dispossessed in the United States failed, New Left radicals increasingly looked beyond

American borders for revolutionary allies. Projecting their romance for the oppressed onto the Third World, from Africa to Cuba, Vietnam, and China, the New Left often ended up excusing or explaining away repression and authoritarianism.

Chapter 6 addresses a paradoxical development that is central to all radical egalitarian movements but that is particularly acute in the case of SDS. In the beginning, SDS was organized along fairly conventional parliamentary lines: majority rule, *Robert's Rules of Order*, and national conventions that elected a president, vice president, and national executive committee. But as egalitarianism became increasingly strong within SDS, these representative structures were dismantled in the name of participatory democracy and antielitism. "No leaders, no structures" was the egalitarian theory; elitism and arbitrary, unaccountable power were increasingly the reality. At national conventions decision making by consensus replaced majority vote, which in practice stripped conventions of their decision-making capacity and thereby transferred decision-making power to the permanent National Office. Annual rotation in office for elected leaders meant concentrating power in the hands of unelected staff, a concentration of power that was furthered by the decision to abolish the offices of president and vice president. These "democratic" reforms produced a leadership that became steadily less accountable to the SDS membership, which in turn made it easier for the leadership to destroy remaining democratic forms. Reforms in the name of more democracy produced less democracy; antielitism produced its opposite.

As an organizational presence, the New Left barely made it out of the 1960s, but its impact on contemporary American social movements and culture has been far more enduring. Critics and defenders of the 1960s agree on this much.[27] Two of the most important contemporary social movements that still carry the imprint of 1960s radicalism are feminism and environmentalism.

Some observers argue that contemporary social movements, while clearly spawned and shaped by the New Left, represent a more democratic egalitarianism, one that has been sobered up by the missteps and errors of the New Left. Sociologist Jean Cohen, for instance, writes that "the new identity in the contemporary movements is consciously distinguished from the two distorting dimensions of the New Left political culture: its revolutionizing and totalizing character." Cohen finds that while new social movements typically reject aspects of "bourgeois industrial paternalist culture," there is "nonethless, a stress on continuity with those elements of civil society . . . that are worth preserving."[28] There is merit to this argument, but contemporary egalitarian movements and thinkers still sometimes manifest a number of the same illiberal tendencies evident in the New Left and in earlier egalitarian movements.

Both the radical environmentalism of Earth First! and the radical feminism of Catharine MacKinnon are a long way from the revolutionary violence of the Weathermen, but both MacKinnon and Earth First! in their different ways reveal some familiar illiberal tendencies of radical egalitarian thought. Characteristic of both radical feminism and radical environmentalism is the tendency to dismiss the choices people make as a product of false consciousness. Under conditions of inequality, MacKinnon insists, female consent is merely male coercion concealed. Female desire is a construction of male dominance. Driving a car, radical environmentalists tell us, is an "addiction," not a real choice. Society implants the acquisitive impulse in us. In both worldviews, people passively imbibe the dominant system's oppressive preferences. A democracy that respects the choices people make has little place in these imaginations; instead, they turn to an enlightened vanguard, whether ecological or feminist, which will be empowered to reconstruct people's values and beliefs in a more "politically correct" direction.

Like 1960s radicals, radical feminists are inclined to denigrate "liberal feminism" as a compromised version of the true faith. Yet the feminist movement, even in its most radical forms, is in many ways a progeny of liberalism. A basic postulate of liberalism, after all, is the equal worth and autonomy of individuals regardless of ascriptive characteristics. That liberal theorists of the past have generally not applied liberal principles to women (or racial minorities) is obvious enough, but that is historically contingent, not inherent in the principles. Indeed, one can justifiably say that insofar as past liberals failed to apply liberal precepts to women, they were to that extent imperfect liberals. Feminism, one might say, is liberalism applied to women. Viewed in world-historical terms, liberalism is a shatteringly radical idea that subverts ascriptive hierarchies, including those erected upon gender.[29]

Yet to reduce feminism to its liberal roots is not quite right either. Feminism's demand that the personal be made political often runs head-on into liberalism's insistence upon recognizing a distinction between public and private spheres of life. For the liberal, as Judith Shklar explains, the boundary between the personal and the political "is not historically a permanent or unalterable boundary, but it does require that every public policy be considered with this separation in mind and be consciously defended as meeting its most severe current standard."[30] Feminists are sharply critical of liberalism because they view the private realm less as a sanctuary from public authority than as the primary source of inequality. Privacy, particularly as it relates to family relations, is seen as impeding efforts to transform the way people think and act in more egalitarian directions. In challenging the autonomy of the private sphere, feminism both makes its most original contribution and runs its greatest risks. At its best, feminism helps us see that where one draws the line between the private and the public, the personal and the political, is itself a political question. But to concede that the personal has political elements is one thing; to insist that the personal is equivalent to the political is to open the way to the politicization of private life. Liberals may concede that privacy and autonomy are a major source of inequalities but will also point out that this is only one of many instances where competing goods collide. The illiberal temptation for feminists is to devalue autonomy, privacy, and the choices men and women make in their own lives. If a woman chooses to live in an unequal relationship (or a relationship that could leave her unequal in the event of divorce), it is tempting to discount such preferences as expressions of an inauthentic self whose consciousness has not yet been raised. To abridge liberty in the name of equality is reason for caution; to abridge liberty in the name of "true" freedom or a higher self is perilous.

Radical environmentalism might seem, at first glance, to have nothing in common with these other egalitarian movements. Radicals in the 1960s, after all, were arguably just as anthropocentric as conservatives in the 1960s. Where previous radicals cared about humans, radical environmentalists supposedly care only about nature. But upon closer investigation, even Earth First!, the paradigmatic radical environmental group, turns out to be thoroughly egalitarian in its organization and ideology, and its infamous misanthropy turns out to be a species of the familiar egalitarian antipathy toward Western industrial capitalism. Earth First!'s sweeping rejection of capitalist civilization seeps into a contempt for the everyday lives of people and prevents its members from making important distinctions between reform and reaction, abuse and legality, democracy and fascism. The illiberalism of the radical environmental movement is also evident in its apocalyptic vision of imminent catastrophe — global warming, nuclear meltdowns, deforestation, and so on. This apocalyptic vision stems not from a bunch of peculiarly risk-averse personalities but rather from the attempt to defend a radical egalitarian way of life and to discredit those competing ways that rely upon bold entrepreneurial experimentation. If no mistakes can be tolerated, then an individualistic trial-and-error process is out of the question. If the dangers to the human race are imminent and cataclysmic, then unprecedented restrictions on individual behavior are not just acceptable but mandatory. Threats of apocalypse together with millennial hopes for the future sustain radical egalitarian commitment at the same time that they erode doubt and hence tolerance, undermining ironically the very value that unpopular minorities like Earth First! are most dependent upon for survival.

The relationship between illiberalism and radical egalitarianism is far too complex and multifaceted to be accurately rendered in these brief capsule summaries. The summaries have been offered as appetizers, not as substitutes for the main course. The path from radical egalitarianism to illiberalism, it is worth underscoring at the outset, is neither invariant nor inevitable. Radical egalitarian values and institutions carry illiberal tendencies and temptations, but they do not guarantee illiberal outcomes.

Moreover, although my focus is on the illiberal "miseries" of radical egalitarianism, we should not forget its liberal "compensations." "Malcontentedness," as Randolph Bourne said, "may be the beginning of promise."[31] Radical egalitarianism is an astringent for the establishment. Incessant criticism of hierarchical and market institutions may be harsh and even unfair, but without that steady drumbeat of criticism those institutions would be less responsive and less accountable. A heightened sensitivity to inequality and injustice, even if gratingly self-righteous or impossibly utopian, can be a useful spur in the side of a complacent or at least pragmatic polity. Indeed, radical egalitarians sometimes justify their millennial rhetoric and impatience with liberal politics in precisely these strategic terms: the real danger in a liberal democratic polity, they argue, is not the occasional excesses of radical social movements but an ossified status quo that shelters injustice in the name of political prudence.[32]

This may be true, but to focus only on strategy and roles is too mechanical, as if habits of mind and styles of thought could be turned on and off as simply as a faucet. The oppositional stance of egalitarian solidarity entails certain social pressures and dynamics that take on a power of their own, shaping attitudes (to borrow Marx's formulation) "behind the back" of individuals.[33] The world becomes divided into the oppressor and the oppressed, the reactionary and the progressive, the corrupt and the pure. Marginalized and out of power, the radical egalitarian grouping is held together by a righteous indignation that serves to highlight the injustices of society. In power, that same righteous indignation can lead to a stunning intolerance of diverse opinions — in the contemporary academic environment this intolerance, ironically, sometimes manifests itself in the name of "diversity."

Before we praise radical egalitarians for their noble if unrealizable ideals, we do well to remember that noble ideals can themselves be the source of ignoble actions. "Our ideals and aspirations," Benjamin Barber sagely cautions, "must be cut close enough to the pattern of the actual to give hope the aspect of the possible." Egalitarian adherents need to examine history closely to see, as Barber suggests, whether "there might be a connection — more than just etymological — between the awesome and awful." The noble idea, to crib again from Marx, contains within it the seeds of its own destruction if that noble idea cannot meet what Barber calls "the test of incomplete realization." It is not enough to declare an idea noble and one's hands clean; one needs to ask what will happen to that uplifting ideal when people behave not like angels but like fallible, biased human beings.[34]

The Nineteenth
and Early Twentieth
Centuries

Radical Abolitionism

PURITY AND VIOLENCE

To make hypocrisy the worst of all the vices is
an invitation to . . . self-righteous cruelty.
   Judith Shklar[1]

We encounter the ever-renewed experience that the
adherent of an ethic of ultimate ends suddenly turns into a
chiliastic prophet. Those, for example, who have just preached
"love against violence" now call for the use of force for the
last violent deed, which would then lead to a state of affairs
in which *all* violence is annihilated.
   Max Weber[2]

In many respects, radical abolitionists were liberal champions. Their
aim, after all, was to root out slavery, the most blatantly illiberal, evil institution in the history of the United States. They insisted that liberal
principles of equal freedom be applied to blacks as well as whites. Moreover, abolitionists, at least while they were a persecuted minority, were a
courageous, unflinching voice for civil liberties. It was slaveholders and
their allies who passed the infamous 1836 Gag Rule, which outlawed
reading of antislavery petitions in Congress, and it was slaveholders who
censored and confiscated antislavery mail coming from the North.[3]
Moreover, it was northern mobs who killed Elijah Lovejoy and vio-
lently terrorized other abolitionists.[4] Wendell Phillips was one of many
radical abolitionists who were initially attracted to the abolitionist cause

less from a concern for slaves than from outrage over the violent assaults on civil liberties perpetrated by northern antiabolition mobs.[5] Yet radical abolitionists' relationship to liberalism was always ambivalent, for the same radical egalitarian commitments that fueled their courageous stance against slavery also contributed to illiberal tendencies within the movement.

Fundamental to radical abolitionism, as with all radical egalitarian movements, was a rejection of hierarchical relations of authority. No person, radical abolitionists insisted, had the right to compel or coerce another person. By liberating individual conscience from the demands of authority, custom, or law, abolitionists could break from established institutions and denounce slavery as an unconscionable evil that must be immediately abolished. This same extreme antiauthority impulse, however, also opened a door to fanaticism, since one might feel justified — indeed required — to do whatever one's individual conscience dictated, no matter what other people might think and no matter the consequences.

The radical abolitionist movement also revealed the characteristic egalitarian tension between the purity of the movement and reform of society.[6] An insistence on moral purity led abolitionists to withdraw (to "come out," in the language of the time) from established institutions such as churches and political parties. Some abolitionists went so far as to create or join utopian communes. But living an exemplary and noncoercive life was insufficient to bring about the end of slavery. To reform society required engagement, not withdrawal. The abolitionists' solution to this dilemma was to organize themselves at the margins of society, distant enough from established institutions to retain their moral purity, engaged enough to help abolish slavery.

Banded together at the margins of society, radical abolitionists constructed a Manichaean conflict between good and evil. Slavery certainly warrants the designation "evil," but this bipolar structure of thought encouraged an illiberal cast of mind that divided the world into hated enemies and cherished friends, the reprobate many and the chosen few. Political coalitions and compromise, so essential to a liberal democratic order, were rejected as inherently corrupting. Joining with those one might disagree with was warned against as "temporiz[ing] with evil."[7]

Radical abolitionists' commitment to moral purity, their rejection of political compromise, and their condemnation of any vacillation, evasion, or hypocrisy nourished a crusading self-righteousness that sometimes spilled over into self-righteous cruelty. While justly condemning the violence of the slave system, they uncritically lauded the "righteous violence" of those like John Brown who took the law into their own hands to deliver the country from sin. Pure motives and a righteous cause justified violent crimes and arbitrary deeds.

The Radical Egalitarianism of Radical Abolitionism

Before exploring the illiberal side of radical abolitionism, it is necessary to establish that the abolitionists were in fact radical egalitarians.[8] From our contemporary vantage point it is tempting to fold radical abolitionism into a developing northern capitalist consensus about the evils of slavery. From this perspective radical abolitionists were not qualitatively different, only more principled or more sensitive to injustice than most of their compatriots. But radical abolitionists were not simply capitalists with a conscience. "Post-1830 abolitionism," as historian Ronald Walters explains, "was a style of life. It defined their role in society, whom they associated with, what they surrounded themselves with, and — for a few — how they died."[9] To live as an abolitionist in the decades before the Civil War was to enact a radical egalitarian culture that in important ways set its adherents apart from the dominant institutions and mores of the North.

To begin with, radical abolitionists did not limit their criticisms to the arbitrary authority relations of slavery. Or, rather, slavery was redefined in such a way that it included, as historian Lawrence Friedman points out, "oppression of man by man in all its forms." The most radical abolitionists, the Garrisonian "nonresistants" or "no-government men," opposed all institutions based on force, including the state itself. Government, the military, jails, political parties, majority rule, voting, oath-taking, officeholding, all of these were part of the slaveholding "spirit." William Lloyd Garrison spoke for these radical abolitionists when he reported that he looked forward to the "happy time, when . . . all rule and all authority shall be put down." The radical abolitionists' aim, then, was not just to liberate the slaves but to emancipate all men and women.[10]

Radical abolitionists' commitment to eradicating authority relations led many of them to question traditional gender roles. In *The Slavery of Sex*, Blanche Hersh points out that "all of the women, and the men, who first spoke out and organized for women's rights were abolitionists." Garrisonian abolitionists were particularly prone to advocate diminishing "distinctions of sex" and to call into question the prevailing conception of the women's sphere as purely domestic. "Never will our governments be wisely and happily administered," concluded Samuel J. May, "until we have mothers as well as fathers of the State." Lydia Maria Child explained to her fellow abolitionist Angelina Grimké that her husband "despised the idea of any distinction in the appropriate spheres of human beings."[11]

Among abolitionists, as historian Ronald Walters points out, "there was a strong undercurrent of criticism of family life, particularly of marriage." Radical abolitionists often viewed marriage as an oppressive institution, not unlike slavery itself. Stephen Foster, a radical Garrisonian, likened "every family" to "a little embryo plantation." When abolitionists did marry, there was an effort among a number of them to structure the marriage as "a partnership of equals." Of the thirty-seven married abolitionist women studied by Hersh, for instance, at least twenty-eight had husbands who supported gender equality and endorsed a woman's right to act in the public realm. Perhaps the abolitionist marriage which most closely approximated the egalitarian ideal was that of Abigail Kelley and Stephen Foster. Both agreed that either could withdraw from the marriage whenever they chose, and the farm they bought after their marriage was deeded to Foster and Kelley jointly. While Abigail was out lecturing, Stephen would often stay home and take care of their farm and child. To an admiring abolitionist friend the Foster home was a place in which there could be "seen the beauty and the possibility of a permanent partnership of equals."[12]

Radical abolitionists' criticisms of the pernicious effects of authority in the family were in sharp contrast with the dominant individualistic culture's glorification of the family as a safe haven from the competitive principles that governed the political and economic spheres. Because egalitarians equated authority with coercion—Abigail Kelley Foster explained that for fear of being tyrannical she was "very conscientious not to use the least worldly authority over her child"[13]—familial relations were natural targets for abolitionist criticism.

The radical abolitionists' assault on authority also manifested itself in the area of religion. Abolitionists lambasted Protestant churches for being "the bulwarks of American slavery." Why had the churches failed them? The most common explanation offered by abolitionists, Walters finds, was that "the problem lay in a desire among clergy to assert their authority." "The ministry," complained one abolitionist, "have grasped and are clinging to power and to prerogative that they have no right to — sheer usurpation, is just as plain." American preachers, argued Theodore

Weld and Angelina Grimké Weld, were guilty of a "truckling subserviency to power, . . . clinging with mendicant sycophancy to the skirts of wealth and influence." When Weld and Grimké married in 1838, they refused to be married by a clergyman. "The nearest thing to an act of authority among the friends who gathered to marry them," writes Lewis Perry, "was that Garrison read a certificate." Even religious revivals, which were once considered a force to convert the world to abolitionism, tended by the 1840s to be seen by abolitionists as "simply another mechanism clergy used to preserve their place in society." Evangelism, Walters observes, was scorned as "a device to perpetuate the churches and to draw in members rather than to regenerate the world."[14]

Faced with a conflict between their commitment to egalitarianism and their church membership, abolitionists frequently withdrew from what they perceived as their "spiritual bondage."[15] Both William Goodell (who wrote an essay in 1843 entitled "Duty of Secession from a Corrupt Church") and Gerrit Smith seceded and then founded their own churches. Having withdrawn from their old denominations that tolerated slavery, a number of Garrisonians, including Foster, Parker Pillsbury, Henry Wright, and Garrison himself, turned to nonresistance — the belief that biblical injunctions against violence meant Christians should renounce all manifestations of force.[16]

The abolitionists' distinctive radical egalitarian vision can also be seen in their often-sweeping criticisms of competitive individualism. Very few, to be sure, repudiated private ownership of property; many showed unbounded enthusiasm for the latest technological advances (as did most European socialists, including Marx); and only a small minority followed European socialists (and southern slaveholders) in condemning "wage slavery." But it does not follow from this that abolitionists, as many historians would have it, were simply "one expression of the bourgeois competitive individualism . . . of antebellum northern society."[17] The abolitionists' social vision combined freedom from institutional restraints with collective fellowship. In their defense of individual autonomy they made common ground with competitive individualists, but in their desire for community, unity, and brotherhood, they departed fundamentally from the competitive individualist ethos.

The distinctive pattern of values and social relations that set radical abolitionists apart from the dominant competitive individualist culture of the North has been described by Lawrence Friedman in his meticulous study, *Gregarious Saints*. "Small groups," Friedman finds, were "at the heart of the immediatist crusade." Faced with a hostile public and possessed of an intense fear of defilement from having "to meet and mingle" with the morally tainted, abolitionists withdrew into "the sanctuary of small informal intimacy clusters" such as the Garrison-led Boston Clique, the circle of Liberty party men who gathered about Gerrit Smith's estate in upstate New York, and Lewis Tappan's evangelical grouping centered in New York City.[18]

These abolitionist groups were characterized, according to Friedman, by an ineradicable tension between "harmonious collectivity" and "unfettered individuality." Historian John Thomas echoes this view that abolitionism simultaneously "contained an anarchic appeal and a collectivist call, a command to shun evil and consult only conscience, and a mandate to join with the like-minded and look outward for perfect fellowship."[19] "A world in ourselves and in each other" is the way one abolitionist characterized their life of minimal authority and strong group boundaries.[20] The combination of strong group ("harmonious collectivity," "collectivist call," "a world in each other") and antiauthoritarianism ("unfettered individuality," "anarchic appeal," "a world in ourselves") defined their distinctively egalitarian way of life.

Lewis Tappan's question "Is it right to be rich?" suggests something of the abolitionists' unease with the competitive individualist's untrammeled pursuit of wealth. Among the Garrisonians, this ambivalence often slipped over into outright hostility. Lydia Maria Child, for instance, lamented that "in Wall-street, and elsewhere, Mammon, as usual, cooly [sic] calculates his chance of extracting a penny from war, pestilence, and famine." Her opinion of bidding and bargaining was equally jaundiced: "Commerce, with her loaded drays, and jaded skeletons of horses, is busy as ever 'fulfilling the World's contract with the Devil.'" Much the same attitude toward the freewheeling bustle of individualism was expressed by Garrison: "Mammon reigns in filthy splendor, and humanity finds none to sympathize with it." Wendell Phillips indicted competitive individualism for its disregard of principle: "It is hard," Phillips said, "to plant the self-sacrifice of a rigid Anti-Slavery, or any other principle, in the heart of . . . a prosperous, industrious, money-loving country, intensely devoted to the love of material gain."[21]

For the abolitionist, explains historian Ronald Walters, slavery was only "the most lurid case of unrestrained greed, . . . a sin that permeated the whole nation." Abolitionists believed that "Northerners as well as Southerners had an excessive love of money and a tendency to warp human relationships into business transactions." "The plantation ideal of defenders of slavery," Walters continues, "had much in common with the Christian utopia of Garrisonian nonresistants. Each was a counterimage, a form of protest against an emerging society in which relationships between humans seemed dictated more by the market-place than by bonds of morality and feeling."[22] The important difference was that abolitionists desired to replace the ethically blind hand of bidding and bargaining with a way of life dedicated to diminishing, rather than legitimating, differences between people.

The marketplace was suspect in the eyes of radical abolitionists because it subverted their vision of a caring community of equals. Radical abolitionists sometimes idealized a simpler, freer, and more cohesive past, where people lived together "in perfect equality, and had no need of laws, or labor." They yearned, in the words of Theodore Weld, for a "freer, larger, more harmonious form of human existence." The ideal they sought was not a world of perfect competition but a world in which "heads and hearts unite in working for the welfare of the human race." Even when abolitionists praised capitalism, as Walters points out, "the capitalism they envisioned was not that of J. P. Morgan; it was socially responsible, almost utopian."[23]

Because radical abolitionists elevated cooperation over competition, rejected existing institutions as corrupt (and corrupting), and harbored an almost limitless faith in man's potential for goodness, some were inevitably attracted to utopian communities. Among the most well known of these communitarian experiments was Adin Ballou's Hopedale Community (or Fraternal Community Number One), founded in 1842. Ballou was converted to abolitionism and nonresistance in 1837 by Garrisonian recruiting agents. His views expressed the orthodox Garrisonian line: he inveighed against "selfish, unscrupulous, and hard-hearted Individualism"; he renounced all authority not based on persuasion; he was appalled at society's "revolting extremes of wealth and poverty"; and he was involved in every reform of his age — peace, women's rights, and temperance, as well as the abolition of slavery. Where he differed was in his determination that true reform could best be achieved in a formal community that had withdrawn from the unregenerate world.[24]

Less successful, and far more radical, was the attempt by the Garrisonian John A. Collins to found a self-sufficient commune on 350 acres in upstate New York. Collins was a close associate of Garrison's and had played an important role in organizing and running various Massachusetts abolition societies. In 1840 Garrison sent the thirty-year-old Collins to England to solicit funds for the financially strapped American Anti-Slavery Society. Collins failed in his assigned mission, but while there he became appalled by the living and working conditions of the English laboring classes. The English system of laissez-faire, Collins explained to Garrison, had created "'a vast and complicated system' of slavery, . . . which gave to the poor subject the appearance of freedom the more successfully to grind him to powder." By the time he left England, Collins had become a convert to Robert Owen's utopian socialism, convinced that the private ownership of property made "man practically an enemy to his species," and that the future of America lay in self-sustaining collectives.[25]

Other followers of Garrison who launched utopian communities included Bronson Alcott in New England, the Brooke brothers in Ohio, and Garrison's own brother-in-law George Benson, who had been a committed abolitionist since the movement's inception in 1831. Another utopian venture was organized by the abolitionist Marcus Spring (who was married to the daughter of Arnold Buffman, one of the original members of the Garrisonian movement). Among the members of Spring's "loving community" at Raritan Bay, New Jersey, was no less a luminary than Theodore Weld.[26]

These "communitarian experiments," John Thomas explains, "in effect were anti-institutional institutions." That is, they were efforts to create radical egalitarian collectivities. Each of these communities, Thomas finds, "veered erratically between the poles of anarchism and collectivism as they hunted feverishly for a way of eliminating friction without employing coercion."[27] Looked at in this way, the organizational dilemma facing these utopian ventures was essentially similar to that which faced all radical abolitionists: that of reconciling, in Friedman's words, "simultaneous cravings for cordial collectivity and pious individuality—for gregarity and sainthood."[28]

Although the great majority of abolitionists doubted the practicality of these self-sufficient communes, many remained intrigued by the models they offered. Garrison, for instance, was a frequent visitor to Benson's community, and Hopedale influenced many abolitionists, serving as it did "as a way-station for all of New England's reformers on their way to or from the endless succession of conventions and conferences for the improvement of American society."[29] Whatever their judgment about the workability of these communal utopias, few Garrisonians questioned the desirability of a more harmonious form of existence in which benevolence replaced selfishness and cooperation would be privileged over competition. In their everyday life, Garrisonians self-consciously tried to build informal, intimate communities of believers and spurned contact with institutions (e.g., political parties and churches) that were morally tainted. Most did not join formal communes because they believed that the "principles of universal Christian brotherhood . . . must be matured in the hearts and lives of individuals, before they can be embodied in any community," but they did not doubt that "when the new organization commences, it will doubtless be in small communities."[30] To withdraw prematurely into self-sufficient communes jeopardized the radical abolitionists' ultimate goal, which was nothing less than "communityzing the whole."[31]

Dirty Hands and the Civil War

The temptation to withdraw from a corrupt world was tempered by the abolitionists' strong desire for reform. The dilemma that faced abolitionists was how to reform a fallen world without incurring "dirty hands."[32] The tension between reform and purity was never greater for the abolitionists than during the Civil War. In the 1830s and 1840s, abolitionists had been an unpopular and persecuted minority, and their stance had been unambiguously oppositional. Radical abolitionists refused to join political parties, support established political leaders, or even vote. They withdrew from corrupting social institutions and social relationships. From the margins of society, they excoriated a complacent America.

With the onset of the Civil War, however, radical abolitionists faced a more morally vexing situation. No longer an isolated, unpopular minority, they found that political leaders now sought out their opinions and their support.[33] The Civil War offered abolitionists a means to crush slavery, and yet the abolition of slavery was not the war's stated aim. How could they lend support to or participate in a war whose objective was only to restore the Union? To support such a war meant becoming complicit in the compromises and expediency that were a necessary part of established political institutions and leadership. It also meant jettisoning long-held pacifist and antimilitarist principles.[34]

The most radically oppositional abolitionists, such as Parker Pillsbury and Stephen Foster, could not bring themselves to compromise their moral integrity in any way. As historian James McPherson remarks, Pillsbury and Foster were so hostile to established authority that they were "temperamentally incapable of supporting any government." In Foster's eyes, "Abraham Lincoln [was] as truly a slaveholder as Jefferson Davis." Pillsbury echoed this view. "I have no higher opinion of Abraham Lincoln, and his Cabinet," he declared, "than I have of the President and Cabinet . . . of the Confederate States."[35] The Union and Confederate governments were equally tainted by the sins of slavery and coercion.

Most abolitionists, however, followed the lead of Garrison and Phillips in initially supporting the war while pressing the North to embrace emancipation. The prospect of emancipation enabled even those who believed "all war to be wicked and unchristian" to "delight that this conflict is upon us." Slavery, after all, was "perpetual war. . . . A single day of Slavery . . . witnessed more wrong, violence, corruption, more actual war, than all that civil war ever could bring." Wendell Phillips agreed that "the bloodiest war ever waged is infinitely better than the happiest slavery which ever fattened men into obedience."[36] Having overridden their deeply held objections to coercion or compromise in any form, radical abolitionists engaged in a desperate search for signs that "the Cause of the North will become the Cause of Truth."[37] To justify their support for the government's war and their own engagement in politics, many radical abolitionists sought to turn the Civil War into a holy war that would usher in an era of perpetual peace and eternal justice.

In a speech announcing his support for the war, Phillips explained his decision by drawing attention to the glorious ends the war would serve. Following the bloodletting and atonement, "the world will see under our banner all tongues, all creeds, all races, — one brotherhood." Yesterday the government had been an agreement with hell; today it was "the Thermopylae of Liberty and Justice."[38] Nor was Phillips alone in this view. The "belief that an affectionate society of free individuals would somehow emerge out of the bloodshed and hatred of war," historian George Fredrickson notes, "was characteristic of the thinking of many abolitionists in 1861."[39] Only a war with such exalted purposes could cleanse their dirty hands.

Abolitionists desperately wanted to believe that the Union's cause would be the cause of eternal truth and justice, but in the first year there were few if any signs of such righteousness emanating from the Lincoln administration. Restoration of the Union, not emancipation of slaves, was the administration's clearly stated policy. The government's refusal to fight a war of emancipation left an indelible stain on the moral purity of the abolitionists who had enthusiastically embraced the war.[40] Their early hopes for a war to redeem a guilty nation redoubled their sense of betrayal. Haunted by the unbearable thought that they were supporting a bloody war that might leave slavery untouched, abolitionists began to back away from their tenuous support for Lincoln. If Lincoln would not launch a holy crusade against slavery, then perhaps another, such as General John C. Frémont, would.

Toward the end of the war's first summer, Frémont issued a proclamation freeing the slaves of every rebel in the state of Missouri. Here, finally, was a leader willing to give the war a great moral purpose that could justify the carnage. Unlike Lincoln, exulted Henry Wright, Frémont had shown himself to be "obedient to the voice of God." General Frémont, Phillips added, deserved to be a leader because he was willing to "launch a thunderbolt" in the service of emancipation. Frémont's proclamation, Gerrit Smith wrote to the president, was "the first unqualifiedly and purely right" step that had taken place during the war. The order, echoed Massachusetts Governor [John] Andrew, gave "an impetus of the grandest character to the whole cause."[41]

As quickly as Frémont raised abolitionists' hopes, Lincoln dashed them. Fearing the effect of Frémont's proclamation on the border states, Lincoln condemned Frémont's order as "simply 'dictatorship'" and immediately modified it to conform to the Confiscation Act of August 6, leaving the abolitionists aghast. In the *Liberator*, Garrison charged Lincoln with a "serious dereliction of duty"; revoking Frémont's order was "timid, depressing, suicidal." Privately Garrison fumed that Lincoln was "only a dwarf in mind." Edmund Quincy believed it to be "one of those blunders which are worse than crimes." Another abolitionist lamented the president's "pigheaded stupidity."[42] The limited armistice between the abolitionists and the Lincoln administration had come to a crashing end.

The president's annual message at the end of 1861, warning against degeneration of the war "into a violent and remorseless revolutionary struggle," met with widespread abolitionist condemnation. In the pages of the *Liberator*, Garrison characterized Lincoln's message as "feeble and rambling." Garrison privately confided his belief that Lincoln "has evidently not a drop of anti-slavery blood in his veins" and concluded by lamenting that Lincoln was "a man of very small calibre." Gerrit Smith publicly assailed the president's address as "twattle and trash." An even more hostile critic called it a "timid, timeserving, commonplace sort of an abortion of a message, cold enough . . . to freeze h-ll over."[43] In a fight against evil, moderation was no virtue.

Radical abolitionists sought out bolder, purer leadership — leadership that would not be constrained by legality nor guided by expediency. General Benjamin Butler, for instance, became an abolitionist hero (despite the fact that he had supported Jefferson Davis for president in 1860) after he declared fugitive slaves who came behind his lines to be "contraband" and put them to work for the Union army. As military governor of New Orleans, writes Irving Bartlett, Butler acted "almost as a law unto himself." The general assumed "entire financial control of the city, hanged a man for hauling down the American flag and told the [women of] New Orleans . . . that if they did not stop insulting his troops they would be treated like common prostitutes."[44] Although long an opponent of capital punishment,[45] Phillips was so enamored with Butler's decisive leadership that he told a crowd that "if I were [Butler] and were to die soon, I would have a tombstone inscribed 'I was the only Major General of the United States that ever hung a traitor; that ever, by the boldness of my action, and the method of the death, told the world it was a Government struggling with rebels, with the right and purpose to put them beneath its laws, at any cost.'" Butler, in Phillips's view, was "almost the only general in our service who acts upon the principle that we are all right and the traitors all wrong."[46] For Phillips, attention to legality was timidity; he desired instead a charismatic leader who would substitute his will for the law in order to achieve an exalted objective.

Like most radical abolitionists, Phillips had no sympathy for the distinction Lincoln consistently made between his own personal opinions about slavery and what the office and laws empowered him to do. Lincoln thought slavery wrong but did not feel that this gave him a license to abolish it except insofar as it was necessary to preserve the Union. As he explained in a public letter toward the close of his first term: "I am naturally anti-slavery. If slavery is not wrong, nothing is wrong. I cannot remember when I did not see, think and feel that it was wrong; and yet I have never understood that the Presidency conferred upon me an unrestricted right to act officially upon this judgment." Indeed the oath to uphold the Constitution, Lincoln insisted, "forbade me to . . . indulge my primary abstract judgment on the moral question of slavery."[47]

Phillips had no such reservations about public officials allowing their political actions to be dictated by their private consciences, even if such action might violate the law. Although Phillips had initially enlisted in the antislavery cause out of concern over violations of free expression, during the war he seemed to forget these civil libertarian concerns almost entirely. "The government," he said, "may safely be trusted, in a great emergency, with despotic power, without fear of harm, or of wrecking the state." Arbitrary, despotic power was inevitable; the only question was whether it would be used to achieve just ends. Phillips thus urged Lincoln and other military leaders to use these despotic powers to abolish slavery.[48]

The chief trouble with Lincoln, in Phillips's view, was that he was a politician, always "casting his eyes over his shoulders to see how far the people will support him."[49] Building public support for government actions was not leadership as Phillips understood that term. Prudence and compromise, in Phillips's view, were simply timidity and weakness. The leadership Phillips sought was of a grander, heroic sort that would bend the nation to the leader's will. Phillips contrasted Lincoln, who "halts and fears" with "a man like Frémont [who would] stamp the lava mass of the nation with an idea."[50] Phillips demanded men with "wills hot enough to fuse the purpose of nineteen millions of people into one decisive blow for safety and for Union."[51] No democratically elected leader who wanted to accommodate a national constituency encompassing a wide array of interests and ideas could meet Phillips's standards of leadership.

Phillips's vision of politics and leadership was often profoundly undemocratic and illiberal. Throughout the war, he sought out leaders who would electrify the nation with decisive, just acts. Such men, he said, "were above words" and were "willing to shake off what are called institutions." They did not need to persuade, and they were not constrained by forms. They simply transformed consciousness through bold, righteous actions. Such great men abolished the need for the rest of us to dirty our hands in the always slow, often unseemly workings of democratic politics. "Out of the millions of refuse lumber," Phillips wrote after John Brown's death, "God selects one in a generation, and he is enough to save a State."[52]

Like many other radical abolitionists, Phillips sought leaders who were willing to destroy and then create anew an entire social system in the South. "The whole social system of the Gulf states," Phillips insisted, "is to be taken to pieces; every bit of it." "We must take up the South and organize it anew." Not just slavery but its entire social and intellectual life must be "annihilated."[53] To Phillips's great credit, he understood that to abolish slavery was not in and of itself sufficient to protect the freedman. Inequalities in economic, social, and political power would soon be used to undermine any formal equality that the law might establish. But

Phillips's appreciation for the ways in which inequalities in one sphere would translate into inequality and domination in other spheres of life was not accompanied by a democratic sensitivity to the question of consent. Phillips and other like-minded abolitionists too often failed to appreciate the extent to which political action required some minimal level of consent and cooperation on the part of white people who lived in the southern states. Raw force, as a believer in "moral suasion" should have been the first to recognize, could not create the just future that abolitionists envisioned.

Phillips's vision of postwar reconstruction seemed to leave little room for democracy and conciliation, let alone reconciliation or forgiveness. "I have no plea for conciliation. I am for conciliation, but not for conciliating the slaveholder. Death to the system, and death or exile to the master, is the only motto." Phillips was hardly the only abolitionist now exulting not just in the destruction of slavery but also in the death of slave owners. Charles K. Whipple, who in the late 1850s had become editorial assistant for the *Liberator*, now called for the "extermination" of southern secessionists and slaveholders even as he insisted that he remained a "peace man." Asked by Henry Richard of the London Peace Society whether he still believed in the power of Christian love, Whipple responded, "You speak of these people as 'our fellow-Christians.' I pray you not to do Christianity so great an injustice. Slaveholders are *not* Christians." Samuel May had come to the same conclusion, that southerners should no longer be seen as fellow citizens or even as fellow Christians. "We must put them down, utterly down, as wicked rebels against God. . . . The Southern Aristocracy must be crushed, if possible annihilated." Upon war's end, May, though like Phillips long an opponent of capital punishment, seemed to suggest that Jefferson Davis should be hanged.[54]

One of the great paradoxes of the Civil War, as Peter Brock points out, is that "it was actually the moderate pacifists, who had opposed the 'no-government' views of the Garrisonian nonresistants, who now in wartime proved the more consistent in their advocacy of peace views." Amasa Walker, for instance, who had helped Garrison and May organize the New England Anti-Slavery Society but had been skeptical of the more anarchist "no government" views, consistently insisted that he expected "nothing good from this or any war, that might not be obtained in a better way."[55] In contrast, Seward Mitchell, a Garrisonian nonresistant and "no-government" man, now decided that war was an "absolute necessity."

Slavery, Mitchell allowed, was the cause of the war, but that was "not going to the *bottom* of our troubles. Slavery is the child, but human government is the parent. Something must come to destroy these governments, and make money worthless; and I am happy to see them dashing out each other's brains. In their self-destruction is the hope of the world."[56] Only the destruction that war could bring seemed capable of realizing the transformative egalitarian vision.

Throughout the war, radical abolitionists justified their support of the war by putting its violence in the service of righteous, even glorious, ends. In the summer of 1862, for instance, Lydia Maria Child wrote to George Julian that she was "convinced that this is the great battle of Armageddon between the Angels of Freedom and the Demons of Despotism."[57] For Sarah Grimké, a committed pacifist for thirty years, this "blessed war" was "the holiest ever waged, [it] is emphatically God's war. . . . The eyes of the nation are being anointed with the eye-salve of the King of heaven."[58] Garrison, too, justified his support for the horrendous violence of the Civil War by telling himself and others that "ours is the cause of God — the cause of man the world over." Having abolished slavery, "we shall all be united as brethren in the spirit of Justice. . . . The North and the South . . . will embrace each other fraternally, and all sectional animosities and rivalries [will] be banished forevermore."[59] William Furness, a devoted nonresistant who prior to the war had sharply criticized John Brown for taking up the sword in defense of liberty rather than trusting to nonviolence, now justified the northern war effort by envisioning an impending age of "millennial splendor" that would be inaugurated by the war. Through the war, God was "binding the North together in ever closer ties of Christian love and fraternal fellowship, . . . ushering in a wonderful new age, a golden age of freedom for all mankind."[60]

That the overwhelming majority of nonresistant abolitionists supported a war which offered the chance to defeat slavery is hardly surprising. What is more puzzling, as Friedman points out is, "why . . . they [had] come to defend force and violence with exultation, even gratification." One answer, I have suggested, lies in the primacy radical abolitionists assigned to purity. Prior to the war, they had defined themselves in opposition to an iniquitous and corrupt government and society. They believed with Phillips that the true reformer must stand "outside of organizations, with no bread to earn, no candidate to elect, no party to save, no object but truth — to tear a question open and riddle it with light."[61] The Civil War, however, drew radical abolitionists into supporting the very political institutions they had hitherto shunned. For some, like Garrison, involvement in the system gradually undermined this oppositional stance; others, like Phillips, sustained their oppositional stance throughout the war. But for virtually all radical abolitionists, the rhetoric of righteous violence was a way of cleansing their "dirty hands."

From Nonviolence to Righteous Violence

The abolitionists' glorification of violence during the Civil War represented a radical departure from their earlier preaching of nonviolence and moral suasion. It is tempting to put this change down to the impact of the horrors and possibilities unleashed by the Civil War. Such an interpretation, however, is not only historically inaccurate,[62] it ignores the important ways in which abolitionists' embrace of righteous violence stemmed from their early commitments to an egalitarian life of noncoercion.

In the beginning, most radical abolitionists were strongly opposed to violence in almost any form. "All the leading abolitionists of my acquaintance," observed the Quaker John Greenleaf Whittier in 1833, "are, from principle, opposed to war of all kinds, believing that the benefits of no war whatever can compensate for the sacrifice of one human life by violence." In that same year, the fledgling American Anti-Slavery Society resolved that abolitionists would never resort to violence or even "countenance the oppressed in vindicating their rights by resorting to physical force."[63] The abolitionists' commitment to nonviolence had never been absolute, however, as their reaction to the killing of the abolitionist editor Elijah Lovejoy in 1837 made evident. After antiabolition mobs had destroyed his printing press three times, Lovejoy, who had started out as a committed Garrisonian nonresistant, resolved to arm himself, his family, and his friends in order to defend his fourth printing press. The very day the new press arrived, a mob gathered to destroy it. After an exchange of gunfire mortally wounded a young carpenter in the mob, the crowd turned ugly. One person in the crowd climbed a ladder to set fire to the warehouse roof, leading both Lovejoy and another man to rush out of the warehouse, pistols aimed at the arsonist. Lovejoy was immediately shot and killed.[64]

A few abolitionists, including the Grimké sisters, Henry Wright, and Samuel May, unequivocally condemned Lovejoy for transgressing the principles of moral suasion. Others, including Wendell Phillips and Lydia Child, unambiguously praised Lovejoy, whom they saw as acting as "the minister of God" and a "terror to evil doers."[65] The overwhelming number of radical abolitionists, however, were deeply ambivalent about the Lovejoy episode. Most, as Friedman observes, mixed extravagant praise with harsh reprimand. They recognized the right of self-defense, admired Lovejoy's bravery, and honored him as a martyr to liberty, but they deeply regretted that, as Garrison put it, he had "resorted to carnal weapons in defence of his rights and the laws of the State, that he became a victim to his mistaken sense of duty."[66]

Even while radical abolitionists praised Lovejoy for his courage in the face of barbarous proslavery forces, most still powerfully reaffirmed their original nonviolent principles. The predominant tone among Garrisonians was one of sorrow and regret that such a "great, noble and good man [had fallen] with a vile implement of human warfare in his hand." In forsaking moral suasion, Garrison and others believed, Lovejoy had "forfeited the protection of God" that attached to those who walked in the righteous path of nonviolence. Although not passing judgment on "how far and under what circumstances it is right to use arms in self-defense," the board of managers of the Massachusetts Anti-Slavery Society reaffirmed their belief that if the doctrine of nonresistance had been adhered to, "victory would, in the providence of God, have been the result; or, if not, that the spilling of the blood of defenceless men would have produced a more thrilling and abiding effect."[67] Nonviolence was reaffirmed as not only right but efficacious.

If the commitment to nonviolence for most radical abolitionists was never absolute, it was still one of the central principles guiding their early political thinking. For Garrison, in fact, the commitment to pacifism predated his interest in antislavery.[68] The Garrisonians' commitment to nonviolence was not merely abstract theory, nor was it something that they preached to slaves but ignored themselves. Outspoken abolitionists faced continual threats of violent reprisal in the 1830s.[69] In October 1835, for instance, Garrison was nearly killed by an enraged mob in Boston and yet resolutely refused to defend himself by arms: "I will perish sooner than raise my hand against any man, even in self-defense," he explained.[70] Other radical abolitionists were more willing to admit self-defense as a justification for violence,[71] but the strong reaffirmation of nonviolent principles in the wake of the Lovejoy episode shows the centrality of nonviolence to radical abolitionist thought and, more specifically, that abolitionists remained strongly if not unambiguously opposed to the use of force for even righteous ends.

Why did the abolitionists' strong, early commitment to nonviolence give way to an embrace of righteous violence? Events, particularly the Fugitive Slave Act of 1850 and the violence of "Bleeding Kansas," played their part, of course. But so, too, did the abolitionists' cultural filters and blinkers.[72] Most important was the radical abolitionists' tendency to frame the conflict over slavery in terms of a Manichaean struggle between the forces of darkness and the forces of light. For radical abolitionists, slavery was more than just an evil institution that brutalized oppressed slaves. It was also a "monster of iniquity" that threatened the freedom of all Americans. The substantial political power of slaveholders was reified into an impregnable, heartless "slave power." As Friedman comments, this "Manichaean good-bad frame of mind . . . allowed immediatists to cultivate necessary emotional distance between themselves and those who were the subjects of their violent thoughts and actions." Constructing a demonic slave power also made it increasingly difficult for abolitionists to believe in the efficacy of moral suasion, which, after all, presupposed a view of the other side as redeemable. Human beings might be persuaded, but only violence could slay a monster. Finally, the abolitionists' Manichaean construction of the conflict worked to undermine their concerns about the morality of the means used to achieve a given end. The question of the morality of the individual act paled in the face of the big question: "Are you for Freedom or are you for Slavery? . . . Are you for God, or are you for the Devil?" Whether one acted on the side of the righteous came to supersede the question of whether the means itself were moral.[73]

The move from nonresistance to righteous violence can be seen particularly vividly in the career of Henry Wright, who had been among the strongest and most vocal advocates of nonviolence during the 1830s and 1840s. Wright's demonization of the slaveholder gradually subverted his initial commitment to nonviolence. So loathsome was the slaveholder — "All around me," he wrote in the *Liberator*, "are the slimy, stealthy, blighting footsteps of the slaveholder" — that he found it difficult to resist the lure of righteous violence. Wright summoned up a monstrous, hegemonic "slave power" that controlled all aspects of federal policy. All federal officers, he believed, were complicit: "Such office-holders in the North should be held up as the earth's vilest enemies, for such they are, in heart and life. . . . [He] should be regarded and treated as the murderer and pirate are regarded and treated. He is a worse enemy to God and man than either. . . . As an officer of a slave-hunting government, a man has no rights which humanity is bound to respect." Since slaveholders and their minions were "the deadly foes of humanity," they all forfeited their rights, even to life: "Away with them all, if to perpetuate their existence and authority, man, physically, socially, or spiritually, must be sacrificed. . . . A baptism of blood awaits the slaveholder and his abettors. So be it. The retribution is just."[74]

For abolitionists like Wright, who had devoted much of their adult lives to the cause of pacifism and nonresistance, justifying violence required, to an extraordinary degree, demonizing and even dehumanizing slaveholders. This dynamic is perhaps most spectacularly evident in the conversion of the zealous nonresistant Charles Stearns, who had gone to Kansas in the mid-1850s to be that state's correspondent for the *National Anti-Slavery Standard* and the *Liberator*.[75] Finding himself almost immediately thrust into the midst of a ferocious border war, he initially refused to arm himself. After ten days of war, however, he suddenly had a change of heart after "becoming convinced that we had not human beings to contend with."

> I always believed it was right to kill a tiger, and our invaders are nothing but tigers. Christ says, "If a *man* smites thee on the one cheek, turn to him the other also." These Missourians are not men. I have always considered that, bad as they were, they had an infinitessimal [*sic*] spark of divinity in them; but . . . our invaders were wild beasts, and it was my duty to aid in killing them off. When I live with men made in God's image, I will never shoot them; but these pro-slavery Missourians are demons from the bottomless pit and may be shot with impunity.

Just as many slaveholders justified enslaving blacks on the grounds that they were subhuman, so Stearns now justified killing slaveholders on the grounds that they were not really human, but rather were "drunken ourang-outans."[76]

Garrison publicly chided Stearns for having been "thoroughly frightened out of his peace principles." The escalating violence in Kansas led Garrison to warn his fellow abolitionists: "Do not get impatient; do not become exasperated; . . . do not make yourselves familiar with the idea that blood must flow." Unlike Stearns, Garrison insisted that the southern slaveholder, though a great sinner, "is a man, sacred before me. He is a man, not to be harmed by my hand nor with my consent. . . . While I will not cease reprobating his horrible injustice, I will let him see that in my heart there is no desire to do him harm."[77] Garrison's heroic insistence on the essential humanity of the slaveholder was difficult to sustain, however, in the face of the incessant demonization of the southern slaveholder. Even Garrison himself, who was among the most consistent nonresistants in the antebellum years, would sound a radically different tone in the wake of John Brown's raid on Harpers Ferry. "Every slaveholder," Garrison would then say, "has forfeited his right to live, if his destruction be necessary to enable his victims to break the yoke of bondage."[78]

In responding to Garrison's public rebuke, Stearns stressed that his violence was no ordinary, sordid violence but a righteous violence. While he was "sorry to deny the principles of Jesus Christ, after contending for them so long," Stearns assured Garrison that "it is not for myself that I am going to fight. It is for God and the slaves."[79] Violence motivated not by self-interest but by an altruistic desire to help the oppressed was a higher, purer sort of violence that could not be weighed in the same scales as the self-interested violence of the slaveholder. The doctrine of nonviolence was "pernicious," the American Peace Society's vice president Gerrit Smith decided, because "it places on the same level the taking of life in the unnecessary and wicked strife of war, and the taking of it in the necessary and righteous work of breaking up a nest of pirates."[80] Violence against slaveholders was righteous and liberating, and was thus completely unlike the slaveholders' institutionalized violence of suppression.[81]

John Brown: A Holy Warrior

The abolitionists' growing attraction to righteous violence was brought into dramatic relief by their reaction to John Brown and his infamous raid on Harpers Ferry in October 1859. Brown was no nonresistant. He had set out for Kansas in 1855 for the express purpose of forcibly resisting the aggression of slaveholders. Brown took his inspiration from the remorseless, vengeful scriptures of the Old Testament. In May 1856, in retaliation for the sacking of Lawrence, a free-soil town, Brown set out with four of his sons and two other supporters to exact revenge on the "border ruffians." Brown's guerrilla band entered three cabins, dragged the unarmed adult males out into the night, and brutally hacked them to death with cutlasses. Though this act was purportedly a retaliation for the burning of Lawrence, most of the settlers killed by Brown's party had not been involved in any attacks on free-soil settlers.

After this brutal massacre, Brown became one of the most notorious figures in Kansas, a notoriety that was only heightened by his leading role a few years later in a raid into Missouri which resulted in the liberation of eleven slaves and the killing of one slave owner.[82]

At the beginning of 1857, Brown embarked on a fund-raising trip to New England. He told the antislavery men he contacted that his mission was to "raise and arm a company of men for the protection of Kansas," but his real aim was the invasion of Virginia. The abolitionists knew "Old Brown" of Kansas as a heroic fighter against the proslavery "border ruffians," but few were willing to credit the allegations of his role in the previous spring's massacre. Eager to believe the best of this antislavery warrior, they accepted Brown's denials at face value and insisted that the allegations against Brown were part of a proslavery plot to discredit him.[83]

Among the abolitionists Brown met on his trip to Massachusetts was Garrison himself. At a reception hosted by Theodore Parker, Garrison and Brown argued about peace and nonresistance. Garrison quoted from the New Testament about love and mercy, Brown from the Old Testament on justice and retribution. There seemed no common ground between Garrison's radical perfectionism and Brown's grim Calvinist theology. Brown scorned Garrison's "milk-and-water" pacifism, yet Garrison, according to Brown's biographer Stephen Oates, was still "rather impressed" by Brown's earnest sense of commitment and his righteousness.[84]

Other New England abolitionists were captivated by Brown. Bronson Alcott, when he met Brown, confided to his journal, "This is the man to do the Deed." George Luther Stearns saw in Brown "a Cromwellian Ironside introduced in the nineteenth century for a special purpose." Stearns's wife was so entranced with Brown's "moral magnetism" that she pressed her husband to sell their horse and carriage, maybe even their entire estate, to aid Brown's "sublime purpose."[85] Emerson, Stearns, and Franklin Sanborn, among others, hardly raised an eyebrow when Brown earnestly told them that it was "better that a whole generation of men, women and children should pass away by a violent death, than that a word of either [the Golden Rule or the Declaration of Independence] should be violated in this country."[86] Such words thrilled many abolitionists, who were dazzled by Brown's combination of righteous commitment and frontier daring.

When the news of John Brown's raid on Harpers Ferry reached the North, the initial reaction of many abolitionists was guarded and even confused. In the initial report of the events in the *Liberator*, Garrison briefly reminded his readers of his well-known opposition to all violence, "even in the best of causes," but he also pointed out that those who gloried in America's revolutionary past could hardly "deny the right of the slaves to imitate the example of our fathers." Brown's raid, Garrison opined, was "misguided, wild, and apparently insane" even if it was also "disinterested and well-intended."[87]

The initial uncertainty as to how to judge Brown's bold action quickly vanished, however. While mainstream Republicans such as Lincoln and William Seward distanced themselves from Brown's fanaticism,[88] abolitionists embraced Brown for his heroic, unselfish act. Only a week after his initial short and ambivalent commentary in the *Liberator*, Garrison wrote a much longer editorial full of praise for Brown. Although still characterizing the raid as "wild and futile" as well as "sadly misguided," Garrison now described Brown in glowing terms. "A more honest, conscientious, truthful, brave, disinterested man (however misguided or unfortunate) does not exist," Garrison proclaimed. Never was there a "more undaunted spirit." For his selfless deed on behalf of the oppressed, Brown deserved "to be held in grateful and honorable remembrance to the latest posterity by all those who glory in the deeds of a Wallace or Tell, a Washington or Warren."[89]

Speaking several months later, on the day of Brown's execution, Garrison went further still. Although insisting he was still "an 'ultra' peace man" who believed in "the inviolability of human life, under all circumstances," he went on to thank God "when men who believe in the right and duty of wielding carnal weapons are so far advanced that they will take those weapons out of the scale of despotism, and throw them into the scale of freedom." Such righteous violence, Garrison explained, was "an indication of progress, and a positive moral growth; it is one way to get up to the sublime platform of non-resistance." Righteous violence would usher in the kingdom of peace. In any event, he added, such violence was "God's method of dealing retribution upon the head of the tyrant."[90] The repressive violence of the oppressor was one thing, the liberating violence of the oppressed quite another.

Henry Wright, long a leading nonresistant, was now among the most extravagant in his praise of John Brown, whom he likened to Jesus Christ. "The sin of this nation," Wright wrote to the Richmond *Enquirer*, was "to be taken away, not by Christ, but by John Brown." Brown, Wright maintained, had been right "in resolving . . . to shoot down all who should oppose him in his God-appointed work." Since there were "but two sides in this conflict" and "you must be wholly for one or the other," it followed that one must either approve Brown's action or support "those kidnapping, piratical hordes of the South."[91] In a bipolar world of good and evil, good men should not just condone but actively celebrate Brown's actions.

Brown's raid had captured the imagination of radical abolitionists, even those such as Wright and Garrison who for decades had been uncompromising apostles of peace. John Brown, as Lewis Perry observes, "confronted [abolitionists] with the possibility that a high motive could sanctify any course of action." The violent deed was sanctified by its sublime purpose. Brown's personal sincerity absolved him of guilt.[92] Again and again Brown's defenders excused or justified his violent actions by pointing to "the purity of his motive and the essential rightness of his object."[93] Because Brown was "true to the light within,"[94] his violent actions had been cleansed in authenticity and inner truth.

Abolitionists were particularly impressed by the selfless character of Brown's acts. Brown, in Emerson's words, was "a true idealist, with no by-ends of his own."[95] He acted not for himself, wrote a contributor in the Liberator, but only for "the weak and the wronged."[96] Garrison echoed this theme: "Brown was a hero, struggling against fearful odds, not for his own advantage, but to redeem others from a horrible bondage."[97] It is one thing to admire those who act in the name of the dispossessed; it is quite another to make motivation the sole or even primary means by which one judges the morality of an action. Down this path lies an illiberal trap in which any atrocity may be justified so long as the motives are selfless and pure.[98] It is an illiberal trap into which radical egalitarians, in part because of their strong antipathy toward self-interest as a motive for action, are particularly prone to fall.

For abolitionists, Brown was an ideal leader because his selflessness and authenticity enabled him to act in the political world without becoming corrupted or compromised by it. His utterances were "perfect words," his soul clean and pure, his actions the embodiment of principle.[99] Thoreau, although never a member of an organized antislavery group, gave expression to the abolitionists' view of Brown when he described him as a man without artifice, a man who "had no need to invent anything but to tell the simple truth."[100] When Brown insisted that certain "Border Ruffians" had "a perfect right to be hung," Thoreau explained that Brown was "not in the least a rhetorician, was not talking to

Buncombe or his constituents anywhere."[101] Unlike mere politicians who might cynically use such rhetoric to inflame the masses, Brown gave voice to the simple truth that emanated from a spotless soul. Brown, the charismatic who knew no law but his own conscience, was the abolitionists' ideal political leader. Throughout the war, as we have already seen, abolitionists sought out political leaders with the same clarity of purpose that might make violence righteous.

Not all abolitionists, however, were so ready to canonize Brown or to justify any means in the service of a righteous end. Adin Ballou, founder of the Hopedale utopian community, was one radical egalitarian whose commitment to nonviolence remained unshaken by Brown's daring raid. Ballou believed that Brown, far from being a Christlike saint, was nothing more than "a well-meaning, misguided, unfortunate zealot." Brown's raid left Ballou "unmoved, except by sorrow for such a deplorable exhibition of mistaken ambition to promote a good end by evil means, and pity for the sufferer who had rashly plunged into a lion's den."[102] Ballou rejected the idea that personal sincerity could make an action right. Brown, Ballou allowed, was "an honest milito-religious zealot, who verily believes himself commissioned of God to pray and fight for the liberation of the slaves."[103] But his sincere enthusiasm did not make his actions right, let alone Christlike.

But Ballou's cautions had little or no effect on the great majority of abolitionists who by this time had become thoroughly captivated by the possibilities of righteous violence. After Brown's raid on Harpers Ferry, notes Friedman, "the notion of righteous violence had become common currency among most immediatists." In canonizing Brown as a holy warrior, most abolitionists did not believe, or at least admit, that they were abandoning their earlier belief in moral suasion and nonviolence. Rather, they persuaded themselves, as Friedman explains, that "when violence was patently righteous, it was consonant with the saintly peace principles of the 1830s."[104] Purity and violence were compatible so long as the violence was inspired by righteous authenticity.

Putting Cruelty First

In *Ordinary Vices* Judith Shklar argues for a politics and political theory that puts "cruelty first," that is, that makes cruelty the most hated of all vices. The "liberalism of fear," as Shklar tags it, is grounded in an appreciation that cruelty is the *summum malum*, the worst thing that human beings can inflict upon one another. The freedom that this sober, skeptical brand of liberalism seeks to secure, Shklar tells us, is "freedom from the abuse of power and intimidation of the defenseless."[105]

The reader may reasonably ask whether the abolitionists did not in fact put cruelty first in a way that few of their contemporaries did. As Elizabeth Clark has recently emphasized, the abolitionists' opposition to slavery was deeply grounded in the humanitarian aversion to pain and cruelty. Abolitionists were leaders in the growing opposition to corporal as well as capital punishment. Abolitionists, Clark argues, extended the standard eighteenth-century liberal critique of excessive state power "to 'private' status relations, including the master-slave, husband-wife, and parent-child pairings." By drawing attention to the personalized violence and cruelty of slavery and in claiming the slaves' right to bodily integrity and autonomy — particularly freedom of movement, the right to marry, the right to refuse sexual relations, and the right to be free of physical abuse — abolitionists played a key role in furthering "the idea that to be free of physical coercion and deliberately inflicted pain was an essential human right."[106]

And yet for all this, radical abolitionists were themselves poor exemplars of Shklar's liberalism of fear, nor can they be said to have consistently put cruelty first. Radical abolitionists, particularly Garrison's Boston clique, tended instead to make hypocrisy the worst of all vices,[107] as is evidenced by their embrace of the doctrine of "disunionism" in the early 1840s. "No Union with Slaveholders" was the slogan; the idea was that the North should secede from the South. Secession would, of course, have left southern slavery untouched while enabling northern abolitionists to cleanse their hands of its sin. The cruelty of slavery would persist unabated, but abolitionists would cease to compromise their purity.

Abolitionists did, as Clark says, try to rouse an apathetic northern populace by highlighting the cruelty of slavery, but the rhetoric of Garrison, Phillips, and other radical abolitionists was generally far more preoccupied with decrying the self-deception, insincerity, and inauthenticity of the North, particularly its leaders. They had withering scorn for those hypocrites who claimed to think slavery was morally wrong and yet still opposed abolition. Hence Garrison's scathing denunciations of the Liberty and Free Soil parties for duping citizens into casting ballots that would only implicate them in the system's corruption.[108] Hence Phillips's vicious attacks upon the Republican Lincoln as a "slave hound," a "huckster," a "spaniel by nature," and a "first rate second rate man."[109] They would unmask their opponents and reveal their villainy.

The radical abolitionists' response to John Brown and General Benjamin Butler also attests to the primacy of hypocrisy within radical abolitionist political thought. Brown was canonized by abolitionists precisely because he embodied the idea of putting hypocrisy first. Brown's moral zeal and uprightness exposed the hypocrisy of the shuffling and timid compromises made by politicians. Brown's own acts of cruelty were forgiven, excused, or denied on account of his authenticity and candor.

Putting cruelty first commits one to rejecting arbitrary authority unconstrained by law.[110] Yet it was exactly the arbitrary, extralegal quality of Brown's act that so inspired the abolitionists' imagination. Virginia was a pirate ship, Wendell Phillips said, and "John Brown sails the sea a Lord High Admiral of the Almighty, with his commission to sink every pirate he meets on God's ocean of the nineteenth century."[111] Since Brown was not an arm of the state, the significance of abolitionists' reaction to Brown can perhaps be dismissed. After all, Shklar herself identifies the liberalism of fear primarily with the avoidance of arbitrary, coercive *state* power. The reaction among radical abolitionists to Butler, however, cannot be so easily dismissed. For Butler's arbitrary rule in New Orleans was precisely the sort of state-sanctioned inducement of fear that Shklar is so concerned to avoid. That many prominent radical abolitionists, most especially Phillips, applauded Butler's high-handed reign suggests how far they were from putting cruelty first.

Radical abolitionists' inability to put cruelty first stemmed in large part from having constructed a bipolar world divided between absolute evil on the one side and pure goodness on the other. As Shklar herself notes, "There is no escape from this Manichaean situation: either for us or against us. And in such struggles everything is permitted." The choice of which side one is on takes precedence over whether or not one judges a particular action to be cruel. Putting cruelty first, as Shklar explains, requires us to refuse "to accept those ideological distortions that make it easy to become zealously cruel."[112] This Phillips and many other radical abolitionists often failed to do.

In the end, radical abolitionism's utopian zeal outstripped its liberalism. Liberalism properly fears governmental power, but a liberalism of fear, as Shklar conceives it, "does not dream of an end of public, coercive government."[113] This, however, was precisely the radical abolitionists' animating dream: "this sublime doctrine of acknowlegeing [*sic*] no government but Gods [*sic*], of loosing myself from all dominion of man both civil and ecclesiastical," as Sarah Grimké described it.[114] Opposed to institutionalized authority of virtually any kind, radical abolitionists often found themselves drawn toward arbitrary or charismatic leaders who disregarded legal or institutional restraints, restraints that are essential to ensure the sort of limited and predictable government that is the foundation stone of liberal democracy. Dreaming of a utopian future helped justify illiberalism in the present.

Illiberal Utopianism
in the Age of Reform

The thing in man which makes him
cruel to a slave is in him *permanently* and
will not be rooted out in a million years.

   Mark Twain[1]

Our ideals and aspirations must be cut close
enough to the pattern of the actual to give hope
the aspect of the possible. Without noble ambitions,
we are yoked to the present as bequeathed to us by a
burdensome and deterministic past; yet with a too exalted
ambition, we are bound to be disappointed, and, what is
worse, in political terms, we are likely to transform our
impatience and frustration into a dictatorship in the
name of the good. . . . Bad as we are, we cannot
afford aims too very much better than we are.

   Benjamin Barber[2]

"The Left," the Polish philosopher Leszek Kolakowski once wrote,
"gives forth utopias just as the pancreas discharges insulin." Utopias, in
Kolakowski's judgment, are something the egalitarian left cannot do
without. Nor did Kolakowski feel that this was something egalitarians
should apologize for. To seek radical or transformative changes in society is, almost by definition, to seek changes that are not "realistic" in the
short term. "Goals unattainable now will never be reached unless they
are articulated when they are still unattainable."[3] To ask egalitarians to
renounce utopia is not just to ask them to give up on fundamental change
but virtually to renounce the egalitarian vision itself.

   Egalitarians may not need to defend themselves against the charge
of utopianism in the sense of unattainable goals (so long, Kolakowski

cautions, as the goal does not "prove so remote from reality that the wish to enforce it would be grotesque" and threaten freedom[4]) but they certainly do need, as Kolakowski emphasizes in a later essay, to concern themselves with utopianism as a vision of the perfectly unified society.[5] High hopes are one thing, the final solution quite another. Utopian visionaries can expand our imaginative horizons, but in seeking the abolition of human conflict (whether between values, groups, interests, or individuals) they seek the end of freedom.[6] Freedom means conflict. Suppressing freedom in the name of unity (or equality) does not eliminate the inevitable conflict of interests or values; it only stifles the legitimate expression of those conflicts, driving them underground, where they can silently fester or savagely erupt.

Dreams of a unity that will dissolve all jarring conflicts are, of course, not unique to the egalitarian left. The hierarchical right, too, has at times been animated by a desire to eradicate conflicts of interest in the name of an organic unity. The promise of science and technology has induced more than a few individuals, liberals very much included, to attempt to transform questions of values, where disagreement is unavoidable, into questions of fact, where correct answers may be found. But if egalitarians are not uniquely vulnerable to the lure of unity, their distrust of conflict and competition, together with their belief in the untapped possibilities of a transformed human nature, renders them particularly susceptible to utopian visions of perfect unity.

Looking Backward to the Future

The first great wave of utopianism washed over the United States in the 1830s and 1840s; the second great wave came in the 1890s, spurred in large part by the publication in 1888 of Edward Bellamy's utopian novel, *Looking Backward*. Over the ensuing decade, *Looking Backward* sold almost half a million copies and powerfully influenced an entire generation of Populist and Progressive reformers.[7] Arguably, no book had a greater impact on those decades that Hofstadter termed "the age of reform," roughly 1890 until the beginning of World War I.[8] Yet oddly, Bellamy is mentioned only once and then merely in passing in Hofstadter's book-length analysis of illiberal reform thought in the Populist and Progressive era.[9] This is a striking omission, for the coexistence of illiberalism and the reform impulse is nowhere more evident than in the pages of Bellamy's *Looking Backward*.

Why does Hofstadter ignore *Looking Backward*, a book of such tower-ing importance to Hofstadter's "age of reform"? Perhaps it is because Bellamy did not readily fit Hofstadter's portrait of the illiberal Populist-Progressive mind, which Hofstadter characterized as antimodern and plagued with resentments against foreigners, intellectuals, and an east-ern seaboard elite. *Looking Backward*, ironically, is not backward-looking. It does not try to recapture a lost agrarian arcadia but to wipe out the shackles of the past.[10] Far from fearing the industrial future, Bellamy's utopian novel portrays technological innovation and industrial consoli-dation as the solution to the ills of modern capitalism. *Looking Backward* has little or nothing in common with the "cranky pseudo-conservatism" of the radical right that so worried Hofstadter,[11] but it does very much foreshadow authoritarian state socialism, even, in some ways, Soviet-style totalitarianism.

The basic plot of *Looking Backward* is easily summarized. Julian West, a well-to-do Bostonian, falls into a hypnotically induced sleep in 1887. He awakens in the year 2000 to find that all of the social problems that had beset late-nineteenth-century America have been solved. Society has peacefully transformed itself from a selfish and anarchic capitalist order to a peaceful and orderly egalitarian society based on cooperation. In this egalitarian utopia, the state owns all property except personal posses-sions, and each citizen receives an equal stipend from the state, no mat-ter the difficulty of the job.[12] State ownership of property dissolves the conflict between worker and capitalist, and equal remuneration abolishes class distinctions. West's guides to this new world are the kindly Dr. Leete and his daughter, Edith.

In a postscript to the novel, Bellamy made it clear that "although in form a fanciful romance," the story was intended "in all seriousness, as a forecast, in accordance with the principles of evolution, of the next stage in the industrial and social development of humanity." Bellamy believed he had divined the laws that governed historical development, and that industrial consolidation, as he has Dr. Leete explain, "only needed to complete its logical evolution to open a golden future to humanity." Un-like Marx, who saw violent revolutionary struggle as the midwife to historical progress, Bellamy envisioned a peaceful unfolding of ineluc-table laws. Bellamy shared with Marx, though, an unshakable conviction that before long history would come to a happy, egalitarian ending in which harmonious cooperation would reign. "The dawn of the new era," Bellamy predicted in his postscript, "is already near at hand. . . . Our children will surely see [the Golden Age], and we, too, who are already men and women, if we deserve it by our faith and by our works."[13]

Bellamy's aim in *Looking Backward*, as Daniel Borus points out, is to create a world in which the principles of solidarity and equality are fully realized.[14] For Bellamy, the two principles are essential halves of a single egalitarian fruit. "Until . . . equality of condition had come to pass," Dr. Leete explains to Julian West, "the idea of the solidarity of human-ity, the brotherhood of all men, could never have become the real con-viction and practical principle of action it is nowadays." Inequality, Leete informs us, is the cause of virtually all crimes and even lying. When people are made social equals and no longer can hope to gain more than another, falsehood vanishes. Even the few criminals who do still exist will almost always admit their guilt.[15] Equality of resources joined with col-lective solidarity makes possible the transformation of human behavior upon which the utopian vision depends.

In the egalitarian utopia created by Bellamy, all contradictions and even tensions have vanished.[16] Men live together as "brethren dwelling in unity, without strife or envying." Problems have been solved once and for all. When Julian asks Dr. Leete how they had managed to settle the labor problem, the good doctor informs his time-traveling guest that "The moment the nation assumed the responsibilities of capital those difficulties vanished. . . . The national organization of labor under one direction was the *complete solution* of what was, in your day and under your system, justly regarded as the insoluble labor problem." A solution, Dr. Leete tells Julian at another point, "which leaves an unaccounted-for residuum is no solution at all." Having definitively solved every prob-lem, Leete tells Julian that they no longer have any need for parties or politicians.[17]

In the year 2000, state legislatures have withered away and a national Congress meets only once every five years. Asked by Julian how the na-tion legislates without state legislatures and with a Congress rarely in ses-sion, Dr. Leete responds that they no longer have much need for legis-lation: "If you will consider a moment, Mr. West, you will see that we have nothing to make laws about. The fundamental principles on which our society is founded settle for all time the strifes and misunderstand-ings which in your day called for legislation."[18] In place of politicians and representative legislatures is the "industrial army," headed by a general-in-chief who also acts as president of the United States. Only retired members of the industrial army are permitted to vote for the president and for the other high-ranking "generals" immediately beneath him, because only those members of society who are no longer in the workforce will have "absolute impartiality . . . and complete absence of self-interest."[19] The political expression of group or individual interests is not permitted in Bellamy's utopia.

The important decisions in the Boston of the future are fundamentally technical in nature and so are best left to the administrative experts who run the industrial army. State or local governments have no place because they would only interfere "with the control and discipline of the industrial army, which, of course, [is] required to be central and uniform." The central administrators envisioned by Bellamy are assumed to possess omniscient knowledge. Knowledge is not something that needs to be discovered; it need only be applied to specific factual questions. The further removed one is from the particular or local situation, moreover, the more omniscient and impartial one's knowledge. "It is easier for a general up in a balloon, with perfect survey of the field, to maneuver a million men to victory than for a sergeant to manage a platoon in a thicket."[20]

The state that Dr. Leete describes has been invested with complete control over the economy. All of industry and commerce have been handed over to the state. The state has become "the sole employer" and unilaterally establishes the conditions of labor.[21] Moreover, the state "provide[s] for *all* [the citizen's] physical and mental needs."[22] From a twentieth-century perspective, it is clear that a state vested with such absolute power over the working lives of its citizens would quickly degenerate into a totalitarian regime.

Yet even as Dr. Leete describes the extraordinary powers to be vested in a centralized state, he insists that the state in the year 2000 has all but withered away.[23] It is a state without jails, military, or tax collectors. The only governmental functions that have been retained from 1887 are the judiciary and the police system, but even here the virtual "absence of crime and temptation to it" means that the number and duties of police officers and judges are kept to a bare minimum.[24] "There is far less interference of any sort with personal liberty nowadays than you were accustomed to," Dr. Leete assures Julian. With the exception of the fundamental law that "every man shall serve the nation for a fixed period," explains Dr. Leete, "our system depends in no particular upon legislation, but is entirely voluntary, the logical outcome of the operation of human nature under rational conditions."[25] In Orwellian fashion,

Bellamy thus ushers in a highly centralized, authoritarian state cloaked in the alluring dress of voluntary cooperation and egalitarian fellowship.

Dr. Leete's "favorite figure" to illustrate the difference between what he describes as the nineteenth century's "age of individualism" and "[the age] of concert" that characterizes life in the year 2000 is the umbrella. In the old days, when "everybody lived for himself and his family, . . . the people of Boston put up three hundred thousand umbrellas over as many heads." In contrast, Leete proudly explains, Bostonians today "put up one umbrella over all the heads."[26] The state thus makes everybody equal in an efficient, orderly manner. In human individuality Bellamy sees only mess and disorder; diversity becomes a form of inequality; and individual choice (what about those misguided souls who *want* to walk — or even sing — in the rain?) is subordinated to state purposes.

If individuality is subordinated by Bellamy, competition and conflict are appreciated even less. In the Boston of 2000, society no longer has a need for lawyers and the adversarial system of justice of which they were a part. Since "the only interest of the nation is to find out the truth," it would make no sense, Dr. Leete explains, to allow those with partial interests to be represented. The accused criminal is thus allowed no advocate. Nor does the system need the check of a jury system, since "no conceivable motive but justice could actuate our judges."[27] Having assumed disinterested altruism on the part of state officials, the checks on state power provided by political competition and conflict become unnecessary and wasteful.

Limitations on state power are also unnecessary because the state is assumed to be nothing more than the expression of a unified, harmonious, popular will. Because the people share the same fundamental interests and views, there is no need to fear a state oppressing one group and favoring another. Those few individuals who do not abide by the rules are regarded as atavistic deviants who are hospitalized if they commit a crime or placed in solitary confinement if they refuse to work as the state dictates (in his follow-up novel, *Equality*, citizens who refuse to cooperate are put on "reservations").[28] The refractory citizens of Boston are treated as sick or insane, just as the Soviet Union treated its own dissidents.

Bellamy's authoritarian — even totalitarian — tendencies are rooted in his hunger for solidarity. In *The Religion of Solidarity*, a statement of personal philosophy written several years before *Looking Backward*,[29] Bellamy counterposed two elements in human nature: solidarity and personality. Solidarity is "the sense of the sublime, of the grand, or whatever may be called the instinct of infinity"; personality, on the other hand, is "the desire of being circumscribed, shut in, and bounded." For Bellamy, "individuality, personality, partiality, is segregation, is partition, is confinement, in fine a prison." True freedom becomes possible only by "losing our personal identity" and becoming "conscious of our other, our universal identity, the identity of a universal solidarity." Individuality, Bellamy continues, "is of so little importance, of such trifling scope, that it should matter little to us what renunciations of its things we make."[30]

In *Looking Backward*, the state is the embodiment of universal solidarity. In subordinating oneself to the state, one is thus realizing one's higher nature, a truer, expansive conception of freedom that is not confined or imprisoned by individuality. As Isaiah Berlin warns, this sort of doctrine leads predictably if not directly to a nightmarish world in which coercion is called freedom and state power is unlimited.[31]

The authoritarian, illiberal soul of *Looking Backward* has been brilliantly dissected by Arthur Lipow in *Authoritarian Socialism in America: Edward Bellamy and the Nationalist Movement* (1982). Lipow persuasively argues that Bellamy betrayed "a deep-going revulsion against individualism in all its forms — not merely against the asocial, egotistical 'individualism' apotheosized by the Spencerians, but against the entire liberal-humanist and democratic tradition as well."[32] But Lipow missteps in trying, at least at times,[33] to root Bellamy's *Looking Backward* in "the entire tradition of conservative political thought."[34] That Bellamy's vision was undemocratic is clear enough, but that does not make him a conservative unless we are to make this true by definition. Bellamy arrives at authoritarian conclusions not by beginning with conservative or hierarchical premises but by striving to realize egalitarian ends. Conservatism has many sins, but it should not be asked to bear the blame for the nightmarish qualities of Bellamy's egalitarian utopia.

Lipow's own analysis makes it clear just how central egalitarianism is to Bellamy's vision. In lectures delivered over a decade before writing *Looking Backward*, Bellamy insisted that "there is . . . enough in the world to support all in abundance if it were equally divided." Justice, Bellamy continued, demands that "the burdens of life as well as the pleasures of life [be] apportioned equally among all."[35] Writing several years after the publication of *Looking Backward*, Bellamy explained what he meant in describing himself as a "New Nationalist." New Nationalists were "socialists who, holding all that socialists agree on, go further, and hold also that the distribution of the cooperative product among the members of the community must be not merely equitable, whatever that term may mean, but must be always and absolutely equal."[36] And in *Looking Backward* itself, all citizens receive exactly equal shares of the national wealth, as they also do in *Equality*.[37]

Bellamy's vision of social order shows no sympathy for the hierarchical gradations in society so dear to late-nineteenth-century conservatives. Indeed, Bellamy explicitly welcomes "the democratic and cosmopolitan movement of modern times" because it "destroys . . . castes and traditional corporations of all sorts." Nor does Bellamy show admiration for the patriarchal familial relations that conservatives typically revere. In fact, in an unpublished outline for "A Reorganization of Society to Extinguish Sorrow," Bellamy proposed essentially abolishing the family. "Parental love," he explained, "is but an effete survival, an aching root of a tooth no longer useful." With society arranged in such a way that it can "provide for [children's welfare] better than the parents possibly could," familial bonds or relationships were no longer useful. In Bellamy's plan, parents would have no intimate relations with their children (except that mothers would still nurse them), and the children's "education and corrections," their "care and maintenance," would be determined and carried out solely by the state.[38] For Bellamy, these intermediary institutions, so dear to conservatives, created partial interests and attachments that impeded identification with the egalitarian whole.

Another telltale sign of Bellamy's egalitarian commitment is the premium he places on authenticity. Adherents of conservative, hierarchical cultures believe that people from different ranks or orders of society should respect the many rules and constraints that govern interactions between different social or political gradations. Guarded feelings are valued. Letting it all hang out would be considered bad form, if not scandalous. In Bellamy's utopian world, though, "artificiality" has been banished. Conversations in the new world, Julian West finds, are marked by "ingenuous sincerity and frankness." Love, too, is "unfretted by artificial barriers created by differences of station or possessions."[39] The egalitarian ideal of authenticity is even more vividly realized in Bellamy's short story "To Whom This May Come," in which the inhabitants of a South Sea island have lost the power of speech but can "communicate perfectly with each other because they can fully read each other's minds. With no secrets, unable to conceal their selfishness, the new society is a totally harmonious one."[40]

If Lipow fails to persuade that Bellamy's political thought is best understood as part of a conservative political tradition, he is on firmer ground when he draws our attention, following Hal Draper, to the "two souls of socialism." For Lipow and Draper, one soul of socialism is bottom-up and democratic, while the other is top-down and authoritarian.[41] The distinction is helpful as a starting place, although allowing for only two souls, one consistently good and the other consistently bad, oversimplifies. Moreover, associating Marx exclusively with the democratic soul, as both Draper and Lipow do, is untenable in view of Marx's embrace of the "dictatorship of the proletariat."[42] The "two souls" idea does, however, help us see that egalitarianism has more than one face; egalitarianism, as I have emphasized already, need not be authoritarian or illiberal (the same, of course, can be said for conservatism).

The illiberalism of Bellamy's egalitarian vision stems in part from Bellamy's tendency to make community abstract and general rather than concrete and local. Egalitarianism is at its most democratic where its commitment to fraternity and solidarity remains fixed on local, small-scale groups or collectivities. The cooperative commonwealth, as Henry Demarest Lloyd explained, "can be made to succeed . . . only by uniting small groups of men engaged in something that brings them together into personal contact daily, so that they know each other and each knows what the other is doing."[43] In attaching the fraternal impulse to abstract, distant entities like the "brotherhood of man" and the "national family,"[44] Bellamy invites unchecked state coercion. For while harmony is difficult to achieve within a family or small group, it is impossible to realize in an entire nation. If a harmony of views is to be achieved at the level of the nation-state, it must be through suppression of dissenting opinions and interests.[45] The "religion of the collective will," as Max Eastman once described it, is a totalitarian temptation for adherents of egalitarianism, a temptation that can be resisted by insisting on the value of local knowledge and democratic politics in face-to-face communities.[46]

Alternatively, egalitarian adherents can avoid the illiberal seduction by elevating individuality and equality over fraternity and community. Eastman had this sort of distinction in mind when he contrasted "libertarian" socialists like himself, who "have not the glimmer of a desire to lose [their] identity in a collection," with those socialists whose "fraternal or gregarious impulse renders [them] tolerant of totalitarianism."[47] Similar in certain respects is Judith Shklar's idea of "negative egalitarianism," which focuses on the inequalities and abuses of political power that stem from gross inequalities in economic wealth.[48] Both Eastman's libertarian socialism and Shklar's negative egalitarianism move egalitarianism away from an emphasis on fraternity and harmony and toward a more open and conflictual politics.

Egalitarianism, then, has liberal as well as illiberal faces, but our best chance to nurture the liberal and democratic side of egalitarianism is to specify more precisely the relationship between egalitarianism and illiberalism. It will not do, as Lipow shows, to treat Bellamy uncritically as a "man of good hope" or his ideas as an expression of "socialist humanism"[49] and to all but ignore the authoritarianism of his political thought. Nor will it do to accept that "Bellamy's limitations belong to his time [while his emancipatory] vision far transcends it and has much to say to ours."[50] Bellamy was certainly a creature of his times, but his illiberalism is more than a historical curiosity and cannot be so neatly separated from his egalitarian commitments. Egalitarianism cannot be strengthened by ignoring the illiberal tendencies that have so often accompanied egalitarian commitments; those who seek a brighter egalitarian future must instead become more self-conscious about the limitations contained *within* the emancipatory vision.

Utopia and Human Nature

Among those enduring limitations must be counted egalitarianism's sunny view of human nature. Human beings are naturally good, egalitarians typically believe, but are corrupted by bad institutions.[51] Remake the institutions and we can reshape human nature. This strongly optimistic view of human nature and human potentiality is the motor that drives the utopian impulse of egalitarians. Without the optimistic conception of human nature, the emancipatory vision collapses.

In moderation, there are obvious virtues to the egalitarian view of human nature. To begin with, such a conception sensitizes us to the ways in which institutions shape incentives and behavior. How one structures the system does shape the ways that human beings act. Moreover, a belief in human plasticity is a good antidote to fatalistic resignation. The presumption that it is possible to change people prevents fatalistic appeals from taking root. However, this optimistic conception of human nature, when carried to extremes, as it frequently is in egalitarian utopianism, has serious pitfalls.

Bellamy's views, at first sight, might not appear to support this characterization of the egalitarian construction of human nature. After all,

Dr. Leete explicitly disavows the notion that his egalitarian utopia rests on a transformed human nature. But as Dr. Leete continues, it becomes clear that he means not to deny that people have changed but rather to insist that institutional change preceded and indeed caused the change in human nature. "The conditions of human life have changed," Dr. Leete explains, "and with them the motives of human action." For Bellamy the altruistic and selfish impulses coexist, but in Boston in the year 2000, institutions have been designed in such a way that the selfish side of human nature has all but atrophied.[52]

The transformation of human nature envisioned by Bellamy becomes evident in the lengthy sermon given by the Reverend Barton toward the end of *Looking Backward*. "Human nature in its essential qualities," Barton explains, "is good, not bad. . . . Men by their natural intention and structure are generous, not selfish, pitiful, not cruel, sympathetic, not arrogant, godlike in aspirations, instinct with divinest impulses of tenderness and self-sacrifice, images of God indeed." Under the old capitalist system, the conditions of life had operated as "a forcing process to develop the brutal qualities of human nature." Selfishness reigned among men because the capitalist system nurtured — indeed demanded — such behavior. Having transformed the system, "it was for the first time possible to see what *unperverted* human nature really was like." Human nature may not have changed, but under the new system all "the depraved tendencies . . . now withered like cellar fungi in the open air, and the nobler qualities showed a sudden luxuriance."[53]

A sympathetic French reviewer of *Looking Backward* found Bellamy's vision "an enchanting 'dream,' but observed that 'unless man's heart be entirely transformed' the dream would remain only a dream."[54] Yet this is not entirely right. The truth is more troubling still. For without the expected transformation in human nature, the dream must become a nightmare. The conception of a redeemed human nature is vital to the egalitarian utopia precisely because in the absence of such change it is impossible to envision a noncoercive utopia. When Dr. Leete insists that "our system depends in no particular upon legislation, but is entirely voluntary," this is then followed in the second half of the sentence by his assurance that this was "the logical outcome of the operation of human nature under rational conditions."[55] If such a transformation in human nature is impossible, then the utopia of perfect harmony can be realized only through a despotic state.

To make altruism not just a noble human motive but *the* motive responsible for running the system may be an idle dream, but more troubling is that it invites unchecked state coercion. At one point a skeptical Julian West asks Dr. Leete what could possibly motivate the labor force to work if everyone received the same amount of money. The doctor answers that "service of the nation, patriotism, passion for humanity, impel the worker as in your day they did the soldier."[56] But of course it is largely state coercion, not love of humanity, that impels the soldier in our day as in Bellamy's. Lurking menacingly behind the voluntary cooperation envisioned by Bellamy is the heavy, unrestrained hand of the state.

The flip side of a redeemed humanity in the future is a corrupted humanity in the present. Believing that capitalism degrades human nature, thwarting humanity's authentic or potential goodness, egalitarians can be tempted to disregard existing preferences, regarding them not as choices freely made but as a reflexive product of a corrupting system. Those who disagree can be dismissed as having been "warped" by "false conditions."[57] Enveloped by false consciousness, people must be made to realize their true or higher natures; they must be forced to be free. Believing that human nature can be changed for the better, egalitarian utopians are tempted to try to remake people in their image, which inevitably means in the image of the state. Here the utopian reform impulse, as Lipow observes, converges with totalitarianism.[58]

The glorious thought of what might be torments the utopian imagination and fuels a loathing of current institutions for perverting natural human goodness. Dreams of human perfectibility are more than just an uplifting vision leading us all to work for a better world; such dreams can also provide reasons to hate the world as it is. Measuring existing institutions against a utopian yardstick can as easily lead to alienation and violent fantasies as it can to constructive reform. The close connection between utopianism and alienated fantasies of violence is nowhere clearer than in Ignatius Donnelly's *Caesar's Column* (1890), a utopian novel that rivaled *Looking Backward* in popularity during the first half of the last decade of the nineteenth century.

The Apocalyptic Vision of Ignatius Donnelly

Ignatius Donnelly was no idle dreamer or scribbler. He was prominently involved in virtually every reform movement in the state of Minnesota during the last third of the nineteenth century. By the late 1880s he had become widely recognized as Minnesota's leading agrarian spokesman. In December 1890, aided by the enthusiastic reception of *Caesar's Column*, he was overwhelmingly elected president of the State Farmers' Alliance of Minnesota. Publication of *Caesar's Column* immediately catapulted Donnelly into a position of national prominence, a position he solidified by authoring the famous preamble to the Populist party's "Omaha Platform" of 1892 and serving as one of the Populist party's most effective orators.[59]

Caesar's Column is the harrowing story of the violent destruction of civilization in the last years of the twentieth century. When the protagonist, Gabriel Weltstein, comes from Africa to visit New York City, he is initially overwhelmed by the affluence and technological wonders of "the great city." But he soon finds, as his host Maximilian tells him, that the "gorgeous shell" disguises a rotten core that is "full of dead men's bones and all uncleanness." Beneath the gleaming surface of "the upper deck of society," he discovers the "dark and stuffy depths of the hold of the great vessel, where the sweating gnomes, in the glare of the furnace-heat, furnish the power which drives the mighty ship resplendent." Almost three-quarters of humanity live in this hellish "Under-World."[60] The downtrodden are kept in this state of abject misery by a brutal plutocracy that ruthlessly exploits the masses through physical terror. The masses have become so degraded by their exploitation that their only thought is bloody revenge and destruction. In gruesome detail, Donnelly paints the violent end that awaits civilization. The plundering plutocracy are eventually overthrown and exterminated, but the mob then turns on its own leaders, devouring them in a violent frenzy that results in the annihilation of civilization.

The grim, desperate horrors of *Caesar's Column* seem worlds apart from the splendid utopia of *Looking Backward*, but they are only different sides of the same coin. Bellamy forecasts the utopia that is possible if we transform our lives with each other; Donnelly forecasts the hell that awaits us if we fail to transform our lives. For both authors, it is the inequalities and atomization created by the capitalist system that are the source of civilization's problems, and for both, redemption in the future lies in solidarity and equality.

Despite the horrible degradation and violence of *Caesar's Column*, Donnelly fully shares Bellamy's view of human nature as naturally good, even sublime. "Mankind," the novel's protagonist insists, is in itself so noble, so beautiful, so full of all graces and capacities; with aspirations fitted to sing among the angels; with comprehension fitted to embrace the universe! Consider the exquisite, lithe-limbed figures of the first man and woman, as they stood forth against the red light of their first sunset — fresh from the hand of the Mighty One — His graceful, perfected, magnificent thoughts! What love shines out of their great eyes; what goodness, like dawn-awakened flowers, is blooming in their singing hearts!

Capitalist society has turned these potential angels into brutes by having, "generation after generation, . . . carefully nursed . . . the little seed of weakness or wickedness." It is the stark contrast between the divine world that could be and the inegalitarian "hell of injustice" that exists which fires Donnelly's moral imagination. Donnelly's optimistic judgment of what humans are capable of, if we can only release "the angel that dwells in human nature," fuels his excoriation of existing institutions and conditions.[61]

Donnelly seemed to hope that by painting an imaginary future in the most gruesome, apocalyptic hues it would spur reform efforts. People would wake up and realize that they needed to act now if they were to avert the doom he forecast. But within the novel itself the terrible conditions he describes have the opposite effect of justifying virtually any action that would contribute to bringing down this inhumane system. The workers' life, as Donnelly envisions it in the future, is

> Toil, toil, toil, from early morn until late at night; then home they swarm; tumble into their wretched beds; snatch a few hours of disturbed sleep, battling with vermin, in a polluted atmosphere; and then up again and to work; and so on, and on, in endless, mirthless, hopeless round; until, in a few years, consumed with disease, mere rotten masses of painful wretchedness, they die, and are wheeled off to the great furnaces, and their bodies are eaten up by the flames, even as their lives have been eaten up by society.

What action, no matter how brutal, would not be justified if it were to help bring an end to this living hell and liberate an "enslaved America"?[62]

This is the philosophy that animates the secret "Brotherhood" that has organized itself for the purpose of overthrowing the plutocracy. Gabriel gives voice to Donnelly's own fears of violent revolutionary action, pleading with the Brotherhood "to stay their hands, to seek not to destroy, but to reform." He reminds them of "the glories of civilization" that would be lost, and laments that the people's "hard fortunes have driven out of their minds all illusions, all imagination, all poetry." In Gabriel's view, the Brotherhood, while clearly on the side of justice, would be incapable of anything beyond destruction. "Who can believe that these poor brutalized men will be capable, armed to the teeth with deadly weapons, and full of passions, hates and revenges, to recreate the slaughtered society?" He trembles at his premonitions of the coming bloodshed: "I could hear the volcanic explosions; I could see the sordid flood of wrath and hunger pouring through these halls; cataracts of misery bursting through every door and window, and sweeping away all this splendor into never-ending blackness and ruin. . . . A hell of injustice, ending in a holocaust of slaughter."[63]

As Gabriel realizes the black depths of the oligarchy's perfidy, however, he becomes more sympathetic to the Brotherhood's purposes. Although still repelled by their violent plans, Gabriel finds himself increasingly attracted to the overwhelming righteousness of their cause. "The rude and begrimed insurgents . . . are the avengers of time — the God-sent — the righters of the world's wrongs — the punishers of the ineffably wicked." After overhearing the ruling oligarchy's terrible plans of destruction, Gabriel chooses to ally himself with Maximilian's "terrible Brotherhood," although still not approving of it. Gabriel decides that "the Plutocrats should no longer cumber the earth with their presence. Men who can cooly plot, amid laughter, the death of ten million human beings, for the purpose of preserving their ill-gotten wealth and their ill-used power, should be exterminated from the face of the planet as enemies of mankind — as poisonous snakes — vermin." Gabriel is still appalled by what Maximilian describes as the "Brotherhood of Destruction," but he becomes enthusiastic about a possible alternative, a "worldwide Brotherhood of Justice," which would make justice "the sole dogma of our society." The goal of this brotherhood, Gabriel explains to a gathering of workingmen, would be to "combine the good . . . against the wicked. It should take one wrong after another, concentrate the battle of the world upon them, and wipe them out of existence. . . . It is not enough to heal the wounds caused by the talons of the wild beasts of injustice; it should pursue them to their bone-huddled dens and slay them." There is "no power in the world," Gabriel insists, that is "too great or too sacred to be used by Goodness for the suppression of Evil." Neither mercy, forgiveness, nor fallibility has any place in Gabriel's brotherhood. Thus while he can still recoil at the total destruction promised by the "Brotherhood of Destruction," one wonders whether the holy crusade against evil envisioned by Gabriel would turn out much better.[64]

My point is not that violence against a plutocracy as evil as the one Donnelly describes is unjustified. On the contrary, such violence clearly can be justified. The point instead is that Donnelly creates a situation so desperate and an oligarchical leadership so evil that the argument for tolerance and democracy and against bloodshed and revolutionary conspiracy necessarily must fail. Conjuring up a purely evil ruling class and a "whole world [that] was corrupt to the very core"[65] makes it possible, if not necessary, to welcome the apocalypse, to justify vengeance in the name of justice. If Donnelly confined these apocalyptic fantasies of a hopelessly corrupt world and a conspiratorial elite to a far-off future, this vision might be of little consequence. But, in fact, Donnelly himself blurs the distinction between the imagined future and the lived present.

In a note to the reader at the beginning of *Caesar's Column*, Donnelly denies that the future he envisions is fantastic. "It is conceded," Donnelly notes, "that [today] life is a dark and wretched failure for the great mass of mankind. The many are plundered to enrich the few." For Donnelly, the problems of civilization are like a hidden cancer that "should be cut out while there is yet time." Any other course, he says, quoting Hamlet, "Will but skin and film the ulcerous place, / While rank corruption, mining all beneath, / Infects unseen."[66] In his preamble to the Omaha Platform of 1892, moreover, Donnelly decried the "vast conspiracy against mankind [that] has been organized on two continents, and is rapidly taking possession of the world." He warned that "the fruits of the toil of millions are boldly stolen to build up colossal fortunes for a few." The world was divided into "two great classes — tramps and millionaires," the plundered and the plunderers. The nightmarish future of *Caesar's Column*, then, was not so different from the America that he imagined all around him.[67]

After the 1896 election, Donnelly's vision of the present became indistinguishable from the dark future imagined in *Caesar's Column*. "Every election," a pessimistic Donnelly confided in his diary, "marks another step downward into the abyss, from which there will be no return save by fire and sword. . . . I tremble for the future." The comment directly echoes Gabriel's own observation that "long established wrongs are only to be rooted out by fire and sword. And hence the future looks so black to me." So dire had circumstances become by 1896 that Donnelly now believed "it will need a god come on earth with divine power, to save [the masses]." Certainly the people could not save themselves since "the bankrupt millions voted to keep the yoke on their own necks." Gabriel is faced with the same dilemma, and it leads to the same antidemocratic and illiberal commitments. Believing the masses lack the intelligence and moral virtue to erect a new world, Gabriel can imagine salvation for the world coming only through divine retribution. "Oh! for the quick-pulsing, warm-beating, mighty human heart of the man of Galilee! Oh! for his uplifted hand, armed with a whip of scorpions, to depopulate the temples of the world, and lash his recreant preachers into devotion to the cause of his poor afflicted children!"[68]

Unlike Bellamy, who believed that the laws of industrial progress would eventually lead to utopia, Donnelly believed that the old order could be destroyed and the new created only through political action. Donnelly was, in this sense, no utopian, but his uncompromising condemnation of the current order, including his disdain for "the bankrupt millions," cannot be understood apart from his utopian sense of what could be reasonably expected from human societies. Gabriel predicts that "the world, released from its iron band, would leap forward to marvelous prosperity; there would be no financial panics. . . . There would be no limit to the development of mankind." The "fingerboard of God," Gabriel insists, "points forward, unerringly, . . . [and] it is still pointing forward to stages, in the future, when men shall approximate the angels."[69] It is because Donnelly believes that a heavenly reign of "universal justice" is possible on earth that he judges existing institutions and conditions so severely.[70]

The utopian hope fuels the deep pessimism. The thought of what might be makes the world that exists unbearable. After the 1896 election Donnelly becomes despondent at the thought that "the sun of triumph [will] never rise." But Donnelly's discovery that a "reign of justice" is beyond humanity's reach does not spur a tragic vision framed by the inherent limitations of humankind. Instead, it fuels conspiratorial visions of an all-powerful, grasping "money power," an almost misanthropic hostility toward a populace "too shallow and too corrupt to conduct a republic," and a deep alienation from established institutions and practices.[71] If the world is too corrupt to be redeemed, then the only option is to withdraw from it, to establish a walled-off egalitarian community beyond the reach of society.

Caesar's Column ends in precisely this way, with a few unspoiled souls, including Gabriel and Maximilian, managing to escape the carnage for "the garden in the mountains," where they establish a utopian enclave. Their first task upon arriving is to erect a thirty-foot-high wall that enables them to exclude all other people.[72] Having walled themselves off from the hellish outside world, the communards begin to establish an egalitarian society. Equality of condition is necessary because, as Gabriel earlier explains to Max, if we should "give one set of men in a community a financial advantage over the rest, however slight — it may be almost invisible — . . . at the end of centuries that class so favored will own everything and wreck the country."[73] Since inequalities must necessarily grow greater, the only way to insure equal opportunities is to mandate equal conditions.

The utopia Donnelly envisions is a harmonious brotherhood of equals, but that does not mean government is absent. Government, according to Gabriel, "is the key to the future of the human race." "We have but to expand the powers of government," Gabriel explains, "to solve the enigma of the world." In Donnelly's utopia there is no distinction between the people and the government. Indeed, the governing body is called "The People." Since government is only an "instrumentality of cooperation," there is no reason to limit the power vested in the hands of the state. Thus the utopia abolishes "all private schools, except the higher institutions and colleges," so that "the whole community grow up together as brethren." Government "owns all roads, streets, telegraph or telephone lines, railroads, and mines, and takes exclusive control of the mails," and is given the power "to fix the rate of compensation for all forms of labor" as well as to "regulate the number of apprentices who shall enter any given trade or pursuit." The state makes all decisions about how new villages or towns are to be designed: the width of roads, the number of trees to be planted, services to be provided, and so on. The preamble to the constitution declares that the "government is intended . . . to insure to every industrious citizen not only liberty, but an educated mind, a comfortable home, an abundant supply of food and clothing, and a *pleasant, happy life.*" The pursuit of happiness is not a right of the citizens that the government should not abridge, but rather a result the government is required to guarantee.[74]

What about those who prefer to live in ways not approved of by the nation? Those "few conservatives" who objected to the reforms, Gabriel tells the reader, were promptly threatened with a "transfer . . . to the outside world." The initially recalcitrant, however, are now "the most vigorous supporters of the new order of things." What about the predators who might be expected to emerge in any human community? "The government," Gabriel answers, "now shuts up every crevice through which they could enter; stops every hole of opportunity; crushes down every uprising instinct of cruelty and selfishness." Donnelly never questions whether a government that can do so much good could not also inflict terrible harm. A government empowered to crush every "instinct" of selfishness could also use that power to crush any other instinct it might wish to eradicate, and soon reduce the imagined "garden of peace and beauty" to a nightmare of oppression no worse than the one from which the protagonists had just escaped.[75]

Islands in a "Shoreless Sea"

Gabriel's flight to an Edenic "garden" anticipated the flight to utopian communities that took place during the 1890s. Historian Robert Fogarty estimates that about forty utopian communities were started up during the 1890s, close to double the number that had been initiated in the previous decade.[76] Among the more significant colonies established were Julius Wayland's Ruskin Colony in Tennessee; the Single-Tax Colony at Fairhope, Alabama; Equality, Burley, and Home Colonies in Washington; and Ralph Albertson's Christian Commonwealth Colony in Georgia. These colonies, together with the explosion of utopian novels in the 1890s, represented what Edward Spann has characterized as "a communitarian revival" during the last decade of the nineteenth century.[77]

The colonies established in the late 1880s and 1890s owed a tremendous amount to the utopian literature of the period, particularly Edward Bellamy's *Looking Backward*.[78] Burley Colony in Washington was described by one of its members as an attempt "to make actual the ideal proposed in Bellamy's 'Looking Backward,'"[79] and members of Kaweah Colony in California reportedly revered *Looking Backward* as the "Bible of the present."[80] Several colonies took their names from the titles or imagined lands of utopian novels, including the colony of Equality in Washington, which was named after Bellamy's sequel to *Looking Backward*. Dissatisfied Equality colonists started up another colony in Washington that they named "Freeland," after Theodor Hertzka's utopian novel of that name,[81] while the colony of Altruria in California took its name from William Dean Howells's *A Traveler from Altruria* (1894).

Although colony-builders frequently found their inspiration in the utopian writings of Bellamy, Bellamy himself disapproved of these social experiments.[82] He felt that utopian colonies were merely distractions and that transformative energies should be targeted at the national level. As Dr. Leete explains near the end of *Equality*, "such experiments led, and could lead, to nothing. Economically weak, held together by a sentimental motive, generally composed of eccentric though worthy persons, and surrounded by a hostile environment which had the whole use and advantage of the social and economic machinery, it was scarcely possible that such enterprises should come to anything practical unless under exceptional leadership or circumstances."[83]

How best to realize the cooperative commonwealth was hotly contested within what historian John Thomas has described as the late nineteenth century's "oppositional culture,"[84] but utopian colonists who shared that culture did not disagree with Bellamy that the ultimate aim was transformation of the entire nation. To be sure, escapism and a desire to belong played their role in the settling of these colonies,[85] but in justifying colonization efforts spokesmen invariably accented the colonies' potential for sparking political transformation. To those critics who felt that Julius Wayland's weekly, the *Coming Nation*, gave too much attention to cooperative ventures and not enough to politics, Wayland responded: "Co-operation is the only politics the people need to know, and when a half dozen colonies founded on economic equality are in successful operation, it will spread like the Australian ballot."[86] Christian B. Hoffman, a Kansas millionare, Populist, and socialist who was deeply involved in the Topolombampo Colony for seven years, believed utopian colonies could be a "fort from which to rally for the emancipation of the race."[87] The goal of California's Kaweah Colony, as described in its deed of settlement, was "to propogate and extend in the world at large the idea of universal and just cooperation." To "be an object lesson that will convert the world," is the way a subscriber to the *Coming Nation* summed up the colonists' aspirations. Leading by example, "our city . . . will . . . soon control the state."[88]

Dreams of egalitarian national transformation emerging from local communitarian settlement were most thoroughly fused in the efforts of the Social Democracy of America and the Brotherhood of the Cooperative Commonwealth (BCC) to colonize a sparsely populated western state. Eugene Debs, who initially was a leading proponent of the colonization idea, believed that by colonizing a state socialists could create a model commonwealth that would quickly become an irresistible model for the rest of the nation. "'From one state the new life will rapidly overleap boundary lines,' generating a great national enthusiasm which would enable 'the great co-operative party' to take control of the United States by 1904."[89] No less optimistic was G. E. Pelton, who had been commissioned by the BCC to find a suitable site for their colonization plans and had selected Skagit County, Washington. Pelton assured Henry Demarest Lloyd that the newly settled Equality Colony was but the "the advance guard of a mighty host."[90]

Lloyd, who was among the most ardent supporters of the BCC, shared this view that utopian communes were an essential aspect of the larger effort to redeem America. In an address delivered at Ruskin Colony in 1898 to celebrate the laying of the cornerstone of a new college, Lloyd lauded "the communes [as society's] pioneers. They are the monasteries in which the light of the new faith is kept burning on the mountain tops until the dark age is over." Lloyd insisted that "these little societies must be generalized into a society which will, like them, extinguish the degrading dependence of the many on the few [and] create the economic equality which is the next step in the historic series which has begun with religious and political equality." But despite the transformative hopes Lloyd invested in communes like Ruskin, it was never clear how utopian communes, no matter how egalitarian or successful, would help bring about "the vast economic revolution" he envisaged. How would the "dark age" of plutocratic dominance come to an end if reformers remained within the walls of the monasteries? Creating "little oases of a people in our desert of persons," as Lloyd expressed it, did little if anything to transform the inhospitable desert.[91] As orthodox Marxists never tired of pointing out, "the establishing of small islands of more or less incomplete communism in the midst of the present sea of capitalistic method of living, only ends in the overwhelming of the islands by the sea."[92]

The obvious mismatch between the grand aspiration (egalitarian transformation of the entire society) and the humble means (the establishment of a handful of tiny egalitarian colonies) led to despair among a number of utopian radicals, including Lloyd himself, who became increasingly despondent about the power of monopoly capital. "I do not see what there is that is going to stand against it," he confessed. Originally Lloyd had hoped that the cooperative colonies would help the people see that the inequities and injustice of capitalism need not be accepted as inevitable. But "the people" in fact showed little interest in the colonies, and indeed were often openly hostile to these ventures. The disappointing public reaction left a depressed Lloyd with the morose sense that he was "swimming in a shoreless sea."[93]

Other utopian radicals reacted to the general public's failure to condemn capitalism and support the cooperative cause by pouring scorn upon ordinary people. Disdain for people dripped from the pages of Wayland's *Coming Nation*. As Wayland surveyed the American landscape he saw "poor dupes," "trained animals," "helpless mental slaves," and "poor deluded mechanisms." If people preferred capitalism or private property, it was because they had been "hypnotized from childhood" and were thus unable "to break the spell that enslaves them."[94] For Wayland it was clear that "the ignorant masses of the world do not know what they think, do not act what they profess, and are tossed, like a rudderless ship, by the schemers who put words into their ears and steal away their reason." But, he condescendingly allowed, at least "they are learning."[95]

A smug elitism suffused Wayland's egalitarianism. Wayland believed that through careful study of the social system, he and people like Bellamy had seen through to "the real character" of the American government. Not all agreed with his diagnosis, of course, but that was because most people had not "advanced in the studies of social forces as I have" and thus still clung to the vain hope that "some relief will be given the country by the coterie of conspirators who are entrenched at Washington. How child-like!" The problem, he explained at another point, is that "the masses have never studied these problems, and they do not know so well as those who have. They do not know the wrongs that injure them, and if they did they do not know that a system can be created that will bring about a remedy." This new order, Wayland believed, "will demand men who have studied the social questions" and who know "the needs of society." Ignorance, he predicted, "is to be dethroned and intelligence given power."[96]

Wayland's dismissive attitude toward ignorant, ordinary citizens was echoed in numerous letters to the *Coming Nation*. A Republican landslide had a simple cause: "It is a lack of intelligence among the common people . . . the common herd." Voting first for the Republicans and then for the Democrats, complained a correspondent from California, voters had shown their "dense ignorance" and an unreasoning "prejudice against the party of Reform."[97] If the people would not accept their diagnosis and cure, then that must be because the people were crude, unthinking, or deluded.

The elitism that sometimes accompanied radical political thought in this period is evident, too, in the thinking of Burnette Haskell, a founder and leader of the Kaweah colony in California. Before founding Kaweah in 1885, Haskell had organized the International Workingmen's Association and had led an unsuccessful effort to unify socialist and anarchist parties in 1883. In Haskell's view, the "masses of working men were densely ignorant, cowardly and selfish, and thus disinclined to learn, to act or to aid others in acting." The people, he insisted, must be "properly led and played upon"; they need "leaders who are able, heroic and self-sacrificing in order to fan the slumbering spark of discontent into a flame." Radicals needed therefore to "concentrate [their] energies upon the task of providing such *leaders* rather than in vainly trying to educate the whole sluggish world before we strike."[98] In beginning Kaweah Colony, Haskell unburdened himself of the "sluggish" workers of the world in order to live among a select few who were bold enough to fashion a just alternative to the capitalist system.

For George Littlefield, who founded Fellowship Farm in Massachusetts, the gap between the inspiring dream of a cooperative commonwealth and the actual practice of local colonization efforts was bridged by visions of inspired, charismatic leaders. For Littlefield, utopian colonies were necessary in order "to escape and keep clear of the enslaving commercial system." But how would collective withdrawal bring the world any closer to overturning a "vampire system that doomed every man to an early death"? This is the same dilemma that left Lloyd feeling he was "swimming in a shoreless sea." Littlefield warded off such desperate feelings by holding out hope for visionary leaders who could spy the opposite shore and transport the people there. These "new Columbuses and Vespuccis and Cabots — have the vision of sagacity so that they see, westward, ho! the Co-operative Islands, and the mainland of the beautiful Co-operative Commonwealth just beyond that." In Littlefield's view, "the best thing for us to do now, and keep on doing, is to live the Golden Rule Life; for out of the midst of Golden Rule folk is to come the Mighty one, the new altruistic Leviathan, who shall lead us into the Co-operative Commonwealth." Repulsed by capitalism and distrustful of democratic politics, utopian radicals saw authoritarian leadership as their only possible rescue from a boundless ocean.[99]

Living with Conflict

The immediate problem facing the utopian colonists was not, as Lloyd had it, "generalizing" the colonies to the larger society but rather simply making the colonies themselves viable. Most of the utopian colonies fell apart in a relatively short span of time. Altruria lasted only one mercurial year; more successful were Ruskin Colony, the Christian Commonwealth Colony in Georgia, the Kaweah Cooperative Commonwealth, and the Washington colonies of Equality, Burley, and Freeland, but none of these lasted more than a decade. These and countless other cooperative colonies fell apart for many and diverse reasons, but central to their failures was the inability to create institutions that could channel conflict and self-interest into harmless or even productive directions.

The utopian colonists had hoped to establish an egalitarian way of life in which discord would give way to harmony, conflict to brotherhood, and self-interest to altruism. They believed that capitalism largely caused the greed and selfish behavior they witnessed all around them, and that it was this avarice that lay at the heart of societal conflict. Do away with capitalism, the colonists reasoned, and the colonies would be essentially free of divisions. Consequently, insufficient thought was given to how the colonies would settle disagreements. Committed to a radical egalitarian way of life and unable to admit the legitimacy of jarring conflict, colonists found themselves ill-equipped to manage, let alone resolve, the conflicts that inevitably did arise.[100]

Perhaps the most closely watched radical experiment of the 1890s was Wayland's Ruskin Colony.[101] The colony's aim was to establish a setting that would allow people to work and live in an "atmosphere of equality and brotherhood." "No member," Wayland promised, "shall have more power or influence in the organization than any other."[102] At Ruskin, all work was of equal value, all meals were provided in a common dining facility, and food, medical care, and housing were provided by the community without charge. Wayland filled the pages of the *Coming Nation* with glowing accounts of Ruskin's many successes, but in fact all was far from well. From the outset, Wayland came under sharp attack from colonists for maintaining ownership of the printing press and control over the *Coming Nation*. The paper, colonists insisted, must be, like everything else at Ruskin, run collectively. Gradually Wayland lost control over the paper, and less than a year after the colony's founding, he left Ruskin bitterly disappointed amid acrimonious accusations of betrayal.[103]

For a little over two years after Wayland's departure, Ruskin Colony seems to have prospered, but it started to come apart toward the latter half of 1897. The charter members who had driven Wayland out now found themselves under attack from newer members for their own reluctance to share power; once again, little of this conflict appeared in the pages of the *Coming Nation*, which continued to portray a perfectly harmonious colony. A. S. Edwards, the man who had been brought in to replace Wayland as editor, now ended up on the losing side of a power struggle, and he and the faction he was aligned with left the colony in the spring of 1898. Edwards was replaced as editor by Herbert Casson, but he, too, soon fell out with the colony and left. In the spring of 1899, Edwards and a number of other charter members brought suit against the colony and asked to have the Ruskin corporation dissolved. After political and legal wrangling, a judge declared the colony hopelessly divided and appointed a receiver to sell the assets at auction.[104] The quest for sweet harmony ended in bitter acrimony.

The fractiousness of Ruskin Colony was repeated elsewhere. Robert Hine, in his study of California's utopian colonies in the late nineteenth and early twentieth centuries, found that the colonies' egalitarian political arrangements, although constructed upon assumptions of altruism and harmony, often worked to exacerbate conflict. These colonies were typically hyperdemocratic: "democracy with the lid off," in the words of one colony leader. Unlike in religious colonies where the leader could single-handedly expel dissenters, expulsion in these secular egalitarian colonies often required a near-unanimous vote of the general assembly. Within the general assembly, moreover, any man in the colony could speak for any amount of time on whatever issue. "The minute books of Icaria and Kaweah and the newspapers of Llano and Altruria," reported Hine, "related interminable sessions airing personal disputes, questioning minor administrative decisions, or seeking individual dispensations." The inability of the general assembly to come to closure and make decisions meant either the colony rapidly unraveled, as in the case of Altruria, or, as at Kaweah, de facto power gradually devolved to the board of trustees as the executive body of the company.[105]

The experience of Llano del Rio Colony, the last and largest of the secular utopian colonies initiated during "the age of reform," is particularly instructive regarding the problem of authority in egalitarian organizations. Llano colony was founded in 1914 by Job Harriman, a leading socialist who had been closely associated with the failed Altruria Colony in the 1890s. In the first decade of the twentieth century, Harriman tried his hand at electoral politics, running as the Socialist party's vice presidential candidate in 1900 and then mounting a serious bid for mayor of Los Angeles in 1911.[106] Harriman's defeat in the mayoral election revived his earlier interest in establishing a successful cooperative colony. Only by showing concretely that socialism could work as an economic system, Harriman argued, would it be possible to persuade Americans to abandon capitalism.[107]

At its high point in the summer of 1917, Llano had about one thousand people living at the southern California colony, a phenomenal rate of growth that seems to have been primarily due to Harriman's stature and his loyal following, particularly but not only in the Los Angeles area. All colony members were to receive an equal wage and to have an equal share of stock in the company.[108] Llano's economic achievements were in many ways quite impressive. The colony managed to irrigate close to two thousand acres of poor soil, and the agricultural yield, while uneven, was adequate. By 1916 the colony was producing about 90 percent of the food it consumed, a statistic which says as much about the low standard of living in the colony as it does about agricultural productivity. An impressive number of industries of various sizes were also developed, including a planing mill, sawmill, brickyard, cannery, and fish hatchery, but only a few handicraft items were ever exported to the outside world. The temporary canvas homes were slowly replaced by more durable adobe homes, and a large dining room, a hotel, industrial buildings and warehouses, and one of the largest rabbitries in the United States were all built within a few years. In addition, the colony also produced a weekly newspaper and did job-printing of other socialist literature.[109]

Although Llano colony was hardly a stunning economic success — poor housing and food and a shortage of water were continual problems — it was the political organization of the colony that was arguably its greatest source of trouble.[110] In Llano, as in most other egalitarian colonies, questions of how to cope with political conflict were given little sustained attention because of the widely shared assumption that serious political conflict would disappear when economic inequalities had been abolished. "If the stream of life were not polluted by the vicious methods produced by the universal conflict of interests," reasoned Harriman, "the hearts and minds of men would be as sweet and gentle and loving as in babyhood." Remove men from "the thorns and thickets and swamps of capitalism," and their natural goodness and cooperative instincts would

quickly reemerge. From the outset, however, Llano colony was characterized not by interpersonal harmony but, as Paul Conkin reports, by
frequent "personal clashes and violent disagreements . . . resulting in a
constant turnover of members."[111]

Having been incorporated, Llano was required by state law to have a
board of directors, but the ultimate source of legislative power resided in
the assembled members of the colony. The General Assembly was thoroughly egalitarian but not particularly well-suited for resolving disagreements or even reaching decisions. For instance, an attempt to write a
constitution that would remedy some of the evident weaknesses in the
colony's political structure foundered after getting bogged down in interminable arguments over details. The untempered egalitarianism of
the General Assembly not only made collective decision making difficult
but also tended to inflame personal jealousies and factional rivalries. The
General Assembly, as one member later recalled, was "democracy rampant, belligerent, unrestricted, . . . an inquisition, a mental pillory, a
madhouse of meddlesomeness . . . , a jumble of passions and idealism —
and all in deadly earnest. . . . It became a [monster] which threatened to
destroy the colony."[112]

The often rancorous character of debate in the Llano General Assembly must be put down in part to a worldview that made no allowance for
legitimate conflict. Since Llano had eliminated conflict between rival interests, disagreements must reflect bad faith, sinister intent, or plain ignorance. Civility and respect become difficult when one construes opposition in terms of betrayal or benightedness. Put positively, recognition
that different groups and individuals have interests can be a profoundly
democratic and even egalitarian idea.[113] In following the elusive grail of
natural harmony and innate goodness, colonists subverted their own
egalitarian and democratic ends.

The subsequent history of Llano colony reveals still more about the
troubling relation between egalitarian utopianism and democratic politics. In the face of serious problems, particularly the inability to obtain a
reliable water source, the Llano colonists (or, more precisely, the most
loyal and committed among them) moved from the California desert to
a new site in Louisiana. From its opening days in the fall of 1917, the
Louisiana colony was beset with tremendous troubles. "The first three
years in Louisiana," Conkin observes, "were marked by poverty, bitter
quarrels, [and] a slow erosion of members." Yet despite this inauspicious
beginning, notes Conkin, Llano went on to "set an endurance record . . .

among the cooperative commonwealth colonies," lasting until 1938 as a successful collectivity.[114]

The key to Llano's longevity was one man, George Pickett. Llano was a dying, desperately poor colony until Pickett assumed almost complete control over the colony's policies in 1920. For the next two decades, Conkin reports, "everything in Llano revolved around the personality and policies of this one man." People either reviled or loved the charismatic Pickett; "he was either an inspired and self-sacrificing leader or an unfair dictator." The constitution consisted of only a brief and vague declaration of principles about cooperation, economic justice, and collective ownership. Its silence on questions of political organization left Pickett free to centralize political authority in the hands of the general manager (himself). Moreover, since the means of production were owned by the colony, Pickett controlled the important power of assigning workers to their jobs. Although Llano maintained democratic forms, it became for all practical purposes "a one-party affair" run by Pickett.[115]

Pickett's authoritarian rule was always justified by appeals to harmony, cooperation, and economic justice for the poor and oppressed. Those who periodically challenged his leadership were denounced for disrupting the harmony of the colony or condemned for lacking the spirit of cooperation. Pickett's hostility to competition and his identification with the weak take on a more sinister hue when one reflects upon his political authoritarianism. As Conkin explains, "He welcomed all disciples, and was happiest with children or with docile old folks. He would never tolerate those who challenged his power or defied his will. Pickett tended to view all the colonists as children, and himself as the great protector."[116]

In 1932 a few younger, rebellious colonists led an attempt to reestablish democracy in Llano. They tried to restore the general assembly and pushed for publication of the colony's financial reports, free speech, and a secret ballot. Pickett responded to this challenge to his authority by having the organizers of the opposition movement expelled from the colony. He justified his actions by arguing that "there should be no MINORITY in such an organization or enterprise as the colony, for the reason that IT ITSELF IS THE MINORITY" within the capitalist system. The threat posed by the external enemy required a "solid phalanx" and the "utmost loyalty" within the colony. Disloyalty in such critical times could not be tolerated; indeed it was treasonable since it threatened the future existence of the colony.[117]

Pickett finally lost control of the colony in a May Day "revolt" in 1935. With Pickett out of the colony at the time, disgruntled colonists instituted a new government and new constitution, one that allowed for secret ballot and voting rights for all workers over eighteen. At first, Pickett seemed inclined to accept his deposing, but then he apparently had a change of heart, precipitating a bitter but largely bloodless civil war within Llano.[118] The end result of this violent feud was bankruptcy and the liquidation of the colony in 1938, exactly fifty years after the original publication of Bellamy's *Looking Backward.*

Llano was the last of the cooperative colonies that owed their inspiration to the utopian vision of Bellamy and other writers of the late nineteenth century. And a telling end point it is. For in Llano one sees in dramatic relief the authoritarianism and intolerance of dissent that may be justified in the name of harmony. The authoritarian, even dictatorial, leadership at Llano was not inevitable, of course, but nor was it a freakish, chance occurrence. The colony's authoritarianism, like Bellamy's, stemmed from an exaggerated aversion to clashing interests and values, and from making a virtual fetish out of cooperation and harmony. Embedded in the ideal of a perfect unity is an invitation for one person to speak for all without considering their opinions or preferences. Recognizing that interests and values inevitably and legitimately clash is necessary to protect against the charismatic or authoritarian leader. Cooperation and harmonious relations are always nice, but they are worth precious little if they come at the expense of democracy and dissent.

The Revolting Masses

FROM WALT WHITMAN TO MIKE GOLD

**Greed is an enemy of equality, but we must
take care in making greed our political enemy
that we do not dismiss human beings along with
their avarice.**

Benjamin Barber[1]

**It is never a good idea for the left to set itself in stark
opposition to the values of ordinary people. The attack on
consumer goods is the work of social critics at the farthest
reach of their willfulness. For men and women deprived
of things are not liberated for radical politics any more
than starving artists are liberated for art. Deprivation is
deprivation; one can't escape from the world of getting
and spending by not getting and not spending.**

Michael Walzer[2]

Egalitarian utopianism is driven by an expansive belief in human potential: liberated from repressive institutions and mores, the human species will reach undreamed-of heights. Accompanying these radiant expectations of human potentiality, though, is often a less-than-charitable view of people as they are. Although egalitarians blame oppressive institutions for the current degradation or depravity of people, their loathing of current institutions often seeps through to disdain for the people themselves, who appear quite content to live lives that to egalitarians seem shallow and inauthentic, materialistic and selfish. The critical distance that egalitarians maintain from society's "mainstream" only exacerbates this elitism.

Egalitarians, though, are ambivalent elitists, quite unlike aristocrats or hierarchists whose disdain for the "bourgeois" lives of ordinary people is relatively unambiguous, reflecting a logically consistent package of antipathies toward liberal capitalism, political democracy, and popular culture.[3] One thinks, for example, of Joseph de Maistre and Charles Maurras in France, or Johann Georg Hamann and Carl Schmitt in Germany.[4] In the United States, a politically weaker and more isolated aristocratic critique of bourgeois liberal democracy emerged among New England Federalists such as Timothy Dwight, southern slaveholders such as George Fitzhugh, and early-twentieth-century reactionaries such as Irving Babbitt and Ralph Adams Cram.[5] The egalitarian distaste for bourgeois society, in contrast, is complicated by a deep desire to identify with "the common people," those ordinary folks who are oppressed or debased by "the system." Egalitarians are bedeviled by an ambivalence toward the people in whose name they act. They both love and loathe "the people," idealize and disdain them.

Walt Whitman: America's "Poet of Democracy"

There is no better (albeit counterintuitive) place to begin exploring the egalitarian ambivalence toward the people than with America's "Poet of Democracy," Walt Whitman. Whitman is typically remembered for his boundless faith in America, the democratic idea, and the common people; his verse has been canonized as among the most vibrant and eloquent celebrations of liberty and equality ever penned in the English language. Whitman's inspiring poetry makes him a hero to people across the political spectrum, but "America's Bard" has a deservedly special place in the hearts and minds of the egalitarian left, for this is where Whitman's own political sympathies and commitments lay.

Whitman, Betsy Erkkila usefully reminds us, was "one of America's most overtly political poets."[6] Before his twenty-first birthday, Whitman had become actively involved in local Democratic politics in Queens County, New York. His idol and mentor was "the glorious [William] Leggett," whose slashing, uncompromising attacks on the rich and inequalities as well as his impassioned calls for working-class solidarity defined the radical, anticapitalist edge of the Democratic party.[7] For a decade Whitman remained active as a radical Democrat and party journalist until he broke with the party over the question of slavery in the late 1840s and joined the short-lived Free Soil party.[8] As Whitman's and the nation's interest turned toward slavery, his sympathies remained with the outsiders and radicals who did not shrink from agitating established institutions. "Agitation," he wrote, "is the test of the goodness and solidness of all politics and laws and institutions. . . . [It] is the most important factor of all — to stir, to question, to suspect, to examine, to denounce. . . . *Vive*, the attack — the perennial assault."[9] Throughout his life and in his poetry, Erkkila writes, Whitman "challenged the traditional hierarchies of power and domination; . . . celebrated the liberation of male and female, sex and the body, workers and poor persons, immigrants and slaves; and . . . placed the values of liberty and equality, comradeship and solidarity at the heart of his democratic songs."[10]

There is, however, a darker side to Whitman's egalitarian vision, a side that has often been obscured from view by Whitman's many champions. His celebration of an almost mythical common people often coexists with disdain for the lives of actually existing people. And for all his paeans to diversity and freedom, there is a disturbing tendency to submerge individuality in an abstract, even mystical, unity. Finally, for all his talk of the value of perpetual agitation, he himself was continually attracted to the idea of having the entire country faithfully follow the word of an inspired, charismatic poet.

Many of these problems are illuminated in Whitman's major prose work, *Democratic Vistas* (1871), the longest and most explicit exposition of his views on American society and politics and of the aims of his poetry.[11] Whitman begins *Democratic Vistas* by celebrating diversity and individuality: "As the greatest lessons of Nature through the universe are perhaps the lessons of variety and freedom, the same present the greatest lessons also in New World politics and progress." Whitman invokes "John Stuart Mill's profound essay on Liberty," singling out for praise Mill's insistence that society allow for the "full play for human nature to expand itself in numberless and even conflicting directions." Yet this opening paragraph serves as prologue to repeated calls for a mystical union that dissolves difference and conflict. Whitman sees the basis of "genuine union" in "the fervid and tremendous IDEA, melting everything else with resistless heat, and solving all lesser and definite distinctions in vast, indefinite, spiritual, emotional power." We cannot look solely at "individualism, which isolates," Whitman explains. "There is another half, which is adhesiveness or love, that fuses, ties, and aggregates, making the races comrades, and fraternizing *all*." The true "master," as distinct from "the common ambition [that] strains for elevations, to become some privileged exclusive, . . . sees greatness and health in being part of the mass." "Would you have in yourself the divine, vast, general law?" Whitman asks. "Then merge yourself in it."[12] Under the influence of Hegel,[13] Whitman repeatedly seeks to dissolve the tension between individuality and community rather than live with it. Synthesis is achieved by absorbing the individual into the "central divine idea of All."[14]

Whitman's rebellious call for perpetual agitation and questioning sits uneasily with his search for ultimate synthesis and unity. The force of his call for the "perennial assault" is also undercut by his insistent search for "a few first-class poets, philosophs, and authors" whom the nation will obediently follow. Whitman invests this elite group of native authors with a shattering, charismatic presence. The great author "penetrates all, gives hue to all, shapes aggregates and individuals, and, after subtle ways, with irresistible power, constructs, sustains, demolishes at will." At times, Whitman likens this new "class of bards" to priests — "The priest departs, the divine literatus comes" — and at other times to despots: "I demand races of orbic bards, with unconditional uncompromising sway. Come forth, sweet democratic despots of the west!" But whatever the specific analogy, invention and even independent thought are clearly reserved for an elevated literary elite; the rest of the nation passively and irresistibly conforms to this new, imposed vision.[15]

The elitism of *Democratic Vistas* coexists uncomfortably with an ostentatious celebration of the common people. Whitman ridicules the pretensions of the upper classes, declaring that "the best class . . . is but a mob of fashionably dress'd speculators and vulgarians." "Refinement and delicatesse . . . threaten to eat us up, like a cancer"; what is needed instead is "a little healthy rudeness." Whitman demands "a programme of culture, drawn out, not for a single class alone, or for the parlors or lecture rooms, but with an eye to practical life, the west, the workingmen, the facts of farms and jackplanes and engineers, and of the broad range of the women also of the middle and working strata." "Long enough," cries Whitman, "have the People been listening to poems in which common humanity, deferential, bends low, humiliated, acknowledging superiors." Whitman's aim is to create a distinctively American poetry that is to be charged with the democratic energies of the people.[16]

If Whitman's political sympathies are with the common people, he shows remarkable contempt for the lives they lead. Turning his "moral microscope" upon America, Whitman sees "a sort of dry and flat Sahara." The cities are "crowded with petty grotesques, malformations, phantoms, playing meaningless antics." Everywhere, "in shop, street, church, theatre, barroom, official chair, are pervading flippancy and vulgarity, low cunning, infidelity." He is struck by "the plentiful meanness and vulgarity of the ostensible masses," the people's "shallow notions of beauty" and their "lack of manners, . . . probably the meanest to be seen in the world." Society is "canker'd, crude, superstitious and rotten."[17] Nor is this disdain for the people something that only came to Whitman late in life. Thirty years earlier, while still an ardent radical Jacksonian, Whitman described his fellow townspeople of Woodbury in the most demeaning manner:

> I am sick of wearing away by inches, and spending the fairest portion of my little span of life . . . among clowns and country bumpkins[,] flatheads, and coarse brown-faced girls, dirty, ill-favored young brats, with squalling throats, and crude manners, and bog-trotters, with all the disgusting conceit, of ignorance and vulgarity.—It is enough to make the fountains of good-will dry up in our hearts, to wither all gentle and loving dispositions, when we are forced to descend and be as one among the grossest, the most low-minded of the human race.[18]

In *Democratic Vistas*, Whitman is particularly disturbed by "the appalling vacuum in our times."[19] The people's lives are shallow and inauthentic. There is a "hollowness at heart. . . . Genuine belief seems to have left us." "What penetrating eye," he asks, "does not everywhere see through the mask? The spectacle is appalling. We live in an atmosphere of hypocrisy throughout. The men believe not in the women, nor the women in the men." The nation's "moral conscience" is "either entirely lacking, or seriously enfeebled or ungrown." Territorial expansion and "materialistic development" have endowed the nation "with a vast and more and more thoroughly appointed body" but left the country "with little or no soul." As he looked at the mass culture produced by democracy Whitman saw sterility, emptiness, lack of meaning, a spiritual void.[20]

A decade before *Vistas*, Whitman had looked to the Civil War to fill the spiritual void left by rampant materialism. In the poem "Beat! Beat! Drums!" Whitman had welcomed the coming of the war as a means to disrupt the mundane patterns of everyday life. He revels in the beat of the drums and blare of the bugles that signal the approaching war.

Beat! beat! drums!—Blow! bugles! blow!
Through the windows — through doors — burst like a ruthless force,
Into the solemn church, and scatter the congregation;
Into the school where the scholar is studying;

Leave not the bridegroom quiet — no happiness must he have now
    with his bride;
Nor the peaceful farmer any peace, plowing his field or gathering his
    grain.[21]

By pulling people away from their merely private pursuits, the war would unify the people, and elevate and ennoble their souls. In "Rise, O Days, from Your Fathomless Deeps," Whitman finds in war the deep spiritual meaning he had long been searching for but had been unable to find in America.

Thunder on! stride on, Democracy! strike with vengeful stroke!
And do you rise higher than ever yet, O days, O cities!
Crash heavier, heavier yet, O storms! you have done me good;
My soul, prepared in the mountains, absorbs your immortal strong
    nutriment;
Long had I walk'd my cities, my country roads, through farms, only
    half satisfied . . .
Hungering, hungering, hungering, for primal energies, and Nature's
    dauntlessness,
I refresh'd myself with it only, I could relish it only;
I waited the bursting forth of the pent fire — on the water and air I
    waited long;
— But now I no longer wait — I am fully satisfied — I am glutted;
I have witness'd the true lightning, I have witness'd my cities
    electric;
I have lived to behold man burst forth, and warlike America rise;
Hence I will seek no more the food of the northern solitary wilds,
No more the mountains roam, or sail the stormy sea.[22]

The Civil War seemed to provide the collective purpose that Whitman had been unable to find either in democratic capitalism or in his own solitary communions with nature. Whitman hoped, as biographer David Reynolds points out, that the war would cleanse "the Augean stables of capitalism and urbanism" and knit the nation together in a spiritual unity.[23] But the immediate postwar years, not to mention the war itself, clearly belied such a dream. Since "not even . . . our fiercest lightnings of the war, have purified the atmosphere," Whitman looked for other ways to remedy the moral emptiness and tawdriness of the American people.[24]

If war would not produce a heroic, morally superior people, then perhaps eugenics would. In *Democratic Vistas*, Whitman proposes to cure America's "deep disease" through a program of national eugenics designed, as Harold Aspiz comments, "to produce an inexhaustible supply of splendid individuals."[25] Whitman envisions the propagation of "new races of Teachers, and of perfect Women, indispensable to endow the birth-stock of a New World." And he eagerly anticipates the time "when fatherhood and motherhood shall become a science — and the noblest science." Careful, selective breeding would produce an "American stock-personality" with "a clear-blooded, strong-fibered physique"— in youth, "fresh, ardent, emotional, aspiring, full of adventure"; at maturity, "brave, perceptive, under control, neither too talkative nor too reticent, neither flippant nor somber; of the bodily figure, the movements easy, the complexion showing the best blood, somewhat flush'd, breast expanded, an erect attitude, a voice whose sound outvies music, eyes of calm and steady gaze, yet capable also of flashing — and a general presence that holds its own in the company of the highest."[26]

Even more important than eugenics in achieving this new American personality are the "mighty poets, artists," Whitman himself very much included. The purpose of his own poetry, *Democratic Vistas* makes clear, is to mold and inspire the common people, "to breathe into them the breath recuperative of sane and heroic life." Whitman's poetic celebrations of the American people are thus not to be understood as a celebration of the actual lives of ordinary people, but rather as a means of making real a mythical people. Whitman himself was quite conscious of the tremendous gap between the ideal and the real American people. Amidst his manuscript notes for *Democratic Vistas* he wrote himself a reminder to "offset the statement of depravity [and] vulgarism . . . of the masses by a full acknowledgment of the latent heroism."[27] For Whitman, the "real PEOPLE, worthy the name" are the people who do not exist, while the actually existing people are the "vulgar," "vicious," and "mean" creatures of an emerging urban, democratic capitalist order.[28]

Whitman's political aims necessitated creating poetry for the people. "I think of art," he once explained, "as something to serve the people — the mass: when it fails to do that it's false to its promises." But in fact Whitman was little read by the common people; he remained, as a contemporary put it, "caviare to the multitude."[29] Among growing numbers of the educated elite, however, Whitman was appreciated and even revered. In particular, Whitman profoundly shaped a host of left-wing literary radicals of the early twentieth century, from Randolph Bourne and Van Wyck Brooks to John Reed and Max Eastman, who tellingly identified himself as an "American lyrical Socialist—a child of Walt Whitman reared by Karl Marx."[30] Centered in New York's Greenwich Village, the "lyrical left"[31] struggled, as befits the children of Whitman, to reconcile their radical commitments with their profound ambivalence toward the common people.

The *Seven Arts*: Waiting for Greatness

"The spirit of Walt Whitman stands behind THE SEVEN ARTS," proclaimed the journal that for a brief twelve-month span stood as the central forum and "pure, distilled essence" of Greenwich Village radicalism.[32] The magazine was founded in 1916 in the Whitmanesque confidence that the nation was "in the first days of a renascent period" and that artists were the ones who would enable America to realize its enormous democratic potential. Inspired by Whitman, the *Seven Arts* rejected genteel art and culture that seemed utterly divorced from life as it was actually being lived in America. It was to be "not a magazine for artists, but an expression of artists for the community." But the journal would not be content to represent American life as it existed. Like Whitman, the *Seven Arts* also aspired to usher in "the coming of that national self-consciousness which is the beginning of greatness."[33] The desire to become a "channel" for art that expressed American life encouraged an identification with and sympathy for the common people, but the desire to lead America to a new national self-consciousness also produced condescension and disdain for them. Measured against an effete and haughty gentility, the masses seemed vital, robust and healthy; measured against an idealized American people of the future, the people seemed vulgar, crude, and puny. Whitman's children found themselves crippled by the same ambiguous feelings toward the people that had handicapped the master.

The chief editor of *Seven Arts* was the poet James Oppenheim, who revered Whitman as "the great poet of America, and better still, the first great poet of democracy." Oppenheim credited "the mighty native bard" with having "sent me out from my dreams to the living America / To the chanting seas, to the piney hills, down the railroad vistas / Out into the streets of Manhattan when the whistles blew at seven / Down to the mills of Pittsburgh and the rude faces of labor." In Whitman's poetry, Oppenheim encountered "a direct taste of things, the sensations of daily

activity, the solidity of buildings, plowed fields, and men and women —
an immense panorama of life." Yet if Whitman seemed to lead Oppenheim to appreciate mundane everyday life "as he found it" and to express
a democratic "faith in all men, low and high," "the mighty native bard"
at the same time taught Oppenheim and the *Seven Arts* to await the next
genius who could interpret and transform American life.[34]

In a strikingly Whitmanesque editorial, Oppenheim suggests that
America — that "colossally energetic and future-working nation"— desperately needs "creators . . . 'powerful persons' to seize and shape the
welter, to project and carry through great tendencies," to visualize and
realize the "limitless possibility of American life." Spurred by "the dream
of the future, the life flowing vividly and rankly around him," the great
artist can harness the energy of the nation and transform it. In a subsequent editorial Oppenheim asks, "What poet and prophet shall clarify
for us and project a vision which shall lead us on to a new nationality?"
He wonders whether Woodrow Wilson "has the stuff of prophecy in
him" (a question he would soon answer emphatically in the negative) and
closes with the call, "A new poet must appear among us."[35] Democratic
deliberation and active participation give way to passively waiting for
artistic inspiration and charismatic leadership. The common people re-
cede until they are no more than a faint glimmer in the brilliant eyes of
the genius. And those eyes are locked on an idealized future uncompli-
cated by real people.

It is this far-off America of the future that stirs Oppenheim's imagination as it stirred Whitman's. As the *Seven Arts*'s final editorial admitted,
"the task we set ourselves was that of understanding, interpreting and expressing that *latent America*, that *potential America* which we believed lay
hidden under our commercial-industrial national organization: that
America of youth and aspiration: that America which desires a richer life,
a finer fellowship, a flowering of mature and seasoned personalities."[36]
Measured against this future race of heroic people, it is no easier for Oppenheim than it was for Whitman to bring himself to like the less than
heroic people who populate the actually existing America. Surveying
popular culture, he finds himself surrounded by "pure trash, pure vulgarity."[37] The masses are "childish and undeveloped." Their lives are
"shallow," lacking "real purposes and meanings."

Oppenheim is sickened by the "flat metallic taste of money," feels "disgust" at "the soft ideal of universal comfort and the ennui of a colorless
social life."[38] Believing that the limitless potential of the American

masses is being strangled by industrial capitalism, Oppenheim and the *Seven Arts* were led away from understanding the lives people actually lived.[39] Instead the people became victims and cripples to be pitied, uncomprehending children to be patronized,[40] or occasionally rebels to be idolized.

America's entry into World War I in the spring of 1917 blackened Oppenheim's Whitmanesque faith in American possibility. The people showed their immaturity, the leaders their perfidy. No longer was America "my outpost nation, my land of the future."[41] But Oppenheim's millennial hope was not so much dashed as transferred to another people, the Russians. One imaginary people was traded for another. In the face of America's betrayal of its promise, Russia was now the last, best hope on earth.

> O the hope of the world were dead, and we were doomed to the
>   undoing of man,
> Were it not for thee Russia, holy Russia,
> Thou glimpse of the splendid sun in the black battle-smoke,
> Thou shining health, thou virtue in the insane death-shambles!
> To thee, the leadership has passed.
> From America to thee has been handed the torch of freedom,
> Thou art the hope of the world, the asylum of the oppressed,
> The manger of the Future.
>
> Rise, ever higher, more splendid,
> Be as the divine dawn sending the rays of thy promised joy into the
>   wilderness of madness,
> Call us with thy clear lips,
> Call us to the Day of Man, to the Planet of Humanity,
> Call us into thy triumphing Revolution. . . .
> Call up the magnificent storm which shall be a throat and a tongue
>   for our dumb thick anguish.[42]

The Russian Revolution offered heroic life, an answer not only to the aimless destruction of war but to the purposelessness and ennui of everyday life. In March 1917, several months before American intervention in the war and before the Bolshevik Revolution, Oppenheim had insisted that "human nature has stronger and angrier hungers than an unrelieved industrialism can meet." Speaking for "our younger generation," Oppenheim declared that "we aspire . . . for something beyond ourselves . . .

and to which we may so give ourselves that life acquires an interest, an intensity, . . . and brings all our submerged powers into play. We aspire to be alive in every part of ourselves"[43] The unfolding Russian Revolution seemed now to offer the chance for authentic, meaningful lives.

Oppenheim impregnates Russia with the same hopes that he had previously vested in "latent America." "We see Russia now as that hopeful chaos, that confusion of the nebula, out of which a new world shapes itself." The Russian people are of Whitmanesque proportions: "nowhere else is there a people who are so intuitively profound, so emotionally quick. They are not held back by cleverness, and success, and organization, and intellectualism." In Russia, moreover, "democracy ceases to be a name for a congeries of conflicting interests and an equality of opportunity to make money, and becomes the organization of their lives." Admittedly, "dark periods of reaction or destruction" may lay ahead, but "it does not matter. In them the fire leaps which may finally fuse us. . . . Beyond the curtain of fire, a little beyond the wall of battle-smoke, there stands waiting and radiant, Revolution. And in her arms is a little child: an inarticulate infant: the new Humanity."[44]

Not all the *Seven Arts* contributors were as enamored with the Russian Revolution or as millennial in their outlook as Oppenheim, but each of the magazine's other major figures — Van Wyck Brooks, Waldo Frank, and Randolph Bourne — shared Oppenheim's Whitmanesque ambivalence toward the people. Brooks penned lengthy essays in seven of the first eight issues of *Seven Arts* and joined as an associate editor after a few months. The *Seven Arts*'s quest for art that was vitally and organically related to American culture owed its immediate inspiration to the publication of Brooks's *America's Coming-of-Age* (1915), a book that Oppenheim told Brooks served as the "prolegomena to our future *Seven Arts* magazine." Indeed many "Young Americans" regarded Brooks as "the principal source of ideas on the cultural life of the United States."[45]

America's Coming-of-Age lamented the lack of a cultural middle ground between the extremes of "highbrow" and "lowbrow," between "desiccated culture" and "stark utility." America was "a prodigious welter of unconscious life, swept by ground-swells of half-conscious emotion," and highbrow arts and letters bore no relationship to this American reality or potential. Lacking the poetic insight that could capture and channel the "unchecked, uncharted, unorganized vitality" of American life, American energies exploded in a destructive and crass commercialism, "richly rewarded trash." Whitman was the sole exception: "Whitman —

how else can I express it?—precipitated the American character. All those things that had been separate, self-sufficient, incoordinate—action, theory, idealism, business—he cast into a crucible; and they emerged, harmonious and molten, in a fresh democratic ideal, based upon the whole personality."[46] Surveying the contemporary American cultural landscape, however, Brooks could find no contemporary Whitman on the horizon.

In his *Seven Arts* essays, Brooks elaborated on these themes, becoming ever more critical not just of American literature but of American society and the American people. Competition had "left us cold and dumb in spirit, incoherent and uncohesive as between man and man, given to many devices, without community in aim or purpose." The "fierce rudimentary mind of America" was like a "primeval monster" who, "relentlessly concentrated in the appetite of the moment, knows nothing of its own vast, inert, nerveless body, encrusted with parasites and half indistinguishable from the slime in which it moves." Brooks's deep distaste for a "mock-efficient, success-loving society" increasingly spilled over into contempt for the people, a majority of whom seemed "quite incapable of living, loving, thinking, dreaming, or hoping with any degree of passion or intensity." The American people, in Brooks's view, were "sultry, flaccid, hesitant," or "blind, selfish, disorderly." "Incapable of wanting anything very much," the people led lives that were barren and empty. The nation, he concluded, was now nearing "the lowest rung of the ladder of spiritual evolution."[47]

So unrelievedly negative was Brooks's portrait of America as "a society given over to acquisition" that it was difficult to discern the substance of America's "latent force." In his second *Seven Arts* essay, "Young America," Brooks insisted that he detected in "all this confused, thwarted, multitudinous welter of spiritual impulse . . . the certain visible sign of some prodigious organism that lies undelivered in the midst of our society, an immense brotherhood of talents and capacities coming to a single birth." Yet how was a civilization so "hideous" to birth such a wonderful new society? How could a "collective spiritual life" be realized in a society in which individualism reigned unchecked? How could the "creative instincts" be unleashed in a society so completely in the grip of an enervating "possessive impulse"? Looking out "over the immense vista of our society," Brooks, quite unlike Whitman, saw "stretching westward in a succession of dreary steppes, a universe of talent and thwarted personality evaporating in stale culture." When he lamented "the latent force that inexhaustibly spends itself in the trivialities of our popular fiction," his obvious disdain for popular expression and taste seemed to overwhelm whatever faith he might have in a latent America. More precisely, the latent America Brooks envisioned seemed to bear no organic relationship to the America that actually existed.[48]

Brooks could not share Whitman's optimism about the American future because, unlike Whitman, Brooks unambiguously rejected industrialism and the division of labor. Brooks himself was conscious of the divergence. In *America's Coming-of-Age*, Brooks suggested that the force of Whitman's cultural criticism was blunted by his "instinct . . . to affirm everything." In the *Seven Arts* essays he became increasingly critical of the man he called "our Homer." The trouble with Whitman, Brooks explained, was that he had failed to "develop along the path he originally marked out for himself." As he became older, "the sensuality of his nature led him astray in a vast satisfaction with material facts, before which he purred like a cat by a warm fire." In Brooks's judgment, Whitman had within himself too large a share of "the naive pioneer nature . . . to develop beyond a certain point," that is, to repudiate industrial development altogether.[49] Admittedly, Whitman's "robust animal humors" had been useful in breaking down "our exclusively Puritan past," but Whitman, great as he was, "knew nothing of what has been made of life, he was unable to imagine what can be made of life, over and above this miraculous animality. . . . Having embraced life, he was unable really to make anything of it." For a positive conception of life Brooks looked instead to the English socialist William Morris, whose "conception of 'joy in labor,' not only released the creative energies of men but held out before them a vision of excellence in labor that mobilized those energies and impelled men to reconstruct their environment in order to give them full play."[50]

Morris offered an unsparing critique of the fundamental premises of industrial capitalism as well as an alluring vision of preindustrial, egalitarian community. For Morris, the division of labor was the central source of society's ills. The industrial process, Brooks agreed with Morris, "devitalized men" because it used not the "whole of a man" but only "small portions of many men."[51] The obvious problem with Morris's nostalgic socialism was how to roll back the tides of modernity. Morris, to his credit, emphatically rejected the scientific planning of Fabianism, insisting that a radical politics must come from below, from "workers reclaim[ing] their own heritage as craftsmen and citizens."[52] Brooks, too, at times tried to follow Morris's lead, insisting in "The Culture of Industrialism" that the work of cultural reconstruction must "begin low . . . before we can begin the exhilarating climb to our own true heights." And his critique of the *New Republic* technocrats imposing their own desires on the public echoed Morris's critique of the Fabian administrative state.[53] But despite the occasional lip service to democracy, Brooks looked primarily to the "electric" genius for cultural change.

Indeed, Brooks was more reliant on great men than Whitman had been because for Brooks the transformation that needed to be brought about was so much more total. If the "tides of enterprise and material opportunity [had] swept away [the] foundation . . . of a living culture," as Brooks believed, then what within American culture was there left to build upon? If industrialism had completely "bowled [America] over," then what cultural resources were the people to rely upon to get back on their feet? European peoples, Brooks believed, had kept alive vibrant traditions that allowed them to resist the ravages of industrialism and to assimilate "the positive by-products of industrialism itself, science and democracy," but America's peculiar curse was that having been born modern it had no comparable sources of cultural resistance.[54] Brooks's tragic analysis of American life, which strikingly resembles Louis Hartz's, left him paralyzed with pessimism or, alternatively, longing for a charismatic genius to create a national identity.

In his final *Seven Arts* essay, "Our Awakeners," a despairing Brooks took solace in the hope that a great artist just beyond the horizon might still lead America out from its barren desert. Germany, after all, had been in a similarly "pulp-like" state at the beginning of the nineteenth century before the great Goethe "not only electrified the German people but obliged it to create an environment worthy of itself." The emergence of an American Goethe was unfortunately being retarded by the influence of American pragmatists like John Dewey and William James, whose "whole training had gone to make them students of the existing fact. . . . Unable to alter the level of human vision, all they could do was to take men on the level where they found them and release their latent capacities on that level — an immensely valuable thing, of course, but not the vital thing for us, because it is the level itself that is at fault in America." To reach a higher level of consciousness, America needed transformative poets, "individuals who . . . repudiate the social organism altogether and, rising themselves to a fresh level, drag mankind after them." Cultural change, as Brooks seemed to envisage it, was a matter of charismatic creators dragging sheeplike multitudes up the mountain.[55] Democracy was nowhere in sight.

Brooks's fellow associate editor, Waldo Frank,[56] was equally inclined to the Whitmanesque wait for a class of artistic prophets to bring the nation to self-consciousness. Frank's vision, though, was more hopeful in part because Frank was more sensitive than Brooks to elements of an organic, oppositional tradition within America. While Brooks waited for the "electric" genius of a Goethe to transform America, Frank detected signs of an emerging cultural consciousness all around him, in the novels of Sherwood Anderson, the photographs of Alfred Stieglitz, the films of Charlie Chaplin, and the political organizing of Bill Haywood.[57] Frank's vision of cultural transformation was more pluralistic and inclusive, and hence more optimistic. "In the scattered corners of the great Darkness, many men light many fitful fires. When once they meet, a flame will blaze across the sky."[58]

In Frank's admiration for Lincoln, too, one finds at least a hint of an appreciation for democratic leadership. "Moral and spiritual eminence" of the sort that Lincoln possessed "does not isolate, it brings a vast capacity for being close to the ranks of men where intellectual genius must hold aloof." Frank notes appreciatively that Lincoln's "mental average kept him close to the crude ore of the American world." Having achieved that "divine average" sung by Whitman, Lincoln was able to mine the strength of the American people, to bring to the surface what Lincoln called "the better angels of our nature." Lincoln's spiritual leadership broke with "the materialistic culture of pioneer America" but was nonetheless "based on the reality of American life — and in terms so simple that they have become the experience of all."[59] But if Lincoln made it seem possible to join prophecy and democracy, the rest of Frank's writings are less encouraging.

More often, the prophetic leadership Frank envisioned is far removed from the people and reduces them to a purely passive role. The prophet mystically gives voice to the American soul, but, as Casey Blake points out, Frank's "romantic ideal of an intuitive bond uniting the prophet and his people merely asserted such a role without explaining how it might work in practice." Of Whitman's prophetic leadership, for instance, Frank wrote: "As with Moses . . . a deep unconscious impulse made the transfer from his own election, to his people. Since he was chosen, his was a chosen people." But who chose or elected the prophet? Democracy rests upon public appeals that can be scrutinized, argued about, and accepted or rejected, not the mystical transfer of unconscious impulses. Politics itself is almost completely absent from Frank's conception of democracy.[60]

The people's failure to follow the artistic prophets of a new American consciousness only fuels Frank's hatred for "an intricate and oppressive system" that has "barred . . . the rightful progress of our spiritual leaders to an audience." But antipathy directed toward the system easily washes over into condescension and even contempt for the people. If the people fail to appreciate, for example, the life-affirming cultural criticism of his colleague, Van Wyck Brooks, who is engaged in the herculean task of "giving America a brain and a nervous system," then that is because the people "are still in the baby stage of playing with their toes." When the people are not pitiful babes, they are passive, brainwashed victims: "the multitude who might naturally catch . . . the solitary voices . . . of great and hardy souls . . . is too enslaved and enfeebled by the poisonous pabulum with which Business persistently has fed it. Adulterate journals, specious magazines, widely touted, saccharinated novels stuff it too full."[61] Mass media and culture are not something created by the people's preferences and interests but rather are "fed" to the people by a powerful elite in order to keep them sedated.

Like many left intellectuals of the period, Frank was contemptuous of popular culture.[62] Broadway theatre —"the Theatre of the whole American Middle-Class"— is "all that is hideous and perverse" in the American middle class. Frank scorns the "vapid, vacant, shifting throng of spending men and women — loosed for a week from the humdrum of their lives — who fill the theatres." Movies, baseball, and Coney Island are all "makeshifts of despair," confirming evidence that "America is a joyless land."[63] In the 1920s Frank would employ this same template to dismiss jazz as simply "the mimicry of our industrial havoc. . . . This song is not an escape from the Machine to limpid depths of the soul. It is the Machine itself!" Jazz's popularity revealed the hegemonic sway of the industrial system, which managed to convert what appeared as dissent into consent.[64] For Frank, popular culture was a sign not of the people's imagination and vitality but of their dull passivity.

Frequently Frank's American people appear as little more than a dumb, docile herd. Admittedly this is the system's fault —"the American powers take every step to preserve them in a state of ignorance, flatulence, complacency which shall approximate the Herd."[65] But Frank's contempt for the stupid animals themselves is never far from view. Of the working people of New York City, Frank has this to say:

> The day's work is done. The houses spew out their human provender, having absorbed what energy they held. The streets rise with the poured human waste, they become choked sluices leading to the subways. In the fetid stations, men and women stand packed as no Western rancher packs his cattle. Masses of them, mute, unangry, wait for the next train to glide in beside them and slough off its loadful. The doors slide open, the brackish human flow pours through, the doors cut like knives the mass within from the discarded mass without. The train crawls with its inert freight.[66]

Having reduced the people to a passive, undifferentiated herd, it is little wonder that Frank has difficulty imagining a genuinely democratic politics. There is no use persuading, let alone bargaining with, cattle or sheep.

Yet even while denigrating the people as a thoughtless herd, Frank, unlike conservatives such as D. H. Lawrence, insisted he was on the side of the people and of democracy. He sustained this stance, as had Whitman, Oppenheim, and Brooks, by differentiating between the people's latent selves and their manifest selves. But "the tragical discrepancy between the vision and the unquickened matter" led Frank as well as others at the *Seven Arts* to seek out other peoples into which they could pour their thwarted egalitarian dreams. If the American people did not justify Whitmanesque hopes, then perhaps other cultures might.[67]

Frank, like Brooks, was particularly attracted to preindustrial cultures. Visiting a Native American settlement, for instance, Frank found that "here, of a sudden, all of a deep great gentle culture swam into my vision — a culture whose spiritual superiority to ours no intelligent man would question." Where the Indian wandered, "his life had the fluidity of fertile streams"; where the Indian settled, he "created beautiful and lasting civilizations." Indian art was "the pure emotional experience of a people who have for ages sublimated their desire above the possessive into the creative realm." And Indian society was an egalitarian utopia: "The uncorrupted Indian knows no individual poverty or wealth. All of his tribe is either rich or poor. He has no politics. He has no dynastic or industrial intrigue. . . . In consequence all his energies beyond the measure of his daily toil rise ineluctably to spiritual consciousness: flow to consideration of his place and part in Nature, into the business of beauty."[68] The perfectly harmonious and undifferentiated Indian culture of Frank's imagination is the cultural life he imagines to be latent in America, waiting to be born.

Frank found the same idealized gemeinschaft among Hispanics in the Southwest. In contrast to the exploitative and rootless American pioneer, the Mexican "sought happiness in harmony with his surroundings: sought life by cultivation, rather than exploitation." Their durable adobe homes symbolize the Mexicans' connections to nature and to each other. Their houses "are of the earth on which they lie: of the earth of these people and of their hands: harmonious, therefore, beautiful." In contrast, the beaten-up, makeshift "gringo" dwellings "suggest impermanence, indifference to nature, absorption in other matters." Although the American looks down on and even despises the "greaser," in Frank's eyes, "the lowly Mexican is articulate, the lordly American is not. For the Mexican has really dwelt with his soil, cultivated his spirit in it, not alone his maize." Unfortunately, "the iron march" of American industry was destroying the beautiful adobe houses and the way of life they symbolized, just as it was burying the Indian culture.[69]

Frank's desire to be on the side of authentic American people sent him to the Midwest at the close of 1919, working as a writer for the Non-Partisan League. Desperate to connect with latent America, Frank visited poor miners in Osage, Kansas: "They are Me," he reported to Sherwood Anderson. "I can look into their eyes, as I look into the eyes of a horse, and into the eyes of myself, and say You are Me. I am You." Impoverished Kansas farmers had the same ringing authenticity. Living close to the soil, these "poor sweet dull brothers" possessed an "earnest and innocent . . . willingness in them to be good and to be right." Frank seemed ready to assume the mantle of agrarian prophet, but his brief brush with American farmers and miners was brought to a quick end by his revulsion at the politicking of the farmers' political organization, the Non-Partisan League. Attending the league's national convention, Frank found, "As I went up in the scale of authority, there gradually faded out all that was sweet and gentle and lovable in the farmers' world. . . . In its place, doctrine, dogma, figures, political manipulation, words. In place of the farmers' world, the usual carpentry of lives." As the latent moved to become manifest, the ideal became corrupted, by politics, by conflict, by life. "Let us be brave," a disillusioned Frank wrote to Anderson, "and admit that political representation will *always, must* always be a game for the tricky, the brutal . . . the shallow." And to Brooks he announced that "politics is a lie. . . . Representative government under any plan will bring into the places of power men who are shallow, plausible, insensitive."[70] So much for democratic politics.

Given Frank's antipathy to conflictual, democratic politics as well as his contempt for mundane American life, it is not surprising that he would be among the many left intellectuals who eagerly invested Soviet Communism with messianic dreams of a transformed humanity. The Russians under Stalin in the first half of the 1930s seemed to have carried out the cultural revolution that Frank had initially hoped might transpire in America. In *Dawn in Russia* (1932), Frank praised Stalin's regime for having invested industrialism with poetic purpose and an almost mystical meaning. Entering a Moscow factory in which a blaring loudspeaker exhorts the workers on, Frank feels he is entering "a new world." The workers appear "to be working more with their minds than their hands, and more with their spirit than with their minds." When their guide stops the workers so the Western visitors may ask some questions, Frank observes that "they seem to emerge from a distant realm . . . like poets suddenly recalled into the surface of a prosaic world." Everywhere else in the world, factory workers are "bent to a task that cut them off from self," but here in Russia are

> happy workers, because here are whole men and women. Although their individual job be a single motion endlessly repeated, although they stand enslaved for hours to the turn of a wheel which they must feed and feed — yet in these dismal halls there is a whole humanity. Dream, thought, love, collaborate in the tedious business of making electric parts, since these toilers are not working for a boss — not even for a living: the least of them knows that he is making a Worker's Union, that he is creating a world.[71]

In Frank's apology for Stalinism, one can see the illiberal consequences inherent in Frank's political thought. A thriving, contentious democratic politics was inconsistent with the mystical cosmic community that Frank sought. The unanimity of "the consciousness of the Whole" could not be achieved without stifling dissent. Desiring to be "ravished by a community," Frank would gladly suspend individual expression and even concerns of injustice. "There will be no time," he wrote in *The Re-discovery of America* (1929), "to clamor for 'rights,' no breath to bewail 'injustice.' Only eyes turned outward see life in these false terms;

there are no rights, and there is no injustice."[72] Moreover, Frank's hostility to mundane life and its towering vulgarity and vacuousness led him on a desperate search for a culture and people willing to don a heroic mantle, and to infuse life with new meaning and beauty. Latent America was buried too deep; the Indians and other indigenous peoples on the continent had been destroyed or corrupted. But the Soviet Union was the future. Inconvenient facts must be ignored, repressed, or explained away, lest one have to settle for the "bloodless death-in-life" of American existence or the low, vulgar contentiousness of American politics.[73]

Randolph Bourne's Radicalism of Fear

No discussion of the *Seven Arts* would be complete without considering Randolph Bourne, whose biting antiwar essays remain the brightest and most enduring legacy of the magazine. Bourne shared many of the assumptions and aspirations of the *Seven Arts* editors,[74] but the essays he wrote for the *Seven Arts* in the latter half of 1917 reveal a distinctively political voice that deserves separate treatment. Although the literary romantic in Bourne admired Whitman as "our divine poet of democracy," his teachers at Columbia University — John Dewey, the historians James Harvey Robinson and Charles Beard, and the anthropologist Franz Boas — developed in Bourne a political and sociological bent of mind that the others on the *Seven Arts* lacked.[75] Bourne shared the literary radicals' distaste for American mass culture — "its leering cheapness and falseness of taste and spiritual outlook, the absence of mind and sincere feeling" — but his deeper commitment to democratic values generally helped Bourne to steer clear of the unabashed elitism of Brooks.[76] And while he shared the group's enthusiasm for what Bourne termed the "beloved community," his fierce independence as well as the pragmatism he learned at Columbia saved him from the mystical holism that consumed Frank and the millennial enthusiasms of Oppenheim.[77]

Bourne's early prewar writings, however, do suffer from many of the same limitations one finds in Frank, Brooks, and Oppenheim. Like so many other literary radicals of the period, Bourne was absorbed with the hopeful quest for egalitarian community.[78] Only within such communities, the young Bourne believed, could Americans heal their alienated and atomized selves. Writing in 1912 as a twenty-five-year-old undergraduate at Columbia, Bourne argued that American society, with its "egotistical" focus on negative rights, "warps and stunts the potentialities of society and of human nature." Only by renovating and renewing

American culture along socialist lines could people participate as "true personalities and full-grown citizens, instead of the partially handicapped persons that society makes them now."[79] In these early years, Bourne expressed a naive faith in socialism. The solution to the problem of class strife was self-evident to Bourne: "Abolish this hostile attitude of classes towards each other by abolishing the class-struggle. Abolish class-struggle by abolishing classes." Problem solved. Socialism would guarantee "freedom and richness in life, joyful labor and a developed humanity," and at the same time "voluntary association and individuality . . . would be of course beautifully guaranteed under Socialist Industrial Democracy."[80] Of course. These early essays are filled with noble, frictionless sentiments that never address, let alone answer, the hard questions, such as how one goes about "abolishing classes" while guaranteeing freedom and individuality.

Like his *Seven Arts* colleagues, Bourne looked abroad for alternatives to the atomized social life of America. After finishing his master's thesis at Columbia in 1913, Bourne was awarded a fellowship that enabled him to spend the next year traveling in Europe. In France particularly, Bourne felt he had found the vital, organic communities he had been seeking. The French, Bourne reported back, "do not slice their souls up as we Anglo-Saxons do." France produced whole men and women who maintained "the directest connection" between their feelings and their "outer expression in speech, gesture, writing, art." In the "group-mind" of the French were the collective resources needed to resist the soul-destroying powers of industrial capitalism. Unlike American society, with its unchecked cult of success, its "class distinctions," and "tired business men," France was "a new world" in which life itself was valued, where "the distinction between the intellectual and the non-intellectual seems to have quite broken down," and where a singularly robust democracy had been achieved in which "you criticized everything and everybody."[81] Bourne's letters tell us little about France but reveal a great deal about his alienation from American society and his communitarian longings.

While in France, Bourne encountered the poet and novelist Jules Romaines, who fascinated Bourne (as well as Frank) as a "Gallicized Whitman." Romaines was the leading light of a school of writers known as the *unanimistes*, who, as Casey Blake explains, were "dedicated to the expression of French folk-consciousness in an urban-industrial setting."[82] Reviewing a book of Romaines's poetry,[83] Bourne seemed to be swept away by the mystical powers of "mass-life," particularly as it expressed itself in the "mystic union" of the city. In "the surge of the mass" was an end to "the isolation that caste and class and sect and fortune have imposed upon us." As Bourne saw it, "the individual, which our western morality and philosophy has for so long glorified, begins to seem to us somehow less real than the mass-life in which we live and move and have our being." Dazzled by "this mysterious power of the city, . . . which welds individuals into a co-operative life," Bourne welcomed "the merging of one's petty individuality and cares into [the city's] throbbing dynamic life."[84] Such passages are Bourne at his most illiberal, desperately desiring to engulf the individual in "the surge of the mass" and sublimate both individual desires and group identities in an amorphous "mass-life."[85]

His distaste for the atomistic separation and messy chaos of American capitalism even led Bourne, despite his democratic radicalism, to admire the Germans' "sense of efficiency," scientific planning, cleanliness, and order.[86] Although disturbed by the war hysteria he witnessed in Germany as well as a "lack of critical sense" among the Germans, Bourne was so deeply impressed by Germany's architecture and town planning (his fellowship had been awarded to study urban planning) that he was willing to forgive the undemocratic decision-making process. Although "undemocratic in political form," Bourne believed that German town planning was "yet ultra-democratic in policy and spirit, scientific, impartial, giving the populace — who seemed to have no sense of being excluded from 'rights'—what they really wanted."[87]

Back in the United States, after the onset of the Great War, Bourne reiterated his abhorrence of "the crass bravado of militarism" in Germany but insisted that still more detestable was "the shabby and sordid aspect of American civilization — its frowsy towns, its unkempt countryside, its waste of life and resources, its stodgy pools of poverty." Germany, he reminded the readers of the *New Republic* (where since his return to the United States he had been a salaried contributor), had given the world Nietzsche and Hegel and had inspired architecture, town planning, and social welfare programs. "German ideals," Bourne insisted, "are the only broad and seizing ones that have lived in the world in our generation." How, he asked, can one not "feel the thrill of their sheer heroic power," so much grander than the "thinner and nicer fare" we Anglo-Saxons are used to. "Whatever the outcome of the war," Bourne predicted, "all the opposing countries will be forced to adopt German organization [and] German collectivism." Indeed, the war had "shattered already most of the threads of their old easy individualism."[88]

These hymns to French gemeinschaft and German collectivism sit uneasily at best with his youthful praise of unbounded individuality in the essays published as *Youth and Life* (1913), the book that established Bourne as perhaps the leading spokesman for Young America. In one of the best essays of the collection, "The Dodging of Pressures," Bourne relentlessly assailed the social pressures that "warp and conventionalize and harden the personality," stunting the growth of true individuality. Here he condemned "the instinctive reaction of the herd against anything that savors of the unusual," and identified "the secret ambition of the group [which was] to turn out all its members as nearly alike as possible." Society, Bourne concluded in an Emersonian flourish, "is one vast conspiracy for carving one into the kind of statue it likes, and then placing it in the most convenient niche it has. But for us, not the niche but the open road, with the spirit always traveling, always criticizing, always learning, always escaping the pressures that threaten its integrity. With its own fresh power it will keep strong and true to the journey's end."[89]

Bourne's political thought in these early years seemed at times to border on incoherence, praising as he does both the settled community and "the open road," the clean and orderly German town and the restless, nonconformist spirit. Bourne both longed to be part of a "beloved community," where he might feel "the liberating forces of democratic camaraderie," and to flee the "blind compressing forces of conventionality" he had experienced in his hometown of Bloomfield, New Jersey. He was torn, feeling "both the tyranny of the herd, and the social hunger for the larger collective life." Bourne could identify the warring impulses but at this stage had little sense of how to reconcile them other than to conjure up a vague ideal of an egalitarian community that would "be measured always in terms of its ability to create and stimulate varied individuality." But this is only to restate the question: How does one get and sustain an egalitarian community that nourishes individuality?[90]

Although Bourne continued to invoke lovingly the "beloved community," in truth he was, as his biographer Bruce Clayton points out, "temperamentally an outsider, not really comfortable in any group." Bourne's longing to belong, "to be 'in' something," may have had its origins in the social unease and isolation caused by Bourne's tremendous physical handicaps: at birth a doctor's forceps had left his face badly disfigured, and at an early age he had contracted spinal tuberculosis that left him a dwarfed hunchback. But these same handicaps may also have been the source of Bourne's strengths as an uncompromising critic of the pretensions and pomposity of received authority. His deformity left him, as Bourne recognized, "truly in the world, but not of the world." While still at Columbia, he confided to a friend that he saw that "my path in life will be on the outside of things, poking holes in the holy, criticizing the established, satirizing the self-respected and contented." From his vantage point at the margins of society, Bourne could speak truth to power in a way that those who were implicated in the "machinery of change" would fail to do.[91]

Bourne's thoroughly oppositional stance was never more needed than in the nationalistic hysteria of hatred and intolerance that swirled around America's entry into World War I in the spring of 1917. In arguably the finest, most compelling writing of his tragically short life, Bourne wrote a series of antiwar essays for the *Seven Arts* between June and October 1917.[92] In the first of these essays, "War and the Intellectuals," Bourne took aim at the liberal intellectuals who justified the war by imagining it as "the war to end all wars" or "the war to make the world safe for democracy." These inflated words might ease their consciences but bore little relationship to the reality of the war. Bourne poured withering scorn upon the halo of "moral spotlessness" and altruism with which intellectuals tried to clothe American involvement. Liberal intellectuals were more than just deluded, however. They were dangerous because they provided the horrors of war with "a certain radiant mirage of idealism." "Idealism," Bourne insisted, "should be kept for what is ideal." Rudely and insistently, Bourne tried to force liberal intellectuals to face the tremendous damage war would do not just to life itself but to truth, dissent, and democracy. A nation flooded with "the sewage of the war spirit," Bourne rightly foresaw, would have little tolerance for searching intellectual inquiry or radical skepticism, but would prefer instead stale dogma and "simple, unquestioning action." In war, "not only is everyone forced into line, but the new certitude becomes idealized. . . . In a time of faith," Bourne reminded his fellow intellectuals, "skepticism is the most intolerable of all insults."[93]

His most bitter and telling blows were reserved for his former teacher and idol, John Dewey.[94] In "The Twilight of Idols," Bourne argued that Dewey was either deluded or misguided: deluded if he "expected a gallant war, conducted with jealous regard for democratic values at home and a captivating vision of international democracy as the end of all the toil and pain"; misguided if he calculated that by adopting a "responsible" prowar position he could influence the direction of the war. "If the war is too strong for you to prevent," Bourne asked, "how is it going to be weak enough for you to control and mould to your liberal purposes?" To see "the war-technique" as something that can be instrumentally used "to remake the world" in the image of democracy is to lack imagination for the "explosive hatred" that war unleashes. "Only a lack of practice with a world of human nature so raw-nerved, irrational, uncreative, as an America at war was bound to show itself to be" could account for Dewey's eager embrace of the war. Bourne, the idealistic voice of Young America, had matured into the worldly voice of realism, chastising "the children of light" for their fanciful enthusiasms and sunny illusions.[95]

World War I led Bourne to rethink his own optimistic assumptions of progress. The story line of his early writings had been a relatively simple narrative of a progressive youth "slowly and surely" shaking off hidebound conventions and outdated mores to usher in a new, more humane society.[96] Bourne now cast his skeptical eye upon the utopian promises of liberal political economy and international socialism alike. The outbreak of war proved that neither increasing commercial interdependence and material affluence nor international solidarity of the working class would bring an end to war. Irrational war no longer seemed to be a vestige of a barbaric past but rather appeared to be integrally woven into the very fabric of human life. In bravely giving up on "that complacent nineteenth-century philosophy of progress," the danger for Bourne was that disillusionment would be followed by despair. But the potential purchase was a much hardier radicalism, a skeptical radicalism without illusions of inevitable progress or final solutions, a radicalism that put fear of the horror and irrationality of war at its core.[97]

Bourne had a thoroughly modern feeling for the horrors and "poison of war." War was the "worst of scourges," its "sinister forces" too volcanic to be coolly and rationally managed. Certain wars might be justified, but Bourne will have no truck with Whitmanesque efforts to justify war on the grounds that it will foster national élan or restore moral purity, no matter how much those qualities might be lacking in society. Those who talked of "the rough rude currents of health and regeneration that war would send through the American body politic" were either fatuous or disingenuous. War might be necessary, but one should not look to it to create liberal democracy at home or abroad. "The luxuriant releases of explosive hatred . . . cannot be wooed by sweet reasonableness, nor can they be the raw material for the creation of rare liberal political structures." The "sure pestilence of war" weighed much more heavily and immediately than vague dreams of distant and uncertain ends.[98]

Bourne's antiwar essays are also distinctive, as Carl Resek notes, in that they "offered none of the usual simplistic interpretations of the conflict. He made no charges against munitions makers, bankers or imperialists."[99] This stands in contrast to his early writings, in which Bourne, like most egalitarian intellectuals of the day, routinely reduced politics to economics. "Our governmental system," he wrote in the *Masses* in 1912, "is at the disposal of the corporation class."[100] Like most egalitarians, the young Bourne believed that the real enemy of egalitarian community and flourishing individuality was corporate capitalism and the cutthroat marketplace, not the state itself. Bourne's antiwar essays, however, are different; they confront the threat that the state itself poses to the "beloved community." Politics, Bourne now understood, could not be reduced to economics. "War," he wrote, "determines its own end — victory, and government crushes out automatically all forces that deflect, or threaten to deflect, energy from the path of organization to that end."[101]

Bourne developed this insight into the autonomy of the state in a long essay entitled simply "The State." War was not "the naive spontaneous outburst of herd pugnacity," nor was it the product of particular economic classes, for they "have too many necessities and interests and ambitions, to concern themselves with so expensive and destructive a game." War, Bourne baldly declares, "could never exist without the State. For it meets the demands of no other institution, it follows the desires of no religious, industrial, political group." War is willed and carried out by the state at the behest not of the majority or even of particular economic classes but in the state's own interests. "War," in Bourne's famous aphorism, "is the health of the State."[102] And also the atrophying of civil society.

Witnessing the mass hysteria and politicization of everyday life ushered in by the war led Bourne to a profound meditation upon the virtues of pluralism.

> The nation at peace is not a group, it is a network of myriads of groups representing the cooperation and similar feeling of men on all sorts of planes and in all sorts of human interests and enterprises. . . . All these small sects, political parties, classes, levels, interests, may act as foci for herd-feelings. They intersect and interweave, and the same

person may be a member of several different groups lying at different planes. . . . To the spread of herd-feeling, therefore, all these smaller herds offer resistance.

In war, however, the state will not countenance these rival loyalties. The state at war "is a jealous God and will brook no rivals. Its sovereignty must pervade every one. . . . The State becomes what in peacetimes it has vainly struggled to become — the inexorable arbiter and determinant of men's business and attitudes and opinions." Pluralistic diversity gives way to unity. All aspects of life become subordinated to the political needs of the state. "Loyalty — or mystic devotion to the State — becomes the major imagined human value. Other values, such as artistic creation, knowledge, reason, beauty, the enhancement of life, are instantly and almost unanimously sacrificed."[103]

Bourne should be forgiven his exaggerations, for his argument, more carefully couched and qualified, is profoundly correct. It is an argument that those who at the time identified themselves as liberals failed to make or even to appreciate, at least until after the war. And it is an argument that today's liberals moved by Judith Shklar's vision of a "liberalism of fear" can hardly fail to appreciate. Bourne is the marginalized voice of radical skepticism pitted against the arrogant certainty of established power. Bourne's is that rare radical egalitarian vision that puts the state first without overlooking economic inequalities, that recognizes "the precariousness of social life" without relinquishing the dream of "a clear and radiant civilization." It is a radicalism that makes war and its attendant repression and cruelty the "most noxious . . . of all the evils that afflict men."[104] In Bourne's sober, skeptical vision there is inspiration for liberals as well as radicals.

Yet one wonders whether Bourne's sober brand of radical egalitarianism can be sustained for long. Increasingly cut off from established institutions, having forsaken the gospel of progress, and lacking a revolutionary force on which to pin his hopes, Bourne rushed headlong into despair and even fatalism. In what was apparently the last essay he wrote before contracting the influenza that killed him in December 1918, Bourne painted a dismal picture of a totally determined social world within which individuals are "entirely helpless," their "puny strength" no match for a hegemonic society. In peace as much as in war, individuals uncritically accept and promulgate "the opinions and attitudes which society provides them with." The people, in Bourne's vision, are completely passive, and rationally so, for there is no possibility of genuine creation or rebellion in a society where human behavior is programmed by, and flawlessly reproduces, the "codes and institutions of society." In such a world, dissent seems pointless; egalitarian resistance gives way to fatalistic resignation.[105]

Mike Gold and the Appeals of Communism

World War I devastated the literary radicals' Whitmanesque faith in the possibility and promise of American life. Bourne's despair was typical. In the decade after the war, Brooks became so despondent that he was plunged to the brink of madness. Asked in 1927 by the *New Masses* what he thought would succeed contemporary American culture, Brooks confessed, "I can't honestly say that I see any improvement, or any likely to come in the near future." Frank, disillusioned and "weary," contemplated suicide. In 1916 Frank had confidently proclaimed that America was "living in the first days of a renascent period"; in 1924 he confided that "now, my inclination draws me to visions of a deathbed that is the one sweetness in which I seem now able to believe: the sweetness of giving-up and of immediate dissolution."[106] Personal agonies mirrored a loss of faith in American life and the American people.

In the postwar era some literary radicals, disgusted with American "normalcy," turned sharply away from political engagement and political criticism, Brooks very much included. Other literary radicals, however, found in Marxism and the Soviet Union a means of keeping alive their Whitmanesque dream of joining art and politics in the service of a transformed, egalitarian future. In describing "How I Came to Communism" for a 1932 *New Masses* symposium, Frank explained how he had "lost my last vestige of faith in the middle-classes, in all middle class action, and in the efficacy of intellectual groups who are identified either openly or indirectly with middle class values." In *Our America*, Frank had quixotically sought "the dynamic force making for revolution" in dying premodern cultures and "a small band of gallant writers," but now, having found Marx ("I accept him wholly," he gushed), he had discovered a firm "methodology" for bringing about a new and just future. In the proletariat Frank found a class that was thoroughly modern yet had "not been hopelessly corrupted by the sources and methods of the capitalistic order." Artists and thinkers, if they are willing "to hope and fight with the masses," need no longer "despair and surrender alone."[107]

The connection between the original Whitmanesque vision and the appeal of Marxism in the 1920s is brought into sharp relief in the person of Mike Gold, the most important and gifted American Communist writer of this period.[108] Gold began the decade writing for the *Liberator*, the reorganized successor of the celebrated radical magazine the *Masses*. Immediately after being appointed a contributing editor in January 1921, Gold highlighted the Whitmanesque roots of his vision. In "Towards Proletarian Art," published in the *Liberator* in February 1921, Gold hailed Whitman as "the heroic spiritual grandfather of our generation" and the people's "divinest spokesman."

> That giant with his cosmic intuitions and comprehensions, knew all that we are still stumbling after.... Walt dwelt among the masses, and from there he drew his strength. From the obscure lives of the masses he absorbed those deep affirmations of the instinct that are his glory. Walt has been called a prophet of individualism, but that is the usual blunder of literature.... His individuals were those great, simple farmers and mechanics and sailors and ditch-diggers who are to be found everywhere among the masses — those powerful, natural persons whose heroism needs no drug of fame or applause to enable them to continue: those humble, mighty parts of the masses, whose self-sufficiency comes from their sense of solidarity, not from any sense of solitariness.

Whitman's genius was to grasp that "a mighty national art cannot arise save out of the soil of the masses." The *Seven Arts*, Gold continued, had failed because its artists had "based their hopes on the studios." Liberating art must be rooted "in the fields, factories, and workshops of America — in the American life." Whitman thus became the prophet of proletarian art and culture.[109]

Notwithstanding Gold's jab at the *Seven Arts*, the Whitmanesque vision he outlined was in important respects strikingly similar to the project conceived by the *Seven Arts* editors. What Gold possessed that the *Seven Arts* veterans no longer did was a Whitmanesque confidence in a transformed future, and this Gold obtained from Marxism. Writing in the spring of 1920, Gold was confident that while "in dark America" the workers did not yet see the banner that had been hung up for them, "there will come a dawn in which they will see it here," just as the workers have in Russia and Europe.[110] He felt hopeful, he explained the following year, not because he was an optimist by nature but rather because he knew he was "fighting on the winning side" of history. "The Revolution is here," he announced matter-of-factly, "and capitalism is doomed, as surely as absolute monarchy was doomed when the Bastille fell." That communism will replace capitalism, and that "there will be all that we have dreamed of . . . is certain as the sun." [111]

Knowledge that they were on history's "winning side" saved Gold and other Communists from the despondency and withdrawal that plagued the likes of Brooks and Frank during America's numbing decade of "normalcy." But such confidence was often purchased at the high price of insufferable arrogance. As the humor columnist for the *New Masses* expressed it in 1934, "From the mere standpoint of being on the inside of history, a Marxist has an immeasurable advantage over everybody else." [112] Gold's slavish following of the party line in the 1930s and 1940s is prefigured in his unshakable conviction that he was on the side of history and righteousness. For Gold, the question of whether one was on the correct side of history came to preempt the question of judging art on its own terms. Art and culture thus increasingly became subordinated to politics rather than productively joined.

The *Liberator*, like its predecessor, the *Masses*, tried to fuse art and politics, in the main fruitfully. But, as Daniel Aaron has pointed out, the conflict between artistic expression and political commitment, gay bohemianism and serious socialism became more difficult to bridge in the 1920s. Gold and the black poet Claude McKay had been appointed as joint executive editors of the *Liberator* at the end of 1921 but almost came to blows. McKay quit, complaining that Gold wanted to turn the *Liberator* into "a popular proletarian magazine, printing doggerels from lumberjacks and stevedores and true revelations from chambermaids." Gold's "social revolutionary passion," McKay felt, led him to sacrifice standards of artistic quality. In the autumn of 1922, with Gold in California, the struggling magazine was turned over to the Communist party, and it slowly became an almost purely political magazine. [113]

Unlike some of the Communist party functionaries who assumed control of the *Liberator* in 1922, Gold believed that art was "a vital part of a revolution." From California he wrote his friend Joseph Freeman, imploring him to help persuade the *Liberator* to keep its columns open to poets. Unhappy with what had happened to the *Liberator*, Gold and others tossed around ideas for "a literary magazine of the revolution," a magazine that would recapture the spirit of irreverent rebellion that had characterized the original *Masses*. After a few false starts, they succeeded in launching such a new magazine, entitled the *New Masses*. The magazine's prospectus, written by Freeman, echoed the *Seven Arts* in calling for American artists and writers to capture the vitality and "potential riches" of American life. As if to underline the continuity with the *Seven Arts*, Waldo Frank was selected as editor in chief. Frank initially accepted before declining the post (though he, along with Brooks, would be listed as contributing editors until 1930), and instead a committee of six, including Gold and Freeman, were chosen to share editorial duties.[114]

Freeman's prospectus had promised a magazine that would "never take itself too seriously. It must be interesting above everything else; fresh, vivid, youthful, satirical, brave and gay; an expression of American youth."[115] This stance was reiterated in an early editorial that echoed the stance of the original *Masses* (and sounded eerily like the young Tom Hayden's conception of the New Left):

> We may as well be frank. We are against dogma, hypocrisy, and rigidity wherever we find it. We are radical, revolutionary, dynamically for change and growth, and we are impatient with liberalism, compromise and reformism. We are as much against the Socialist puritan as we are against the capitalist puritan. We are as much against a labor-union bureaucrat as we are against Mussolini. Smug formulas and complacent institutions we will attack lustily wherever they seem to stand in the way of human freedom. That kind of crusade is lots of fun.[116]

But despite these good intentions, the *New Masses* never came close to recapturing the irreverence or humor of the original *Masses*. On the contrary, it increasingly became a vehicle for Communist party dogma, particularly after Gold was given sole editorial control in the summer of 1928.[117]

With Gold now at the helm, the *New Masses* became a faithful follower of the Communist party line, but to focus on the dictates of a foreign Communist party is to miss the indigenous sources of Gold's thought.[118] Soviet manipulation certainly cannot explain Gold's insistent emphasis on proletarian art during the 1920s, since it was not until 1928, with the expulsion of the Trotskyists and the commencement of the "Third Period" in the Soviet Union, that the proletarian culture movement become elevated to a central plank of international communism. Until the Communist party called for an "intensification of the class war on the cultural front" in 1928, the U.S. Communist party had shown limited interest in art or literature, as illustrated by the fate of the *Liberator* after the magazine was handed over to them in 1922. Indeed, during the 1920s Gold often complained that American Communists disdained intellectuals and looked down on art as "a childish self-indulgence, not useful, not functional."[119]

Gold's positions, at least prior to 1930,[120] were driven less by party directives than by inner conviction and a Whitmanesque romance with Russia.[121] Gold saw in Russia a realization of Whitman's original vision of an art that was dynamically related to the people's lives. "The Russian revolutionists," Gold wrote in 1921, "have been aware with Walt that the spiritual cement of a literature and art is needed to bind together a society." The Russians were carrying out what Whitman had called for: an art rooted in and growing out of the inherent vitality of the masses. In a 1926 review of Trotsky's *Literature and Revolution* in the *New Masses*, Gold hailed Soviet Russia for having rescued art by connecting it to real life.

> Art is . . . a heroic spirit that moves in the streets and public squares, that marches in the Red Army, lives with the peasants, works side by side with the factory workers. . . . Art is no longer snobbish or cowardly. It teaches peasants to use tractors, gives lyrics to young soldiers, designs textiles for factory-women's dresses, writes burlesque for factory theatres, does a hundred other useful tasks. . . . Art, that was once the polite butler of the bored and esthetic, has become the heroic and fascinating comrade of all humanity.[122]

In Russia art was no longer a useless, decorative ornament but an organic part of the revolutionary struggle.

Gold's drive to politicize art had strong organic roots in Whitman's own understanding of art. In an interview posthumously published in one of the last issues of the *Seven Arts*, Whitman dismissed the idea of "art for art's sake" as "a horrible blasphemy — a bad smelling apostasy." Literature, Whitman told his friend Horace Traubel, must be understood as "a weapon, an instrument, in the service of something larger than itself" rather than as an end in itself to be "worshipped [or] adored." Shakespeare, according to Whitman, "stood for the glory of feudalism." Feudalism and its literature "has had its day," but today "it has no message for us: it's an empty vessel: all its contents have been spilled."[123]

Gold faithfully echoed Whitman's critique. He poured scorn upon "those awful, awful cliches" that "Art is Eternal. Art is never *useful*. Art has nothing to do with propaganda. Art is above the battle. Art is Free, etc., etc." Art, he insisted, was necessarily "a Class Weapon." The creation of great art, Gold insisted, could only occur when an artist was in the service "of something greater than one's own neurotic fluctuations." Proletarian art was "never pointless. It does not believe in literature for its own sake, but in literature that is useful, has a social function. . . . Every poem, every novel and drama, must have a social theme, or it is merely confectionary."[124] Gold felt the same way about bourgeois literature that Whitman had about feudal literature: it was a hollow shell that had no meaning for the masses.

In more subtle hands the idea that art had political or sociological dimensions could be fruitful and revealing, but for Gold the notion freed him to substitute political judgments for literary ones. Possessing the correct politics became more important than the literary merits of a work. As early as 1921 Gold had insisted that "no one, who speaks for the right wing in any age, can rise to nobility and passion," although during the 1920s he generally held to a more supple understanding of the relationship between art and politics.[125] As the decade wore on, Gold became ever more dismissive of those he considered bourgeois writers, culminating in a savage attack in 1930 on Thornton Wilder, who epitomized for Gold the bourgeois writer who, though he wrote "perfect English," had "nothing to say in that perfect English." To those who tried to separate out the message from the style or craftsmanship of the writing, Gold exploded that such a distinction was "classroom nonsense." "There is no 'style'— there is only clarity, force, truth in writing. If a man has something new to say, *as all proletarian writers have*, he will learn to say it clearly in time." Bourgeois writers could have nothing to say about America, ranted Gold, because "the great magnetic continent belongs to the masses, to the workers." Having subordinated art to politics, Gold could dismiss T. S. Eliot as "anti-people, and fascist-minded" and Sherwood Anderson as a treasonous "cockroach aristocrat" while heralding an undistinguished novel by a young radical author as a "significant class portent," representing yet one more "victory against capitalism."[126]

Gold's pioneering call for a proletarian art owed far more to Whitman than to Marx (who never mentioned the idea), Lenin (who knew better than to romanticize the people), Trotsky (who opposed the program out of fear it would restrict imaginative expression), or even Stalin (who endorsed it only after 1928). Gold's romantic invocation of the masses in "Towards Proletarian Art" strongly echoed Whitman and the *Seven Arts*. The masses were the vital life source into which artists must plunge themselves to avoid spiritual sterility. "The masses are still primitive and clean, and artists must turn to them for strength again. . . . We must lose ourselves again in their sanity. . . . The primitive sweetness, the primitive calm, the primitive ability to create simply and without fever or ambition, the primitive satisfaction and self-sufficiency — they must be found again. The masses know what Life is, and they live on in gusto and joy." Submerged in the "mass-life," the proletarian artist achieved a depth of understanding that was denied to the isolated, individualistic artist of the capitalist world who must "brood and suffer silently and go mad." The problem with intellectuals today, Gold continued, is that they "have become contemptuous of the people and are therefore sick to death." [127]

For all Gold's ostentatious identification with the masses, his portrayal of existing mass culture is every bit as negative as that offered in the *Seven Arts*. Indeed, Gold's version of American popular culture often sounds almost indistinguishable from that promulgated by the Harvard-bred Brooks. "We have two art-philosophies in this country," Gold explained in the *Liberator*, "and both are decadent and incapable of lusty, life-bringing fertilization." On the one hand was highbrow art that was "hollow" and defeatist, disconnected from life. On the other hand was the lowbrow, "the school represented completely by the *Saturday Evening Post* [whose writers] feed the masses the opium of a cheap romanticism, and turn their thoughts from the concrete to the impossible." In their "every line . . . may be found the devout acceptance of the capitalist system." The aesthete highbrow looks to art to escape the abominations of this world; the commercial lowbrow art is used to "gild the filth in which we live." [128] Like Frank, Gold reconciled his populist identification with the masses and his dislike for their chosen forms of entertainment by turning the people into hapless victims. To editors who claimed to be "giving the people what they want," he scoffed, "Pimps, dope peddlers and gold-brick merchants have the same apology for their professions." [129] A decade later, in the *New Masses*, Gold again pressed the drug addiction analogy.

> They say the people want it. . . . Cocaine peddlers have the same alibi. . . . The coke fiend does not "want it" — he has the misfortune to form a terrible habit, and instead of helping to cure him, certain shrewd businessmen keep him in bondage. The people want news — they read newspapers — it is a normal taste — but the capitalists who own newspapers have fastened the habit of cheap crime and sports

news upon the people. Mass degradation pays — it forms a habit — the slaves demand their daily dope — it is given to them by the Hearst and Scripps coke peddlers — by the tabloids.

In Russia, in contrast, there was not one word of crime news, which demonstrated to Gold that the people, when freed from the capitalist dope peddlers, did not want to hear about crime.[130]

Gold's unflattering portrayal of the American people was virtually identical to that offered by Brooks, Bourne, and Frank. The masses, as Gold envisioned them in America, had been "hypnotized" by a hegemonic "capitalist culture" that was "present in every short story, every piece of newspaper reporting, every advertisement, child's primer, popular jazz song." The main purpose of capitalist culture, Gold explained, was "to dope the masses; keep them childish; fill their minds with any nonsense that will divert them from thinking." Americans seemed to Gold to be inert, lifeless, bored. The American people, he continued, "find nothing to live for except money-making. That becomes boring in time. Americans are overworked and bored. So their amusements verge on delirium." His colleague Joseph Freeman was blunter still: "Most people today are dead." It was thus the duty of those precious few who were alive to wake the people from their listless stupor.[131]

It was such attitudes that led Floyd Dell, one of the mainstays of the old *Masses*, to forsake the *New Masses*. He found in them a "hatred for the human race, mistaken as a hatred for the bourgeoisie."[132] While Gold was certainly no joyless Communist,[133] his all-consuming hatred of "this vast empire of cheapness and shallowness and hypocrisy that forms the current America" made it difficult for him to sympathize with the real people who inhabited and collaborated with this ghastly system. After the stock market crash, for instance, he relished listening to "the recent music of the victim's howls and tears." The barber or street cleaner who dabbled in Wall Street were pathetic vermin, "cockroach capitalists."[134]

Like the *Seven Arts* contributors, Gold reconciled his idealized celebrations of the life-affirming "mass-life" with his dark portrayals of an American cultural wasteland by imagining a molten American life beneath the hardened crust. So, for instance, Gold condemned jazz, much as Frank had, as a debased crutch of capitalism foisted upon unsuspecting blacks. Gold was confident, though, that "among the masses the Negro will at last find his *true* voice. It will be a voice of storm, beauty and pain, no saxophone clowning, but Beethoven's majesty and Wagner's might, sombre as the night with the vast Negro suffering, but with red stars burning bright for revolt." Once capitalism was abolished, the authentic voices of the masses would be heard as they were now being heard in Soviet Russia. The "gaudy, fleshy, dollar-hunting Broadway" would give way to "the eternal theatre — that voice of the masses, that forum of mass-beauty, of mass-revolt, hope and despair."[135]

Latent America was as "heroic" and "brave" as present America was mundane and petty. Gold, again much like Whitman, envisioned the birth of a "new race" of "Supermen." In the *Liberator*, Gold predicted that "out of our death shall arise glories, and out of the final corruption of this old civilization we have loved shall spring the new race — the Supermen."[136] After visiting Russia for the first time in 1924, Gold wrote to Upton Sinclair that he had found "everything beginning, life young and hopeful and strong. . . . [It is] the earth in the throes of the birth of a new race of giants."[137] Gold's attachment to the people, like Whitman's and the *Seven Arts*'s, was not to an existing people but to a heroic people yet unborn.

In far-off Soviet Russia, Gold was free to imagine that the latent potential of the masses was at last becoming manifest. Not all American literary radicals, of course, became the apologists for Stalinism that Gold became. For every Gold who justified Stalin's show trials and stood by the Hitler-Stalin pact,[138] there were many other radicals who sharply repudiated Stalin and the Communist party during the 1930s. For some true believers, such as Joseph Freeman and Granville Hicks, the disassociation from Soviet communism was slow and traumatic; for others less involved to begin with, withdrawal was quick if not painless. Those who were rebels at heart, such as Max Eastman and Floyd Dell, repudiated the Communist party at relatively early signs of stifling orthodoxy and cant. Others stayed on longer before finally repudiating the party or, as in V. F. Calverton's case, before the party repudiated them. Gold's experience sheds little light, then, on when and why radical literary intellectuals repudiated the party, but it reveals a great deal about why, as Daniel Aaron notes, "Russia [had] become for so many [literary radicals] the holy land."[139]

Although Gold's enthusiastic embrace of communism was not widely shared by the literary left of the 1920s, his disgust with American life certainly was. Writing in 1926, in only the second issue of the *New Masses*, Gold gave voice to a sentiment prevalent at the time among literary radicals: "No humane and sensitive artist," he insisted, "can assent to this vast

Roman orgy of commercialism, this wholesale prostitution of mind, this vast empire of cheapness and shallowness and hypocrisy that forms the current America." The problem with America, Gold and many other literary radicals believed, was that ordinary life lacked great challenges. "In ordinary times," lamented Gold, "writers are never tested by events. They live in a kind of parliamentary peace, and nurse, like liberals, all manner of delusions." Only with war or revolution, Gold felt, can writers see reality with clarity. American life had been dulled by the "virus of success." The "simple souls who save their money, plod to offices, and plan college careers for their children" led insipid, uninspired lives. Social life, Soviet Russia proved to Gold, could be heroic. Russia touched the prosaic and infused it with purpose. The Revolution transmuted even "vouchers, day books and index cards" into a soaring poetry of freedom.[140]

The attraction of Soviet Russia for American literary radicals, as the case of Gold and the *New Masses* helps us see, cannot be put down simply to the collapse of capitalism during the Great Depression. For many literary radicals, their romance with Russia and, more important, their alienation from the mundane, atomized existence of American society preceded the economic wreckage that followed the stock market crash of October 1929. "It wasn't the depression that got me," Malcolm Cowley explained in the *Daily Worker*. "It was the boom." It was "the tripe demanded by the present order, stultified and corrupted," "the life of conventionality, artificiality, and personal ambition," the "organized stupidity" of America.[141] For these radicals, the Great Depression did not cause their disillusionment with American capitalism so much as give them exhilarating hopes of radical change. As Edmund Wilson recalled, "to the writers and artists of my generation who had grown up in the Big Business era [of the 1920s] and had always resented its barbarism . . . these years [of the Great Depression] were not depressing but simulating. One couldn't help being exhilarated at the sudden and unexpected collapse of that stupid gigantic fraud."[142] It was against the backdrop of the complacent affluence and "money culture" of the 1920s, not the desperate, grinding poverty of the 1930s, that Soviet Russia first attracted the interest of a diverse host of left intellectuals, including John Dewey, Lincoln Steffens, John Dos Passos, Theodore Dreiser, Joseph Freeman, and V. F. Calverton.[143]

Even during the 1930s, as Richard Pells has emphasized, it is striking how the radical critique of American society was "in many ways an elaboration of attitudes that had flourished in the 1920s. . . . Writers continued to focus on the intrinsic *anarchy* of private enterprise — not only its inability to produce and distribute goods efficiently but its more basic failure to endow the country with any coherent purpose or mission beyond the making of money."[144] Visiting Soviet Russia in the 1930s, radicals praised a Russia "untrammeled by conventions," a people virtually lacking in "pettiness or meanness," endowed with a heroic purpose that gave a coherent meaning and moral purpose to their lives.[145] The Soviet Union not only offered the idea of economic equality but, more important, held out a heroic, moral purpose lacking in the atomized and mundane selfishness of liberal capitalism.[146]

Toward the New Left

Every new generation is prone to think that it is uniquely positioned to begin the world anew. Certainly this is true of the student radicals of the early 1960s who, in identifying themselves as a "New Left,"[147] intended to signal that theirs would be a movement free of the problems that had indelibly scarred the "Old Left." For the New Left, the term "Old Left" conjured up visions of hidebound labor unions, sectarian political conflict, dogmatic doctrinal disputes, and a blinding obsession with communism. Yet in important respects the New Left was not new at all. New Left rhetoric often sounded much like the Old Left when it was young. From its rejection of the "stale dogmas of Marxism" and its contempt for liberals to its search for a counterculture and countermorality different from that of the conventional middle class, the New Left of the 1960s unknowingly mimicked the aspirations and rhetoric of the literary left of the 1910s and 1920s.[148]

Among the more striking similarities between the young Old Left of the 1910s and 1920s and the New Left of the 1960s is a disdain for the mundane lives of ordinary people. Just how central this disdain was to the New Left can be gleaned from two of the seminal and most widely distributed speeches of the early New Left: Tom Hayden's at the University of Michigan in March 1962, published as "Student Social Action," and Mario Savio's at a sit-in during the Free Speech Movement at the University of California, Berkeley, in 1964, which appeared in print as "An End to History."[149]

"Student Social Action" begins as an attack on the paternal university, specifically the doctrine of in loco parentis that university administrators invoked to justify treating students as children. It ends, however, as much more than a critique of authoritarian administrators; it becomes instead a blistering indictment of the passivity and mindlessness of the entire student body and American society more generally. Linked only by "the *functional* bond of being students" rather than "the *fraternal* bond of being people," Hayden's fellow students suffered "a terrible isolation of man from man only dimly disguised in the intensity of twist parties." Private life had become a pathetic "place of systematic study schedules, two nights a week for beer, a steady girl, early marriage." Hayden deplored this "profound detachment from the cooperative and public life, this buckling down to make a safe buck and a safer life." In today's society, lamented Hayden, "there is no . . . conception of personal identity except one made in the image of others, no real urge for personal fulfillment except to be *almost* as successful as the very successful people." Hayden heaped praise upon the few "creative minorities" who had managed to shatter "the crust of silence," and dripped contempt for the vast majority who remained in a state of "petrifaction," wedded to "the old, stultified order."[150]

In "An End to History" Mario Savio's immediate target is an unresponsive, impersonal, and authoritarian university bureaucracy. As in Hayden's speech, though, specific grievances with the university blossom into a broader assault on American society and the meaningless lives of the masses. Savio complains, as does Hayden, that American "society provides no challenge. . . . [It] is simply no longer exciting." The jobs and lives of the overwhelming majority of Americans are dismissed by Savio as "intellectual and moral wastelands." Savio scorns "the utopia of sterilized, automated contentment," this "chrome-plated consumers' paradise" that is American society. Faced with this "bleak scene," Savio, again like Hayden, takes heart that an alive, chosen few are now "coming to the front" and showing "they will die rather than be standardized, replaceable and irrelevant."[151]

Savio and Hayden both reduced the rich textures of private life to a drab passivity, complacency, isolation, and silence. In the oppositional groupings that by 1965 would become lumped together as "the movement," the New Left radicals found a life "charged with intensity," an excitement and public purpose that stood in marked contrast to "the American bleakness" that stifled them.[152] Here they could give themselves to a purpose that transcended the narrow self.[153] As Jack Newfield saw at the time, the movement offered the radicals of the 1960s what William James called "the moral equivalent of war."[154] Such attitudes might seem fitting in the context of the heroic struggle for black civil rights in the

Deep South, but ridiculing the preferences and values of ordinary people as mindless, meaningless, and boring ultimately undercut the New Left's aspirations to build a genuinely democratic popular movement that would fundamentally change America, just as such attitudes had crippled radicals earlier in the century. Condescension and disdain for the masses are hardly a solid foundation for a mass movement.

Disdain for the lives of ordinary people was, of course, not the only reason the New Left recapitulated many of the pathologies and failures of earlier leftist movements.[155] In the next three chapters, I take a closer look at the ideology and social organization of the New Left in an attempt to understand why it so quickly succumbed to the very problems its leaders initially so eloquently warned against. By 1968, for instance, the New Left had become enmeshed in sectarian fights and doctrinal battles that were every bit as byzantine and dogmatic as those that had crippled the Old Left. At the beginning of the decade, Marxism had been widely seen within the New Left as outmoded and even slightly old-fashioned,[156] yet by 1968 Marxism had become a sort of "unofficial language" within New Left organizations such as Students for a Democratic Society (SDS).[157] The close of the 1960s, moreover, saw SDS' early commitment to participatory democracy give way to vanguard fantasies. And far from condemning oppression wherever they found it, many in the New Left went to great lengths to excuse and sometimes even to glorify repressive political regimes around the world. These are the puzzles I explore in Part II.

SDS, the New Left, and the 1960s

The Illiberal Turn

TOM HAYDEN, SDS, AND

THE NEW LEFT

In the minds of all fundamentalists, porousness makes
for corrosiveness. A porous society is an impure society.
The impulse is to purge impurities, to wall off the
stranger.

    Todd Gitlin[1]

The heretic is the saint who wants to have some
truck with the outside.

    Mary Douglas[2]

October 8, 1969. After nightfall in Lincoln Park, Chicago. Tom Hayden
speaks through a bullhorn to a crowd of two or three hundred people
armed with helmets, chains, pipes, and baseball bats. The group has
promised to visit on Chicago "four days of rage" and has vowed to "tear
pig city apart." Hayden tells the assembled crowd of Weathermen that
he and the rest of the "Chicago 8" (who were standing trial on charges of
conspiracy for their role in street riots the previous year) support them
and back their efforts to "intensify the struggle and end the war." Shortly
thereafter, the crowd of disaffected college students and former members of Students for a Democratic Society (SDS) set off on a rampage,
smashing the windows of parked cars, hurling rocks and bricks through
apartment windows, and fighting with police.[3]

A decade earlier Tom Hayden, having just graduated from the University of Michigan, had drafted a "manifesto of hope"[4] that would define the principles and agenda of a fledgling organization called Students for a Democratic Society. This manifesto, the *Port Huron Statement*, unambiguously embraced nonviolence: "We find violence to be abhorrent because it requires generally the transformation of the target, be it a human being or a community of people, into a depersonalized object of hate." The *Port Huron Statement* insisted, too, that "the brutalities of the twentieth century teach that means and ends are intimately related, that vague appeals to 'posterity' cannot justify the mutilations of the present."[5] What went wrong? How did Tom Hayden and the New Left get from Port Huron to the streets of Chicago? How could a movement that warned against transforming people into depersonalized objects of hate end up referring to policemen as "pigs"? Why did a movement that argued against justifying present harms in the name of some glorious future end up doing precisely that? How did an organization that began with a principled commitment to nonviolence end by enthusiastically embracing revolutionary violence? How did the New Left get from a humane "manifesto of hope" to the senseless violence of the "days of rage"?

In the Beginning

SDS began life as the student affiliate of the League for Industrial Democracy (LID), an organization which, as James Miller puts it, had become "a tax-exempt sinecure — a kind of dignified retirement home for aging social democrats." The main tenets of the LID in the 1950s were a commitment to the American labor movement, the liberal welfare state, and anticommunism, tenets echoed in the affiliated student organization, then called the Student League for Industrial Democracy (SLID). As the 1950s wore to a close, SLID seemed well on its way to extinction — in 1958 it had only three barely functioning chapters, and only thirteen delegates attended its national convention that year. Yet only two years later it emerged with new leadership, new ideas, new energy, and a new name — Students for a Democratic Society.[6]

With the help of a ten-thousand-dollar grant from Detroit's United Automobile Workers in the summer of 1960, SDS was able to hire Alan Haber as a full-time national officer. A graduate student at the University of Michigan, Haber possessed enormous energy and dedication, a keen intelligence, and a vision of where he wanted to take SDS. Haber's plan was to create a "radical democratic organization" of students that would both serve as a "think tank" for the student movement — organizing conferences, publishing newspapers, disseminating literature — and be politically active, supporting and participating in pickets, sit-ins, freedom marches, boycotts, and protest demonstrations.[7]

Haber hoped to break from the nonpolitical, educational orientation of SLID as well as from the union-oriented, anticommunist liberalism of LID, but he did not seem to think radicalism and liberalism were mortally antithetical. In the spring of 1961, for instance, Haber could speak of the need to build a "radical liberal force" in America,[8] and in December of that same year he wrote of "the liberal, left, activist community."[9] The following spring, SDS defined itself as "an association of young people on the left . . . bringing together liberals and radicals." The organization's aim was to put forth "a radical, democratic program counter posed [sic] to authoritarian movements both of Communism and the domestic Right."[10] Haber and SDS in fact set up a "Liberal Study Group" at the National Student Association (NSA), the aim of which was to provide an informal meeting place where NSA delegates could discuss issues "of particular importance to liberals and radicals of the university community."[11] At this early stage, then, liberals and radicals were generally seen as different but on the same side, as allies instead of enemies.[12]

Haber was the organizational brains behind the early SDS; Hayden provided the rhetorical passion and proved to be the more lasting and important influence. Hayden began his senior year (1960–1961) at the University of Michigan ensconced as editor of the *Michigan Daily*, a post he used to call for increased student activism, university reform, civil rights, and world peace.[13] Gifted as Hayden was with the written word, he was never content with words alone. He was the prime mover behind the establishment of VOICE, the first independent student political party at Michigan, and in the spring of 1961 he was persuaded to join SDS.[14] After graduating in June, Hayden was selected to be the organization's field secretary and headed south to publicize the emerging civil rights movement, particularly the heroic organizing efforts of the Student Nonviolent Coordinating Committee (SNCC). In a number of reports, sent to Haber in New York and then mimeographed and distributed across campuses, Hayden helped fix the brutality and injustice of southern society in the consciousness of thousands of college students.[15]

Like Haber, Hayden initially conceived of SDS as an organization that drew strength from both liberals and radicals. While still a senior in college, Hayden had written an article for *Mademoiselle* that described

SDS as well as the sit-ins and Freedom Rides in the South as part of "the liberal student movement." As Hayden became more actively involved in SDS, he began to distinguish more sharply between the terms "liberal" and "radical." Yet at the end of 1961 he could still think of putting together a book of essays by students and young faculty with an aim to "re-generating liberal-radical political discussion." In fact, a chapter of that book was to address "the liberal community in historical perspective," which Hayden envisioned as a history of "the Left." And in the spring of 1962, Hayden spoke of the importance of SDS "touching the adult liberal-socialist community." [16]

Hayden's early ambivalence toward liberalism and liberals is best captured in his "Letter to the New (Young) Left," published at the end of 1961 in *Activist*, an Oberlin-based New Left journal. The letter began with a laundry list of specific "challenges" confronting American society, including "the persistence of a racism that mocks our principles," "the endless repressions of free speech and thought" in universities, "the decline of already-meager social welfare legislation in the face of larger defense appropriations," "the failures of the welfare state to deal with the hard facts of poverty," "the ugliness and ill-planned nature of our cities," the "incredibly conservative Congress," and "the drift of decision-making power away from directly representative, legislative or executive institutions into corporate and military hands." The challenges he identified were for the most part fairly typical of conventional left-liberal thinking of the time. [17]

Yet Hayden identified with radicalism rather than liberalism because he felt that liberalism had become poisoned with the "liberal realism" of Reinhold Niebuhr, Seymour Lipset, Daniel Bell, Richard Hofstadter, and the Americans for Democratic Action (ADA). "Behind the facade of liberal realism" Hayden discerned "an inhibiting, dangerous conservative temperament." Realism was just a pretext for not acting to change unjust institutions or practices. These individuals and organizations were, in fact, "false liberals," who were "eviscerating the great optimistic tradition of liberalism from the Enlightenment to the twentieth century." Hayden still hoped that student radicalism might help to re-create an optimistic, hopeful liberalism in the tradition of Thomas Jefferson. [18]

Hayden chastised liberal philosophy for having "dealt inadequately with the twentieth century," but he also insisted on the paramount importance of "the general ideals of Western humanism, particularly, the freedoms of speech, thought, and association." Rival schools of thought did not escape criticism either. Although Hayden thought that "Marx the humanist . . . has much to tell us," he also insisted that Marx's "conceptual tools are outmoded and his final vision implausible." Even C. Wright Mills, whom Hayden admired above all other American intellectuals, came in for criticism. Hayden found Mills "appealing and dynamic in his expression of theory in the grand manner," but he lamented that Mills's "pessimism yields us no . . . path out of the dark, and his polemicism sometimes offends the critical sense." [19]

Although Hayden rejected counsels of pessimism and defeatism, his idealism was hardly a rejection of pragmatism. Hayden disavowed abstraction in favor of pragmatic experimentation. "It is in the test of their practical meaning," Hayden insisted, "that we must make our judgment [between ways of organizing social life] — not between good and evil, but the more difficult distinction between better or best, or the hardest choice of all, that of the necessary evil." And while Hayden aimed to change, even transform, society rather than just "assuaging . . . its continuing ills," it was a transformation to be brought about incrementally rather than through sudden revolution. "Our gains," he warned, "will be modest, not sensational. It will be slow and exhaustingly complex, lasting at the very least for our lifetimes." [20]

Radicalism, in Hayden's formulation, seemed to be virtually equivalent with searching, open, intellectual inquiry. He rejected dogmatism, which he defined as a style "which employs stereotypes, untested concepts, easy answers, ritualistic language." Radicalism as a style, Hayden explained, "presumes a willingness to continually press forward the query: Why? Radicalism finds no rest in conclusions; answers are seen as provisional, to be discarded in the face of new evidence or changed conditions." Radical change would come about by exposing social ills and taboos to "the sunlight of the inquiring mind." Radicalism seemed like a first-rate university seminar. [21]

In a talk given at the University of Michigan the following spring, Hayden invoked liberal principles to attack the university doctrine of in loco parentis, that is, that "the college stands in the same position to its students as that of a parent." Anticipating themes that were to gain national prominence in the Berkeley Free Speech Movement of 1964, Hayden insisted that the university should not be "the moral guardian of the young" and that college students should not be forced to relinquish their First Amendment freedoms of speech, press, assembly, even privacy. Moreover, "When and where a law is thought unjust and improper, the responsible citizens and institutions affected by the law should challenge it. *That is the relevance of constitutionalism and liberal democracy.*[22] Far from being seen as the enemy of the student movement, liberal democracy provided the language that Hayden used to challenge the legitimacy of paternalistic relations in the university.

Given that Hayden, Haber, and many of the others involved in founding SDS began with a deep commitment to intellectual inquiry,[23] to the freedom of individuals to think and to speak, and to pragmatic, even incremental, experimentation, the later evolution of SDS and the New Left is stranger still. How could a movement that began by embracing free speech as a central principle end up by shouting down opponents in public forums and embracing Herbert Marcuse's scathing critique of "repressive tolerance"? How did a movement that began by celebrating experimentation and decrying dogma end up mouthing stale, simplistic slogans?[24] How did a decade that began with Hayden approvingly quoting Camus on the need "to insist on plain language so as not to increase the universal falsehood"[25] end up in the obscurantism of impenetrable Marxism, most evident in the ponderous rhetoric of the Weathermen? How did a group that began by decrying "the institutionalized worldwide dynamic of epithet and counter-epithet [and] the objectifying of human beings and nations into 'enemies'" end up so thoroughly immersed in a Manichaean cosmology that divided the world into good and evil, the movement and the system?[26] How did an organization that began by defining itself in part as liberal end up excoriating liberalism as the most pernicious of political afflictions? How did it all happen?

The Usual Explanations

The conventional explanations of this transformation in SDS and the New Left more generally proceed in one of two ways. One is to focus on generational change, on the entrance into SDS beginning in 1965 of "a younger, more alienated, more committed" radical.[27] A generation untouched by the *Port Huron Statement* is portrayed as diverting or perverting what had begun as a humane, reformist organization.[28] A second route is to explain this shift in terms of changes in the external environment. Those in SDS, according to this argument, were radicalized by the increasing repressiveness and violence of state and society — the invasion of the Dominican Republic; riots in Watts and other cities across the country; the assassination of the Kennedys, Malcolm X, and

Martin Luther King; police repression of the Chicago, Columbia, and Berkeley student protests; and most of all the escalation of the war in Vietnam.[29]

These two modes of explanation are distinct but not at all incompatible. Indeed, most of the time the generational explanation is woven together with an emphasis on the radicalizing force of objective events.[30] They are commonly found together in the same narrative because both modes of explanation absolve the original New Left vision and commitments of responsibility for the subsequent development of SDS and the New Left. Neither explanation is without validity, and taken together they explain much about the development of the New Left. Yet both explanations are incomplete.

The radicalizing nature of events seems at first to explain a great deal, if not everything. As the violence of the Vietnam War escalates, so too does the violence of the protesters; as the great hopes of mainstream liberalism are murdered, so students' hope in liberalism is extinguished. Some analysts evidently feel that to explain the ideological development of SDS it is enough to list the events of the 1960s. Kirkpatrick Sale, for instance, suggests that "it takes no very special perception to discover the reasons for [SDS'] leftward swing [in 1963 and 1964]" and proceeds to list a series of events: the assassination of John Kennedy, the ascension of Lyndon Johnson, the murders of SNCC workers in Mississippi, and the refusal of the Democrats to seat the Mississippi Freedom Democratic party at the 1964 convention.[31] But the meanings of these and other events are socially constructed. We cannot hope to build a satisfying explanation of the New Left's ideological development from a laundry list of events.

It is important to be clear about what is and is not being claimed here. I am not denying that historical events were critically important in the radicalizing of the New Left. Without the escalation of the war in Vietnam, the intense bitterness toward America would not have spread as it did. Vietnam not only turned SDS into a mass organization (which, given its radically egalitarian organizing principles, created or at least exacerbated many of its pathologies) but also helped those with a darker, more apocalyptic vision of American society triumph over more balanced voices. Events did matter, of course, but so did the perceptual filters through which those events were interpreted and acted upon. And the perceptual screens that those in the New Left brought to events were strongly shaped by their commitment to a radical egalitarian way of life.

The generational explanation is also inadequate. The escalation of the Vietnam War did produce a tremendous influx of new members into SDS early in 1965, and these new recruits did differ from the SDS "old guard" in that they were less intellectual, less eastern, and less Jewish.[32] But the new recruits did not tend to be hardened radicals. As Jeffrey Shero, a leader of the younger breed of SDSer, explained in a working paper prepared for the 1965 summer convention, "The bulk of new membership is found among the liberal-humanist student population. . . . Most join SDS because it appears stimulating, or alas! cool; or are attracted to a specific project." As Shero saw it, the problem was not an insufficiently radical old guard, but rather that "older members . . . with their radical perspective . . . tend to allienate [sic] or at least have difficulty communicating their views to inexperienced people." He was confident, however, that these new recruits would "become more radical" as they become involved with others in SDS and "develop greater understanding of what change entails."[33] It was not so much a younger generation that radicalized SDS, but SDS that helped radicalize a new generation.

The disjunction between the "old guard" and the "new breed" of radical has, in any event, been greatly exaggerated.[34] The younger generation of radicals who dominated SDS after 1965 might have been less intellectual but they were committed, by and large, to the same radical egalitarian way of life that Hayden and others of the old guard had so persuasively articulated. When Shero and other younger radicals insisted in 1965 that the National Office be democratized, they were only making the old guard live up to their own rhetoric of participatory democracy. And in 1968, when Mark Rudd insisted that occupying Columbia University buildings was "participatory democracy . . . put into practice," he was only echoing Hayden's own rhetoric.[35]

Finally, a generational explanation cannot begin to account for why the old guard itself became more radical and illiberal over time. This is a problem that comes into particularly sharp relief as we examine the development of Hayden's thought.[36] The evolution of Hayden, the most famous of the old guard, raises serious questions about the thesis that the illiberalism of the later New Left was attributable to a new generation of more alienated radicals who took over SDS in the middle to late 1960s. Hayden's development also points to problems with explanations that focus on events alone, for Hayden's radicalization *preceded* most of the events usually cited as causal factors, including and most especially the escalation of the war in Vietnam.

Both the objective events and generational explanations are incomplete because they pay insufficient attention to the initial organizational choices and value commitments within SDS, and the way these early choices and commitments shaped subsequent ones. Particularly important for SDS' evolution was the decision to separate the organization from the inegalitarian mainstream. From "the decision to disengage," as Hayden termed it in 1961, came a heightened sense of isolation and alienation from society, as well as a growing tendency to pose conflicts in terms of "us" and "them," the forces of good versus the forces of reaction.

"The Decision to Disengage"

The New Left's desire to separate itself off from an inegalitarian system is evident in embryonic form from the outset of the 1960s, although initially that impulse was held in check by a strong countervailing desire to be an effective force for social change.[37] In "A Letter to the New (Young) Left," Hayden accepted that "an essential phase of radicalism is the decision to disengage oneself entirely from the system being confronted (segregation for example) so that the structure sustained by our former attitudes can no longer endure." Though recognizing withdrawal as an "essential phase," Hayden worried that the radical impulse would be dissipated unless those who withdrew also constructed institutions of their own. Hayden's model of radicalism was not the individual withdrawal of support preached by Thoreau, but rather collective disengagement and the creation of counter-institutions. The New Left, Hayden insisted, must not just reject existing institutions but also "visualize and then build structures to counter those [structures] which we oppose."[38]

In draft notes for the *Port Huron Statement*, Hayden elaborated on the problems posed by disengagement. The pursuit of "effectiveness" must lead the individual to accept the system's mores, to "dress, talk, eat and sleep conventionally." Such a person inevitably becomes "indistinguishable from the established power order." Thus the need for disengaging from the system. Yet Hayden warned, too, that the individual who strives to remain "only honest and clear . . . tends to be encased in an ivory tower, uncontaminated by the exigencies of life which might test the value of his theoretic judgments." Hayden had in mind not only university faculty but also the "American Socialist movements"; "what else is sectarianism," Hayden asked, "if not a compulsion to be honest and clear without regard for the consequence?" The dilemma, as Hayden framed it, was that "it is necessary to work within social and political structures so as to grasp and influence their dynamic. It is necessary to work outside the same structure so as to be critical and unfettered." To be effective and honest, SDS thus needed to position itself close enough to the "centers of power" to be effective, but remote enough to retain the capacity for "radical honesty."[39]

In "A Letter to the New (Young) Left," Hayden had presented the "decision to disengage" as a tactical one: withdrawing support from the system was necessary to undermine and then transform the system. But in his draft notes for the *Port Huron Statement*, Hayden shifted his ground: the decision to disengage was now framed largely in terms of the radical's own need to remain pure or honest. Although Hayden continued to insist that the search for honesty must be balanced against the need for effectiveness, he also added, in a memo to the SDS Executive Committee, that "where honesty and short-range effectiveness are in conflict, we should be reluctant to forsake honesty."[40] If, as the *Port Huron Statement* maintained, honesty and fraternity were systematically thwarted by American society,[41] then disengagement from society would seem to be a necessary step if the New Left hoped to realize the values of brotherhood, authenticity, and equality that were articulated at Port Huron.

In the summer of 1962, though, disengagement from society remained largely rhetorical. Many members of SDS may have felt themselves "at odds with society,"[42] but they were not in fact disengaged from that society. They did not dress much differently from their fellow middle-class students or even from their middle-class parents.[43] Relations with family members were sometimes strained but not usually severed.[44] SDS continued to work with liberal, reformist student organizations as well as with its parent organization, LID. Older liberals, though suspect, were still seen as potentially valuable allies.[45]

The desire to be pure without being irrelevant or impotent helps explain why so many within SDS were so strongly attracted to community organizing among the poor and dispossessed. In the year following the *Port Huron Statement*, SDS became plagued by uncertainty about what an organization should do beyond discussing problems and issuing papers.[46] Organizing the poor seemed to offer a way out of the organizational dilemma Hayden had outlined so starkly in the spring of 1962.[47] By working to organize those outside of the system, SDS members could engage the world while still preserving their own integrity and honesty. The establishment of the Economic Research and Action Project (ERAP) in September 1963 finally gave Hayden and others in SDS a way to act effectively in the world without becoming corrupted by it.[48]

SDS began the summer of 1964 with ERAP projects in ten cities. Many of SDS' most important leaders and activists were involved in these projects: Hayden and Carl Wittman in Newark; Todd Gitlin, Bob Ross, and Lee Webb in Chicago; Paul Potter and Sharon Jeffrey in Cleveland; and Nick Egleson in Philadelphia.[49] For those SDSers who lasted any length of time, ERAP was a defining experience.[50] In a number of the projects, including Newark and Cleveland, staff members all lived, ate, and slept under the same roof. Allies in the community were initially sought out — a union organizer or social worker here, a local parish or civil rights organization there — but for the most part ERAP-ers separated themselves from established organizations in the community.[51] Their communal living and spartan lifestyle, Hayden recalls in his memoirs, "separated us clearly from any other would-be organizers, missionaries, or social workers these poor had ever seen." Indeed the "wall of separation," as Hayden calls it, extended to romantic involvements as well: "There were relatively few liaisons between staff and community people," Hayden recounts, which "only intensified the need for what affection and intimacy was possible among ourselves."[52]

After six months in Newark, Hayden traveled to New York for SDS' annual winter meeting of the National Council. Hayden told the SDS executive council that all American institutions, organizations, and rules were "tainted" and that "one [could] not use these products without the taint coming off on one's hands."[53] If American society was corrupting, those who advocated contact with it put the rest of the group at risk. In the latter half of 1964, Steve Max, Jim Williams, and others who advocated working through electoral politics to realign the party system had not been particularly influential within SDS, but they had nevertheless been given the leeway to pursue their own projects, specifically the Political Education Project (PEP). This time it was different. Amidst rumors of "plots against the organization" and accusations of sellout, SDS axed PEP and painted Max and Williams as apologists for corporate liberalism. It was, as Paul Booth admitted, "the prime example of sectarianism in SDS. We destroyed them." Max attributes the rejection of his vision of political action to "the youth culture that was coming up then, kids who were into drugs and the new culture and who felt they were past electoral politics — we were trying to show what was wrong with Congress and they already felt Congress was irrelevant to them." But this generational analysis is misleading, since most of the old guard, particularly Hayden and the ERAPers, already rejected the notion that SDS should work through electoral channels.[54]

By the end of 1964, the trade-off between influence and honesty initially posed by Hayden seemed to have become almost totally forgotten (even — or especially — by Hayden himself). In its place arose a crescendo of calls for "counter-institutions," "parallel structures," even a "counter-society" that would remain uncorrupted by the inequities of the larger society.[55] The metaphor or phrasing differed, but the idea was the same, whether it was Staughton Lynd describing the "building of a brotherly way of life even in the jaws of Leviathan" or a Swarthmore chapter of SDS speaking of creating "moral communities within an amoral society." As Lynd approvingly summarized the mood in SDS: "What is most clear at the moment is the call reminiscent of the Radical Reformation to 'come out of Babylon.'"[56] The quest for purity was driving out pleas for influence.

The Hayden of 1962 had stressed the need "to work within social and political structures so as to grasp and influence their dynamic," "to be involved enough within the structural mainstream to be influential." And in drafting the 1963 convention document, Hayden articulated the need for "a new left which is insurgent, locally-based, and constructively involved in liberal issues and movements." Even the following spring, with the ERAP projects set to get under way, Hayden could still suggest that a "secondary purpose" of a radical movement, which would include "radical individuals and organizations from the worlds of established labor, religion and education," would be "to spur liberalism" into action.[57]

By the end of 1964, however, Hayden had essentially given up on working with established liberal groups; his attention instead became increasingly absorbed with the prospect of creating a movement that operated entirely outside the "structural mainstream." Toward the end of ERAP's first summer, Hayden counseled his fellow ERAP organizers that "we should recognize that the people are the only source of support we should seek. . . . We want a movement and that means, for now, the development of activity *outside* of all existing institutions, except those in the area of civil rights." No established group, he cautioned, "has an interest in a movement of the poor for social change," and so we "cannot enter into . . . political bartering [with established institutions] without violating the basic trust we have with the neighborhood people." Only by accepting these "new and totally unstable roles" was it possible to transcend "the stalemate of liberalism and America in general."[58]

Hayden's shift in emphasis is probably most evident in a review he wrote of Howard Zinn's *SNCC: The New Abolitionists* at the end of 1964. Hayden had admired SNCC since its founding in 1960, but the grounds on which he now praised it dramatically shifted. His 1961 reports from Mississippi had stressed SNCC's courage in the face of vicious brutality and their commitment to put their bodies on the line for what they believed. Now, writing in the Newark ghetto, Hayden highlighted "SNCC's position as an effective force largely un-integrated into American society."[59] SNCC's strength, Hayden now wrote, "comes from the humanism of a rural people who are immune to the ravages of competitive society." SNCC's significance lay not in its fight against segregation but rather in its "construction of alternative institutions — freedom schools, cooperatives, the FDP — which carry at least the seeds of a new consciousness."[60]

Transforming society, Hayden had decided by 1965, meant "building institutions [community unions, freedom schools, free universities] outside the established order which seek to become the genuine institutions of the total society."[61] Indeed, at a National Council meeting in April 1965, Hayden went so far as to suggest that SDS call a new Continental Congress that would represent all the people "who feel excluded" from decision making in America. Such a Congress might become "a kind of second government, receiving taxes from its supporters, establishing contact with other nations, holding debates on American foreign and domestic policy, dramatizing the plight of all groups that suffer from the American system."[62] This extraordinary proposal symbolizes the extent to which Hayden, and subsequently much of the rest of the New Left, allowed the search for effectiveness to be trumped by the desire for purity.[63]

The Fear of Co-optation

Some in SDS recognized and occasionally drew attention to the dangers of separating themselves from the larger society,[64] but these reservations went largely unheeded or unappreciated, sometimes even by those voicing them. As those in SDS became increasingly committed to their vision of an uncorrupted, noncoercive community, their understanding of what threatened their way of life changed. Southern conservatives were no longer the "common enemy,"[65] as they had been in 1962 and 1963; now it was northern liberals. The integrity of the "beloved community" was endangered not by congressional deadlock but by "corporate liberalism,"[66] not by reactionary repression from the domestic right but by coalition and co-optation from the liberal reform establishment. Overt repression not only was relatively easy to identify but served to knit the group more closely together. Co-optation was more insidious, more difficult to detect, and more destructive of group cohesion. No part of the system was seen to be more pernicious than its "spongelike genius for either absorbing or merchandizing all dissent,"[67] and no element of the system was more reviled than the liberal.[68]

Hayden's and SDS' growing disdain and even contempt for liberals and liberalism cannot be laid primarily at the door of the Vietnam War. To begin with, Vietnam gave SDS an issue upon which radicals could reach common ground with many liberals.[69] Moreover, at the crucial transformative period, Hayden's attention, like most of the rest of SDS involved with ERAP, was fixed on questions of race and poverty, not on Vietnam. Much more important than Vietnam in creating the New Left's disenchantment with liberals was the Democratic party's refusal in August 1964 to seat the national convention delegates from the SNCC-inspired Mississippi Freedom Democratic party (MFDP). More distressing still, the most respected members of the liberal community, including Martin Luther King, Jr., Joseph Rauh, and Bayard Rustin, urged the MFDP to accept the Johnson administration's compromise of two at-large delegates.[70] This proposed compromise only reinforced Hayden's growing sense (expressed several months before the Atlantic City convention) that liberalism was often not that different from "sophisticated conservatism."[71] More than that, Atlantic City helped convince Hayden and many others within SDS that the most well-meaning and sympathetic liberals, by drawing radicals into compromising positions, posed the greatest threat to their egalitarian principles and honesty. In the minds of most SDSers, the Atlantic City compromise asked them to choose between selling out SNCC, the New Left's model of moral courage and egalitarian élan, and turning their back on established liberal leaders and organizations. For most the choice was really no choice at all. Purity and honesty, as Hayden had said back in 1962, must take precedence over compromise and effectiveness.

SDS' growing estrangement from liberalism in 1964 is not simply a matter of disappointed expectations. For the New Left's growing antipathy to liberalism stemmed as much from liberalism's successes as from its failures.[72] Johnson's War on Poverty together with the passage of the landmark Civil Rights Act posed a fundamental challenge to SDS' identity.[73] The danger with such liberal programs, as a paper prepared for the summer 1964 SDS convention said, was that "corporate liberalism may produce economic programs that *appear* to be the same as those of the insurgent movements."[74] To distinguish genuinely radical egalitarian programs from those liberal "tokenist" reforms that were designed only to co-opt dissent and shore up the system, SDS felt impelled to place increasing emphasis on "the question of power and participation."[75] At the same time, SDS became increasingly critical of liberal democratic structures and norms — political conflicts in America were "sterile, rhetorical, and meaningless," elections had "an aura of unreality without meaningful choice," and intellectual freedom was a sham.[76] Twentieth-century American liberalism was "committed to a manipulative, undemocratic" politics.[77] For many SDSers, defining their own identity increasingly meant rejecting, even demonizing, liberalism.

The ERAP organizing experience helped accelerate SDS' tendency to define itself in opposition to liberalism. It was the organized liberal groups in the inner cities — the social workers, welfare department staff, labor unions, church organizations — that most threatened to compromise SDSers' "radical honesty" and draw them into the system. ERAP's aim, after all, was not just to ameliorate the conditions of the poor but to build "a genuine movement of the poor aimed at an all-out assault on the economic and political priorities of this country."[78] One of the topics on the agenda for the initial ERAP Training Institute, held in June 1964, was how to "prevent co-optation of our movement by more 'respectable' established liberal groups."[79] The difficulties ERAP had in mobilizing the urban poor were often put down to the ability of liberal politicians and organizations to buy off dissent.[80] Liberals thus threatened the organizational integrity of SDS not only by tempting radicals into the system but also by ameliorating the discontent necessary to mobilize and radicalize the oppressed.

The escalation of the Vietnam War began to have its own substantial impact on SDS in the early months of 1965, particularly after the commencement of bombing in February. Over the next several years, the horror of President Johnson's war in Vietnam would help to transform the New Left's already well-developed antipathy toward liberals into a deep and visceral loathing. But Vietnam's most immediate impact upon SDS was to spur a huge influx of new members. If issues of race and poverty raised the problem of co-optation for SDS, Vietnam raised the danger of dilution. These new members might be opposed to the war, but were they really radical? "Most students," as Jeff Shero worried, were like "the bulk of America . . . tied to the status quo." "If a chapter is over-expanded by taking in too many moderates," Shero warned, "its radical nature will be lost."[81] Expansion, then, was fraught with the same dangers to SDS' organizational integrity as co-optation.

As SDS continued to expand through the first half of 1965, there emerged a heightened concern with boundaries and purity, with selling out, with false friends.[82] For example, Bayard Rustin, a prominent black pacifist who had served time on a chain gang and had been one of the prime movers behind the 1963 march on Washington, was excoriated after he not only advocated coalition politics[83] but also opposed the 1965 march on Washington, which he feared was becoming "a frenzied, one-sided anti-American show."[84] In a stinging open letter, published in *Studies on the Left*, Staughton Lynd accused Rustin of "apostasy" and of "betray[ing]" his own and the movement's positions and "set[ting] the stage for a government witch-hunt."[85] In a subsequent issue, sociologist Herbert Gans was sharply critical not only of Lynd's attack on Rustin but also of Hayden's editorial attacking his coeditors at *Studies* for their advocacy of a "radical center." Lynd's and Hayden's jointly written reply to Gans shows that they felt the main threat to their egalitarian vision came less from opponents than from false friends. SDS and SNCC, they wrote, have been engaged in "a continuous fight to prevent being destroyed organizationally, not by the ultra-right or the Johnson Administration but by persons who supposedly have the same goals."[86]

By the summer of 1965, most in the New Left now divided the world into "the movement" on the one side and "the system" or "the establishment" on the other side — and liberals not only were on the side of the system, they were its ideological and political core. As "liberal" became a term of abuse, those like Rustin who sought to work with the system were cast out as threats to the purity of the movement. "Of course, such a person has become corrupted," explained one activist. "In trying to become part of the power structure, he is forced to lose his militancy; he forgets the people he should be fighting for. He has been taken over by the system." "Courting 'persons in public life,'" argued another, "guarantees an early death by incorporation."[87] Those who did not oppose the system were its minions, either conscious or unwitting. Throughout the New Left ran a dread that "the energies of militant community people and activists will be absorbed and channeled in [some] new 'sophisticated' direction" by the system.[88] The system's protean capacity for co-optation meant that the New Left felt compelled to invest enormous energy in patrolling the behavior of fellow radicals, making sure that their commitment to the movement did not waver or become diluted by compromise and accommodation.

The consequences of the fear of co-optation were sometimes perverse in that more oppressive social structures could become preferable to less oppressive social structures. In *Studies on the Left*, Hayden's then-girlfriend Connie Brown reported on an ERAP community-organizing conference held in Cleveland in February 1965. Brown relates a debate between those who felt that higher welfare payments and a higher standard of living in the North "meant that things got better as you go north" and others (who seemed to be in a definite majority) who believed "that things get worse, because the poor are being bought off, and their vision clouded by minor concessions." At one point in the meeting a black man from a northern city got up to discuss programs aimed at getting dropouts back into high school. The man took the position that poor people should try "to enter the small cracks in American society open to them." These views met with a chilly reception from the other participants at the meeting. Brown commented:

> In order to survive in the northern cities, to adjust, to enter the tiny crack, the poor man must blind himself to innumerable absurdities, and in doing so, he distorts his vision of himself and of the world he lives in. In the south, where things are "wide open," it is difficult for the poor Negro to blind himself. Presumably for this reason, the people from Mississippi were able to cut through again and again to the absurdities that lie at the root of the innumerable adjustments that the northern poor people did not even know they had made.

Unambiguous repression, as in the South, was preferable because it made it easier for people "to 'cut loose' from the thin but powerful strings that tie them to a society that offers them almost nothing." It became easier, then, to see the need for an alternative movement and "the forging of a new identity."[89]

The Good Inside and the Monstrous Outside

Evident in such thinking is the growing pressure within SDS to create a version of American society that could justify and hence sustain their egalitarian way of life. SDS' increasing focus on the hidden dangers and evils of the American system stemmed in large part from its egalitarian mode of organizing. The often-trying life inside the collectivity was justified by exaggerating the horrors of life outside the group. Life inside might be frustrating, members reminded each other, but how much more awful was life on the outside.[90]

The day-to-day social interactions within ERAP were particularly important in this regard. ERAP projects were generally structured in a radically egalitarian fashion, without formal leadership roles and with decisions reached through consensus.[91] In Cleveland, for instance, meals were communal and cooking was shared equally within the group.[92] Individuals did have different roles, but to avoid creating a status hierarchy, people were designated as "keepers" ("broom keeper" and "research keeper," for example) rather than as directors.[93] "The general internal functioning of [the group]," the project's opening report explained, "could best be described . . . as 'loosey-goosey.' In many senses, authority is evenly dispersed throughout the group."[94]

The egalitarian structure of these groups quickly created tensions. The insistence that actions be taken collectively and that decisions be reached by consensus made for prolonged, trying meetings. As Sharon Jeffrey remembers, "We had long, long discussions — twelve hours. Eighteen hours. Six or seven weeks into the summer, we had a twenty-four-hour discussion to decide whether we could take off *one* day and go to the beach."[95] Similar problems surfaced in Newark: "The problems of operating a staff of 45 in a democratic manner," reported the Newark project, "are much greater than anybody seemed to realize at first. Although many of us regard voting as undemocratic, there is a real question about whether we can afford to take 8 hours to attain a consensus on every issue."[96]

Little wonder that only a few ERAP projects lasted more than a year or two. As frustrations with dissension and interminable meetings mounted, many individuals packed up and left.[97] Those who stayed on justified their decision to themselves and to each other by converting ERAP into a heroic struggle against a monstrous enemy. Nothing else could justify the almost total commitment of self. "I never went to a movie," Jeffrey recalls, "I never went out to dinner. I didn't go to the beach. I didn't do any restful things. I didn't do anything on my own. Everything was with the group."[98] The need to justify personal sacrifice together with the need to halt others in the group from leaving created enormous pressures to believe that those inside the group were righteous and those outside vile.[99] How ERAPers chose to live with each other thus explains much of why ERAP was such a radicalizing experience for those who, like Hayden, remained in it for any length of time.[100]

Internal tensions were not limited to ERAP, however. The 1964 SDS convention, unlike the previous two summer conventions, had been unable to agree on a common statement, and debate was often inconclusive and sometimes rancorous.[101] Immediately after the September 1964 National Council meeting, Gitlin confided to Robb and Dorothy Burlage that he was concerned that "organization cohesion was now under fire by strong, if indecipherable, conflicts," which manifested themselves in "strong language and disintegrative caucusing." SDS' steady growth, Gitlin worried, was "eclipsing . . . the friendship base of the 'original' SDS."[102] The word "faction" began to be used regularly within the organization,[103] and the December National Council meeting of that year played out the intensely acrimonious factional fight between those few like Max, who advocated involvement in electoral politics, and most of the rest of SDS, who by now rejected such a course.[104]

By the time of the 1965 summer convention, which came on the heels of the tremendous membership surge that followed the SDS-sponsored antiwar march in April 1965, these internal tensions reached the breaking point. The 1965 convention, according to Sale, was the first in which "most of the people were unknown to each other."[105] Paul Booth described it as "a loony convention: everyone was loony."[106] Workshops debated whether or not to have a chairman, and "full plenary sessions of 250 people were chaired by members picked at random with no regard to ability."[107] Meetings turned into meandering, even rambling, sessions on whatever topics individuals chose to bring up.[108] Efforts to draw up policy statements were denounced as "statementism."[109] An attempt to craft a statement on foreign policy got nowhere; "the resolution that finally passed," reports Sale, "ended up being a denunciation of foreign policy resolutions."[110] "The lack of structure," several participants complained, meant that "everyone talked about everything" and no decisions were reached.[111]

The tremendous growth in SDS membership during the fall of 1964 and 1965 together with the organization's increasing hostility to all authority and structure meant that SDS found it ever more difficult to agree on what it favored. Collective decisions, never easy in SDS, now became excruciatingly difficult, if not impossible. Unwilling to rely upon the kind of rules and structures that most large organizations (and SDS was now a very large organization) use to function effectively, those in SDS were impelled to hold their organization together by focusing increasing attention on the boundary separating the movement from the system. SDSers now regularly demonized the outside world in a way that had been relatively uncommon in the New Left prior to the middle of 1964.

The demonization of America did not, of course, occur all at once. Different individuals followed different trajectories, and yet there was an unmistakable collective shift in 1964 and 1965. As "the movement" increasingly became an all-encompassing source of identification and as the lives of those in SDS became increasingly absorbed by and defined in terms of the alternative institutions and social relationships that constituted the movement,[112] the sense of distance from American society grew. Indeed, that sense of separation from American society *had* to grow in order for New Left radicals to sustain their countercultural lives with each other.

In the afterglow of Port Huron, SDS officers had issued "An Open Letter to the Student Community," which stated that "we are honestly and openly critical of *our* society." Similarly, in drafting the 1963 *America and the New Era* statement, Hayden and Richard Flacks spoke of how reform from the top failed "to cope effectively with *our* fundamental economic and social problems." By the middle of 1965 the identification of American society as "us" had all but vanished from the New Left. After the spring of 1965, Gitlin recalls, "whenever I spoke of my country and its government, the pronoun ['we'] stuck in my throat." America had become "them."[113]

Here as elsewhere, Hayden's evolution was a bellwether of the future development of SDS. The ambivalence toward American society that characterized Hayden's early thought had all but vanished by the beginning of 1965. His relationship with his father, which had been strained by his early activism, now "descended into a complete break."[114] His condemnation of the American system became increasingly sweeping and strident. In the spring of 1962 Hayden had written that "a central fatal fact about the United States" is that "it is a republic, not a democracy, and nearly everyone wants to keep it that way." By the beginning of 1965 Hayden had accepted Marcuse's view of the United States as "the most flexible of totalitarianisms."[115] America, Hayden now insisted, was a "rotten society." He seemed seized with revulsion at the thought of America. "Mississippi," he wrote, "is not an isolated wasteland left outside of 'mainstream America.' It is more nearly a deliberate creation of the nation's liberal political and economic elites and, as such, raw testimony to the *unspeakable qualities* of ordinary American life."[116]

By the spring of 1965 this view of American society as fundamentally rotten or sick had become widespread within SDS.[117] Rapidly receding was talk of coping with America's "problems" or even of "correcting" American society.[118] In its place emerged a language of corruption, cleansing, and, later, violence. According to one sympathetic observer, the New Left's aim was "to wash away so many of America's false totems, and cleanse so many of its rotted institutions."[119] This shift in language and style of thought emerged out of and justified the decision to build egalitarian groups at the margins of society. Only a view of the larger society as morally contaminating could justify the New Left's disengagement. And having constructed a view of America as "a profoundly inegalitarian, diseased society" and "a fundamentally rotten system," many members of SDS came to believe that only drastic, revolutionary transformation would suffice.[120]

By the spring of 1965 the future illiberal trajectory of the New Left was clearly discernible although not yet inevitable. Writing in the 1965 summer issue of *Dissent*, Irving Howe spotted in the New Left an "extreme, sometimes unwarranted, hostility toward liberalism," "an unconsidered enmity toward something vaguely called the Establishment," an "equally unreflective belief in 'the decline of the West'" "a crude, unqualified anti-Americanism," and "a vicarious indulgence in violence, often merely theoretic."[121]

Turning to Violence

In his memoirs Hayden suggests that the illiberalism and violence of the later New Left must be understood as a reflection of the ills of America. "We ourselves," he laments, "became infected with many of the diseases of the society we wished to erase." Hayden insists that the New Left arrived at violent confrontation in the streets "not out of political preference but only as a last resort" after having exhausted conventional channels. Once in the streets, moreover, the New Left's resort to violence, according to Hayden, was primarily in reaction to the brutality and violence initiated by police.[122]

There is no need to downplay police brutality in Chicago, Berkeley, Newark, and Columbia, or the violence of American society generally, to see that Hayden's account is inadequate. For Hayden's formulation leaves out altogether the internal organizational and ideological dynamics of the New Left that contributed to its turn to violence. The focus on police brutality neglects the ways in which the New Left, before it ever ended up in the streets, had come to embrace violence. Nor was this turn to violence a matter of a few misfits taking over SDS in its later years, for a number of early SDSers, including Hayden, were at the forefront of this violent turn.

The New Left's turn to violence was not just a reflection of the general level of violence in American society but was rooted in the way those in the New Left had chosen to organize themselves. The New Left took to the streets not because, as Hayden claimed at the time, "no institution is changeable from within," but rather because their intense fear of co-optation had left them without the allies necessary to effect social change.[123] They had not tried the system and found it wanting; rather, fearing that the system would co-opt or tame them, they had looked outside the system to the poor and dispossessed. When these groups responded not as egalitarians but as fatalists, the New Left was left alone. And absent allies in the larger population, New Left students often found violent confrontation in the streets to be the only way to achieve the social transformation they sought.

By 1965 SDS leaders had become convinced that they faced an oppressive, "totalitarian" system equipped with virtually limitless techniques for co-opting dissent. Writing in the spring of 1965, Hayden drew explicitly upon Marcuse's analysis of "one-dimensional society," warning that "almost everyone develops a vested interest of some kind in the American system as a whole, and from within the system there are virtually no legitimate places from which to launch a total opposition movement."[124] This mode of thinking, which had become commonplace within the New Left by the end of 1965,[125] led the New Left to oscillate between a defeatism on the one hand (evident in Hayden's essay "The Ability to Face Whatever Comes," written at the outset of 1966) and a longing for violent confrontation on the other.[126]

Moreover, if the system was as rotten and diseased as those on the New Left believed it to be, by mid-1965 it was difficult to resist the argument that any means would be justified in bringing it to an end. "There is nothing sacrosanct about the fabric of our society," Hayden had written as early as December 1963, "if the fabric is a snarl and a strangling cord." Using a different metaphor, another radical reminded his fellows, "If the eye be jaundiced, pluck it out. If the society is rotten, rid thyself of it."[127] The more ominous America became in the eyes of the New Left, the more irresistible became the arguments in favor of violence; the more righteous the movement, the easier to sanction its use of almost any means. After all, something so bad could hardly be made worse, and something so good could hardly act badly. Having demonized the system and cloaked the movement in purity, the slide toward righteous and even senseless violence was difficult to halt.

The division between the good inside and the monstrous outside produced its logical corollary: a dichotomy between the righteous violence of the New Left and the oppressive violence of the system. This line of thought was most fully elaborated by Marcuse in his 1967 lecture "The Problem of Violence and the Radical Opposition." "The concept of violence," Marcuse explained, "covers two different forms: the institutionalized violence of the established system and the violence of resistance, . . . [the] violence of suppression and [the] violence of liberation." "The violence of revolutionary terror," Marcuse continued, "is very different from that of the White terror, because revolutionary terror as terror implies its own abolition in the process of creating a free society, which is not the case for the White terror."[128] Violence aimed at liberating man was on a different moral plane than violence aimed at repressing man. Marcuse only made explicit a reasoning process that suffused the New Left by the mid-1960s.[129] The use of violence was justified, many in the New Left comforted themselves, because theirs was a violence to end all violence, a liberating and righteous violence that would rid the world of a system that deformed and destroyed people. Such glorious ends justified, even ennobled, violent means.

Forgotten were their own early warnings about the ways in which means shape ends. In 1961 Hayden had insisted that social movements must reject "the illusions and super-truths that in this century have licensed revolutionaries to use any means, often violent ones, to gain their ends." The same theme was worked into the *Port Huron Statement,* which accepted that "the brutalities of the twentieth century teach that means and ends are intimately related, that vague appeals to 'posterity' cannot justify the mutilations of the present." The early SDS and SNCC leadership were steeped in Camus, for whom "the great event of the twentieth century was the forsaking of the values of freedom by the revolutionary movement."[130] Hayden's charismatic counterpart in SNCC, Bob Moses, was profoundly influenced by Camus's warning that "those who revolted against oppression might in the process become 'executioners'—in fact or in attitude—after having rebelled successfully against their 'victim' status." The problem, as Moses posed it, was whether "you can move Negro people from the place where they are now the victims of this kind of hatred, to a place where they don't in turn perpetuate this hatred."[131] The emphasis on countercommunities in part grew out of the New Left's conviction that the means needed to be intimately related to ends, that in order for "there [to] be progress toward a new and integrated society . . . some small model of the new and envisioned society [must be] built within the old."[132]

By 1964, though, leaders of both SNCC and SDS already sounded radically different than they had in 1961 and 1962. Within SNCC, which was organized as a tightly bound egalitarian collective, Camus was fast giving way to Frantz Fanon as patron saint.[133] Where Camus warned against the individual rebel succumbing to the "temptation of hatred" and becoming an executioner, Fanon taught that true psychological liberation for the oppressed would come only if the oppressed seized their independence through violent, armed struggle with the oppressor. For Camus, hateful means necessarily foreshadowed hateful ends; for Fanon, horrible violence was the only means capable of realizing true liberation. To invoke Fanon and Camus in this way is not to explain the shift in SNCC's orientation in terms of abstract political theorizing. Those in SNCC did not shift because they read *Wretched of the Earth*; rather, they read and reread *Wretched of the Earth* because its message spoke to and reinforced their egalitarian mode of organizing in a way that Camus's message of individualistic rebellion, which Camus portrayed as the antithesis of collective revolution, did not.

A similar although somewhat later metamorphosis occurred within SDS, a transformation symbolized by the newfound attraction Hayden and his fellow ERAPers felt for the Bertolt Brecht poem "To Those Born Later." Pinned up in the ERAP office in Newark were the poem's foreboding lines:

Even the hatred of squalor
Makes the brow grow stern.
Even anger against injustice
Makes the voice grow harsh. Alas, we
Who wished to lay the foundations of kindness
Could not ourselves be kind.
But you, when at last it comes to pass
That man can help his fellow man,
Do not judge us
Too harshly.

Or, as soon-to-be SDS president Greg Calvert, drawing out the logical implications of this style of thought, would put it in 1966: "Our freedom is not to be free but to be a force for freedom." In an interview many years later, Hayden conceded that the Brecht poem, by placing ends over means, "justifies anything. You have no flaws. They're all written off to historical necessity."[134]

To accent the transformation that occurred within the New Left is not to accept that revolutionary violence was something foreign grafted onto the original New Left at a later stage by a new breed of radicals. Nor is it to accept that the New Left's turn to revolution came only in the late 1960s as a reaction to an unprecedented series of horribly violent events — the assassinations of Martin Luther King and Robert Kennedy, the "police riot" at the Chicago convention, the Tet offensive, and on and on. Events did matter and so did the new breed of radical, but these explanations miss the ways in which the longing for total revolution, to use Bernard Yack's phrase,[135] was rooted in the egalitarian commitments and organization of the early New Left. Contrary to the account of Sale and others,[136] an identification with revolutionary action permeated the New Left long before 1968 or even 1966, and most of the SDS old guard were no less at home with calls for revolutionary change than were the newer members.[137]

Indeed, the attraction to revolutionary transformation and a righteous violence that would redeem America and even the world had been there in some ways from the outset. It was evident in Hayden's widely circulated 1961 report, "Revolution in Mississippi," in which he reported approvingly that those students in SNCC "have decided not only to protest but to seek social transformation as well, and that is revolution. They have decided it is time right now . . . to give blood and body if necessary for social justice, for freedom, for the common life, and for the creation of dignity for the enslaved, and thereby for us all." It was there, too, in Hayden's hope that these SNCC activists would be harbingers of "a revolution that would reduce complexity to moral simplicity . . . [and] give man back his 'roots,'" and in his extravagant praise of the "beautiful fury" of the sit-ins. It was evident, too, in the tremendous attraction that Todd Gitlin and his Harvard friends felt toward Barrington Moore's message in the fall of 1962 that "protest . . . has to take the form of destructive criticism of a destructive system," and that saving the world required "simultaneous revolutions in the United States and the Soviet Union."[138] All this came before Vietnam was even a glimmer in the radical eye.

Even during ERAP's sunny inaugural summer, a number of the organizers seemed attracted to violent confrontation as a means of revealing the underlying power realities. In August 1964, for instance, the Newark project reported back to the ERAP national headquarters, "In general we saw the possibility of a riot as a good opportunity for confrontation over some basic issues."[139] Indeed, ever since the 1963 manifesto *America and the New Era*, which had spoken hopefully of "a new anger" generating "the new insurgency," there had been a lot of loose talk within SDS about living "the insurgent way of life." Long before Watts, some in SDS looked with hope to "the explosion of mass demonstrations in Northern cities" as a way of opening up "the possibilities of a political transformation."[140]

The language of revolution and violent confrontation was also evident in the Berkeley Free Speech Movement that shook the campus in the autumn of 1964. "What happened at Berkeley this fall," wrote one participant, "can with some justice be regarded as a scale model revolutionary movement within the University community." In an open letter to the Berkeley students, Bradley Cleveland urged, "There is only one proper response to Berkeley from undergraduates: that you organize and split this campus wide open! From this point on, do not misunderstand me, my intention is to convince you that you do nothing less than begin an open, fierce, and thoroughgoing rebellion on this campus." In confronting police, students found egalitarian community: "the students of a large, anonymous university lost, for a moment, their feeling of being strangers to one another. Different in their motives, they lost their fear of difference in a common feeling of rebellion, and in a sense of equality in banding together."[141]

It was in the summer of 1964, not the summer of 1968, that the Swarthmore SDS chapter drew up a draft statement for the National Convention, which spoke approvingly of "revolutionary change . . . coming from islands of transformed society within the old . . . [that] spread by force of example or by guerrilla warfare until they control the whole country." In this model, the best examples of which were identified as "the agrarian revolutions of Cuba and China," "revolutionary forces initially establish themselves in one area, and build up a community of people for whom revolution becomes a major part of their lives. As they spread out to other areas they capture local centers of government and set up their own administration and carry out large parts of their program." Though conceding that this method alone could not effect change in the United States, the authors of this statement did see such a method as a necessary part of change in America. In particular they saw it as a powerful model for the ERAP projects in the ghettos, where people were exploited, powerless, and alienated.[142]

By far the most important source of inspiration for SDS' ERAP projects, though, was not guerrillas in Cuba but SNCC organizers in the South. By 1964 SNCC's moral standing and influence within SDS was at its peak,[143] but the organization SDS looked to for guidance and inspiration had drifted far from the unambiguous endorsement of nonviolence contained in its founding statement of purpose.[144] By 1964 SNCC was far more impressed with Fanon than Ghandi, and many had come to associate nonviolence with weakness and the liberal reformism of Martin Luther King. Even those in SNCC who retained a principled commitment to nonviolence, such as John Lewis, seemed to call for what sounded at times like violent revolution. Addressing the march on Washington in August 1963, Lewis boasted: "We will march through the South, . . . the way Sherman did. We shall pursue our own 'scorched earth' policy and burn Jim Crow to the ground — nonviolently. We shall crack the South into a thousand pieces and put them back together in the image of democracy."[145] A few months later, in November 1963, Bob Moses explained SNCC's aims this way: "Only when metal has been brought to white heat can it be shaped and molded. This is what we intend to do to the South and the country, bring them to white heat and then remold them."[146] Although both Lewis and Moses were adherents of nonviolence, their rhetoric betrays the revolutionary's faith in being able to create justice through destruction. It was a faith shared by Hayden, who in late 1964 found inspiration in "the possibility that [SNCC offered] for construction," which he explained "is the craft of mending as you tear, building as you destroy, seeding the present with the future while rooting out the past."[147]

Hayden and others in SDS were particularly impressed with the revolutionary potential of SNCC's experimentation with extralegal methods and institutions. "What if the [Freedom Democratic party]," Hayden asked rhetorically, "is the only political party which is *legal* in America and what if the so-called laws are made and administered by men who are criminals because they trade nonchalantly in human life?" What if, echoed Lynd, blacks of Nashoba County, Mississippi, recognized only the authority of their own "Freedom Sheriff" rather than that of the white sheriff responsible for the murders of three civil rights workers in 1964? "What if the Freedom Sheriff impanneled [*sic*] a Freedom Grand Jury which indicted Sheriff Rainey for murder?"[148] What if, indeed? Would not lawless violence against the state be justified?[149] If established law is simply a cover for murdering innocent citizens and protecting criminals, both Hayden and Lynd seemed to intimate that "the people" should then take the law into their own hands.

Lynd, to be sure, still insisted that "so long as revolution is pictured as a violent insurrection it seems to me both distasteful and unreal." Lynd's call in the summer of 1965 was explicitly for a "nonviolent revolution" (which, he argued, was "the only long-run alternative to coalition with the marines"). Yet this Quaker apostle of nonviolence (and Yale professor of history) could at the same time fantasize about forcibly seizing the seat of government.

> As the crowd [at the April 17 march on Washington] moved down the Mall toward the seat of government . . . it seemed that the great mass of people would simply flow on through and over the marble buildings, that our forward movement was irresistibly strong, and that even had some been shot or arrested nothing could have stopped that crowd from taking possession of its government. Perhaps next time we should keep going, occupying for a time the rooms from which orders issue and sending to the people of Vietnam and the Dominican Republic the profound apologies which are due.

In such imaginings it is difficult to tell where nonviolent revolution leaves off and violent revolution begins.[150]

After a trip to Vietnam with Hayden at the close of 1965, the line seemed to disappear altogether. Lynd and Hayden came back from the trip with a glowing account of guerrilla warfare as a revolutionary experience. "Guerrilla war," they wrote, "means to begin with, that in the process of taking over the state one creates a replica of the larger society one hopes to build in the microcosm of a remote rural 'base.'" These revolutionaries, far from being bellicose and destructive, "seemed the gentlest people we had ever known." In armed struggle, "the revolutionary learns to fight with one hand and build a new society with the other, to break through Camus' distinction between the 'rebel' interested in present positive action and the 'revolutionary' concerned with distant visions, and to be both at once."[151] In guerrilla warfare, Lynd and Hayden found an ideal model of a tightly bounded egalitarian organization.[152] "The twentieth century guerrilla," they wrote, "finds himself forced by circumstance to live out even before the 'first stage' of socialist construction many relationships which Marxist theory prescribes only for the Communist 'final stage': equality of income (food is scarce, and everyone eats from the same pot), a blending of manual and intellectual labor (Mao kept a garden in Yenan); an emphasis upon the power of human will to overcome objective difficulties." Here was a model ERAP project; here were radicals, indeed, revolutionaries, "mak[ing] history,"[153] living a life of equality, not getting bogged down in endless meetings or resting content with getting a traffic light put up or improving garbage collection.

Returning to Newark, Hayden became impressed by the revolutionary possibilities of "an American form of guerrilla warfare based in the slums." Through "persistent, accurately-aimed attacks, which need to be on human life to be effective," Hayden suggested that the "conscious guerrilla" could "disrupt the administration of the ghetto to a crisis point" and potentially "create possibilities of meaningful change."[154] Such violence, Hayden argued, was justified because it was a necessary — though not a sufficient — condition for transforming American society.[155] Rebellion, for Hayden, meant "people transcend[ing] their pettiness to commit themselves to great purposes,"[156] and a riot represented "people making history." For many of those who joined in the five days of rioting in Newark in July 1967,[157] it was a "celebration of a new beginning [in which] people felt as though for a moment they were creating a community of their own."[158] For these people, Hayden insisted, the violence of the riot "is far less lawless and far more representative than the system of arbitrary rules and prescribed channels which they confront every day." [159]

At the Democratic convention in Chicago the following summer, Hayden went from justifying the guerrilla violence of others to orchestrating guerrilla violence of his own. The story of Hayden acting out the role of the "conscious guerrilla," donning disguises and appearing and disappearing in ridiculous cat-and-mouse games with police, has been superbly told by James Miller in *Democracy Is in the Streets*. Miller shows us a Hayden reciting the tired Maoist slogan "Dare to struggle, dare to win," fulminating about "the new Nazis," and setting up an apocalyptic confrontation between "a police state and a people's movement"; a Hayden who promises to "make sure that if blood flows, it flows all over the city" and afterward fantasizes that he and others had been "participants in the creation of a new society in the streets . . . with its own natural laws, structures, language and symbols"; [160] and, finally, a Hayden who, several months later, on trial for his role in inciting violence in Chicago, goes out into a cold October night to egg on the remorseless Weathermen as they prepared to set off on a violent rampage through the streets of Chicago.

"The Temptation of Hatred"

Hayden's personal and intellectual development from Port Huron to the streets of Chicago (and then Berkeley) is about something more than an individual succumbing to "the temptation of hatred." [161] It is that, too, but its meaning must also be sought in the sociocultural dynamics of radical egalitarian ideas and organization. To write, as Hayden does in his memoirs, that "claiming love as our motivation, we could not subdue hate; . . . thinking we could build a new world, we self-destructed in a decade; . . . questing for community, we met our egos," obscures the relationship between the original hopes and the ultimate outcome, the social relations sought and the destruction that resulted. It is a dangerous mistake to reduce the violence and illiberalism of the late New Left to oversized egos getting in the way of cooperation or hate subduing love. Dangerous because it encourages the false hope that maybe next time, if only we can hold our egos in check or if love can conquer hate, things might turn out differently. A mistake because individual psychology or psychopathology cannot account for the illiberal turn of the New Left. [162] Whatever the truth about his personal demons, one is still left to explain why his message appealed to so many others. An explanation of the illiberalism of the late New Left, in short, must be rooted in the organizational and ideological dynamics of radical egalitarianism.

Hayden wishes us to see the illiberalism and violence of the later 1960s, including his own, as a turning away from and rejection of the innocent idealism of the *Port Huron Statement*.[163] But this cordoning off of the original ideals from later actions is untenable, for what came later was generated in part by the attempt to live by the egalitarian values spelled out in the *Port Huron Statement*. The years immediately following the *Port Huron Statement* saw an intense effort on the part of those in SDS to live by the egalitarian commitments articulated at Port Huron, an effort nowhere more evident than in the egalitarian groupings of the ERAP projects. From the effort to live by these egalitarian commitments emerged patterns of belief and behavior that no one originally anticipated or planned, patterns that often contradicted and undermined other values articulated in the *Port Huron Statement*, including the abhorrence of violence, the insistence that means and ends be intimately related, the desire for a realignment of the party system, and a sympathetic if not uncritical attitude toward liberalism and liberal reform.[164]

Any number of desirable values may be piled upon each other in a document or speech, but social relations with other human beings are not so forgiving. Living the life of egalitarian community generates certain pressures and dilemmas that force people to choose between values. Having opted for a life of radical egalitarianism, as SDS had by 1964, the New Left found its original desire to realign the party system preempted by its growing desire to retain an uncorrupted purity at the margins of society. Alliances with left-liberal-labor groups were increasingly seen as tainting. The less willing SDS was to work with other groups to effect change, the more institutions seemed unchangeable and the more violent confrontation in the streets seemed the only alternative.

At the same time, the group (whether conceived narrowly as SDS or more broadly as "the movement") increasingly became the individual's locus of identity. As the movement became ever more self-enclosed, the New Left's worldview increasingly became one of "us" versus "them," the good if vulnerable inside and the malignant, predatory outside.[165] This Manichaean worldview was compounded by radical egalitarian organizational principles (particularly rule by consensus), which meant that both locally and nationally SDS had a difficult time reaching agreement and making collective decisions. Justifying the often-trying life on the inside created enormous social pressures to further demonize the outside world. This helped to create a sense of solidarity within SDS but also helped to foster a perception that even the most violent means were justified in transforming such a fundamentally rotten and destructive society. The Weathermen were, of course, not the only or inevitable product of Port Huron and ERAP, but Todd Gitlin is exactly right in detecting that the Weathermen

> were the pure New Left in a way — self-enclosed, contemptuous of liberalism, romantic about Third World revolutions, organized in small squads. . . . The whole movement had been self-enclosed for a long time, progressively more so into the late Sixties, for turning toward revolution usually meant turning away from family and the wrong friends, dropping contact with disquieting ideas, confounding books, critical magazines. . . . The Weathermen developed this hermetic tendency to a coarse art. The revolutionary loop closed.[166]

5

Romancing the Oppressed

THE NEW LEFT AND THE LEFT OUT

Whenever there is a contest between the oppressed
and the oppressor . . . God knows that my heart must
be with the oppressed, and always against the oppressor.
  William Lloyd Garrison [1]

I had reduced everything to the simple theory that the
oppressed are always right and the oppressors are
always wrong: a mistaken theory, but the natural
result of being one of the oppressors yourself.
  George Orwell [2]

In a "Letter to the New Left," written in 1960, C. Wright Mills acidly derided the "labor metaphysic." It was a phrase, Dick Flacks later recalled, that was "constantly reverberating" within SDS. The idea that the working class was the chosen agency for bringing about revolutionary change, Mills argued, was an outdated legacy bequeathed by a "Victorian Marxism." Loudly echoing Mills, Tom Hayden told the SDS executive council in 1962 that the working class "is just not the missionary force we can count on." In his master's thesis on Mills, Hayden went further still, insisting that "there is no country, no class, no vanguard to count on for freedom." Lacking a revolutionary vanguard class, Hayden counseled that "changing society meant committing to the laborious, democratic process of organizing diverse social groups.[3]

In *The Communist Manifesto*, Marx and Engels had posited that capitalism would become ever more polarized "into two great hostile camps," with the increasingly oppressive bourgeoisie on the one side and the increasingly immiserated proletariat on the other. This polarized schema left little room for those who were neither affluent property owners nor propertyless workers. Hence Marx and Engels's tremendous scorn for the lumpenproletariat, the "scum, offal, refuse of all classes" who lacked any positive place in their envisioned process of historical development. And, too, the polarized schema explains Marx's impatience with the peasantry (which he likened to "a sack of potatoes") and with "the idiocy of rural life." The peasantry and especially the lumpen proletariat seemed to be equipped only for "the part of a bribed tool of reactionary intrigue."[4]

The early New Left seemed to depart dramatically from the bipolar schema of classical Marxism. Not only did the New Left begin by rejecting the proletariat as "The Necessary Lever,"[5] but they reached out to the very groups that Marx and Engels had so brusquely pushed aside as historically marginal or retrograde. New Left intellectuals moved to push the poorest and most downtrodden members of society back onto the historical stage. Theirs was to be a movement that would include poor rural blacks, the homeless and dysfunctional, chronically unemployed youths, and later even Third World peasants.

SDS' commitment to kicking the "labor metaphysic" and to organizing the most excluded and least advantaged groups in society was institutionally realized in September 1963 when it established the Economic Research and Action Project (ERAP).[6] The initial objective of ERAP was to organize unemployed youths in the ghettos and slums of urban America. The decision to focus on organizing the urban poor was spurred by a belief that the ranks of the unemployed and dispossessed were poised to swell as a result of increasing automation, the inevitable end of the postwar boom, and cutbacks in military spending.[7] This dire prediction was peddled by a number of prominent left intellectuals and economists in 1963[8] and was immediately seized upon by those in SDS who were seeking a way for the organization to do more than just issue provocative position papers.[9]

Academic forecasts of impending economic crisis, however, are not sufficient to explain why the best and the brightest within SDS flocked to the ghettos in the summer of 1964. One explanation frequently proferred is middle-class guilt;[10] another, more flattering, is compassion.

Without denying the powerful role that guilt and compassion played in the New Left, one needs to ask why these emotions or impulses took the form they did. Were those who joined ERAP more guilt-ridden than the rest of their generation? Perhaps, but if so the answer begs the question of why some students felt guilty about their privileged position in a system while other similarly situated middle-class students apparently did not. Were those who went to the ghettos more compassionate than those who did not? Possibly, but more important are the competing social definitions of what counts as compassion. The leap between individual psychological traits and social action is just too large; to bridge that gap, we must turn to the cultural commitments that structure and shape individual choices.

The Egalitarian Dilemma

SDS' commitment to organizing the poor cannot be understood apart from its commitment to an egalitarian way of life and its rejection of established institutions that were structured upon principles of competitive individualism and hierarchical bureaucracy. The dilemma facing the New Left, as we saw in the previous chapter, was how to effectively achieve social change while retaining the capacity for "radical honesty." This tension between the purity of the movement and the reform of society haunts not only the New Left but virtually all egalitarian social movements that aim not only to change their own lives but to transform the larger society as well. Withdrawing into self-enclosed egalitarian communes sustains the group's purity but leaves society unredeemed. Reaching out to established groups or organizations creates the potential for egalitarian social change but at the risk of compromising the group's purity. The New Left, like many egalitarian movements before it, attempted to resolve this dilemma by seeking an alliance with the poor and dispossessed who were outside of or marginal to established institutions.[11] By participating in a "movement of all the powerless and exploited,"[12] the New Left hoped to gain the power to transform established institutions while still remaining outside of those institutions. ERAP, in short, gave the members of SDS a way to act in the world without becoming corrupted by it.

An alliance with the poor offered the New Left more than the negative attraction of avoiding compromises with a corrupting system. For in the lives of the marginal and the oppressed, many in the New Left detected an authentic, unspoiled voice of opposition, honed outside the dominant value system. Peering into the eyes of the oppressed, the New Left saw the reflection of their own preference for a noncoercive, egalitarian community.

The economically marginal and vulnerable attracted the New Left, moreover, because here was a group that in their everyday lives exposed the injustice of American institutions. Like egalitarians the world over, the New Left looked to the oppressed for an indictment of existing institutions and as a lever to help bring about a more just world. These "victims of the system"[13] knew firsthand the oppression of the system, and because they were the most oppressed they also had the greatest interest in overturning that system. Out of the grievances and the anger of the oppressed, the New Left hoped to create a "new insurgency" that would undermine the "establishment" axis of competitive individualism and hierarchy.[14]

For all their desire to be a genuinely *New* Left, then, sixties radicals in fact re-created much of the basic structure of thought that characterized past egalitarian movements. Much like the Russian populists,[15] the American abolitionists,[16] the Young American critics Randolph Bourne and Waldo Frank, and a string of other egalitarian intellectuals, including the early Marx,[17] the New Left invested the poor with an uncorrupted authenticity and goodness. In addition, the New Left ended up ascribing to the poorest and most downtrodden members of society the same transformative potential that Marx and Engels had assigned to the proletariat. In this chapter, I describe the ways in which the New Left romanticized the poor and the marginal, and show how this contributed to pushing many in the New Left down some of the very same illiberal tracks they had begun the decade warning against.

"The Strength of Being Poor"

The New Left's romance with the poor was powerfully shaped by the civil rights movement, in particular the Student Nonviolent Coordinating Committee's (SNCC) experience mobilizing poor blacks in the rural South. In the struggle of Mississippi sharecroppers New Left radicals justifiably saw courage in the face of repression and terror. Admiration for particular individual or collective acts, however, often spilled over into a wildly romantic view of disenfranchised and excluded blacks as an unsullied repository of natural goodness.

In 1961 Hayden was selected as SDS' field secretary and headed south to publicize the emerging civil rights movement. In a number of powerful factual reports sent to the membership, Hayden dramatized both the heroic organizing efforts of SNCC and the unconscionable brutality and injustice of southern society.[18] From the outset Hayden had been impressed by this "*pure*, good struggle," which he felt had the potential to spark revolutionary changes in the entire society.[19] What dazzled Hayden was not only the courageous resistance to segregation and terrorism that he witnessed in the South, but increasingly also the possibility that poor, rural blacks embodied an authentic "humanism" that was "immune to the ravages of competitive society." In a review of Howard Zinn's influential book, *SNCC: The New Abolitionists* (1964), Hayden explained that the source of the "special character of [SNCC's] revolt" was not only their "consciousness of persevering through historical suffering" but also the fact that Mississippi sharecroppers lived in

> a place remote enough from urban industrial society to make possible the beginning of a counter way of life. In these rural areas, contact among Negroes is veined thickly with direct human issues — the worth of men is likely to be measured by what they do, not as much by the labels and organizational imagery they project. Since the society is largely pre-industrial, men tend to have a direct and coherent relation to their work which contributes also to the integrity of their personality and social relations.

Because they were marginal to the system, rural blacks possessed the "honesty" and "insight" that those trapped in society's "framework of lies" could not achieve.[20]

Jack Newfield's *A Prophetic Minority* (1966) portrayed rural Mississippi blacks in the same romantic hue. In contrast to "urban impersonalization and the alienation of mass society," there was a "human generosity and vitality that exists among rural Mississippi Negroes." In Amite County, Newfield marveled, "people are judged not by their manners, or their fathers' income, or what fraternity they belong to, but by their integrity, their work, and their courage." Although Newfield conceded that the lives of poor blacks in the South are perhaps too often sentimentalized, this did not prevent him from continuing on in the same vein: "There is a special quality to the Negroes of Amite County that is missing elsewhere [that in part] comes from living in a totally rural environment, removed from the criminality, corruption, and violence in the cities . . . and in part . . . comes from a people that has achieved an authentic nobility in one hundred years of stoic suffering."[21]

In the unspoiled lives of poor blacks, many in the New Left saw a model of the "authentic" human relationships called for in the *Port Huron Statement*. Without "the fraud and glitter of a distorted prosperity," it seemed possible for poor blacks "to remove the barriers that prevent human beings from making contact with one another." Here were "simple people living lives of relative inner peace, love, honor, courage and humor." Down here, many a white student reported, were "beautiful," genuine people who "have not forgotten how to love." Students identified with "unsophisticated" blacks "who come off the land," SNCC organizer Bob Moses explained, because the poor "simply voice, time and time again, the simple truths you can't ignore because they speak from their own lives."[22]

In "Some Notes on Education," a memo written and circulated within SNCC in 1965, SNCC's first executive secretary Jane Stembridge marveled at the goodness, freedom, and truth manifest in the lives of rural Negroes, who had "the strength of being poor." Blacks living in the South "maintained a closeness with the earth [and] a closeness with each other in the sense of community developed out of dependence." Middle-class whites like herself, in contrast, had from the earliest moments of their lives "been made to feel shame and guilt by the institutions of childhood." Every institution of middle-class life, from the family to the public school to the churches, "worked . . . to see that we are completely smashed as ourselves." Segregation had thus ironically "freed the Negro from a society which enslaves the self."[23]

Blacks' exclusion from the system meant that they were relatively free from the system's destructive influences.[24] Exclusion from the mainstream opened up space for alternative definitions of justice and freedom. As SDSer Norm Fruchter saw it, "The rural southern Negro has been so systematically excluded from and oppressed by the majority society that his clear desire is for his freedom, and . . . he does not define that freedom according to the values and aspirations accepted in the majority society." Contained within their oppression were thus the seeds of liberation, not only for blacks but for all of society. Casey Hayden recalls the feeling: "We loved the untouchables. We believed the last should be first, and not only should be first, but in fact *were* first in our value system. They were first because they were redeemed already, purified by their suffering, and they could therefore take the lead in the redemption of us all."[25] Indeed, this was the preeminent virtue of the poor, whether urban or rural, black or white. The "radical potential of the poor," as Todd Gitlin expressed it, was that they were "less tied to the dominant values." Unlike the working class, the poor had not had their consciousness molded by the system.[26]

Staughton Lynd's experience as the first director of the Mississippi freedom school project shaped his belief that "alienated poor people" share with "alienated intellectuals" a "vision of community" that was fundamentally at odds with the dominant social definitions and institutions. They share "the vision of a band of brothers standing in a circle of love," as well as "the idea that states may have quarrels with each other but that people don't." "Both the Negro Baptist fieldhand in Mississippi and the intellectual activist," Lynd elaborated, "have in view an ideal community, they have a vision of how people ought to relate together. In the back of the mind of each is a picture of a blessed community, something like a family but bigger, something like a seminar except that people act as well as talk, something like a congregation except that people work together as well as pray together."[27]

This hope that in the poor lay the seeds of a new egalitarian society had been expressed by Hayden and Carl Wittman in "An Interracial Movement of the Poor?", the paper that was intended to serve as the initial road map for the ERAP projects. "Among the uneducated, the poverty-stricken, and the segregated," they wrote, "there is . . . an absence of vested interests in continued exploitation and possibly the seed for a different society." They pointed with hope to the successes of organizing efforts in Maryland, where Wittman and other students had worked with SNCC. "After months of cooperation," Hayden and Wittman noted, "the residents of the second ward of Cambridge, Maryland, not only discuss basic flaws in the system and verbalize what their economic and social rights are, they also have developed institutions and patterns of behavior which are foreign to middle-class America."[28] This was the alluring promise of the poor: that their authenticity and suffering would show the way to building an egalitarian society that was fundamentally different from the dominant institutions and social relations.

"The Radical Potential of the Poor"

ERAP had been conceived, in Hayden's words, as "a northern parallel to SNCC."[29] While SNCC mobilized impoverished blacks in the rural South, SDS would organize the chronically unemployed youth of urban America. Together they would build an interracial movement of the poor that would help to transform American society.

After the ERAP idea had been approved by the SDS National Council in September 1963, SDS immediately sent a University of Michigan undergraduate, Joe Chabot, to Chicago to test out the viability of organizing unemployed youths. Chabot spent the fall on the northwest side of Chicago but met only with frustration. In November a dispirited Chabot reported back to the National Office:

> I have not been accepted by any group of older teenagers of this neighborhood. They don't understand me. They are suspicious of me as well as everyone else who tries to have anything to do with them. . . . There is nothing to make them think socially at this time and nothing to give them confidence that in action their lives can improve. The kids feel totally at sea when an idea of joining together to press your demands is raised. They accept their state although dissatisfied.[30]

Among these unemployed youth Chabot found not the voice of authentic opposition but rather a pervasive culture of distrust, hostility, and fatalism. This pattern of unrequited love would dog the ERAP projects.

The SDS leadership seemed undaunted by Chabot's experience. Encouraged by rent strikes (largely led by blacks) in several major cities and especially by the success that Swarthmore students, led by Wittman, were having in organizing and working with blacks in Chester, Pennsylvania, SDS moved ahead with ERAP. That December they rejected Al Haber's plea not to succumb to the "cult of the ghetto" and voted decisively (20–6) to follow Hayden's lead in making ERAP the centerpiece of SDS. The plan now, following the counsel of Hayden and Wittman, was to allow each project to decide which groups of poor people to organize and which issues to organize around.[31] By the following summer ERAP projects were under way in Baltimore; Boston; Chester; Chicago; Cleveland; Hazard, Kentucky; Louisville; Newark; Philadelphia; and Trenton.

The ERAP experiment began with heady optimism. The aim of organizing the poor was not just improving their lives but creating a "new society" of "shared abundance" through the mobilization of "an aroused community of dispossessed people."[32] In formulating plans for ERAP during the spring of 1964, the organizers-to-be pointed with great excitement to what they felt was "an increasing tendency for hitherto inarticulate groups within the society to forcefully express demands for an end to the conditions of poverty." Students who wished to challenge established institutions and transform society thus needed to capitalize on and channel "this upsurge of the poor."[33]

The initial reports from these projects reveal the fantastic hopes that many in ERAP initially invested in the downtrodden. From Philadelphia came the confident report that, "starting on the issue of unemployment, we also reach the people who are the most degraded and oppressed of this society, who therefore are likely to be the best lever for the conversion of this social hierarchy into something new and better." This view was echoed by then SDS president Todd Gitlin in an SDS working paper, "The Battlefields and the War," issued in April 1964. "We have chosen," Gitlin announced, to organize those who inhabit "communities of the under-America," where "people live materially deprived, politically alienated and used, and victimized by social and economic institutions beyond their comprehension and reach." These are the people who are most "strongly afflicted with the rottenness of our society" and as such "are best capable of exorcising that rot." Only through "insurgent movements of poor people," echoed Richard Rothstein, will "America . . . ever be shaken from [continuing down] its path to a very rigidly stratified society."[34]

It did not take many months living among the desperately poor to see that the "dispossessed" were unlikely candidates to usher in the hoped-for new society.[35] They were too disorganized, too distrustful, too alienated, too apathetic. They blamed themselves rather than society. They distrusted collective action. Organizers found these people could sometimes be mobilized around such issues as obtaining a new streetlight, improving recreation areas, or improving housing conditions, but the gap between helping poor people in their everyday lives and transforming society remained vast.[36] Rather than leading to revolution or even radical reform, organizing the poor seemed only to distract attention and energy away from the root ills of American society.[37] Still, even as it became increasingly evident to many within SDS that the urban poor were neither the vanguard of the revolution nor even a particularly sympathetic constituency, many prominent leaders within SDS found it difficult to give up on the idea that a radical movement should begin with the most disadvantaged and most oppressed.

In his widely read essay "The Politics of 'the Movement,'" published at the beginning of 1966 at a time when ERAP was widely seen as having failed,[38] Hayden described an "awakening . . . taking place among the poor in America." Although Hayden acknowledged and even stressed some of the obstacles to organizing in northern ghettos, this did not stop him from describing the movement as aiming "at a transformation of society led by the most excluded and 'unqualified' people." Hayden could not relinquish his dream of a movement based on the poor because the poor, who are "victimized from every direction," provided the evidence privileged students needed to reveal "the system's inhumanity." Working among the poor put students in "a position from which to expose the whole structure of pretense, status, and glitter that masks the country's real human problems."[39]

The next year, with the ERAP experiment now clearly in ruins, Gitlin published an influential paper entitled "The Radical Potential of the Poor." In it he argued that the poor's marginal position in society gave them firsthand experience of the brutality of the system, thus making them an untapped "source and reservoir of opposition to the final rationalization of the American system." To organize the poor was thus "to keep the country open to authentically different values and styles." It was "in the culture of poverty" that the New Left needed to seek "a culture of resistance." Because the poor are "less tied to the dominant values" and "are less central to the economy that creates and expresses those values," Gitlin felt "the poor are probably . . . better equipped to understand — and find *new* ways of understanding — the class structure of American society than are most organized workers."[40]

Although priding itself on having kicked the Old Left's "labor metaphysic," the New Left succumbed to a poverty metaphysic every bit as problematic. The New Left had firmly rejected the Old Left idea that workers were the motor force of history, but they retained the basic Marxist faith that in the rebellion of the oppressed lay the seeds of a just future society. Hayden could warn against seeing the working class as a "missionary force" and yet at the same time lionize poor blacks for "giv[ing] blood and body . . . for social justice, for freedom, for the common life, for the creation of dignity for the enslaved, and *thereby for us all*."[41] The Old Left had insisted that the interests of the working class were the interests of all humanity; the New Left largely wrote off the co-opted working class but still clung tenaciously to the Marxist dream that in the struggle of the downtrodden lay the salvation of all. The savior now, though, was the poor rather than the proletariat.[42]

Occasionally New Left leaders self-consciously disavowed such a belief. In "The Ability to Face Whatever Comes" (1966), for example, Hayden cautioned that radicals had to grasp that there was "no active agency of radical change — no race, no class, no nation — in which radicals can invest high hopes as they have in previous times." But the belief in the oppressed as the radical agent of change could not be easily quashed, for to give up on the oppressed was to abandon hope in a redeemed future. So only a page after issuing his caution, Hayden fell back on the hope that it was in the lives of the outcasts that radicals would uncover the true extent of oppression in American society. He urged radicals to "identify with all the scorned, the illegitimate and the hurt" and to organize these people "whose visible protest created basic issues: who *is* criminal? who *is* representative? who *is* delinquent?" It was only among the excluded, as Hayden wrote elsewhere, that radicals would find "not just people who want 'more' but people who want 'no more' of a rotten society; not just people who are satisfactorily accommodated but remain humanitarian, but people who are beyond accommodation because their alienation is so great."[43]

Many in the New Left could not give up on the oppressed and outcast because in the alienation of the poor they found reflected and justified their own feelings of alienation from the system. A shared experience of alienation and "exclusion from the power structure," they argued, laid the foundation for a truly radical movement of poor people and students.[44] Both the ghetto poor and the young, agreed the editors of *Studies on the Left*, "unite in the powerlessness, the impotence, irrelevance, and despair attendant on the realization that what one feels, believes, and demands are neither shared nor acted on by the overwhelming majority of one's society." This "differently experienced alienation" was "the tie between the militancy in the ghettos and the unrest of students."[45] "Students and poor people," explained Hayden, "make each other feel real." Students could help the poor overcome their feelings of inadequacy and fear, and the poor could "demonstrate to the students that their upbringing has been based on a framework of lies." This was what had been so exhilarating to Hayden about students working in the South, "becoming one with . . . the masses of hungry, aspiring, utopian peoples intervening in history for the first time."[46]

Unrequited Love

But the South was not the North. A central tenet of the ERAP projects had been that the poor, whether in the North or South, black or white, "share a common tragedy in being locked out of all relevant chan-nels of decision-making."[47] In their "common need for jobs, incomes, and control of their lives" lay the basis for "a natural alliance among all poor [people]."[48] "One oppression, one movement" was the theory;[49] the reality was that the Mississippi Black Belt and the West Side of Chicago were worlds apart, as those who had worked as organizers for any length of time in the two areas quickly learned.

One such person was Hayden's ex-wife, Casey Hayden. She had been the first white person to be invited to work for SNCC, but rising per-sonal and racial animosities within SNCC had led her to join the Chicago ERAP project in the spring of 1965. After only a few months of organizing poor whites in Chicago, she was forced "to question whether students can organize on a large scale in poor white areas on the pattern of the Southern movement." In one of the last issues of the *ERAP Newsletter*, Hayden explained to her fellow ERAPers why she thought the SNCC model could not work in the North. First, "the clarity of the issues"—for example, voter registration, desegregation, and Klan vio-lence, which SNCC depended on—was lacking in the North, where or-ganizing centered around more diffuse and less morally compelling is-sues such as condemned housing, recreation facilities, and welfare. Second, in the South, fostering a sense of solidarity among those being organized was relatively easy because "identifying an enemy" (Bull Con-nor, White Citizens Councils, or the Klan) was relatively straightfor-ward. In the North, in contrast, "instead of identifying an oppressor, people identify problems." Blame was diffused or internalized. Third, where SNCC organized there were "literally no institutions to provide relief to Negroes," while the North was dotted with institutions that "ac-commodate poor people." SNCC had defined its task as "to organize, not to build coalitions" because locally there were "no allies to be trusted" and nationally there was "enough support . . . to provide adequate funds and political pressure." In contrast, organizing a movement of poor people alienated local allies and liberal sources of money because they are "right there in Chicago, judging and periodically threatened by our work." Finally, and perhaps most important, Hayden found that the people she was organizing were different. Unlike southern blacks, Hay-den found that "the people we're working with [in Chicago] . . . [have] no group experience of working together on problems." "People in this area," she said, "don't belong to anything and nothing belongs to them."[50] Discouraged by the lack of progress, Hayden left the Chicago project after less than six months.

Hayden's experience with ERAP was typical, even if the experience she brought with her was not. Most of the students who joined ERAP were totally ill-prepared for the distrust and apathy that characterized the ghetto poor. These middle-class students, as Kirkpatrick Sale observes, "expected the poor to be natively intelligent, informed, angry at the circumstances of their lives, prepared to unite against a common enemy . . . and instead they found the poor . . . ignorant, passive, atomized and fragmented, and with a whole set of quite different values."[51] On campus, all one needed was an outrage and a few leaflets and one had a full-scale demonstration. In the ghettos, simply getting a handful of people together to discuss their community's problems counted as a tremendous triumph. Reflecting on ERAP's first summer, Rennie Davis commented:

> An organizer can spend two or more hours with a single individual. Through hundreds of conversations, slowly clusters of unemployed contacts are made and identified on city maps. One person in a large unemployment area is approached about having a meeting: he agrees, but hasn't the time to contact neighbors. So the JOIN worker calls every nearby unemployed by phone or sees them in person. Thirty people are contacted; eight turn out. One is a racist, but his arguments get put down by the group. One (maybe) is willing to work and has some sense of what needs to be done. The others go round and round on their personal troubles. The process is slow.[52]

The excruciatingly slow progress of ERAP organizing was in stark contrast to the spectacular success of the SDS-organized march on Washington in April 1965, in which thousands of people were mobilized to protest the Vietnam War with only a fraction of the effort and manpower that had gone into ERAP. Although the Cleveland and Baltimore projects lasted into 1966 and the Newark and Chicago projects survived until 1967, the summer of 1965 was ERAP's last hurrah. By the end of 1965 ERAP was generally recognized to have run aground, and it ceased from that point on to be of much consequence within SDS.[53]

Not that ERAP failed to accomplish anything. ERAP organizers could point to small victories that improved the lives of the ghetto poor in tangible ways — landlords occasionally forced to make housing improvements, somewhat better garbage collection, red tape cut for welfare recipients, and the like.[54] But none of this kind of activity seemed to move ERAP any closer to "an interracial movement of the poor" that could fundamentally transform society in an egalitarian direction. After a year of organizing in one of the more successful projects, a Cleveland organizer confessed that their organizing had generally been limited to "building personal relationships" rather than creating an organization. "People who have been here a year," he reported, "seem frustrated with building personal relationships with no action resulting." The group's frustration was particularly acute since none of the relationships that had been built had reached "the point where there is real commitment, understanding, and frankness."[55]

The students' unrequited love for the ghetto poor stemmed, most obviously, from the fatalistic cultural bias and atomized and arbitrary social relations of the urban underclass.[56] As more than one SDS organizer came to understand, for many impoverished people living in the ghetto, distrust of collective action was a rational response to a capricious and often violent social environment. "For them as individuals, or even as small groups," wrote an ERAP organizer in Hoboken, "the best course is to go along with the game, cover up mistakes, lie, give the boss a line, don't mess with the cops, keep your mouth shut." If they participate in a protest and fail, "they get fired, if they win, they still have to work at the same stuff and live in almost the same way: They won't be much better off. . . . It may be true that if everyone who feels screwed thought things could change, they could. But seeing as how almost no one thinks they can be, they can't and no one will perceive that they can be. Someone who does is a fool."[57]

But the distrust and apathy of the culture of the underclass was only part of the reason for the pattern of unrequited love that ERAP encountered. ERAP's failures stemmed also from the fact that what ERAP wanted the poor to be — avenging angels against the inequalities of capitalism and an alternative source of values to middle-class consumerism — was not what most of the poor wanted, namely, to join the American middle class and purchase a part of the American dream. The *America and the New Era* statement, written in the summer of 1963 by Tom Hayden and Richard Flacks, had expressed the hope that an "insurgent politics" could produce "constituencies expressing, for the first time in this generation, the needs of ordinary men for a decent life."[58] The problem was that when New Left radicals met ordinary Americans, most of the radicals didn't seem to like what they found.

Hayden expected the poor to aid student organizers in "attacking power structures" and certainly did not want student organizers helping the poor adapt to societal norms. The attraction of the poor, after all, was that "the poor everywhere build up their own styles and mechanisms for staying clear of the majority society." Hayden had contempt for those social reformers who tried to bring "ghetto residents into the 'mainstream' of competitive society."[59] As Richard Rothstein explained to ERAP director Rennie Davis: "We no more want poor people integrated so they become like the middle class, than we want Negroes to feel they should try to be like whites."[60] The problem for ERAP was that most ordinary poor people did not want to stay clear of the middle class so much as they wanted to have the things the middle class had.

Most ordinary people, ERAP organizers soon found out, were less interested in "social change" than they were in preserving property values and making their neighborhoods safer.[61] Faced with such middle-class aspirations, Hayden and others in the Newark project reacted by redefining and narrowing their constituency. They wrote off the "deserving poor," "people with developed middle-class aspirations, who see their needs on a narrow self-interest basis, who identify with middle-class authority figures," and turned instead to the "genuine poor" who lived in the most dilapidated areas of Clinton Hill.[62]

Here among the desperately poor, Hayden and his coworkers in ERAP could find clear evidence of rejection or withdrawal from middle-class society. Here were people, as Hayden wrote, who "share a deep alienation from people with official authority, complicated language and a middle class or parliamentary style."[63] The difficulty for ERAP organizers was that if these people distrusted parliamentary procedures and official authority, as they undoubtedly did, they were hardly any more enthusiastic about participatory democracy and radical students. Their distrust of bureaucrats and lack of opportunity to compete as individualistic entrepreneurs did not make them egalitarians. If these poor people had given up on the hope that through individual effort they could lift themselves out of poverty, they were even more skeptical about the possibility of transforming their environment through collective action.

The failure to mobilize the urban underclass against the establishment left some within ERAP totally dispirited, bereft of all hope for radical social change.[64] More adjusted their views of what could be expected from such community organizing, becoming satisfied to improve individual lives even if that did not lead to the revolution.[65] For most who worked in ERAP, though, the poor's failure to fulfill its radical potential was taken as further evidence of the system's oppressiveness and pervasiveness. The poor's middle-class aspirations, their support for the Vietnam War,[66] and their pattern of self-blame[67] all showed how hegemonic the system really was. Not even the outcasts of society had escaped its deforming grip. Most of those who worked in ERAP emerged with the conviction that things were even worse than they had initially thought, and that the system needed drastic and immediate change.

Later in the 1960s this unrequited love would lead some within SDS to turn to Leninism. If the oppressed could not respond to egalitarian overtures because they were in the grips of a hegemonic system, then radicals would have to make the revolution on behalf of the victimized.[68] But in the immediate wake of ERAP's collapse, those on the New Left were inclined not so much to give up on the oppressed as to seek out other oppressed groups that existed outside of the system, that acted out an alternative source of values, and that could thus provide a model for egalitarian revolution. Unable to find such people in the United States, they increasingly looked to the people of the Third World, particularly in Vietnam and Cuba.[69]

"The Other Side"

This shift from the urban poor to Third World peasants as the repository of unspoiled virtue and revolutionary potential is perhaps most dramatically evident in the person of Tom Hayden. His first reactions to the failures of ERAP had been defensiveness and denial — understandably so, since the idea had originally been his. Throughout 1965 he held to the belief that the urban poor could be a catalyst for social change. As project failures mounted, denial was followed by depression and even fatalistic resignation. If organizing the urban poor wasn't going to produce a revolution, then perhaps the best radicals could hope for was "the ability to face whatever comes." But even as Hayden's faith in the urban underclass was waning, a new love emerged to take its place: the oppressed people of Vietnam.

In late December 1965, with the bulk of the SDS leadership at a special "rethinking conference" in Illinois,[70] Hayden accompanied Staughton Lynd and Herbert Aptheker on a trip to North Vietnam. In his memoirs Hayden explains that he hoped to "bring back an image of the Vietnamese as human beings" that would help to counteract stereotypes of the "faceless Vietcong" propagated by the U.S. government and media.[71] This admirable desire to show the Vietnamese as real people, however, was preempted by Hayden's even stronger need to romanticize the oppressed and to identify with their revolutionary struggle against the oppressor.

In *The Other Side*, an account of the trip he wrote together with Lynd, Hayden presented the Vietnamese as more superhuman than human.[72] Their gentleness, patience, even serenity were the outward expressions of calm determination and heroic fearlessness.[73] The Vietnamese people, Hayden came away thinking, were quite simply "the most extraordinary people now living in the world, setting a standard of morality and sacrifice for the whole world."[74]

Much as Hayden had identified his own sense of alienation with the exclusion of the urban underclass and, before that, the black sharecropper, he now felt a keen solidarity with the oppression and struggle of the Vietnamese people. "We felt they were like us," Lynd and Hayden wrote, "that their cause was ours as well."[75] In "the lives they encountered in . . . Hanoi and [in] the lives of the rebellious poor of the United States," they discerned the common problems and insights of "the colonized and excluded." So eager were Lynd and Hayden to identify with the Vietnamese that they could write that "colonial American town meetings and current Vietnamese village meetings, Asians peasants' leagues and Black Belt sharecroppers' unions have much in common, especially the concept of a 'grass-roots' democracy or 'rice-roots' democracy."[76]

Hayden projected onto Vietnamese village life his own longing for egalitarian community. Here was a society that was "organized but not bureaucratic," in which people had a feeling of community unlike anything he knew in America. Here was a society of equals, men and women close to nature, not restricted by convention and artifice. The "human socialism" of the Vietnamese "was evident in unembarrassed hand clasps among men; the poetry and song at the center of man-woman relationships; the freedom to weep which we observed in everyone from guerrillas to generals, from peasants to factory managers — as the Vietnamese speak of their country." Here, Hayden concluded, "we began to understand the possibilities for a socialism of the heart."[77]

To Hayden and others on the New Left, the Vietnamese seemed to be "whole" human beings, not "split" like commercialized Westerners.[78] In contrast to the "empty" nature of American lives and careers,[79] Hayden saw in the Vietnamese "a people who somehow manage to practice a *rich* life in the center of violence."[80] Just as Hayden had looked to organizing poor communities in the United States as "a concrete task in which the split between job and values can be healed,"[81] so he now looked to the Vietnamese struggle for a model of a meaningful and whole life. The Vietnamese, Hayden found, "have learned how to build life even while in war. Production goes on, arts and music, poetry, romantic life, not during intervals between fighting but as the fabric of which the struggle is maintained."[82]

Looking for Love in All the Wrong Places

In Newark or Cleveland, the day-to-day experience of living among the urban underclass had served as a powerful if only partial check upon fantasies about the inherent goodness or revolutionary potential of the poor. But far-off nations about which few people in the movement had any direct, personal knowledge left Hayden and others almost totally free to project their own egalitarian cultural bias onto the oppressed.[83] Perhaps nowhere was this projection dynamic more evident than in the New Left's romance with the tiny embattled island just ninety miles off the U.S. coast.

Cuba was vital to the New Left imagination because here, close to home, was an inspiring example of an oppressed people and a band of committed egalitarian radicals together overthrowing an exploitative system. The "Fidelista," as one admiring student radical explained, knows "the meaning of misery and exploitation, of disease and illiteracy, of unemployment and squalor in the midst of plenty, of graft and corruption."[84] Freed from the oppression and inequality of Batista's authoritarian rule, Castro's Cuba was defiantly constructing a new egalitarian future despite the opposition of the Yankee colossus to the north. Leaders of the New Left, including those who, like Paul Potter, had traveled to Cuba in the immediate wake of Batista's fall, immediately sensed that "we and the Cuban revolutionaries were somehow fighting the same battle."[85] There were, echoed another, "remarkable . . . ideological similarities between the Cuban and campus revolutions."[86]

Particularly important in propagating this message was C. Wright Mills's widely circulated polemic, *Listen, Yankee* (1960). The importance of the Cuban revolution, Mills stressed, was that it showed that egalitarian transformation was still possible. Prior to Castro's revolution, "people had given up hope [that] a revolution against Yankee imperialism can win." "Everyone thought the days of the guerilla were over," but in this "moment of Cuban truth, [people] are seeing that they are not over." The Cuban revolution revealed that "guerilla bands, led by determined men, with peasants alongside them, and a mountain nearby, can defeat organized battalions of . . . tyrants equipped with everything up to the atom bomb." The revolution, moreover, did not just replace one set of rulers with another, but rather was "working out a brand-new social and economic order in Cuba, . . . from top to bottom, and in all spheres of our lives."[87]

Other influential early reports from Cuba came from the radical pacifist Dave Dellinger. Writing in *Liberation* at the end of 1960, Dellinger reported that in revolutionary Cuba he had "seen man's cynical and self-destructive inhumanity to man being replaced by the spirit and practice of a kind of brotherhood that is unknown to those of us who live in a country whose idealism is behind it and where the 'rights' of property override the rights of human beings." The revolution had seemingly erased "the artificial distinctions of class and status" that had previously plagued Cuba. Hierarchy had been dissolved in an "exhilarating atmosphere of freedom, self-reliance, and individual initiative." Instead of top-down commands, there was "a tremendous sense of participation, of people running their own revolution and running their own lives." Dellinger's enthusiasm for the egalitarian Cuba he witnessed was significantly tempered, however, by a nagging concern that Cubans did not seem to show any interest in establishing elections. "The people may be getting what they want," Dellinger warned, but "politically Cuba is under the control of a small group of idealists who formulate the laws and broad policy. . . . The history of politics makes it clear that it is dangerous for even 'good' men to hold this kind of power for any length of time."[88]

As the authoritarian implications of Cuba's political arrangements became clearer, criticisms of Castro by Dellinger and others became more rather than less muted. Writing in 1962, Dellinger allowed that Cuba's "political superstructure is faulty" but comforted himself and his readers with the thought that "no 20th century framework has been developed for holding the government in check or making it responsible to those it governs." Moreover, Dellinger now argued that "the day-to-day relationships in the cooperatives and the factories express a revolutionary egalitarianism which . . . serves as a *de facto* check on any overriding ambitions of a political elite." Because Cuban society had become suffused with radical egalitarian principles and practices, Cubans would no longer allow a domineering or arrogant political elite to reverse the revolution's progress. And what glorious progress there had been! In the factories and collectives there were "no status differences of any kind (and only slight differences in salary)." Human relationships in Cuba were now "far and away superior to those of either the Soviet Union or the United States." In closing, Dellinger allowed himself to hope that Cuba's "egalitarian practices . . . may some day help inspire a similar revolution in this country."[89]

Dellinger returned to Cuba in 1964, and in his subsequent report, again published in *Liberation*, his earlier skepticism about Cuban political arrangements seemed to have almost totally vanished. Dellinger stressed that "the amazing success of the Revolution in providing houses, schools, hospitals, food, clothing, socially useful work, dignity, freedom, and an atmosphere of social solidarity and brotherly love [carried] a whole new message of desperately needed hope." Even if the Cuban revolution were to be overturned by American military might, "the people would never forget the glorious years they have had, the discovery they have made that human nature does not have to be selfish and cruel, and brotherhood an empty slogan frustrated by the economic and political realities of the system."[90] Cuba was a beacon to the oppressed everywhere, showing them that egalitarianism worked.

During his visit, Dellinger had been profoundly moved by watching the May Day celebration in Havana. Here the formerly oppressed and apathetic were engaged and mobilized. Dellinger found himself overwhelmed by "the jubilant workers, male and female — most of them with the faces of the obviously honest and long-suffering poor" who now "feel free for the first time in their lives." It was

> the kind of communal thanksgiving that never takes place any more in the United States. . . . It was as if the black people of Mississippi and Harlem (and the inhabitants of all the other slums, ghettoes, and Appalachias) were holding a great festival to celebrate five years of freedom and happiness. . . . To understand the mood of this laughing, singing, exuberant crowd . . . you would have to imagine that the Negroes had done far more than to break out of their ghettoes and desegregate the schools, restaurants, parks, and employment agencies. You would have to imagine that in the process of doing this they and their white allies had developed a spirit of brotherhood which made it

impossible for them to be satisfied with integrating into the existing commercial culture and engaging in its selfish competition for personal profit and prestige. You would have to imagine that those who clung to capitalism had emigrated and the rest of the population was engaged in the infinitely more exciting business of working out a whole new society in accord with deepest yearnings for brotherhood.[91]

You would have to imagine, in other words, egalitarianism having raised up the oppressed, and competitive individualism and hierarchy vanquished.

In contrast to his 1960 report, in which Dellinger had expressed concerns about the absence of political democracy in Cuba, Dellinger now dismissed such objections as a presumptuous imposition of Western standards on a Third World culture. "It is both arrogant and provincial," Dellinger announced, "for residents of the United States to insist that the liberation of Cuba and other Latin American countries can only take place if they adopt the same forms of economic and political organization that liberated the eighteenth century white American colonists." If the political "forms" of the Cuban revolution were different from what most Americans were accustomed to associating with democracy and freedom, that was the Americans' problem, not the Cubans'. The "Popular Assemblies" of Cuba, Dellinger reported, "constitute a far more effective and dynamic form of 'democracy' or popular participation in decision-making than has existed in the United States for some time." American political institutions, though they may have been liberating at one stage, had "gradually lost [their] original content and become the forms of a constrictive pseudo-democracy and pseudo-freedom instead." Indeed, they had become "instruments of coercion and repression."[92]

As the New Left invested the oppressed island of Cuba with its deepest dreams and hopes, it became ever more difficult to allow criticism of the Cuban reality. When confronted with disturbing events or trends in Cuba, those in the New Left increasingly went to extraordinary lengths to overlook, excuse, justify, or explain them away. Responding to one Cuba skeptic, Dellinger explained that "it is not *prima facie* evidence of totalitarian tyranny if Cubans try to head off sabotage in the normal manner, by reporting suspicious events and meetings to local officials." Dellinger played down the importance of elections — he and many others didn't ordinarily find it worth voting in the United States, and of how much value was an institution that could make Lyndon Baines Johnson president? In any event, Dellinger reassured himself, "there are probably more elections in Cuba than in any other country in the world."[93] When Castro arrested and put on trial forty Communists, Dellinger denied this was a purge, pointing to the fact that "the men were accused of stealing secret documents." Does any non-Communist country, Dellinger asked, "permit spying or conspiracy with a foreign government to overthrow the existing regime?"[94]

As evidence of political repression and authoritarianism became more plentiful, the New Left's claims on behalf of Cuba seemed to become ever more exaggerated. The Cuban revolution would not only "make a marvel of [Havana]," James Higgins reported in *Liberation* in 1968, but would, "in mankind's future, [be] a wonder of the world." Reaching new heights of absurdity, Higgins announced, "Babies and adults, human relationships, the condition of human beings, are of first importance to the Cuban Revolution. Everybody — the professionals, the authorities, the people themselves — participate in the study of the program. It is not too much for me to argue the proposition that the babies participate, too." If there were aspects of Cuba that were less than satisfactory, that was because of the evil influence of the United States. "Everything no good in Cuba," Higgins asserted, "originated in the United States."[95]

This combination of stunning naïveté (about Cuba) and hardened cynicism (about the United States) was evident, too, in Gitlin's reports from his own visit to Cuba at the end of 1967. At the same time that Gitlin and his fellow SDSers were denouncing U.S. imperialism in the most scathing terms, Gitlin could relate the following Castro speech without any hint of unease or concern. "There could be nothing more honorable for this country," Castro told a huge gathering in the Plaza de la Revolución, "than for its sons to know how to fight to death, spilling even the last drops of their blood for the liberation of the peoples, which is the liberation of humanity." To Gitlin, Castro was not "stirring up the masses" but rather just expressing the people's sentiments. "If we think [this policy] has to be implanted, like somebody else's heart, we are talking about the American experience, not the Cuban."[96] In America such a speech would make the political leader a warmongering tool of the military industrial complex; in the mouth of Castro it only gave voice to the courageous sentiments of a noble and valiant people.

Cuba, in Gitlin's view, was everything the United States was not. Cuba was "a refuge from [the] nationalist smugness" that afflicted the United States. It was a country completely devoid of racism. "When I tried to explore the history of racism in Cuba," Gitlin commented, "I had the feeling I was asking Martians to comment on an earthly sin." Cuba showed that "vast bureaucracy is not an inevitable, uncombattable [*sic*] feature of economic development." And in Cuba, unlike in the United States, "the best minds are unalienated from their people." By working as laborers in the fields in "the spirit of hard, purposeful communal work," Cuban poets and artists found themselves able to produce "the most liberated art imaginable, [and] the most stunning poetry." Cuba was "breaking . . . the pecuniary impulse" that governed American relationships. In place of American "money mindedness" and egotism, Cuba was creating "the spirit of community and common ownership, the habits of critical thinking within a frame of common enterprise, [and] the blending of discipline and individuality." In short, Gitlin concluded, "Cuba stands as a model of what it is [the American] system wants to discredit and destroy."[97]

Like Dellinger, Gitlin insulated the Cuban revolution from criticism by insisting that to understand it in American terms of formal civil liberties, electoral processes, or economic statistics was to "imprison" it. Such measurements "miss that powerful, transfusing, distinctive tone, those qualities of the ordinary life of ordinary Cubans which simply defy description in the securely narrow categories of liberal thought. They miss fraternity; they miss ease within discipline; they miss the spirited critical consciousness at the very center of revolutionary life." Liberal doubt, Gitlin continued, "cannot encompass the enormity of the revolution; it asks the wrong or the most inane and naive questions." The Cuban revolution was "at another level of experience altogether," and to gage it by Western standards made no more sense than measuring weight with a ruler.[98]

Many in the New Left seemed unable or unwilling to question a revolution that had come to define their deepest aspirations and identities — students, Hayden wrote in the aftermath of the 1968 confrontation at Columbia University, were, "in Fidel Castro's words, 'guerrillas in the field of culture.'"[99] Many New Left radicals found it difficult to confront honestly the more troubling and even sinister developments in Cuba without calling into question their most fundamental cultural commitments and identities. It was perhaps easier to overlook or excuse repression, purges, and authoritarianism than to face the dark underbelly of radical egalitarianism.

"We Are Free Only to Choose Sides"

In its romance with Cuba, Vietnam, and the Third World more generally, the New Left succumbed to one of the oldest and least lovely patterns of left political thought, a pattern in which the failings of liberal democratic nations are mercilessly criticized while, as Raymond Aron pointed out over forty years ago, "the worst crimes [are tolerated] as long as they are committed in the name of the proper doctrines."[100] Whatever the oppressed had done, many in the New Left reasoned, it did not begin to compare with what the oppressor had done to the oppressed. One should never therefore "blame the victim," whether that victim was Cuban, Vietnamese, or African American. The morality of individual acts, in any event, paled in comparison with the appalling immorality of an oppressive system. Complex judgments about the morality of individual actions were thus dwarfed by the conversation-closing retort, "Which side are you on?"[101]

Typical of this mode of reasoning, which pervaded the New Left by the late 1960s, was Carl Oglesby's response to Barbara Deming's call for nonviolence. The former SDS president attacked Deming for presuming to judge the actions of the oppressed. "The structure of oppression and unprovoked vengeance in our culture," Oglesby wrote, "has conferred upon its victims a definitive and all-but-inexhaustible claim upon the loyalty of by-standing radicals." White radicals have no business offering advice to, let alone judging, those "victims who have paid and paid and paid." No matter what these oppressed groups did, the task of white radicals was "to support the victim in his struggle in the ways in which the victim asks for support." At a minimum, Oglesby concluded, radicals should not publicly say or do anything that might help the enemy. "What criticisms I may have," Oglesby suggested, "are reserved for private conversations and will never take the form of demands." However deplorable or heinous, the victims' words and actions should be justified, excused, or ignored, but never criticized, because "history . . . is the terrain in which we are free only to choose sides."[102]

And for the New Left, by the latter half of the 1960s, there were only two sides to choose from. There was "the system," which was rotten, diseased, even criminal, and there was "the movement," which was the source of virtually all that was meaningful and good in the lives of New Left radicals.[103] Having summoned up a world in which there were basically only two sides — good, moral victims and an evil, oppressive system — the New Left deprived itself of the capacity to make moral judgments about individual actions. The oppressed were always right.[104] The question of whether one was on the correct side superseded the question of whether an action by a particular individual or group of individuals was morally acceptable. Free only to choose sides, the New Left inadvertently forced itself to condone reprehensible rhetoric and sometimes even brutal actions.

Explaining the Illiberalism of the New Left

What does it tell us that the New Left so quickly fell prey to many of the same tendencies of the old Marxian left that it had so recently warned against? Scornful of Marxism's simplistic bipolar conflict between bourgeoisie and proletariat, why did the New Left then construct a Manichaean battle between the oppressor and the oppressed, the system and the movement, that was every bit as destructive of the moral ambiguity and rich complexity of life? Contemptuous of Marx's vain quest for deliverance from "a class in bourgeois society which is not a class of bourgeois society,"[105] why did the New Left then seek an equally improbable salvation in those oppressed and marginal groups thought to be outside of the system's deforming grip?

One possible explanation is that the New Left's failure is a sign of Marxism's strength. The story of the New Left, from this perspective, is a story of the New Left's tragic failure to transcend the inherited categories of Marxism. There is perhaps something to this argument, but it is unsatisfactory in several respects. First, as a matter of intellectual genealogy it greatly overstates Marx's importance in the early New Left. The structure of Hayden's political thought, to take a particularly important example, was shaped by Mills and Camus, not Marx and Engels.[106] Second, and more fundamental, this approach mistakes the species (Marxism) for the genus (egalitarianism).[107] Marx was hardly the first egalitarian thinker to invest the oppressed and the marginal with redemptive power. The hope that "the last shall be first" has echoed throughout the ages.[108] The New Left's problem was not that the structure of its thought failed to transcend Marxism, but rather that shunning and even ignoring Marxist ideas and thinkers could not shield the New Left from the cultural dilemmas that lie at the heart of radical egalitarianism.

Others have sought the answer to the New Left's romance with the oppressed and its subsequent illiberal turn in psychodynamics and psychopathology. Perhaps, as Stanley Rothman and S. Robert Lichter have suggested, identification with the oppressed provided a means by which aggressive, self-aggrandizing individuals disguised or denied their own power drive and narcissism. The New Left's romance with the oppressed and its hatred of authority, in this view, were thus the externalization of unresolved inner conflicts.[109] Particular individuals in the New Left may indeed have had psychopathic tendencies, but a psychological explanation cannot explain why idealization of the oppressed and demonization of the system became a widely *shared* belief system among an otherwise diverse group of personalities.[110] To account for the shared illiberalism of the later New Left one must understand the ways in which the commitment to a radical egalitarian culture shaped the ways that those in the New Left perceived the world.[111]

Adherents of the New Left invested the oppressed with transformative and redemptive qualities not because they had read Marx or because they disliked their parents, but rather because the oppressed seemed to offer a solution to a fundamental organizational dilemma that confronts all radical egalitarian movements: how to transform the world in an egalitarian direction without becoming compromised or co-opted by established institutions. The oppressed, in other words, fulfill a cultural need for egalitarians by offering the social basis for the imagined transformation of society while also allowing egalitarians to retain what anthropologist Mary Douglas calls a "wall of virtue" against what is perceived to be a coercive and inegalitarian system.[112]

Egalitarian sympathy for the oppressed is genuine, but the cultural function of this attraction often serves to distort a noble sentiment. The oppressed are made the crucible into which egalitarians pour their deepest hopes for a just future. At the same time that radical egalitarians condemn the system for dehumanizing the poor, they themselves are often guilty of making the oppressed superhuman, or turning ordinary people into abstractions, symbols, or even, more dangerously, instruments of the egalitarian vanguard. Hayden and other ERAPers, it must be stressed, were cognizant of the need to avoid a "manipulative approach" toward the poor. The poor, Hayden insisted, must not be treated as "the shock troops" of the revolution but must instead articulate their own needs, develop their own programs, and learn to lead themselves.[113] This was the New Left at its most democratic.

And yet for all SDS' self-conscious internal debate about whether it had the right to impose its vision on the poor,[114] the organization eventually did succumb to the vanguard seduction when the masses failed to respond as nascent egalitarians. This development was predictable, although certainly not inevitable, because SDS' interest was not in the poor per se but in using the poor as a lever to transform the system. If the oppressed could not be made to see their true needs through "the propaganda and falsehoods that are constantly around them,"[115] then many in the organization came to the conclusion that the revolution would have to be made for them.

Where the oppressed did challenge the system in ways that were consistent with New Left expectations, the temptation was to overlook or explain away their crimes. So strong was the will to believe in the oppressed that even thugs such as Huey Newton could become egalitarian heroes.[116] Particularly problematic was the New Left's long-distance romance with the Third World.[117] Here the desire to find an unsullied ally in the struggle against a coercive system drowned out the New Left's early insistence on a radicalism that questioned all premises. Hayden had opened the decade by defining the "radical spirit" as one "that buys nobody's dogma and lives off nobody's myth,"[118] and yet Hayden and many other New Left radicals ended the decade by buying into the most simplistic myths about Third World revolutionaries.

That even the most well-intentioned, well-read, and self-conscious New Left activists so often failed to avoid the pathologies they knew had warped past egalitarian movements suggests the phenomenon is deeper than individual failings or contingent circumstances. The illiberalism of the New Left must be understood at least in part as a consequence of a shared commitment to a radical egalitarian way of organizing social life. From that basic commitment, other choices followed, some consciously, others quite unintentionally. Enduring cultural dilemmas, not just individual pathology or intellectual inheritance, lay at the root of the illiberal turn of the New Left.

When More (Democracy) Is Less

The trouble with socialism is
that it would take too many evenings.

　Oscar Wilde

Socialism means the rule of the men with the most
evenings to spare. . . . If only some citizens participate in
political life, it is essential that they always remember and
be regularly reminded that they are . . . only some. This isn't
easy to arrange. The militant in the movement, for example,
doesn't represent anybody; it is his great virtue that he is self-
chosen. . . . But since he sacrifices so much for his fellow men,
he readily persuades himself that he is acting in their name.
He takes their failure to put in an appearance only as a
token of their oppression. He is certain he is their
agent, or rather, the agent of their liberation.

　Michael Walzer[1]

The year 1965 was critical in the development of SDS and the New Left. The ERAP projects were largely failing. SNCC was turning from integration to black power. And most important of all, the escalation of the Vietnam War was transforming a face-to-face organization into a mass movement. The SDS leadership responded to these developments by calling a "Rethinking Conference," which was held at the end of 1965 in Champaign-Urbana, Illinois. An SDS pamphlet announcing the meeting drew attention to a disturbing and paradoxical development within the organization: "We scream 'no leaders,' 'no structures,' and seem to come up with implicit structures which are far less democratic than the most explicit elitism. How did we get here?"[2] How did an organization that rejected authority end up with unaccountable, arbitrary leaders?

How, moreover, did an organization intensely committed to bottom-up participatory democracy end up after 1968 as a top-down Leninist organization?

Reversing the "Iron Law of Oligarchy"

Among the most celebrated theories of social science is Robert Michels's "iron law of oligarchy."[3] Observing the development of labor and socialist parties in Europe, Michels showed how what began as decentralized, egalitarian organizations metamorphosed into centralized, hierarchical bureaucracies. Growth in organization inevitably meant a taming of the initially radical or revolutionary impulse as the conservative need to maintain and expand the organization displaced the original objectives of transforming society in a more egalitarian direction.

The story of SDS seems in many ways to be Michels's law in reverse. The organization began with relatively traditional representative and parliamentary structures of decision making. The 1962 Port Huron convention was conducted according to *Robert's Rules of Order*; credentials were carefully monitored; voting delegates wore special colored badges and elected a president, vice president, and National Executive Committee (NEC); the NEC was authorized to hire a full-time staff; and between conventions, interim policy decisions were to be made by a National Council composed of the NEC and chapter representatives.[4] Far from inexorably evolving in a more bureaucratic direction, SDS systematically dismantled the few formal, bureaucratic structures there had been in favor of greater participation and local control.[5] To combat "the stability of leadership" Michels had observed among European socialist parties, SDS insisted on annual rotation in office.[6] In the spring of 1965, the national ERAP office was dismantled because it smacked of bureaucratic hierarchy, and the office staff, including director Rennie Davis, went to work in local ERAP projects.[7] That summer, the SDS National Convention moved to abolish the SDS National Office but decided such a momentous decision should be put to the membership. The convention did decide, however, to eliminate the position of national secretary as part of a larger effort to democratize the internal and external functioning of the National Office. Each office worker was paid the identical wage, and everyone in the office lived and ate together in the same apartment. At the same time, the role of the president was downgraded (the convention had tried to abolish it but that proposal was subsequently rejected by the membership), and within two years the office would be abolished altogether.[8] All of this was carried out in the name of anti-elitism and greater democracy.

From the outset, the SDS leadership self-consciously strove to avoid the deadening bureaucratization described by Michels.[9] Participatory democracy, the central defining idea of the early New Left, was so critically important exactly because it promised to steer the New Left clear of the centralized, hierarchical structures that characterized the trade unions and political parties of the Old Left. The aim of the New Left, Tom Hayden explained, was to avoid depending on "fixed leaders, who inevitably develop interests in maintaining the organization (or themselves) and lose touch with the immediate aspirations of the rank and file." Instead, the New Left would "build a movement where 'everybody is a leader.'"[10]

Leadership was inherently elitist, and a flagrant violation of egalitarian norms. "Leaders mean organization, organization means hierarchy, and hierarchy is undemocratic."[11] "We don't believe in leadership," explained one SDSer, "because so many organizations have been sold out by leaders."[12] Those in the New Left constantly reminded each other of the dangers presented by leaders. One poem, entitled simply "Leaders," warned, "Beware of leaders, heroes, organizers / Watch that staff. Beware of structure freaks."[13] No one, particularly within ERAP, would admit to being a leader.[14] There were "rotating coordinators," "facilitators," and "keepers," but no leaders.[15] Followership was even redefined as leadership. "The term 'leader,'" Hayden announced, is "coming to mean anyone whose commitment is with us, daily, all the way."[16]

The same antipathy to leaders was, if anything, even more pronounced within SNCC. James Forman echoed the familiar New Left refrain, "We don't believe in leadership." "The people on the bottom don't need leaders at all," explained Robert Moses. "What they need is the confidence in their own worth and identity to make decisions about their own lives." Decision making was supposed to be egalitarian and consensual. Casey Hayden recalls "talking about circles. Instead of lines, boxes, and hierarchy in the diagrams of how to organize SNCC, I was drawing circles indicating people working together with the circles overlapping other circles as we all generated programs and things to do together." SNCC was sustained by the radically egalitarian hope that they were helping to create a world in which everyone would participate equally and in which people would "not even have to do such things as vote or have leaders or officers."[17]

The New Left harbored enormous faith in the power of spontaneous cooperation and improvisation from below. Many people felt, as Carol McEldowney reported, that "when there were decisions to be made, people would find ways to get together and make them, and that we shouldn't create structures." For the New Left, a movement without leaders was a deeply moving and beautiful experience. After the 1967 march on Washington, one participant exulted in the "massive improvisation from below, unplanned by leaders." Another marveled, "There was no leadership; that was what was so beautiful." Formal roles and institutional structures were believed to be neither necessary nor sufficient for realizing democracy. As SDSer C. Clark Kissinger noted in 1965, "SDS has tended to speak of democracy as an intangible quantity whose presence or absence is far more related to notions of community and trust than to formalized structures." Democracy, the New Left believed, is "ensured not by structures but by the will of the people involved to be democratic."[18]

A movement without leaders or structures: that was the New Left's alluring ideal. The reality, however, was quite different. Despite or rather because of their best efforts, the New Left increasingly suffered from the exercise of arbitrary and unaccountable power by an ever more unrepresentative elite. Reforms in the name of more democracy produced less democracy; antielitism produced its opposite.[19]

Charisma as a Substitute for Formal Authority

From the outset, the New Left's antipathy toward formal authority and organizational structure created powerful pressures within the movement to invest particular individuals with charisma. Charisma substituted for the authority of office in organizations such as SDS and SNCC that spurned the standard operating procedures and formal leadership roles by which most bureaucratic organizations resolved conflict. By creating charismatic stars, New Left groups could avoid routinized procedures and formal structures while still providing the ideological direction necessary for the group to reach decisions, take action, and survive.[20]

Charisma was particularly important within SNCC, the most egalitarian of the early New Left organizations. In the early years, SNCC was fiercely egalitarian in its ethos and social relations. Decisions were reached not by voting but through hours of discussion aimed at forging a consensus. Structure and leadership, to many SNCC members, meant manipulation, even exploitation.[21] SNCC's thoroughgoing egalitarianism meant it was often difficult to reach agreement on goals, strategies, or tactics. Investing charisma in particular individuals allowed SNCC to make decisions in the absence of formal leadership roles.

The most notable of the early SNCC charismatics was the soft-spoken Robert Moses.[22] As Emily Stoper reports, Moses "could shape the course of a meeting by his mere presence. He had a talent for waiting without saying a word for the point when a debate had reached an impasse and then standing up and in one clear statement saying precisely what most of the people said and resolving the issue." "If it was Bob who said it," one SNCC member recalls, "you knew it had to be done." Many SNCC members have testified to the towering charismatic appeal of Moses. "If Bob walked into a room or joined a group that I was in," SNCC staffer Mary King recalls, "I felt my chest muscles quicken and a sudden rush of exhilaration. He inspired me and touched me. I trusted Bob implicitly and . . . considered him prophetic."[23] Any number of SNCC workers and volunteers likened Moses to Jesus Christ,[24] and local people in Mississippi referred to him as "Moses in the Bible."[25] He became, John Lewis remembers, "the all-perfect and all-holy and all-wise leader."[26]

Within SDS the comparable person was Tom Hayden. Numerous reports attest to the charisma that those in SDS and the ERAP projects invested in Hayden. SDSer Bob Ross confessed, "Many of us spend a lot of time worrying whether Hayden would approve of what we're doing." Journalist Andrew Kopkind, who had been deeply affected by his visits to Hayden's Newark project in the mid-1960s, later allowed that for him and for many of his friends "Tom Hayden remained a touchstone in our lives. . . . Years afterwards, when pondering a political or existential decision I would flash on Hayden and guess what he'd say, or think, or do." Radical intellectuals aligned with the New Left seemed to hope, as Steven Roberts reported, "that just by being near [Hayden] they might imbibe the vibrations of true radicalism."[27]

The New Left's weakness for the visionary, charismatic leader stemmed not only from internal organizational dynamics but also from its commitment to the sort of sweeping social changes that were unlikely to be produced by a political system biased toward incrementalism. From the outset, the New Left's hope for dramatic, revolutionary change brought with it a longing for visionary leaders, even as their shared egalitarian ideology warned against leadership. In his 1961 "Letter to the New (Young) Left," Hayden lamented that "we have no real visionaries for our leaders. . . . What is desperately needed . . . is the person of vision and clarity, who sees both the model society and the pitfalls that precede its attainment, and who will not destroy his vision for short-run gains, but, instead, hold it out for all to see as the furthest dream and perimeter of human possibility." Interviewed twenty-five years later, Hayden's attraction to the charismatic, visionary leader remained strong. "Parliamentary leaders are prosaic," Hayden explained,

> visionary leaders are poetic. The prosaic leader elicits participation primarily on the level of an occasional vote. The poetic leader elicits curiously greater participation from people who are in fact not just an anonymous mass of followers. At the same time that they're followers in one sense, they are doing more than voting. They are involved in neighborhood or union or political associations, they're reading, they're studying, they're arguing, they're developing — even though they seem to have been triggered by an authoritarian or dominating kind of leader.[28]

The New Left's longing for a visionary leader or heroic organizer who would transcend the mundane political roles and expectations that characterized American society also manifested itself in admiration for Fidel Castro (and Mao and Che Guevara). For those on the New Left who admired Castro (and there were precious few who did not), personal vision was more important than institutional process and structure; indeed, the latter must be sacrificed because they were only an obstacle to reaching the promised land as visualized by the leader. Even as skeptical a person as C. Wright Mills could uncritically accept the claim that in order to work out "a brand-new social and economic order" the Cubans had "to have leaders with the power to act fast and not to be hampered . . . with some 'political system'—whatever that may mean." Mills wrote glowingly of "Fidel's antibureaucratic personality" and of his "way of going about things, of getting things done, without red tape and without delay." Castro, Mills marveled, "explains and he educates, and after he speaks almost every doubt has gone away." As long as the visionary Castro (whom Mills characterized as the most "democratic force in Cuba") remained in power, Cuba was "going to be all right."[29]

Castro was uncritically admired from afar, but the New Left's own leaders were not so fortunate. Even for those invested with the charismatic aura of a Hayden or a Moses, exercising leadership in the intensely antiauthority organizations of the New Left was tremendously trying and stressful.[30] Every organizer or leader was vulnerable to accusations of "manipulation." Cries of manipulation, Richard Rothstein notes, seemed to arise within ERAP projects "whenever we might otherwise have been on the verge of action or decision."[31] Many of those in SNCC and ERAP, Rothstein continues, adhered to "the image of an organizer who never organized, who by his simple presence was the mystical medium for the spontaneous expression of the 'people.'"[32] Leaders adapted to the antiauthority bias by adopting a self-abnegating leadership style in which they led without seeming to. Moses, for example, would typically crouch in the corner or speak from the back of the room,[33] while Hayden often tried to avoid the appearance of leadership by posing questions rather than giving answers.[34] However, this leadership style only served to intensify fears within the group of "hidden agendas" and disguised manipulation.

More important for our purposes than the suspicion and distrust engendered by the ambiguous roles of participatory democracy is the way in which the need to hide or deny leadership led to unaccountable, even arbitrary, power. "The self-abnegating style of participatory democracy," as Gitlin came to recognize, "didn't eliminate leadership, only disguised it. The de facto leaders were still influential; followers were swayed willy-nilly. Diffident leaders in disguise couldn't be held accountable, and ended up more manipulative than when they stood up tall, made their authority explicit, presented solid targets."[35] "What is more undemocratic," asked Paul Booth in his final report as national secretary, "than a leader who denies he is a leader, refuses to organize meetings in which he can let the other people know what's going on, [and] refuses to file a report in the [National Office] so that other people can know what he did?"[36] SNCC executive secretary James Forman agreed: "Just because you don't have a structure and you don't have leaders doesn't mean that nobody is running things. It just means you don't know who is running it."[37] Pretending that there were no leaders made holding leaders accountable more difficult.

Accountability Lost

Throughout 1965 there was ample evidence in both SNCC and SDS that extreme hostility to structure and bureaucracy actually created a vulnerability to unaccountable and arbitrary power. Historian Clayborne Carson relates how in the spring of 1965, SNCC underwent intense debate about the work being done within the organization. Many within SNCC, including Casey Hayden, Mary King, and even Bob Moses, were accused of "floating" between projects and of being on a "freedom high." This concern, Carson reports, led the central Atlanta office to begin "a person-by-person evaluation, lasting almost two days, of the activities of over one hundred staff members." However, since there were no "procedures for supervision or rules governing staff assignments and behavior, the assessments were often arbitrary or inconsistent and sometimes based merely on reputations." The result of this personnel review was a purge of the "freedom high" faction within SNCC, leaving power in the hands of the self-described "hard liners," who favored a "disciplined," centrally administered organizational structure.[38] Not for the last time, the New Left had a striking demonstration of how reflexive opposition to all bureaucratic structures and procedures created not freedom and equality but rather an invitation to arbitrary and authoritarian power.[39]

The limitations of participatory democracy were also prominently on display in the SDS National Office, where at the urging of the newly elected vice president, Jeff Shero, a much-heralded "experiment in office democracy" had been instituted. Since the division of labor was inegalitarian and elitist, the National Office decided that every staff member would perform clerical duties. As James Miller recounts, "All staffers would share responsibility for processing the mail; the person who sent the last copy of a document would be responsible for mimeographing, collating and stapling another batch. But nobody liked to mimeograph, collate and staple. Nobody liked to stuff envelopes. Consequently, nobody did these things . . . [and] virtually no mail was processed." Communications to the membership about what the National Office was doing virtually ceased, and piles of requests for SDS literature and applications for membership went unopened and unanswered. Most ironic of all, the National Office failed to send out the membership referendum on whether to have national officers. By the end of the summer even the National Office was forced to admit that the office was in "a general state of collapse and failing to perform the most rudimentary functions." By "democratizing" the office, SDS had managed to cut off the flow of communication between leaders and followers that is so indispensable to democratic control and accountability.[40]

Some members of SDS hoped to use the December 1965 Rethinking Conference to raise tough questions about the paradoxes and limitations of participatory democracy that were becoming increasingly evident. Paul Booth, who had been installed as national secretary in the fall of 1965 in order to bring some order to the chaos of the National Office, was particularly anxious to get SDSers to acknowledge the limitations of participatory democracy and then to "re-create accountability mechanisms." "We are now too large," Paul Booth explained, "to proceed along the lines of consensus." Voting was necessary, Booth insisted, to make decisions and to create accountability. Booth chastised SDS for tending "to believe in the false view that structure in itself is harmful" and for indulging in the fanciful wish "that leadership doesn't have to exist."[41]

Booth's warnings fell on largely unreceptive ears. Most SDSers seemed far more inclined to agree with Robert Pardum (who would be elected education secretary in 1967) that the problem was that SDS hadn't yet taken participatory democracy seriously enough. In a paper entitled "Organizational Democracy," prepared for the Rethinking Conference, Pardum gave voice to the complaint that "participatory democracy is nonexistent within the national office structure. [Working for SDS] is like getting saved by a traveling preacher, who you later find out is a drunkard and beats his wife."[42] The organization's problems, SDS tried to reassure itself, were rooted not in its egalitarian commitment to participatory democracy but rather in its failure to root out the last vestiges of hierarchy and structure.

The 1965 Rethinking Conference not only revealed the dominance of antistructure sentiment within SDS but also dramatically showcased the problems that participatory democracy posed in large-scale organizations. The attempt to make SDS national meetings ever more open and democratic — rotating chairmen, voting on the honor system, small group discussions and seminars — had the effect of making decisions increasingly difficult to reach,[43] which created tremendous frustration and even despondency. One participant described the December conference as "a morass, a labyrinth, a marathon of procedural amendments, non sequiturs, soul-searching and maneuvering, partying and arguing, plenaries which went nowhere, proposals unheeded, undebated; terminology which only the most in of the ingroup could comprehend, much less care about. . . . Pages and pages of proposals, prospectuses, amendments, workshop resolutions, recommendations, counter-recommendations, hasseling, and dancing to the Beatles." Todd Gitlin agreed that the National Council meeting had been a "disaster" and reported that "feelings ranging from discomfort to boredom to distaste to nausea to utter rejection seemed almost universal."[44]

Although discontent with this and other national meetings was commonplace, few within SDS seemed willing at this point to identify participatory democracy as a major source of the organization's ills. Don McKelvey, for instance, complained that "at these national meetings, decisions don't get made," and yet announced that he was becoming increasingly opposed to "representative democracy [which] is virtually bound to encourage manipulation and elitism as a political style." "Without direct democracy," he added, "the people have at best only formal power."[45] National Council meetings and national conventions, McKelvey recommended, should be "built around small group meetings" rather than large plenary sessions. For Gitlin, the National Council's problems were due to the "shallowness of debate." "Slogans and symbols," he complained, "replace[d] analysis and hard thinking." What SDS needed, Gitlin believed, was more time to have "a serious, hard, agonizing honest talk about elitism, experience, competence, decision-making, personal styles, etc." Gitlin's suggestions brought a biting rebuke from Steve Max, one of the organization's long-standing skeptics about participatory democracy. "Workshops," Max responded, "[don't] resolve anything. . . . It is decisions that we need — explicit, clear statements with which people can agree or disagree." The National Council, Max insisted, must "conceive of itself as a decision-making body."[46]

But for the National Council to act as a decision-making body was increasingly difficult as the organization grew in size. The original SDS constitution had set the ratio of voting National Council delegates to SDS members at roughly twenty-five to one. In an SDS that numbered in the hundreds and strictly limited voting (and, initially, speaking) to those who were properly credentialed, National Council meetings were manageable (barely). But as the membership of the organization ballooned to five thousand plus, meetings of the National Council also increased in size. To increase the ratio between delegates and members, as Clark Kissinger proposed,[47] was rejected as a violation of participatory democracy. Moreover, at the same time that dramatic organizational growth was making representative democracy more necessary, parliamentary structures and processes were becoming ever more deeply reviled. Voting was increasingly dismissed as "the archaic project of an individualist age" or as symptomatic of an "authoritarian" age. *Robert's Rules of Order* were denounced as hopelessly bourgeois and outmoded. "There's no point," one SDSer complained, "in having our hands tied by a reactionary rule-system like Robert's [*Rules of Order*]."[48]

The rapid growth in the size of the membership of the National Council, combined with the increasingly pronounced disdain for representative democracy and parliamentary procedures (including such "embarrassingly bourgeois" practices as checking voting credentials[49]), created a situation in which the National Council was essentially stripped of the decision-making power that the SDS constitution had given it. As National Council meetings became monopolized by interminable debates and esoteric discussion,[50] real policy-making power shifted inexorably to the permanent National Office. In the name of greater democracy, SDS had in fact shifted decision-making power further away from the membership base and exacerbated the gap between the national leadership and the rank-and-file membership.

This paradoxical development within SDS has been diagnosed by Richard Rothstein in his incisive 1972 retrospective, "Representative Democracy in SDS." As Rothstein shows:

> Beginning in 1963, under the banner of "democratic" reform, the representative structure of SDS was dismantled. As each representative institution in the organization was destroyed, the organization became, in fact, less democratic. This increasing lack of democracy was seen by SDS members as further evidence of the failure of representative structures and fueled the flames of new "democratic" reform movements to destroy the remaining representative institutions within the organization. Thus, destruction of democratic forms led to less democracy, and less democracy to the destruction of democratic forms.[51]

Among the earliest democratic reforms to undermine democratic control was annual rotation of office. Rothstein points out that when Hayden stepped down in June 1963 after his year as president in favor of Todd Gitlin, then almost totally unknown, Hayden "continued to provide ideological and programmatic leadership." But rotation made Hayden's "leadership less publicly accessible to the SDS membership, less responsible to the organization, and required the establishment of the fiction of Gitlin's powers to disguise the hidden manipulation of the actual leadership which was being exercised." Moreover, the principle of rotation extended well beyond the presidency, through every level of the organization. Members of the National Executive Committee (which was selected by the membership at the national convention) stopped running for reelection, and there were enormous social pressures on the organization's "heavies" to withdraw from leadership roles.[52]

Annual rotation in office for elected leaders was designed to maximize participation and to ensure that the organization did not become overly reliant on any one leader or set of leaders. The unintended result, however, of the extreme discontinuity in leadership that strict rotation created was to concentrate de facto power in the hands of the national staff. The SDS constitution designated the president (who was elected at the national convention) as "the spokesperson of SDS," but increasingly the president became a figurehead, while real power passed to the national secretary (who was appointed by the National Council as "the chief administrative official") and the National Office staff he hired. Moreover, neither the National Council nor any other body had the supervisory authority or capacity to oversee the National Office, leaving the latter with tremendous freedom to control the organization's agenda.[53]

The Leninist Turn

The pattern of "democratic" reforms producing a leadership that was steadily less accountable to the SDS membership continued into 1967 and 1968. At the national convention in the summer of 1967, the National Office presented a plan to eliminate the presidency and vice presidency, and to democratize itself by creating three equal officers: "a National Secretary in charge of the National Office and responsible for implementing national programs, an Education Secretary for internal education and chapter communications, and an Inter-organizational Secretary acting as liaison with other political groups." The purpose of the reform was to make the national secretary, which had become in any event the real locus of decision-making power in SDS, a position that would be elected by the entire organization at the national convention. It was also hoped that creating three equal officers would do away with "the hierarchical structure of president–vice president as well as the . . . division between administrative and political jobs." The convention delegates debated the measure for less than an hour before voting by an overwhelming margin to accept the reorganization plan.[54]

No one present seemed to anticipate the undemocratic consequences that would follow from such a seemingly egalitarian reform. Although the reforms were designed to eliminate hierarchy, Kirkpatrick Sale points out that the actual effects "were to concentrate even more power in the hands of the National Secretary, who could now operate almost without restrictions." The result, too, was "to make the NO even more of a closed-off world" and "to permit the leadership to go its own way virtually unchecked until the next convention." The plan called for the National Council to "elect administrative bodies" to review the decisions made by the National Office, but this quickly became seen as too hierarchical and bourgeois, and was replaced, as Richard Rothstein recounts, by "the notion that the national staff should be responsible only to a 'national collective' appointed and organized by the staff itself." In the name of combating hierarchy and elitism, SDS had managed to create an organizational structure that lacked institutional safeguards against the abuse of authority by national officers.[55] In the name of greater democracy, SDS had weakened democratic control and created an organization that was ripe for capture by committed antidemocrats.

The depth of the gulf between the leadership and membership had become increasingly troubling. In December 1967 the national secretary, Mike Spiegel, openly acknowledged the "tendency for the NO to become further and further alienated from the membership." Spiegel's explanation of the problem was superficial, however. He attributed the growing gap between the membership and the leadership to the National Office's need to insure its own survival in the face of a repressive society. While the National Office certainly was harassed on a regular basis by the Chicago police and had its headquarters smashed once by unknown attackers, this hardly began to explain the organizational problems that afflicted SDS.[56]

More fundamental was the National Office's growing sense of itself as a revolutionary vanguard. It came to envision itself both as "a bastion against the forces of a repressive society" and as the leader of what Carl Davidson identified as the organization's "shock troops."[57] "The people around the NO," Sale reports, "became an increasingly close-knit group: a number of the staff lived and slept together in nearby apartments in a quasi-communal style." Longtime SDSer Steve Weissman, who in the fall of 1967 worked in Ann Arbor with the Radical Education Project, recalled that the National Office, which "had always thought of itself as just trying to keep things going... [now] became... a collective unto itself."[58]

Greg Calvert was probably the most influential architect of the Leninist turn within SDS. Calvert, who served as national secretary between the summers of 1966 and 1967, was the first national officer to openly question participatory democracy and to insist on the need for a radical separation of organizational means and ends. The attempt "to create community in the midst of an anti-communitarian world" had failed, Calvert insisted, ending up as "either a fruitless mutual-titillation society or as disruptive self-destructive chaos." The New Left's vision of the beloved community had been "correct," but the revolutionary movement itself could not be a beloved community. "We are not the beloved community," Calvert intoned; "we can only hope to become the revolutionary community of hope which will give birth to the beloved society. . . . Our freedom is not to be free but to be a force for freedom."[59] Lenin could hardly have put it better.

Calvert elaborated upon his critique of participatory democracy in an article published in *New Left Notes* at the end of 1967. While participatory democracy was appealing as "a vision of the good society," it was totally ineffective "as a style and structure for serious radical work." Calvert noted that at the level of local chapters the avoidance of formal leadership roles meant "elitist manipulation by individuals or cliques which can operate freely because there is no defined leadership responsibility"; long, formless meetings only led to "the disillusionment of large numbers of new recruits who find it impossible to participate in the manipulated mass meetings"; and the emphasis on spontaneity frustrated "serious activists because neither serious organizational forms nor long-range programs are developed." The answer to the organization's ills, Calvert argued, was a "responsible collective leadership which can be held accountable to its constituency." Only then could it become a truly "revolutionary organization" capable of transforming America.[60]

Though Calvert couched his plea in terms of increasing accountability, he failed to spell out the institutional mechanisms that would insure accountability to the membership. How could leaders remain accountable to followers without emulating the sort of prosaic parliamentary structures of representative democracy that the New Left by this point widely derided as symptomatic of an authoritarian America? It was all very well to rhetorically reject "rigid authoritarianism and dogmatic elitism," but what organizational structures would insure that "responsible collective leadership" did not become a euphemism for a revolutionary Leninist vanguard? And although Calvert endorsed the ultimate objective of a "non-repressive society of equals," his radical divorce of means and ends augured well for neither means nor ends.[61]

Calvert's diagnosis of the ills of participatory democracy, particularly in a large-scale organization, was compelling in many ways, yet his embrace of the Leninist faith that revolutionary ends and means could be readily separated was a fundamental mistake from which flowed deeply illiberal consequences, as Calvert himself later came to recognize.[62] What had helped save the early New Left from the temptations of Leninism was the insistence that means and ends were necessarily joined, that "the character of the future society is determined by the character of the movement which forges it."[63] The ERAP organizers repeatedly bumped up against the limitations of participatory democracy, yet they consistently rejected the idea of themselves as a vanguard. Their adherence to the idea that the aim of organizing was "to replace ourselves with community people running their own movement"[64] helped ERAP to resist the insulting notion of the masses as simply the "shock troops" for the revolution. And while ERAPers did distinguish between the people's "felt" needs and their "true" needs,[65] their insistence that a popular movement must be based on needs articulated by the people themselves checked the potentially authoritarian impulse to discount "felt" needs as false consciousness.[66]

By abandoning SDS' commitment "to anticipate the lineaments of a future society" in their own organization,[67] Calvert and others kicked the door wide open to the most antidemocratic and illiberal impulses of radical egalitarianism. SDS rapidly succumbed to the utopian fallacy that realizing the beloved community in which all would participate as equals could be postponed to a distant future, and that a hierarchical, disciplined, revolutionary organization could achieve that egalitarian end.[68] The radical separation of means and ends envisioned by Calvert allowed SDS to be taken over in 1968 by various Marxist-Leninist factions and quasi-military cadres that represented a fundamental perversion of the organization's original participatory, egalitarian ideals. Once SDS was in the hands of self-described "revolutionary communists" such as Bernardine Dohrn, concerns with democratic process were systematically subordinated to the revolutionary struggle.[69]

It would be a mistake, however, to view this antidemocratic turn within SDS as simply an unfortunate error of a few misguided or fanatical leaders. Indeed, a central lesson of SDS' experience in the 1960s is that antidemocratic results are intimately connected to the pursuit of radical egalitarian conceptions of democracy. To begin with, as we have seen, the rejection of formal structures and leadership roles allowed for the concentration of power in the hands of an unaccountable and unrepresentative elite who were then able to take the organization in explicitly antidemocratic directions. Moreover, SDS' development must be understood not only in terms of the Leninist path Calvert and others chose but also in terms of the paths that SDS had already foreclosed. The widely shared antipathy within SDS (and SNCC) to bourgeois representative institutions and procedures resulted in framing the choice in terms of participatory democracy versus democratic centralism. When participatory democracy failed, there was only vanguardism left.

And fail participatory democracy inevitably must, at least in a mass organization.[70] Participatory democracy might work tolerably, even superbly, well in a small, face-to-face organization of like-minded friends, but SDS had long since outgrown that phase. Calvert was surely right that participatory democracy could not and was not working in an organization that, by the end of his term as national secretary, claimed thirty thousand members.[71] The rapid increase in the organization's size meant that if SDS was to avoid the vanguard seduction, members needed to rethink their reflexive antipathy to representative structures. In particular, participatory democracy and representative institutions and structures needed to be seen not as mutually exclusive but as complementary, with different strengths and weaknesses.[72] For the overwhelming majority of SDS activists, however, the prosaic parliamentary structures that characterized American society were dismissed as the death of real democracy and of meaningful participation. Only after SDS had been devoured by its warring Marxist-Leninist factions — the Weathermen, the Revolutionary Youth Movement, Progressive Labor — and flamed out in a senseless orgy of violence did former SDSers begin to reconsider some of the virtues of a less heroic, even mundane, model of representative democracy.[73]

Rethinking Organization and Democracy

"Who says 'organization' says oligarchy." The New Left leadership read and absorbed this most-quoted sentence from Robert Michels's masterwork. Fearing elite control, they sought to avoid organizational structures. Under Michels's influence, the New Left tried to do without bureaucracy, structure, and leadership so as to facilitate participation, democracy, and egalitarian community. And yet seeking to learn from Michels, they ended up with something quite different and much worse than the organizational timidity and bureaucratic elitism he predicted. Assiduously striving to avoid Weberian bureaucracy, SDS and SNCC ultimately ended up with a Leninist vanguard.

SDS' evolution suggests a weakness in Michels's famous proverb and, indeed, in his entire argument. For Michels, the tragedy is that over time the structure of successful radical parties will increasingly come to resemble the parliamentary structures of the established parties. The egalitarian party will never succeed, he predicts, "in becoming more than an ineffective and miniature copy of the state organization."[74] Yet not all state organizations are created alike. Michels fails to appreciate adequately the distinction between a personalistic and arbitrary authoritarianism and impersonal, rule-bound bureaucracies, between accountable elites subject to democratic control through competitive elections and unaccountable elites free from popular control. Michels's focus on the transformation from radical egalitarianism to hierarchical elitism slights these critically important differences in modes of elite rule.

For the New Left, particularly as it became a mass organization, these were differences that needed to be taken into account. If bureaucracy is bad, arbitrary authoritarianism is worse. If voting in competitive elections means settling for an unheroic politics in which elites rule, at least it protects against unlimited power. If, as Michels rightly saw, it is not possible to sustain radical egalitarianism in a successful mass organization, then egalitarians would do better not to try vainly to defy Michels's "iron law" but instead to nurture the sort of organizational structures and leadership roles that best preserve democratic control and accountability and prevent authoritarianism or Leninist vanguardism.

Egalitarianism Today

Radical Feminism

THE PERSONAL IS POLITICAL

The little utopia of the family is the enemy—
indeed the principal enemy—of the beloved community.
   Lewis Mumford[1]
[The home is] that open grave where so many women
hide waiting to die.
   Andrea Dworkin[2]

Among the most important legacies of the 1960s and the New Left is the contemporary feminist movement.[3] Of course, feminism, even its more radical variants, long predates the 1960s. In the decades before the Civil War, radical abolitionists such as Stephen Foster and Abigail Kelley assailed the patriarchal family structure and the "slavery of sex,"[4] while nineteenth-century utopian communities strove to construct alternatives to the conventional bourgeois family, in some cases forbidding marriage in favor of "free love," in others separating children from their parents so the young could be raised by the collective rather than the "isolated household."[5] The term "feminism" itself came into widespread usage in the United States during the early 1910s, at the height of Progressive ferment.[6] Those who identified themselves as "feminists" in the

1910s sharply distinguished the new "feminism" from the old "suffragism." For these new self-described feminists, the vote was seen not as an end in itself but as a means to achieve what one activist described as a "complete social revolution" in gender relationships.[7] Their aim was not only the political inclusion of women but a radical restructuring of private relationships between the sexes. For these early-twentieth-century feminists, the personal was political.[8]

Feminism, then, was not born moderate and then radicalized by the 1960s. From its inception, the term "feminism," in the minds of both its proponents and its opponents, has been linked with radicalism and even socialism.[9] "Feminism," as Nancy Cott explains, "was born ideologically on the left of the political spectrum, first espoused by women who were familiar with advocacy of socialism and who, advantaged by bourgeois backgrounds, nonetheless identified more with labor than with capital."[10] Max Eastman and Floyd Dell, both self-proclaimed feminists and socialists, frequently used the pages of the *Masses* to plead the case for the emancipation of women, and Randolph Bourne saw Greenwich Village feminism as a leading edge in the radical assault on deadening bourgeois conventions.[11]

Although the radical feminism that took shape in the late 1960s had much in common with Greenwich Village feminism, it was the nonfeminist social movements of the 1960s that were most important in shaping the egalitarian structure and ideology of the early radical feminist groups. Indeed the term "radical feminism," which did not enter the vocabulary of the women's movement until the summer of 1968, is itself a mark of the influence of the late New Left on the women's movement. For many women radicalized by the protest politics of the 1960s, the unadorned term "feminist" conjured up not liberating images of Greenwich Village bohemian radicalism but rather, in the words of Shulamith Firestone, the repressive visage of the "granite-faced spinster obsessed with the vote." Feminism was seen as "one of those horribly discredited terms" that smacked of the sort of liberal reformism which by 1968 most New Leftists found completely anathema.[12] Much as the word "feminism" had emerged in the 1910s in contradistinction to mere suffragism, so now the term "radical feminism" was preferred because, as Alice Echols reports, the term "differentiated [the radicals] from the reformist branch of the women's movement."[13]

Early-twentieth-century feminists had insisted the personal was political, but the immediate origins of that contemporary feminist rallying cry lie in the 1960s New Left. It was Tom Hayden, speaking at the University of Michigan in the spring of 1962, who had issued a ringing call for "a re-assertion of the personal," and it was the *Port Huron Statement*, in the summer of 1962, that summoned a new left to "give form to . . . feelings of helplessness and indifference, so that people may see the political, social, and economic sources of their private troubles and organize to change society." Hayden and others in the early New Left, as Echols writes, "reconceptualized apparently personal problems — specifically their alienation from a campus cultural milieu characterized by sororities and fraternities, husband and wife hunting, sports, and careerism, and the powerlessness they felt as college students without a voice in campus governance or curriculum — as political problems." The New Left thus paved the way for feminism by expanding political discourse to include personal relations and by encouraging people to find personal fulfillment in the movement.[14]

Having endorsed the movement's scathing indictment of American racism, capitalism, and imperialism, many radicalized women now turned egalitarian rage back upon the movement's own sexism with devastating effect. Men were the oppressors; women the oppressed. Some New Left males tried to argue that issues of gender only detracted from the "real" issues of race, class, and war, but met with only limited success. By insisting that equality begins at home in personal relationships, radical feminists seized the egalitarian high ground, "radicalizing the left by expanding the definition of radical to include feminism."[15] Having hoisted the movement "heavies" on their own egalitarian petard, radical feminists began to organize themselves into small groups modeled on the egalitarian participatory principles of the New Left. The trouble with the New Left, radical feminists believed, was that it had been insufficiently egalitarian; allowing gender inequalities and patriarchy to flourish had made a mockery of the New Left's egalitarian principles. Radical feminists were determined to take equality seriously, and no radical feminist group took equality more seriously than The Feminists.

Organizing The Feminists

The National Organization for Women (NOW) was the stepchild of Title VII of the 1964 Civil Rights Act, which outlawed discrimination in employment on the basis not only of race, creed, and national origin, but also sex. NOW's primary mission was to provide an organizational presence in Washington and in the states to see to it that the newly created

Equal Employment Opportunity Commission enforced Title VII's prohibition against sex discrimination. Although NOW's 1966 founding statement of purpose did not ignore inequities in the family and marriage, its primary focus was on "tak[ing] action to bring women into full participation in the mainstream of American society now." NOW's founding statement articulated precisely the sort of liberal integrationist agenda that the egalitarian New Left was already in the process of rejecting in the area of black civil rights.[16] The clash between liberal and radical feminist was a conflagration waiting only for a spark.

That spark came in the person of Ti-Grace Atkinson, who had been elected president of the New York chapter of NOW in December 1967. Although raised a Republican, Atkinson became radicalized after her enrollment in the mid-1960s as a philosophy graduate student at Columbia University — a vital center of New Left activism that in the spring of 1968 became virtually synonymous with radical student protest after radical students, led by members of SDS, "liberated" the university, taking a dean hostage, occupying university buildings, and bringing normal campus life to a standstill for almost a week.[17] Six months after the revolt at Columbia, Atkinson tried to bring the New Left's demanding brand of participatory democracy to the New York chapter of NOW. First, she and her allies proposed eliminating all offices on the grounds that they were inherently unequal and thus oppressive; defeated on that proposal, Atkinson then called for abolishing elections and choosing officers by lot, frequent rotation of office to equalize power relations within the organization, and diffusing power by increasing the number of persons within each office. Defeated here as well (by a two-to-one margin), Atkinson charged her opponents with only wanting "women to have the opportunity to be oppressors, too" instead of desiring "to destroy oppression itself." Told by Betty Friedan that NOW's goal was "to get women into positions of power," Atkinson retorted that feminism's aim should be "to get rid of the positions of power, not get up into those positions. The fight against unequal power relationships between men and women necessitates fighting unequal power everyplace: between men and women (for feminists especially), but also between men and men, and women and women, between black and white, and rich and poor." Having failed to dismantle her own position of power, Atkinson resigned as president, explaining that "by holding this office I am participating in oppression itself."[18]

Following her resignation, Atkinson founded the "October 17th Movement," soon to be renamed "The Feminists." Unlike the hierarchically structured NOW, the new group's internal power relationships were to mirror or, more precisely, prefigure the group's egalitarian aspirations for restructuring society.[19] To that end the group immediately instituted a system of lots to equalize power within the group. Within less than a year, however, the commitment to internal democracy was becoming threatened by a zealous policing of group boundaries and radical commitment. By the summer of 1969, Echols reports, Atkinson and other members were "pushing for The Feminists to become a disciplined, revolutionary, vanguard group with strict membership and attendance regulations and even more draconian rules to ensure egalitarianism." With half of its membership absent, the group passed a number of restrictive regulations. It was mandated, for instance, that "no other activity may supersede work for the group." Individuals who missed meetings were disciplined, either by forfeiting voting privileges or through expulsion. All tasks were now to be distributed by lot, and those women with strong writing or speaking skills were asked "to withdraw their names from the 'privileged' lot where those tasks were assigned so that others could cultivate these skills."[20] Most controversial of all, the group declared a quota on the number of married women who could belong to the group, since marriage was "inherently inequitable" and "rejection of this institution both in theory and in practice [was] a primary mark of the radical feminist." No more than a third of the membership, the group decided, could be women "in either a formal (with legal contract) or informal (e.g., living with a man) instance of the institution of marriage." These new rules were immediately denounced by some members, most prominently Anne Koedt, as "fascistic." Koedt and all the married women promptly left the group, leaving Atkinson and her allies to consolidate their authoritarian brand of radical egalitarianism.[21]

For The Feminists, the quota measure was necessary because married women were necessarily "hostages" or "prisoners" of their husbands. Women who were "locked into men" would not be able to take the truly radical measures that would be necessary to liberate women. By "rejecting marriage and fidelity," Pam Kearon explained, "we are cutting off our retreat from radical feminism and creating the necessity for female unity and trust." Marriage undermined the solidarity of the group and the feminist consciousness of individual members, because married women would "go home to discuss the meetings with their husbands." Marriage was the principal site in which women "internalized their oppression"; it was monogamous relationships that produced women who were "messed up" as well as "messed over." Married women, it was felt, were necessarily "damaged" and would thus contaminate "the thinking of the group."[22]

Having driven out the politically incorrect, The Feminists now turned to realizing their egalitarian vanguard. Differences undermined egalitarian unity, so Pam Kearon and Karen Mehrhof proposed a uniform as a way of making all members equal.[23] But despite the rhetoric of absolute equality, some women were more equal than others. Formal authority having been done away with, informal resources such as personal stature, charisma, and verbal virtuosity became the coin of the realm. In an effort to limit the charismatic power of the loquacious Atkinson, the group adopted "the disc system," whereby each member was given the same number of chips at the beginning of a meeting and was required to relinquish one chip every time she spoke. Once out of chips, the member could no longer participate. Atkinson technically abided by the system, but now, as one member lamented, "each time she spoke, she spoke for so long."[24]

Atkinson's growing stature as a leader in the feminist movement not surprisingly created tensions and resentments within the egalitarian grouping. In the spring of 1970 The Feminists passed a resolution taking Atkinson to task for permitting the mass media to define her as the leader of the group. To make sure that the group was genuinely "leaderless," the group resolved that "all contact with the media on feminist issues by a member of The Feminists is to be decided upon by the group and chosen by lot." Any member "appearing on the media" was to be identified by group affiliation rather than name. Violators would be expelled from the group. Atkinson responded by condemning the resolution and withdrawing from the group she had founded only eighteen months before.[25]

With Atkinson gone, the group continued to pass more rules designed to define standards for appropriate radical feminist conduct. Members late to meetings were penalized, digressions during meetings were not permitted, alcohol and drugs were forbidden before and during meetings. And now the group voted to exclude all married women from membership — entirely a symbolic gesture since married women were hardly beating down the doors to join. Kearon and Mehrhof, who had been instrumental in Atkinson's downfall, now found themselves the object of egalitarian resentment; within a year they, too, would depart the group.

With the personnel changes, the group's interest in being the vanguard of the radical feminist movement waned. The Feminists evolved instead into a countercultural support group absorbed with female mysticism and reclaiming a matriarchal past — someday, they now hoped, women would "rule the world." The group developed a religious ritual that involved wine and marijuana as sacraments, "Momma" as the chant, and a huge, anatomically correct, papier-mâché man that they would frenetically tear apart. Toward the end of 1973, roughly two years after Atkinson's departure, the group dissolved.[26]

This brief history of The Feminists contains in capsule form some of the troubles that beset the women's liberation movement (and the New Left more generally) in the late 1960s and early 1970s. Throughout the movement, leadership talents were underutilized or wasted because of resentments about violations of equality. "Every time you opened your mouth," recalls Patricia Mainardi, "someone told you to shut it. Every time you tried to write something someone told you you shouldn't. So, finally you went away." An obsession with internal equality meant, as Elinor Langer observed, that "no one could be smarter than anyone else, or prettier, or more talented, or make more money, or do anything significant on her own." The movement's equality line, Rita Mae Brown lamented in early 1972, had "become a tyranny of personal conformity. Imagination, inspiration, and efficient political organization are suspect and throttled."[27] Moreover, virtually all these groups suffered constant and acrimonious divisions and schisms between different personalities and factions. So fractured was the women's liberation movement that in 1972 Nora Ephron could write that it made "the American Communist Party of the 1930's look like a monolith."[28] The humane hope for a world in which everyone was treated equally mutated into matriarchal fantasies about "the restoration of female rule."[29] Cut off from public support, radical feminist groups often oscillated between revolutionary vanguardism and countercultural withdrawal, between total structurelessness and collective authoritarianism.[30] In these and other ways, radical feminist groups such as The Feminists reproduced the illiberal trajectory of the male-dominated, radical egalitarian groups.

False Consciousness and Consciousness-Raising

Central to the radical feminist movement of the late 1960s and early 1970s was the "consciousness-raising" group. The aim of consciousness-raising, according to its principal architects in the pioneering women's liberation organization, New York Radical Women (NYRW),[31] was to "awaken the latent consciousness that . . . all women have about our oppression." The hope was that by sharing personal experiences and problems women would become radicalized. Much like ERAP organizers who had tried to mobilize the urban poor and SNCC organizers who mobilized rural blacks, NYRW hoped that through these meetings oppressed women would see that what they had constructed as isolated personal problems were in fact systemic social problems requiring collective action.[32]

The problem of false consciousness has long bedeviled the left, especially in its Marxist varieties. The assumption that large groups of people are blinded by a false consciousness has often been a handmaiden to repressive antidemocratic policies and regimes. The idea of false consciousness offers a convenient justification for discounting, dismissing, or even suppressing the preferences and beliefs of others. After all, if one begins from the premise that a small cadre of people know what is in the best interests of a large group of people, then it is a relatively short step to the conclusion that this enlightened cadre is justified in preventing people from pursuing their own conceptions of the good life.

The consciousness-raising group offers a potentially democratic resolution to the problems that accompany ideas of false consciousness. In consciousness-raising groups, women would talk about their own personal experiences and feelings, and learn to empathize with the experiences of others. The direction and policies would emerge spontaneously from within the group. Kathie Sarachild, who apparently coined the term "consciousness-raising," advocated a process in which women "share our feelings and pool them. [We should] let ourselves go and see where our feelings lead us. Our feelings will lead us to ideas and then to actions."[33] True consciousness, then, becomes the pooled feelings and experiences that emerge from the group.

If consciousness-raising was potentially democratic and even liberating, it sometimes seemed in practice and even in conception to be little better than a crude reeducation camp in which participants were guided to predetermined conclusions. Sarachild's own account of the consciousness-raising group reveals both the experimental side of consciousness-raising and its more closed doctrinaire face. At times, Sarachild described the consciousness-raising group as exemplifying the inductive "scientific method of research" in which we "test all generalizations and reading we did by our own experience."[34] Elsewhere in Sarachild's explication of consciousness-raising, however, it becomes clear just how distant consciousness-raising was from open-ended inquiry, scientific or otherwise. In Sarachild's seminal 1968 article, "A Program for Feminist Consciousness-Raising," she outlined eleven "classic forms of resisting consciousness." The list included "shunning identification with one's own oppressed group and other oppressed groups," "self-cultivation, rugged individualism, seclusion, and other forms of go-it-alonism," "excusing the oppressor (and feeling sorry for him)," "thinking one has power in the traditional role," "belief that one has found an adequate personal solution or will be able to find one without large social changes," and "self-blame."[35] To raise one's consciousness, in other words, meant thinking like those radical feminists who had organized the consciousness-raising groups.

Nor was Sarachild shy about confronting those women within the group whom she felt were showing these classic signs of denial. Sarachild aggressively challenged the neophytes who failed to identify with other women sufficiently or who did not indict male oppression. To those who resisted making the right radical feminist noises "She'd say, 'what *aren't* you saying?' and [proceed] to ask twenty five questions." Admirers thought this style "brilliant," but others, as Echols notes, understandably found it "more intimidating than illuminating." Even those sympathetic to Sarachild acknowledged she could be "really obstreperous and not listen to people."[36] And why should she listen? For what could one learn from those who were in denial about the truth, which, according to Sarachild, was that "our personal limitations are really prisons built by the privileged and that these prisons are locked by brainwashing and guarded by military police power"?[37] To Sarachild, the truth was simple and self-evident. "Truth," she explained, "is in the interest of the oppressed and against the interest of the oppressor." The choices facing individual women were thus equally simple. Women could either side with "the male chauvinist interests" or with "the interests of women and humanity as a whole." In this bipolar world drained of ethical dilemmas, value trade-offs, tragic choices, or ironic, unintended consequences, people are of interest not for the stories they can tell or the choices they have made but only for the side they can be cajoled, persuaded, or manipulated into adopting. "Taking sides is what it's all about," she concludes. And "since the radical's commitment is not to a method but to a side, she will use any method which serves her people [and] . . . any means that make the advance possible." Consciousness-raising, in Sarachild's conception, is less an open, democratic method of inquiry than a forced march toward the correct line.[38]

Not every consciousness-raising group, of course, had this politically doctrinaire flavor. In practice, many enabled women to explore and express ambivalent and confused feelings. As Ann Snitow has noted, "The good c-r groups allowed material that contradicted the fantasy feminist answers." But Snitow, a founding member of New York Radical Feminists, also recalls visiting many other consciousness-raising groups where "people were hysterically scrambling to get the line down so they could be stamped" as politically correct. The problem, as Snitow shrewdly dissected it, was that "the c-r questions structured the answers."[39] For instance, Sarachild reported that NYRW decided that "one of the questions . . . we would bring at all times to our studies would be — who and what has an *interest* in maintaining the oppression in our lives."[40] Such questions, of course, had the acceptable answers already encoded.

Apparently more open-ended and indeterminate was the formulation of consciousness-raising advanced by NYRW cofounder Pam Allen in her widely reprinted 1970 essay, "Free Space." Allen, who had been active in SNCC before joining NYRW, felt that consciousness-raising groups should provide women "a *non-judgmental* space in which to express themselves."[41] Sarachild and Carol Hanisch worried that consciousness-raising so conceived would become simply an "uncritical support group."[42] Instead of the personal being made political, the political would be transformed into the personal (this was designated as the "right liberalism error" by Sarachild)[43] and individual therapy would be substituted for an analysis of "the *objective* reality" of women's oppression.[44]

But in Allen's formulation, at least, the consciousness-raising group was far from an uncritical support group.[45] The nonjudgmental space mentioned by Allen applied only to the initial phase of "opening up," which was designed to foster group unity; it was the "beginning of sisterhood, the feeling of unity with others, of no longer being alone." But "carried to an extreme," Allen acknowledged, this focus on "the individual's expressive needs . . . can become self-indulgence." Women could not be permitted to "remain only on the subjective level"; their stories must be challenged and "subjected to the processes of analysis and abstraction." Only through analysis and abstraction could women move from the subjective level to an understanding of "the *objective* condition of women and the many forms that oppression takes in the lives of women."[46]

Before proceeding to the third stage of analysis and abstraction, the group went through a second stage of "sharing." Here Allen's account is essentially indistinguishable from Sarachild's, and it suffers from a similar problem of predetermined ends precluding genuinely open inquiry. Like Sarachild, Allen explains that the group arrives at an "understanding of the social conditions of women by pooling descriptions of the forms oppression has taken in each individual's life." As is also the case with Sarachild, the conclusions are preordained. "The personal is political" is not an empirical discovery but a carefully protected premise couched as a conclusion. "After sharing," Allen reports, "we *know* that women suffer at the hands of a male-supremacist society and that this male supremacy intrudes into every sphere of our existence." After sharing, women will understand that their problems "are not personal at all" and thus "attention can turn to finding the real causes of these problems," which are of course political. Perceiving the real nature of women's oppression requires going "beyond our personal experiences" to an objective process of analysis and abstraction that allows women "to look *objectively* at new experience and analyze it *correctly*." [47]

For all its alluring rhetoric of indeterminate and never-ending investigation and discovery, the consciousness-raising group was often erected upon a rigid juxtaposition of false consciousness on the one hand and, on the other, a true, liberating consciousness that reflected a correct understanding of objective conditions. Anne Forer, for instance, a prime mover behind the early NYRW consciousness-raising sessions, [48] spoke of consciousness-raising in exactly these terms. Women's authentic consciousness, she suggested, had been "replaced by a false consciousness." Women's "true individual awareness" had been rendered "somehow not really operative, either it [had] been blocked or stymied or repressed or just overloaded with so much shit." The aim of consciousness-raising, then, was to allow women to identify those people and institutions that were responsible for women's false consciousness. "False consciousness," according to Forer, "must be exposed and made to yield its power over us. When it is exposed and destroyed in this way *real* consciousness can take its place." [49]

Far from being a way out of the false consciousness trap laid by orthodox Marxism, the original radical feminist conception of consciousness-raising was deeply steeped in the Marxist understanding and even language of false consciousness and objective conditions. Indeed,

Sarachild, Shulamith Firestone, and the other radical feminists associated with NYRW and later the Redstockings[50] frequently employed the Marxist vocabulary of class to describe women. The Redstockings' 1969 manifesto described women in exactly the terms Marx used to describe the proletariat. "Women are an oppressed class. Our oppression is total, affecting every facet of our lives. . . . [It is only an] illusion that a woman's relationship with her man is a matter of interplay between two unique personalities, and can be worked out individually. In reality, every such relationship is a *class* relationship, and the conflicts between individual men and women are *political* conflicts that can only be solved collectively." The manifesto went on to explain that the "chief task at present is to develop female class consciousness" through both consciousness-raising and public actions.[51] Similarly, in her 1968 paper "A Program for Feminist Consciousness-Raising," Sarachild explained that consciousness-raising "is a program planned on the assumption that a mass liberation movement will develop as more and more women begin to perceive their situation *correctly* and that, therefore, our primary task right now is to awaken 'class' consciousness in ourselves and others on a mass scale."[52] And just as Marx believed that the proletariat's total exclusion from social life made it a liberating, universal class, so Sarachild believed that "the seeds of a new and beautiful world society lie buried in the consciousness of this very class [women] which has been abused and oppressed since the beginning of human history."[53]

Radical feminism's reliance on the structure and language of Marxism is particularly ironic in view of the statement of principles issued by NYRW as well as the 1969 manifesto of the Redstockings. "We cannot rely on existing ideologies," intoned the Redstockings, "as they are all products of male supremacist culture. We question every generalization and accept none that are not confirmed by our experience." No less incongruous is the NYRW's statement: "We are critical of all past ideology, literature and philosophy, products as they are of male supremacist culture. We are re-examining even our words, language itself."[54] Much like the male-dominated New Left, radical feminists trumpeted a radical skepticism while displaying doctrinaire certainty. And also like the New Left, radical feminists insisted that they represented a total break from the leftist past at the same time that they settled into well-worn egalitarian grooves. Believing that no one else had traveled down the path they had chosen, radical feminists, like SDS before them, failed to learn from the signs and markers along the road of radicalisms past.

Had they reexamined past ideologies and current words more deeply, radical feminists might have been more sensitive to the self-defeating fallacy of assuming, as Marx did, that a category of people making up a majority of the population suffer from the same and hence a unifying oppression.[55] So, too, radical feminists might have been more skeptical about hoping for the emergence of "real consciousness," "authentic selves," or total liberation.[56] Such a "longing for total revolution" is deeply rooted, as Bernard Yack has shown, in the political thought of Rousseau, Schiller, and Marx, among others.[57] Believing that nothing short of total revolution in the subpolitical sphere of social interaction could liberate their true or authentic selves, radical feminists often tended, as Echols notes, "to interpret every success a defeat." Political reforms were routinely rejected as appeasement that left the real roots of an oppressive system in place. So, for instance, in *The Dialectic of Sex*, Shulamith Firestone rejected child-care centers because they "buy women off," while other radical feminists denounced the Equal Rights Amendment as "paper offerings" by "the system . . . try[ing] to appease us." "Our demands," the radical feminists continued, "can only be met by a total transformation of society which you cannot legislate, you cannot co-opt, you cannot control." "It's all or nothing," insisted Ti-Grace Atkinson. Having rejected all partial reforms or even partial revolutions, radical feminism's ecstatic hopes of total transformation often degenerated into an immobilizing hopelessness, or what feminist Robin Morgan tagged as "futilitarianism."[58]

Finally, a close examination of their own language and its historical roots might have warned them away from building a movement upon the idea of false consciousness. The assumption that the overwhelming masses of women suffered from false consciousness not only brought with it a blinding hatred for those people or interests held responsible for distorting women's true consciousness, but also, and more important, encouraged a disdain or at least condescension toward women, especially nonmovement women. It was difficult if not impossible to respect the choices women had made if one believed they had been brainwashed, programmed, conditioned, or indoctrinated or were otherwise out of their minds.[59] And it was certainly difficult to build a mass movement among ordinary women when radical feminists groups such as Cell 16 insisted that those women who wanted children merely showed they had "not achieved sufficient maturity and autonomy," or when the New York–based group WITCH (Women's International Conspiracy from

Hell) disrupted the Bridal Fair at Madison Square Garden, singing, "Here come the slaves / off to their graves" and releasing white mice into the Garden.[60] Such open contempt for "unliberated" women prompted socialist-feminist writer Barbara Ehrenreich to worry about "a feminism which talks about universal sisterhood, but is horrified by women who wear spiked heels or call their friends, 'girls.'"[61] But radical feminist disdain for unliberated women should hardly surprise us, for it is exactly parallel to the contempt Marxists have long shown toward workers who prefer toasters and lawn mowers to revolutionary overthrow of the bourgeoisie. It is a contempt for people rooted in the certainty that they do not understand their "true situation."[62] The belief in false consciousness lures radicals away from dialogue and persuasion and pulls them toward smugness and condescension.

What's Love Got to Do with It?
The Radical Feminism of Catharine MacKinnon

By the early 1970s the radical feminist groups, consumed by dissension within and among groups, were in disarray or had ceased to exist. New York Radical Women had dissolved in 1969, the Redstockings in 1970, the D.C. Women's Liberation group in 1971. The year 1972 witnessed the end of the New York Radical Feminists, a group established by Firestone and Koedt in 1969, and the disbanding of The Furies, a Washington, D.C., based lesbian feminist collective that had been established in 1971. Cell 16, which had been created in 1968, disbanded in 1973, and that same year also saw the dissolution of The Feminists as well as Bread and Roses, a socialist feminist group founded by Meredith Tax and Linda Gordon in 1969. Almost none of the important radical feminist groups established during the 1960s were still intact by the time Richard Nixon resigned the presidency in 1974.[63]

But while most of the original radical feminist groups quickly disappeared, radical feminist commitments and beliefs did not. In part, they became embodied in (and modified by) new institutions: self-help groups, coffeehouses, women's centers, feminist bookstores, academic women's studies programs, rape crisis centers, battered women's shelters, and various single-issue organizations.[64] Moreover, much of the radical feminist outlook (especially the belief that there was an important political dimension to personal life) and methods (including consciousness-raising) became adopted (or, as radical feminists sometimes complained, co-opted) by national feminist organizations, most notably the National

Organization for Women.[65] Finally, many of the pioneering radical feminists influenced other women through their writings: Shulamith Firestone's *The Dialectic of Sex* (1970), Kate Millett's *Sexual Politics* (1970), Robin Morgan's anthology *Sisterhood Is Powerful* (1970), and Susan Brownmiller's *Against Our Will: Men, Women, and Rape* (1975), to mention just a few.

Among the most important contemporary heirs of radical feminist commitments is the legal theorist Catharine MacKinnon. MacKinnon came to political consciousness at the very moment that radical feminism was flowering, graduating from Smith College with a B.A. in government in 1969, the same year that the Boston-based Bread and Roses as well as the New York Radical Feminists and Redstockings were founded. After graduation she moved on to Yale University, which in the early and mid-1970s was "a hotbed of political activism and 'consciousness-raising.'" In a 1991 interview, MacKinnon traced her "intellectual and political roots" to her years as a graduate student at Yale, where "she worked with the Black Panthers, studied martial arts,[66] opposed the Vietnam War and found a focus in the nascent women's movement."[67]

MacKinnon reports that she "first heard about [the women's movement] from the liberated issue of *Rat*," a leftist underground paper that was taken over by the female staff members in January 1970.[68] It was from the early women's movement that MacKinnon readily admits she "learned everything I know." Among the things she says she learned were that sexual "intercourse [was] a strategy and practice in subordination," that "love . . . was a lust for self-annihilation that bound women to their oppression," and that "the ruling concept of freedom, especially sexual freedom, unpacked and unmasked [was] a cover for the freedom to abuse." She also learned "not [to be] taken in by concepts like consent," and to take the "women's side in everything."[69] And, finally, she learned that "the logic" of the Miss America Pageant and "snuff" movies has the same results: both turn women into sexual objects. "Miss America is the foreplay, turning a woman into a plaything. *Snuff* is the consummation, turning a woman into a corpse."[70] Although MacKinnon has been reluctant to talk specifically about her personal history,[71] her book, *Toward a Feminist Theory of the State* (1989), which she began writing in 1971, documents the enormous influence early radical feminism has had on her thinking. Among the early radical feminist works that appear are Roxanne Dunbar's *Female Liberation as the Basis for Social Revolution* (1968), Pat Mainardi's "The Politics of Housework" (1969), Pam Allen's

"Free Space" (1970), Meredith Tax's "Woman and Her Mind: The Story of Everyday Life" (1970), and Irene Peslikis's, "Resistance to Consciousness" (1970), as well as Millett's *Sexual Politics* and Firestone's *Dialectic of Sex*. In the preface to *Toward a Feminist Theory of the State*, MacKinnon justifies her referencing of the "original (movement-based) expressions of [feminist] ideas" wherever possible because "academic reformulation of feminist insights has too often added little of substance." Indeed, it is the women's movement of the 1970s, she insists, that made "most of the groundbreaking contributions to feminist theory."[72]

In MacKinnon's political thought one can see the potential illiberalism of radical feminism in perhaps its starkest and certainly its most influential contemporary form. For MacKinnon, under conditions of inequality one cannot meaningfully distinguish between consent and coercion. What appears to be consent is only coercion disguised as consent by male power. "Male dominance," MacKinnon argues, is "metaphysically nearly perfect. Its point of view is the standard for point-of-viewness, its particularity the meaning of universality. Its *force is exercised as consent*."[73] Drawing nearer to MacKinnon's specific interests, "[sexual] intercourse under conditions of gender inequality" becomes "an issue of forced sex."[74] That is, since consent is coercion disguised, even consensual sex cannot be reliably distinguished from forcible rape. Consent can only have real meaning when disparities of power are eliminated.

What about women's own desires, sexual or otherwise? According to MacKinnon, these desires are socially constructed by men. "Sexual desire in women," MacKinnon explains, "at least in this culture, is socially constructed as that by which we [women] come to want our own self-annihilation. . . . Femininity as we know it is how we come to want male dominance, which most emphatically is not in our interest."[75] Even the thoughts women have are not really their own. What "women have been and thought is what they have been permitted to be and think." If (as Carol Gilligan contends) women value care, for instance, it is only because "men have valued us according to the care we give them."[76] Women, in short, do not live in a world of their own creation; rather, they live in a world constructed of, by, and for men. Women are what men have told them to be.[77] Women's every feeling, thought, or impulse is thus not to be trusted, since such emotions and thoughts were put there by men to service their own interests.[78]

Who is to be trusted, then? Not men, obviously. And not, it would seem, women, the mass of whom are plagued with false consciousness, wanting that "which is not in our interest," preferring activities and relationships that are in reality part of a "system that is killing us."[79] How can one dismantle a system of oppression that so successfully imposes its own definition of reality upon the oppressed? Democracy under such conditions would only perpetuate oppression. Indeed, democracy itself may only be an ingenious way to disguise male power. Marxists often resolved the false consciousness dilemma by staking hope on a revolutionary vanguard, but at least Marx believed that the "progressive immiseration" of the proletariat would make the working class increasingly aware of its own oppression and thus would form the basis for a genuinely democratic mass movement, if one was prepared to wait. In MacKinnon's theory, there is no such democratic hope. The system of male dominance is virtually impregnable because its harms are made "invisible."[80] Like most totalistic systems of thought that are premised upon hegemonic false consciousness, the only options seem to be fatalistic resignation or a vanguard willing to seize state power and impose its new, liberating definition of reality.

Like the original radical feminists, MacKinnon attempts to escape either authoritarian or futilitarian conclusions by appealing to consciousness-raising. This was, after all, the site in which MacKinnon herself had first begun to perceive the unspeakable truth of male power and to "unmask . . . [the] realities hidden under layers of valued myth." Consciousness-raising, according to MacKinnon, is the "feminist method" or "way of knowing." By establishing an egalitarian community, women are able to discuss their experiences honestly and openly and to shatter the silence imposed upon them by male power. Through the creation of a closed, nonhierarchical community, the consciousness-raising group moves "the reference point for truth and thereby the definition of reality as such." The consciousness-raising method allows women to establish a "women's point of view" with its own standards of verification."[81]

But MacKinnon's formulation of consciousness-raising runs into familiar problems. Although MacKinnon begins by describing consciousness-raising as a "method," she soon proceeds to define consciousness-raising in terms of substantive conclusions. "To raise consciousness," we learn, "is to confront male power in its duality: as at once total on one side and a delusion on the other. In consciousness raising, women learn they have learned that men are everything, women their negation, but the sexes are equal. . . . [It] becomes clear for the first time that women are men's equals, [but] everywhere in chains."[82] Consciousness-raising, in MacKinnon's formulation, is not a method for investigating the conditions of women but rather a means by which others can be made to see the world the way MacKinnon does. Consciousness-raising is MacKinnon's conclusions in the guise of method.

What of those women within the consciousness-raising group who resist MacKinnon's conclusions that "the male perspective is systemic and hegemonic," that neutrality or objectivity are simply the male perspective disguised, or that the love or desire women feel toward men has been implanted by a malevolent system of male dominance? Such women, from MacKinnon's perspective, are deluded, having not yet escaped the pervasive, hegemonic grip of the male perspective. But MacKinnon recoils from saying these or any other women suffer from "false consciousness" because that is to posit "objective ground," and objectivity, she insists, is an illusion foisted upon women by male power. MacKinnon claims that the feminists can escape this dilemma by "creating a new process of theorizing and a new form of theory," but in fact she offers nothing that allows her to escape this dilemma. And given her unflattering portrait of women as "only walking embodiments of men's projected needs," it is hard to see how she can tolerate, let alone respect, their preferences and desires.[83]

Moreover, given the enormity of the feminist task — nothing less than dismantling "the most pervasive and tenacious system of power in history"[84] — small groups of women coming together to discuss their problems are clearly nowhere close to adequate. Not surprisingly, then, MacKinnon's own frequent forays into the political world have made little use of consciousness-raising. Rather, MacKinnon has relied upon the state and the law to advance her preferred policies. Over the last decade or so she has been increasingly and most visibly involved in efforts to restrict pornography. In the mid-1980s Minneapolis and Indianapolis both passed antipornography ordinances drafted by MacKinnon and Andrea Dworkin, which defined pornography as a form of sex discrimination and therefore actionable as a civil rights violation. The U.S. Supreme Court subsequently struck down the Indianapolis ordinance (Minneapolis's mayor vetoed that city's ordinance),[85] but in Canada MacKinnon has had more success. In *Butler v. the Queen* (1992), the Canadian Supreme Court agreed with MacKinnon and Dworkin that materials that are "degrading" or "dehumanizing" to women should be outlawed. MacKinnon immediately hailed the decision as "a stunning victory for women [that] is of world historic importance."[86]

Given MacKinnon's own views about the systemic and hegemonic character of male power, it is not clear why she should celebrate placing more power in the hands of a male-dominated state.[87] And, indeed, the subsequent history of enforcement under *Butler* has confirmed what civil libertarians had predicted: such laws enhancing state power to censor materials would hurt rather than help disadvantaged and unpopular minorities. Indeed, the first successful prosecution under the new law was of a lesbian and gay bookshop. The *Butler* decision, according to Canadian bookstore managers, has "increased censorship in Canada by customs, police, and lower courts, and . . . the predominant targets have been gay, lesbian, and women's literature." In the most delicious irony of all, *Butler* was used by customs officials to justify seizing two books written by Andrea Dworkin, *Women Hating* and *Pornography: Men Possessing Women*, because they "illegally eroticized pain and bondage."[88]

MacKinnon's failure to anticipate the actual effects of *Butler* stems from her belief that the First Amendment, under conditions of gender inequality, merely protects the voices of the powerful and the privileged.[89] The First Amendment, she says, does nothing for the disadvantaged and silenced, while buttressing the power of those who already have a voice. "Speech . . . belongs to those who own it, mainly big corporations. . . . The more the speech of the dominant is protected, the more dominant they become and the less the subordinated are heard from."[90] Thus freedom of speech perpetuates domination and impedes the achievement of substantive equality. MacKinnon ignores the ways in which the First Amendment might actually benefit (and perhaps benefit most) those who have the least power and are thus most vulnerable to intrusion by the state.[91]

MacKinnon wants the state to abandon its pose of neutrality, which in reality is only a guise for male dominance. She has only contempt for the law's "studied inability to tell the difference between oppressor and oppressed."[92] (Interestingly, when the ideological chips are down, her commitment to social constructionism seems to evaporate — the identities of the oppressed and the oppressors are not socially constructed or contested; rather, they are self-evident givens that should be obvious to all.) Since neutrality is just the male perspective disguised, law should abandon all pretense to treating everyone equally and should explicitly take up the side of the disadvantaged.[93] Words should be redefined so that what has hitherto appeared as partiality would now seem to be impartiality. So, for example, "no distinction would be made between nondiscrimination and affirmative action."[94] Words should come to mean whatever the oppressed say they mean; after all, at present words only mean whatever the oppressors say they mean.

Despite MacKinnon's searing indictment of the liberal state, she shows remarkably little concern about investing that state with enormous power. Once the state has been put on the side of the oppressed and downtrodden, MacKinnon apparently feels there will be no reason to fear its power.[95] Since restrictions on state power in the form of the public/private divide, the First Amendment, private property, and equality before the law are merely thin disguises for male power, MacKinnon seems to believe it self-evident that women will be better off in a society without such protections against state power. The fact that women have not fared any better, and arguably worse, in those societies lacking such liberal principles and institutions is never acknowledged by MacKinnon.[96]

MacKinnon's rather cavalier attitude toward state power becomes even more disturbing when one considers her persistent efforts to collapse the distinction between words and actions, attitudes and behavior, thought and deed. "Distinguishing speech from conduct in the inequality context," MacKinnon argues, is simply incoherent. "To say it is to do it, and to do it is to say it. . . . Speech acts. . . . Acts speak."[97] For MacKinnon, the harm of pornography is not just that it leads to violence against women,[98] for pornography *is* itself violence against women, all women. Pornography is "not harmless fantasy"; rather, it "institutionalizes the sexuality of male supremacy" by constructing the way men see women.[99] MacKinnon's logic is faulty—just because the categories of words and actions or thoughts and deeds overlap does not mean that it is incoherent to draw any distinctions between these categories.[100] The political consequences of such reductive logic, moreover, are dangerous. If the behavior is a reflexive response to a stimulus (MacKinnon likens pornography to "saying 'kill' to a trained guard dog"[101]), or if fantasizing rape cannot be distinguished from actual rape, then it is not enough for the state to regulate the behavior. The state must control the thought as well. As Thelma McCormack has pointed out, by collapsing "the distinction between dream and deed, fantasy and act, thought and behavior," MacKinnon justifies "an elaborate system of social control." It is this aspect that makes MacKinnon's thought look not just authoritarian but totalitarian.[102]

MacKinnon's authoritarian tendencies are evident, too, in the way she reacts to criticism. After the Feminist Anti-Censorship Task Force

(FACT) submitted a legal brief (signed by fifty prominent feminists, including Kate Millett, Adrienne Rich, and Betty Friedan) that attacked the Indianapolis ordinance for "reinforcing rather than undercutting central sexist stereotypes," MacKinnon accused FACT of "fronting for male supremacy." "The Black movement," explained MacKinnon, "has Uncle Toms and Oreo cookies. The labor movement has scabs. The women's movement has FACT." In an angry, uninhibited 1985 speech to the National Conference on Women and the Law, published as "On Collaboration," MacKinnon lashed out at "so-called" feminist women lawyers who, she charged, were defending pornographers simply to legitimate "their relatively high position among women under male supremacy." Such women were traitors to their sex and had no business calling themselves feminists.[103]

MacKinnon's intemperate attacks on other feminists have met with strong criticism. Indeed, many of the sharpest, most incisive criticisms of MacKinnon have come from those who identify themselves as on the left. The *Nation*, in particular, has published scathing reviews of each of MacKinnon's three recent books.[104] In one of those reviews, written in 1990, Wendy Brown helpfully situates MacKinnon's concerns in the context of the radical feminism of the early 1970s, even going so far as to suggest that "in both argument and audience, much of *Toward a Feminist Theory of the State* is flatly dated." MacKinnon, Brown suggests, "is fighting an anachronistic battle." Feminism, according to Brown, has now moved well beyond the limitations so evident in the thought of MacKinnon and the early radical feminists. Brown's effort to distance the left and feminism from MacKinnon is evident from her opening sentence, in which she describes MacKinnon as "widely known as the Meese Commission's favorite feminist."[105] If Brown is correct that contemporary left feminism has outgrown or transcended the antidemocratic or illiberal tendencies of Catharine MacKinnon, then perhaps MacKinnon does not warrant the attention we have accorded her.

But although Brown is right to root MacKinnon in the radical feminism of the early 1970s, she underestimates MacKinnon's influence among contemporary feminists and ignores the positive reviews her work has received from a long line of important feminists, including Alison Jaggar, Carole Pateman, Patricia Williams, and even Gloria Steinem.[106] Also slighted is the fact that throughout the latter half of the 1980s and into the 1990s she has remained a superstar on the college lecture circuit — and it is feminists, not friends of Ed Meese, who have invited and applauded her. Overlooked too is the popularity of MacKinnon's books and her prominence in feminist anthologies and syllabi, as well as the tremendous influence she exerts among "critical race" theorists, who have borrowed directly from MacKinnon in developing their critiques of the First Amendment and liberal legalism.[107, 108]

The point is not to tar all of contemporary feminism or even radical feminism with the brush of Catharine MacKinnon. MacKinnon's position on pornography has certainly been repudiated by many lesbian feminists and by the more individualistic or libertarian strand within radical feminism (Ellen Willis, for instance), as well as by liberal feminists such as Nadine Strossen and Betty Friedan. But other troubling aspects of MacKinnon's thought are shared more widely by feminists teaching today in women's studies programs in the United States. A substantial number of academic feminists, for instance, echo MacKinnon's view that women have effectively been "silenced" by patriarchal institutions; hence the emphasis in women's studies programs on nurturing women's lost "voice" in a nonhierarchical setting. MacKinnon's critique of objectivity as a male social construction is also widely shared within many women's studies programs, as is her disdain for liberals and her tendency to dismiss feminism's critics as enemies of women. The next section examines more closely the illiberal effects that these shared premises have had in some women's studies programs.

Women's Studies: Politicizing the Classroom

One of the primary institutional loci for the transmission of radical feminist values and commitments has been women's studies programs.[109] University courses on women were among the earliest fruits of the women's movement. Before 1968, courses explicitly about women were rare, yet by 1971–1972 there were over one thousand college-level women's studies courses in the United States. The following academic year, at least seventy colleges and universities had established programs in women's studies.[110] In the subsequent years, women's studies' offerings and programs have proliferated at an astonishing rate, so that today there are over six hundred undergraduate and several dozen graduate programs. And it is not women's studies programs alone that have institutionalized feminist values and beliefs on campus. At the University of Minnesota, for example, there exists not only a Women's Studies Department but also a Center for Advanced Feminist Studies, the Center for Women in International Development, the Center for Continuing

Education for Women, and the Humphrey Center on Women and Public Policy.[111]

The ideology and even social organization of many women's studies programs reflect the strong egalitarian bias of the early radical feminist movement. One woman, a founder of the National Women's Studies Association (NWSA) and director of a women's studies program for over a decade, recalls her experience in the program in ways that directly echo the organizational trials and tribulations of the radical feminist movement in the early 1970s. She remembers the tremendous "antipathy for traditional governance procedures." The program was run "in accordance with the feminist principle of operating as a collectivity, regardless of rank or position." No distinctions were made between staff and faculty, for instance. A "huge fight" erupted over the use of the word "director," which the program's staffers felt connoted too much power. Instead for "many, many years" she was called a "coordinator." "They didn't want anyone to have any power in that position," she recalls; "they didn't want 'stars.'" The director/coordinator found that she had "to hide [her] own ideas and abilities to some extent, because of this notion of 'leveling'—that we are all the same." Egalitarian envy was exacerbated by the large differences in professional accomplishments and salary that the university's meritocratic principles necessitated. The program, she notes, had a terrible time dealing with envy and conflict, since "the rhetoric of the women's movement . . . was 'sisterhood,' and that meant no conflict, which was ridiculous," as anybody who has a sister would be quick to attest. Unwilling to allow that rivalry and competition between sisters was legitimate, not to mention unavoidable, the first impulse was to suppress conflict, "sweeping problems under the rug." But conflict could not be wished away, and the program became mired in disabling rounds of "argument and . . . antagonism and self-interrogation and daily confrontation." Since true sisters would not disagree, it was assumed that disagreements were evidence of bad faith, insufficient radicalism, or petty self-interest. Hence the desire to denounce and cast out the ideologically impure who were polluting the egalitarian collective.[112]

Egalitarian collectives, as anthropologist Mary Douglas argues, typically attempt to resolve internal tensions and build group cohesion by focusing on an external enemy, building up the boundary between "us" and "them."[113] The description of the organizational dynamics of many women's studies programs offered by Daphne Patai and Noretta Koertge in *Professing Feminism* nicely illustrates Douglas's thesis. "Separatism," as

Patai and Koertge observe, "has been a dominant theme since the inception of Women's Studies."[114] But separatism sustained by demonizing the outside (usually, in this case, "patriarchy")[115] affects the internal dynamics of the group as well. The "us-versus-them opposition," Patai and Koertge observe, "is replicated within the original grouping [and] policing actions get under way."[116] "Petty surveillance" of how women within the group dress, look, and behave "becomes a mechanism for maintaining group solidarity, because it separates authentic members from questionable ones." Condescension toward the prefeminist or hostility to the nonfeminist outside the group can easily become a searching-out of the false feminists within.[117]

Egalitarian structure and distrust of leadership roles are evident in many women's studies classrooms, where the authority of the teacher is often de-emphasized. Feminist pedagogy encourages classes to operate on principles of "equalitarianism, a critique of the traditional teacher/student authority relationship, and student empowerment."[118] As one generally appreciative student noted, "Many [women's studies] professors say, 'This is your classroom, this is your discussion. I'm here as another participant, not as a leader.'"[119] Karen Lehrman, who visited women's studies programs at four prominent universities, reported in *Mother Jones* that "many teachers try to divest the classroom of power relations. They abandon their role as experts, lecturing very little and sometimes allowing decisions to be made by the group and papers to be graded by other students." In a few classes taught by graduate students, Lehrman found herself unable to "figure out who the teacher was until the end."[120] The aim of the egalitarian classroom is to provide "liberated zones" or "safe spaces" where previously "silenced" women will feel safe to speak out.[121] Passive victims will become egalitarian soldiers in the battle against patriarchy.

A widely touted "model" women's studies syllabus that was developed by twelve Rutgers University professors illustrates how early radical feminist ideas have imprinted themselves on the curriculum of contemporary women's studies. Among the course's chief goals is to "challenge and change the social institutions and practices that create and perpetuate systems of oppression." Even more revealing, the two poles of early radical feminist activism — direct, disruptive actions and consciousness-raising groups — become requirements for the course. Close to one-third of the student's grade is based on (1) "performing some 'outrageous' and 'liberating' act outside of class" and (2) "forming small in-class consciousness-raising groups."[122]

The consciousness-raising emphasis on personal experiences is a particularly important part of women's studies programs.[123] During the early 1970s, consciousness-raising was sometimes criticized by feminist "politicos" as well as by liberal feminists such as Betty Friedan for substituting group therapy for political action.[124] Consciousness-raising, unless it was properly politicized, could become merely a montage of personal grievances and frustrations. For those trying to build a political movement, the danger of consciousness-raising was that people might lose sight of the political in the personal. When the privileging of personal experiences is transferred to the educational domain, consciousness-raising becomes more troubling still if feel-good therapy drives out rigorous intellectual inquiry.[125] Personal experience can be a valuable way to engage students and connect them to material, but education also entails teaching students to question the representativeness of their own life experiences and, more important, to evaluate arguments based on evidence or logic rather than on the basis of strongly held personal prejudices or feelings.

An additional danger, as a self-study by the Wellesley women's studies program obliquely acknowledges, is that by encouraging students to relate material to their own personal lives, students come to feel that "to be critical of someone's ideas is to be critical of them as a person."[126] Patai and Koertge point out that "as long as positions are not too far apart . . . everybody feels validated and cozy. But as soon as sharp conflicts arise, absent the normal modes of conflict resolution — striving for personal detachment, trying to look at the evidence objectively, . . . attempting to be as methodical and logical as possible — the result is likely to be not just a breakdown in sisterly connectedness, but outbursts of extreme rudeness and insoluble conflict."[127] The chances of such outbursts are exacerbated by the fact that feminist pedagogy, again drawing upon the consciousness-raising model, encourages the "freeing up" of repressed anger and rage — indeed, for some radical feminists the expression of anger seems to be almost "a measure of one's feminist commitment . . . a sign of one's authenticity."[128] "The feminist classroom," explain five women's studies professors from the University of Massachusetts, "welcome[s] the intrusion/infusion of emotionality — love, rage, anxiety, eroticism — into intellect as a step toward healing the fragmentation capitalism and patriarchy have demanded from us."[129] Combine the unleashing of rage with egalitarian inhibitions about teachers intervening in the classroom and one can see why feminists have often expressed concerns about "horizontal hostility" or "hazing within the community."[130]

Reducing education to therapy is bad, but more worrying still is the way that consciousness-raising can be used to politicize education. If what counts as a raised consciousness is believing that women are oppressed by a system of patriarchal domination,[131] then those who believe that such a premise is misleading are condescended to as victims of false consciousness[132] or dismissed as part of an antiwoman "backlash."[133] The charge that they "just don't get it" functions in a similar way by allowing feminists to dismiss opponents as politically benighted rather than engaging opposing arguments. When the aim is conversion to a particular worldview, disagreement becomes labeled as "resistance."[134] Student objections or complaints can be put down to improper socialization or unenlightened thinking. Giving the politically correct answer can become more important than cogency of argument, mastery of material, creativity, or effort.

From the outset, women's studies programs have been conceived as "the academic arm" of the women's movement.[135] As the preamble to the constitution of the NWSA explains: "Women's Studies owes its existence to the movement for the liberation of women; the feminist movement exists because women are oppressed.... Women's Studies is the educational strategy of a breakthrough in consciousness and knowledge.... Women's studies, then, is equipping women to transform the world to one that will be free of all oppression ... [and is] a force which furthers the realization of feminist aims."[136] From its inception, then, women's studies programs have had a dual purpose: the educational goal of studying women and the political goal of recruiting women to the feminist movement and remedying social injustice.[137] The danger is that in conflating academics and activism, education may be reduced to indoctrination.

Feminists often brush aside concerns about the dangers of confusing education with politics by insisting that all knowledge is political.[138] Following MacKinnon and countless other feminist theorists, those within women's studies programs typically acknowledge that "feminist teaching is ideological and even political" but insist that this is no different than "other so-called 'objective' and 'apolitical' teaching" that occurs in the rest of the curriculum.[139] Those who write about feminist pedagogy often place the term "objectivity" in quotation marks as a way of signaling their skepticism that such a thing exists. What appears or claims to be objective knowledge is merely knowledge constructed from the (white) male point of view.

But if all knowledge is socially constructed, does that mean that all perspectives are equally valid? Some postmodern feminists seem inclined to this radically relativist position, but most feminists reach quite different conclusions. The feminist premise that sexuality is socially constructed, for instance, is often harnessed to a static view of an omnipresent male dominance. Like MacKinnon, these feminists lack an anthropological interest in the myriad differences in the way sexuality is understood across cultures and history; instead, there is a bipolar division in which the social construction of the oppressive heterosexual male is counterpoised to the liberating construction of the oppressed female. Social constructionism here leads not to cultural relativism but to an unmasking of the lies and coercion at the heart of the hegemonic patriarchal culture. Sexuality is socially constructed, but some social constructions are clearly superior to others. Similarly, while the idea that existing knowledge as well as reason and logic itself are patriarchal social constructions is widespread within women's studies,[140] many feminists are simultaneously drawn to the idea that the most oppressed groups enjoy privileged epistemologies or ways of knowing that give them a superior understanding of social and scientific reality.[141]

The dilemma of teaching social constructionism while avoiding relativism and sustaining political and ideological commitment is explored in a revealing manner by Alison Jaggar, the first occupant of a state-endowed chair in women's studies at Rutgers University and subsequently director of women's studies at the University of Colorado, Boulder. "Prevailing knowledge," Jaggar argues, purports to be "value free" but in fact merely "reflects the interests and values of the dominant class and gender." There is no "neutral, Archimedean point outside the social world." Does this mean, then, that feminism only "represents one among many competing points of view and that a just resolution of public policy issues is most likely to be reached if all points of view are heard and allowed to compete in the marketplace of ideas"? Not at all, for this would be to fall into "the liberal idea" of treating all positions as "equally worthy of consideration." Feminism is not just one point of view but a privileged position of knowledge. "From the feminist perspective," for instance, "*one can know almost a priori* that approaches to public policy that fail to examine the specific policy implications for women are quite inadequate and do not merit valuable class time." While Jaggar insists that "impartiality," defined as being "open-minded," is quite consistent with feminist commitment, she then proceeds to vitiate this claim by adding that "a genuinely impartial consideration of contemporary social life must generate *inevitably* a commitment to feminism."[142] To preach feminism to the exclusion of all other perspectives is legitimate because to be genuinely impartial and open-minded is to accept feminism into your heart.

To question feminism is to show oneself to be close-minded. Hence the ground rules established by the Center for Research on Women at Memphis State University (now the University of Memphis) and subsequently used, among other universities, at Rutgers, Minnesota, and Penn State. These ground rules stipulate that every student in the course must (1) "acknowledge that oppression (i.e., racism, sexism, classism) exists" and (2) "acknowledge that one of the mechanisms of oppression (i.e., racism, sexism, classism, heterosexism) is that we are all systematically taught misinformation about our own groups and about members of both dominant and subordinate groups." Students are thus warned off from questioning whether oppression is a fruitful way of describing the experiences of affluent, middle-class Western women.[143] And since we are required to assume that we are systematically deceived about the real nature of oppression, the only question becomes which of the familiar suspects — men, patriarchy, capitalism, the media, advertisers, the West, colonialism — are responsible for this systematic misinformation. If these initial ground rules jeopardize open inquiry by politicizing education, others demean and trivialize the learning process by turning the classroom into a closed and uncritical support group. In this category is the requirement that we must "assume that people (both the groups we study and the members of the class) always do the best they can," an assumption that is self-evidently false, and the restriction that "if members of the class wish to make comments that they do not want repeated outside the classroom, they can preface their remarks with a request and the class will agree not to repeat the remarks."[144]

The latter restriction is justified on the grounds that it will help to create a safe haven within the class where people will be more willing to speak their mind. This laudable goal, however, is sometimes undercut by the politicized character of some women's studies classes. "Before there was a name for it," reports a prominent ex–women's studies professor,

"I certainly experienced what we now call political correctness in Women's Studies in the sense of not being able to speak freely. I think there's a lot of fear about being publicly denounced. . . . People are so ready to pounce." Another prominent veteran of women's studies programs complains of a "relentless dogmatism" among women's studies students and faculty.

> Any criticism is because you're homophobic, or you're a patriarchalist in disguise, or you're this or you're that. . . . Politics is driving out their ability to think! . . . What "feminist process" in the classroom winds up being is a push toward conformism and toward silencing dissent. It's all done under the rubric of being nice and open, and not being an authoritarian, old-fashioned type of teacher. But this winds up being tremendously more coercive.

For one thing, if the teacher refuses to exert her authority, then militant students are free to intimidate and "silence" less assertive students.[145] Another disillusioned feminist laments that while "we — women, feminists, lesbians, whatever — so often make statements or wear buttons proclaiming 'Question Authority' or 'Question Everything' . . . we rarely, if ever, question feminism. . . . Questioning the authority of feminism or the heavyweights within the movement is akin to heresy, and is basically treated as such." Feminism, she concludes, has "been just as conformist and stifling of creative thought as the most right-wing religious groups." Yet another women's studies professor observes, "The hard-line feminist [students] . . . simply dismiss the teacher as not feminist enough or not the right kind of feminist for them. Their unwillingness to examine their own ideas is one of the things that clearly sets the Women's Studies students apart from the others."[146]

Systematic data from Wellesley College support these alarming if anecdotal reports from the disillusioned.[147] In 1990 the women's studies program at Wellesley undertook a self-study that focused, among other things, on the question of whether students felt "pressure to give 'politically correct' answers." (The survey was carried out before the term "politically correct" became a political football in the mass media, which perhaps explains why the Wellesley program was willing to ask such a question.) The self-study found that 30 percent of students in women's studies courses said they "felt silenced or at risk expressing unpopular opinions," compared with less than half that number among those in non–women's studies courses. In one particularly egregious case, nineteen of the twenty-five women's studies students affirmed that they felt pressured to give politically correct answers. As one survey respondent explained, "Students at Wellesley don't want to hear about women who choose more traditional roles such as wife and mother. To support such a choice is to be 'politically incorrect' in a women's studies class." These sentiments were echoed by another student who commented that "there seems to be a party line on feminist issues that we had better not waver from. However, it is masked in a feeling of openness."[148]

These reports of politicized classrooms reveal what is obscured by the slogan "All knowledge is political." Namely, although all knowledge may be biased, some knowledge is more biased than others. Pristine objectivity is impossible — the point is a virtual truism in the philosophy of science and certainly not a revolutionary feminist discovery — but that does not mean there are no differences between education and political indoctrination. Any theory unable to distinguish indoctrination from education, propaganda from scholarship, is intellectually vacuous and politically dangerous.[149] Recognizing the political biases of existing knowledge is a valid and useful intellectual enterprise; reducing knowledge or scholarship to politics debases scholarship and justifies indoctrination.

Education, then, is not reducible to the political or the personal. Politicizing education subordinates individual creativity to political dogma; personalizing education subordinates reasoned argument to emotional outburst. Whether politicized or personalized, the education of students is poorly served.[150] Failure to appreciate and respect the differing values, competencies, and loyalties that are appropriate to different spheres of life has consequences not only for how radical feminists conceive of education and scholarship but for how they understand the family as well.

Justice in the Family

Almost all feminists accept that "the personal is political," but they diverge markedly in their understanding of that slogan's meaning. Radical feminists typically adopt a highly literal interpretation. For them, "the personal is political" has meant rejecting altogether liberalism's project of carving out a nonpolitical, private domain that would limit government intervention.[151] For Shulamith Firestone, the family needs to be smashed by having childbearing and child rearing diffused "to the society as a whole."[152] For MacKinnon, the privacy right is simply "male supremacist." "Men's realm of private freedom," she argues, "is women's realm of collective subordination. . . . For women, the private is the distinctive sphere of intimate violation and abuse, neither free nor particularly personal."[153] If the family is, as Andrea Dworkin has it, an "open grave" for women, the line between public and private is not to be renegotiated or moved but obliterated altogether.[154] Who needs privacy if it is synonymous with oppression?[155]

Other feminists, uncomfortable with abolishing a linchpin of liberal democratic freedom, have adopted a less literal interpretation of "the personal is political." Here one finds an effort not to do away with the public/private boundary but to shift or redefine it. Among the feminists who take this tack is Stanford University political theorist Susan Okin. Okin's project is to create a strongly egalitarian feminism that is nonetheless consistent with liberal democratic principles and institutions, that challenges and rethinks the public/private dichotomy without diminishing the value of privacy or giving up on the institution of the family.[156] A close examination of Okin's political thought, particularly as it is developed in her important book *Justice, Gender, and the Family* (1989), serves to illuminate the ambivalent relationship between feminism and liberalism.

In contrast to MacKinnon, who is unsparingly critical of all things liberal Okin aims to extend liberal universalistic principles of justice to include women.[157] Okin explicitly endorses "fundamental principles of liberalism." She supports liberalism because it takes seriously "that we live in an age of a great plurality of beliefs, preferred ways of life, conceptions of the good. . . . It values the individuality that is promoted and preserved by the respect for personal preferences and for the need for privacy; it promotes the opportunity of persons to live their own lives and to seek out their own conceptions of the good; and it is well aware of the dangers that can result from the imposition of supposed 'community values.'" Moreover, she accents "the vast debts of feminism to liberalism," singling out such basic tenets of liberalism as "the replacement of the belief in natural hierarchy by a belief in the fundamental equality of human beings, and the placing of individual freedoms before any unified construction of 'the good.'" Without this liberal tradition, Okin reminds us, "feminism would have had a much more difficult time emerging."[158]

Okin's liberal feminism, however, should not be confused with a classical liberalism content with procedural equality. Okin is strongly committed to a substantive vision of equality in which life chances are thoroughly equalized.[159] Liberalism, she explains, is "not only *compatible* with a significant degree of socialization of the means of production and redistribution of wealth — indeed it *requires* it." Her vision of a just future, moreover, goes well beyond women and men being treated equally under the law. "A just future," she explains, "would be one without gender. In its social structures and practices, one's sex would have no more relevance than one's eye color or the length of one's toes." The "disappearance of gender," she reiterates, "is a prerequisite for the *complete* development of a nonsexist, fully human theory of justice."[160]

For Okin, the central defect of liberal political theory and practice has been its failure to apply principles of justice to the family.[161] The family, in Okin's view, is the root cause of gender inequalities in society. The unequal distribution of benefits and burdens within the family places women at a tremendous disadvantage, particularly in the event of a divorce. Inequalities in the domestic sphere translate into inequalities in the political and economic spheres. Moreover, the family is "a school of justice" where children learn how to interact with others.

> It is essential that children who are to develop into adults with a strong sense of justice and commitment to just institutions spend their earliest and most formative years in an environment in which they are loved and nurtured, *and* in which principles of justice are abided by and respected. What is a child of either sex to learn about fairness in the average household with two full-time working parents, where the mother does, at the very least, twice as much family work as the father? What is a child to learn about the value of nurturing and domestic work in a home with a traditional division of labor in which the father either subtly or not so subtly uses the fact that he is the wage earner to "pull rank" on or to abuse his wife?

If women are to be equal in politics, work, or any other sphere, they must first become equal within the family.[162]

Okin's lucid book represents a powerful, unsettling challenge to liberalism, a challenge that is made all the more compelling by her willingness to engage contemporary liberal theorists in a sustained and serious dialogue.[163] Okin forces liberals to pay close attention to the ways in which the privacy of the home can shield and perpetuate inequalities and injustices. But while Okin's feminist critique strongly brings to light the enduring tension between privacy and equality, she is too inclined to regard this as a contradiction within liberalism that can ultimately be resolved through egalitarian transformation. It is at this point that Okin's feminist and egalitarian commitments outrun her liberal sensibilities. Okin's critique of contemporary liberal theorists for slighting or ignoring the family is illuminating and often persuasive, but her own positive vision is more troubling.

In her conclusion, Okin acknowledges that achieving a just family is "a complex question" because it involves a conflict between "personal freedom" and "social justice." She allows that "the way we divide the labor and responsibilities in our personal lives seems to be one of those things that people should be free to work out for themselves," yet also insists that "because of its vast repercussions it belongs clearly within the scope of things that must be governed by principles of justice."[164] Here Okin seems to speak a liberal language of balancing liberty and equality, yet this acknowledgment of competing values is almost completely forgotten in other parts of her discussion where the value of privacy becomes almost totally subordinated to equality.[165]

Justice, Okin repeatedly tells us, requires "the demolition of gender," "the abolition of gender," "the disappearance of gender."[166] But if we are to respect privacy, how is this abolition to be achieved? Since appropriate gender relations are fiercely contested in our society, Okin acknowledges that the state "cannot simply dictate and enforce the abolition of gender." Having made this concession, however, she goes on to insist that "neither may [the state] favor gender, or even *allow* gendered practices that make women and children vulnerable."[167] But if the gendered division of labor within "the vast majority of households in the United States today"[168] renders women and children vulnerable, as Okin compellingly argues at book length, then calling on the state not to allow such "gendered practices" seems tantamount to calling for the state to abolish gender. Perhaps there are a few "gendered practices" that do not leave women vulnerable, but there is nothing in Okin's analysis to suggest what these might be. Indeed, the thrust of Okin's entire argument has been to suggest that everything from giving dolls to girls and trucks to boys, to parents spending unequal amounts of time on unpaid household work leaves women and children vulnerable, particularly in the event of a divorce.[169] Despite Okin's occasional nod to the value of privacy and respecting individual freedom, her call for the state to forbid all "gendered practices that make women and children vulnerable," if taken seriously, is a virtually unlimited license for the state to intervene in the family.

To be sure, as Okin and many other feminists have shown, there are many ways that the state now structures family life, and even a number of things it disallows, such as polygamy or gay marriage.[170] But because the family is in important respects regulated by the state does not mean, as Okin says, that "the very notion that the state can choose whether or not to intervene in family life makes no sense."[171] This particular verbal sleight of hand, common among feminist theorists, obscures the fact that it is not at all meaningless to talk about more or less state intervention in the family. There is a massive difference in the extent of state power and intrusiveness that is required by the government telling people they cannot have more than one spouse at a time and the government telling parents they must share doing the dishes or must give Sally a tool set.

The radical, even illiberal implications of Okin's political thought are obscured by the moderate nature of her reform proposals. The reforms she proposes include day care, parental leave, and divorce reform, all of which are well within the tradition of liberal reform. Even her most egalitarian reform — requiring alimony and child support to equalize the standard of living of the two postdivorce households for a period of years at least equal to the number of years of the marriage — is no threat to liberal democratic institutions and is a creative if debatable way to recognize the contributions of the spouse who works within the household.[172] But none of Okin's reforms move us particularly far toward her goal of a genderless society; indeed, equalizing postdivorce income arguably makes it easier for families to continue gendered practices while still minimizing the economic vulnerability of women in the case of divorce.

It is Okin's implausible, indeed utopian, vision of a genderless future, not her particular reform proposals, that is fraught with illiberal dangers.[173] Okin imagines a future where "childbearing would be so conceptually separated from child rearing and other family responsibilities that it would be a cause for surprise, and no little concern, if men and women were not equally responsible for domestic life or if children were to spend much more time with one parent than the other."[174] But in a society where preferences vary and individual choice is allowed, such variation is exactly what one *would* expect. Even if the genderless egalitarian family became the norm, we surely would not expect all families to be clustered closely around this mean. What Okin seems to foresee is not only a new mean but a mean around which there is little or no deviation. Every family would resemble every other in its equal division of domestic responsibilities and roles. Equality becomes uniformity.

Moreover, how are we to reach this imagined future? Given the entrenched nature of gender differences, such a change, as Okin concedes, "is unlikely simply to happen. Only legal, political, and social changes can bring it about." What are we to do, however, with those recalcitrant folks who do not share Okin's view of a just family? Sometimes Okin strikes a tolerant pose: we must "respect people's views and choices" while trying to "encourage and facilitate the equal sharing by men and women of paid and unpaid work, of productive and reproductive [*sic*] labor." But only two pages later, Okin adopts a strikingly less tolerant view of those who do not adhere to her egalitarian vision of the family. Here Okin announces that we have no obligation to respect traditional "approaches to marriage that view it as an inherently and desirably hierarchical structure of dominance and subordination." Even if the parties to the marriage prefer to live in a hierarchical relationship, we should not allow it "for the sake of the children."[175] One wonders who will decide which families are structured in unacceptably hierarchical ways and what will count as evidence of dominance and subordination. Cause for concern and even alarm is heightened when one notices Okin's earlier argument that "gender . . . is a prime and socially all-pervasive case of dominance."[176] If gender itself is a case of dominance, then to proscribe dominance is to proscribe gender. All gendered differences and inequalities in the division of labor become forms of behavior that society cannot tolerate.

If liberals remain skeptical of feminists brandishing "the personal is political" slogan, it is not necessarily because "they just don't get it." Rather, it may be that liberals distrust feminist intolerance of those private relationships they do not like, and worry that the slogan encourages feminists to call for dramatically increased state intervention in the private sphere without acknowledging that is what they are doing.[177] Liberals need not object to striking a different balance between the private and public, liberty and equality, but they are rightfully alarmed when the tension is assumed away as an unreal or false dichotomy, or when privacy is simply put on hold until equality is achieved.

Earth First! and the Misanthropy of Radical Egalitarianism

It is often hard to tell when . . . a movement has passed
beyond the demand for important and necessary reforms
to the expression of a resentment so inclusive that it embraces
not only the evils and abuses of a society but the whole society
itself, including some of its more liberal and humane values.

   Richard Hofstadter[1]

Consider the countries you have visited, all of which
you have left behind. Each was devoted to the pursuit of a
worthy objective. . . . Yet each pursued its favoured goal to the
exclusion of the others and in the process sacrificed countless
individual humans at the altar of its abstract ideal. . . . The
alternative is to see that none of these ideals is worth
anything without the others. Only then will you create
a world fit for humans, and also . . . for owls.

   A Wise Owl[2]

The 1960s was a decade of demonstrations. Demonstrators marched on Washington in August 1963 to show support for passage of the proposed Civil Rights Act. SDS organized the 1965 march on Washington to express opposition to the Vietnam War. In 1967 Stop the Draft Week climaxed in the massive march on the Pentagon. At the time of his assassination, Martin Luther King, Jr., was planning another march on Washington, this time by the poor to demand an "Economic Bill of Rights." In the summer of 1970 thousands of women across the country marched in the Women's Strike for Equality called by NOW. Yet the largest demonstration of all from this era was not over civil rights for blacks, women's rights, Vietnam, or poverty, but the environment. As many as 20 million people across the nation are estimated to have taken part in what was tagged "Earth Day."[3]

Earth Day, April 22, 1970, had its origins in Wisconsin Senator Gaylord Nelson's 1969 call for a national environmental "teach-in" on college campuses, on the model of the antiwar teach-ins. To some committed sixties radicals, Earth Day seemed like an establishment plot, designed to divert attention from the "real" issues of war, race, and poverty.[4] Anything so popular, the reasoning went, could hardly be radical or subversive. Many radical activists, though, as Terry Anderson points out, saw Earth Day as another way to draw attention to "a sick business establishment: Businessmen were greedy so they profited from bombs and kept wages for women and minorities low; they were irresponsible so they poured their refuse into streams."[5] Pollution of the environment was yet one more way in which corporate capitalism poisoned America.

Few Americans agreed with the radical diagnosis of American capitalism, but Earth Day did powerfully dramatize Americans' growing concern over environmental degradation, particularly air and water pollution. In the wake of Earth Day, polls showed that Americans identified the environment as among the most important domestic problems facing the country.[6] New environmental groups proliferated, and established groups saw their memberships skyrocket. The venerable Sierra Club, which had only about 20,000 members in 1960, grew to 170,000 members by 1975; over that same fifteen-year period the Audubon Society mushroomed from 40,000 members to 275,000.[7] Among the many environmental groups born in the first half of the 1970s were Zero Population Growth, Negative Population Growth, Greenpeace, Environmental Action, Worldwatch Institute, Earthwatch, the Environmental Policy Institute, the Cousteau Society, and even Environmentalists for Full Employment.[8] Politicians responded to the expressions of public concern with a bonanza of environmental legislation: the National Environmental Policy Act of 1969, the Marine Protection Act of 1972, the Endangered Species Act of 1973, the Safe Drinking Water Act of 1974, the Toxic Substances Control Act of 1976, and the Resource Conservation and Recovery Act of 1976, as well as the Clean Air Act Amendments of 1970 and the Clean Water Act Amendments of 1972.[9]

As the federal government got into the environmental protection business in a serious and sustained way, particularly with the establishment of the Environmental Protection Agency in 1970, the large environmental organizations increasingly set their sights on lobbying Washington, D.C. With influence and success inevitably came charges of selling out, of being too bureaucratic, too compromising, too distant from the grass roots, too concerned with organizational maintenance at the expense of environmental advocacy.[10] Environmentalism had entered the mainstream, but in bargaining with the establishment, many activists believed, environmentalism was losing its radical edge, indeed its very soul. In their rush to be respectable, environmental lobbyists were forgetting to put the earth first.

Among those who felt that "the system" was corrupting environmentalism's soul was the Wilderness Society's chief lobbyist, Dave Foreman. The trouble, as Foreman saw it in the late 1970s, was that environmental lobbyists were "less part of a cause than members of a profession"; enhancing their salary and prestige was more important to them than protecting the environment.[11] Disgusted with the compromises being made by the Wilderness Society and other mainstream environmental organizations, Foreman quit and, together with four other disaffected environmentalists, founded a new group, Earth First! Theirs was to be a radical organization that would speak truth to power, an organization in which there would be no bureaucracy and no lobbyists, only grassroots activists committed to putting the earth first.[12] "NO COMPROMISE IN THE DEFENSE OF MOTHER EARTH" became the banner on the *Earth First! Journal*'s masthead, directly echoing the *Liberator*'s "NO COMPROMISE WITH SLAVEHOLDERS."[13]

Earth First! stirs strong passions on all sides. Heroes to some, terrorists to others. Life-affirming, says David Brower; misanthropic, according to many others.[14] To loggers in the Northwest, they are "communist hippies"; to some eastern environmentalists, they seem to embody a redneck "isolationist frontier ethic."[15] Some dismiss Earth First! as irrelevant; others see it as having played an important role in changing people's consciousness about the environment as well as in making the demands of other environmental organizations seem more moderate.

As the group (or, more precisely, confederation of groups) took shape during the 1980s, it became identified with its most controversial tactic: tree-spiking, or driving nails into trees in order to discourage their cutting or at least to increase the cost of cutting to the timber industry.[16] Tree-spiking, however, was only one of many "monkeywrenching" tactics that Earth First! utilized to defend mother earth from rapacious developers and greedy capitalists. In regular "Dear Nedd Ludd" columns in the *Earth First! Journal* and then in *Ecodefense: A Field Guide to Monkey-wrenching* (1985), Foreman provided detailed instructions on how to disable tractors, snowmobiles, and power lines, how to jam locks and make smoke bombs, and, of course, how to avoid detection.[17] Earth First! also became infamous for some outrageous remarks, including several columns by "Miss Ann Thropy" (actually Christopher Manes, author of the best-selling *Green Rage*) suggesting that AIDS could be a boon to the environment by dramatically reducing human population, and an interview with Foreman in which he opined that the best way to deal with famine in Ethiopia was "to just let nature seek its own balance, to let the people there just starve."[18]

In view of Foreman's right-wing background (in college he had supported Barry Goldwater) and the undisguised misanthropy of some Earth First!ers,[19] the reader may well wonder what Earth First! has to do with radical egalitarianism. One might expect adherents of a "biocentric" or "ecocentric" (as opposed, in the language of the movement, to "anthropocentric") worldview simply not to care much about the shape of human relationships. Indeed, this is exactly the basis for the frequent charge of misanthropy leveled at Earth First! A number of Earth First!ers certainly have seemed relatively unconcerned about how humans live with each other (or, indeed, whether they live at all),[20] but the great majority of Earth First!ers, and radical environmentalists generally, are strongly committed to a radical egalitarian vision of human relationships.

The Egalitarianism of Earth First!

Strong evidence of the egalitarianism of Earth First! emerges from a survey conducted recently by Dan Metz of Willamette University.[21] Over 70 percent of Earth First! respondents agreed that the country needed "a fairness revolution to make the distribution of goods more equal." Only 14 percent disagreed. Over two-thirds felt that "the world would be a more peaceful place if its wealth were divided more equally among nations," while fewer than one in five disagreed. Three-quarters believed that "we should seek to eliminate all forms of inequality, hierarchy and domination,"[22] seven in ten agreed that "big corporations are responsible for most of the problems of the world," and better than eight in ten thought that "we should all participate in every decision that directly affects us." On each of the five items designed to tap egalitarianism, then, Earth First!ers scored extremely high, far higher than the general public or mainstream environmental groups.[23]

Indeed, Earth First!ers' egalitarianism was as strong as or stronger than the egalitarianism of members of the Earth Island Institute, a radical environmental organization that self-consciously defines itself as working at the intersection of social justice and ecology issues. On the "fairness revolution" item, Earth First!'s mean score was 5.2 (out of a possible 7), a half point higher than Earth Island's mean score of 4.7. On two other items, "big corporations" (EF mean 4.8, EI mean 4.5) and "participate in every decision" (EF mean 5.6, EI mean 5.2), Earth First!ers also scored marginally higher in their egalitarianism. On the only other egalitarian statement posed to both groups, "peaceful place," the mean scores of Earth First (5.0) and Earth Island (5.1) were essentially identical.[24]

Also noteworthy is the finding that Earth First!ers (mean score 5.6) were little different from Earth Islanders (mean score 5.4) in their concern with "environmental racism." Members of both groups overwhelmingly endorsed the idea that "people of color suffer disproportionately from environmental degradation." This is particularly remarkable since Earth Island, through its Urban Habitat program, has made the issue of environmental racism a centerpiece of its agenda. Putting the earth first, these results suggest, does not mean ignoring social justice or the oppressed.

That the primary hue of Earth First! is egalitarian rather than simply anarchist can be seen from the responses to the statement "Individuals should be free to pursue their own interests and preferences without too much regard for what the community thinks is right." Despite the well-publicized anarchism of some Earth First!ers, only about one in four Earth First!ers agreed with this statement. The survey also found, not surprisingly, that Earth First!ers are strongly critical of competitive capitalism. Only about 15 percent agreed that competitive markets were "the best way to supply people with the things they want," accepted that "people who are successful in business have a right to enjoy their wealth as they see fit," or endorsed the idea that society would be a "better place if there was much less government regulation of business."

Confirmation of the close connection between deep ecology and radical egalitarianism emerges from a larger survey of another radical environmental organization, the Voluntary Human Extinction Movement. This survey found a robust correlation ($r = .41$) between egalitarianism, as measured by a five-item scale, and deep ecology, as measured by a single statement, "All living organisms deserve to be treated equally." For those coded as "very strong" and "strong" egalitarians, the mean scores on the deep ecology item were 5.8 and 5.5, respectively, while the mean deep ecology scores for those coded as "moderate" or "weak" egalitarians were 4.7 and 3.6, respectively. Put another way, almost 60 percent of those who were weak egalitarians rejected the deep ecology statement, while only 13 percent of those who were very strong egalitarians rejected it.[25] In sum, the evidence from this survey supports the thesis that deep ecology and radical egalitarianism are strongly linked.

These findings may come as a surprise to those accustomed to following the often acrimonious philosophical debate between theorists of "deep ecology" and "social ecology." Countless environmental philosophy texts use this distinction to structure the narrative. On the one side are the deep ecologists, who espouse a biocentric philosophy that "places the welfare of the wilderness and the planet before that of human beings," while on the other side are the social ecologists, who endorse a "left-libertarian philosophy which sees social transformation as the key to saving the environment."[26] Social ecologists such as Murray Bookchin have dismissed deep ecologists as "vague," "formless," and "a bizarre mix of Hollywood and Disney," as well as antisocial and antihuman. Several leading Earth First!ers, Bookchin has insisted, are "barely disguised racists, survivalists, macho Daniel Boones, and outright social reactionaries."[27] Not to be outdone, deep ecologists have attacked Bookchin as a "fat old lady" and an "unintelligible grouch." Bookchin and the social ecologists are accused by deep ecologists of possessing a "Faustian ambition to seize control of evolution" and a "shallow" commitment to the environment.[28]

And yet for all the hostility that the leading exponents of these two rival philosophies have often shown for each other, they share a tremendous amount of common ground.[29] Both sides are fervently committed to saving the wilderness and are agreed that this can only occur if there is a radical transformation in the way people live with each other and with the earth. The social transformation imagined by social ecologists and deep ecologists typically entails abolishing hierarchical relations of domination in favor of more small-scale, noncoercive, egalitarian relationships. Moreover, both sides are extremely hostile to capitalism, consumerism, and especially multinational corporations, which are seen as root causes of social injustice as well as ecological devastation.

The close connection between ecocentrism and radical egalitarianism is less surprising if we think of deep ecology, as Roderick Nash encourages us to do, as the radical egalitarian impulse extended to nonhuman animals or even plant life.[30] The effort to eliminate or reduce distinctions between human beings and other organisms is part of the same radical egalitarian impulse that has sought to reduce differences between rich and poor, black and white, men and women, old and young, adults and children.[31] "EQUAL RIGHTS FOR ALL SPECIES," read an Earth First! banner unfurled at the foot of the Lincoln Memorial in Washington, D.C.[32] "Civil rights for all people," Mike Roselle explains, means civil rights for "the tree people, rock people, deer people, grasshopper people and beyond . . . to its logical conclusion, the single-celled parasite people."[33] And just as the social movements to abolish distinctions between people carried with them the emotionally charged vocabulary of racism, sexism, and ageism, so the radical environmentalists have hurled accusations of "speciesism" and even "sentientism."[34] The aim remains liberation of the exploited and oppressed, but for radical environmentalists it is lions and lizards, mountains and rivers that are the most "oppressed members of our planetary society."[35]

Earth First!'s radical egalitarianism was strongly evident in its 1990 Redwood Summer campaign, which was self-consciously modeled upon the civil rights movement's Freedom Summer of 1965.[36] The brainchild of Judi Bari, a self-described child of the sixties,[37] Redwood Summer was designed as "a season of non-violent direct action" to save northern California old-growth forests from destruction. Redwood Summer would be "the rallying point for people of conscience," just as Freedom Summer in Mississippi had been a quarter-century earlier. Earth First!ers would be "freedom riders for the forests," which, as one California Earth First!er wrote, was "in the spirit of demanding equality not just for human beings, but for all living things."[38]

A frequent refrain in the pages of the *Earth First! Journal* is that the domination of nature is inextricably tied up with the domination of people. Only when we treat each other better will we treat the earth better, and vice versa. "Seeing the Earth as merely something to be exploited leads to seeing humans in the same way," explained Bill Weinberg. As one *Earth First! Journal* contributor put it, "We recognize the inherent connection between the suppression of women and minorities, and the suppression of other lifeforms." When Earth First!ers speak, as they frequently do, of "subverting the dominant paradigm," they have in mind these habits of domination that structure all human interaction. "The habit of exploitation," Stephanie Mills reminded her fellow Earth First!ers, "is indivisible." And because they are indivisible, "the end to the human destruction of nature," the *Earth First! Journal* staff affirmed, "must coincide with an end to the oppression of human by humans."[39]

For the great majority of Earth First!ers, a commitment to radical egalitarianism goes hand in hand with a commitment to saving the earth. The overwhelming majority of Earth First!ers in the Metz survey agreed that we can only save the planet by "radically transforming" the way human beings relate to each other.[40] Loss of wilderness and biodiversity, for Earth First!ers, is a product of an entire social system, and therefore the goal must be transforming that system. The group's objectives, explains one Earth First!er, must include "not only revolutionary changes in our attitudes and actions toward the environment but in our social [and political] structure . . . as well." Far from ignoring human power structures, then, putting the earth first necessarily entails opposing Western industrial civilization, multinational corporations, and consumer capitalism.[41]

Toward the end of the 1980s some within Earth First!, including Foreman, feared that the group's commitment to wilderness issues was being diluted by growing attention to social issues.[42] Trying to delimit the scope of the organization, Terry Morse suggested that "a social issue should be considered an Earth First! issue insofar as it impacts wilderness and biodiversity. Social issues which do not meet this criterion should be acknowledged, but left for the Greens and the New Left to deal with."[43] Such a distinction proved difficult to maintain, however, because it flew in the face of a central tenet of deep ecology, namely, that "everything is connected to everything else."[44] "Because all things are inter-connected," the argument went, "to be successful in our campaigns against any oppression we must be committed in the fight against all oppression."[45] The rallying cry "subvert the dominant paradigm" presupposed this systemic unity. Perceiving the hidden connections between what appeared to most other people to be discrete problems, between, say, eating a hamburger and the destruction of the rain forests, or logging and the oppression of women, is, after all what made Earth First!ers radical and set them apart from those whom they scorned as merely "environmental reformists."

Those Earth First!ers who argued that the group should limit itself to preserving wilderness and have nothing to do with "anthropocentric" political and social issues lost out not only because the majority of Earth

First!ers were strongly egalitarian but also because efforts to limit the organization to preservation of wilderness and biodiversity were at odds with the sweeping indictment of modern industrial society that lay at the heart of Earth First!'s message.[46] If corporate capitalism was killing the planet, then one could not defend the planet without opposing competitive capitalism and working to put "a nonexploitative culture" in its place. As Bari argued:

> Our society is so destructive that any wilderness we may preserve may be destroyed by acid rain, drought, or the greenhouse effect. . . . The only way to preserve wilderness [then] is to find a way to live on the earth that doesn't destroy the earth. In other words, EF . . . is also a social change movement. . . . It doesn't make sense to bemoan the destruction of nature while supporting the system that is destroying it. . . . We need to build a society that is not based on the exploitation of the earth at all — a society whose goal is to achieve a stable state with nature for the benefit of all species.[47]

If the capitalist system ineluctably destroys wilderness, as virtually all Earth First!ers believe, then to save the wilderness necessarily requires overthrowing capitalism and creating a new nonexploitative society.

The strongly egalitarian attitudes of Earth First!ers are matched by the radical egalitarian structure of the groups they have established. Earth First!ers reject not only "the authority of the hierarchical state"[48] but also hierarchical authority within their organization. They understand, as Dave Foreman has explained, that "if you organize yourself like a corporation, you start to think like a corporation."[49] Each Earth First! group is completely autonomous — there is no national or central office (the closest thing is the *Earth First! Journal*, the location of which has been periodically moved). Indeed, Earth First! does not consider itself an organization at all, because the term denotes authority and hierarchy. Earth First!, explains the *Journal*'s business manager, Karen Wood, "is not an 'organization,' but a 'movement.' The difference is that we do not have a central hierarchy. There is no president, no executive director. There are individual activists and autonomous local groups."[50] One of the root problems with mainstream environmental organizations, in the eyes of Earth First!ers, is that they have become bureaucratic and hierarchical, and therefore inimical to real change.[51]

The *Earth First! Journal* is run as an egalitarian collective. There is an editorial staff but no editor in chief. Work is shared relatively equally, and decisions are made by consensus.[52] Similarly, the annual Earth First! Round River Rendezvous, where Earth First!ers get together to build morale, exchange information, and discuss future directions, is organized along egalitarian lines. All Earth First!ers are invited to what one participant described as a "semi-organized anarchy";[53] meetings are convened in circles so that no one has a privileged place,[54] and decisions are reached by consensus.[55] There are no elections or voting.[56] In 1990, having decided to select a temporary committee to oversee a *Journal* staff that some felt was not sufficiently responsive to the membership, a committee was selected by having people interested in serving step inside the circle. When about twenty people stepped in, they were asked to weed themselves down voluntarily, which they did until twelve were left. Rather than make a decision about which of these twelve would best represent members' views, the group opted to take the twelve-person committee, figuring that "some will drop out or not do the work." The committee, of course, promised "to work by consensus not only among ourselves but with the current staff."[57]

This nonhierarchical structure is typical of the radical environmental movement generally. The Earth Island Institute explains that "central to the concept of Earth Island is the belief that action should take place over bureaucracy." To that end it sets up a number of small, autonomously operating projects that informally collaborate and share ideas and resources with each other.[58] The more radical Native Forest Network describes itself as "a global autonomous collective of forest activists, indigenous peoples, conservation biologists and nongovernmental organizations [which] functions on a consensus basis and is non-violent, non-hierarchical, and non-patriarchal."[59] The Cathedral Action Forest Group, too, operates by consensus and has a "permanent workers circle" instead of a board of directors.[60] And Critical Mass rides (the aim is to choke the streets with bicycles in order to slow or bring to a halt auto traffic, or the "auto-cracy") "have no rules except those the group agrees to."[61] Even the Sea Shepherds, a renegade Greenpeace offshoot that is often referred to as the "Earth First! navy,"[62] have tried to realize egalitarian relationships in their organization, although the need for expertise at sea, together with the authoritarian predispositions of the group's founder, "Captain" Paul Watson, has meant egalitarian principles have been sacrificed. Still, according to Rik Scarce, author of *Eco-Warriors*, the Sea Shepherds' "ideal vision of decision-making authority is through a consensus process, with everybody agreeing on a course of action."[63]

For those who are activists, a group like Earth First! is not just one more organization to join but instead a defining part of the person's identity. "There are no 'members' of Earth First!," explains an Earth First! primer, "only Earth First!ers."[64] A letter from a recent recruit evokes the invisible yet powerful boundaries separating Earth First! members from nonmembers and the intense emotional bonds that tie Earth First!ers together. Joining Earth First!, the letter writer recounts, was like walking into "the middle of a spiritual catapult." At the outset of the EF! Northwest Rendezvous,

> There is a strange distance I feel with the first people I meet at the parking area. . . . I know that they know that I am not already "on the inside" of EF! It is obvious . . . I am not "one of them." [By the end of the rendezvous, however, I have broken through.] Now I am "on the inside." Inside the perimeter fence of the Brave New World. With the primitives. Wild ones. Unclones. All My Relations. Time has all but stopped. *My skin is an illusionary boundary.* . . . I am now in the elusive "other side". . . . I can't go back. [Now] I have something . . . worth dying for. . . . I have joined the rebel alliance. . . . I now have deliberate purpose: Save the Earth.[65]

The importance of group solidarity within Earth First! is also emphasized in the *Earth First! Primer*, which explains that "Earth First!ers invariably . . . feel isolated and alone before coming together as a group. Nothing is more empowering or more fulfilling than acting in defiant and creative consort with other like-minded people."[66]

In sum, Earth First! combines intense group solidarity with extreme opposition to hierarchical authority in a paradigmatically radical egalitarian way. Earth First!'s concern for ecosystems and wildlife sets it apart from previous egalitarian movements, but the group's concern for the environment is inextricably bound up with its radical egalitarian commitments. Earth First!ers care passionately about trees, grizzly bears, mountains, and hawks, but they also care just as profoundly about how human beings should live with each other.

Native Greens
The inadequacy of the conventional characterization of Earth First! as misanthropic comes into sharp relief when one examines Earth First!'s view of Native Americans and tribal peoples throughout the world. Most of the people in Earth First! have extremely favorable, even

romanticized, views of indigenous peoples, who are seen as offering a model of how to live with the earth and with each other in nonexploitative ways. The misanthropy of Earth First!ers is typically reserved for the people in Western industrialized nations. "If ever there was a species which deserved to go extinct," writes *Earth First! Journal* staffer John Green, "*Homo sapiens euroamerican* is it."[67] This pattern of hostility toward one's own society combined with an uncritical attitude toward oppressed peoples is a common characteristic of radical egalitarian movements, as we saw in chapter 5. The difference between the 1960s New Left and radical environmentalism is that where the former sought inspiration and hope in the lives of poor southern blacks, the Vietnamese, and Cubans,[68] radical environmentalists look for wisdom and redemption in the lives of Native Americans and indigenous tribes throughout the world.[69]

Whatever else may have changed since Earth First!'s founding in 1980, its strong identification with indigenous peoples has remained relatively constant. Earth First!'s first public act was to erect a plaque in honor of an Apache chief at the site where the Apaches had massacred an entire mining camp. The plaque paid tribute to the Apache's valiant efforts "to protect these mountains from mining and other destructive activities of the white race." Siding with the Indians was necessary, explained Christopher Manes, because the Indians practiced "earth-harmonious ways of life," whereas "Western culture" stood for the "foolhardy exploitation of nature." Fifteen years later, at the 1995 Activist conference, Earth First!ers discussed ways of "supporting campaigns of indigenous and oppressed peoples" and forming "the natural link between EF! and indigenous struggles" in the battle "to bring down the multinational corporations . . . that threaten the Earth, her creatures and peoples."[70]

Indigenous peoples are generally portrayed by Earth First!ers as the first ecologists,[71] living in harmony with the natural world. "For thousand of years," we are told, "indigenous people lived in harmony with the crystal clear springs of central Texas." "For tens of thousands of years," another Earth First!er tells us, "humankind thrived in blissful balance with the rest of the then-wild world." These peaceful and harmonious ways of living on the earth are unfortunately being systematically destroyed by the "exploitative lifestyle" of Western industrial civilization.[72] "Wherever you go," agrees another Earth First!er, "the Natives know what's best for the land, and the white European invaders know best how to destroy it."[73] "Instead of a Peace Corps," Dave Foreman has suggested, "what we need is a reverse Peace Corps. Instead of North America and Europe teaching the rest of the world how to live, we needed some Australian aborigines and bushmen and Eskimos and Kayapo Indians and Penan tribespeople to come to teach us how to live."[74]

Indigenous peoples are seen as exemplary not only for their "earth-harmonious" way of life but also for their often heroic resistance to Western industrial civilization.[75] Because "primal peoples and wild species" are both being destroyed by the same underlying force — namely, Western industrial capitalism — many Earth First!ers have elevated indigenous peoples into something closely akin to Marx's universal class.[76] In protecting their homeland, indigenous peoples necessarily strike a blow against industrial capitalism and for the liberation of all those who inhabit the earth.[77]

Indigenous peoples, moreover, are seen by many within Earth First! and the deep ecology movement more broadly as providing an exemplary model of small-scale egalitarian communities. This attitude is reflected in William Devall and George Sessions's widely read treatise, *Deep Ecology*, in which North American Indians are praised for "teach[ing] us the viability of communal societies based on mutual aid between people" and thus providing an alternative to "the modern western version of isolated individuals forever competitive, aggressive, and untrusting of other people."[78] Indeed, the lives of indigenous peoples, as imagined by at least some Earth First!ers, seem like nothing so much as the leisurely communist utopia envisioned by Marx in which people might hunt in the morning, fish in the afternoon, and debate in the evening. Tim Haugen, for instance, insists that "the lives of the so-called 'primitives' are much easier than those of 'modern man' (not to mention modern woman)." In those traditional cultures that have not been forced off their lands by European expansion and colonialism, there is a "pattern of short work days and roughly every other day off, with free time devoted to 'dancing, wrestling, . . . informal recreation, . . . loafing.'"[79] Dolores La Chapelle has also emphasized the ways in which the lack of specialization in "traditional primitive cultures" allows for the flourishing of "healthy multiple personality structures." Modern Western societies, in contrast, tend to produce drab, monocultural personalities.[80]

This view of primal societies as the first egalitarians is developed in great detail in Wm. H. Kotke's apocalyptic treatise, *The End of Empire*. Primal societies, according to Kotke, "tend to be egalitarian, non-coercive, and non-hierarchical." They did not have jails or police, and tribal society invariably operated through "consensus government." In many tribes, Kotke explains, "no action is taken unless everyone agrees." Unlike our competitive, grasping culture of "muted desperation," the culture of primitive tribes was "distinctly peaceful and emotionally positive," and characterized by sharing, cooperativeness, and concern for others.[81]

This view of indigenous peoples is by no means limited to Earth First! or to the deep ecology movement. Many radical environmentalists believe indigenous peoples are a repository of knowledge about how to live with the earth and with each other in nonexploitative ways. Social ecologist Murray Bookchin, for instance, admires "non-hierarchical, organic, tribal societies" for their "absence of coercive and domineering values," as well as for their view of nature as "a fecund source of life and well-being" and "as a community to which humanity belongs."[82] More abstruse but otherwise similar is ecofeminist Carolyn Merchant's portrait of "Native American Society" as characterized by a "total participatory consciousness," "equality of all senses," "reciprocity between humans and nature," and a "steady state" society. "Industrial Society," in contrast, is characterized by male domination of nature and women, the sublimation of sexuality, "disembodied intellect," and "dualistic thinking."[83] More crudely still, bioregionalist Kirkpatrick Sale contrasts the "nature-hating culture" of the Europeans with the "nature-loving culture" of indigenous peoples.[84]

The journal of the Earth Island Institute presents a similarly undifferentiated conception of indigenous peoples as an untapped reservoir of wisdom about the natural world.[85] Just as Earth First!er Mike Roselle speaks of "tribal peoples . . . as a link back to a sustainable way of life," so the editor of the *Earth Island Journal*, Gar Smith, hopes that "indigenous cultures of our Earth can show us the way back home."[86] Indigenous tribes are regularly praised in the *Earth Island Journal* for providing "an important perspective on the natural world and knowledge about how we might exist in less destructive ways with our environment."[87] Indigenous peoples become "less a relic of the past than an outpost of the future," an inspiring model of how we might reshape our social relations in a more sustainable and egalitarian way.[88]

Radical environmentalists also emphasize the rich participatory culture of indigenous tribes.[89] According to Jerry Mander, for instance, the Iroquois Confederacy is an exemplar of successful participatory democratic governance. Unlike in the United States, where the most important decisions are left to a few meeting in secret, the Iroquois insisted that all decisions of great importance be made only after "first going back to all of the people in the confederacy." "The basic strength of Iroquois governance comes from its trust in and dependence upon the participation of all the people." Mander can think of no "native society in which any war chief could undertake military action without long meetings of the entire tribe."[90]

Radical environmentalists, in sum, are not misanthropes. Far from hating all people, most radical environmentalists, like radical egalitarians the world over, go to great lengths to see only the best in those who are perceived to be oppressed victims of the system. Judging by what they choose to praise in others, the overwhelming majority of radical environmentalists, far from shunning human companionship, seek to realize egalitarian social relationships. Their vision of the good society is generally not misanthropic withdrawal into hermitude, but rather deep involvement in a close-knit, noncoercive community in which all participate as equals.[91]

Consumed Souls

If the charge of misanthropy in its familiar guise is wide of the mark, what then are we to make of Earth First!'s often-expressed disdain for the lives of ordinary human beings? Not lack of concern with how people live with each other but rather an intense concern to make the world a radically more egalitarian place lies at the heart of radical environmentalists' contempt for "Homo sapiens euroamerican." Viewed in this light, radical environmentalists' contempt for people's lives no longer seems so novel; instead it begins to appear as another manifestation of the sort of radical disdain for ordinary people that we explored in chapter 3.

Earth First!ers see America as a vapid, vulgar, materialistic society. Indeed, no aspect of American society is more harshly and unrelentingly criticized by Earth First!ers than what they perceive as its wasteful, mindless consumerism. Western consumerism is seen as the root cause of nature's destruction. "Our consumption habits," one Earth First!er says, "are eating the planet alive."[92] Only by radically reducing consumption in Western societies, Earth First!ers believe, can we save the earth and create a more meaningful and equitable world.

To dramatize the depths of their disgust with consumer society, members of one Earth First! group held a "puke-in" at a Seattle-area shopping mall. They shared an emetic and then, "as the drug took effect and they began vomiting, they unfurled signs and shouted anti-consumerism messages at the strolling holiday shoppers."[93] The vulgarity of this incident shocked a number of veteran Earth First!ers, but even those, such as Howie Wolke, who criticized the puke-in as a tactical blunder because it alienated people, still endorsed the basic premise of the "insanity of modern consumerism."[94] Most Earth First!ers would prefer to find less offensive ways to express their opposition to consumer capitalism, but there are few who do not share the protestors' disgust with it.[95]

Earth First! reverberates with the deep-ecology refrain "simple in means, rich in ends."[96] Those who "live more frugally on the material side of life," deep ecologists explain, are thereby "enabled to live more abundantly on the psychological and spiritual side of life."[97] Conversely, those who accumulate material possessions must necessarily be psychologically impoverished and spiritually bereft. This oft-repeated axiom of deep ecology and quintessentially egalitarian sentiment is morally equivalent to the obverse belief held by late-nineteenth-century social Darwinists that material wealth was a sure indicator of inner virtue and that material poverty signified spiritual deprivation. The external signs of inner virtue are reversed, but the effects in both cases are the same — contempt for the great majority of people whose lives lack the external marks of inner grace. If there is a difference, it is that the radical environmentalists' disdain is untempered by the compassion and charity that social Darwinists sometimes showed toward those unfortunate souls.

Earth First!ers feel much the same sort of withering (and elitist) scorn for American consumerism that Marx felt for things bourgeois.[98] America, one Earth First!er writes derisively, is a "nonculture." "Everyone's dressed the same . . . the same neon bright white socks, sneakers, shorts and striped (going up and down) shirts from K Mart (Walmart)."[99] An Earth First! poem, "The Marketplace or Yuppie Hell," speaks of

> Happy consumption.
> Balloons for the kiddies. . . .
> All are identical
> Homogenized into one
> Consumptive greedy culture. . . .
> Clean swept bricks and dying trees. . . .
> You are doomed to walk these
> Dead barren streets

Seeking to buy happiness.
It will not replace the sacred
You will remain empty
and dead.[100]

Our consumptive society is an artificial and emotionally empty world, full of "cosmetic smiles" and plastic people. Our consumptive habits have consumed our very souls.[101]

What most Americans call freedom Earth First!ers typically identify as slavery. In abundance and variety of goods, Earth First!ers see not freedom of choice but "enslavement to [a] technocratic, consumerist society."[102] People are shackled by their material possessions. The American dream of "homes, vehicles, electronics . . . [has] reduced them to wage slaves."[103] Earth First!ers argue that Americans are slaves to their desires, desires which have been artificially manufactured by the capitalist system. "The system," writes Tim Haugen, "may be unequaled in providing things, [but] it constantly rebuilds the illusion of deprivation, perpetuating bondage to the system."[104] Freedom as it is currently experienced in America is largely illusory. Genuine freedom can come about only by breaking the chains that imprison the wild self within, the self that has not become addicted to comfort, the self that has only spontaneous, natural needs to fulfill.

Except for the automobile, probably no possession is more reviled by Earth First!ers than the television.[105] "The connection between TV and [society's] promotion of over-consumptive lifestyles cannot be stressed enough," writes Earth First!er John Potter. "The television experience," Potter continues, "is almost identical to hypnotism," and in that hypnotic state audiences are bombarded with "the prime message of television advertising [which] is consume, consume, consume."[106] When not stimulating consumers to buy more, the television is pacifying the masses. "They will settle their swollen carcasses down on their new couch," sneers *Earth First! Journal* staffer John Green, "activate their new glowing god . . . and become mesmerized for a few hours, days, weeks, etc." In this catatonic state, they do not even notice that "all around them, the dozers roar, the chainsaws scream, the cash flows, and a beautiful, fragile world most will never know, never care about, spirals toward oblivion."[107] Hypnotized or mesmerized, the message is the same. The masses of people are shallow, easily manipulated pawns of a hegemonic system.[108]

Important as it is, television is only one mechanism by which "the dominant mindset" reproduces itself.[109] Virtually every institution in society, from the public schools to the press, is seen as complicit. Echoing Herbert Marcuse, Earth First!ers have launched an attack on a hegemonic system that has brainwashed people into wanting what the system needs rather than what they as individuals truly need. In a typically Marcusian lament, one Earth First!er writes of the "constant brainwashing we all undergo every day living within the dominant culture"; another complains of "the mass brain washing [that occurs] via the public school systems of America," while yet another refers to the "brainwashed drudges slaving away" and calls for people to "rid [themselves] of [their] mainstream American values."[110]

Radical environmentalists who travel down this well-worn Marcusian path find it difficult to resist the illiberal implications waiting around the corner. If people's preferences reflect not their own volition but rather an imposed hegemonic cultural system, then is it not legitimate to force people to be free? Why respect people's choices if they do not reflect their "true" needs but rather the needs that "the system" has foisted upon them? If driving a car is not a choice but an "addiction," as Guy Claxton calls it,[111] then should we not treat car addicts as we would heroin addicts: take the stuff away, if not all at once then at least gradually? Coercion becomes liberation. Force becomes freedom.

The Ecological Vanguard

Radical environmentalists' scorn for the choices people have made usually goes hand in hand with their sense of themselves as an ecological vanguard.[112] They are a beacon of ecological sanity in a sea of apathy and greed. The problem, as Earth First!ers see it, is that they "share the planet with *unenlightened* people who think . . . that nature's value can be determined by a price tag."[113] In their more democratic moments, Earth First!ers believe that this brings with it the responsibility to persuade the American public that they are wrong. Too often, however, Earth First!ers seem interested less in persuading than in showing disdain for the misguided and unenlightened. Rarely do they question whether the issue is appropriately framed as a battle between the enlightened few and the unenlightened many.

The Earth First! cognitive world is made up not of uncertain facts and difficult value trade-offs but of absolute truth and moral righteousness on the one side and pathetic delusion and grubby greed on the other. For them, persuasion often amounts to little more than revealing immanent truth. The aim, as one Earth First!er explains, is "to brush away the false gods of credit cards, food preservatives, and convenience stores from before their eyes."[114] Base materialism, another Earth First!er confidently tells us, "must give way to superior values."[115] On the one side, we are repeatedly told in the pages of the *Earth First! Journal*, are the amassed forces of "selfishness, shortsightedness, and greed," while on the other are the much smaller number of "forward-thinking people who are not under the spell of greed."[116]

Disagreement becomes dismissed as ignoble or insincere. For Earth First!er Robert Streeter, for instance, it is axiomatic that "nobody with any ecological vision and respect for other life forms would argue that we have not exceeded Earth's carrying capacity for humans."[117] Those who disagree are, by definition, ecological neanderthals not worth taking seriously. In much the same spirit, Earth First! editor John Davis insists that "any reasonable person who reads [Christopher Manes's *Green Rage*] must needs renounce industrial society."[118] That there could be different readings of the facts or different perspectives on the issues is not possible if we are reasonable people who respect life. Disagreement can thus be put down to sordid motives or pathetic ignorance.

Throughout the pages of the *Earth First! Journal*, the masses of people are derided as hopelessly ignorant about the natural world. They fail, Maria Quintana explains, to "become intimate with their bioregion; they live insulated from their physical environment by air-conditioning; they never learn about our ecosystems, wonder what type of landscapes originally occupied the land their houses are built on, or the native plants that should grow there. They know little about the urgent ecological threats to our region."[119] If the masses know little, they feel even less. Lacking direct contact with the wild earth, the common people are unable to appreciate the earth's majesty. "Most folks," Mark Davis assures us, "will never care about the Earth, or be fortunate enough to really understand the sacredness of life and the incredible beauty and richness of the wild."[120] The small efforts people might make to become more ecologically conscious are occasionally applauded but are often met with utter condescension. Quintana, for instance, ridicules those who "consider themselves good little environmentalists if they participate in curbside recycling."[121]

Earth First!ers seem at times to simply write off the "90 percent of the population, living in their apathy and consumerism."[122] One Earth

First!er, for instance, speaks of the difficulty of fighting the tremendous forces of inertia caused by the "brain-dead suburban voter" who doesn't seem to care even if his "own habitat is next in line for destruction."[123] Another Earth First!er describes America as "a nation of zombies, pacified by media and shopping malls, kept too busy 'making ends meet,' caught in a rat race that never ends."[124] No need to pay attention to the objections of the brain dead or zombies.

Given the herd's inattention and ignorance, many Earth First!ers ask themselves the next logical question: Why should people's judgments be trusted or respected? "Modern humans are so disconnected from the natural environment," reasons one Earth First!er, "that we [in contrast to both animals and people in a wild, natural setting] are no longer capable of making sensible choices about reproduction."[125] Perhaps, then, others who are more directly in touch with nature and her needs should make those decisions for us. "So many humans are becoming consumer zombies," another Earth First!ers argues, that we cannot possibly "expect the population of our earth to understand the actions and attitudes of those who put the Earth First!" The desensitized masses can no longer hear the earth's cries, but "the souls of those [of us] who are 'alive' [can hear] . . . the plants and animals, the birds and insects cry out in a seemingly unconscious appeal."[126] Only Earth First! activists have "felt those trees and critters pumping their life into our blood."[127] By virtue of their unmediated contact with the wild earth, Earth First!ers can speak for the earth in a way that the rest of us cannot.

Earth First!ers are hardly alone in succumbing to this radical hubris. The environmental historian Donald Worster, for instance, betrays the same belief in an ecological vanguard who can discern the earth's true needs. For Worster, the "common people [have] become a herd," living as "docile masses governed by clocks." Having become "lifelong wards of the corporation and the state, [they have] absorbed and internalized the ruling ideas completely . . . [and] have lost the capacity for critical thought. Genuine freedom is for the average citizen an unknown ideal." In contrast, those possessed of "liberated reason can reveal what a river or a valley needs for its own realization, what values it may have beyond serving as a means to profit or amusement, what moral claims it makes on humans. When set free from its bondage to money and power, reason can determine which uses of the earth are worthy and truly necessary, and which are not."[128]

Earth First!ers envision themselves as a vanguard "acting out . . . the will-of-the-planet."[129] "We are the Earth in defense of Herself," is a continual refrain among Earth First!ers.[130] As a vanguard they represent that which ordinary people cannot yet understand, or speak for constituencies that are unable to express themselves. They hear and give expression to "the voice of the earth." "The voice of the forest," one Earth First! protester reported, "came through these people [who had blockaded a Forest Service road]—and it rang strong and true."[131] Through their direct actions, Earth First!ers give voice to all "those who cannot speak for themselves—the trees, wolves, salmon, spotted owls, grizzly bears, and on and on."[132]

If the earth or the forests or future generations cannot speak for themselves, neither can they give consent to the vanguard's action. Claiming vanguard status thus becomes a way of avoiding the democratic need to gain consent for one's actions. To claim to speak for those who cannot consent is to claim for oneself a privileged and unassailable position in the argument.[133] Certainly no democratic majority, no matter how overwhelmingly large, can be relevant. As Paul Watson explains, "If 'majority' is defined as all those whose numbers are yet to be born for say, the next millennium, . . . then, the present opinions of the majority of the now, suddenly become the minority opinion. . . . [Moreover, since] we as one species are clearly a minority as opposed to the majority of species that actually inhabit a forest . . . arguments about abandoning tree spiking based on present majority opinion are not relevant."[134] Empowered to speak for all living creatures and for all those not yet born, the ecological vanguard need not bother itself with such mundane matters as democracy.

Trashing Western Civilization

Radical environmentalists' privileged feelings of moral superiority coexist uneasily with their critique of human arrogance. At their best, Earth First!ers teach a valuable message of humility and modesty. Their criticisms of capitalism, their skepticism about industrial progress, even their insistence on the moral claims of nonhuman life may all be healthy antidotes to human arrogance. To see human beings as just one small part of a much larger web of life is profoundly humbling. Yet Earth First!ers separate themselves so completely from society that their healthy distrust of social mores easily becomes contempt for people; useful suspicions of power and politics become corroded by unchecked conspiratorial fantasies of omnipotent and sinister power.[135] Hostility toward "the system" becomes so all-encompassing that one ends up unable to make distinctions between better and worse, between a society's faults and its more noble and humane features.

Too many Earth First!ers indiscriminately reject the whole of Western industrial civilization — the good, the bad, and the indifferent. For most of them, "the anthropocentric imperialism of Western civilization" is the source of virtually all that is wrong with the world. "Western industrial civilization," writes one Earth First!er, "is a killing machine." The Enlightenment has been a "holocaust." Everything would be fine again if we could simply "shake off this awful thing called Western culture which has now, inevitably, brought the world to the brink of ecocide." "We need to disassemble civilization," one Earth First!er advises; another urges that "our industrial culture must be dismantled."[136]

In this alienated mind-set, even the problems plaguing the non-Western world, such as overpopulation, grinding poverty, and environmental degradation, become the fault of the West. Since those in the West consume so much more than those in the Third World, overpopulation is really a First World problem. "Although the average Kenyan woman bears eight children in her lifetime, since the average American uses over 100 times the earth's resources as a Third World citizen, one American baby is more costly to the Earth than the Kenyan woman and all her babies." And in any event, it is the West and specifically the United States that, "through military persecution and colonial exploitation, . . . [causes] misery, poverty, and hence, overpopulation" in the world. Famine and hunger in the Third World is the result of "traditional, self-supporting agriculture in the Third World countries [being] systematically ruined in favor of a Western-oriented agriculture." Moreover, it is the Western nations, through mass consumption and corporate greed, that are responsible for environmental degradation in Third World countries. Even their authoritarian governments are our fault. "It must also be remembered," explains one Earth First!er, "that the ecologically destructive elite groups from Japan, Brazil, El Salvador, etc. only exist because of the crucial economic, political, and military aid that has been provided by the affluent white male elite of North America and Europe."[137] Such sentences say more about the alienation of Earth First!ers from their own society than they do about the nature of the ecological problems facing Third World countries.

The language Earth First!ers use to describe the West and the American political system specifically is so exaggerated and hyperbolic that careful distinctions become almost impossible to draw. They are up against a "murderous system," "industrial totalitarianism," a "planetary Empire of Growth and Greed."[138] Earth First!ers do battle with an "industrial monster that is devouring the planet," "an all-devouring entity that feeds . . . on the earth itself," a "profit monster [that] . . . gobbles up victims, human and otherwise."[139] The system is both evil and omnipotent; nothing bad happens without the system willing it. When somebody almost killed Earth First! activists Darryl Cherny and Judi Bari by blowing up their car, one Earth First!er immediately seized on this as an example of "state-sponsored violence."[140] Many Earth First!ers inhabit a conceptual world in which there are no tragedies, only conspiracies; a world where problems are never due to human beings' limitations, frailties, or even perversities but rather are an intended product of systemic malevolence.

Sweeping hostility toward the system erodes the ability to make important distinctions between reform and reaction, abuse and legality, democracy and fascism. Every institution seems to be infested with the same malevolent spirit of greed and violence. "The Nazi spirit is still alive," one Earth First!er writes. "In the FBI. In MAXXAM. In Congress. In the Supreme Court. In the New World Order."[141] If the United States is "becoming a police state," then it is hardly surprising to find the editor of the *Earth First! Journal* recommending "Nepal and Mongolia, as well as Eastern Europe and Russia" as democratic models that the United States might emulate.[142] Those who work within the political system to improve the environment become just another prop of the system. "Earth First!," the *Earth First! Primer* proudly reported, "has survived attacks by the timber and mining industry, the FBI, moderate professional environmentalists and other agents of the system." Reformist environmentalists become indistinguishable from the forces of reaction. "The Sierra Club," one Earth First!er tells us, "[has] far more in common with the Wise Abuse Movement than the grassroots of the environmental movement." Greenpeace becomes "just an example of eco-corporations, eco-business." These mainstream environmentalists are nothing more than "a passive instrument of government authority" or, alternatively, they are the puppet of "the shadowy syndicate of mega-foundations."[143] When it is unable to distinguish meaningfully between

Standard Oil and Greenpeace, the FBI and the Supreme Court, the Sierra Club and James Watt, radical environmentalism may be said to have passed beyond the demand for important and necessary reforms toward, as Hofstadter says, "the expression of a resentment so inclusive that it embraces not only the evils and abuses of a society but the whole society itself, including some of its more liberal and humane values."[144]

Apocalypse and Authoritarianism
in the Radical Environmental Movement

In the wake of the Oklahoma City bombing, we learned a great deal about the apocalyptic and millennial visions of radical right groups, as well as their conspiratorial fears of an imminent takeover of a "one world government." These fantasies have been treated by the media with the concern and scorn they deserve, and a few commentators have even managed to introduce some much-needed historical perspective by noting how congruent these contemporary styles of thought are with the "paranoid style" that Richard Hofstadter dissected over thirty years ago.[3] Yet radical right-wing militia groups and religious fundamentalists hardly have a monopoly on such apocalyptic visions. Indeed, over the last quarter century few have more consistently peddled an apocalyptic vision of the future than radical environmentalists.

To identify an apocalyptic vision is not to deny that there are pressing and even massive environmental problems, just as to talk of a paranoid style is not to deny that there are conspiratorial acts.[4] Determining how much of a threat a particular phenomenon — whether global warming, pesticides, or deforestation — poses to life on earth can be addressed only by careful empirical study. My aim here is not to sift through the relevant scientific evidence but to examine the worldview of those radical environmentalists who, across a range of environmental issues, consistently embrace the most apocalyptic interpretation of environmental problems.[5] The focus is on a style of thought that, as Hofstadter says, "traffics in the birth and death of whole worlds, whole political orders, whole systems of human values."[6]

Concerns over imminent environmental disaster cannot be explained by levels of information about the actual dangers of particular risks, nor can they be reduced to psychological predispositions such as risk aversion. Studies have repeatedly shown that concerns over environmental risks are not related to risk aversion in other domains of life.[7] Those who lose sleep over the greenhouse effect, for instance, are not any more likely to fret about the dangers of flying on an airplane. Risk perception, as Mary Douglas and Aaron Wildavsky have argued, is embedded in cultural orientations.[8] Apocalyptic warnings of imminent environmental catastrophe are part of the attempt to defend a radical egalitarian way of life and to discredit competing ways of living that rely upon bold entrepreneurial experimentation. After all, if people become persuaded that nature is fragile and that the slightest misstep may result in cataclysmic consequences for the human species, then it becomes difficult to resist arguments and policies that would rein in the acquisitive entrepreneur in the name of the collectivity.

But there is more than just the normal, healthy clash of cultural biases involved here. For apocalyptic and millennial visions can also have strongly illiberal consequences. If nature is so unforgiving that no mistakes can be tolerated, then not only an individualistic trial-and-error process but even democracy itself becomes put into question. If the future can be made perfectly harmonious, then error, democracy, and even dissent become intolerable or unnecessary. If the dangers to the human race are potentially cataclysmic, then can society afford the normal processes of political bargaining and compromise? Such dangers perhaps even justify restrictions on basic individual liberties. Indeed, in the face of impending doom would it not be legitimate for individuals or even the state to use any means necessary to save the earth?

William Ophuls and the Specter of Authoritarianism

In some respects, the story of environmental doomsayers is quite familiar. The late 1960s and early 1970s witnessed a flood of articles and books by environmentalists prophesying imminent doom. Predictions of nuclear annihilation, population explosion leading to mass starvation, "diatom blooms" leading to the extinction of all important marine animal life, climate change (the fear back then was global cooling) causing a catastrophic die-off of species all received tremendous publicity.[9] Critics of these "prophets of doom" often noted the religious flavor of these jeremiads, and environmentalists themselves were often sharply critical of the illiberal and antidemocratic conclusions that some theorists drew from their apocalyptic premises.

Among the most important of these early prophets of doom was William Ophuls. Ophuls began from the conventional apocalyptic premise that the world had reached the ecological brink. If we did not act soon, Ophuls believed, we could easily experience "an ecological crash" that would extinguish "perhaps billions of humans and [shake] the structure of our civilization to its foundations."[10] What distinguished Ophuls's work from that of most of the other doomsayers of the time was not his dire forecasts of impending oblivion, but rather his bold effort to spell out in detail "the political, social, and economic implications of the crisis."[11]

From apocalyptic premises, Ophuls pressed unabashedly authoritarian conclusions. Ophuls held out little hope that people would voluntarily change their destructive ways. "We as a society simply do not know the score and seem unlikely to learn it anytime soon," a pessimistic Ophuls concluded. If changes in individual conscience were inadequate to avoid the coming ecological tragedy, then it seemed that the only effective solution was to establish "a government possessing great powers to regulate individual behavior in the common interest." Ophuls had in mind here much more than simply strengthening the Environmental Protection Agency or beefing up enforcement of the Clean Water Act. In Ophuls's view the current political process, because it was "supremely responsive to our wills," could not be counted on to pursue the environmentally correct policies that could avert the coming environmental crisis.[12]

"In the face of deep crisis," Ophuls concluded, "democracy may simply not be a valid system of politics." How likely is it, Ophuls asked, that our elected leaders will be environmentally competent when they are "selected by an incompetent electorate"? For Ophuls, the pressing need to avoid the coming cataclysm means that democracy is no longer a luxury we can afford. "The closer your situation resembles being embarked on a ship making a perilous voyage," reasoned Ophuls, "the greater the rationale for placing power and authority in the hands of the few who know how to run the ship." If we are to avert destruction, we must defer to those who grasp the profound dimensions of the environmental problems we face. "It will require an extraordinarily high degree of competence to run this over-burdened, hard-pressed spaceship," Ophuls goes on to explain. "In such a situation, political equality as we know it and simple majority rule cannot be retained if we wish to ensure our survival."[13]

Not only democratic politics but basic liberties will have to be sacrificed as well. Ophuls is forthright about the fact that creating an ecologically sustainable society will mean "the loss of rights we now possess."[14] He unreservedly embraces Rousseau's formula that "man must be 'forced to be free'"; that is, Ophuls explains, he must be "made obedient to his real self-interest, which is the common good or the general will." Again invoking Rousseau, he suggests that "a certain minimum level of ecological virtue must be imposed by our political institutions." Ecological scarcity, he continues, means that "the individualistic basis of society, the concept of inalienable rights, the purely self-defined pursuit of happiness, liberty as maximum freedom of action, and laissez faire itself all become problematic, requiring major modification *or perhaps even abandonment* if we wish to avert inexorable environmental degradation and eventual extinction as a civilization."[15]

Ophuls's authoritarianism is sustained by his faith in the ability of an elite to identify and follow "*objective* ecological values." If we want to survive, Ophuls tells us, "then to a large extent objective ecological values must dominate our personal prejudices and interests, and some particular interests will have to be *suppressed* in the interest of the whole." Ophuls has nothing but disdain for liberal democratic politics, which seem, he says, to be based on the notion "that one man's values are just as good as another's."[16] Leaving aside the question of whether liberal democracy is in fact founded upon such absolute relativism, it is certainly skeptical, and rightly so, of any person's claim to have discovered the one, true, objectively correct set of values. That way, liberalism teaches, lies the road not to "a benign Leviathan," run by "technocratic pilots [running] the ship in accordance with technological imperatives," as Ophuls evidently hopes,[17] but to a much more ominous totalitarianism. History also tells us, moreover, that totalitarian or even authoritarian governments have generally been much poorer at protecting the environment than have democratic governments.[18]

To those who would suggest that the authoritarian cure is worse than ecological collapse, Ophuls offers first contempt and then pathos. He can admire the ancient Greeks who died in defense of their "noble ideal of public life in the polis," but how can one admire our refusal to give up a life of "slovenly affluence"? In any event, he closes, the choice is illusory, for the "closely-impending ecological crash" will bring with it, whether we like it or not, "the establishment of a de facto Leviathan."[19] The best we can do, then, is to try to shape that Leviathan in a relatively benign direction.

Ophuls's sweeping rejection of liberal democracy and his unabashed authoritarianism touched off immediate criticism within the community of leftist academics and environmentalists. David Orr and Stuart Hill, for instance, questioned the ability of large-scale, hierarchically structured institutions to solve the ecological problems that Ophuls identified. Decentralization, they suggested, would likely allow for more resilient and flexible responses. Richard Barnet and Roger Holsworth reaffirmed the value of participation in keeping government responsive to the environmental concerns of its citizens. An elite unresponsive to popular pressures, they argued, was likely to be less ecologically sensitive rather than more. Still others vigorously reasserted the value of bargaining and compromise in maintaining a free society and a healthy environment.[20]

Judging from this vigorous reaction to Ophuls (as well as Ophuls's own softening of his authoritarian message in subsequent writings),[21] one might conclude that the environmental movement quickly outgrew its early preoccupation with apocalyptic warnings and had come firmly to reject illiberal and antipolitical arguments. Robyn Eckersley suggests as much, arguing that the controversy surrounding the authoritarian solutions put forth by Ophuls and others "encouraged the search for more deepseated cultural transformations along with alternative, nonauthoritarian institutions that would foster a more cooperative and democratic response to the environmental crisis."[22] But this conclusion is misleading; radical environmentalists continue to adhere to apocalyptic visions of the future that lead many of them, despite strong egalitarian and antiauthoritarian predispositions, down illiberal and antipolitical paths.[23]

Apocalypse Now

A quick survey of recent radical environmental writings is enough to show how pervasive the apocalyptic vision remains. In his 1990 bestseller *Green Rage*, Christopher Manes luridly summons up the looming apocalypse. We are facing, he says, a "biological meltdown," "an environmental crisis unparalleled in history," and ultimately "the threat of ecological extinction." Mainstream politicians have left us with "dying forests, dead rivers, and nightmarish industrial landscapes." Only if we are ready "to dismantle industrial society" will we be able to avert the coming catastrophe.[24]

Dave Foreman's message is the same. There is no way, Foreman says, that the earth can sustain a population of five billion people given the destructive "worldview they have and the economic and industrial imperatives they live under." What will happen instead is that "the system is going to collapse of its own corruption." It is unavoidable, Foreman believes, that "there will be "a major ecological collapse [and] a concomitant die-off of the human population." The next twenty years, he concludes somberly, "aren't going to be very pleasant." Foreman's predictions are dire, but they are intended to spur activism, not fatalism. We are morally impelled to work for wilderness preservation, Foreman insists, "so that there is something to come back after human beings . . . destroy their civilization."[25]

Such apocalyptic views are commonplace among Earth First!ers. All Earth First!ers see "biological collapse looming on the horizon."[26] Our profligate way of life has placed in jeopardy not just the survival of particular species but all life on earth. Summing up what Rik Scarce describes as the Earth First! "consensus position," Judi Bari predicts that "the Earth is going to rise up and throw us off. . . . I'm sure life will survive that [collapse], but I don't know that humans will."[27] The future, most Earth First!ers believe, is bleak but not beyond redemption if we act immediately and uncompromisingly. "It's plain to see," one Earth First!er explained to the court at his sentencing for illegally blockading a timber road, "that the Earth is dying [and] our species is committing suicide." Ecotage, the Earth First!er explained to the judge, was thus life-affirming, providing hope for "an alternative to rape, consumption and death."[28]

More systematic evidence of Earth First!ers' fears of environmental collapse comes from the Metz survey, which found that 90 percent of Earth First!ers endorsed the apocalyptic statement that "our present civilization is headed for collapse, and is poised to carry the rest of the world down with it." Only 5 percent rejected this idea. Similarly, 95 percent of Earth First!ers believed that "the oceans are gradually 'dying' from oil pollution and dumping of waste," with only 4 percent again dissenting. On both items, well over half of Earth First!ers agreed in the strongest possible terms.

This apocalyptic vision is not limited to the deep-ecology wing of the radical environmental movement. In fact, the "Civilization headed for collapse" item was taken essentially verbatim from the writings of social ecologist Brian Tokar."[29] For Tokar, as for all radical environmentalists, invoking the apocalypse is intended to stir people to action. We are at the "brink of ecological collapse," he says, and must therefore change our "ecologically-disastrous way of life" before it is too late. To save the earth, Tokar urges that "the destruction of many — possibly most — of the defining institutions of modern society should be actively encouraged by earth-loving people."[30]

The *Earth Island Journal* is full of apocalyptic warnings of coming ecological calamity. "The bounty of the ocean, once thought to be unlimited, is 'heading the same way as . . . the buffalo.'" "Undersea ecocide . . . threatens to disrupt 'the ecological balance of the oceans with unforeseen results.'" Chlorine is a "chemical demon" systematically destroying the fragile ozone layer, and the resulting ultraviolet radiation coming in is now so high that "we could have a second Jonestown worldwide. By our political indolence, we're committing suicide right now." "We're living in a sea of lead. . . . Several generations of Americans may have already been damaged by chronic low-level exposure." "Everything is going to crescendo soon. . . . The end is closer than we ever realized."[31] And on and on.

These apocalyptic forebodings are shared by the Earth Island membership. A survey of Earth Island's northwest membership found that 92 percent endorsed the idea that "the oceans are gradually dying." Asked whether they thought that "if things continue on their present course, we will soon experience a major ecological catastrophe," better than nine in ten again agreed. Eighty-six percent of Earth Island respondents assented to the even more alarming proposition that the "unrelenting exploitation of nature has driven us to the brink of ecological collapse," while 84 percent felt that "what human beings are currently doing to nature can be fairly characterized as an ecoholocaust."[32]

Earth Island's titular head, David Brower, the charismatic granddaddy of radical environmentalism, takes his apocalyptic message wherever he goes. "The Earth is rapidly going downhill," he tells audiences.[33] In introducing his latest environmental project, the Global CPR Service, David Brower insists on the need for an immediate "U-turn that will avoid the abyss toward which humanity is speeding." Only radical transformation in the way we treat each other and the earth can prevent our "global home" from being "irretrievably mutilated" and forestall "vast human misery."[34] "We are entering a 20-year period," Brower tells us in his latest book, "that can either spell the end of beautiful trees as we know them, or that can save them."[35]

The apocalyptic, as Hofstadter observes, "constantly lives at a turning point: it is now or never."[36] "Half the species on Earth will die unless we act now," warns Randall Hayes of the Rainforest Action Network.[37] Tomorrow will be too late. "Species are dying at a catastrophic rate; pollution and greenhouses . . . pose a dire threat: we must act now," urges Daniel Coleman, a cofounder of the Green movement in North Carolina who helped draft the national Green platform.[38] Time is forever just running out. "There is no time," warns Christopher Manes. "It is the eleventh hour," says another. "It's later than you think." "There simply is not the time." "We have only ten years to save our planet." "We're midway through the decisive decade for life on Earth." And so on.[39]

Intended to spur action, these warnings of imminent danger can sometimes appear almost paralyzing. Every action, even apparently pro-environmental actions, seems to add to the degradation of the environment and endanger our lives.[40] "Every time you turn on an electric light," Helen Caldicott warns, "you are making another brainless baby."[41] "Every bite of a hamburger," an Earth First!er cautions, "is a vote for the mindless machinery of exploitation and death that eats up diversity and spits out deforestation, soil erosion and water pollution."[42] Computers, we are told in the *Utne Reader*, "cause disease and death in their manufacture and use, enhance centralized political power, and remove people from direct experience of life." Photography should be jettisoned because it destroys biodiversity. Most "environmentally themed T-shirts," the *Earth Island Journal* tells us, are "not environmentally correct" and actually contribute to the pollution problem. Even recycled toilet paper, we learn, kills the forests. "By supporting these products," one Earth First!er chastizes his fellow radical environmentalists, "you are not entirely free of participation in the military-industrial-toilet-paper-earth-raper complex."[43] Just "being part of this society," laments another, "demands endless and constant compromises of my environmental ethics. Every time I use electricity, flush the toilet, or get in the car, I am knowingly contributing to the degradation."[44] If every gesture or action, no matter how well-intentioned, only brings us closer to the brink of ecological collapse, one might expect apocalyptic visions would breed fatalism or at least withdrawal into solitude.

The longing for the purity that only withdrawal can bring is a perennial egalitarian impulse, as we saw in chapters 1 and 4. The temptation to form small countercultural communes is pervasive among radical environmentalists,[45] but that desire is always in tension with the strong desire to remake society.[46] It is social transformation, not resignation or quiescence, that is the intended aim of radical environmental apocalypticism, as indeed it is with most apocalypticism. As Hofstadter points out, such "apocalypticism . . . runs dangerously near to hopeless pessimism, but usually stops short of it. . . . They portray that which impends but which may still be avoided."[47] The drumbeat of danger tells of the terrible cataclysm to come if we do not mend our ways. If we do transform our lives, however, the radical environmental message often becomes positively millennial. If we can avoid doom we may enter paradise.

The Millennium Tomorrow

Radical environmentalists have sometimes been criticized for being interested only in survival rather than in the nature of the "good life."[48] Such criticism is largely misplaced. The apocalyptic message of radical environmentalists is very much part of the contest over the good life. The apocalypse is invoked by radical environmentalists to persuade people to reject industrial capitalism, the quintessentially "bad life," in their view, and to embrace a more egalitarian and communitarian way of life. When the "Club of Rome" invoked "a spirit of survival," it was to ask for global redistribution of wealth from the fortunate to the less fortunate,[49] and when Ophuls threatened oblivion it was to persuade people to make "the switch from rugged individualism to a communitarian ethic."[50] The language of survival, in short, is employed as a spur toward egalitarian collectivism.

Most radical environmentalists believe we presently stand at a crossroads. One road, of course, leads to assured destruction, but the other road, environmentalists generally believe, leads not to a minimally acceptable politics of bare survival but to a flourishing of natural diversity and human potential. Typical of this framing of the issue were R. A. Falk's two "alternative pathways to the future," one of which progressed from the politics of despair through desperation, catastrophe, and ultimately annihilation, the other of which moved from the "decade of awareness" through mobilization, transformation, and finally the "era of world harmony."[51] The choice facing us, as Brian Tokar frames it, is "between purification and destruction."[52] In a similar vein, environmental historian Donald Worster foresees two possible scenarios: one in which "the power elite will go on appropriating every available drop of water for its canals and pipelines, while providing the masses with a few dribbles." The other possibility is that a "new spirit of restlessness and challenge," inspired by the protests of the 1960s, may create a new "questioning mood" in which the previously quiescent masses at last seek "a freer, more human scale in [their] relationship with nature." The choice, as Worster poses it, is between true liberation or continued domination, destruction, and apathy.[53]

The radical environmentalist jeremiad thus relies not only on predictions of destruction and doom but also on utopian hopes for an emerging future that will "have no place for exploitative values, destructive technologies, and dehumanized relationships."[54] The utopian vision of radical environmentalism was prominently on display at the First International EcoCity Conference held in Berkeley in 1990. The opening address, delivered by Richard Register, president of Urban Ecology, told the audience that there had never before been a more auspicious moment for building "healthier ecological and social arrangements than we have experienced for hundreds of years, perhaps ever." Continuing in our present ways, of course, "guarantees environmental collapse," but learning to build in "balance with nature makes it possible for humanity to live in a way that permits all people — and all species — the opportunity and fullness of life." In these "whole, vital, [and] healthy" ecocities, at last human beings "can coexist in harmony with all other life forms on our home planet."[55]

For other radical environmentalists, the promise of the future lies not in new, transformed ecological cities but rather in the abandonment of cities altogether. Edward Abbey, for instance, the literary inspiration for

Earth First!, foresaw "the coming restoration of a higher civilization: scattered human populations modest in number that live by fishing, hunting, food-gathering, small-scale farming and ranching." This bucolic paradise would be accompanied by the withering away of the state. "The military-industrial state," Abbey predicted, "will disappear from the surface of the Earth within fifty years." Moreover, the "regime of technology" would come to an end, and people would "assemble once a year in the ruins of abandoned cities for great festivals of moral, spiritual, artistic and intellectual renewal." We would be "a people for whom the wilderness is not a playground but their natural and native home."[56]

David Brower's warnings of apocalypse, to take another prominent example, are typically accompanied by a soaring optimism about the alternative future that is still possible. The Earth Island "credo," penned by Brower, talks hopefully of ushering in "a new Renaissance." "The old [Renaissance] found a way to exploit," Brower writes. "The new one has discovered the Earth's limits. Knowing them, we may learn anew what compassion and beauty are, and pause and listen to the Earth's music." In this future world we will "be part of an enduring harmony, trying hard not to sing out of tune."[57] As with most utopias, the attraction of harmony threatens to drown out the wayward individual.

Greens like Daniel Coleman hold out the prospect for a similarly glorious future. "In the ecological society, in the just society," Coleman rhapsodizes, "time is what all people have in abundance. Recast in terms of the cycles of nature, . . . time is no longer associated with power and control but rather with sharing and care. The democratization of time can return time to its organic context." Coleman cautions that it will take time to grow this new ecological society but predicts that if we show "respect for natural processes and rhythms" and begin to plant the seeds "of cooperation, community, and democracy in the context of life-affirming values,"[58] we will be ready to harvest his imagined "ecological society" in the not so distant future.

Social ecologists like Brian Tokar and Murray Bookchin have painted the future in even more strikingly utopian hues. In a "true ecological society," as Tokar envisions it, "the institutions that ruthlessly exploit resources, despoil the earth and repress people's deepest desires would be replaced with free, fully participatory forms evolved to foster the fullest relationship of humanity-in-nature." Similarly, Bookchin imagines a future in which "hierarchy, in effect, would be replaced by interdependence, and consociation would imply the existence of an organic core that meets the deeply felt biological needs for care, cooperation, security, and love. Freedom would no longer be placed in opposition to nature, individuality to society, choice to necessity, or personality to the needs of social coherence."[59] All contradictions, oppositions, and conflict would give way to a harmonious unity.

The future, as most radical environmentalists hope to experience it, then, is far from a minimalist politics of mere survival. If we take the right "sustainable" path, we can finally realize an egalitarian utopia of public-spirited citizens living in harmony with nature and with each other. Centralized, stifling bureaucratic structures will be replaced by small-scale decentralized institutions that allow for diversity and creativity. Ugly, discordant competition will give way to beautiful, harmonious community. Today's extravagant disparities in income will give way to a shared frugality and modesty. The future is green and egalitarian.

The promise of a future ecotopia is central to the radical environmental message, but there is little agreement on how we will get there or how soon. For most, the future is up to us and still very much in the balance — hence the urgency with which the message is delivered. An ecotopian future is possible if we are willing to forsake the path of destruction for a more sustainable and equitable path. Others seem more confident that history is on their side, and that we are at the beginning of an ecological revolution that will fundamentally change the way people understand their relationship to nature and society.[60] Still others, particularly in Earth First!, believe that the coming millennium will arrive only through cataclysm.

A particularly striking elaboration of this idea is Wm. H. Kotke's *The Final Empire: The Collapse of Civilization and the Seed of the Future* (1993). Kotke believes that "world society is trapped within a system of cultural assumptions and patterns of behavior from which it cannot extricate itself." In Kotke's view, "there is no way out. There will be a collapse of civilization." But Kotke's apocalyptic message is only a prelude to the coming rebirth of paradise. "Within the compost of the fallen empire," explains Wolf Hardin, who enthusiastically reviewed the book for the *Earth First! Journal*, "lies the certainty of seed. . . . In the collapse of Tula and Babylon there resides the *world perfect*." As Kotke himself explains it, "the crisis of our era offers us paradise. It offers us the opportunity to shed the tensions and dangers of civilization so that we may create a new world." The egalitarian ecotopia envisioned by Kotke is a blueprint for "life in balance, including the re-creation of deliberate, non-hierarchical tribes, and earth-friendly foraging and sedentary models."[61]

Although radical environmentalists differ over our chances of realizing a sustainable ecological society and how that future society is likely to be reached, virtually all agree that the path to destruction is so clearly marked for all who care to read the signs that no one could inadvertently travel the wrong road. Only base greed, blind selfishness, or unthinking addiction to comfort could lead one to take a path so clearly destructive. With alternatives so obvious and so stark—a just, harmonious ecological society on the one side, and death and destruction on the other—there is a temptation to denigrate the choices people make, to patronize, to "reeducate," or to coerce those who so clearly have gone astray. The binary choice radical environmentalists pose between apocalypse and millennialism thus justifies authoritarian politics.

The Authoritarianism of Apocalypticism

The most self-consciously democratic environmentalists have recognized the potentially illiberal and antidemocratic consequences that can spring from an apocalyptic and millennial pattern of thought. Daniel Coleman, for instance, cautions that although things are undeniably desperate, the sense of urgency should not be used to justify political actions that would short-circuit the necessarily "slow process of building an ecological society from the grassroots." Similarly, Kirkpatrick Sale emphasizes that although "we do not know, and cannot, how long we have before the apocalypse," that only means we should begin the process of change immediately. The process itself, though, must be "slow, steady, continuous, and methodical, not revolutionary or cataclysmic" if the movement is not to do "irreparable violence to its own values." This is the democratic face of radical environmentalism.[62] But there is another face, an antidemocratic face that is more congruent with the enveloping sense of apocalypse that pervades radical environmental thinking.

A striking illustration of the top-down authoritarianism that can stem from environmental apocalypticism is a 1993 paper by Laura Westra published in the journal *Environmental Values*. Westra begins from the premise that people left to themselves will follow their shortsighted self-interest and lead us down the path of collective destruction. To avert this catastrophe, it is necessary that our laws be given "ecological eyes," an idea that she says entails choosing "laws and regulations . . . according to an ideal goal or 'good,' rather than represent the haphazard implementation of voters' preferences." Echoing Ophuls, she asks whether it is "right to have uneducated voters ultimately decide questions that might affect all life on earth." Majoritarian rule, Westra concludes, at least "in its present (as yet uneducated) state, is inimical to environmental values."[63]

If voters cannot be trusted to choose environmental policies, even indirectly through elected officials, then who is to be entrusted with that decision? Again like Ophuls, Westra searches out disinterested guardians who are apart from and above the political process: "some sort of Platonic philosopher queen," governmental experts, or a modified jury system that might weigh all the expert advice. These agents of environmental truth have "an obligation to be paternalistic, that is, to implement the less dangerous choices as *morally right*, even if (temporarily) unpopular and thus not perceived as a social 'good' by 'informed' citizens."[64] Without ever referring to Ophuls, Westra still lands in the same authoritarian boat.

Westra pushes her logic further still, for even governmental experts, she sees, represent the partial views of particular nation-states. And since what is at stake is the viability of life in the entire world, each part of which is organically connected to every other part, national identities and interests only obstruct our ability to pursue the "global 'good.'" Nationalism, Westra writes, "in its present form should be obsolete, and . . . competitive, divisive laws and regulations should no longer be supported." Westra proposes global organizations that would be charged with dispassionately and objectively overseeing and protecting global life-support systems. How these bodies are selected or who they represent seems not to concern Westra, since presumably they would be ministering to the earth's needs. To those who worry that such omnipotent, unelected global bodies might endanger civil liberties, Westra offers the assurance that "the imperative of protection and interference ought to be in force only when life-sustaining systems are at peril." But, of course, ascertaining when "life-sustaining systems" are "at peril" is in large part a contested political question that cannot help but involve deep questions of values.[65] And it is democratically elected politicians, not distant technocrats, whom we want settling or at least trying to mitigate these inevitable conflicts over values.[66]

The illiberal dynamic of apocalypticism is also evident in William Catton's influential book *Overshoot*, which argues that the human race has overshot the earth's carrying capacity and predicts that "now we must expect [a] crash." The need to reduce human consumption is so urgent, Catton argues, that it justifies extreme measures. In an overpopulated and resource-depleted world, Catton insists that it is essential "to discredit and wind down the want-multiplying industry [of advertising], perhaps even legally suppress it." Freedom of speech, Catton continues, should not be allowed "to authorize irresponsible encouragement of habitat destruction." Averting ecological disaster would mean that the First Amendment provision for "unabridged freedom of speech and press" would need radical "reinterpretation (if not outright alteration)."[67]

Those like Paul Ehrlich who feel that a "population explosion" threatens life on the earth think it a quite modest proposal to suggest aggressive proenvironmental indoctrination in public schools. Ehrlich, for instance, suggests that "the importance of small families can be discussed, and happy, successful families in classroom stories and films should never be shown with more than two children."[68] An Earth First!er carries this mode of reasoning a step further, suggesting that "to leave the decision to breed a matter of personal choice, is to encourage the [ecologically] irresponsible to breed." Instead, the state should limit every woman to one child.[69] An Earth Island Institute member suggests that before being allowed to have children, individuals should have to "prove [they] will be . . . fit parent[s] and raise [their] kids with an environmental consciousness."[70]

With catastrophe looming, it is easy to feel that there is no time for politics or discussion. "The earth is dying all around us," explained one Earth First!er. "There is no time to argue."[71] Political compromise becomes a luxury that we can no longer afford or something that nature will simply not allow anymore. As Jamie Sayen, director of Earth Island's Northern Appalachian Restoration Project, suggests, "We do not have the biological freedom to ignore, or to cut a compromise with, the ecological crisis that now grips us. . . . We can repeal a tax law, but not the law of gravity."[72] Ecological survival trumps political democracy.

Believing that the earth is heading for a cataclysmic collapse makes it much easier to justify defending the earth "by any means necessary."[73] Indeed, according to Dave Foreman, "it *forces* you to consider any and all means of resisting that destruction." Such extraordinary and illegal actions "not only can be morally justified but [are] morally required.[74] Faced with "habitat on the brink of extinction," explains Karen Pickett, "higher laws come in to play."[75] Indeed, for some Earth First!ers, "'No compromise in defense of mother earth' might just mean compromising

EVERYTHING ELSE WE BELIEVE IN for the sake of Her."[76] Other values — compassion, kindness, decency, empathy — must be subordinated in the name of defeating the forces of greed and averting the apocalypse.

Such sentiments are not confined to a few environmental philosophers or irate letter writers to the *Earth First! Journal*. The Metz survey shows widespread support for antidemocratic ideas, as well as the close connection between these ideas and apocalypticism. Among members of the Voluntary Human Extinction Movement, 84 percent agreed (only 10 percent disagreed) that "on many environmental questions, the stakes are simply too high to leave issues to the normal process of political bargaining and compromise," seven in ten agreed (two in ten disagreed) that "we are morally obligated to resort to whatever means necessary in order to defend the earth from destruction," and 62 percent agreed (30 percent disagreed) that "if we are to save the environment, we will have to give up certain basic rights we now enjoy." Among the Earth First! subset of the VHEMT sample, the percentages agreeing to these statements rose substantially to 92 percent, 83 percent, and 68 percent, respectively.

Using a two-item measure of apocalypticism ("Civilization headed for collapse" and "Oceans are dying") and a three-item measure of illiberalism (made up of the three statements listed in the previous paragraph), we find a massively strong correlation ($r = .54$) between apocalypticism and illiberalism. Illustrated another way, among the most apocalyptic VHEMT members (that is, those who agreed in the strongest possible terms to both the "Oceans are dying" and the "Civilization headed for collapse" items), 58 percent scored high on the illiberalism scale while only about one in ten of those who ranked low on the apocalyptic index ranked high on the illiberalism scale. Only 6 percent of the most strongly apocalyptic VHEMT members scored low on the illiberalism scale, while two-thirds of the nonapocalyptic VHEMT members scored low on illiberalism.[77] The survey evidence, in sum, confirms that acceptance of apocalyptic scenarios about the future of the environment makes environmentalists vulnerable to illiberal, antidemocratic, or antipolitical arguments.[78]

Dead Certainties

Apocalyptic and millennial rhetoric is difficult if not impossible to reconcile with liberal democracy or even laborious grassroots organizing. Such rhetoric is more congruent instead with the calling of a holy war or crusade. "Since what is at stake is always a conflict between absolute good and absolute evil," Hofstadter explains, "the quality needed is not a will-ingness to compromise but the will to fight things out to a finish, . . . not the usual methods of political give-and-take, but an all-out crusade."[79] Radical environmentalists imagine themselves involved in nothing less than "a war to save the planet." They are "eco-warriors," "earth war-riors," "warriors of the rainbow," even "nonviolent warriors," engaged in "the most sacred crusade ever waged on earth," defending the globe against "the unholy assault [of] the industrial state." "Our fight," echoes another, "is the holiest fight of all! To save life itself!" The call goes out for an "Eco-Jihad." "For the sake of the living and all who are yet to live," they tell each other, "we must prevail."[80]

Having embarked on a crusade against evil, they find it difficult to make room for skeptics or to tolerate doubters. Fanaticism sets in. "This is ji-had," explains Earth First!er Mike Roselle. "There are no innocent by-standers, because in these desperate hours, bystanders are not innocent." "This is a revolution," echoes another Earth First!er. "You're either on the bus or off the bus. There is no middle ground of this struggle!"[81] Those who vacillate or who seek to accommodate opposing views are complicit in the destruction and no less guilty than the butchers them-selves. Reformist environmentalism becomes almost worse than reaction or no action, since it serves only to muddy the clearly drawn battle lines between good and evil.[82]

The tendency toward fanaticism has not gone unnoticed or uncriti-cized within the radical environmental community. Not long before he left Earth First!, Dave Foreman voiced his growing concern over what he saw as a tendency among his fellow radical environmentalists to move from "a position of opposition" to "creating a dualistic world of *Us* ver-sus *Them*." In a remarkable essay published in the *Earth First! Journal*, Foreman warned that

> when we create such a world, our opponents become the enemy, be-come the *other*. . . . In such a dichotomous world, they lose their hu-manness and we lose any compulsion to behave ethically or with con-sideration toward them. In such a psychological state, we become true believers and any action against the enemy is justified. One needs only to look at Adolf Hitler or the Ayatollah Khomeini to see the results to one's psyche of holding this attitude.

Restoring the moral complexity of the world enabled Foreman to pull back from the misanthropic hard edge of radical environmentalism. No longer "so sure of myself," Foreman found it more difficult to demonize others. Perceiving others not as evil but as "potential supporters" allowed the political question of "how you gain support for your goals and actions" to became relevant for him again. Having grown dubious about the chances of "creating a new society with a new morality," Foreman now seemed less willing to justify "any means necessary" to achieve his ends and became more respectful of "the rules or customs of this society."[83]

Foreman's message seemed to fall largely on deaf ears. His criticisms of Earth First! were seen as apostasy and as further evidence of the system's immense powers of co-optation. "If the Police State can turn the most revered 'No Compromise' ecowarrior into an opportunist extraordinaire," one particularly excited Earth First!er wrote, "then who can be trusted?"[84] Although still deeply committed to wilderness preservation, Foreman soon gravitated toward the reformist environmentalism he had previously scorned.[85] Foreman's departure and the resulting schism within Earth First! helped fuel an even more apocalyptic and conspiratorial outlook among many Earth First!ers.[86] The rhetoric often became indistinguishable from that of the contemporary radical right: there were the warnings of "One World Government,"[87] of federal "jackboots . . . coming down on more necks," and even of "a new Dark Age descend[ing] over the Republic."[88]

Even when the content of the rhetoric differs from that of the radical right, as it mostly does,[89] the style of thought remains remarkably similar. Both the radical right of the militias and the radical left of Earth First! share an illiberal habit of mind that Norman Cohn diagnosed in *The Pursuit of the Millennium*, his seminal study of the millennial sects of medieval and Reformation Europe. It is a style of thought characterized by a view of one's group "as the Elect, wholly good, abominably persecuted yet assured of ultimate triumph; the attribution of gigantic and demonic powers to the adversary; the refusal to accept the ineluctable limitations and imperfections of human existence, such as transience, dissention, conflict, fallibility whether intellectual or moral; . . . systematized misinterpretations, always gross and often grotesque . . . ruthlessness directed towards an end which by its very nature cannot be realised — towards a total and final solution."[90] It is a mind-set characterized not by the lively doubt of radicalism at its best but by the dead certainties of the alienated fanatic.

Doubt, as Raymond Aron says, is the seed of tolerance. Nobody, of course, has a greater stake in nurturing tolerance than the radical groups that exist at the ideological margins of society. Without its protective cover, their ideas and their very existence are likely to be systematically repressed rather than just periodically harassed or constantly ridiculed. Although dependent on society's tolerance, radical groups at the figurative margins of society are themselves difficult places in which to plant the skepticism of which Aron speaks. It is a difficult life — they suffer real and sometimes imagined persecution at the hands of the state, and they may be asked to give up much in the way of material comforts or social acceptance to live the radical way of life. The apocalyptic and millennial visions help keep such groups together — individuals leaving or the group splitting are particularly a problem where, as in the case of Earth First!, the group completely rejects formal authority or hierarchical sanctions of any kind. The invocations of apocalypse and the millennial hopes help sustain radical egalitarian commitment but also erode doubt and hence tolerance, ironically undermining the very value they are most dependent on for survival.

CONCLUSION

A history that does not grapple with the reasons for and consequences of failure will not take the current Left very far.

   Michael Kazin[1]

Protecting old-growth forests is far different from abolishing slavery, just as eradicating sexism is not the same as opposing a war or protesting the inequities of capitalism. Separated by time and place, each radical egalitarian movement is in many ways distinctive, even unique. From a contemporary perspective, nineteenth-century American radicals may appear to be apologists for patriarchal families or insensitive to environmental destruction. Yet for all their different policy concerns and widely divergent historical contexts, these disparate movements and individuals often display striking similarities in political style and sensibility. Most notably, radical egalitarians consistently adopt an oppositional posture vis-à-vis dominant institutions and mores. Their aim is not just to reform abuses or remedy specific injustices but to transform radically the dominant culture; their central dilemma is how to transform society yet remain uncorrupted by it. They are trapped, as Daniel Bell has written of the American socialist movement, "by the unhappy problem of living '*in* but not *of* the world.'"[2] By withdrawing to the margins, egalitarians maintain their purity, but at the risk of irrelevance. To bring about fundamental social change means moving closer to the centers of power, but at the cost of having their cause co-opted or their message diluted. From this core organizational dilemma stem several illiberal tendencies, most especially the tendency to construct a Manichaean view of the world as a battle between righteousness and iniquity.

MANICHAEANISM AND POLITICAL CORRECTNESS

The radical egalitarian life is rarely easy. Resources are usually scarce, and the individuals and groups are often despised, ridiculed, harassed, or just ignored. Abolitionists in the 1830s and 1840s were denounced as fanatics, shunned by their neighbors, assaulted by angry mobs, and occasionally suppressed by government policy (the infamous Gag Rule, for instance). Utopian colonists were often regarded as crazies and sexual perverts, and were harassed by local citizens and occasionally by local or state governments. Radicals who opposed intervention in World War I were ostracized and risked imprisonment. Civil rights workers were denigrated as "nigger-lovers," radical feminists were shunned as "bra-burners," and Earth First!ers are ridiculed as "tree-huggers." External attacks help cement commitment to the group but also promote a view of the outside world as benighted or malign.

The dynamic of opposition and denunciation, confrontation and repression, reinforces the tendency for the oppositional grouping to reject "the system" as hopelessly corrupt. The boundaries separating the inner purity of the group from the outside world are zealously policed by the elect. Deviations from a politically correct orthodoxy are denounced and perhaps even punished. Distrust of the outside turns into an inward search to root out false friends, to expose and expel the "oreos" (black on the outside, white on the inside) or "radishes" (red on the outside, white on the inside) of the movement. Small differences in doctrine or outlook are amplified into heresy. Rather than fighting the system, the movement becomes consumed with disabling sectarian battles.

IDEALIZING THE OPPRESSED

Because radical egalitarians are a small minority and the dominant culture is seen as hopelessly corrupt, egalitarians cast around for oppressed groups who can help them imagine and bring about revolutionary change. Remote from power, the oppressed are seen as being uncontaminated by the dominant ethos of society. Their exclusion and oppression invest them with a purity and heroic nobility that make them a window on the transformed future. With these hopeful eyes, Waldo Frank turned to the Native American settlements and Hispanics in the Southwest, Tom Hayden fixed upon poor Mississippi sharecroppers and urban outcasts, and contemporary radical environmentalists turn to long-suffering indigenous peoples. Some of what goes under the rubric of "multiculturalism" today is yet another manifestation of the egalitarian romance with the oppressed "other."

At times this egalitarian romance with the oppressed is only foolish, but at times it can be more pernicious. Both the Old Left and the New Left tended to romanticize not only powerless groups within American society but also powerful groups in other societies. The Old Left's romance with Soviet communism ended with tawdry apologies for Stalinist repression, just as the New Left's romance with Third World revolutionaries led them to excuse or overlook political repression and acts of brutality. Romancing the "other" allows egalitarian groupings to "keep hope alive," but at the high cost of the intellectual honesty and radical skepticism that egalitarian intellectuals rightly prize.

MILLENNIAL FAITH AND APOCALYPTIC FOREBODINGS

The romance with the oppressed "other" and the construction of a bipolar battle between good and evil emerge out of an oppositional consciousness shaped by giving primacy to purity. But it is not purity alone that pushes the egalitarian along illiberal tracks. As important is the egalitarian's perfectionist faith, the belief that people are naturally good and that established institutions systematically thwart people's almost infinite potential for goodness. At its best, this optimistic conception of human nature can motivate idealistic action aimed at reform of real abuses; at its worst, millennial faith in a perfectible human nature can lead to forcibly remaking people in the image of the revolutionary.

Extravagant hopes of what is possible torment the radical egalitarian mind, feeding a desperate unhappiness with current institutions and practices. A politics that merely seeks to avoid cruelty, to allow people to live peaceably with each other, or even to remedy injustices, seems woefully inadequate to those who believe human beings can usher in something approaching a heaven on earth. Utopian visions of unrealized human potential go hand in hand with apocalyptic warnings of the cataclysm that will befall us if we fail to heed the signs. The apocalyptic prophecies, whether conjured up by nineteenth-century agrarian radicals such as Ignatius Donnelly or twentieth-century radical environmentalists, are designed to scare people out of their complacency, specifically to shake their confidence in the unplanned anarchy of competitive markets or the unresponsive indifference of hierarchical institutions. Apocalypse is the cultural stick, but for the radical egalitarian, as opposed to, say, the survivalist, the stick is always in the service of a bright vision of a humanity redeemed, in touch with nature and with each other, living simply, close to the land, and without coercion or inequality.

The inspiring dream and the apocalyptic nightmare converge on the terrain of authoritarian politics. The looming threat of widespread death and destruction leaves no time for democratic politics or liberal reform.

By the same token, a future so bright justifies the authoritarian urge to disregard the expressed preferences of people in favor of what is so clearly in their long-run interests. They may not understand now, but when we get them to the chosen land they or their descendants will thank us and excuse our excesses. Where the costs of choosing the wrong path are so monumentally disastrous and the benefits of choosing the right road so wonderfully liberating, it is tempting not to allow people to make mistakes for themselves but instead to "force them to be free."

AUTHORITARIAN AND CHARISMATIC LEADERSHIP

The authoritarian implications of the apocalyptic and millennial visions can in some instances be held in check by the strong antiauthority views of most radical egalitarians. Yet the egalitarian antiauthority ethos can itself be a cause of arbitrary or authoritarian leadership, as we saw in examining abolitionists, utopian colonists, the New Left, and radical feminists. The attempt to build a way of life that minimizes formal structures of authority can leave a vacuum that may be filled with informal and therefore unaccountable leaders. Charisma becomes a substitute for authority. Tearing down official leaders and formal structures can, paradoxically, leave radical egalitarian movements with implicit structures and leaders that are less democratic.

The ideal that we should all participate in every decision that directly affects us is a profoundly democratic one, but carried to extremes the ideal can undermine democratic institutions. More democracy can lead to less. In small groups with limited aims and minimal disagreements, having each person participate in and consent to every decision may be workable. But in large-scale social movements committed to sweeping change and characterized by vigorous differences of opinion, adherence to strict egalitarian norms of participatory democracy almost invariably incapacitates the movement. Repeated failure to reach decisions discredits the process and strengthens the hand of the self-appointed revolutionary vanguard willing to disregard democratic forms in pursuit of egalitarian ends.

In surveying the history of radical egalitarianism in America, it is striking how often one finds the active search for the charismatic leader or genius who will disregard convention and law. Although this longing for "men of magnetic force"[3] is hardly limited to radical egalitarian movements, the affinity does seem particularly striking among radical egalitarians, particularly given their emphasis on equality and participation. The relative lack of formal structures within egalitarian movements helps to explain why charismatic leaders find the space to flourish within such movements, but it does not account for the active seeking-out of the disruptive charismatic leader we find among Wendell Phillips, Edward Bellamy, Walt Whitman, Van Wyck Brooks, and others. To understand egalitarians' penchant for the charismatic prophet one has to appreciate not only their obvious antipathy for established institutions and practices, but also the mammoth mismatch between radical egalitarian hopes, which involve nothing less than the total restructuring of society, and radical egalitarians' influence, which is usually meager, positioned as they generally are at the political margins. The charismatic genius, much like the oppressed "other," is sought out to close this gulf between the ideal and the real. Through sheer force of inspiration, the charismatic leader has the power to stir the sluggish masses, tear down corrupt institutions, and forge a bright new world. The charismatic substitutes for the hard work of democratic organizing and democratic politics.

THE FALSE-CONSCIOUSNESS TRAP

A scarlet thread running throughout the radical egalitarian thought surveyed in this book is a barely concealed contempt for the choices most people make in their everyday lives. The masses of people are assumed to make decisions that do not express their "true" preferences or their authentic selves, but rather reflect the hegemonic value system — whether capitalist, materialist, patriarchal, or anthropocentric — they have passively imbibed. It is the system and not ordinary people who draw the brunt of egalitarian wrath, but having reduced people to passive automatons, deluded fools, or naive dupes, egalitarians have scant reason to treat people or their preferences with respect. Pity is about the best one can expect; condescension, ridicule, and disdain are the more likely and less lovely reactions to what radical egalitarians write off as false consciousness.

The term "false consciousness" conjures up the specter of Marxism, but the concept is not unique to orthodox Marxism. If Marxian socialism has by and large failed to plant deep and lasting roots in American soil, that does not mean the concept of false consciousness has been any less important to the American left than it has been to the left in other nations. Marx dismissed Henry George as an "utterly backward" crank, but both Marx and George believed they had discovered the fundamental truth of the social order that, in George's words, lay "hid from the great masses of men."[4] The certain knowledge that one possesses the truth need not mean forsaking politics, but politics becomes limited to the prophetic mode, awakening people to an a priori truth, rather than a process of mutual persuasion and accommodation during which both sides adjust their views and learn from rival arguments.

FROM RADICAL SKEPTICISM TO RADICAL CERTAINTY

The radical egalitarian typically begins as the radical skeptic determined to rid people's minds of accepted cant. Radical intellectuals of the early twentieth century intended to be "freely experimental, skeptical of inherited values, ready to examine old dogmas, and to submit afresh its sanctions to the test of experience." Hayden described the early New Left in similar terms as a movement that would "buy nobody's dogma" and would regard all answers "as provisional, to be discarded in the face of new evidence or changed conditions." The feminist Redstockings promised to "question every generalization and accept none that are not confirmed by our experiences." Explaining the "New Cultural Politics of Difference," Cornel West sounds the same theme when he insists on a "demystificatory criticism" that "always keeps open a sceptical eye to avoid dogmatic traps, premature closures, formulaic formulations, or rigid conclusions."[5] This, at least, is the original promise.

But radical egalitarians often have a difficult time maintaining their commitment to a genuinely radical skepticism. To start with, skepticism does not coexist easily with the utopian faith and transformative aspirations that are so fundamental to the radical egalitarian sensibility. Under the pressure of radical egalitarian commitments, radical skepticism often gives way to radical certainty. Commitment to the cause trumps intellectual skepticism; "in a time of faith," as Randolph Bourne wrote, "skepticism is the most intolerable of all insults."[6] A few like Bourne stand out for their ability to maintain a critical distance from their own egalitarian allegiances, but for every Bourne there are more like Hayden or Mike Gold who succumb to the very sort of dogmatic thinking they began by criticizing.

A corollary to this radical certainty is an anti-intellectualism, specifically an impatience with intellectuals who raise doubts or questions that might impede radical action. We see this impatience in Hayden's lament that "intellectuals are placed at vantage points which, described as seats of reason, actually function to immunize the senses and turn incoming truths into trickling, instead of tidal currents." Righteous action stems

not from a life of learning but from trusting one's gut reactions, the un-
tutored heart, the instinctive "law of love." Simple justice requires simple
thoughts, which is why, as Hayden expresses it, "it is sometimes foolish
to judge the open mind, the questioning spirit, as ipso facto good."[7]

POLITICIZING THE PRIVATE AND DEPOLITICIZING THE PUBLIC

We have repeatedly bumped up against the egalitarian tendency to
denigrate the private realm as a bastion of antisocial activities and behaviors. The private sphere, whether in the form of the cohesive family
or the atomistic marketplace, poses a dual problem for the collectivist
egalitarian: first, freedom of action in the private realm generates inequalities and, second, it weakens collective solidarity. The egalitarian
response is frequently to politicize what had previously been regarded as
private, thus limiting individual freedom in the name of equality or fraternity (or, more dangerously, the liberation of the true self).

Efforts to redefine the boundary between public and private are not
necessarily illiberal. The precise boundary between the personal and
public spheres, as Judith Shklar has commented, is "not historically a
permanent or unalterable boundary. . . . The important point for liberalism is not so much where the line is drawn, as that it be drawn."[8] New
Deal liberal reform, for example, renegotiated the boundaries between
private and public in such a way as to involve government more in what
had previously been seen as purely private economic exchange. The result was a more interventionist state that struck a different balance between liberty and equality. Welfare-state liberalism is less libertarian
than nineteenth-century liberalism, but it is not illiberal so long as the
value of privacy is cherished and the boundary between public and private remains a core value against which every public policy is scrutinized.

The illiberal road is embarked upon when the private realm is systematically demeaned as a prison or dungeon (Edward Bellamy) or a grave
(Andrea Dworkin) thwarting the true self. The desire becomes not to
shift the line between public and private so much as to erase it, since the
boundary only serves to protect and legitimate selfishness and coercive
inequalities. The dream, as in Bellamy's *Looking Backward*, is to "banish
artificiality" so that private thoughts become indistinguishable from
public acts. Artistic expression without political purpose, as Mike Gold
saw it, is degenerate or useless, and political purpose is sufficient or at
least necessary to judge artistic merit. Disgust with the materialism and
atomism of private life leads Walt Whitman to rejoice that civil war

would disrupt "the solemn church and scatter the congregation," enter "the school where the scholar was studying," and not even leave "the bridegroom quiet with his bride." Public commitment drives out mere private enjoyment. Individuality perfected is individuality lost in the collectivity; as Henry Demarest Lloyd expressed it, the highest social good is "the fusion of perfected individuals in social action — the melting of the grains of sand into the perfect glass."[9]

Egalitarian antipathy for atomized individualism can lead not only to politicizing the private but also, ironically, to depoliticizing the public sphere. The egalitarian quest for harmonious fellowship, for a world without strife or wasteful competition, has a natural affinity with strongly antipolitical and even antidemocratic sentiments in which conflict is seen in terms of an illegitimate selfishness rather than in terms of the legitimate and inevitable conflict of rival interests and visions. In this illiberal variant one finds the cohesive, egalitarian family raised up as a model for the egalitarian polity.[10]

"UNSELFISH CRIMES"

In the aftermath of the French Revolution, the German romantic Friedrich von Schlegel warned of a new era of "unselfish crimes."[11] Altruism can be noble, of course, just as self-interest can be sordid. But von Schlegel saw that those who claimed to act in the name of mankind, or the earth, or the children, or the future, or equality, could be more self-righteous and fanatical than those who freely admitted to acting out of self-interest or group interest. "It is easier," Stephen Holmes points out, "to be cruel . . . when you act in the name of others, or in the name of an ideal, or even for the benefit of your victim, than when you act for your own sake." The greater the disdain for self-interest, the greater the vulnerability to "selfless cruelty."[12]

The history of radical egalitarianism in the United States has nothing that compares with the selfless cruelty of the Khmer Rouge or the Cultural Revolution, in part because radical egalitarians have never come to power in this country as they did in Cambodia and China. But one does find among American radical egalitarians, from the radical abolitionists of the 1830s to the radical environmentalists of today, a tendency to justify violent or high-handed acts by appealing to pure or selfless motives. So Charles Stearns assured Garrison that he went to Kansas to fight slaveholders "not for myself [but] for God and the slaves."[13] John Brown's violent deeds were cleansed by his pure, selfless motives.

Similarly, radical environmentalists justify their sometimes illegal actions on the grounds that they are free of self-interest. They act not for themselves but for the rain forests, the desert, the redwoods, the grizzly bear.

Acts of selfless cruelty are certainly not confined to the left. Operation Rescue, for instance, justifies its violence in the name of the unborn and the Lord. Zealotry knows no ideological boundaries. But adherents of radical egalitarianism are particularly prone to the "unselfish crime" precisely because they have so little tolerance or sympathy for selfishness and self-interest. Believing that selfishness is almost criminal, radical egalitarians too readily assume that selflessness must be virtuous, even righteous. The dichotomy they draw between malevolent selfishness and benevolent altruism betrays a lack of appreciation for human irrationality that is neither benevolent nor self-seeking.[14] The dark side of the left is integrally connected, then, to the left's tendency to ignore or deny the dark side of humanity.

What Does Egalitarianism Have to Do with It?

Some readers may accept the existence and even importance of this illiberal style in America and yet may still wonder what egalitarianism or even radical egalitarianism has to do with it. Perhaps the illiberalism of the left that we have observed is better explained as a response to objective events. One variant of this interpretation would be to attribute the failures and pathologies of the egalitarian left largely to external repression rather than to internal dynamics. As Herbert Marcuse insisted, "The movement [of the 1960s] did not die, it was murdered!" Official repression certainly played an important role in the development of the New Left, but Todd Gitlin is right when he says that, viewed in comparative or historical perspective, "the repression of the late Sixties and early Seventies was mild."[15] The New Left's embrace of violence cannot be understood apart from the violence visited upon the movement ("the police riot" in Chicago, for example), but neither can it be understood apart from the New Left's own ideological and organizational dynamics. Hayden's claim that student radicals "arrived at a confrontational stance not out of political preference but only as a last resort" is misleading because separation from and confrontation with "the system" was central to the New Left's mode of organizing from its earliest stages.[16]

Obviously, history without events and context is incomplete. But the events themselves are also insufficient to explain why particular people construed or constructed those events in the way they did. Little in political life is self-evident, like a wall of water rushing down the street that everybody flees. Since for the most part the individuals and groups described in this book have behaved in ways that are often markedly different from the rest of the population, it seems safe to say that to understand these individuals and groups we need to understand the perceptual screens through which they viewed the world and defined their interests. Whether those screens are shaped in important ways by a radical egalitarian way of life is the critical question.

An alternative explanation for the illiberal pathologies of these radical egalitarian groups is that the groups inadvertently mirrored the larger values and pathologies of the society. Their illiberalism thus reflects not so much the dark side of egalitarian ideas and modes of organizing as a failure to transcend fully the pathological values and commitments of the dominant culture. The sectarian fights and authoritarianism of the New Left or radical feminists, in this explanation, reflect not the weaknesses of radical democracy but rather the failure of egalitarian adherents to shake off the competitive, self-seeking values of a hegemonic culture. What destroys the dreams of the left is the inegalitarian culture into which everyone is socialized.

If this is true, the prospects for change seem bleak indeed. If even the most radical challenges to established institutions are in the iron grip of a hegemonic culture, then it hardly seems worth the effort. Resignation and withdrawal would seem the most rational responses. More likely, this belief would lead to one last search for those marginal groups that are so excluded and downtrodden that they have escaped the blighting touch of the dominant value system, or, perhaps, a redoubled effort to purge oneself and one's ranks of the hegemonic mind-set, or maybe even a last desperate assault on a horribly unjust system. The real danger with this sort of explanation is that it reproduces the radical egalitarian bias without understanding the weaknesses of that bias any better. Blaming a hegemonic system, whether patriarchal, racist, or capitalist, is unlikely to serve the left's own interests in understanding and learning from its own weaknesses and failures. More specifically, it justifies building up the boundaries protecting internal purity while ignoring the ways in which a successful social movement, as Leon Fink points out, necessarily "must draw in constituencies attached to traditional values."[17]

A different and more testable version of this objection is to question whether this illiberal style is distinctive to radical egalitarianism. Weren't the bipolar cosmology and the crusading self-righteousness of the radicals abolitionists, for instance, mirrored in the overheated rhetoric of the southern "fire-eaters"? Weren't the millenial hopes of redemption and apocalyptic visions of cataclysm a commonplace of northern political culture during the Civil War? Weren't the exaggerated condemnations of self-seeking materialism and the quest for collective harmony frequent refrains among late-nineteenth- and early-twentieth-century American conservatives? Wasn't the New Left's Manichaeanism an inverted reflection of a cold war America that divided the world into absolute good and absolute evil, the free world versus totalitarian communism? Wasn't the violence of the Weathermen a reflection of a peculiarly violent American society? And so on.

The objection is well taken, and no short answer can possibly resolve the issue.[18] Ultimately the question raised is an empirical one that can be settled only by carefully comparing the political thought and actions of Stephen Foster or Wendell Phillips with those of Abraham Lincoln or William Henry Seward, or Edward Bellamy with William Graham Sumner, or Randolph Bourne with Woodrow Wilson, or Tom Hayden with Lyndon Johnson. That is a task for another book, but a few words of clarification are necessary now.

First, it is worth reiterating that there are multiple routes to an illiberal end point, and radical egalitarianism is certainly not the only illiberal route. Authoritarian or hierarchical conservatism takes one down an illiberal path much more quickly and surely. Theodore Roosevelt's desire for a "splendid little war" that would hone the flabby muscles of a materialist nation is a monument to the illiberal spirit of hierarchical conservatism, as is the Alien and Sedition Act pushed through by the Federalist party in the 1790s. Second, there is no need to deny that radicals were shaped by dominant American institutions and values. No radical movement is able to separate itself totally from the larger society's mores and customs, yet American radicals generally did create and inhabit what historian John Thomas has described as an "oppositional culture." They defined themselves, intellectually, politically, and often socially, in terms of an oppositional consciousness.[19] Many conventions of the day they left unchallenged, of course, but it is striking how often radicals attacked inegalitarian institutions, beliefs, and practices that were unrelated to the original impetus for organizing. Radical abolitionists, for instance, attacked not only slavery but also a wide range of hierarchical institutions, including churches, political parties, and traditional family structures, as well as the amoral bidding and bargaining of the competitive marketplace.

Even if one concedes that these radicals were not just capitalists with a conscience, it hardly settles the role of egalitarianism. Perhaps it is not radical egalitarianism but rather radical Protestantism that explains the crusading moral absolutism and millennialism so often encountered in this book.[20] Certainly we know from historian Stephen Foster that radical Protestantism in its original form "all too easily passed over into a millenarianism that led to the dictatorship of the regenerate."[21] Protestantism as an explanation works relatively well in making sense of the abolitionists and even the late-nineteenth-century utopian reformers,[22] but in the more secular contemporary period such an explanation becomes more strained. If a Manichaean cosmology and crusading moralism are due to an inherited Protestant past, how does one explain that the New Left was disproportionately Jewish, and that its leading figure, Tom Hayden, was Catholic, and a product of a Catholic parochial school at that? Compared with the rest of the public, New Left activists were not only less Protestant but also less religious. Radical feminists, moreover, are not notable for their religiosity, and Earth First! is more pagan than Protestant.

A fallback position is to argue that Protestantism is so pervasive that it has become "generalized far beyond its denominational or even specifically religious base."[23] On this reading, Americans are all sectarian Protestants at heart, whether they are Jewish, Catholic, atheist, or pagan. But this retreat has several notable problems. First, and most fundamentally, it makes the thesis virtually nonfalsifiable. If we find that non-Protestants in America are also moralistic or believe in "the perfectibility of man and of civil society,"[24] then this becomes evidence of Protestantism's deep subterranean influence rather than its weakness as an explanatory factor. If non-Protestants are as likely as Protestants to believe human beings are perfectible, this suggests not the power of Protestantism but rather that the explanation must lie in factors other than Protestantism.

An additional problem with this fallback position is that the pathologies that afflicted the American New Left, including demonization of the system and a sectarian purism, were not unique to the United States. As Paul Berman has recently pointed out, the illiberal trajectory of the New Left was not unique to America but characterized the New Left student movements throughout the non-Communist world. Berman reports,

The New Left in the United States followed the world pattern exactly, beginning with the beginning.... Almost everywhere, the movements began by promising to construct a new kind of democratic or libertarian socialism. And almost everywhere ... the democratic and libertarian aspects dropped away, in part or in whole, by the end of the sixties or the early seventies, and the protests and merry carnivals degenerated into guerrilla mayhem and Dostoyevskian persecutions, and the specter of left-wing dictatorship arose.[25]

Egalitarian student radicals in Catholic France during the 1960s were no less crusading or Manichaean than American student radicals of the same decade. Although separated by different national and religious traditions, the New Left in Europe and the United States shared a commitment to a radical egalitarian way of life, and with that shared preference came common organizational and ideological dilemmas and pathologies.

There is a further problem with invoking a disembodied Protestant spirit that exists totally apart from social or institutional relations. Permanently lodging Protestant zeal "deep in the American consciousness" begs too many questions.[26] How does such zeal lodge there in the first place? What stops such traditions from being dislodged or pried loose from the collective memory? To explain why some Americans have expressed a fervent commitment to transforming a corrupt and selfish society into a virtuous and cooperative commonwealth, it is not sufficient to invoke distant Puritan ancestors or ethereal Protestant spirits. One needs also to ask about the social and political experiences that create an affinity for this style of thought. If Mary Douglas is right that "it takes a certain kind of social experience to start to worry about the problem of evil," then we need to think systematically about types of social experiences.[27]

Douglas suggests that "where a man is expected to build his own career by transacting with all and sundry as widely as possible, ... men are not set on either side of a line dividing sheep from goats." Under these competitive conditions, people "are seen to be unequally endowed with talents, but the inequality is random, unpredictable and unconnected with moral judgment." Rigid boundaries separating good from evil would be dysfunctional to the individualistic entrepreneur, as they would serve only to impede individual transactions. It is in strongly bounded but internally egalitarian collectivities, Douglas argues, that rigid distinctions between "pure, good men and utterly vile men" will flourish. The central organizational dilemma for people who wish to live a collective, egalitarian life is how to keep the group together in the absence of coercive sanctions. Belief in an evil and corrupt outside world serves to knit together the members of the group by reminding them of their precarious position as a "city on the hill." The rigid dichotomy between a good inside and an evil outside thus serves to legitimize their preferred pattern of social relations.[28]

Even where sectarian Protestantism clearly and identifiably shaped language and thought, as is the case with the abolitionists, Douglas's emphasis on social organization remains illuminating as a complementary mode of analysis. Sectarian Protestantism is itself a form of radical egalitarianism, that is, a way of life combining strong group boundaries with a rejection of hierarchical relationships. Viewed in this way, radical Protestantism becomes an instance of a more general phenomenon, thereby directing our attention to what it was about radical Protestantism that sustained a preoccupation with moral purity and corrupting evil. Religion ceases to become a conversation stopper, the explanation of last resort, but rather itself becomes opened up to cultural analysis.

Toward a Liberal Egalitarianism

In recent years, a number of left-leaning intellectuals have begun trying to formulate a "radical liberalism" or "egalitarian liberalism."[29] The aim is to nurture an egalitarian sensibility attuned to economic injustices and social inequalities but simultaneously appreciative of the core components of liberalism: constitutionalism; representative government; free and competitive elections; toleration; freedom of conscience, expression, and assembly; freedom to buy and sell in the market; and separation of state and civil society. In Benjamin Barber's recent formulation, this is an egalitarianism that "must act as democrats first and as social egalitarians second," an egalitarianism that insists "that without the safeguards of liberalism, no struggle for inclusion will be worth winning."[30]

This is an important intellectual enterprise that promises to look the failings of authoritarian socialism square in the face, and asks how one can combine egalitarian redistribution with liberal democracy. Egalitarians are right to insist that liberalism should not be equated with a laissez-faire philosophy of minimal government.[31] Certainly, redistributive or welfare measures are not inherently illiberal. A society with a progressive income tax is not any less liberal than a society with a flat tax. Equality and liberty are certainly often in conflict, but so are virtually all of the social goods we desire in this world. Liberal democracy requires that we acknowledge and balance these rival values and interests, not that we always resolve this tension by coming down on the side of liberty over equality. The libertarian who insists that each step taken in the direction of equality must lead inevitably to the final extinction of liberty betrays an absolutist, even illiberal, sensibility that is little different from the radical egalitarian who insists that liberty is meaningless until we have true equality.[32]

A heightened sensitivity to the inevitable and profound inequalities generated by capitalist markets is arguably needed more today than ever before. The collapse of communism has left liberalism ascendant across most of the industrial world, but, as Ira Katznelson has recently cautioned, "liberalism's current welcome hegemony . . . invites a certain complacency about liberalism's effectuality and prospects."[33] A self-congratulatory and self-satisfied liberalism may be even more inclined to slight or ignore the great inequalities that are inevitably produced in a capitalist economy. Given the strength of capitalist values, at least in the United States, it is perhaps unlikely that society will overlook the merits of competitive markets and private property (both of which are indispensable to a liberal polity),[34] and decidedly more probable that the American polity (although not American universities, where anticapitalist sentiment runs strong) will downplay or ignore the limitations of competitive capitalism.

Joseph Schumpeter, no friend of egalitarianism, wrote of capitalism's enormous capacity for "creative destruction." Today, capitalism's defenders are eager to embrace the creative side of the market but lack Schumpeter's unflinching honesty in acknowledging the market's need to destroy in order to create. Newt Gingrich and other Republican leaders are fond of blaming the breakdown of close-knit communities and families on the Great Society and the New Left of the 1960s (usually conflating these two radically different phenomena), but the uncomfortable truth is that any such "breakdown" has as much or more to do with the creative destruction of a market system that encourages the free mobility of persons and capital. In such a society, the egalitarian voices of fraternity and community ("it takes a village") as well as the more hierarchical visions of ordered community will continue to resonate in American life. And rightly so.

The inherent problems with capitalism, not to mention the inherent limitations of hierarchical institutions and values (there are inherent problems, of course, with *any* set of human arrangements or institutions), mean that there is always a need for advocates of egalitarianism in liberal politics. The moral outrage of the egalitarian draws the political system's attention to cruelty, humiliation, and abuse that those in positions of power would often just as soon ignore. A liberal democracy needs strong and even strident egalitarian voices to shatter the hypocrisies and smug indifference that often envelop ruling groups. A voice of outrage cannot always be expected to be a voice of civility and moderation, and yet neither must it be the illiberal and antidemocratic voice that it has too often become.

Liberal egalitarianism is absolutely not an oxymoron. It must begin, though, with the recognition that it is liberal democracy's virtue, as Barber insists, that "its expectations are so earthbound," just as it is "communism's vice that its values are so stratospheric." Liberal egalitarians will put "politics first, then economics; a prudent democracy and a limited government, and then, once power is accountable and limited, its use on behalf of social justice."[35] Not inequalities per se, but the vulnerability to abuse and cruelty that comes with poverty and dependency should be the focus of liberal egalitarianism. Even more important, liberal egalitarianism must privilege politics over purity. Egalitarianism becomes most pathological when purity becomes an end in itself and the limitations, ambiguities, and paradoxes of life are brushed aside or crammed into an impoverished victimology. Finally, a liberal egalitarianism would have no place for the illusion that the political arena can be usefully understood as a place where the benighted forces of reaction square off against the enlightened few. Instead, liberal egalitarianism would recognize that political life necessarily involves trade-offs between rival values. "In the world we live in," Leszek Kolakowski teaches, "contradictions cannot be reconciled. . . . Contradictions pursue us as long as we act in a world of values, which simply means for as long as we live."[36]

NOTES

PREFACE

1. Martin Duberman, "Bloom Buried," *Nation*, October 7, 1996, p. 25 (review of Lawrence W. Levine, *The Opening of the American Mind: Canons, Culture, and History* [Boston: Beacon Press, 1996]).

2. See "Which Side Are You On?", an SDS pamphlet in SDS Microfilm, Series 4B, No. 169, Wisconsin State Historical Society, Madison.

3. Harvey C. Mansfield, "The Legacy of the Late Sixties," in Stephen Macedo, ed., *Reassessing the Sixties: Debating the Political and Cultural Legacy* (New York: Norton, 1997), 34.

4. Cf. Daphne Patai and Noretta Koertge's experience in writing *Professing Feminism: Cautionary Tales from the Strange World of Women's Studies* (New York: New Republic Books, 1994), a book that is sharply critical of women's studies programs. In a prologue ("On Airing Dirty Linen") they report that "even the people who basically agree with us [about the problems of women's studies programs] often remarked during interviews how important it is not to criticize feminism in a way that would give legitimacy to the political and religious right" (xiv). When they told colleagues what they were up to, they were immediately met with "expressions of concern about . . . the possible appropriation by political enemies of any open critique of feminism" (xvi).

5. George Orwell, "Through a Glass, Rosily," in *The Collected Essays, Journalism and Letters of George Orwell: In Front of Your Nose, 1945–1950*, ed. Sonia Orwell and Ian Angus (New York: Harcourt Brace Jovanovich, 1968), IV:34.

6. Cf. Jackson Lears's comment about the late Christopher Lasch: "Lasch insisted on darkening the American progressive tradition, but that was his way of toughening it" (Jackson Lears, "The Man Who Knew Too Much: The Grim Optimism of Christopher Lasch," *New Republic*, October 2, 1995, 44). Similar in spirit are the reflections of Lasch's mentor, Richard Hofstadter, who, in the introduction to *The Age of Reform: From Bryan to FDR* (New York: Vintage, 1955), described himself as "criticizing largely from within . . . the Populist-Progressive tradition." His aim, he explained, was "to reveal some of the limitations of that tradition and to help free it of its sentimentalities and complacencies" (12, 15).

7. More surprising and worthy of further attention, though, are the ways in which some contemporary conservatives have adopted a Manichaean outlook and moral absolutism that resemble nothing so much as the New Left they so abhor. The demonization of President Clinton and, even more so, Hillary Clinton by some right-wing

activists is comparable to the New Left's rabid loathing of Lyndon Johnson and Richard Nixon. Republican Majority Whip Tom Delay's description of the Environmental Protection Agency as "the gestapo of government" ("Morning Edition," August 2, 1995, National Public Radio) is the sort of indiscriminate and overheated rhetoric that was a staple of late 1960s radicalism. These points are made by Todd Gitlin in his Afterword to Macedo, ed., *Reassessing the Sixties*, especially 287–88, but Gitlin goes too far in claiming that "today virtually all the terrible simplifiers are on the right" (285).

8. T. W. Adorno et al., *The Authoritarian Personality* (New York: Harper, 1950). Herbert McClosky and Alida Brill, *Dimensions of Tolerance: What Americans Believe About Civil Liberties* (New York: Russell Sage, 1983), chapter 7. Paul M. Sniderman et al., "The Fallacy of Democratic Elitism: Elite Competition and Commitment to Civil Liberties," *British Journal of Political Science* 21 (1991), 349–70.

9. See Ira Katznelson, *Liberalism's Crooked Circle: Letters to Adam Michnik* (Princeton, N.J.: Princeton University Press, 1996), 16; Stephen Holmes, *Passions and Constraint: On the Theory of Liberal Democracy* (Chicago: University of Chicago Press, 1995), 1–2, 13–41; and Stephen Holmes, *The Anatomy of Antiliberalism* (Cambridge, Mass.: Harvard University Press, 1993), 3–4.

10. Judith N. Shklar, "The Liberalism of Fear," in Nancy Rosenblum, ed., *Liberalism and the Moral Life* (Cambridge, Mass.: Harvard University Press, 1989), 21. Also see Oren M. Levin-Waldman, *Reconceiving Liberalism: Dilemmas of Contemporary Public Policy* (Pittsburgh, Pa.: University of Pittsburgh Press, 1996), xi.

11. Cf. Hofstadter: "What appeals to me in the New Conservatism, in so far as anything does at all, is simply the old liberalism, chastened by adversity, tempered by time, and modulated by a growing sense of reality" (*Age of Reform*, 15).

12. Shklar, "Liberalism of Fear," 27, 21. Also see Bernard Yack, "Liberalism Without Illusions: An Introduction to Judith Shklar's Political Thought," in Yack, ed., *Liberalism Without Illusions: Essays on Liberal Theory and the Political Vision of Judith N. Shklar* (Chicago: University of Chicago Press, 1996), 1–13.

13. Shklar, "Liberalism of Fear," 31. Judith N. Shklar, *Ordinary Vices* (Cambridge, Mass.: Harvard University Press, 1984), 29. Also see Holmes, *Passions and Constraint*, especially 254, 17.

14. Cf. Avishai Margalit: "Why characterize the decent society negatively, as non-humiliating, rather than positively, as one that, for example, respects its members? . . . The moral reason stems from my conviction that there is a weighty asymmetry between eradicating evil and promoting good. It is much more urgent to remove painful evils than to create enjoyable benefits. Humiliation is a painful evil, while respect is a benefit. Therefore eliminating humiliation should be given priority over paying respect" (*The Decent Society* [Cambridge, Mass.: Harvard University Press, 1996], 4).

15. Isaiah Berlin, *The Crooked Timber of Humanity: Chapters in the History of Ideas* (New York: Vintage, 1992), 13, 17. Also see Leszek Kolakowski, "Marxist Roots of Stalinism," in Robert C. Tucker, ed., *Stalinism: Essays in Historical Interpretation* (New York: Norton, 1977), especially 284, 296; and Joseph Schwartz, *The Permanence of the*

Political: A Democratic Critique of the Radical Impulse to Transcend Politics (Princeton, N.J.: Princeton University Press, 1995).

INTRODUCTION

1. Lewis Coser and Irving Howe, "Authoritarians of the 'Left,'" *Dissent* 2 (Winter 1955), 40.

2. Richard Hofstadter, *The Age of Reform: From Bryan to FDR* (New York: Vintage, 1955). In the *Social Sciences Citation Index* between 1991 and 1995, the *Age of Reform* was the most frequently cited of Hofstadter's many books. In fact, it was cited as many times as his two next most frequently cited books (*Social Darwinism in American Thought* and *Anti-Intellectualism in American Life*) combined. A 1993 poll of subscribers to the *Journal of American History* asked which three or four books had most influenced them, and found that *The Age of Reform* ranked behind only the Bible, Tocqueville's *Democracy in America*, E. P. Thompson's *The Making of the English Working Class*, and Hofstadter's own earlier book, *The American Political Tradition*. When subscribers were asked which three or four historical monographs they most admired, *Age of Reform* ranked eighth, well ahead of any of his other books, including *The American Political Tradition*. See Appendix 3 in the *Journal of American History* 81 (December 1994), especially 1203, 1206, as well as David Thelen, "The Practice of American History," *Journal of American History* 81 (December 1994), 953. Also see Daniel Joseph Singal, "Beyond Consensus: Richard Hofstadter and American Historiography," *American Historical Review* 89 (October 1984), 988.

3. Hofstadter, *Age of Reform*, 20, 21, 16.

4. Vernon L. Parrington, *Main Currents in American Thought*, 3 vols. (New York: Harcourt, Brace, 1930). Daniel Aaron, *Men of Good Hope: A Story of American Progressives* (New York: Oxford University Press, 1951).

5. See David Thelen, "Social Tensions and the Origins of Progressivism," *Journal of American History* 56 (September 1969), 323–41, especially 330–34; and Gerald W. McFarland, "Inside Reform: Status and Other Evil Motives," *Soundings* 54 (Summer 1971), 164–76. Also see Leonard L. Richards, *"Gentlemen of Property and Standing": Anti-Abolition Mobs in Jacksonian America* (New York: Oxford University Press, 1970), especially 140–44.

6. Michael Paul Rogin, *The Intellectuals and McCarthy: The Radical Specter* (Cambridge, Mass.: MIT Press, 1967).

7. See, for example, Walter T. K. Nugent, *The Tolerant Populists: Kansas Populism and Nativism* (Chicago: University of Chicago Press, 1963), and C. Vann Woodward, "The Populist Heritage and the Intellectual" (1959), in Woodward, *The Burden of Southern History*, rev. ed. (Baton Rouge: Louisiana State University Press, 1968), 141–66.

8. Hofstadter, *Age of Reform*, 22.

9. See, for example, Victor Christopher Ferkiss, "Populist Influences on American Fascism," *Western Political Quarterly* 10 (June 1957), 350–73.

10. Richard Hofstadter, *The Paranoid Style in American Politics and Other Essays* (New York: Vintage, 1967). The other three essays were more loosely tied together under the heading "Some Problems of the Modern Era." Of those, only the last essay, "Free Silver and the Mind of 'Coin' Harvey," extended the argument of *The Age of Reform* in a way that contributed to our understanding of the illiberalism of the left.

11. Hofstadter, *Paranoid Style*, vii.

12. Mark E. Kann, *Middle-Class Radicalism in Santa Monica* (Philadelphia: Temple University Press, 1986), 249.

13. David Donald, "Toward a Reconsideration of the Abolitionists," in Donald, *Lincoln Reconsidered: Essays on the Civil War Era*, 2d ed., enl. (New York: Vintage, 1961), 19–36.

14. Cf. Bertram Wyatt Brown's comment that "the term *paranoia* condemns as much as it explains. . . . Psychiatric metaphors, no matter how sophisticated in definition, carry uncomfortable risks and limitations" (*Yankee Saints and Southern Sinners* [Baton Rouge: Louisiana State University Press, 1985], 98).

15. Hofstadter, *Paranoid Style*, ix.

16. Hofstadter more clearly distinguished "projective politics" from "status politics or cultural politics" in "Pseudo-Conservatism Revisited: A Postscript" (1962), in Daniel Bell, ed., *The Radical Right* (New York: Anchor Books, 1964), 100. In this postscript he regretted the "excessive emphasis on what might be called the clinical side of the problem" (100). Similarly, in *The Paranoid Style*, Hofstadter admitted that his earlier formulation "overstressed clinical findings" (67).

17. Mary Douglas, "Introduction to Grid/Group Analysis," in Mary Douglas, ed., *Essays in the Sociology of Perception* (London: Routledge and Kegan Paul, 1982), 7.

18. The category of egalitarianism is one of four categories derived from Mary Douglas's typology of "grid" and "group." The other types are competitive individualism, hierarchy, and fatalism. The categories and typology are elaborated, among other places, in Mary Douglas, "Cultural Bias," in Douglas, *In the Active Voice* (London: Routledge and Kegan Paul, 1982), 183–254; Mary Douglas and Aaron Wildavsky, *Risk and Culture* (Berkeley: University of California Press, 1982); Douglas, *Essays in the Sociology of Perception;* Jonathan Gross and Steve Rayner, *Measuring Culture: A Paradigm for the Analysis of Social Organization* (New York: Columbia University Press, 1986); Aaron Wildavsky, "Choosing Preferences by Constructing Institutions: A Cultural Theory of Preference Formation," *American Political Science Review* 81 (March 1987), 3–21; Steve Rayner, "The Rules That Keep Us Equal," in James G. Flanagan and Steve Rayner, eds., *Rules, Decisions, and Inequality in Egalitarian Societies* (Aldershot, Eng.: Avebury, 1988), 20–42; Michael Thompson, Richard Ellis, and Aaron Wildavsky, *Cultural Theory* (Boulder, Colo.: Westview Press, 1990); Michiel Schwartz and Michael Thompson, *Divided We Stand: Redefining Politics, Technology and Social Choice* (London: Harvester Wheatsheaf, 1990); Mary Douglas, *Risk and Blame: Essays in Cultural Theory* (London: Routledge, 1992); Richard J. Ellis, *American Political Cultures* (New York: Oxford University Press, 1993); and Dennis J. Coyle and Richard J. Ellis, eds., *Politics, Policy and Culture* (Boulder, Colo.: Westview Press, 1994).

19. Thomas Sowell, *A Conflict of Visions: Ideological Origins of Political Struggles* (New York: Quill, 1987), 88.

20. This is not to say that egalitarians desire absolute equality of condition. As Thomas Sowell explains, both process-oriented and results-oriented visions of equality "recognize degrees of equality, so the disagreement between them is not over absolute mathematical equality versus some degree of equalization, but rather over just what it is that is to be equalized" (*A Conflict of Visions*, 122). Also see Ellis, *American Political Cultures*, chapter 3.

21. See John H. Schaar, "Equality of Opportunity and Beyond," in Roland Pennock and John Chapman, eds., *Equality* (New York: Atherton, 1967), 228–49.

22. James Miller, *"Democracy Is in the Streets": From Port Huron to the Siege of Chicago* (New York: Touchstone, 1987), 90.

23. Max Eastman, "Motive-Patterns of Socialism," *Modern Quarterly* 11 (Fall 1939), 46.

24. Among the more obvious groups that I have left out are the Socialist party and the Industrial Workers of the World (IWW). Particularly relevant are Daniel Bell, *Marxian Socialism in the United States* (Princeton, N.J.: Princeton University Press, 1967), and Aileen Kraditor, *The Radical Persuasion, 1890–1917: Aspects of the Intellectual History and the Historiography of Three American Radical Organizations* (Baton Rouge: Louisiana State University Press, 1981).

25. See the sage warnings in Ronald G. Walters, "The Boundaries of Abolitionism," in Lewis Perry and Michael Fellman, eds., *Antislavery Reconsidered: New Perspectives on the Abolitionists* (Baton Rouge: Louisiana State University Press, 1979), 8; and Lewis Perry, *Radical Abolitionism: Anarchy and the Government of God in Antislavery Thought* (Ithaca, N.Y.: Cornell University Press, 1973), 297, 320.

26. Richard Hofstadter, *The Progressive Historians: Turner, Beard, Parrington* (New York: Vintage, 1970), 465; also see Hofstadter, *Age of Reform*, 22.

27. See Stephen Macedo, ed., *Reassessing the Sixties: Debating the Political and Cultural Legacy* (New York: Norton, 1997).

28. Jean L. Cohen, "Strategy or Identity: New Theoretical Paradigms and Contemporary Social Movements," *Social Research* 52 (Winter 1985), 668–69.

29. See Karen Orren, *Belated Feudalism: Labor, the Law, and Liberal Development in the United States* (Cambridge: Cambridge University Press, 1991).

30. Judith N. Shklar, "The Liberalism of Fear," in Nancy Rosenblum, ed., *Liberalism and the Moral Life* (Cambridge, Mass.: Harvard University Press, 1989), 24.

31. Randolph Bourne, "Twilight of Idols," in Olaf Hansen, ed., *Randolph Bourne: The Radical Will, Selected Writings, 1911–1918* (Berkeley: University of California Press, 1992), 347.

32. This is the argument of the admiring portrait of Wendell Phillips ("The Patrician as Agitator") in Richard Hofstadter, *The American Political Tradition* (New York: Vintage, 1973), and of Aileen Kraditor's analysis of the Garrisonian abolitionists in *Means and Ends in American Abolitionism: Garrison and His Critics on Strategy and Tactics, 1834–1850* (New York: Pantheon, 1969).

33. Jon Elster, *Making Sense of Marx* (Cambridge: Cambridge University Press, 1985), 18. Also see Thompson, Ellis, and Wildavsky, *Cultural Theory*, 58.

34. Benjamin R. Barber, "An Epitaph for Marxism," *Society* 33 (November/December 1995), 23, 25.

CHAPTER 1. Radical Abolitionism

1. Judith N. Shklar, *Ordinary Vices* (Cambridge, Mass.: Harvard University Press, 1984), 44.

2. Max Weber, "Politics as a Vocation," in H. H. Gerth and C. Wright Mills, eds., *From Max Weber: Essays in Sociology* (New York: Oxford University Press, 1946), 122.

3. Russell B. Nye, *Fettered Freedom: Civil Liberties and the Slavery Controversy, 1830–1860* (East Lansing: Michigan State College Press, 1949).

4. Leonard L. Richards, *"Gentlemen of Property and Standing": Anti-Abolition Mobs in Jacksonian America* (New York: Oxford University Press, 1970).

5. See Silvan S. Tomkins, "The Psychology of Commitment: The Constructive Role of Violence and Suffering for the Individual and for His Society," in Martin Duberman, ed., *The Antislavery Vanguard: New Essays on the Abolitionists* (Princeton, N.J.: Princeton University Press, 1965), 283, 292–94.

6. This tension between "the purity of the church and the reform of society" is highlighted in the context of New England puritanism and those political cultures that evolved from puritanism in J. David Greenstone, *The Lincoln Persuasion: Remaking American Liberalism* (Princeton, N.J.: Princeton University Press, 1993), especially 265–74.

7. Lawrence J. Friedman, *Gregarious Saints: Self and Community in American Abolitionism, 1830–1870* (Cambridge: Cambridge University Press, 1982), 1.

8. Much of the material in this section has been adapted from Richard Ellis and Aaron Wildavsky, "A Cultural Analysis of the Role of Abolitionists in the Coming of the Civil War," *Comparative Studies in Society and History* 32 (January 1990), 89–116; and Richard J. Ellis, *American Political Cultures* (New York: Oxford University Press, 1993), 16–20.

9. Ronald G. Walters, *The Antislavery Appeal: American Abolitionism After 1830* (Baltimore: Johns Hopkins University Press, 1976), 33.

10. Friedman, *Gregarious Saints*, 63–64; Lewis Perry, *Radical Abolitionism: Anarchy and the Government of God in Antislavery Thought* (Ithaca, N.Y.: Cornell University Press, 1973), 57–58; Garrison quoted in John Demos, "The Antislavery Movement and the Problem of Violent 'Means,'" *New England Quarterly* 37 (December 1964), 513. Also see "William Lloyd Garrison Repudiates the Government of the United States," in John L. Thomas, ed., *Slavery Attacked: The Abolitionist Crusade* (Englewood Cliffs, N.J.: Prentice-Hall, 1965), 76–79. On the extreme anti-authority views of radical abolitionists, in addition to Perry, *Radical Abolitionism* and Friedman, *Gregarious Saints*, see also George M. Fredrickson, *The Inner Civil War: Northern Intellectuals and the Crisis of the Union*, chapter 1; Stanley M. Elkins, *Slavery: A Problem in American Institutional and Intellectual Life*, 3d ed. (Chicago: University of Chicago Press, 1976), part IV; and Peter Brock, *Radical Pacifists in Antebellum America* (Princeton, N.J.: Princeton University Press, 1968), chapter 3, especially 89.

11. Blanche Glassman Hersh, *The Slavery of Sex: Feminist-Abolitionists in America* (Urbana: University of Illinois Press, 1978), vii, 224; Friedman, *Gregarious Saints*, 142 and chapter 5 passim.

12. Walters, *Antislavery Appeal*, 93. Perry, *Radical Abolitionism*, 230. Hersh, *Slavery of Sex*, 219, 225. Also see Dorothy Sterling, *Ahead of Her Time: Abby Kelley and the Politics of Anti-Slavery* (New York: Norton, 1991).

13. Walters, *Antislavery Appeal*, 72.

14. Ibid., 41, 43, 44. Perry, *Radical Abolitionism*, 106. Also see Robert H. Abzug, *Passionate Liberator: Theodore Dwight Weld and the Dilemma of Reform* (New York: Oxford University Press, 1980), 199–200; Fredrickson, *Inner Civil War*, 8–9; and John R. McKivigan, *The War Against Proslavery Religion: Abolitionism and the Northern Churches, 1830–1865* (Ithaca, N.Y.: Cornell University Press, 1984).

15. Perry, *Radical Abolitionism*, 105. Walters, *Antislavery Appeal*, 47.

16. Walters, *Antislavery Appeal*, 48, 45–46. Perry, *Radical Abolitionism*, 57.

17. Jonathon A. Glickstein, "'Poverty Is Not Slavery': American Abolitionists and the Competitive Labor Market," in Lewis Perry and Michael Fellman, eds., *Antislavery Reconsidered: New Perspectives on the Abolitionists* (Baton Rouge: Louisiana State University Press, 1979), 198n6. Also see John Ashworth, *Slavery, Capitalism, and Politics in the Antebellum Republic* (Cambridge: Cambridge University Press, 1995), chapter 3, especially 191.

18. Friedman, *Gregarious Saints*, 97, 4. Lawrence J. Friedman, "'Pious Fellowship' and Modernity: A Psychosocial Modernity," in Alan M. Kraut, ed., *Crusaders and Compromisers: Essays on the Relationship of the Antislavery Struggle to the Antebellum Party System* (Westport, Conn.: Greenwood Press, 1983), 241. A decade after the Civil War, Wendell Phillips recalled fondly "the large and loving group [the Boston Clique] that lived and worked together . . . [and had been] all the world to each other" (Friedman, *Gregarious Saints*, 66).

19. Friedman, *Gregarious Saints*, 68. John Thomas, "Antislavery and Utopia," in Duberman, *Antislavery Vanguard*, 247.

20. Friedman, *Gregarious Saints*, 44. James Brewer Stewart, *William Lloyd Garrison and the Challenge of Emancipation* (Arlington Heights, Ill.: Harlan Davidson, 1992), 129.

21. Walters, *Antislavery Appeal*, 111, 119, 113. After the Civil War, Phillips would go much further and call for "the overthrow of the whole profit-making system" (quoted in Richard Hofstadter, *The American Political Tradition* [New York: Vintage, 1973], 202).

22. Walters, *Antislavery Appeal*, 112, 148. Also see Daniel J. McInerney, "'A State of Commerce': Market Power and Slave Power in Abolitionist Political Economy," *Civil War History* 37 (June 1991), 101–19. "In the eyes of [abolitionist] reformers," McInerney shows, "the slavepower built a world on the model of the market: it merchandised mankind, encoded accumulation, and systematized selfishness" (107). "The slavepower," in the abolitionists' indictment, "dominated economic relations, internalized the mercenary standards of the marketplace, . . . made the market the measure of all things, [and] . . . hoped to subordinate the polity and society completely to the principles of economic transaction" (102–3).

23. Friedman, "'Pious Fellowship' and Modernity," 242. Thomas, "Antislavery and Utopia," 263. Ronald G. Walters, *American Reformers, 1815–1860* (New York: Hill and Wang, 1978), 37. Walters, *Antislavery Appeal*, 127.

24. Thomas, "Antislavery and Utopia," 249–52. Walters, *American Reformers,* 49–50.

25. John L. Thomas, *The Liberator: William Lloyd Garrison* (Boston: Little, Brown, 1963), 312–13. Thomas, "Antislavery and Utopia," 254–57.

26. Thomas, "Antislavery and Utopia," 260–63, quotation at 263.

27. John L. Thomas, "Romantic Reform in America, 1815–1866," *American Quarterly* 17 (Winter 1965), 678.

28. Friedman, *Gregarious Saints,* 67.

29. Thomas, *The Liberator,* 315. Thomas, "Antislavery and Utopia," 251.

30. An anonymous contributor to the *Liberator,* quoted in Arthur Bestor, *Backwoods Utopias,* 2d ed. (Philadelphia: University of Pennsylvania Press, 1970), 19.

31. Quoted in Walters, *American Reformers,* 77. Also see Aileen S. Kraditor, *Means and Ends in American Abolitionism: Garrison and His Critics on Strategy and Tactics, 1834–1850* (New York: Vintage, 1967), 252.

32. For insightful reflections on "the problem of dirty hands," see Michael Walzer, "Political Action: The Problem of Dirty Hands," *Philosophy and Public Affairs* 2 (Winter 1973), 160–80.

33. On the wartime popularity and prestige of the abolitionists, see James M. McPherson, *The Struggle for Equality: Abolitionists and the Negro in the Civil War and Reconstruction* (Princeton, N.J.: Princeton University Press, 1964), 81–90, 127–32, 299–300.

34. Some of the material in this section has been adapted from Richard Ellis and Aaron Wildavsky, *Dilemmas of Presidential Leadership: From Washington Through Lincoln* (New Brunswick, N.J.: Transaction Publishers, 1989), 188–93.

35. McPherson, *Struggle for Equality,* 103–4, 59–60; also see 10.

36. William Lloyd Garrison, Jr., Moncure Conway, and Wendell Phillips, quoted in ibid., 52, 55. Also see Gerritt Smith, quoted in Brock, *Radical Pacifists,* 240; and Samuel May, Jr., quoted in Friedman, *Gregarious Saints,* 210.

37. Gerrit Smith to Garrison, September 2, 1861, quoted in McPherson, *Struggle for Equality,* 60. The government, Garrison assured another abolitionist, "is entirely in the right" (Garrison to T. B. Drew, April 25, 1861, quoted in ibid., 52).

38. Phillips, "Under the Flag," delivered in the Music Hall, Boston, April 21, 1861, before the 28th Congregational Society, in Wendell Phillips, *Speeches, Lectures and Letters,* 2 vol. (Boston: Lee and Shepard, 1891), 1:400, 414. Also see Irving Bartlett, *Wendell Phillips: Brahmin Radical* (Boston: Beacon Press, 1961), 238–39.

39. Fredrickson, *Inner Civil War,* 69.

40. This was the language Phillips himself used in the pages of the *Liberator,* where he warned that unless the war was prosecuted for the purpose of removing slavery it would leave the "bloodiest stain of the century" (July 12, 1861, cited in Bartlett, *Wendell Phillips,* 241).

41. *Liberator,* October 11, 1861, p. 164. Bartlett, *Wendell Phillips,* 245. McPherson, *Struggle for Equality,* 72–73.

42. J. G. Randall, *Lincoln the President: Springfield to Gettysburg,* 2 vols. (New York: Dodd, Mead, 1945), 2:22. *Liberator,* September, 20, 1861; Garrison to Oliver Johnson, October 7, 1861; *National Anti-Slavery Standard,* September 28, 1961; and

B. Rush Plumly to Salmon Chase, October 19, 1861; all quoted in McPherson, *Struggle for Equality*, 73–74.

43. *Liberator*, December 6, 1861; Garrison to Oliver Johnson, December 6, 1861; and Gerrit Smith to Thaddeus Stevens, December 6, 1861; all quoted in McPherson, *Struggle for Equality*, 94; S. York to Lyman Trumbull, December 5, 1861, quoted in Randall, *Lincoln the President*, 2:27.

44. Bartlett, *Wendell Phillips*, 261.

45. See Phillips, "Capital Punishment," plea before a committee of the Massachusetts Legislature, March 16, 1855, in *Speeches, Lectures and Letters*, 2:77–109.

46. *Liberator*, February 13, 1863, quoted in Bartlett, *Wendell Phillips*, 262. Wendell Phillips, "The State of the Country," speeches in New York, January 21 and May 11, 1863, in *Speeches, Lectures and Letters*, 1:556; also see 1:551.

47. "Letter from President Lincoln," *Liberator*, May 6, 1864, p. 73. Cf. Lincoln's comments to a delegation from the Religious Society of Progressive Friends in which he agrees with the memorialists that "slavery was wrong" ("Interview with the President on Emancipation," *Liberator*, June 27, 1862, p. 102).

48. Phillips, "The War for the Union," lecture delivered in New York and Boston, December 1861, in *Speeches, Lectures and Letters*, 1:436. Cf. the comments by Charles Whipple, the *Liberator*'s editorial assistant: "[Lincoln's] arrests of manifest allies of the enemy, his suppression of treasonable newspapers, and his interference with the numerous movements by which aid and comfort have been given to rebels in arms, have never been half so frequent or half so effective as the exigencies of the country demand. It is absurd to expect war to be carried on otherwise than by violent and arbitrary rule. What we have a right to demand is that this arbitrary rule shall accomplish the things needful for the party or the cause that uses it." Whipple hopes that the coming election will put "in place of [Lincoln] some better man who would rejoice to use the power which war gives a president to *crush* that wickedness, and to establish liberty in its place" (*Liberator*, June 10, 1864, p. 95).

49. Phillips, "The State of the Country," in *Speeches, Lectures and Letters*, 1:552. Cf. Charles Whipple's complaint that Lincoln was a man without "back-bone" who was "content merely to follow the shifting indications of public opinion" (*Liberator*, January 8, 1864, p. 6). Not all abolitionists remained so critical of Lincoln. Garrison was the most prominent abolitionist to come to respect both Lincoln's political skill and his antislavery convictions. After Lincoln's Emancipation Proclamation, Garrison, along with many other abolitionists, became generally supportive of Lincoln. Moreover, as Garrison became more friendly toward Lincoln, he also began to temper and then to jettison altogether his oppositional stance. As a prelude to a well-earned retirement, Garrison introduced a resolution in 1865 calling for the dissolution of the American Anti-Slavery Society, since passage of the Thirteenth Amendment had abolished slavery. Garrison's resolution was defeated by better than a two-to-one margin as the abolitionist delegates overwhelmingly sided with Phillips, who argued that the society must carry on its work to secure equal rights for the freedman.

50. Phillips, "The Cabinet," speech at Abington, in the Grove, August 1, 1862, in *Speeches, Lectures and Letters*, 1:457.

51. Phillips, "The War for the Union," in *Speeches, Lectures and Letters,* 1:435.

52. Wendell Phillips, "The Puritan Principle and John Brown," delivered in the Music Hall, Boston, December 18, 1859, before the 28th Congregational Society, in *Speeches, Lectures and Letters,* 2:297.

53. T. Harry Williams, *Lincoln and the Radicals* (Madison: University of Wisconsin Press, 1941), 9. Phillips, "The State of the Country," in *Speeches, Lectures and Letters,* 1:547, 534–35.

54. Phillips, "The State of the Country," 532. *Liberator,* August 28, 1863, quoted in Brock, *Radical Pacifists,* 256–57. Donald Yacovone, *Samuel Joseph May and the Dilemmas of the Liberal Persuasion, 1797–1871* (Philadelphia: Temple University Press, 1991), 174, 176.

55. Brock, *Radical Pacifists,* 258–59.

56. *Liberator,* March 13, 1863, p. 44.

57. Brock, *Radical Pacifists,* 248.

58. *Liberator,* January 15, 1864, quoted in Brock, *Radical Pacifists,* 247.

59. Speech of William Lloyd Garrison, delivered at the annual meeting of the Massachusetts Anti-Slavery Society, January 30, 1863, in the *Liberator,* February 6, 1863, p. 22.

60. William Furness, "A Word of Consolation for the Kindred of Those Who Have Fallen in Battle," a discourse delivered September 28, 1862, quoted in Brock, *Radical Pacifists,* 243–44, and Friedman, *Gregarious Saints,* 216. The last sentence is Brock's paraphrase of Furness. Cf. Charles Sumner's grandiloquent proclamation that as a result of the war, "slavery will give way to freedom; but the good work will not stop here. . . . As the whole wide-spread tyranny begins to tumble, then, above the din of battle, sounding from the sea and echoing along the land . . . will ascend voices of gladness and benediction" (Allan G. Bogue, *The Earnest Men: Republicans of the Civil War Senate* [Ithaca, N.Y.: Cornell University Press, 1981], 154). Also see Sumner's "Grandeur of the Cause," reprinted in the *Liberator,* November 18, 1864, p. 186.

61. Friedman, *Gregarious Saints,* 214. Bartlett, *Wendell Phillips,* 391.

62. See Demos, "Antislavery Movement and the Problem of Violent Means," in Perry, *Radical Abolitionism,* chapter 8; and Friedman, *Gregarious Saints,* chapter 7, both of whom show how abolitionists had accommodated themselves to violence well before the onset of the Civil War.

63. Friedman, *Gregarious Saints,* 198. Also see Brock, *Radical Pacifists,* especially chapter 3; and Valerie H. Ziegler, *The Advocates of Peace in Antebellum America* (Bloomington: Indiana University Press, 1992), especially 48–50, 56–65.

64. Richards, *Gentlemen of Property and Standing,* 108–10. Brock, *Radical Pacifists,* 90. Friedman, *Gregarious Saints,* 200.

65. Friedman, *Gregarious Saints,* 200–201. Brock, *Radical Pacifists,* 91–93.

66. Friedman, *Gregarious Saints,* 201. Perry, *Radical Abolitionism,* 75. Also Brock, *Radical Pacifists,* 91.

67. Friedman, *Gregarious Saints,* 200–201. Brock, *Radical Pacifists,* 92. Also see Perry, *Radical Abolitionism,* 75.

68. Brock, *Radical Pacifists,* 223.

69. Richards, *Gentlemen of Property and Standing.*

70. Brock, *Radical Pacifists,* 90.

71. Friedman, *Gregarious Saints,* 199.

72. See Perry: "This accommodation to violent means took place on a highly abstract level. No wave of slave revolts forced revaluations of violence. . . . There were episodes of white resistance to the Fugitive Slave Law, but fewer than the nonresistants hoped. . . . Rather than being dragged along by history, nonresistants were in advance of the violence of their times. To account for their accommodation to the use of force, we must inspect the intellectual loopholes in their doctrine" (*Radical Abolitionism,* 239).

73. Rev. Frederick Frothingham, *Liberator,* June 26, 1857, p. 101. Friedman, *Gregarious Saints,* 197. Charles Sumner, quoted in David Brion Davis, *The Slave Power Conspiracy and the Paranoid Style* (Baton Rouge: Louisiana State University Press, 1970), 61.

74. *Liberator,* July 17, 1857, p. 116. *Liberator,* November 13, 1857, p. 184. Also see *Liberator,* July 3, 1857, p. 108.

75. Perry, *Radical Abolitionism,* 240, 242–44.

76. Ibid., 240–41. Also see Brock, *Radical Pacifists,* 233.

77. Brock, *Radical Pacifists,* 234.

78. Garrison, "The Tragedy at Harper's Ferry," *Liberator,* October 28, 1859, in William E. Cain, ed., *William Lloyd Garrison and the Fight Against Slavery: Selections from The Liberator* (Boston: Bedford Books, 1995), 154.

79. James M. McPherson, *Battle Cry of Freedom: The Civil War Era* (New York: Oxford University Press, 1988), 204.

80. Brock, *Radical Pacifists,* 230; also see 229 and McPherson, *Battle Cry of Freedom,* 204.

81. See Herbert Marcuse, "The Problem of Violence and the Radical Opposition," in Marcuse, *Five Lectures: Psychoanalysis, Politics and Utopia* (Boston: Beacon Press, 1970), 90.

82. Stephen B. Oates, *To Purge This Land with Blood: A Biography of John Brown* (New York: Harper Torchbook, 1972), 132–37, 261–64. Paul Finkelman, "Preface: John Brown and His Raid," in Finkelman, ed., *His Soul Goes Marching On: Responses to John Brown and the Harpers Ferry Raid* (Charlottesville: University Press of Virginia, 1995), 5, 6–7.

83. Oates, *To Purge This Land with Blood,* 184. Finkelman, "Preface," 5–6. Even after Brown's leading role in these heinous crimes had been definitively established, his defenders continued to seek ways to excuse and justify these brutal premeditated murders. For instance, writing in 1909, W. E. B. Du Bois, who has become something of a saint himself among certain leftist scholars today, ridiculed the "timid [who] rushed to disavow the deed." Du Bois argued that John Brown's "blow" (the same word Du Bois uses to describe the raid on Harpers Ferry) "freed Kansas by plunging it into civil war, and compelling men to fight for freedom which they had vainly hoped to gain by political diplomacy" (W. E. Burghardt Du Bois, *John Brown* [New York: International Publishers, 1962], 157). The bloodiest and most despicable deeds are justified by a righteous purpose. "To acquit, even to respect [John Brown],"

John T. Morse, Jr. commented in 1886, "it is only necessary to admit the sincerity of the belief" (Gilman M. Ostrander, "Emerson, Thoreau, and John Brown," *Mississippi Valley Historical Review* 39 [March 1953], 714).

84. Oates, *To Purge This Land*, 186. Brock, *Radical Pacifists*, 235.

85. Perry, *Radical Abolitionism*, 253–54. Oates, *To Purge This Land*, 237, 204.

86. Ostrander, "Emerson, Thoreau, and John Brown," 720. Bertram Wyatt Brown, "'A Volcano Beneath a Mountain of Snow': John Brown and the Problem of Interpretation," in Finkelman, *His Soul Goes Marching On*, 23. Oates, *To Purge This Land* 197, 395n21; also 258.

87. Paul Finkelman, "Manufacturing Martyrdom: The Antislavery Response to John Brown's Raid," in Finkelman, *His Soul Goes Marching On*, 41. Fredrickson, *Inner Civil War*, 41. Perry, *Radical Abolitionism*, 259.

88. Oates, *To Purge This Land*, 310. Finkelman, "Manufacturing Martyrdom," 41.

89. Garrison, "The Tragedy at Harper's Ferry," 153–54.

90. Garrison, "John Brown and the Principle of Nonresistance," *Liberator*, December 16, 1859, in Cain, *Garrison and the Fight Against Slavery*, 156–57. Also see Friedman, *Gregarious Saints*, 211.

91. Perry, *Radical Abolitionism*, 258. Brock, *Radical Pacifists*, 238.

92. Perry, *Radical Abolitionism*, 252, 258.

93. "John Brown as a Hero," *Liberator*, July 2, 1859, p. 190.

94. Perry, *Radical Abolitionism*, 248.

95. Ostrander, "Emerson, Thoreau and John Brown," 720. Oates, *To Purge This Land*, 197. Emerson went on to say: "[Brown] charms us, because it indicates that a man loves an idea better than all things in the world, that he is thinking neither of his bed, nor his dinner, nor his money, but will venture all to put in act the invisible thought of his mind" (Fredrickson, *Inner Civil War*, 40).

96. "John Brown as a Hero," *Liberator*, July 2, 1859, p. 190.

97. Garrison, "The Tragedy at Harper's Ferry," 154.

98. See Ostrander, "Emerson, Thoreau, and John Brown," 714.

99. William Henry Furness, quoted in Finkelman, "Manufacturing Martyrdom," 43. Thoreau described the martyred Brown as the "embodiment of principle" (Perry, *Radical Abolitionism*, 256). Du Bois writes of Brown's "clean and pure soul" (Du Bois, *John Brown*, 338). Also see Wendell Phillips, "Harper's Ferry" and "The Puritan Principle and John Brown," in *Speeches, Lectures and Letters*, 1:263–88, 2:294–308.

100. Perry, *Radical Abolitionism*, 256. Similarly, Emerson described Brown as a man "so transparent that all men see him through" (Ostrander, "Emerson, Thoreau, and John Brown," 720). Cf. Du Bois: "Such a light was the soul of John Brown. He was simple, exasperatingly simple; unlettered, plain, and homely. No casuistry of culture or of learning, or well-being or tradition moved him in the slightest degree" (*John Brown*, 340). In fact, Brown was an inveterate and skilled liar who managed to deceive most of New England about his past role in "Bloody Kansas" and about his future plans for the invasion of Virginia.

101. Ostrander, "Emerson, Thoreau, and John Brown," 721.

102. Brock, *Radical Pacifists*, 239. Also see Friedman, *Gregarious Saints*, 209.

103. Perry, *Radical Abolitionism*, 265; also see 266–67.

104. Friedman, *Gregarious Saints*, 214, 212.

105. Shklar, "Putting Cruelty First," in *Ordinary Vices*, 7–44. Judith Shklar, "The Liberalism of Fear," in Nancy Rosenblum, ed., *Liberalism and the Moral Life* (Cambridge, Mass.: Harvard University Press, 1989), 27, 29.

106. Elizabeth B. Clark, "'The Sacred Rights of the Weak': Pain, Sympathy, and the Culture of Individual Rights in Antebellum America," *Journal of American History* 82 (September 1995), 490, 488, 463. Clark explicitly invokes Shklar's essay, "Putting Cruelty First," on pages 488–90.

107. Following her opening chapter, "Putting Cruelty First," Shklar analyzes the dangers of putting hypocrisy first in the next chapter, "Let Us Not Be Hypocritical."

108. Stewart, *Garrison and the Challenge of Emancipation*, 124–26. William E. Cain, "Introduction: William Lloyd Garrison and the Fight Against Slavery," in Cain, *Garrison and the Fight Against Slavery*, 29–30.

109. Ellis, *American Political Cultures*, 83.

110. Shklar, *Ordinary Vices*, especially 237. Shklar, "Liberalism of Fear," 29.

111. Phillips, "Harper's Ferry," in *Speeches, Lectures, and Letters*, 1:272.

112. Shklar, *Ordinary Vices*, 21.

113. Shklar, "Liberalism of Fear," 29.

114. Sarah Grimké to Gerrit Smith, June 28, 1837, in Gilbert H. Barnes and Dwight L. Dumond, eds., *Letters of Theodore Dwight Weld, Angelina Grimké Weld and Sarah Grimké, 1822–1844*, 2 vol. (Gloucester, Mass.: Peter Smith, 1965), 1:408. Also see Brock, *Radical Pacifists*, 89.

CHAPTER 2. Illiberal Utopianism in the Age of Reform

1. A comment entered into one of Mark Twain's notebooks while he was writing *A Connecticut Yankee in King Arthur's Court*. Quoted in Kenneth Roemer, *The Obsolete Necessity: America in Utopian Writings, 1888–1900* (Kent, Ohio: Kent State University Press, 1976), 78.

2. Benjamin R. Barber, "An Epitaph for Marxism," *Society* 33 (November/December 1995), 23.

3. Leszek Kolakowski, *Toward a Marxist Humanism: Essays on the Left Today* (New York: Grove Press, 1968), 70.

4. Ibid. More compelling still is the Russian radical Alexander Herzen's warning that "a goal which is infinitely remote is no goal, only . . . a deception. Do you truly wish," Herzen asks, "to condemn the human beings alive today to the sad role . . . of wretched galley slaves who, up to their knees in mud, drag a barge . . . with. . . . 'progress in the future' upon its flag?" Isaiah Berlin pursues Herzen's question: "The one thing that we may be sure of is the reality of the sacrifice, the dying and the dead. But the ideal for the sake of which they die remains unrealised. The eggs are broken, and the habit of breaking them grows, but the omelette remains invisible" (Isaiah Berlin, *The Crooked Timber of Humanity: Chapters in the History of Ideas* [New York: Vintage, 1992], 16).

5. Leszek Kolakowski, "Marxist Roots of Stalinism," in Robert C. Tucker, ed., *Stalinism: Essays in Historical Interpretation* (New York: Norton, 1977), 297.

6. See Bernard Crick, *In Defense of Politics*, 2d Pelican ed. (New York: Penguin, 1982).

7. Asked in 1935 to draw up a list of the twenty-five most influential books published in the last half century, both Charles Beard and John Dewey ranked *Looking Backward* second only to Marx's *Das Kapital*. On *Looking Backward*'s titanic influence on "the age of reform," see Elizabeth Sadler, "One Book's Influence: Edward Bellamy's 'Looking Backward,'" *New England Quarterly* 17 (December 1944), 530–55. Bellamy's influence on the Populists specifically is documented in Christine McHugh, "Edward Bellamy and the Populists: The Agrarian Response to Utopia, 1888–1898" (Ph.D. diss., University of Illinois at Chicago Circle, 1977). Bellamy's influence on the Industrial Workers of the World (IWW) and the turn-of-the-century labor movement is accented in Franklin Rosemont, "Bellamy's Radicalism Reclaimed," in Daphne Patai, ed., *Looking Backward, 1988–1888: Essays on Edward Bellamy* (Amherst: University of Massachusetts Press, 1988), 147–209. On Bellamy's influence on utopian literature and utopian communities in the 1890s, see Roemer, *Obsolete Necessity;* and Robert S. Fogarty, *All Things New: American Communes and Utopian Movements, 1860–1914* (Chicago: University of Chicago Press, 1990), especially 15, 134–35, 189. On the Nationalist Movement that was spawned by Bellamy's novel, see Arthur Lipow, *Authoritarian Socialism in America: Edward Bellamy and the Nationalist Movement* (Berkeley: University of California Press, 1982); and Edward K. Spann, *Brotherly Tomorrows: Movements for a Cooperative Society in America, 1820–1920* (New York: Columbia University Press, 1989), especially chapter 12.

8. Richard Hofstadter, *The Age of Reform: From Bryan to FDR* (New York: Vintage, 1955), 67. At times Hofstadter seems to include the New Deal years in his definition of "the age of reform" (3), but the focus of his study is almost completely on "the Populist-Progressive age." He treats the New Deal not just as a "new phase of reform" (4) but as qualitatively different from the Populist-Progressive era of reform.

9. Hofstadter says only that Donnelly's *Caesar's Column* was "possibly inspired by the success a few years earlier of Bellamy's utopian romance *Looking Backward*, which called forth a spate of imitators during the last decade of the century" (*Age of Reform*, 67).

10. Cecilia Tichi, Introduction, in Edward Bellamy, *Looking Backward: 2000–1887* (New York: Penguin, 1982), 12. All subsequent page references to *Looking Backward* refer to this edition.

11. Hofstadter, *Age of Reform*, 19.

12. Lipow, *Authoritarian Socialism*, 24.

13. Bellamy, *Looking Backward*, 232, 65, 234.

14. Daniel H. Borus, "Introduction: Edward Bellamy's Utopia in His Time and Ours," in Edward Bellamy, *Looking Backward, 2000–1887* (Boston: Bedford, 1995), 14.

15. Bellamy, *Looking Backward*, 125, 151–53.

16. This might seem to be true by definition of utopian visions. But utopias need not have a static, predetermined end point. William Morris's utopian novel, *News*

from Nowhere, which was written in reaction to *Looking Backward*, explicitly rejected the idea of a predetermined end or perfect world. See Borus, "Introduction," 27.

17. Bellamy, *Looking Backward*, 205, 69, 111, 68; emphasis added. Also see Roemer, *Obsolete Necessity*, 137.

18. Bellamy, *Looking Backward*, 156.

19. Ibid., 145.

20. Ibid., 155, 143.

21. The state decides, for instance, the length of the work week for each occupation. Citizens are free, within limits, to choose their occupation, and "it is the business of the administration to see that . . . the number of volunteers for any trade is exactly the number needed in that trade" (Bellamy, *Looking Backward*, 71). The state insures that "all trades shall be equally attractive" (72) by varying the number of hours required for each job. The more popular jobs are given longer hours, the less popular jobs shorter hours. Dr. Leete denies this entails state coercion, since people are choosing their occupations but, of course, if a citizen prefers a job that few other citizens prefer he will be coerced into working fewer hours than he might otherwise like. The untenable assumption that underpins Leete's analysis is that all people will prefer leisure to work.

22. Ibid., 65, 67; emphasis added.

23. See Milton Cantor's unpersuasive claim that "Bellamy's nationalism . . . depended upon a central unitary government, which was yet another deviation from the orthodox Marxist view of the state as withering away" ("The Backward Look of Bellamy's Socialism," in Patai, *Looking Backward*, 33–34). In fact, though, Marxism, orthodox or otherwise, contains the same unresolved contradiction between a utopian hope for the withering away of the state and an economic agenda that envisions and requires all power to be vested in the hands of a central state.

24. Bellamy, *Looking Backward*, 155–56, also 150, 167.

25. Ibid., 100–101, also 67–68.

26. Ibid., 122–23.

27. Ibid., 152, 154.

28. Ibid., 150–51. Borus, "Introduction," 23. John L. Thomas, *Alternative America: Henry George, Edward Bellamy, Henry Demarest Lloyd and the Adversary Tradition* (Cambridge, Mass.: Harvard University Press, 1983), 342.

29. John Thomas describes *The Religion of Solidarity* as "the psychological substructure" upon which *Looking Backward* was built (Introduction, in Bellamy, *Looking Backward* [Cambridge, Mass.: Harvard University Press, 1967], 13). Bellamy himself described it as "the germ of what has been ever since my philosophy of life" (Lipow, *Authoritarian Socialism*, 44; also see 44n96). Also see McHugh, "Bellamy and the Populists," 114–16, 126n63.

30. Edward Bellamy, *The Religion of Solidarity*, in Joseph Schiffman, ed., *Edward Bellamy: Selected Writings on Religion and Society* (New York: Liberal Arts Press, 1955), 14, 9, 17. Lipow, *Authoritarian Socialism*, 44–46. Also see Thomas, *Alternative America*, 158.

31. Isaiah Berlin, "Two Concepts of Liberty," in Berlin, *Four Essays on Liberty* (New York: Oxford University Press, 1969). Also relevant is Nancy L. Rosenblum's

warning that "connection with 'everything which exists' is no actual connection at all. Fusion supplants relationship" (*Another Liberalism: Romanticism and the Reconstruction of Liberal Thought* [Cambridge, Mass.: Harvard University Press, 1987], 47).

32. Lipow, *Authoritarian Socialism*, 162.

33. At other times, however, Lipow clearly situates Bellamy and Bellamyism on the egalitarian left. For example, he writes, "The tendency of students of the appeal of authoritarian political movements has been to limit their analysis to the 'right.' This has obscured the important role that the type of reaction described by [Eric] Fromm has played in the appeal of anticapitalist currents on the 'left'. . . . There is no reason, however, why Fromm's analysis must be limited to right-wing movements" (ibid., 164).

34. Ibid., 279. At another point, Lipow describes "the elaborate authoritarianism of *Looking Backward* [as] a reflection of conservative antidemocratic ideas" (33), and at yet another juncture he describes Bellamyism as "a collectivistic variation upon the conservative reform theme" (14).

35. Ibid., 40.

36. Quoted in Daphne Patai, "Introduction: The Doubled Vision of Edward Bellamy," in Patai, *Looking Backward, 1988–1888*, 13. Also see Lipow, *Authoritarian Socialism*, 77n54.

37. Bellamy, *Looking Backward*, 87. Edward Bellamy, *Equality* (1897; reprint ed., New York: Greenwood Press, 1969), 120. Also see Lipow, *Authoritarian Socialism*, 24, 56, 284.

38. Lipow, *Authoritarian Socialism*, 48, 50. Also see Thomas, *Alternative America*, 159–60, 254–55.

39. Bellamy, *Looking Backward*, 58, 134.

40. Lipow, *Authoritarian Socialism*, 51.

41. Ibid., ix.

42. Lipow stresses that Marx insisted that domination could end only as the result of a "process of self-emancipation in which men transformed themselves and made themselves fit for self-rule as they transformed society" (ibid., 52). Lipow then faults Bellamy because his "agents [of change] could have no particular self-interest to serve" (52). But what is Marx's proletariat but a "universal class" without particular or partial interests? Marx's vision of a proletariat that in striving for its own liberation necessarily produces freedom for all is no less utopian than Bellamy's vision, and the authoritarian implications ("the dictatorship of the proletariat") are no less troubling (on Marx's utopianism see the excellent discussion in Axel van den Berg, *The Immanent Utopia: From Marxism on the State to the State of Marxism* [Princeton, N.J.: Princeton University Press, 1988], especially 43–77). At another point, Lipow borrows from Marx's criticism of the early utopian socialists to condemn Bellamy's collectivist utopia as only the "positive annulment of private property," whereas true or "humanistic communism" would result in the "positive transcendence" of property (*Authoritarian Socialism*, 77). But why should we believe that Marx's vision of "positive transcendence" is any less utopian than Bellamy's vision of "positive annul-

ment," and why should we assume the implications for authoritarian state power would be any different? On the connection between Marxism and Stalinism, see Kolakowski, "Marxist Roots of Stalinism."

43. Thomas, "Utopia for an Urban Age: Henry George, Henry Demarest Lloyd, Edward Bellamy," *Perspectives in American History* 6 (1972), 143. Also see Thomas, *Alternative America*, 286.

44. Bellamy, *Looking Backward*, 111, 124.

45. "Except for despotism," Leszek Kolakowski writes, "there is no other technique known to produce a unity of society; no other way of suppressing the tension between civil and political society but the suppression of civil society; no other means to remove the conflicts between the individual and 'the whole' but the destruction of the individual" ("Marxist Roots of Stalinism," 296).

46. Max Eastman, "Motive-Patterns of Socialism," *Modern Quarterly* 11 (Fall 1939), 54. Also see J. L. Talmon, *The Origins of Totalitarian Democracy* (1951; reprint ed., New York: Norton, 1970).

47. Eastman, "Motive-Patterns of Socialism," 54. Lipow, *Authoritarian Socialism*, 172.

48. Judith N. Shklar, *Ordinary Vices* (Cambridge, Mass.: Harvard University Press, 1984), 29. Also see Stephen Holmes, *Passions and Constraint: On the Theory of Liberal Democracy* (Chicago: University of Chicago Press, 1995), 254, 17.

49. Lipow, *Authoritarian Socialism*, 3. Daniel Aaron's influential study is *Men of Good Hope: A Study of American Progressives* (New York: Oxford University Press, 1951). In his Foreword to *Looking Backward* (New York: Signet, 1960), Eric Fromm characterizes Bellamy's vision as one of "humanistic socialism" (xix).

50. Patai, "Introduction," 19.

51. See Michael Thompson, Richard Ellis, and Aaron Wildavsky, *Cultural Theory* (Boulder, Colo.: Westview Press, 1990), especially 33–34.

52. Bellamy, *Looking Backward*, 68.

53. Ibid., 203; emphasis added. The view that capitalism nurtured "egotistic lusts" (Roemer, *Obsolete Necessity*, 77) was a widely shared premise of egalitarian thought during this "age of reform."

54. Roemer, *Obsolete Necessity*, 56.

55. Bellamy, *Looking Backward*, 101.

56. Ibid., 89.

57. William Dean Howells, *Letters from an Altrurian Traveller*, quoted in Roemer, *Obsolete Necessity*, 62.

58. Lipow, *Authoritarian Socialism*, 169.

59. Hofstadter, *Age of Reform*, 67. Norman Pollack, ed., *The Populist Mind* (Indianapolis: Bobbs-Merrill, 1967), 469–70. Martin Ridge, *Ignatius Donnelly: The Portrait of a Politician* (Chicago: University of Chicago Press, 1962), 277–78. Donnelly was deeply immersed in the language of antimonopoly in a way that was never true for Bellamy. At the same time, Donnelly's political vision, as it developed during the 1880s and 1890s, became increasingly shaped by a communitarian language of solidarity and harmony. That Donnelly, at least by 1890, hoped to transcend rather than

simply restore competition is evident by the utopia he imagines at the close of *Caesar's Column*.

60. Ignatius Donnelly, *Caesar's Column: A Story of the Twentieth Century*, ed. Walter B. Rideout (Cambridge, Mass.: Belknap Press, 1960), 34.–35. Cf. the imagery offered by Jack Newfield, writing about America in the 1960s: "Beneath this nation's gleaming surface of computers, Hilton hotels, and super-highways, there are latent volcanoes of violence. . . . Riot and assassination are symptoms of the disease in our society below the Disneyland facade. The New Radicals will rub these hidden sores until they bleed, or until the Great Society begins to heal the one in five who are poor, and the millions who are voteless, powerless, victimized, and mad" (*A Prophetic Minority* [New York: New American Library, 1966], 209).

61. Donnelly, *Caesar's Column*, 71, 42, 297; also see 35.

62. Ibid., 40–41.

63. Ibid., 73, 68, 70–71, 62.

64. Ibid., 258, 145, 174, 170, 169.

65. Ibid., 159.

66. Ibid., 4–5. In a letter to a publisher who rejected *Caesar's Column*, Donnelly affirmed his belief that "the evil tendencies of our age . . . are dragging civilization rapidly and certainly to its own funeral" (Donnelly to A. C. McClurg, December 31, 1889, quoted in Ridge, *Ignatius Donnelly*, 266).

67. The Omaha Platform, in Pollack, *Populist Mind*, 60–61. Also see Ridge, *Ignatius Donnelly*, 247. Nor was Donnelly alone in imagining the nation in these Manichaean, apocalyptic terms. In the *Coming Nation*, a leading radical newspaper of the 1890s, Julius Wayland conjured up a world of unspeakable oppression and impending doom. The laboring masses, "sullen and angry," were "oppressed and enslaved by the drones, the useless" members of society. The "present state of society," Wayland wrote, is "ominously suggestive of speedy collapse and chaos in the near future" (*Coming Nation*, December 2, 1893). Also see Fogarty, *All Things New*, 217–18.

68. Paul Glad, *McKinley, Bryan, and the People* (New York: Lippincott, 1964), 197. Donnelly, *Caesar's Column*, 68, 169.

69. Donnelly, *Caesar's Column*, 108, 188.

70. Ibid., 100; also see 5.

71. Glad, *McKinley, Bryan, and the People*, 197.

72. Donnelly, *Caesar's Column*, 300; also see 305–6.

73. Ibid., 102.

74. Ibid., 112, 304, 303, 306–9; emphasis added.

75. Ibid., 309–10, 313.

76. Fogarty, *All Things New*, 229–31. Fogarty counts thirteen colonies starting operation in the 1860s, thirty in the 1870s, twenty-four in the 1880s, forty in the 1890s, and twenty in the opening decade of the twentieth century (227–32).

77. Spann, *Brotherly Tomorrows*, 231.

78. On Bellamy's influence on utopian colonies, see Fogarty, *All Things New*, 15, 134–35, 139, 216, 248n78; Lipow, *Authoritarian Socialism*, 87–88; Roemer, *Obsolete Necessity*, xii, 3; and Elliott Shore, *Talkin' Socialism: J. A. Wayland and the Role of the*

Press in American Radicalism, 1890–1912 (Lawrence: University Press of Kansas, 1988), 59, 41.

79. Spann, *Brotherly Tomorrows*, 240; also see Fogarty, *All Things New*, 12.

80. Robert V. Hine, *California's Utopian Colonies* (New Haven, Conn.: Yale University Press, 1966), 162; also see 163–64, 85–86.

81. Charles Pierce Le Warne, *Utopias on Puget Sound, 1885–1915* (Seattle: University of Washington Press, 1975), chapter 4; also see Fogarty, *All Things New*, 165.

82. Spann, *Brotherly Tomorrows*, 229. Lipow, *Authoritarian Socialism*, 88n80. Fogarty, *All Things New*, 15, 163. Hine, *California's Utopian Colonies*, 86. Henry George was equally disapproving of the single-tax colonies that were inspired by his ideas. Like Bellamy, George felt such communes were bound to fail and would discredit his theories. See Paul M. Gaston, *Man and Mission: E. B. Gaston and the Origins of the Fairhope Single Tax Colony* (Montgomery, Ala.: Black Belt Press, 1993), 4, 87, 91.

83. Bellamy, *Equality*, 351.

84. Thomas, *Alternative America*, 366.

85. Hine, *California's Utopian Colonies*, 167–69.

86. *Coming Nation*, December 30, 1893.

87. Fogarty, *All Things New*, 224; also see 129–31. On Hoffman's life see Patricia Michaelis, "C. B. Hoffman, Kansas Socialist," *Kansas Historical Quarterly* 44 (Summer 1975), 166–82.

88. Hine, *California's Utopian Colonies*, 87. Spann, *Brotherly Tomorrows*, 232.

89. Spann, *Brotherly Tomorrows*, 239. Unfortunately, the colonization plan could not keep even Debs's enthusiasm, let alone the nation's. In June 1898, the majority within SDA voted to proceed with the colonization plan, but the minority bolted the convention to form the Social Democratic party, and Debs sided with the bolters. See Spann, *Brotherly Tomorrows*, 241; and Fogarty, *All Things New*, 163–64.

90. G. E. Pelton to Lloyd, December 14, 1897, in Le Warne, *Utopias on Puget Sound*, 55. Also see Fogarty, *All Things New*, 164.

91. "Henry D. Lloyd's Address," June 19, 1898, in *Coming Nation*, July 3, 1898. Also see Thomas, *Alternative America*, 345.

92. Marx's daughter, Eleanor Aveling, quoted in Spann, *Brotherly Tomorrows*, 228.

93. Thomas, *Alternative America*, 344–45.

94. *Coming Nation*, October 21, 1893; December 23, 1893. "The average American," Wayland explained, "is as ignorant of the real character of this government as is the lowest type of Russian of his. Both are taught to believe his the grandest, greatest country on earth, to believe in private ownership of land and machinery, to denounce any who question these theories — and the ruling classes do the rest. Of the two, I believe the American is the most easily duped" (December 2, 1893).

95. Ibid., January 6, 1894.

96. Ibid., December 2, 1893; January 6, 1894; October 21, 1893; September 23, 1893. Cf. the sentiments expressed by a colonist at Llano: "We are bonded together, the few elect, who will lead the grand parade of freedmen and freedwomen. . . . By our example we will teach the inert multitude of the unenlightened to join actual freedom's procession" (*Llano Colonist*, December 3, 1927, quoted in Paul K. Conkin,

Two Paths to Utopia: The Hutterites and the Llano Colony [Lincoln: University of Nebraska Press, 1964], 120).

97. *Coming Nation*, December 2, 1893.

98. Chester McArthur Destler, *American Radicalism, 1865–1901* (1946; reprint ed., Chicago: Quadrangle Books, 1966), 84–85, 87.

99. Fogarty, *All Things New*, 217–18, 215. Cf. Spann, who describes the utopian hope "that some Good King Utopus would work the social miracles that men in general could not achieve" (*Brotherly Tomorrows*, 163).

100. Cf. Lewis A. Coser's conclusion: "Conflict tends to be dysfunctional for a social structure in which there is no or insufficient toleration and institutionalization of conflict. . . . What threatens the equilibrium of such a structure is not conflict as such, but the rigidity itself which permits hostilities to accumulate and to be channeled along one major line of cleavage once they break out in conflict" (*The Functions of Social Conflict* [New York: Free Press, 1956], 157).

101. Shore, *Talkin' Socialism*, 68.

102. Spann, *Brotherly Tomorrows*, 232. Shore, *Talkin' Socialism*, 59.

103. Shore, *Talkin' Socialism*, 60–66. John Egerton, *Visions of Utopia: Nashoba, Rugby, Ruskin, and the "New Communities" in Tennessee's Past* (Knoxville: University of Tennessee Press, 1977), 70–73.

104. Shore, *Talkin' Socialism*, 69. Egerton, *Visions of Utopia*, 76, 78–79. Also see Frederick A. Bushee, "Communistic Societies in the United States," *Political Science Quarterly* 20 (December 1905), 632–35.

105. Hine, *California's Utopian Colonies*, 170–71, 87–88, 122–23.

106. Ibid., 114–17. Conkin, *Two Paths to Utopia*, 103, 106–7. Harriman's 1911 mayoral defeat, according to both Hine and Conkin, was caused by a widely publicized confession coming just five days before the election. Two union organizers, the McNamara brothers, had been accused of the bombing of the *Los Angeles Times* building that had killed twenty men. Socialist and labor leaders flocked to the defense of the brothers, and Harriman himself was involved as one of the chief counselors for the defense. The guilt or innocence of the McNamara brothers was the biggest issue in the campaign, and their shocking confession immediately before the election destroyed Harriman's chances. Even so, Harriman received 35 percent of the vote.

107. Hine, *California's Utopian Colonies*, 117.

108. The wage plan quickly broke down. In part this was because the promise of a four-dollar-per-day wage plus guaranteed security seemed to attract the wrong sort of person to the colony, the sort "whose ideals were [not] sufficiently lofty to carry them through the dry years of cooperative hardship." But the scheme also broke down because the wage was to be paid "when and if the company realized excess profits." Since the colony never made such a profit, a healthy skepticism about the value of the wage "payment" quickly set in. Before too long the wage system was superseded by a system more like the one at Altruria, where the community essentially guaranteed each member the necessities of life regardless of his credit account (Hine, *California's Utopian Colonies*, 120).

109. Conkin, *Two Paths to Utopia*, 109–10. Hine, *California's Utopian Colonies*, 118, 121–22, 124.

110. Hine, *California's Utopian Colonies*, 122. Conkin, *Two Paths to Utopia*, 112–13.

111. Conkin, *Two Paths to Utopia*, 112, 109.

112. Hine, *California's Utopian Colonies*, 122–23. Also see Conkin, *Two Paths to Utopia*, 127–28.

113. This argument is brilliantly elaborated in Holmes, *Passions and Constraint*, chapter 2.

114. Conkin, *Two Paths to Utopia*, 114, 125.

115. Ibid., 129–30, 134, 120–21.

116. Ibid., 132.

117. Ibid., 139–41.

118. Ibid., 143–47.

CHAPTER 3. The Revolting Masses

1. Benjamin R. Barber, "An Epitaph for Marxism," *Society* 33 (November/December 1995), 25.

2. Michael Walzer, *The Company of Critics: Social Criticism and Political Commitment in the Twentieth Century* (New York: Basic Books, 1988), 123.

3. The aristocratic roots of the scorn for "bourgeois" life are accented in Paul E. Corcoran, "The Bourgeois and Other Villains," *Journal of the History of Ideas* 38 (July–September 1977), 477–85.

4. See the chapters on Schmitt and de Maistre in Stephen Holmes, *The Anatomy of Antiliberalism* (Cambridge, Mass.: Harvard University Press, 1993), 13–60; Isaiah Berlin, "Joseph de Maistre and the Origins of Fascism," in Berlin, *The Crooked Timber of Humanity* (New York: Knopf, 1991), 91–174; Isaiah Berlin, *The Magus of the North: J. G. Hamann and the Origins of Modern Irrationalism* (London: John Murray, 1993); and J. S. McClelland, ed., *The French Right: From de Maistre to Maurras* (New York: Harper Torchbooks, 1971).

5. On the Federalists and southern slaveholders, see Richard J. Ellis, *American Political Cultures* (New York: Oxford University Press, 1993), chapter 6, and the sources cited therein. On Cram, see T. J. Jackson Lears, *No Place of Grace: Antimodernism and the Transformation of American Culture, 1880–1920* (New York: Pantheon, 1981). On Babbitt, see Russell Kirk, *The Conservative Mind: From Burke to Eliot* rev. ed. (Chicago: Gateway, 1960), 477–91.

6. Betsy Erkkila, *Whitman the Political Poet* (New York: Oxford University Press, 1989), 7.

7. Ibid., 19. David S. Reynolds, *Walt Whitman's America: A Cultural Biography* (New York: Knopf, 1995), 66–67.

8. Erkkila, *Political Poet*, 6, 19–20, 52. Reynolds, *Whitman's America*, 83.

9. Reynolds, *Whitman's America*, 139.

10. Erkkila, *Political Poet*, 7. In Erkkila's account, Whitman sometimes sounds close to an Americanized Marx, who "imagined a 'real culmination' of the American republic, in which the values of liberty and equality, shared wealth and general

property ownership, productive labor and local control, independence and cooperation would offer a road to the democratic future different from the capitalist road in
which the few profit at the expense of the many and at the expense finally of the republic itself" (307). Also see Gregory Jay, "Catching Up with Whitman," *South Atlantic Quarterly* 57 (January 1992), 91–92.

11. Much of *Democratic Vistas* was originally written in response to Thomas Carlyle's "Shooting Niagara; and After?," a bitter attack on democracy published in the
United States in 1867. Although Whitman originally intended to "counterblast" Carlyle's attack, he came to find that in fact he shared many of Carlyle's concerns about the
ills of democracy (Erkkila, *Political Poet*, 247), as he freely acknowledged in a footnote
in *Vistas* (465). Carlyle, Whitman later admitted, performed a "needed service." "His
rude, rasping, taunting, contradictory tones — what ones are more wanted amid the
supple, polish'd, money-worshipping, Jesus-and-Judas equalizing, suffrage sovereignty echoes of current America?" (Reynolds, *Whitman's America*, 479).

12. Walt Whitman, *Democratic Vistas*, in *Complete Poetry and Selected Prose of Walt
Whitman*, ed. James E. Miller, Jr. (Boston: Houghton Mifflin, 1959), 455, 460, 469;
emphasis added.

13. Reynolds, *Whitman's America*, 480–81. Erkkila, *Political Poet*, 248–49.

14. Quoted in Erkkila, *Political Poet*, 253; also see Reynolds, *Whitman's America*,
483.

15. Whitman, *Democratic Vistas*, 458, 457. Reynolds, *Whitman's America*, 483.

16. Whitman, *Democratic Vistas*, 461, 478, 479, 491. Cf. Whitman's earlier declaration of solidarity with the common people: "I will not descend among professors
and capitalists — I will turn the ends of my trousers around my boots, and my cuffs
back from my wrists, and go with drivers and boatmen and men that catch fish or
work in the field. I know they are sublime" (Erkkila, *Political Poet*, 48). Also see
Reynolds, *Whitman's America*, 325.

17. Whitman, *Democratic Vistas*, 462, 499, 462, 461, 463.

18. Reynolds, *Whitman's America*, 68–69.

19. Whitman to Edward Dowden, January 18, 1872, quoted in Thomas Bender,
*New York Intellect: A History of Intellectual Life in New York City from 1750 to the Be-
ginnings of Our Own Time* (Baltimore: Johns Hopkins University Press, 1988), 155.

20. Whitman, *Democratic Vistas*, 461–62; also see 457.

21. Walt Whitman, *Drum Taps* (New York: Grosset and Dunlap, 1936), 5–6.
This poem was written after the early Union defeat at Bull Run (Reynolds, *Whitman's
America*, 407). Also see George M. Fredrickson, *The Inner Civil War: Northern Intel-
lectuals and the Crisis of the Union* (New York: Harper and Row, 1965), 67.

22. Whitman, *Drum Taps*, 17–19. Also see Reynolds, *Whitman's America*,
419–20.

23. Reynolds, *Whitman's America*, 418. On romantic glorification of militarism,
see Nancy Rosenblum, *Another Liberalism: Romanticism and the Reconstruction of Liberal Thought* (Cambridge, Mass.: Harvard University Press, 1987), chapter 1.

24. Reynolds, *Whitman's America*, 479–80. The quotation is from several lines
that Whitman added to the poem "Respondez" for the 1871 edition of *Leaves of Grass*.

25. Whitman, *Democratic Vistas*, 461. Harold Aspiz, "The Body Politic in *Democratic Vistas*," in Ed Folsom, ed., *Walt Whitman: The Centennial Essays* (Iowa City: University of Iowa Press, 1994), 106.

26. Whitman, *Democratic Vistas*, 456, 480, 460, 480.

27. Ibid., 460, 463. Aspiz, "The Body Politic," 110. In *Democratic Vistas* he heeded his warning, criticizing literature for failing to make a "fit scientific estimate and reverent appreciation of the People—of their measureless wealth of *latent* power and capacity" (466, emphasis added). In his notes, Whitman also cautioned himself to "beware of the too strong contradiction between the eulogiums [?] of the rank and file 'the grand common stock' . . . and the statement of depravity of the common classes" (Aspiz, "The Body Politic," 110).

28. Aspiz, "The Body Politic," 109. Whitman, *Democratic Vistas*, 498–99.

29. Reynolds, *Whitman's America*, 5. Whitman himself was painfully aware of his failure to touch the masses. Toward the end of his life, he confided to a friend: "The people: the crowd—I have had no way of reaching them. I needed to reach the people . . . but it's too late now" (Reynolds, *Whitman's America*, 6).

30. John Patrick Diggins, *The Rise and Fall of the American Left* (New York: Norton, 1992), 94. Whitman's life, Eastman wrote, "was the greatest life lived in America" ("Menshevizing Walt Whitman," *New Masses* [December 1926], 12). On Whitman's tremendous influence on early-twentieth-century radicals, see Leslie Fishbein, *Rebels in Bohemia: The Radicals of The Masses, 1911–1917* (Chapel Hill: University of North Carolina Press, 1982), 39–41, and Daniel Aaron, *Writers on the Left* (New York: Avon, 1965), 24–25.

31. See Diggins, *Rise and Fall of the American Left*, chapter 4; and Edward Abrahams, *The Lyrical Left: Randolph Bourne, Alfred Stieglitz, and the Origins of Cultural Radicalism in America* (Charlottesville: University Press of Virginia, 1986).

32. "The Spirit of Walt Whitman Stands Behind The Seven Arts," *Seven Arts* (May 1917), vii. Henry F. May, *The End of American Innocence: A Study of the First Years of Our Own Time, 1912–1917* (Chicago: Quadrangle, 1959), 322. Historian Thomas Bender describes Whitman as the "patron saint" of the *Seven Arts*, noting that "he was invoked in nearly every article in the first issue" (*New York Intellect*, 242). In 1932 Waldo Frank, cofounder of *Seven Arts*, recalled that "Our 'master' was Walt Whitman" ("How I Came to Communism: A Symposium," *New Masses* [September 1932], 6–7). James Oppenheim, writing in 1930, agreed that "we stemmed from Walt Whitman" ("The Story of the *Seven Arts*," *American Mercury* [June 1930], 158).

33. Editorial, *Seven Arts* (November 1917), 52–53. These words are from the journal's prospectus, which, according to Van Wyck Brooks, was penned by Waldo Frank. The prospectus was reprinted in the unsigned editorial from the inaugural issue. See Casey Nelson Blake, *Beloved Community: The Cultural Criticism of Randolph Bourne, Van Wyck Brooks, Waldo Frank, and Lewis Mumford* (Chapel Hill: University of North Carolina Press, 1990), 126, 132, 320n17.

34. "The Seven Arts Chronicle for May: The Fifth-Month Poet," *Seven Arts* (May 1917), 118–19. James Oppenheim, "Memories of Whitman and Lincoln,"

Seven Arts (May 1917), 10. The "Seven Arts Chronicle for May" is not signed but was almost certainly written by Oppenheim.

35. James Oppenheim, Editorial, *Seven Arts* (January 1917), 268–69. Oppenheim, Editorial, *Seven Arts* (April 1917), 630. In an earlier editorial, Oppenheim rhapsodizes about "the great artist" who "could unify a nation and express a national entity. . . . To the low he gave their own lowness, but also the overtones, the promptings and leadership toward the higher. To the high he gave height, but also depth. He offered the thin abstraction and the monstrous welter of passion: philosopher, merchant, sailor and thief could go to him for a sense of the life that included and transcended their own" ([December 1916], 155).

36. "To the Friends of the Seven Arts," *Seven Arts* (October 1917). In asking why Whitman was still so neglected in America, Oppenheim answers, "Perhaps the reason lies in the fact that our life is still unself-conscious. Whitman makes it conscious, and we do not recognize it. Or perhaps, and more probably, it is that he pictures an ideal America, an America still far off" ("The Seven Arts Chronicle for May," 119).

37. James Oppenheim, Editorial, *Seven Arts* (December 1916), 153. Also see Paul R. Gorman, *Left Intellectuals and Popular Culture in Twentieth-Century America* (Chapel Hill: University of North Carolina Press, 1996), 59.

38. James Oppenheim, "The Strong Young Modern," *Seven Arts* (December 1916), 194. Oppenheim, Editorial, *Seven Arts* (June 1917), 201. Oppenheim, Editorial, *Seven Arts* (March 1917), 504–5.

39. Cf. Waldo Frank's later recollection of the ethos that animated the *Seven Arts:* "We were all sworn foes of capitalism, not because we knew it would not work, but because we judged it, even in success, to be lethal to the human spirit" (Blake, *Beloved Community*, 124). Also see Waldo Frank, "Vicarious Fiction," *Seven Arts* (January 1917), 297.

40. Oppenheim's condescension is most vividly on display in his essay "The Strong Young Modern," a critique of Walter Lippmann's call for "realism." The people need false dreams and utopian visions, Oppenheim argues, just as children need fairy tales. "You can no more take their utopias, heavens, holy Maries, resurrections and immortality from them, than you can ask them to write H. G. Wells novels" (*Seven Arts* [December 1916], 194). Lippmann's reply is printed in the subsequent issue, January 1917, 304–5.

41. James Oppenheim, "America," *Seven Arts* (March 1917), 466.

42. James Oppenheim, Editorial, *Seven Arts* (August 1917), 491.

43. James Oppenheim, Editorial, *Seven Arts* (March 1917), 504–5.

44. James Oppenheim, Editorial, *Seven Arts* (July 1917), 342–43.

45. Oppenheim and Lewis Mumford, quoted in Bender, *New York Intellect*, 241, 239.

46. Blake, *Beloved Community*, 114, 116, 117. Gorman, *Left Intellectuals and Popular Culture*, 57–58.

47. Van Wyck Brooks, "Young America," *Seven Arts* (December 1916), 146–47. Van Wyck Brooks, "Our Awakeners," *Seven Arts* (June 1917), 243, 237, 236. Van Wyck Brooks, "The Culture of Industrialism," *Seven Arts* (April 1917), 666, 658, 655.

48. Van Wyck Brooks, "Our Critics," *Seven Arts* (May 1917), 113. Brooks, "Young America," 151, 147. Brooks, "Culture of Industrialism," 663, 656; also see 666. Van Wyck Brooks, "Toward a National Culture," *Seven Arts* (March 1917), 540. Also see Brooks, "Our Awakeners," 240, 246.

49. Blake, *Beloved Community*, 117. Van Wyck Brooks, "The Splinter of Ice," *Seven Arts* (January 1917), 272. Brooks, "Culture of Industrialism," 657. In *Democratic Vistas*, Whitman wrote, "I perceive clearly that the extreme business energy, and the almost maniacal appetite for wealth prevalent in the United States are parts of amelioration and progress, indispensably needed to prepare the very results I demand." And in a letter from that same period, he explained to a Danish correspondent that "I see that the only foundations and *sine qua non* of popular improvement & Democracy are *worldly & material success established first*, spreading & interweaving everywhere — *then* only, but surely for the masses, will come spiritual cultivation & art" (Reynolds, *Whitman's America*, 483; also see 482).

50. Brooks, "Our Awakeners," 241; also see 240.

51. Brooks, "Culture of Industrialism," 662. Blake, *Beloved Community*, 109. The first quote is from Brooks, the latter two are from Morris. On Brooks's socialist/egalitarian inclinations, see Blake, *Beloved Community*, 79, 105–8.

52. Blake, *Beloved Community*, 109.

53. Brooks, "Culture of Industrialism," 665. Brooks, "Our Awakeners," 246.

54. Brooks, "Splinter of Ice," 273. Brooks, "Culture of Industrialism," 662–63. Also see Brooks, "Toward a National Culture," 539–40, 544–45.

55. Brooks, "Our Awakeners," 237–38, 242–43. Also see Blake, *Beloved Community*, 105, 110–11, 143.

56. Frank cofounded the *Seven Arts* along with Oppenheim. Although he wrote relatively little for the journal, at least after the first few issues, Frank was arguably the most important figure in defining its identity. Indeed, according to Brooks, Frank was the magazine's "real creator." See Blake, *Beloved Community*, 126.

57. On Anderson see Waldo Frank, "Emerging Greatness," *Seven Arts* (November 1916), 73–78, Waldo Frank, *Our America* (New York: Boni and Liveright, 1919), 136–44, and Blake, *Beloved Community*, 146–47. On Stieglitz see Frank, *Our America*, 180–87, 230; and Blake, *Beloved Community*, 146–48. On Chaplin see Frank, *Our America*, 214–15; and Blake, *Beloved Community*, 273–74. On Haywood see Frank, *Our America*, 230. Also see Blake, *Beloved Community*, 142–43.

58. Frank, *Our America*, 201. In truth, Frank is not terribly consistent. Within the space of a few pages he can sound Whitmanesque themes of confidence — "in the direct column of advance, poets and artists still swarm in from farm and provincial city. . . . Their bulk shall be resistless. They make loam for the growing prairie. . . . The soil stands ready to be turned" (228–29) — and then voice pessimistic laments worthy of Brooks — "The solitary voices seek each other out across the American wastes, and no one else attends them" (209). Frank's more Whitmanesque vision is also evident from the fact that Frank never takes Whitman to the woodshed in the manner that Brooks does. Frank's view of Whitman, like Oppenheim's, is almost totally celebratory. See Frank, *Our America*, especially 9, 71, 222, and chapter 8.

59. Frank, *Our America*, 50–51, 56. Also see Blake, *Beloved Community*, 172–73. "Better angels of our nature" is from Lincoln's second inaugural address.

60. Blake, *Beloved Community*, 173; also see 170, 174, 255, 266, 274–75. Frank, *Our America*, 204.

61. Frank, *Our America*, 227, 210, 196, 209.

62. See Gorman, *Left Intellectuals and Popular Culture*. Gorman does not take up Frank, focusing instead on Brooks and a few other lesser contributors to the *Seven Arts*, but his argument fits Frank exactly.

63. Frank, *Our America*, 216–17, 175.

64. Frank, "The Comedy of Commerce" (1925), in *In the American Jungle*, 118–19, quoted in Blake, *Beloved Community*, 272. Blake rightly points out how much this resembles the views of Theodore Adorno and Herbert Marcuse. It is also uncannily like the contemporary wing of literary and cultural studies represented by Sacvan Bercovitch, among others, which interprets virtually every expression of dissent as "ultimately" (the key weasel word) an act of consent to Americanism. For a critique of this strain of Bercovitch's thought, see Ellis, *American Political Cultures*, 170–74.

65. Frank, *Our America*, 210; also see 211–12, where he explicitly likens the American people to a herd of sheep.

66. Frank, *Our America*, 173. Passages such as this led other literary radicals like Matthew Josephson and Malcolm Cowley to criticize Frank "for betraying his Whitmanesque heritage by disdaining the vibrant new popular culture of the American city" (Blake, *Beloved Community*, 270). But while Frank is certainly more critical of the urban masses than Whitman — nothing in Whitman's thought compares to the passage quoted in the text — Frank's disdain for the people is strongly rooted in Whitman's own thought, as we have seen.

67. Frank, *Our America*, 205. On Lawrence see Blake, *Beloved Community*, 174.

68. Blake, *Beloved Community*, 174. Frank, *Our America*, 109, 114.

69. Frank, *Our America*, 94–96, 105. Also see Blake, *Beloved Community*, 276–77.

70. Blake, *Beloved Community*, 175–77.

71. Waldo Frank, *Dawn in Russia* (New York: Charles Scribner's Sons, 1932), 133–35. Also see Blake, *Beloved Community*, 277–78; and Paul Hollander, *Political Pilgrims: Travels of Western Intellectuals to the Soviet Union, China, and Cuba, 1928–1978* (New York: Oxford University Press, 1981), 109. In another revealing passage, Frank contrasts the Russian muzhiks he had met on his visit with the sophisticated Westerners who accompanied him on the train ride from Berlin back to Paris. Frank's disgust at his companions' lack of understanding of Russia triggered him to ruminate, "We know others only insofar as we know ourselves. The peasant, the unsophisticated toiler, have a self-knowledge humble but authentic. This, our western culture has merely covered and destroyed with a patina of lies. And that is why there is more hope in the uncultured workers of all races: more hope, not because we idealize or romanticize their sodden state, but because the finished product of modern rationalist-capitalist culture is hopeless" (*Dawn in Russia*, 230).

72. Frank, *Our America*, 72. Blake, *Beloved Community*, 278, 275; also 248.

73. The phrase "bloodless death-in-life" is actually from Van Wyck Brooks,

"Enterprise," *Seven Arts* (November 1916), 58, but the sentiment is as typical of Frank as of Brooks.

74. These shared aspirations and assumptions are splendidly accented in Blake, *Beloved Community*.

75. Randolph Bourne, "Maurice Barres and the Youth of France," *Atlantic Monthly* (September 1914), 399. Biographer Bruce Clayton remarks that Bourne had "read more E. A. Ross [a prominent social scientist at the University of Wisconsin] than Walt Whitman" (Bruce Clayton, *Forgotten Prophet: The Life of Randolph Bourne* [Baton Rouge: Louisiana State University Press, 1984], 124). On Ross, see Eldon Eisenach, *The Lost Promise of Progressivism* (Lawrence: University Press of Kansas, 1994). On the influence of his Columbia teachers on Bourne, see Clayton, *Forgotten Prophet*, 67–70; Carl Resek, Introduction to Randolph S. Bourne, *War and the Intellectuals: Collected Essays, 1915–1919*, ed. Carl Resek (New York: Harper Torchback, 1964), x–xi; and Bender, *New York Intellect*, 234–35.

76. Randolph Bourne, "Trans-National America," *Atlantic Monthly* (July 1916), in Olaf Hansen, ed., *Randolph Bourne: The Radical Will, Selected Writings, 1911–1918* (Berkeley: University of California Press, 1992), 255. Particularly revealing is Bourne's essay, "The Heart of the People," where he admits that "as a would-be democrat, I should like to believe passionately in the movies," but finds that he must "resist the stale culture of the masses" just as "we resist the stale culture of the aristocrat" (*New Republic* [July 3, 1915], in Bourne, *War and the Intellectuals*, 171, 174). Also see the acute analysis in Gorman, *Left Intellectuals and Popular Culture*, 62–65.

77. On the influence of the pragmatism of William James ("James has settled so many of my own worries," Bourne wrote to a friend in 1913, "that I preach him as a prophet") and John Dewey, see Clayton, *Forgotten Prophet*, 69–73, 126–27; Randolph Bourne, "John Dewey's Philosophy," *New Republic* (March 1915), in Hansen, *Radical Will*, 311–15. Bourne borrowed the phrase "beloved community" from Josiah Royce (Blake, *Beloved Community*, 117).

78. On Bourne's attachment to egalitarian community, see Blake, *Beloved Community*, especially 51–52, 69–70, 74–75, 77, 80.

79. Randolph Bourne, "The Doctrine of the Rights of Man as Formulated by Thomas Paine," in Hansen, *Radical Will*, 246. Randolph Bourne, "In the Mind of the Worker," *Atlantic Monthly* (June 1914), quoted in Blake, *Beloved Community*, 77.

80. Randolph Bourne, "Law and Order," *Masses* (March 1912), in Hansen, *Radical Will*, 354. Randolph Bourne, "Socialism and the Catholic Ideal," *Columbia Monthly* (November 1912); and Randolph Bourne, "The Next Revolution," *Columbia Monthly* (May 1913), quoted in Abramson, *Lyrical Left*, 42. Also see Bourne, "The Doctrine of the Rights of Man," 246.

81. Blake, *Beloved Community*, 83–84.

82. Ibid., 84. Also see Bourne to Carl Zigrosser, March 6, [1914], in *The Letters of Randolph Bourne: A Comprehensive Edition*, ed. Eric J. Sandeen (Troy, N.Y.: Whitson Publishing, 1981), 225. Bourne elaborates the comparison with Whitman: "There is much in the work of M. Romains that suggests Walt Whitman, divinest of poets, and the 'unanimistes' do acknowledge his influence. But he is a Whitman industrialized, and, if I may say it, sociologized; for besides the push of industrial

invention and energy that throbs though [Romaines's] poetry, there is a strong intellectual fibre running through him, the fibre of sociological science which Whitman of course could not have. To us Americans this poetry . . . should come as a fulfillment of Whitman, who, prophetic before his time, was submerged in our cult of an individualistic capitalism" ("A Sociological Poet," in Hansen, *Radical Will*, 522–23).

83. Bourne sent the essay to the *Atlantic Monthly* (where by this time he had already published over a half dozen articles), but the article was never published. Bourne himself anticipated the rejection, telling a friend, "I doubt very much whether it will suit; it must strike the normal American as very bizarre, for he is not used to feeling so keenly the social reverberations, the power of the group, and the intoxication of camaraderie" (Bourne to Carl Zigrosser, March 6, 1914, in Bourne, *Letters*, 225). Also see Clayton, *Forgotten Prophet*, 111–12.

84. Bourne, "A Sociological Poet," 521–23. Like Whitman and his progeny, Bourne's rhapsody was less a celebration of the city as it was than the city as it was becoming. "Does it not," Bourne asked, "suggest the stirrings of a new civilization, socialized and purified? In this garish, vulgar, primitive flow of Broadway, are not new gods being born?" (522).

85. Compare this with a letter from 1914 that displays the same desire to lose himself in a mystical group: "The world universal seems to begin to take form as social; your spiritual man is my social man, vibrating in camaraderie with the beloved society, given new powers, lifted out of himself, transformed through the enriching stimulation of his fellows,— the communion of saints,— into a new being, spiritual because no longer individual. This . . . *hunger* [is] thwarted and unsatisfied by the chaos of society split up into separate, mutually uncomprehending groups" (quoted in Olaf Hansen, "Affinity and Ambivalence," in Hansen, *Radical Will*, 28–29). Also see the troubling essay he wrote for the *Atlantic Monthly* ("Maurice Barres and the Youth of France [September 1914], 394–99) in praise of Maurice Barres, whose mystical nationalism would later be an important influence on the extreme right in France. As Blake points out, "Bourne's essay suggests the need for caution in enlisting nationalist notions of tradition, mutuality, and organic culture for a democratic communitarianism" (Blake, *Beloved Community*, 312–13n13; also see Abramson, *Lyrical Left*, 50–51).

86. See Abramson, *Lyrical Left*, 51; Blake, *Beloved Community*, 85, 94, 98–99; and Clayton, *Forgotten Prophet*, 115–16.

87. Hansen, "Affinity and Ambivalence," 46.

88. Randolph Bourne, "A Glance at German 'Kultur,'" *Lippincott's Monthly Magazine* (February 7, 1915), quoted in Clayton, *Forgotten Prophet*, 138. Bourne, "American Use for German Ideals," *New Republic* (September 4, 1915), in Bourne, *War and the Intellectuals*, 48–52. Also see Bourne, "The Disillusionment," in Hansen, *Radical Will*, 406.

89. Randolph Bourne, "The Dodging of Pressures," in Hansen, *Radical Will*, 115, 128, 131, 133. Also see Clayton, *Forgotten Prophet*, 86.

90. Bourne, "A Sociological Poet," 520–21. Bourne, "The Dodging of Pressures," 131. Bourne's most compelling answer to this question would appear in "Trans-National America," which celebrated a cosmopolitan multiculturalism that

would nurture the group identities that would enable individuals to resist the "tasteless, colorless . . . uniformity" of mass society and popular culture (Hansen, *Radical Will*, 254).

91. Clayton, *Forgotten Prophet*, 159. Blake, *Beloved Community*, 73. Abramson, *Lyrical Left*, 34. Bourne to Alyse Gregory, July 24, 1915, in Bourne, *Letters*, 311.

92. "Never was his prose so charged, his tone so taut, his arguments so strong," judges Michael Walzer, "as in the essays that he wrote for *Seven Arts* between June and October 1917" (*Company of Critics*, 55).

93. Randolph Bourne, "War and the Intellectuals," *Seven Arts* (June 1917), in Hansen, *Radical Will*, 311–12, 307, 315, 309.

94. In criticizing Dewey, Bourne was not abandoning pragmatism so much as accusing Dewey himself of abandoning the pragmatic spirit. Thus in "Twilight of Idols," Bourne opens and closes by appealing to "the spirit of William James" (*Seven Arts* [October 1917], in Hansen, *Radical Will*, 336, 347). Also see Robert B. Westbrook, *John Dewey and American Democracy* (Ithaca, N.Y.: Cornell University Press, 1991), especially 197, 206–8.

95. Bourne, "Twilight of Idols," 339, 336–37. Clayton, *Forgotten Prophet*, 265.

96. Bourne, "The Dodging of Pressures," 132. Also see Clayton, *Forgotten Prophet*, 86.

97. Bourne, "The Disillusionment," 396–99, 404. Faint remnants of that progressive faith are evident in Bourne's halfhearted closing paragraph, in which he hopes the war may teach us "the insane peril of leaving about loose and omnipotent in the world antiquated institutions to shatter at any moment the order and beauty we are realizing" and shake "us out of our fatuous complacency of shibboleths and creeds, and [make] us long for a clear and radiant civilization as a lover desires his bride" (407). This essay was never published.

98. Bourne, "Twilight of Idols," 336–38. Bourne, "The Disillusionment," 397. Bourne, "War and the Intellectuals," 308.

99. Resek, Introduction, in Bourne, *War and the Intellectuals*, xi.

100. Bourne, "Law and Order," 354. Also see Bourne, "The Doctrine of the Rights of Man," 245.

101. Randolph Bourne, "War Diary," *Seven Arts* (September 1917), 535–47, in Hansen, *Radical Will*, 324.

102. Randolph Bourne, "The State," in Hansen, *Radical Will*, 370–71, 360. The essay was written during 1918 and was unfinished at the time of his death. Oppenheim published it posthumously in *Untimely Papers* (New York: B. W. Huebsch, 1919).

103. Bourne, "The State," 366–67, 359, 361. In a similar vein, Bourne wrote to Van Wyck Brooks that "the war has brought an immense and terrifying inflation to the political sphere, so that for most people non-governmentalized activity has ceased almost to have significance" (Bourne to Van Wyck Brooks, March 27, 1918, in Bourne, *Letters*, 412).

104. Bourne, "The Disillusionment," 407. Bourne, "War and the Intellectuals," 317.

105. Walzer, *Company of Critics*, 63. Randolph Bourne, "Old Tyrannies," in Hansen, *Radical Will*, 171, 173. The essay was given its title by Oppenheim, who pub-

lished it posthumously in *Untimely Papers*. Cf. Bourne's essay "For Radicals," in *Youth and Life* (Boston: Houghton Mifflin, 1913).

106. Blake, *Beloved Community*, 239, 246, 255. "Are Artists People?" *New Masses* (January 1927), 5. Editorial, *Seven Arts* (November 1916), 52.

107. Waldo Frank, "How I Came to Communism: A Symposium," *New Masses* (September 1932), 6–7.

108. For the judgment of Gold as the most important literary Communist, see Alan M. Wald, *The New York Intellectuals: The Rise and Decline of the Anti-Stalinist Left from the 1930s to the 1980s* (Chapel Hill: University of North Carolina Press, 1987), 47. Gold's contemporary, V. F. Calverton, writing in 1932, judged Gold to be "the second most important revolutionary writer in this country," behind only John Dos Passos (James D. Bloom, *Left Letters: The Culture Wars of Mike Gold and Joseph Freeman* [New York: Columbia University Press, 1992], 2). Also see Robert Wolf's contemporary judgment, quoted in Daniel Aaron, *Writers on the Left* (New York: Avon, 1965), 429n5; as well as Stanley Burnshaw's reminiscence quoted in Alan M. Wald, *Writing from the Left: New Essays on Radical Culture and Politics* (London: Verso, 1994), 72. Edmund Wilson believed Gold the most "naturally gifted" of the Communist writers (Aaron, *Writers on the Left*, 259), a judgment echoed by Bender in *New York Intellect*, 246. Also see Bloom, *Left Letters*, 7, 57.

109. Irwin Granich [Michael Gold], "Towards Proletarian Art," *Liberator* (February 1921), 22–24. Gold did voice one criticism of Whitman: "He made but one mistake. . . . He dreamed the grand dream of political democracy, and thought it could express in completion all the aspirations of proletarian man . . . [but] political democracy failed to evoke from the masses . . . all the grandeur and creativeness Walt knew so well were latent in them" (22–23). Gold also has words of praise for Whitman in "Let It Be Really New!" *New Masses* (June 1926), 26; "America Needs a Critic," *New Masses* (October 1926), 7; "The Ninth Year," *New Masses* (November 1926), 5; and "Wilder: Prophet of the Genteel Christ," *New Republic* (October 22, 1930), in Loren Baritz, ed., *The American Left: Radical Political Thought in the Twentieth Century* (New York: Basic Books, 1971), 195. More ambivalent is Gold's essay, "Three Schools of U.S. Writing," *New Masses* (September 1928), where he praises Whitman but repeats in more emphatic terms his earlier criticism: "Now . . . Walt Whitman's IDEA [of Democracy] is dead. That is why he sounds now, in moments, so old-fashioned, so naive and soft" (13).

110. Irwin Granich [Michael Gold], "Spiritual Pikers," *Liberator* (April 1920), 47. Also see Irwin Granich [Michael Gold], "Under Two Flags," *Liberator* (October 1920), 19. At the close of "Spiritual Pikers," Gold does have a moment of doubt, acknowledging that perhaps "we will lose after all." But this is only a prelude to rejecting liberal reformism: "We would rather lose everything than gain that which the liberals gain."

111. Michael Gold, "Hope for America," *Liberator* (December 1921), 14–15. Also see Michael Gold, "The American Famine," *Liberator* (November 1921), 5, as well as Michael Gold, "Girl by the River," *New Masses* (August 26, 1926), 20, and Gold, "America Needs a Critic," 7: "The revolution of the workers today will inevitably lay its hand on our own culture, and make it over anew. How could it be otherwise?"

112. Richard H. Pells, *Radical Visions and American Dreams: Culture and Social Thought in the Depression Years* (1973; reprint ed., Middletown, Conn.: Wesleyan University Press, 1984), 174; also see 175.

113. Aaron, *Writers on the Left*, 109–13, quotation on 111. On McKay, see Aaron, *Writers on the Left*, 101–2.

114. Ibid., 116, 113, 115, 118–20.

115. Ibid., 119.

116. Michael Gold, "On Being Radical" *New Masses* (May 1927), 3, quoted in Aaron, *Writers on the Left*, 219. The original *Masses* contained a statement in every issue, written by Max Eastman, declaring that it was "a magazine with a sense of humor and no respect for the respectable: frank, arrogant, impertinent. Searching for the true causes; a magazine directed against rigidity and dogma wherever it is found" (ibid., 39). On Hayden's similar declarations, see chapter 4 of this book.

117. On the contrast between the *Masses* and the *New Masses*, see the judgments offered in Fishbein, *Rebels in Bohemia*, 207; Diggins, *Rise and Fall of the American Left*, 155–57; Bender, *New York Intellect*, 246; and Aaron, *Writers on the Left*.

118. Among Daniel Aaron's great accomplishments in *Writers on the Left*, as Alan Wald writes, is to root "the leftist literary tradition in indigenous trends in U.S. culture beginning with the pre–World War I literary rebellion championed by the *Masses*" (Wald, *Writing from the Left*, 19; also see 87). Also good on this score is James Burkhart Gilbert, *Writers and Partisans: A History of Literary Radicalism in America* (New York: John Wiley, 1968), and Pells, *Radical Visions and American Dreams*.

119. Gorman, *Left Intellectuals and Popular Culture*, 112, 117. Gold, "Three Schools of U.S. Writing," 14. Also see Michael Gold, "John Reed and the Real Thing," *New Masses* (November 1927), 7; Michael Gold, "American Jungle Notes" *New Masses* (December 1929), 8; and Aaron, *Writers on the Left*, 116, 231.

120. In November 1930, the Second World Plenum of the International Bureau of Revolutionary Literature, which Gold attended, issued a number of explicit instructions to the *New Masses*, including the need to make itself "in every respect the cultural organ of the class-conscious workers" (Aaron, *Writers on the Left*, 238). To be sure, in Gold's case conformity and inner conviction were so closely merged, at least prior to the Popular Front period that commenced in 1935, that telling them apart was rarely easy. But when in 1932 he could inform his longtime friend and associate, V. F. Calverton, that "publishers wanted some quotation [for your book], but I'd rather not until you get yourself cleared up with the Party," Gold had clearly subordinated individual conscience and integrity to party directives (Leonard Wilcox, *V. F. Calverton: Radical in the American Grain* [Philadelphia: Temple University Press, 1992], 129).

121. The term "romance" is appropriate in view of Gold's description of Russia as "fresh, as new and beautiful as first love" ("The Ninth Year," *New Masses*, [November 1926], 5). After returning from Russia in 1924, Gold told Upton Sinclair that in Russia everything was "so simple and real. . . . one sheds one's years there" (Aaron, *Writers on the Left*, 161–62).

122. Granich [Gold], "Towards Proletarian Art," 23. Gold, "America Needs a Critic," 7. Also see Aaron, *Writers on the Left*, 224.

123. Horace Traubel, "With Walt Whitman in Camden," *Seven Arts* (September 1917), 633, 630, 632.

124. Gold, "America Needs a Critic," 7. Gold, "Three Schools of U.S. Writing," 13. Michael Gold, "Notes of the Month," *New Masses* (September 1930), 5. Also see Gorman, *Left Intellectuals and Popular Culture*, 117.

125. Michael Gold, "Two Critics in a Bar-room," *Liberator* (September 1921), 31. As late as December 1929, though, Gold could still come to the defense of his friend Upton Sinclair by insisting, "It is almost impossible to approach literature and art in the party spirit. . . . It is a mistake to judge [Sinclair] solely as a member of the Socialist party. A writer must in the last analysis be judged by his work; not by his private morals or party affiliations" (*New Masses* [December 1929], 23).

126. Michael Gold, "Notes of the Month," *New Masses* (April 1930), quoted in Aaron, *Writers on the Left*, 254. *New Masses* (June 1930), 22, quoted in Aaron, *Writers on the Left*, 256; emphasis added. Michael Gold, "Out of the Fascist Unconscious," *New Republic* (July 26, 1933), quoted in Aaron, *Writers on the Left*, 283. Michael Gold, *Hollow Men* (1941), 21, quoted in Wald, *New York Intellectuals*, 94; also see 95. Michael Gold, "Renegades: A Warning of the End," in *Mike Gold: A Literary Anthology*, ed. Michael Folsom (New York: International Publishers, 1972), 264–65. Michael Gold, "A Letter to the Author of a First Book," *New Masses* (January 9, 1934), 25, quoted in Pells, *Radical Visions and American Dreams*, 172. Also see Gold, "Wilder: Prophet of the Genteel Christ." Stinging criticisms of Gold's reductive approach to art can be found in Aaron, *Writers on the Left*, 136 (Robert Sage), 218 (Ernest Walsh), 421–22n19 (E. E. Cummings). Best of all, perhaps, is Philip Rahv's put-down of proletarian realism as the "literature of a party disguised as the literature of a class" (Bender, *New York Intellect*, 246; also see Wald, *New York Intellectuals*).

127. Granich [Gold], "Towards Proletarian Art," 22, 21. Gorman, *Left Intellectuals and Popular Culture*, 112. Also see Aaron, *Writers on the Left*, 218, 283.

128. Gold, "Two Critics in a Bar-room," 30–31. Also see Gorman, *Left Intellectuals and Popular Culture*, 113–14.

129. Michael Gold, "Thoughts of a Great Thinker," *Liberator* (March 1922), in Folsom, *Gold: A Literary Anthology*, 114. Also see Gorman, *Left Intellectuals and Popular Culture*, 115.

130. Michael Gold, "Toward an American Revolutionary Culture," *New Masses* (July 1931), 12.

131. Ibid. Gold, "American Jungle Notes," 8. Freeman, quoted in Aaron, *Writers on the Left*, 101. Paul Gorman has shown that such unflattering portraits of the people and contempt for their preferred modes of entertainment pervaded the *New Masses* and the Communist left more generally. Harry Alan Potamkin, film critic for the *New Masses*, argued that images in film "become the beliefs of the impressionable audience, whose mind [*sic*] receives the suggestions like wax and retains them like marble." Hollywood films, Lewis Jacobs opined, were a "stupefying opiate." In the *New Masses*, Philip Sterling described how "the magic sounds" of popular music had hypnotized America into fighting in World War I, and predicted that in the next war the latest and even more potent techniques of popular music would "din a new message of mass suicide to unprecedented numbers of workers over the radio and

through the talkies." The masses, in Sterling's view, were lemminglike, to be led wherever the capitalist pipers might wish to take them (*Left Intellectuals and Popular Culture*, 121, 119, 121; also see 109).

132. Aaron, *Writers on the Left*, 234.

133. When Upton Sinclair approached Gold in 1924 about starting up a revolutionary literary magazine to replace the *Liberator*, Gold cautioned his friend: "It is like being asked by a pure young girl in marriage when one is a battered old roue with five or six affairs on hand. I am immoral, Upton, I drink, smoke, swear, loaf, sneer, shoot pool, dance jazz, shake the shimmy, ride box-cars, and do most everything. . . . After I have been with good people, formal people, however revolutionary, for more than a month or two, I want to bust loose and do something wild. . . . I'm a good Red, etc. and take that seriously enough, but . . . I can't be as pure, fervent and puritanical as yourself, Upton, and I would not want to be. The mass of humanity, stupid or intellectual, is fond of any kind of fun, sensuality, relaxation, sport and frivolity, and I am one of them. . . . I love humor, joy and happy people; I love big groups at play, and friends sitting around a table, talking, smoking, and laughing. I love song and athletics and a lot of other things. I wish the world were all play and everybody happy and creative as children. That is Communism, the communism of the future" (Aaron, *Writers on the Left*, 115, 117). Such sentiments would seem to bode well for a radicalism that did not take itself too seriously, and that identified and kept in touch with existing people rather than an idealized folk of the egalitarian imagination. That Gold nonetheless ended up bedazzled by a mythical Soviet Russia and became a shameless apologist for Stalinism becomes an even more intriguing puzzle.

134. Gold, "Let It Be Really New!" 20. Gold, "American Jungle Notes," 8. Also see Michael Gold, "Faster, America, Faster," *New Masses* (November 1926), 7–8.

135. *New Masses* (December 1926), 23, quoted in Aaron, *Writers on the Left*, 218. Michael Gold, "Notes of the Month," *New Masses* (February 1930), 3, emphasis added. Gold, "American Jungle Notes," 9. Also see Gorman, *Left Intellectuals and Popular Cultures*, 134.

136. Michael Gold, "Palm Sunday in the Coal Fields," *Liberator* (May 1922), 9, in Baritz, *American Left*, 181. Granich [Gold], "Towards Proletarian Art," 20. On Jack London's similar vision of a future "race of supermen," see Aaron, *Writers on the Left*, 38.

137. Aaron, *Writers on the Left*, 162.

138. See, for example, Gold, "Renegades: A Warning of the End," 274–76. Also see Aaron, *Writers on the Left*, 392.

139. Aaron, *Writers on the Left*, 402.

140. Gold, "Let It Be Really New!" 20. Gold, "America Needs a Critic," 7. Granich [Gold], "Spiritual Pikers," 46. Michael Gold, "Loud Speaker and Other Essays," *New Masses* (March 1927), 5–6. Aaron, *Writers on the Left*, 224.

141. Gilbert, *Writers and Partisans*, 92. Aaron, *Writers on the Left*, 167, 90.

142. Gilbert, *Writers and Partisans*, 93.

143. Dewey visited the Soviet Union in 1928 and reported very favorably on his "Impressions of Soviet Russia" in a five-part series for the *New Republic* at the end of that year. Russians, Dewey found, were striving to create the sort of "integrated life"

that was systematically thwarted by America's "money culture" (quoted in Pells, *Radical Visions and American Dreams*, 31–32; also see 66). Dewey's *New Republic* reports were published the next year as *Impressions of Soviet Russia and the Revolutionary World: Mexico-China-Turkey* (New York: New Republic, 1929). Dreiser spent eleven weeks in Russia in 1927, and his generally favorable though not uncritical assessment was published as *Dreiser Looks at Russia* (New York: H. Liveright, 1928). See Aaron, *Writers on the Left*, 159–60. John Dos Passos visited Russia in 1921 and again in 1928, and believed Russia offered unprecedented opportunities for "unstagnant lives," although his impressions, like Dreiser's, were mixed with strong criticisms, especially about the terroristic methods of the secret police. See Aaron, *Writers on the Left*, 160–61. Steffens visited Russia in 1917, 1918, and 1923; he wrote glowingly of the Soviet Union in *Moses in Red* (1926) and in his *Autobiography* (1931). See Aaron, *Writers on the Left*, 85, 143–48. Calverton visited Russia in 1927 and published his favorable impressions in the pages of the *Modern Quarterly*, which he edited, and the *New Masses*, as well as in a book, *The Bankruptcy of Marriage* (1928; reprint ed., New York: Arno Press, 1972). Freeman visited the Soviet Union in 1926; see Aaron, *Writers on the Left*, 148–56. "Almost every day during the twenties," reports Aaron, an article or essay appeared in the American newspaper and periodical press attacking, defending, analyzing, or describing the Soviet Union (*Writers on the Left*, 157).

144. Pells, *Radical Visions and American Dreams*, 98.

145. Hollander, *Political Pilgrims*, 135, 120–21. Aaron, *Writers on the Left*, 169–70.

146. Cf. John Maynard Keynes: "Communism is not a reaction against the failure of the 19th century to organize optimal economic output. It is a reaction against its comparative success. It is a protest against the emptiness of economic welfare, an appeal to the ascetic in us all" (Hollander, *Political Pilgrims*, 121–22).

147. On the evolution of the term "New Left" see Maurice Isserman, *If I Had a Hammer . . . : The Death of the Old Left and the Birth of the New Left* (New York: Basic Books, 1987), 173–74.

148. The quotation is from Randolph Bourne, "The Price of Radicalism" (1916), in Hansen, *Radical Will*, 299. On the young Old Left's desire for a counterculture and countermorality, see Pells, *Radical Visions and American Dreams*, xv. Also see Robert Cohen, *When the Old Left Was Young: Student Radicals and America's First Mass Student Movement, 1929–1941* (New York: Oxford University Press, 1993).

149. Hayden's speech was distributed as a pamphlet by SDS at the 1963 National Student Association Congress. In 1966 alone, James Miller reports, SDS printed ten thousand copies of the speech. "Apart from *The Port Huron Statement* itself," judges Miller, "it was one of the most widely circulated radical pamphlets of the Sixties" (*"Democracy Is in the Streets": From Port Huron to the Siege of Chicago* [New York: Touchstone, 1987], 100). Savio's "An End to History" was originally published in the December 1964 issue of *Humanity*, and was reprinted in virtually every edited collection of New Left speeches and writings that appeared during the 1960s. It is reprinted, for example, in Massimo Teodori, ed., *The New Left: A Documentary History* (Indianapolis: Bobbs-Merrill, 1969), 158–61; Mitchell Cohen and Dennis Hale, ed., *The New Student Left: An Anthology*, rev. and exp. ed. (Boston: Beacon, 1967), 248–52; and Paul Jacobs and Saul Landau, *The New Radicals: A Report with Documents*

(New York: Vintage, 1966), 230–34; as well as Seymour Martin Lipset and Sheldon S. Wolin, eds., *The Berkeley Student Revolt* (New York: Anchor, 1965), 216–19; and Michael V. Miller and Susan Gilmore, eds., *Revolution at Berkeley* (New York: Dell, 1965), 239–43.

150. Thomas Hayden, "Student Social Action: From Liberation to Community," in Cohen and Hale, *New Student Left*, 280, 282, 287–89. The passage beginning "There is no willingness" was used virtually verbatim in the *Port Huron Statement*, which Hayden drafted. See Teodori, *The New Left*, 169. Cf. Hayden's 1961 "A Letter to the New (Young) Left" (Cohen and Hale, *New Student Left*, 4), in which he spoke of having "turned with trembling and disgust from the Americans who do recognize peril and recoil into shelters full of the comforting gadgets the culture has produced." War, Hayden mused, "ironically, would be cathartic — though the release would be grimly brief."

151. Savio, "An End to History," in Teodori, *The New Left*, 161. In the same vein, Larry D. Spence contemptuously dismissed "the vacuous suburban ranch," "the mortgaged home, the gadgeted housewife, and the communal martinis" ("Berkeley: What It Demonstrates," *Studies on the Left* 5 [Winter 1965], 67). Also see Michael Nagler, "Berkeley: The Demonstrations," *Studies on the Left* 5 (Winter 1965), 56.

152. Todd Gitlin, *The Sixties: Years of Hope, Days of Rage* (New York: Bantam, 1987), 101, 105. Also see Howard Zinn, *SNCC: The New Abolitionists* (Boston: Beacon Press, 1965), 15; and *America and the New Era* (1963), as quoted by Richard Rothstein, "Evolution of ERAP Organizers," in Priscilla Long, ed., *The New Left: A Collection of Essays* (Boston: Porter Sargent, 1969), 276.

153. Cf. James Oppenheim's plea: "[We] cannot now be content alone with factory-work, or business, or the flat metallic taste of money. We aspire . . . for something beyond ourselves, . . . and to which we may so give ourselves that life acquires an interest, an intensity, . . . and brings all our submerged powers into play. We aspire to be alive in every part of ourselves" (Editorial, *Seven Arts* [March 1917], 505). In notes Hayden drafted for the *Port Huron Statement*, he valiantly wrestled with some of the difficulties posed by the yearning he felt for an "attachment to a consuming cause or a transcendent form of being." People in an authoritarian or even totalitarian regime, Hayden thought, "can be mobilized by a sense of mission, an identity with some transcendent cause," but could "a non-totalitarian society generate the same elan, mission, purposefulness?" ("Manifesto Notes: Problems of Democracy," Convention Document #2, March 19, 1962, p. 5, SDS Microfilm, Series 1, No. 6, Wisconsin State Historical Society, Madison). Was it possible to build a more exciting, more meaningful politics without eroding or destroying individual freedoms?

154. Jack Newfield, *A Prophetic Minority* (New York: New American Library, 1966), 212. Newfield himself disparages "the desert of the 1950's" (123) and the "sterile suburbs" (32).

155. See Isserman, *If I Had a Hammer*, 174.

156. See Hayden, "Letter to the New (Young) Left," 3, 6. Also see C. Wright Mills, "Letter to the New Left," in Long, *The New Left*, 22.

157. Gitlin, *The Sixties*, 383.

CHAPTER 4. The Illiberal Turn

1. Todd Gitlin, *The Twilight of Common Dreams: Why America Is Wracked by Culture Wars* (New York: Henry Holt, 1995), 223.

2. Mary Douglas, *Natural Symbols: Explorations in Cosmology* (1970; reprint ed., New York: Pantheon, 1982), 117.

3. James Miller, *"Democracy Is in the Streets": From Port Huron to the Siege of Chicago* (New York: Touchstone, 1987), 311–13; Todd Gitlin, *The Sixties: Years of Hope, Days of Rage* (New York: Bantam, 1987), 393–94; Kirkpatrick Sale, *SDS* (New York: Random House, 1973), 602–8.

4. Tom Hayden, *Reunion: A Memoir* (New York: Random House, 1988), 74. Hayden also used this same phrase in notes he made toward the end of 1961 for a book of essays he planned to pull together on the New Left ("Proposed Book of Essays," [n.d.], SDS Microfilm, Series 1, No. 11, Wisconsin State Historical Society, Madison).

5. The *Port Huron Statement*, in Massimo Teodori, ed., *The New Left: A Documentary History* (Indianapolis: Bobbs-Merrill, 1969), 168, 166.

6. Miller, *Democracy Is in the Streets*, 29. Sale, *SDS*, 30. Maurice Isserman, *If I Had a Hammer . . . : The Death of the Old Left and the Birth of the New Left* (New York: Basic Books, 1987), 204. The name change from SLID to SDS formally occurred on January 1, 1960 (Isserman, *If I Had a Hammer*, 204).

7. Sale, *SDS*, 24–25. Isserman, *If I Had a Hammer*, 206.

8. Haber to Nathaniel Minkoff, April 15, 1961, cited in Sale, *SDS*, 24, 698. Minkoff was chairman of the board of LID, and at the time Haber had just been fired as SDS field director (he was soon reinstated after the LID Executive Committee had a change of heart). Haber's phraseology must thus be seen in part at least as an effort to mollify LID elders.

9. Al Haber, "Professionals and Social Change Project," December 1961, SDS Microfilm, Series 1, No. 3. In an exchange in the spring of 1962 with Nick Bateson, an English New Leftist who was disturbed by what he saw as the liberal as opposed to leftist slant of SDS, Haber struggled with the shifting meaning of these words. Haber's interest was in creating an organization that was home to both "leftists" (like Bateson) who tend "to focus on structural change" and "liberals" who tend to focus on values and what the good society should look like. The leftist, Haber conceded, "has theory, the liberal doesn't"; the leftist, moreover, tends to be more politically active and aware. Yet Haber was insistent "that the leftists [should] not predominate." Leftists, Haber felt, were "more alienated [than liberals] from (in a dysfunctional sense) American society and institutions of change." Moreover, since leftists were a small minority on campuses they "should not dominate an organization that preports [*sic*] to be broad." SDS, Haber concluded, must include the "left," but "the main portion of membership and dominant image of the organization will be liberal." "Aims and Purposes of SDS: Some Comments," [n.d.], SDS Microfilm, Series 1, No. 6. At the time, Bateson was chairman of the New Left Club at Chapel Hill, North Carolina, as well as a member of the SDS National Committee.

10. "What Is the S.D.S.?" [n.d.], SDS Microfilm, Series 1, No. 6. This statement defining SDS was issued in the spring of 1962. The proposed agenda for the SDS meeting in December 1961 started from the premise that "an organization on the left . . . must bring together liberals and radicals" (Proposed Agenda, Students for a Democratic Society Organization Discussion, December 29–31, 1961, Ann Arbor, Michigan, SDS Microfilm, Series 1, No. 3). Also see "Draft Constitution," May 20, 1962, SDS Microfilm, Series 1, No. 6; and "An Open Letter to the Student Community," issued by the officers of SDS in the wake of Port Huron, SDS Microfilm, Series 1, No. 24.

11. SDS Convention Bulletin, April 25, 1962, SDS Microfilm Series 1, No. 6. Also see Al Haber, "Memorandum on the National Student Association Congress, Re: Organization of a 'liberal study group,'" SDS Microfilm Series 1, No. 21.

12. Al Haber and Jerry Schwinn, for instance, wrote a paper that spoke of "the liberal and radical community" ("Peace Research in the University," [n.d.], p. 7 SDS Microfilm Series 1, No. 24). The same words were used in the letter by National Secretary Jim Monsonis (May 1, 1963, SDS Microfilm, Series 2A, No. 2) that accompanied a leaflet announcing the 1963 SDS convention. That radicals and liberals were seen as distinct is also clear. At the first official convention of SDS in New York, held in June 1960, "a major area of concern throughout the discussions," according to a published account, "was the distinction between liberal activity, which attempts to realize the American Dream, and radical activity, which proposes fundamental changes in that dream and which suggests alternatives" (Miller, *Democracy Is in the Streets*, 38).

13. Hayden, *Reunion*, 42. Miller, *Democracy Is in the Streets*, 50–51.

14. Miller, *Democracy Is in the Streets*, 53. Hayden, *Reunion*, 43. VOICE was modeled after SLATE in Berkeley, where Hayden had visited in the summer of 1960.

15. Sale, *SDS*, 35–36. Miller, *Democracy Is in the Streets*, 59–60.

16. Tom Hayden, "Who Are the Student Boat-Rockers?" *Mademoiselle* (August 1961). Copy in SDS Microfilm, Series 1, No. 11. Hayden, form letter to SDS community, December 5, 1961, SDS Microfilm, Series 1, No. 3. Tom Hayden, "Proposed Book of Essays," [n.d.], SDS Microfilm, Series 1, No. 11. Comments from Tom Hayden in partial reply to [Questions from Betty Garman], in "Aims and Purposes of SDS: Some Comments," SDS Microfilm, Series 1, No. 6. Even as late as the spring of 1964, Hayden can still be found making reference to "the liberal-radical community." See Hayden to Sumner Rosen, March 31, 1964, SDS Microfilm, Series 2B, No. 9.

17. Thomas Hayden, "A Letter to the New (Young) Left," in Mitchell Cohen and Dennis Hale, eds., *The New Student Left: An Anthology*, rev. and exp. ed. (Boston: Beacon Press, 1967), 2–3. Sale, *SDS*, 36–37.

18. Hayden, "Letter to the New (Young) Left," 3–4; emphasis added. The previous fall, in a *Michigan Daily* editorial, Hayden had credited the students' sense of idealism not only to Ghandi and Camus but also to "Mill and classic liberalism" and "Jefferson's attitude on liberty" (Miller, *Democracy Is in the Streets*, 51). In September 1962, Hayden still maintained that "SDS stands for the best values of the liberal

community" ("President's Report," in *SDS Membership Bulletin*, No. 1 (1962–1963), p. 3, SDS Microfilm, Series 4A, No. 19).

19. Hayden, "Letter to New (Young) Left," 3, 6. The title of Hayden's piece was self-consciously modeled on Mills's own "Letter to the New Left," which had been published the year before in the *New Left Review*. On Mills's influence on Hayden, see Miller, *Democracy Is in the Streets*, chapter 4.

20. Hayden, "Letter to the New (Young) Left," 7–8.

21. Hayden, "Letter to the New (Young) Left," 5–6. Thomas Hayden, "Student Social Action: From Liberation to Community," in Cohen and Hale, *The New Student Left*, 282. Similar in spirit was Al Haber's conception of radicalism as "getting people to think," and his withering disdain for leftist organizations "suffocating under a blanket of slogans, euphemisms and empty jargon" (Haber to Charles Van Tassel, July 31, 1958, quoted in Miller, *Democracy Is in the Streets*, 30–31). At the first SDS convention in June 1960, the official account stressed that there was general agreement on what one participant called "Cartesian radicalism," i.e., the constant asking of "Why?" (Miller, *Democracy Is in the Streets*, 39).

22. Hayden, "Student Social Action: From Liberation to Community," 273–74; emphasis added.

23. "An Open Letter to the Student Community," issued by SDS Officers after Port Huron, supported transforming our "universities . . . into places of intellectual excellence" and upheld the ideal of "academic freedom in a university free from state authority" (SDS Microfilm, Series 1, No. 24).

24. Hayden's early draft notes for the *Port Huron Statement* declared: "I am proposing that we cease in the use of the slogans, the slams, the 'tyranny of categories'" ("Manifesto Notes: A Beginning Draft," Convention Document #1, March 19, 1962, p. 3, SDS Microfilm, Series 1, No. 6).

25. Hayden, "New Student Action in a World of Crisis," the *Michigan Daily*, September 16, 1960, quoted in Miller, *Democracy Is in the Streets*, 51.

26. Thomas Hayden, "President's Report," *SDS Membership Bulletin*, No. 1 (1962–1963), p. 3, SDS Microfilm, Series 4A, No. 19.

27. Sale, *SDS*, 204; see also 204–6, 211, 213, 215.

28. Hayden, *Reunion*, 259, 275–79.

29. SDS' *America and the New Era* (1963) argued that people were "increasingly being radicalized as they experienced the events of the new era" (Sale, *SDS*, 92).

30. The best example is Kirkpatrick Sale's *SDS*, which, as James Miller notes, "is justifiably regarded as the standard history of [SDS]" (*Democracy Is in the Streets*, 379n1).

31. Sale, *SDS*, 123–24.

32. Ibid., 204.

33. Jeffrey Shero, "Bulletin Proposal," 1965 SDS National Convention—Working Paper, SDS Microfilm, Series 2A, No. 16.

34. Interestingly, Stanley Rothman and S. Robert Lichter's study suggests strong similarities in the motivations and personality orientations of early and late New Leftists (*Roots of Radicalism: Jews, Christians, and the New Left* [New York: Oxford University Press, 1982], chapter 8).

35. Miller, *Democracy Is in the Streets*, 291. In the process of making his argument for a dramatic generational and ideological break between the "old guard" and the "new breed" of younger radicals, Sale quotes from Greg Calvert's report on the draft program in January 1967. The draft program was vital, the soon-to-be SDS president argued, because "it talks about the kind of struggle which has been most meaningful to the new left — the revolutionary struggle which engages and claims the lives of those involved despite the seeming impossibility of revolutionary social change — the struggle which has the power to transform, to revolutionize human lives whether or not it can revolutionize the societal conditions of human existence. . . . It offers no clear path to power, no magic formula for success, only struggle and a new life. No promise is made, only the hope that struggle and confrontation with the existing system of humanity will create freedom in the midst of life-destroying society" (Sale, *SDS*, 315–16). Far from this being the distinctive voice of a new generation, it directly echoed Hayden's language and thoughts, particularly Hayden's essay from early 1966, "The Ability to Face Whatever Comes." Moreover, the move "from protest to resistance" and the emphasis on putting "bodies on the line" (Sale, *SDS*, 316), which characterized the draft resistance program in 1966 and 1967, was already there in Hayden's 1961 report, "Revolution in Mississippi," especially p. 21, SDS Microfilm, Series 4B, No. 159.

36. The generational explanation looks more plausible if we focus on Paul Booth or Al Haber; indeed, Sale, when making the generational argument, often quotes from these two as representative of the old guard. But Booth, as Sale admits, "had always been in the careful center of SDS" (*SDS*, 224), and Haber, who was substantially older than Hayden, Gitlin, Potter, and the rest of the old guard, was, from at least December 1963 on (when he lost decisively to Hayden over the issue of ERAP), a marginalized voice whose Cassandra-like warnings were almost uniformly ignored. When Haber, for example, warned in the fall of 1965 about "a certain hostility or intolerance to people whose vocation is not obviously 'radical' and who pursue interests apart from the organizing objectives of the 'movement,'" this was not, as Sale would have it, the old guard doing battle with the newer generation (*SDS*, 222); rather, it was an isolated Haber once again taking aim at the direction Hayden and much of the rest of the old guard had taken SDS. Certainly Haber's criticism is more true of Hayden than of any other person in SDS.

37. The tension between these two desires was perceptively identified by Dick Flacks in "Some Problems, Issues, Proposals," 1965 SDS National Convention — Working Paper, SDS Microfilm, Series 2A, No. 16. Flacks counterposed "existential humanism," i.e., the desire to live a life of egalitarian community "unencumbered by the conventional barriers of race, status, class, etc.," and "radical transformation of the social order," i.e., the desire to redistribute wealth and power in the larger society (p. 1). Flacks's judgment in the summer of 1965 was that SDS and SNCC "have so far done a pretty good job of maintaining the necessary tension between these two orientations" (p. 2), although his paper also made clear his feeling that the organization was tending to become overly concerned with "existential humanism" at the expense of social change. My own view is that by the middle of 1965 the balance had already been thrown badly out of kilter, with purity and disengagement driving out

effectiveness. The desire to effect social change remained strong within SDS, but political action that entailed involving oneself in what were seen as relations of manipulation and compromise had become increasingly taboo and difficult to defend.

38. Cohen and Hale, *The New Student Left*, 7. Hayden continued, "This extends from the concrete formation of a national student organization to the conceptual — for the time being — formation of a different society."

39. [Tom Hayden], "Politics, the Individual, and SDS," SDS Microfilm, Series 1, No. 6. Also see the discussion in Miller, *Democracy Is in the Streets*, 99; Miller mistakenly identifies the title as "Politics, the Intellectual, and SDS." In a memo to the SDS Executive Committee that same spring, Hayden phrased the dilemma this way: "We want to be involved enough within the structural mainstream to be influential, but detached enough from it to maintain personal intellectual independence and perspective" (Hayden to SDS Executive Committee, others, Re: Manifesto, [n.d.], SDS Microfilm, Series 1, No. 6).

40. Hayden to Executive Committee, others: Re: Manifesto, SDS Microfilm, Series 1, No. 6.

41. "The Port Huron Statement," reprinted as an appendix in Miller, *Democracy Is in the Streets*, 332, 335.

42. Hayden, "Proposed Book of Essays," [n.d], SDS Microfilm, Series 1, No. 11.

43. Sale, *SDS*, 116–17.

44. Indeed, a number of early SDSers who came from liberal or socialist families found that their activism met with unqualified parental approval. Sharon Jeffrey, for instance, who reports that "the things I was doing — sympathy strikes, civil rights demonstrations, *The Port Huron Statement*—were applauded by my parents" (Miller, *Democracy Is in the Streets*, 185). Hayden's early activism, on the other hand, met with considerably less enthusiasm from his blue-collar Catholic parents, who felt their son was throwing away his education and life (*Reunion*, 126).

45. In his first President's Report, for instance, published in the *SDS Membership Bulletin* in September 1962, Hayden asked for "the aid of [liberal] intellectuals older and more experienced than ourselves," but also expressed SDS' fear that "the liberal movement today moves tragically . . . 'from the picket line to the picket fence'" (SDS Microfilm, Series 4A, No. 19).

46. Sale, *SDS*, 97.

47. This was a dilemma he continued to worry about into the next year. In a long letter to fellow SDSer Steve Johnson in the spring of 1963, Hayden wrote that "we want both independence and access to the establishment. . . . We do not choose to be the Young Democrats, we choose instead to be respected and welcome in every sector, especially the liberal ones, of the Establishment, without merging our identity and theirs." Engagement with liberal organizations carried with it the risk of leading "to our co-optation into the wrong ranks"; creating "the counter-community" carried with it the danger that it might be devoid of politics and "become a ghetto from the world" (May 10, 1963, SDS Microfilm, Series 2A, No. 25).

48. The model for ERAP, at least in Hayden's mind, was the Student Nonviolent Coordinating Committee (SNCC). SNCC, as Hayden admiringly reported to Haber in the fall of 1961, was engaged in a "*pure*, good struggle, the kind that can bring hope

to Africans and Asians and the rest of the hungry people and it's a struggle that we have every reason to begin in a revolutionary way across the country" (Milton Viorst, *Fire in the Streets: America in the 1960s* [New York: Touchstone, 1981], 181; emphasis added).

49. Sale, *SDS*, 114.

50. "Like malaria, or a war," Sale writes, "it was something that no one who went through would ever forget" (*SDS*, 150).

51. There were substantial differences between ERAP projects in the extent to which they sought to work with established groups. The JOIN project in Chicago, which allowed staff to have separate apartments and thus did not have the same level of intense group interaction as, say, Cleveland or Newark, was much more willing and able to work with community groups than were most of the other projects. The Newark project (NCUP), on the other hand, almost immediately alienated established liberal organizations and individuals who were initially sympathetic to their goals of community organizing (see Douglas Eldridge, "Militant Groups Stirs Controversy," *Newark News*, February 5, 1965, SDS Microfilm, Series 2B, No. 26; Stanley Aronowitz, "When the New Left Was New," in Sohnya Sayres et al., eds., *The 60s Without Apology* [Minneapolis: University of Minnesota Press, 1984], 22–23). The Cleveland project began by visiting established community groups but quickly came to the conclusion that these organizations "seemed to have a vested interest in what did exist" (Report from the Cleveland Community Project, June 20–28, 1964, p. 8, SDS Microfilm, Series 2B, No. 2). After an entire summer the Cleveland project could "boast of only one real active ally" and "several really good friends: only one in the labor movement, and the rest from left backgrounds" (Cleveland-Continuation of Projects, p. 4, SDS Microfilm, Series 2B, No. 2).

52. Hayden, *Reunion*, 130.

53. Sale, *SDS*, 160. The words are Sale's paraphrase of remarks made by Hayden at the meeting.

54. Sale, *SDS*, 111–13, 157–58. At the December 1964 meeting, Hayden reportedly stood up in the middle of arguments and posed questions such as: "Suppose parliamentary democracy were a contrivance of nineteenth century imperialism and merely a tool of enslavement?" (Sale, *SDS*, 159; Miller, *Democracy Is in the Streets*, 225). Even Al Haber, a bitter critic of ERAP and its "cult of the ghetto," had urged SDS members not to vote in 1964. See Al Haber and Barabara Haber, "Taking Johnson Seriously: A Response to Richard Flacks," SDS Microfilm, Series 2B, No. 24.

55. See David Bernstein to Carl Wittman, January 25, 1965, SDS Microfilm, Series 2B, No. 20, in which Bernstein asks Wittman to write a working paper on "the 'counter-society' theory," an idea "that has been talked around quite a bit, but about which nothing has been written." See also Carol McEldowney's proposed agenda for the ERAP summer institute, which suggests that "the suggested framework for debate is that of building [a] counter-society and counter-institutions" (May 19, 1965, p. 7, SDS Microfilm, Series 2B, No. 18). Also see the Chester Report (submitted by Vernon Grizzard), August 1964, p. 1, SDS Microfilm, Series 2B, No. 2, which praises "Mao's efforts in China and Castro's in Cuba to set up a separate society in an area of the country [as] extended cases of the method of example." Also see Helen Garvy

to Robb Burlage, June 4, 1965, SDS Microfilm, Series 2A, No. 14; as well as Steve Johnson, 1965 National Convention—Working Paper, SDS Microfilm, Series 2A, No. 16, a paper that refers to "counter-government," "counter-people," "counter-politics," "counter-economy," "counter-Madison," "counter-welfare legislation," "counter-Constitutional Convention," "counter-poverty program," and "counter-property ethic," in addition to a "counter-society."

56. Staughton Lynd, "The New Radicals and 'Participatory Democracy,'" in Teodori, *The New Left*, 233, 229; originally published in *Dissent* 22 (Summer 1965). SDS 1964 Convention, Draft Statement #1, submitted by members of the Swarthmore College Chapter of SDS, p. 3, SDS Microfilm, Series 2A, No. 9.

57. [Hayden], "Politics, the Individual, and SDS," SDS Microfilm, Series 1, No. 6. Hayden to SDS Executive Committee, others, Re: Manifesto, [n.d.], SDS Microfilm, Series 1, No. 6. Tom Hayden, "Outline of Draft of the [1963] SDS Convention Document," SDS Microfilm, Series 2A, No. 2. Eugene Feingold and Tom Hayden, "Politics 1965—Corporatism and Crisis," [n.d.], p. 12, SDS Microfilm, Series 4B, No. 157.

58. "Memo: to all the guys on ERAP, From: Tom [Hayden]," [n.d.], pp. 7, 12, 5, SDS Microfilm, Series 2B, No. 1. Tom Hayden and Carl Wittman, "Summer Report, Newark Community Union," in Teodori, *The New Left*, 133.

59. Hayden, "SNCC: The Qualities of Protest," *Studies on the Left* 5 (Winter 1965), 113. Similarly, SDSer Norm Fruchter praised SNCC's "notion of a counter-community, which builds institutions and relationships based on assumptions about identity, personality, work, meaning, and aspirations not accepted in the majority society" ("Mississippi: Notes on SNCC," *Studies on the Left* 5 [Winter 1965], 76). This was subtly but critically different from "An Open Letter to the Student Community," issued by the officers of SDS in the wake of the *Port Huron Statement*, which had talked of "forming a 'counter-community' outside the authority structure of their *immediate* environment" ("Section on Civil Rights," SDS Microfilm, Series 1, No. 24; emphasis added). In the 1962 letter, SNCC is praised for remaining outside the racist authority structures of the Deep South and for being "the major focus of student integration activity in the South"; in contrast, the 1965 statements by Hayden and Fruchter see SNCC as a model countercommunity because it remains separate from and unintegrated into American society as a whole.

60. Hayden, "SNCC: The Qualities of Protest," 123, 119, 120. Contrast this with the liberal universalism apparent in a letter Hayden wrote in 1961: "I am quite rigidly opposed to provincialism, no matter how pleasant its flags or warm its handshakes. . . . Provincialism, call it regional pride or whatever you will, is the anathema of integration" (Hayden to Robb Burlage, November 10, 1961, SDS Microfilm, Series 1, No. 11).

61. Tom Hayden, "The Politics of 'the Movement,'" *Dissent* 23 (January/February 1966), 87. Also see Staughton Lynd, "Coalition Politics or Nonviolent Revolution?" in Teodori, *The New Left*, 197–202.

62. Hayden, "The Politics of 'the Movement,'" 87. Also see "Call for a Congress of Unrepresented People to Declare Peace in Vietnam," and "Correspondence from

Tom Hayden," *ERAP Newsletter*, July 10, 1965, SDS Microfilm, Series 2B, No. 24. Also see Miller, *Democracy Is in the Streets*, 234; and Sale, *SDS*, 194.

63. For strong criticism of Hayden's idea on these grounds, see Paul Cowan's open letter to Hayden, circulated as a working paper at the 1965 SDS national convention, SDS Microfilm, Series 2A, No. 16. Sale reports that Hayden's idea "was too bizarre even to go to a committee and was soon dropped," but also adds that the idea "continued to lead an underground life on the left for the next several years" (Sale, *SDS*, 194).

64. In 1964, for example, Steve Max sounded alarms about the danger of SDS "breaking social and organizational connections with other parts of the campus," which would result in "isolation from the campus, . . . a slow growth rate, and a lack of leadership people" ("The Rock-Pile Theory and SDS," 1964, SDS Microfilm, Series 2A, No. 7). And Ken McEldowney, in a 1965 working paper, warned that "the quest for community — soul — whole man" led SDS and particularly the ERAP projects to "elite — isolation — in-groupism." A strong sense of community is "the type of society we would like to live and operate in," but "community can also be defined in terms of who is in it and who is out." How, McEldowney asked, is such a community expanded? "How does a counter-society grow?" (Miller, *Democracy Is in the Streets*, 215). Much later, in 1967, Todd Gitlin cautioned that a community-organizing project "must resist the temptation to cut itself off from the whole society." The dangers, Gitlin pointed out, included sectarian politics and apolitical posturing ("The Radical Potential of the Poor," in Teodori, *The New Left*, 142). Also see David Garson, "Comments on Working with Other Groups," SDS 1965 National Convention — Working Paper, SDS Microfilm, Series 2A, No. 16.

65. "An Open Letter to the Student Community," issued by the officers of SDS immediately after the *Port Huron Statement*, SDS Microfilm, Series 1, No. 24. Even in 1963, Hayden and Richard Flacks, in their draft statement of *America and the New Era*, lamented "a conservative Congress, securing the status quo by restricting the labor and left movements" (June 7, 1963, American Scene Document [draft], Part I — Analysis, SDS Microfilm, Series 2A, No. 3). Also see Tom Hayden, "The Dixiecrats and Changing Southern Power: From Bourbon to bourbon," August 1963, SDS Microfilm, Series 4B, No. 150, an earlier version of which was presented at an SNCC conference in the spring of 1963.

66. The term "corporate liberalism" was commonly used within SDS by the 1964 summer convention. See, for example, Jim Williams, "Amendment on Political Action," which was passed and became part of the convention statement on "SDS & the 1964 Elections," SDS Microfilm, Series 2A, No. 9. Also see the ERAP Report from Boston PREP, July 22, 1964, p. 1, SDS Microfilm, Series 2B, No. 2. The term "corporate liberalism" had been used in the *America and the New Era* document adopted at the previous year's convention. The 1963 document stated that "the capture of liberal rhetoric and the liberal political base by the corporate liberalism of the New Frontiersmen means that the reformers and the democratically oriented liberals are trapped by the limitations of the Democratic Party, but afraid of irrelevancy outside it" (Teodori, *The New Left*, 179).

67. Jack Newfield, *A Prophetic Minority* (New York: New American Library, 1967), 209; also see 211.

68. In January 1965, a worried Paul Potter wrote, "Tom seems to be moving closer and closer to a position that the liberal establishment (if not all liberals) constitutes the most dangerous enemy we confront" (Paul Potter to Clark Kissinger, Tom Hayden, Carl Wittman, Rennie Davis, Dick Flacks, Todd Gitlin, Paul Booth, January 22, 1965, quoted in Gitlin, *The Sixties*, 165). Also see Helen Garvy's lament that "we seem to be going farther and farther from liberals" (Helen Garvy to Robb Burlage, June 4, 1965, SDS Microfilm, Series 2A, No. 14). Interestingly, Potter himself, in a 1964 working paper entitled "The Intellectual and Social Change," had described the leading liberal organization, Americans for Democratic Action, as "an amalgamation which in its very effectiveness led to the co-optation of more intellectuals into the power structure, rather than the freeing of the intellectuals from the burdens of an oppressive university system" (Cohen and Hale, *The New Student Left*, 17).

69. Paul Booth noted as much in a working paper prepared for the 1965 summer convention, in which he sketched out the possible future strategies for SDS. Booth's "Model A" envisioned SDS focusing on the Vietnam War, which "has proven to be a subject on which wide debate could easily be awakened" and an area in which "we are really penetrating and moving liberals to actions in large numbers." As the war continues, Booth wrote, "this becomes more and more true" (Paul Booth, "Summer Projects," Working Paper—1965 SDS Convention, SDS Microfilm, Series 2A, No. 16). Cf. Gitlin, *The Sixties*, 177.

70. Sale, *SDS*, 124.

71. Eugene Feingold and Tom Hayden, "Politics 1965—Corporatism and Crisis," [n.d.], p. 2, SDS Microfilm, Series 4B, No. 157.

72. Or rather, what liberals defined as success the New Left increasingly defined as failure. Thus from SNCC's perspective the Selma march was a "failure" (Mary King, *Freedom Song: A Personal Story of the 1960s Civil Rights Movement* [New York: William Morrow, 1987], 480), and President Lyndon Johnson's "invocation of the title of the movement anthem [We shall overcome]" could make them "depressed . . . annoyed [and] sickened" (King, *Freedom Song*, 478). Cf. the account in Gitlin, *The Sixties*, especially 177, 256, or Sale, *SDS*, 123–24.

73. The Civil Rights Act, according to one paper prepared for the 1964 summer convention, was a typically "tokenist" liberal response to conflict. Indeed, "the liberal establishment, national and local, responds to most of [the Negro Freedom Movement's] activities by attempting to dull the edge of their thrust" (Charles Capper and Kim Moody, "The Case for the Third Party: A Critique of American Liberalism," June 1964, prepared for the 1964 Convention of Students for a Democratic Society, p. 9, SDS Microfilm, Series 2A, No. 9). Similar in spirit was an editorial in the Summer 1964 issue of *Studies on the Left*, which noted that "the most forward looking forces in the black movement have identified the white liberal as their main enemy. This expresses their understanding that the liberal political and economic systems and liberal ideology comprise the basis of corporate rule. The 'power structure' of American society is not controlled, of course, by the ardent white liberal in

the ranks nor by his ideological mentors, who, aware or unaware, serve corporate power by helping to co-opt movements of political protest and to divert forces from the development of alternative political power bases" ("Civil Rights and the Northern Ghetto," *Studies on the Left* 4 [Summer 1964], 12).

74. Capper and Moody, "Case for the Third Party," p. 9, SDS Microfilm, Series 2A, No. 9. Corporate liberalism, Capper and Moody continued, was "committed to the absorption of conflict. . . . Whether it appears in terms of civil rights demonstrations or a revitalized labor movement, conflict is to be absorbed by token solutions . . . rhetorical abstractions . . . [and] manipulation from above" (p. 2). This paper echoes in many ways the analysis put forth in *America and the New Era*, the statement of principles drafted by Flacks and Hayden and subsequently agreed to at the previous year's convention. That 1963 document insisted that Kennedy's New Frontier was "the central agency for strategy and decision-making for the American Establishment." The Kennedy administration's policies as well as its "style" were alleged to "flow from its necessary commitment to the preservation of the ongoing system"; its purpose was "adjusting to the revolutions of the new era in order that the old order of private corporate enterprise shall be preserved and rationalized." These "efforts to dampen social conflict and prevent popular upsurge" through "reforms [that] emanate from the top . . . limit drastically the possibilities for real reform and innovation in the society." The policies of the Kennedy administration, the 1963 document concluded, can be characterized as "aggressive tokenism" (Teodori, *The New Left*, 175–78).

75. Capper and Moody, "Case for the Third Party," p. 9, SDS Microfilm, Series 2A, No. 9. Gitlin correctly observes that "as civil rights and antipoverty reforms became national policy, the idea of participatory democracy grew . . . more prominent" because in part "it had the virtue of distinguishing us from managerial liberals" (*The Sixties*, 258).

76. "Intellectual freedom . . . absent-mindedly tacked on to the corporatist base, is too often similar to Norman Mailer's idea of freedom of the press — every reporter having the right to tell his own lies" (Capper and Moody, "Case for the Third Party," p. 3, SDS Microfilm, Series 2A, No. 9).

77. Ibid., p. 10.

78. Rennie Davis, "Report from Ann Arbor," July 2, 1964, in ERAP Project Report, June 20–July 1, 1964, p. 2, SDS Microfilm, Series 2B, No. 2. Also see Economic Research and Action Project, June 1964 SDS Convention Statement on Community Organizing, SDS Microfilm, Series 2A, No. 20; "Prospectus for Conference on Community Organizing for Economic Issues," to be held on April 10–12, at the University of Michigan, sponsored by ERAP and the Michigan chapter of SDS, p. 2, SDS Microfilm, Series 2B, No. 2; "Background of the Institute [on Organizing for Social Action]," to be held June 7–June 14 sponsored by ERAP, SDS Microfilm, Series 2B, No. 17; Prospectus for Cleveland Community Project, [n.d.], SDS Microfilm, Series 2B, No. 16; SDS Economic Research and Action Project: An Introductory Statement," SDS Microfilm, Series 2B, No. 26; Jeff Goodman, "Organizing the Poor on their own Behalf," SDS Microfilm, Series 2B, No. 26; and Philadelphia ERAP Report, June 16–24, 1964, p. 5, SDS Microfilm, Series 2B, No. 2.

79. Training Institute of the Economic Research and Action Project, June 6–11, 1964, SDS Microfilm, Series 2B, No. 17. Also see Rennie Davis, Report from Ann Arbor, July 2, p. 1, SDS Microfilm, Series 2B, No. 2.

80. The Chester Report, for instance, attributed many of its difficulties to "a terrifically efficient buy-off machine that seems to steal issues and programs from the civil rights–social change movement faster than we can find them" (Chester Report, September 28, 1964, p. 1, SDS Microfilm, Series 2B, No. 2). At the same time, SDS continued to seek financial support from liberal organizations and foundations for their various projects. Their attitude toward these supporting institutions, however, became increasingly cynical and manipulative. After pulling together a prospectus to be submitted to various liberal foundations, Rennie Davis confided, "There's a lot of bull shit. It sort of brings the best bull from various prospectuses plus a patch of my own into a large tank for the liberals to dive in" (To Dick [Flacks] and Paul [Potter], March 13, 1965, SDS Microfilm, Series 2B, No. 16). Desperate for financial support, ERAP's leaders decided that "money (however dirty) should be taken" (Ann Arbor Report, ERAP National Committee Meeting, Cleveland, Ohio, November 7–8, p. 4, in *ERAP Newsletter*, November 16–23, 1964, SDS Microfilm, Series 2B, No. 24). Cf. Hayden's quite different, appreciative reaction to the five thousand dollars that Walter Reuther and the United Auto Workers gave to SDS in 1963. See Tom Hayden to Todd Gitlin etc., August 2, 1963, SDS Microfilm, Series 2A, No. 23.

81. Jeffrey Shero, "SDS, Organization and the South," [n.d.], SDS Microfilm, Series 2A, No. 130. The paper appears to have been written in the fall of 1964.

82. The search for false friends is a constant theme in egalitarian groups; hence we hear of the radish (red on the outside, white on the inside) or the oreo (black on the outside, white on the inside). See Douglas, *Natural Symbols*, chapter 8.

83. See Bayard Rustin, "From Protest to Politics," *Commentary* 39 (February 1965), 25–38. In June 1965, an exasperated Helen Garvy could write, "We need to talk about the nature of coalitions — not just yell out — we don't like them" (Helen Garvy to Robb Burlage, June 4, 1965, SDS Microfilm, Series 2A, No. 14).

84. Rustin also opposed the 1965 march, held on April 17, because he objected to SDS' unwillingness to exclude Communists from the march. Up until this point, Rustin had been extraordinarily supportive of SDS and its ERAP projects, particularly Hayden's Newark project, which he visited in October 1964 (see C. Clark Kissinger to Rennie Davis, October 26, 1964, SDS Microfilm, Series 2B, No. 6). An SDS fund-raising letter that went out in the winter of 1964 included a blurb from Rustin praising SDS for "its program of study and research [that] helps to move all of us to the point where we can hope to see the emergence of a new and vital grouping of forces on the Democratic Left" (SDS Microfilm, Series 2B, No. 16). And when Hayden faced trumped-up charges of assault and battery, Rustin helped initiate a defense committee in Hayden's behalf and sent a telegram to Newark's mayor urging his administration to support Hayden (Tom Hayden, Dear Friend letter, February 16, 1965, SDS Microfilm, Series 2B, No. 13).

85. Staughton Lynd, "An Open Letter to Bayard Rustin," *Studies on the Left* 5 (Spring 1965), 70. This from someone who, according to Gitlin, had a "sweet-tempered generosity [that] was the stuff of movement legend" (*The Sixties*, 266).

Lynd elaborates on his criticisms of Rustin in "Coalition Politics or Nonviolent Revolution?"; 197.

86. Herbert Gans, "The New Radicalism: Sect or Action Movement," *Studies on the Left* 5 (Summer 1965), 126–31. Tom Hayden and Staughton Lynd, "Reply to Gans," *Studies on the Left* (Summer 1965), 135. See Greg Calvert's attack on SDS National Secretary Paul Booth for his "Build, Not Burn" speech, which Calvert scored as "the greatest formula ever devised for selling out the radical movement and playing into the cooptive hands of the establishment" (Sale, *SDS*, 235).

87. Barbara Brandt, "Why People Become Corrupt," March 28, 1965, in Paul Jacobs and Saul Landau, eds., *The New Radicals: A Report with Documents* (New York: Random House, 1966), 128. Peter Lathrop, "Teach-ins: New Force or Isolated Phenomenon?" *Studies on the Left* 5 (Fall 1965), 52. Lathrop is criticizing Arnold Kaufman, Hayden's teacher at Michigan and an early exponent of participatory democracy. On Kaufman's influence on Hayden, see Miller, *Democracy Is in the Streets*, 44, 94–95.

88. Danny Schechter, "Reveille for Reformers: Report from Syracuse," *Studies on the Left* 5 (Fall 1965), 87–88. Compare with Todd Gitlin's lament that the "media and publishing houses are sufficiently open to drain off energies that would otherwise look for and to us as academic vehicles — initially — and perhaps subsequently as a political one" (Gitlin to Richard Rothstein, November 16, 1964, SDS Microfilm, Series 2B, No. 38).

89. Connie Brown, "Cleveland: Conference of the Poor," *Studies on the Left* 5 (Spring 1965), 72.

90. This dynamic of egalitarian groups is more fully elaborated in Mary Douglas, "Cultural Bias," in Douglas, *In the Active Voice* (London: Routledge, 1982), as well as in Douglas, *Natural Symbols*.

91. See Sale, *SDS*, 146; and Jacobs and Landau, *The New Radicals*, 30–31.

92. The planning of menus and shopping for food, though, was done by a three-woman committee of "potatoe [*sic*] keepers" (Report from the Cleveland Community Project, June 20–28, 1964, pp. 1, 6, SDS Microfilm, Series 2B, No. 2).

93. Report from the Cleveland Community Project, June 20–28, 1964, p. 1, SDS Microfilm, Series 2B, No. 2, p. 1. Also see Carol McEldowney's letter regarding the ERAP summer institute, May 19, 1965, especially pp. 1, 4–5, SDS Microfilm, Series 2B, No. 18.

94. Report from the Cleveland Community Project, June 20–28, 1964, p. 6, SDS Microfilm, Series 2B, No. 2. Also see Miller, *Democracy Is in the Streets*, 198. Similarly, the Chester project reported that "this group has a loose structure" (Chester Report, October 29, 1964, *ERAP Newsletter*, November 6, 1964, SDS Microfilm, Series 2B, No. 24).

95. Miller, *Democracy Is in the Streets*, 207. Also see Report from Cleveland Community Project, June 20–28, 1964, p. 1, SDS Microfilm, Series 2B, No. 2.

96. Newark Report, section on "Staff Democracy Problems," *ERAP Newsletter*, July 23, 1965, SDS Microfilm, Series 2B, No. 24.

97. From Chicago, for instance, came reports of a "lack of a consensus among the staff members about the project's strategy" (Chicago Project, September 25,

1964, p. 1, SDS Microfilm, Series 2B, No. 2), poor turnouts at meetings of the community, and a lack of a "clear notion of what the criteria of success for a project like this is," (Chicago Report, October 5, 1964, pp. 1, 2, SDS Microfilm, Series 2B, No. 2). Too often, Lee Webb reported to ERAP director Rennie Davis, "meetings turn into discussion groups, nothing is decided, and everyone is exhorted to come back next week to decide what to do" (Lee Webb to Rennie Davis, Report from Chicago Project, July 17, 1964, SDS Microfilm, Series 2B, No. 38). For dissension in the Chester project, see Chester Report, July 31, 1964, p. 4, SDS Microfilm, Series 2B, No. 2; Chester Report, September 28, 1964, pp. 1–2, SDS Microfilm, Series 2B, No. 2; Helen Garvy to Paul Potter and Rennie Davis, October 10, 1964, SDS Microfilm, Series 2A, No. 22.

98. Miller, *Democracy Is in the Streets*, 207; also see 198–99. "The frustrations of organizing and lack of clearly defined roles for people," reported the ERAP office in Cleveland, "caused them to turn to each other and the group as the primary source of morale and reinforcement" ("ERAP Reports, Cleveland: To Build Democracy," *New Left Notes*, April 22, 1966, p. 6).

99. Reflecting on his own experiences as a community organizer, Paul Booth suggests that "people who do community organizing are almost impelled to a sectarian attitude. . . . What makes community organizing viable is that you have a certain number of people willing to work incredibly long hours for almost no money, in order to be involved in something that they can totally mold. You have an overwhelming need as an organizer to justify your personal sacrifices by taking an ideological position that only doing exactly what you are doing is right and that everything else is wrong" (Miller, *Democracy Is in the Streets*, 224).

100. Cf. the explanations advanced in Sale, *SDS*, 145; and Richard Rothstein, "Evolution of the ERAP Organizers," in Priscilla Long, ed., *The New Left: A Collection of Essays* (Boston: Porter Sargent, 1969), 274.

101. In a working paper prepared for the 1965 convention, Jeremy Brecher suggested certain guidelines for debate. "An ounce of this sort of prevention at the last convention," Brecher advised, "would have saved a pound of rancorous flesh." Brecher wanted to avoid the "feeling we had last year of a roomful of frustrated children who couldn't make their toys work right" (Jeremy Brecher, "Some Notes on the 1965 SDS Convention," SDS Microfilm, Series 2A, No. 14). Also see Robb Burlage's letter to the SDS National Office in which he refers to the "mess of last summer's Pine Hill dead-end" (Robb Burlage to Helen [Garvy], Clark [Kissinger], NO-ers, et al., April 25, 1965, SDS Microfilm, 2A, No. 14). Also see Miller, *Democracy Is in the Streets*, 194.

102. Gitlin to Robb and Dorothy Burlage, September 12, 1964, in Todd Gitlin, *The Whole World Is Watching: Mass Media in the Making and Unmaking of the New Left* (Berkeley: University of California Press, 1980), 134–35.

103. Miller, *Democracy Is in the Streets*, 223. Gitlin, *The Whole World Is Watching*, 134.

104. Miller, *Democracy Is in the Streets*, 224–26. Sale, *SDS*, 154–58.

105. Sale, *SDS*, 204. Also see Gitlin, *The Sixties*, 189, and Jeremy Brecher, "Some Notes on the 1965 SDS Convention," SDS Microfilm, Series 2A, No. 14.

106. Sale, *SDS*, 204.

107. Steve Max, quoted in Sale, *SDS*, 207.

108. Sale, *SDS*, 207. Miller, *Democracy Is in the Streets*, 239. Jacobs and Landau, *The New Radicals*, 31.

109. Sale, *SDS*, 208. Later that fall Paul Booth proposed instituting a "key list" mailing, which would include all the chapters and all the ERAP projects. This suggestion ran into objections on the grounds that the term "key list" was elitist — so the name was changed to "worklist" (Miller, *Democracy Is in the Streets*, 247). The denunciation of "statementism" as well as the rejection of the term "key list" foreshadows the egalitarian hypersensitivity that would characterize what in the 1990s would come to be termed "political correctness."

110. Sale, *SDS*, 208. As Gitlin points out, even the 1963 convention, which produced the *America and the New Era* document, failed to say much about foreign policy. At that convention, Gitlin chaired a workshop on foreign policy: "There we debated the degree to which 'American imperialism' could be held responsible for tyranny and poverty in the Third World. . . . In the end, with no consensus in sight, we decided not to write a report at all" (Gitlin, *The Sixties*, 130–31).

111. Richie, Neil, and Nina, "Comments on Michigan," *ERAP Newsletter*, July 23, 1965, p. 4, SDS Microfilm, Series 2B, No. 24.

112. The evidence of this almost total identification with "the movement" (or with SDS, SNCC, ERAP, NCUP, JOIN, or FSM) is not difficult to find. "The movement today," Casey Hayden recalls, "is commonly known as the civil rights movement, but it was considerably more than that. To me, it was everything: home and family, food and work, love and reason to live. When I was no longer welcome there, and then when it was no longer there at all, it was hard to go on" (Casey Hayden, preface to Mary King, *Freedom Song*, 7; also see 74, 297, 495). "We could not imagine any life without the movement," Todd Gitlin recalls; when, as Gitlin described it, "the movement no longer held any life for us," he, like many others, became disoriented and "depressed." "Having lost faith," Gitlin wrote a friend at the time, "I don't know just what I believe in now" (Gitlin, *The Sixties*, 396–97). Sharon Jeffrey told James Miller, "This was my family. I never even thought about what I would do if I wasn't living and organizing in Cleveland with this group of people I loved. In the midst of individualism, we were trying to be very *group*" (Miller, *Democracy Is in the Streets* 207). Staughton Lynd affirmed that "all members of the [radical] project regard the Movement — the task of social change — as their principal work, the axis of their lives" ("Resistance: From Mood to Strategy," in Teodori, *The New Left*, 311). For Jack Weinberg, the Free Speech Movement had "been the most complete experience of my life, the most all-encompassing. . . . It gave me a sense of comradeship we had not known existed" (Wini Breines, *Community and Organization in the New Left, 1962–1968: The Great Refusal*, 2d ed. [New Brunswick, N.J.: Rutgers University Press, 1989], 27).

113. "An Open Letter to the Student Community," SDS Microfilm, Series 1, No. 24; emphasis added. American Scene Document (draft) Part II — Program for Action, SDS Microfilm, Series 2A, No. 3; emphasis added. Gitlin, *The Sixties*, 187. Gitlin attributes this change to events in Santo Domingo a week after the march on

Washington. Without questioning the importance of this event in Gitlin's life, it also seems fair to say that the event itself was less important than the perceptual screen that led Gitlin and other New Left radicals to interpret almost any exercise of U.S. military might as an act of oppression. After all, in a working paper published a year before, in April 1964, Gitlin had already spoken of "the rottenness of our society" ("Battlefields and the War," in Cohen and Hale, *The New Student Left*, 126).

114. Hayden, *Reunion*, 179; also 272. Just how complete that break was can be gleaned from the fact that Hayden's young sister was raised by their father "without the knowledge that she had a brother" (272). Cf. Jeff Shero's recollection that for many students who joined SDS in late 1964 and 1965, "to join SDS meant breaking with your family, it meant being cut off—it was like in early Rome joining a Christian sect" (Sale, *SDS*, 206).

115. Tom Hayden to SDS Executive Committee, others, Re: Manifesto, p. 5, SDS Microfilm, Series 1, No. 6. Tom Hayden, Norm Fruchter, Alan Cheuse, "Up from Irrelevance," *Studies on the Left* 5 (Spring 1965), reprinted in Teodori, *The New Left*, 209. Also see the editorial, "After the Election," *Studies on the Left* 5 (Winter 1965); and Herbert Marcuse, *One-Dimensional Man: Studies in the Ideology of Advanced Industrial Society* (Boston: Beacon Press, 1964), especially 3. Hayden had used the word "totalitarian" in a paper he wrote at the end of 1963, but he then used the word in a quite un-Marcusian manner and to describe only the South: "Poverty, terror, mockery, and hypocrisy create an all but totalitarian system [in the South] which is given patent by the whole society" ("Liberal Analysis and Federal Power," SDS Microfilm, Series 4B, No. 152). Earlier still, in draft notes for the *Port Huron Statement*, Hayden used the term in the conventional manner to describe Soviet-style dictatorships ("Manifesto Notes: Problems of Democracy," Convention Document #2, March 19, 1962, p. 5, SDS Microfilm, Series 1, No. 6).

116. Hayden, "SNCC: The Qualities of Protest," 123, 115; emphasis added. Also see Hayden, "The Politics of 'the Movement,'" 75. This view of the South as a microcosm of the whole American system rather than as an aberration soon suffused the New Left, with SNCC leading the way here as elsewhere. See, for example, Stokely Carmichael, "Who Is Qualified?" in Andrew Kopkind, ed., *Thoughts of the Young Radicals* (New York: Pitman, 1966), 28.

117. See Sale, *SDS*, 191. In the summer of 1965, SDSer Donald McKelvey described American society as "rotten to the very core" ("Pacifism, Politics and Nonviolence," *Liberation* 10 [August 1965], 24).

118. American Scene Document (draft) Part II—Program for Action, SDS Microfilm, Series 2A, No. 3. Joan Wallach, "Chapter Programming," December 1963, SDS Microfilm, Series 2A, No. 6. Cf. Lynd, "Resistance: From Mood to Strategy," in Teodori, *The New Left*, 311.

119. Newfield, *Prophetic Minority*, 48.

120. Norm Fruchter, "Reply to Rabinowitz," *Studies on the Left* 5 (Spring 1965), 94. Eric Mann, quoted in Sale, *SDS*, 191. Also contributing to the New Left's faith in revolutionary transformation was an optimistic view of human perfectibility. As Hayden explained, his goal in the Newark ghetto had been "to release the potential of people who were bottled up by the system" (Hayden, *Reunion*, 133). Specialization

and hierarchy, Hayden believed, kept "people from reaching their maximum potential for responsibility and activity" ("SNCC: The Qualities of Protest," 123). "'Human nature' is not an evil or corrosive substance to be feared or contained," Hayden wrote in his draft notes for what would become the *Port Huron Statement*. "Rather, it represents a potential for material and spiritual development which, no matter how lengthily or rapidly unfolded, can never be dissipated. The liberation of this individual potential is the just end of society" (Hayden, "Manifesto Notes: Problems of Democracy," Convention Document #2, March 19, 1962, SDS Microfilm, Series 1, No. 6). Transform the institutions, Hayden predicted, and "a new kind of man emerges" ("Up from Irrelevance," 212). Also see Jane Stembridge, "Some Notes on Education," which can be found in the New Left Collection at the Hoover Institution of War, Revolution and Peace, Stanford University.

121. Irving Howe, "New Styles in 'Leftism,'" in Howe, ed., *Beyond the New Left* (New York: McCall, 1970), 23–27.

122. Hayden, *Reunion*, xviii, 324. Miller, *Democracy Is in the Streets*, 274. Also see Hayden's testimony before the National Commission on the Causes and Prevention of Violence in October 1968, as reported in Gitlin, *The Sixties*, 285.

123. Miller, *Democracy Is in the Streets*, 295.

124. Hayden, Fruchter, and Cheuse, "Up From Irrelevance," 211. Cf. Marcuse: "By virtue of the way it has organized its technological base, contemporary industrial society tends to be totalitarian. For 'totalitarian' is not only a terroristic political coordination of society, but also a non-terroristic economic-technical coordination which operates through the manipulation of needs by vested interests. It thus precludes the emergence of an effective opposition against the whole" (*One-Dimensional Man*, 3). In academia today, this phenomenon is labeled "hegemony."

125. See Jacobs and Landau's report that "the real task visualized by this group, a vision which most of the SDS shares, is to gain freedom from the 'one-dimensional society' which controls by terror, welfare, and vested interests" (*The New Radicals*, 37). Also see McKelvey, "Pacifism, Politics and Nonviolence," 24; Staughton Lynd, "Radical Politics and Nonviolent Revolution," *Liberation* 11 (April 1966), 16; and Norm Fruchter and Robert Kramer, "An Approach to Community Organizing Projects," *Studies on the Left* 6 (March/April 1966), especially 31. Also see Gitlin, *The Sixties*, 246. In an essay published in *Dissent* in the summer of 1965, Lynd described American society as "domestic totalitarianism" (Teodori, *The New Left*, 233); and Richard Rothstein, in early 1965, indicted the "totalitarian . . . assumptions of liberal politics" ("A Short History of ERAP," p. 3, SDS Microfilm, Series 2B, No. 21).

126. This same oscillation is evident in the thinking of Marcuse himself. Compare the defeatism of *One-Dimensional Man* with the longing for liberating violence in his lecture "The Problem of Violence and the Problem of Opposition," published in *Five Lectures: Psychoanalysis, Politics, and Utopia* (Boston: Beacon Press, 1970).

127. Tom Hayden, "Liberal Analysis and Federal Power," p. 3, SDS Microfilm, Series 4B, No. 152. Ronnie G. Davis, "Guerrilla Theatre: A Way of Life," in Teodori, *The New Left*, 396.

128. Marcuse, "The Problem of Violence," 90, 103. Marcuse had earlier introduced the distinction between "revolutionary and reactionary violence" in "Repres-

sive Tolerance," in Robert Paul Wolff, Barrington Moore, Jr., and Herbert Marcuse, *A Critique of Pure Tolerance* (Boston: Beacon Press, 1965), 103; also 107–8, 117. Cf. Staughton Lynd and Thomas Hayden, *The Other Side* (New York: New American Library, 1966), chapter 10; and Carl Oglesby, "Revolution: Violence or Nonviolence," *Liberation* 13 (July/August 1968), 37. Also see Nigel Young, *An Infantile Disorder? The Crisis and Decline of the New Left* (Boulder, Colo.: Westview Press, 1977), 233–34.

129. SDSer Donald McKelvey, for instance, argued that "the difference between Batista's violence against Castro and Castro's against Batista is the vastly different social effects of the victory of each. The negative effects of violence in making (and continuing) a revolution can be offset by the positive effects of the creation of . . . a society where men are not impelled by social conditions to be physically and psychologically violent to others." Violence can be justified "by changes in the social structure which tend toward creating nonviolent men." Moreover, "in seeking a thoroughgoing and fundamental liberation of men who have been constantly violenced [*sic*], we frequently must expect — and accept — violence as part of the process of liberation" (McKelvey, "Pacifism, Politics and Nonviolence," 23, 24). Also see Dave Dellinger, "Cuban Contradictions: A Response to David Wieck," *Liberation* 10 (June–July 1965), 41.

130. Tom Hayden, "Who Are the Student Boat-Rockers?" *Mademoiselle* (August 1961), copy in SDS Microfilm, Series 1, No. 11. The *Port Huron Statement*, in Teodori, *The New Left*, 168, 166. Newfield, *Prophetic Minority*, 149. On Camus's influence, see Hayden, *Reunion*, 76–77.

131. Richard H. King, *Civil Rights and the Idea of Freedom* (New York: Oxford University Press, 1992), 174–75.

132. Anne and Carl Braden, "Is There a Significant Place for the White Southerner in the Integration Struggle," a Discussion Paper for Consideration of Student Conference at Chapel Hill, N.C., May 4–6, 1962, SDS Microfilm, Series 1, No. 4. Also see Don McKelvey, quoted in Breines, *Community and Organization*, 53; and Norm Fruchter, "Mississippi: Notes on SNCC," *Studies on the Left* 5 (Winter 1965), 79; as well as Young, *An Infantile Disorder?*, especially 272.

133. On the influence of Fanon within SNCC see King, *Freedom Song*, 169–72, and King, *Civil Rights and the Idea of Freedom*, chapter 7.

134. Miller, *Democracy Is in the Streets*, 312. Sale, *SDS*, 309, 150.

135. Bernard Yack, *The Longing for Total Revolution: Philosophical Sources of Social Discontent from Rousseau to Marx and Nietzsche* (Princeton, N.J.: Princeton University Press, 1986).

136. Sale leaves the reader with the mistaken impression that it was not until the spring of 1967 that "the people around SDS began toying with the idea of revolution" (*SDS*, 335). Only then, Sale contends, was there "a willingness . . . to confront the idea of sweeping and total change in the institutions of America" (*SDS*, 336). Perhaps the entire dichotomy between reform and revolution is inadequate in view of Hayden's initial defense of the ERAP concept on the grounds that short-run reforms could lead to revolution. Arguing against Haber, who felt ERAP would get bogged down in small, incremental reforms and thus divert SDS from its role as a radical organization, Hayden successfully made the case that "radical organization for short

run goals could empty the system so that the demands . . . for justice would outweigh the system. Tokenism should be replaced by a revolutionary trajectory in which each step progressed from the next. . . . The search for influence can be viewed as a demand for reforms now and the presence of radicals was necessary to prevent the trend to being bought-out. The proposal can be summarized by the risk that day to day reforms can lead to revolution" (National Council Minutes, December 30, 1963, SDS Microfilm, Series 2A, No. 6).

137. Back in 1961 Hayden had reported to Haber on a "crazy new sentiment" growing in the South, that this was "not a movement but a revolution, that our identity should [be] with the new nations around the world and that beyond lunch counter desegregations there are more serious evils which must be ripped out by any means: exploitation, socially destructive capital, evil political and legal structure, and myopic liberalism which is anti-revolutionary. Revolution permeates discussion like never before" (Hayden to Haber, "Re: SNCC meeting, Jackson, Mississippi, September 14–17, 1961," quoted in Miller, *Democracy Is in the Streets*, 60). Also see Clayborne Carson, *In Struggle: SNCC and the Black Awakening of the 1960s* (Cambridge, Mass.: Harvard University Press, 1981), 176; Milton Viorst, *Fire in the Streets: America in the 1960s* (New York: Touchstone, 1981), 181; Howard Zinn, *SNCC: The New Abolitionists* (Boston: Beacon Press, 1964), 13; Jacobs and Landau, *The New Radicals*, 147; and Todd Gitlin, "Student Political Action, 1960–1963: The View of a Participant," September 1963, p. 10, SDS Microfilm, Series 4B, No. 115. In his report, Hayden urged SDS to learn to "speak their revolutionary language without mocking it" (Carson, *In Struggle*, 176); by 1965 most of the SDS "old guard" had done so. References to "the revolution," "revolutionary change," and "revolutionary society" suffuse SDS thinking by 1965. See, for example, To: ERAP staff and friends, From: Cleveland Project, Re: Summer Institute, May 5, 1965, p. 6, SDS Microfilm, Series 2B, No. 18; Vernon Grizzard to Rennie Davis, August 13, 1964, SDS Microfilm, Series 2A, No. 24; "Memo: to all the guys on ERAP, From: Tom [Hayden]," p. 12, SDS Microfilm, Series 2B, No. 1; David Bernstein to Carl Wittman, January 25, 1965, SDS Microfilm, Series 2B, No. 20. Sharon Jeffrey, an ERAP organizer in Cleveland, told James Miller that part of the attraction of the ERAP projects was that she and others were "excited by the idea of toppling the American society" (Miller, *Democracy Is in the Streets*, 190). Early in 1966, Richard Flacks, hardly the most radical of the old guard, called for "permanent revolution against overweening power" (Flacks, "Is the Great Society Just a Barbecue?" in Teodori, *The New Left*, 195; also see the interview with Flacks in Jacobs and Landau, *The New Radicals*, 163).

138. Tom Hayden, "Revolution in Mississippi," p. 21, SDS Microfilm, Series 4B, No. 159. Editorial written by Hayden for the *Michigan Daily* in September 1960, quoted in Miller, *Democracy Is in the Streets*, 51. Tom Hayden, "Political Analysis," SDS Microfilm, Series 1, No. 17. Gitlin, *The Sixties*, 100.

139. Newark Report, August 2, 1964, p. 2, SDS Microfilm, Series 2B, No. 2. Cf. the lament from Trenton: "Since Trenton is a liberal city, we have had difficulty creating confrontations" (ERAP Report, Trenton, August 1964, p. 2, SDS Microfilm, Series 2B, No. 2).

140. "SDS: America and the New Era," in Teodori, *The New Left*, 180. David Bernstein to Carl Wittman, January 25, 1965, SDS Microfilm, Series 2B, No. 20. Tom Hayden, "Civil Rights in the United States," p. 4, SDS Microfilm, Series 4B, No. 149. This paper appears to have been written early in the winter of 1963–1964.

141. Michael Nagler, "Berkeley: The Demonstrations," *Studies on the Left* 5 (Winter 1965), 55. Bradley Cleveland, "A Letter to Undergraduates," in Teodori, *The New Left*, 151. Joseph Paff, Bill Cavala, and Jerry Berman, "The Student Riots at Berkeley: Dissent in the Multiversity," in Cohen and Hale, *The New Student Left*, 239.

142. SDS 1964 Convention, Draft Statement #1, submitted by members of the Swarthmore College Chapter of SDS, pp. 2–4, SDS Microfilm, Series 2A, No. 9. In a book sympathetic to the New Left published in 1966, Jack Newfield summed up SDS as a "guerilla band of participatory democrats" (*Prophetic Minority*, 146).

143. On SNCC's importance to SDS as a model of a tightly knit, egalitarian group operating outside of and in opposition to the values and practices of the dominant society, see Gitlin, *The Sixties*, 128, 165; Hayden, *Reunion*, 124; Breines, *Community and Organization*, 80; Sale, *SDS*, 97, 98–99, 210; and Carson, *In Struggle*. One of the few flaws in James Miller's superb account of the New Left is that he is too eager to discount SNCC's influence on SDS. Miller is correct that participatory democracy as a doctrine was not derived from SNCC, but SNCC was still critically important in the development of SDS because it provided a model of an egalitarian collective working to transform society while remaining outside of it.

144. As Hayden reported at the close of 1963, "There are many civil rights leaders who believe that violence or every disruption short of violence is now necessary to make this nation choose between paralysis and progress" ("Liberal Analysis and Federal Power," p. 3, SDS Microfilm, Series 4B, No. 152).

145. John Lewis, "A Serious Revolution," in Teodori, *The New Left*, 102. "Get in," Lewis continued, "and stay in the streets of every city, every village and every hamlet of this nation, until true Freedom comes, until the revolution is complete" (101–2).

146. Gitlin, *The Sixties*, 146. Also see King, *Freedom Song*, 103–4, 479.

147. Tom Hayden, "SNCC: The Qualities of Protest," 124. Also see Gitlin, "Power and the Myth of Progress," in Teodori, *The New Left*, 191.

148. Hayden, "SNCC: The Qualities of Protest," 119. Lynd, "Coalition Politics or Nonviolent Revolution?", 199–200. Carson, *In Struggle*, 178. Also see Paul Jacobs, "Shadows of Freedom," December 1964, SDS Microfilm, Series 2B, No. 21, which called for setting up "another court system, complete with judges and juries, . . . a shadow court system" (p. 6).

149. After all, as one SNCC member put it in terms that had by 1965 become conventional wisdom for the New Left, "The 'order' of the country is based on people being taught to relinquish the right to order their own lives. The claiming of this right is disorderly; disorder which has to be, if real order is to happen" (Charles Cobb, "Whose Society Is This," in Kopkind, *Thoughts of the Young Radicals*, 16; this article originally appeared in the *New Republic*, December 18, 1965).

150. Lynd, "Coalition Politics or Nonviolent Revolution?", 199, 202. It becomes

even harder when Lynd quotes Fanon approvingly to the effect that "no one takes the step of planting a bomb in a public place without a battle of conscience" (Lynd and Hayden, *The Other Side*, 192). More strained still is Lynd's attempt to claim Fanon as an exponent of nonviolence: "In the best tradition of nonviolence [Fanon asserted]: 'What we Algerians want is to discover the man behind the colonizer. . . . We want an Algeria open to all'" (193). Also see Staughton Lynd, "A Radical Speaks in Defense of SNCC," *New Left Notes*, September 25, 1967, pp. 3, 7, 8.

151. Lynd and Hayden, *The Other Side*, 146, 188. Cf. Lynd, "Coalition Politics or Nonviolent Revolution?", 200.

152. See Miller, *Democracy Is in the Streets*, 267.

153. Lynd and Hayden, *The Other Side*, 146–47, 68.

154. Tom Hayden, *Rebellion in Newark: Official Violence and Ghetto Response* (New York: Vintage, 1967), 69–71. When a congressional committee confronted Hayden with comments he had made to the effect that "urban guerrillas are the only realistic alternative at this time to electoral politics and mass armed resistance," Hayden tried to distance himself from these remarks by claiming that what he had "said was that we have to function as political guerrillas. . . . A political guerrilla is a person who uses the political concepts of guerrilla warfare without the weapons or the guns. The political concept of guerrilla warfare is to make yourself at one with the people you are trying to organize, be among them, go through their day-to-day existence, live on the same budget as they do, and organize them into a political force" (*Rebellion and Repression: Testimony by Tom Hayden Before the National Commission on the Causes and Prevention of Violence, and the House Un-American Activities Committee* [New York: Meridian Books, 1969], 74).

155. Hayden, *Rebellion in Newark*, 71–72.

156. Hayden, "The Ability to Face Whatever Comes," 41. Also see Hayden's comment describing "those moments [in the revolutionary process] when individuals overcome themselves, or people suddenly feel the deep emotional meaning of solidarity and community" (Lynd and Hayden, *The Other Side*, 191).

157. Hayden explained the Newark riot this way: "The authorities had been indifferent to the community's demand for justice; now the community was going to be indifferent to the authorities' demand for order" (*Rebellion in Newark*, 26).

158. Ibid., 69, 32. Also see the interview with Eric Mann, a staff member of NCUP, in *New Left Notes*, July 24, 1967, pp. 1, 6. Even in his memoirs, written twenty years later, the romance for violence is still not totally expunged. On the Newark riots Hayden writes: "There was exhilaration and no sense of guilt. . . . There was an order of sorts within this 'breakdown of law and order.' . . . Looked at from the inside, this apparently irrational explosion was a classic case of a 'festival of the oppressed.' . . . The riot was a rite of passage from feelings of servitude to the proud psychic independence of 'black power'" (Hayden, *Reunion*, 153–54).

159. Hayden, *Rebellion in Newark*, 3, 69. In an article written shortly before his trip to Vietnam, Hayden described the radical's need to overcome the poor's "sense of inadequacy and embarrassment which destroys the possibility of revolt" ("The Politics of the Movement," 84). Observing Hayden over the course of 1964 and

1965, Jack Newfield came to the conclusion, in what was obviously meant as a compliment, that Hayden, "may someday write an American version of Fanon's *The Wretched of the Earth*" (*Prophetic Minority*, 122).

160. Miller, *Democracy Is in the Streets*, 298, 303, 308–9.

161. In his memoirs, Hayden frames the issue in these terms; indeed, he begins his book with this quotation from Camus (*Reunion*, ix, xvi).

162. Cf. Rothman and Lichter, *Roots of Radicalism*.

163. Hayden, *Reunion*, 201–2, 259, 275–79. At times Hayden goes beyond wishing to erase any connection between the *Port Huron Statement* and the later New Left, and tries to distance himself from the more violent and militant episodes and personas of the late 1960s. For instance, Hayden portrays himself as a "fascinated" bystander at Columbia who just happened to get caught up in events (*Reunion*, 274). In this same vein, he insists that there was "a world of difference" between Columbia student leader Mark Rudd and himself: "While I had experienced the religious and reformist South at his age, he had already visited revolutionary and socialist Cuba as part of an SDS contingent." But SNCC, which was Hayden's baptism in radical politics, was hardly reformist, as Hayden's own reports stressed. Moreover, by 1968 Hayden had been to North Vietnam twice. Hayden contrasts his own "intense intellectual development in formulating the *Port Huron Statement*" with Rudd's view that "'SDS intellectuals' [were] impediments to action" (*Reunion*, 275). What Hayden neglects to tell the reader is that in 1963 Hayden had written that "intellectuals are placed at vantage points which, described as seats of reason, actually function to immunize the senses and turn incoming truths into trickling, instead of tidal, currents," and insisted that "it is sometimes foolish to judge the open mind, the questioning spirit, as ipso facto good" ("Liberal Analysis and Federal Power," p. 1, SDS Microfilm, Series 4B, No. 152). And when Hayden says he "sensed in Mark an embryo of fanaticism" (*Reunion*, 275), it is hard not to recall Irving Howe's identical reaction to the young Hayden, who struck Howe as "the most rigid, perhaps even fanatical" of the SDS leaders (Gitlin, *The Sixties*, 172), or Joan Baez's later remark that "when the revolution does come, the one to shoot me is going to be Hayden" (Steven V. Roberts, "Will Tom Hayden Overcome?" *Esquire* 70 [December 1968], 178).

164. The *Port Huron Statement*, in Teodori, *The New Left*, especially 166, 168, 170–71.

165. The attraction of this dichotomy between the vulnerable inside and a predatory outside can be seen in the language of a proposal which was adopted nearly unanimously by the SDS National Council in the spring of 1968. The delegates declared their intent to "fight all the aspects of a racist culture that *the system attempts to inject into us*" (Sale, *SDS*, 419; emphasis added).

166. Gitlin, *The Sixties*, 382, 395.

CHAPTER 5. Romancing the Oppressed

1. Peter Brock, *Radical Pacifists in Antebellum America* (Princeton, N.J.: Princeton University Press, 1968), 237.

2. George Orwell, *The Road to Wigan Pier* (New York: Harcourt Brace Jovanovich, 1958), 148. This quotation also serves as a lead into Michael Walzer's "The Obligations of Oppressed Minorities," in Walzer, *Obligations: Essays on Disobedience, War, and Citizenship* (Cambridge, Mass.: Harvard University Press, 1970), 46. Also see Walzer's splendid essay, "George Orwell's England," in Walzer, *The Company of Critics: Social Criticism and Political Commitment in the Twentieth Century* (New York: Basic Books, 1988), 121.

3. C. Wright Mills, "Letter to the New Left," in Priscilla Long, ed., *The New Left: A Collection of Essays* (Boston: Porter Sargent, 1969), 22, 25. James Miller, *"Democracy Is in the Streets": From Port Huron to the Siege of Chicago* (New York: Touchstone, 1987), 177, 262. To: SDS executive committee, From: Tom Hayden, Re: manifesto, p. 2, SDS Microfilm, Series 1, No. 6. Thomas Hayden, "Letter to the New (Young) Left," in Mitchell Cohen and Dennis Hale, eds., *The New Student Left: An Anthology*, rev. and exp. ed. (Boston: Beacon Press, 1967), 8. The article originally appeared in *The Activist* (Winter 1961).

4. Karl Marx and Friedrich Engels, *Collected Works* (New York: International, 1976), 6:485, 488, 494; 11:149, 187. The first quotation and last two quotations are from *The Communist Manifesto;* the other two are from *The 18th Brumaire.* My thinking about the role of the lumpenproletariat in Marx's and Engels's thought is indebted to the penetrating discussion in Sammy Basu, "'Self-Ownership' and 'Friendship': The Liberal Individualism of La Boétie, Overton, and Stirner" (Ph.D. diss., Princeton University, 1993), 505–8. Also see Robert L. Bussard, "The 'Dangerous Class' of Marx and Engels: The Rise of the Idea of the Lumpenproletariat," *History of European Ideas* 8 (1987), 675–92.

5. Mills, "Letter to the New Left," 22.

6. The program, somewhat ironically, was started with the help of a five-thousand-dollar grant from the United Auto Workers to fund "an education and action program around economic issues" (Kirkpatrick Sale, *SDS* [New York: Random House, 1973], 96, 101–2).

7. As ERAP's "Introductory Statement" put it, "we can expect for the indefinite future a growing army of unemployed and unemployables" (SDS Economic Research and Action Project, "An Introductory Statement," p. 1, SDS Microfilm, Series 2B, No. 26, Wisconsin State Historical Society, Madison). Also see Swarthmore Political Action Committee, "Chester, PA.: Community Organization in the Other America," December 1963, p. 9, SDS Microfilm, Series 2B, No. 25.

8. The most influential statement of this view was Ray Brown, "Our Crisis Economy: The End of the Boom," paper delivered at conference Unemployment and Social Change, Nyack, New York, June 1963. The conference was attended by many in SDS, and the paper was widely circulated that fall as an SDS pamphlet. Also see the "Triple Revolution Statement," which was issued in February 1964 as a press release and signed by many leading left intellectuals including Michael Harrington, Gunnar Myrdal, Robert Theobald, Linus Pauling, and Robert Heilbroner, as well as by SDSers Tom Hayden and Todd Gitlin. The statement was later published in *Liberation* 9 (April 1964), 9–15. For further background information, see Sale, *SDS*, 99–100; and Miller, *Democracy Is in the Streets*, 170, 192.

9. Sale, *SDS*, 96–97.

10. See, for example, ibid., 143; Todd Gitlin, *The Sixties: Years of Hope, Days of Rage* (New York: Bantam, 1987), 165; and Stanley Rothman and S. Robert Lichter, *Roots of Radicalism: Jews, Christians, and the New Left* (New York: Oxford University Press, 1982), 12. The Orwell quotation that begins this chapter also points, of course, to the importance of guilt in the middle-class romance with the oppressed.

11. The theoretical reasons for the egalitarian attraction to the oppressed (or what Aaron Wildavsky calls "fatalists") are sketched out in Aaron Wildavsky, "Change in Political Culture," *Politics, the Journal of the Australasian Political Studies Association* 20 (November 1985), 95–102, especially 99–100. Also see Michael Thompson, Richard Ellis, and Aaron Wildavsky, *Cultural Theory* (Boulder, Colo.: Westview Press, 1990), especially 95–96; and Richard J. Ellis, "The Social Construction of Slavery," in Dennis J. Coyle and Richard J. Ellis, eds., *Politics, Policy, and Culture* (Boulder, Colo.: Westview Press, 1994), especially 117–20.

12. Tom Hayden, "The Politics of 'the Movement,'" *Dissent* 23 (January/February 1966), 81.

13. Tom Hayden and Staughton Lynd, "Reply to Gans," *Studies on the Left* 5 (Summer 1965), 133.

14. The idea of a "new insurgency" was introduced in the document *America and the New Era*, which had been drafted by Richard Flacks and Tom Hayden and then adopted as the official SDS statement at the SDS convention in June 1963. The document is reprinted in Massimo Teodori, ed., *The New Left: A Documentary History*, (Indianapolis: Bobbs-Merrill, 1969), 172–82.

15. The Russian Populists, Isaiah Berlin writes, "looked upon [the peasants] . . . as embodiments of simple uncorrupted virtue, whose social organisation . . . was the natural foundation on which the future of Russian society must be rebuilt" (Berlin, "Russian Populism," reprinted in *Russian Thinkers* [Harmondsworth, Eng.: Penguin, 1978], 211). Also see Franco Venturi, *Roots of Revolution: A History of the Populist and Socialist Movements in Nineteenth Century Russia* (New York: Universal Library, 1966), for which Berlin's essay was originally written as an introduction.

16. Abolitionists typically described the "African race" as "gentler and less selfish," "humbler [and] more noble" than Caucasians. See Lewis Perry, *Radical Abolitionism* (Ithaca, N.Y.: Cornell University Press, 1973), 107, 233; quotation from James Russell Lowell at 233. Abolitionists, writes historian George M. Fredrickson, "tended to see the Negro more as a symbol than as a person, more as a vehicle for romantic social criticism than as a human being with the normal range of virtues and vices" (*The Black Image in the White Mind: The Debate on Afro-American Character and Destiny* [New York: Harper and Row, 1971], 109). Also see Richard Ellis and Aaron Wildavsky, "A Cultural Analysis of the Role of Abolitionists in the Coming of the Civil War," *Comparative Studies in Society and History* 32 (January 1990), 104.

17. In an early newspaper article, "Debates on the Law on Thefts of Wood," written in 1842 for the *Rheinische Zeitung*, Marx had written of the poor as "the elemental class of human society" in whose customs there was an "instinctive sense of right." The dispossessed's natural needs and urges were also inevitably "rightful" needs and urges (*Collected Works*, 1:233–34). Also see Heinz Lubasz, "Marx's Initial

Problematic: The Problem of Poverty," *Political Studies* 24 (March 1976), especially 31, 33, 41. On the more general tendency in certain strands of Western political thought to see a natural uncorrupted goodness in the poor or marginal, see John M. Ellis, "The Western Tradition of Political Correctness," *Academic Questions* 5 (Spring 1992), especially 24–27.

18. Sale, *SDS*, 36. Miller, *Democracy Is in the Streets*, 57–61.

19. Hayden to Al Haber, quoted in Milton Viorst, *Fire in the Streets: America in the 1960s* (New York: Touchstone, 1979), 181; emphasis added.

20. Hayden, "SNCC: The Qualities of Protest," *Studies on the Left* 5 (Winter 1965), 113, 119.

21. Jack Newfield, *A Prophetic Minority* (New York: New American Library, 1967), 94.

22. Howard Zinn, *SNCC: The New Abolitionists* (Boston: Beacon Press, 1965), 237; also see 12. Elizabeth Sutherland, ed., *Letters from Mississippi* (New York: McGraw-Hill, 1965), 48–49; also see 17, 46–47, 51, 96, 226. Gitlin, *The Sixties*, 163. Also see Doug Rossinow, "'The Break-through to New Life': Christianity and the Emergence of the New Left in Austin, Texas, 1956–1964," *American Quarterly* 46 (September 1994), 324.

23. Jane Stembridge, "Some Notes on Education," 3, 5–6. This document was kindly provided by Clayborne Carson, and can be found in the New Left Collection at the Hoover Institution on War, Revolution and Peace at Stanford University. Similar in spirit were some of the "Letters from Mississippi" written by participants in the Freedom Rides in the summer of 1964. Reported one: "The Mississippians and the SNCC staff members . . . are the ones who are really free. More free, certainly, than the Southern white imprisoned in his hatred for the Negro" (*Letters from Mississippi*, 17). Another noted, "One sees a freedom here that is so much more than just the ironical fact that the enslaved people are, at least relatively, the liberated ones. Some 'white' people sit at their feet wondering at this sorrow freed and made beautiful, sensing dimly in themselves a similar pain" (17). Also see Mary King, *Freedom Song: A Personal Story of the 1960s Civil Rights Movement* (New York: William Morrow, 1987), 140.

24. In celebrating the marginal position of poor blacks, the New Left created a dilemma for itself, for was not the aim of the civil rights movement to integrate southern blacks into the system? Yet to integrate southern blacks would destroy their unspoiled beauty and undermine their radical potential. Some activists were not unaware of this tension. As one participant in the Freedom Rides admitted, "There is some strong ambivalence which goes with this work. I sometimes fear that I am only helping to integrate some beautiful people into modern white society with all of its depersonalization." He assured himself that it wasn't "19th century pastoral romanticism" that he felt but rather "a genuine respect and admiration for a culture which, for all the trouble, still isn't as commercialized and depersonalized as is our Northern mass culture" (*Letters from Mississippi*, 47–48). This romanticized view of poor blacks, together with a growing antipathy in the New Left to the commercialized North, with "its white snaring suburbs . . . [and] its millions of insulated consciences" (Tom Hayden, "The Dixiecrats and Changing Southern Power: From Bourbon to

bourbon," August 1963, p. 1, SDS Microfilm, Series 4B, No. 150), helped to undermine the goal of integration and pave the way for the flowering of black power and racial separatism.

25. Norm Fruchter, "Mississippi: Notes on SNCC," *Studies on the Left* 5 (Winter 1965), 76–77. Casey Hayden, Preface to Mary King's *Freedom Song*, 8. Also see Stokely Carmichael, "Who Is Qualified?" in Andrew Kopkind, ed., *Thoughts of the Young Radicals* (New York: Pitman, 1966), 28–29; and Ronald Radosh, "The White Liberal's Crisis," *Studies on the Left* 4 (Summer 1964), 118–19.

26. Gitlin, "The Radical Potential of the Poor," in Teodori, *The New Left*, 137. Also see Norman Fruchter and Robert Kramer, "An Approach to Community Organizing," *Studies on the Left* 6 (March/April 1966), 35.

27. Staughton Lynd, "Radical Politics and Nonviolent Revolution," *Liberation* 11 (April 1966), 18; the text is from a speech delivered March 26, 1966, at rallies in Chicago and Madison.

28. Carl Wittman and Thomas Hayden, "An Interracial Movement of the Poor?" in Cohen and Hale, *The New Student Left*, 196–97. Also see Sale, *SDS*, 104.

29. Tom Hayden, *Reunion: A Memoir* (New York: Random House, 1988), 124.

30. Sale, *SDS*, 103.

31. Ibid., 105, 107.

32. Economic Research and Action Project, June 1964, SDS Convention Statement on Community Organizing, SDS Microfilm, Series 2A, No. 20. Prospectus for Cleveland Community Project, [n.d.], SDS Microfilm, Series 2B, No. 16. Also see Jeff Goodman, "Organizing the Poor on their own Behalf," SDS Microfilm, Series 2B, No. 26. Just how high ERAP's hopes initially were can be gleaned from "An Introductory Statement" that outlined the organization's vision of the future: "America is entering a New Era. Automation is the agent of a New Industrial Revolution. The abundance made possible by new technology can eliminate the economic basis of exploitation. Man can be freed from insecurity, exhausting labor and from the dehumanizing struggle for material survival in an economy of scarcity. Men's creative energies can be released for self development, and for self government. A democracy of participation, at last, becomes possible. . . . Automation is revolutionary not only in its creative potential, but also in its destruction of this full employment mechanism." Automation thus simultaneously created the constituency for revolutionary transformation (i.e., the unemployed and underemployed) at the same time that it made such a transformation in lifestyle technologically possible (SDS Economic Research and Action Project: An Introductory Statement, SDS Microfilm, Series 2B, No. 26).

33. "Prospectus for Conference on Community Organizing for Economic Issues," to be held on April 10–12, at the University of Michigan, sponsored by ERAP and the Michigan chapter of SDS, p. 2, SDS Microfilm, Series, 2B, No. 2. Identical language is used in "Background of the Institute [on Organizing for Social Action]," to be held June 7–14, sponsored by ERAP, SDS Microfilm, Series 2B, No. 17. Richard Flacks also speaks of "the upsurge of the poor" in the draft statement he submitted to the 1964 SDS convention, held June 11–14, 1964, Draft Statement #2, p. 9, submitted by Richard Flacks, SDS Microfilm, Series 2A, No. 9. Also see the

form letter sent out late in the summer of 1964 by ERAP National Director Rennie Davis, which spoke of the urban poor as "a dynamic force" that could help lead "a fresh assault on the economic injustices of our cities and towns" and turn attention to "the fundamental structural obstacles to Negro freedom" (SDS Microfilm, Series 2B, No. 14). In a similar vein was a confidential staff report by Rennie Davis that spoke of creating "a genuine movement of the poor aimed at an all-out assault on the economic and political priorities of this country" (Rennie Davis, "Report from Ann Arbor," July 2, 1964, in ERAP Project Report, June 20–July 1, 1964, p. 2, SDS Microfilm, Series 2B, No. 2). Also see Hayden, *Reunion*, 123; and Richard Rothstein, "JOIN Organizes City Poor," April 1964, SDS Microfilm, Series 2B, No. 9.

34. Philadelphia ERAP Report, June 16–24, 1964, p. 5, SDS Microfilm, Series 2B, No. 2. Gitlin, "The Battlefields and the War," in Cohen and Hale, *The New Student Left*, 125–26. Richard Rothstein, untitled working paper, prepared for an SDS-sponsored Conference on Community Movements and Economic Issues, Ann Arbor, Michigan, April 10–12, 1964, SDS Microfilm, Series 2B, No. 9. This premise that it was the most deprived who were the best agents of change did not go unchallenged within ERAP. See, for instance, Kimberly Moody's critique, "Can the Poor Be Organized?" in Cohen and Hale, *The New Student Left*, 153–59.

35. See, for example, Report from Cleveland, July 27, 1964, p. 2, SDS Microfilm, Series 2B, No. 2; and Cleveland, August 1964, SDS Microfilm, Series 2B, No. 2.

36. As a result, organizers sometimes felt the need to dissemble about their real or long-term aims in order not to frighten off those they were trying to organize. ERAP director Rennie Davis, who envisioned a "world beyond the welfare state" in which "the small community [was] tied in . . . to a country that guarantees a set income" and in which there was "democratic control and use of our economic resources for brotherly and creative ends" (Rennie Davis to Robb Burlage, May 2, 1964, SDS Microfilm, Series 2B, No. 17; Rennie Davis, "Introduction," p. 2, SDS Microfilm, Series 2B, No. 26), felt that it was important that organizers address "the question of 'openness' or honesty with regard to the long-term goals of the project [and] *when conspiracy may be needed to achieve those goals*" (Rennie Davis to Richard Flacks, August 16, 1964, SDS Microfilm, Series 2B, No. 38, emphasis added; this question had been placed on the agenda for the Training Institute of the Economic Research and Action Project, June 6–11, 1964, SDS Microfilm, Series 2B, No. 17). Radical organizers often reported that "there are things which we felt were true that we do not feel we can discuss in the community at this time" (John Bancroft, "The Newsletter," *ERAP Newsletter*, August 27, 1965, p. 6, SDS Microfilm, Series 2B, No. 24). Among the more ridiculous products of this felt need to disguise their radical-socialist goals was a short-lived "secret" newsletter that was circulated among ERAP staff with instructions that "the person whose name is last on the list is responsible for destroying the newsletter" ("Peace, Land and Bread: Not a People's Paper," SDS Microfilm, Series 2B, No. 38).

37. The question of how ERAP organizing could lead to fundamental social change was asked with increasing frequency and urgency during 1965. So, for instance, David Bernstein inquired of Carl Wittman how "a series of workable neighborhood democracies, local insurgency movements, [can] result in a revolutionary

and just society formed in their image" (Bernstein to Wittman, January 25, 1965, SDS Microfilm, Series 2B, No. 20). Also see Carol McEldowney, [untitled letter regarding ERAP institute], May 19, 1965, p. 7, SDS Microfilm, Series 2B, No. 18; Cleveland Report, July 23, 1964, p. 6, SDS Microfilm, Series 2B, No. 2; Cleveland Report, July 27, 1964, p. 5, SDS Microfilm, Series 2B, No. 2; Report from Newark, July 24, 1964, p. 2, SDS Microfilm, Series 2B, No. 2; and Cleveland: Continuation of Projects, [n.d.], p. 3, SDS Microfilm, Series 2B, No. 2.

38. According to Sale, "By the end of the summer of 1965, ERAP had proven itself to be a failure" and "the collapse of ERAP [was] generally acknowledged by the end of 1965" (*SDS*, 142, 147).

39. Tom Hayden, "The Politics of 'the Movement,'" 81, 87, 83, 81, 85–86.

40. Todd Gitlin, "The Radical Potential of the Poor," 137, 143, 137, 143–44. Among the most acute analysts of the New Left's tendency to romanticize the poor is Gitlin himself in his memoirs, *The Sixties*, especially 164–65, as well as earlier in "The Dynamics of the New Left," *motive* 31 (November 1970), 43. "A strain of radical intellectuals," Gitlin writes, "has insisted not only that simple people, especially peasants, are entitled to justice but that they are unspoiled repositories of wisdom, insulated from the corruptions of modern urban commercial life; that despite the injuries meted out to them, or perhaps because of those injuries, they remember something about living which the prosperous have forgotten. The ideals of equality and fraternity meet in the presence of the noble savage" (*The Sixties*, 164). In his memoirs Gitlin acknowledges, "I felt the force of the spirit of pastorale myself, or its literary equivalent" (ibid., 166).

41. To: SDS executive committee, From: Tom Hayden, Re: manifesto, p. 2, SDS Microfilm, Series 1, No. 6. Tom Hayden, "Report on McComb, Mississippi," p. 15, SDS Microfilm, Series 1, No. 11; emphasis added.

42. See Raymond Aron, *The Opium of the Intellectuals* (New York: Norton, 1962), chapter 3.

43. Tom Hayden, "The Ability to Face Whatever Comes," in Kopkind, *Thoughts of the Young Radicals*, 40–41. Hayden, "SNCC: The Qualities of Protest," 123. Also see Tom Hayden, "Community Organizing and the War on Poverty," *Liberation* 10 (November 1965), 18. In his memoirs Hayden concedes, albeit obliquely, that he continued to search for the chosen agent of change. "*Even more than myself*," Hayden writes, "Rennie [Davis] had long searched for some sort of moral agency, whether an organization or class of people, who could redeem the world. For a time it had been our generation, then the dispossessed of Appalachia, now he was pulled to the Vietnamese, whose suffering and dedication surpassed his understanding" (Hayden, *Reunion*, 219; emphasis added).

44. Hayden, "The Ability to Face Whatever Comes," 40; also see 38. Also see "Call for a Congress of Unrepresented People to Declare Peace in Vietnam," *ERAP Newsletter*, July 10, 1965, SDS Microfilm, Series 2B, No. 24; "Afterthoughts on Washington," p. 11, *ERAP Newsletter*, August 14, 1965, SDS Microfilm, Series 2B, No. 24; Kay Moller, "Prospectus for the White Southern Student Project," SDS Microfilm, Series 2B, No. 2; Lynd, "Radical Politics and Nonviolent Revolution," 18; Lynd and Hayden, *The Other Side*, 236. This premise did not go unchallenged within

SDS. In the spring of 1965, for instance, Robb Burlage urged those in SDS to ask themselves whether "there are real links — requisites for united movement — between the 'alienation' of the student or intellectual and the 'alienation,' displacement, and powerlessness of the poor" (Burlage to Helen [Garvy], Clark [Kissinger], NOers, et al., April 25, 1965, SDS Microfilm, Series 2B, No. 14).

45. From the Editors, "After the Election," *Studies on the Left* 5 (Winter 1965), 20. Cf. Herbert Marcuse: "Opposition is concentrated among the outsiders within the established order. First it is to be found in the ghettos among the 'underprivileged,' whose vital needs even highly developed, advanced capitalism cannot and will not gratify. Second, the opposition is concentrated at the opposite pole of society, among those of the privileged whose consciousness and instincts break through or escape social control" (Herbert Marcuse, *Five Lectures* [Boston: Beacon Press, 1970], 84).

46. Hayden, "The Politics of 'the Movement,'" 86, 83–84. Hayden, "SNCC: The Qualities of Protest," 119. Thomas Hayden, "Student Social Action: From Liberation to Community," in Cohen and Hale, *The New Student Left*, 288.

47. Jeff Goodman, "Organizing the Poor in Their Own Behalf," SDS Microfilm, Series 2B, No. 26. Goodman's article essentially summarizes and repeats the thinking of Hayden and Rennie Davis. The opening report from the new West Oakland project stressed that "Oakland is not much different from Louisiana or Mississippi" (*ERAP Newsletter*, July 17, 1965, SDS Microfilm, Series 2B, No. 24).

48. SDS Pamphlet, "A Movement of Many Voices," SDS Microfilm, Series 2B, No. 26.

49. This expression is adapted from Gitlin, who summarizes the attitude as "one oppression, one revolution" (*The Sixties*, 185).

50. Casey Hayden, "Notes on Organizing Poor Southern Whites," *ERAP Newsletter*, August 27, 1965, pp. 7–10, SDS Microfilm, Series 2B, No. 24. Also see Sara Evans, *Personal Politics: The Roots of Women's Liberation in the Civil Rights Movement and the New Left* (New York: Knopf, 1979), 132–33.

51. Sale, *SDS*, 143. Even those who did not romanticize the poor's native intelligence still expected to find an anger that could be harnessed and directed. So Al Haber, for instance, could write that "the problem is finding ways to direct the energy of hostility and alienation (which is basically a healthy rejection of a society that fails to meet their needs) into modes of action which, on the one hand, do not compromise with the system and on the other hand, effectively challenge and undermine the structure of power under which these people suffer" (To: the SDS worklist, From: Al Haber, Re: ERAP, [n.d.], SDS Microfilm, Series 2B, No. 2).

52. *SDS Bulletin*, September, 1964, quoted in Sale, *SDS*, 132–33. Also see Sharon Jeffrey's testimony, cited in Miller, *Democracy Is in the Streets*, 199; as well as Evan Metcalf in Cleveland to Larry Gordon and Nick Egleson, *ERAP Newsletter*, July 23, 1965, SDS Microfilm, Series 2B, No. 24.

53. Sale, *SDS*, 142, 147.

54. Ibid., 135, also 148.

55. Evan Metcalf in Cleveland to Larry Gordon and Nick Egleson, *ERAP Newsletter*, July 23, 1965, SDS Microfilm, Series 2B, No. 24.

56. On fatalism as a cultural bias see Mary Douglas, "Cultural Bias," in Douglas,

In the Active Voice (London: Routledge, 1982); Thompson, Ellis, and Wildavsky, *Cultural Theory;* and Richard J. Ellis, *American Political Cultures* (New York: Oxford University Press, 1993), chapter 7.

57. Nick Egleson in Hoboken to Joe Eyer and Brenda Porster, "Correspondence: In the Factory," *ERAP Newsletter,* July 23, 1965, SDS Microfilm, Series 2B, No. 24.

58. "America and the New Era," in Teodori, *The New Left,* 181; also see Students for a Democratic Society, "A Letter to Young Democrats," SDS Microfilm, Series 2A, No. 130.

59. Hayden, "SNCC: The Qualities of Protest," 121. Hayden, "Community Organizing and the War on Poverty," 17. Cf. Casey Hayden's indictment of welfare "caseworkers [who] act as agents of the middle class values of the state. . . . Recipients are supposed to be reshaped to meet society's demands and norms and then pushed back into the system." Her aim as an organizer, in contrast, was "building a group of women whose allegiance is to us and each other against the system" (Casey Hayden, "Chicago's Welfare Work," *ERAP Newsletter,* August 27, 1965, pp. 1–2, SDS Microfilm, Series 2B, No. 24).

60. Richard Rothstein to Rennie Davis, March 15, 1965, p. 2, SDS Microfilm, Series 2B, No. 35.

61. Sale, *SDS,* 141.

62. Hayden, "Community Organizing and the War on Poverty," 18. Stanley Aronowitz, "When the New Left Was New," in Sohnya Sayres et al., eds., *The 60s Without Apology* (Minneapolis: University of Minnesota Press, 1984), 23.

63. Hayden, "Community Organizing and the War on Poverty," 19.

64. See, for example, Evan Metcalf in Cleveland to Larry Gordon and Nick Egleson, *ERAP Newsletter,* July 23, 1965, SDS Microfilm, Series 2B, No. 24. Also see Sale *SDS,* 147.

65. See, for example, the unidentified community organizer quoted in Paul Jacobs and Saul Landau, eds., *The New Radicals: A Report with Documents* (New York: Vintage, 1966), 179.

66. On the poor's support for the Vietnam War and the government, and the ERAP organizers' reaction to the poor's disappointing attitudes, see the revealing account by Sharon Jeffrey, "Vietnam in Poor Black and White Communities," *ERAP Newsletter,* August 14, 1965, SDS Microfilm, Series 2B, No. 14.

67. See Wini Breines, *Community and Organization in the New Left, 1962–1968* (New Brunswick, N.J.: Rutgers University Press, 1989), 145, 148. Hayden, "The Politics of 'the Movement,'" 84.

68. See the relevant remarks in Gitlin, *The Sixties,* especially 384, 389, 289–90.

69. This is not to say that SDS gave up on the urban poor altogether — far from it. Even after the collapse of ERAP, some in SDS continued to court the alienated poor. The feeling persisted among some that "there is radical potential in these communities" and that "it is our job as radicals to reach out to the poor and working whites and bring them into the movement." The need to believe in the radical potential of the poor overrode the hard experience of failure in the ERAP projects. "We

should not conclude that because ERAP failed, organizing poor and working whites will fail," insisted two organizers with experience in Chicago's JOIN project. Rather, ERAP's failure pointed to the need for a different kind of organizing, one in which "rather than moving a project — office, large number of people, etc. — into a neighborhood," a small number of people would unobtrusively "submerge themselves in that community" (Bob Lawson and Diane Sager, "A Perspective for Community Organizing," 1967, SDS Microfilm, Series 4B, No. 213).

70. Sale, *SDS*, 248.

71. Hayden, *Reunion*, 180. Curiously, Hayden also says that "most of my memories of the Vietnamese experience are collective ones, a whole society more than specific individuals" (184).

72. Hayden admits as much in an interview with James Miller: "I think I was too motivated by anger at feeling excluded, and so I overidentified with the really excluded, like the Vietnamese. It skewed my judgment as to what was possible, or even necessary. I made the Vietnamese more than human" (Miller, *Democracy Is in the Streets*, 269). Also see Hayden, *Reunion*, 184.

73. Hayden, *Reunion*, 183. Also see Lynd and Hayden, *The Other Side*, 56–57.

74. Tom Findley, "Tom Hayden: Rolling Stone Interview, Part 1," *Rolling Stone*, October 26, 1972, 48. Also see Gitlin, *The Sixties*, 272–73.

75. Lynd and Hayden, *The Other Side*, 9. "Without knowing much about the particulars of Vietnam," Gitlin writes, "many of us [assumed] that the Vietnamese revolutionaries were a more victimized and better organized version of ourselves" (*The Sixties*, 185).

76. Lynd and Hayden, *The Other Side*, 236, 200. Cf. Dave Dellinger's remark that "the 'Popular Assemblies' that take place in Cuban factories, cooperatives, schools, and housing projects . . . fulfill a grass-roots, democratic function similar to that formerly provided in the United States by the New England town meeting" (Dave Dellinger, "Cuba: Seven Thousand Miles from Home" [1964], reprinted in Dellinger, *Revolutionary Nonviolence: Essays by Dave Dellinger* [Garden City, N.Y.: Anchor Books, 1971], 167).

77. Lynd and Hayden, *The Other Side*, 200; Hayden, "A Visit to Hanoi," 26. Also see Lynd and Hayden, *The Other Side*, 73, 62–63.

78. See, for example, Susan Sontag, quoted in David Caute, *The Fellow Travelers: Intellectual Friends of Communism* (New Haven, Conn.: Yale University Press, 1988), 394.

79. Hayden, "Politics of 'the Movement,'" 85. Also see Hayden, "Student Social Action."

80. A speech delivered by Hayden at the International Days of Protest, March 25–26, 1966, quoted in Lynd and Hayden, *The Other Side*, 56.

81. Hayden, "Politics of 'the Movement,'" 85. Cf. "An Open Letter to ERAP Supporters and New Organizers," written in the fall of 1964, in which Hayden boasted of having "created lives for ourselves in Clinton Hill of a deeper sort than days can measure" (SDS Microfilm, Series, 2B, No. 26).

82. Hayden's verbatim notes taken while on his trip to Vietnam, quoted in Lynd and Hayden, *The Other Side*, 84.

83. Writing in the summer of 1965, Paul Potter expressed his worry that people in SDS "actively identify with the National Liberation Front and the Viet Cong . . . although the complexities of making judgments about those forces on the basis of confused, incomplete and almost universally ideologically distorted information remains [*sic*] as difficult as ever" ("SDS and Foreign Policy," SDS Microfilm, Series 2A, No. 16; quoted in Gitlin, *The Sixties*, 188–89).

84. Dale L. Johnson, "On the Ideology of the Campus Revolution," originally published in *Studies on the Left* (1961), reprinted in Jacobs and Landau, *The New Radicals*, 98.

85. The quotation is Gitlin's description of what Potter was saying about Cuba in the early 1960s (*The Sixties*, 102; also see 122).

86. Johnson, "On the Ideology of the Campus Revolution," 97.

87. C. Wright Mills, *Listen, Yankee: The Revolution in Cuba* (New York: Ballantine Books, 1960), 114–17.

88. Dave Dellinger, "Cuba: America's Lost Plantation" (1960), in Dellinger, *Revolutionary Nonviolence*, 127–28, 140–41, 148.

89. Dave Dellinger, "A 20th Century Revolution?" (1962), in Dellinger, *Revolutionary Nonviolence*, 150, 154.

90. Dellinger, "Cuba: Seven Thousand Miles from Home," 162, 159, 176.

91. Ibid., 168–69, 174–75.

92. Ibid., 166–67.

93. Dave Dellinger, "Cuban Contradictions (A Response to David Wieck)", *Liberation* 10 (June–July 1965), 45. Other intellectuals on the left reconciled themselves to the more disturbing aspects of Cuba's political system in similar ways. See Caute, *Fellow Travelers*, 408, 415; and Mills, *Listen, Yankee*, 117.

94. Dave Dellinger, "Cuba: The Revolutionary Society," *Liberation* 13 (March 1968), 9.

95. James Higgins, "Episodes in Revolutionary Cuba," *Liberation* (March 1968), 25, 21.

96. Todd Gitlin, "Cuba and the American Movement," *Liberation*, (March 1968), 14.

97. Ibid., 15, 17. Todd Gitlin, "The Texture of the Cuban Revolution," *New Left Notes*, February 12, 1968, pp. 4–5.

98. Gitlin, "The Texture of the Cuban Revolution," 4.

99. Tom Hayden, "Two, Three, Many Columbias," in Teodori, *The New Left*, 345.

100. Aron, *Opium of the Intellectuals*, ix. Also see Paul Hollander, *Political Pilgrims: Travels of Western Intellectuals to the Soviet Union, China, and Cuba, 1928–1978* (New York: Harper and Row, 1983).

101. See the SDS Pamphlet, "Which Side Are You On?" SDS Microfilm, Series 4B, No. 169.

102. Carl Oglesby, "Revolution: Violence or Nonviolence," *Liberation* 13 (July/August 1968), 37. Cf. Ronald Radosh's discovery that members of the group that traveled with him to Cuba in 1973 revealed a psychological attitude much like the visitors to Russia in the 1920s and 1930s. "To criticize Cuba, they argued, was to aid

the Revolution's enemies. . . . The job of North American radicals is to 'offer political support,' not to indulge in the bourgeois luxury of independent criticism; radicals should not 'arrogantly assert [their] individual right to pursue [their own] sense of truth'" ("The Cuban Revolution and Western Intellectuals," in Ronald Radosh, ed., *The New Cuba: Paradoxes and Potentials* [New York: William Morrow, 1976], 41–42).

103. Gitlin, *The Sixties*, 396–97. Mary King, *Freedom Song*, 7, 74, 297, 495. Staughton Lynd, "Resistance: From Mood to Strategy," in Teodori, *The New Left*, 311.

104. A thoughtful essay on this danger is Michael Walzer's "The Obligations of Oppressed Minorities" and particularly the short appendix, "On the Responsibility of Intellectuals," in Walzer, *Obligations*, 46–73.

105. Marx, quoted in Aron, *Opium of the Intellectuals*, 69.

106. On Hayden's intellectual development, see the early chapters of Miller, *Democracy Is in the Streets*.

107. Cf. David W. Lovell, *Marx's Proletariat: The Making of a Myth* (London: Routledge, 1988), 4, and Aron, *Opium of the Intellectuals*, xii.

108. See Lovell, *Marx's Proletariat*, 11; also 225n25; and Aron, *Opium of the Intellectuals*, 66.

109. Rothman and Lichter, *Roots of Revolution*, 166. Also see E. Victor Wolfenstein, *The Revolutionary Personality* (Princeton, N.J.: Princeton University Press, 1967). Cf. Kenneth Keniston who, in *Young Radicals: Notes on Committed Youth* (1968), saw the New Left's identification with the oppressed as evidence of a psychologically healthy "empathy" and "nurturant identification with the underdog" (Rothman and Lichter, *Roots of Revolution*, 65; also see Sale, *SDS*, 101).

110. Even Rothman and Lichter admit that in their own sample "most student radicals were not authoritarians" (*Roots of Rebellion*, 389). For a critique of Rothman and Lichter's evidence, see Richard Flacks's review in *Society* 21 (January/February 1984), 89–92. On the inadequacy of psychological explanations more generally, see Mary Douglas, *Natural Symbols: Explorations in Cosmology* (New York: Pantheon, 1982), 119; as well as Ellis and Wildavsky, "A Cultural Analysis of the Role of Abolitionists," 95; and Lewis Coser and Irving Howe, "Images of Socialism" (1954), reprinted in Nicolaus Mills, ed., *Legacy of Dissent: Forty Years of Writing from Dissent Magazine* (New York: Touchstone, 1994), 31–32.

111. In describing the idealization of the oppressed or the demonization of the system as a widely shared belief system, I am not saying that every SDS activist accepted these views. Al Haber, Steve Max, and Kim Moody, among others, for instance, sharply challenged the romance with the oppressed almost from the outset. And certainly there were people within SDS who were sympathetic to the idea of working with the liberal-labor establishment. In general, those with stronger Old Left backgrounds — Steve Max is a prime example — seemed to be more skeptical of the version of the New Left represented by Hayden and those like him.

112. Wildavsky, "Change in Political Culture," 100.

113. Memo: to all the guys on ERAP, From Tom [Hayden], p. 4, SDS Microfilm, Series 2B, No.1.

114. See, for example, "Training Institute of the Economic Research and Action Project, June 6–11, 1964," SDS Microfilm, Series 2B, No. 17; and To: ERAP staff and friends, From: Cleveland Project, Re: Summer Institute, May 5, 1965, p. 3, SDS Microfilm, Series 2B, No. 18.

115. *ERAP Newsletter,* June 30, 1965, p. 4, SDS Microfilm, Series 2B, No. 24. Also see Jeremy Brecher to Rennie Davis, *ERAP Newsletter,* November 6, 1964, SDS Microfilm, Series 2B, No. 24; and S.P.A.C., "Chester, PA.: Community Organization in the Other America," December 1963, p. 4, SDS Microfilm, Series 2B, No. 25.

116. Peter Collier and David Horowitz, "Baddest: The Life and Times of Huey P. Newton," in *Destructive Generation: Second Thoughts About the Sixties* (New York: Summit, 1990), 141–65. Gitlin, *The Sixties,* 350–51.

117. Gitlin comments perceptively on the roots of "the New Left's Third World turn" in *The Sixties,* 262–63.

118. Hayden, "Proposed Book of Essays," SDS Microfilm, Series 1, No. 11. Also see Miller, *Democracy Is in the Streets,* 39.

CHAPTER 6. When More (Democracy) Is Less

1. Michael Walzer, "A Day in the Life of a Socialist Citizen," *Dissent* (May/June 1968), reprinted in Nicolaus Mills, ed., *Legacy of Dissent: Forty Years of Writing from Dissent Magazine* (New York: Touchstone, 1994), 106, 109, 110.

2. Wini Breines, *Community and Organization in the New Left, 1962–1968: The Great Refusal* (New Brunswick, N.J.: Rutgers University Press, 1989), 83.

3. Robert Michels, *Political Parties: A Sociological Study of the Oligarchical Tendencies of Modern Democracy* (1911; reprint ed., New York: Free Press, 1962).

4. Richard Rothstein, "Representative Democracy in SDS," *Liberation* 16 (February 1972), 11. C. Clark Kissinger, "Notes on Structure," p. 2, SDS Microfilm, Series 4B, No. 198.

5. In the margins of a draft of *"Democracy Is in the Streets": From Port Huron to the Siege of Chicago* (New York: Touchstone, 1987), where James Miller made this point in the context of ERAP, Hayden scrawled: "It was the reverse of the usual organizational dynamic of centralism, bureaucracy, stagnation, etc" (399n63). Also see Breines, *Community and Organization,* 51.

6. Michels, *Political Parties,* part 2, chapter 1. Rothstein, "Representative Democracy in SDS," 12. "The longer the tenure of office," Michels warned, "the greater becomes the influence of the leader over the masses, and the greater therefore his independence" (120).

7. Miller, *Democracy Is in the Streets,* 213. Rothstein, "Representative Democracy in SDS," 16–17. The previous fall ERAP had abolished its project directors, and the ERAP Committee (which consisted of seven people elected by the SDS National Council plus the project directors) was replaced by meetings of the entire ERAP staff. See C. Clark Kissinger, "Notes on Structure," SDS Microfilm, Series 4B, No. 198.

8. Miller, *Democracy Is in the Streets,* 242, 245–46. Breines, *Community and Orga-*

nization, 82. C. Clark Kissinger, "Notes on Structure," SDS Microfilm, Series 4B, No. 198.

9. According to SDSer Richard Rothstein, "the influence of Michels' *Political Parties* was strong in the thinking of early SDS. Michels, together with Mills, was most quoted in 1962, and his description of inevitable bureaucratization in traditional organizations provided the chief framework for analysis of both the domestic trade union movement and the Old Left Communist Party here and in the U.S.S.R." ("Representative Democracy in SDS," 11).

10. Tom Hayden, Norm Fruchter, and Alan Cheuse, "Up from Irrelevance," *Studies on the Left* 5 (Spring 1965), quoted in Massimo Teodori, ed., *The New Left: A Documentary History* (Indianapolis: Bobbs-Merrill, 1969), 212. Also see Tom Hayden, *Reunion: A Memoir* (New York: Random House, 1988), 139.

11. Paul Jacobs and Saul Landau, eds., *The New Radicals: A Report with Documents* (New York: Vintage, 1966), 31. Hayden wondered aloud: "What if 'lines of authority' are harnesses made by the system and what if 'spokesmen' turn out to be coffin nails standing upright until they can be hammered down to keep the dead from returning?" (Hayden, "SNCC: The Qualities of Protest," *Studies on the Left* 5 [Winter 1965], 119).

12. Jesse Allen, "Newark: Community Union," *Studies on the Left* 5 (Winter 1965), quoted in Jacobs and Landau, *The New Radicals*, 174.

13. From an underground newspaper, *The Seed*, quoted in Breines, *Community and Organization*, 36.

14. Observing the Cleveland ERAP project, Jacobs and Landau report, "It is difficult to single out those who hold authority. Leaders, elected or *de facto*, hem and haw when they are called leaders, for traditional authority and arbitrary decision-making are incompatible with the values of the SDS staff" (Jacobs and Landau, *The New Radicals*, 30–31).

15. In a similar antiauthority vein, recently selected editor (and soon-to-be SDS president) Greg Calvert informed readers that "editing *New Left Notes* means encouraging people to write about issues of serious concern without encouraging any one viewpoint: it means being a *non-editor*" ("on being a non-editor," *New Left Notes*, August 5, 1966, p. 1). Also see Johnny Bancroff to Jeff Shero, *ERAP Newsletter*, August 19, 1965, SDS Microfilm, Series 2B, No. 34.

16. Tom Hayden, "An Open Letter to ERAP Supporters and New Organizers," SDS Microfilm, Series 2B, No. 26.

17. David J. Garrow, *Bearing the Cross: Martin Luther King, Jr., and the Southern Christian Leadership Conference* (New York: Morrow, 1988), 423. Bruce Payne, "SNCC: An Overview Two Years Later," in Mitchell Cohen and Dennis Hale, eds., *The New Student Left: An Anthology*, rev. and enl. ed. (Boston: Beacon Press, 1967), 90. Casey Hayden, Preface to Mary King, *Freedom Song: A Personal Story of the 1960s Civil Rights Movement* (New York: William Morrow, 1987), 9. SNCC volunteer, quoted in Clayborne Carson, *In Struggle: SNCC and the Black Awakening of the 1960s* (Cambridge, Mass.: Harvard University Press, 1981), 154.

18. Carol McEldowney, "Report on Michigan," *ERAP Newsletter*, July 23, 1965, p. 3, SDS Microfilm, Series 2B, No. 24. Breines, *Community and Organization*, 33.

Nancy Zaroulis and Gerald Sullivan, *Who Spoke Up? American Protest Against the War in Vietnam, 1963–1975* (New York: Holt, Rinehart and Winston, 1984), 138. C. Clark Kissinger, "Notes on Structure," p. 1, SDS Microfilm, Series 4B, No. 198.

19. This is the theme of Richard Rothstein's insightful essay, "Representative Democracy in SDS." I have relied upon Rothstein's account throughout this chapter.

20. This argument is developed further in Richard J. Ellis, "Explaining the Occurrence of Charismatic Leadership in Organizations," *Journal of Theoretical Politics* 3 (July 1991), 305–19. Also see Aaron Wildavsky, "A Cultural Theory of Leadership," in Bryan D. Jones, ed., *Leadership and Politics: New Perspectives in Political Science:* (Lawrence: University Press of Kansas, 1989), 87–113; and Michael Thompson, Richard Ellis, and Aaron Wildavsky, *Cultural Theory* (Boulder, Colo.: Westview Press, 1990), 206. A starkly different explanation for the New Left's "star system" is offered by Todd Gitlin in his influential work, *The Whole World Is Watching: Mass Media in the Making and Unmaking of the New Left* (Berkeley: University of California Press, 1980). Gitlin faults the dominant "cultural apparatus's structured need for celebrity" (146), a process that he sees as rooted in competition, upward mobility, "a certain vacuum of social principle, [an] absence of clear values beyond private attainment, . . . great social inequality, . . . impersonal, commodified relationships and mass manipulation" (148). According to Gitlin it was this "all-permeating," competitive individualist cultural system, of which the mass media was an integral part, that "insisted that the movement be identified through its celebrities" (147, 153). Although Gitlin is correct that the media played an important role in personalizing and even sensationalizing the movement (the media does the same, it should be noted, in its coverage of even the Congress and the president), he understates (although does not ignore) the ways in which the movement itself, because of its radical egalitarian rejection of formal leadership roles, was attracted to, needed, and sustained charismatic stars.

21. Emily Stoper, *Student Nonviolent Coordinating Committee: The Growth of Radicalism in a Civil Rights Organization* (Brooklyn, N.Y.: Carlson Publishing, 1989), 71, 81.

22. Other charismatic figures within SNCC included Charles Sherrod in southwest Georgia and Bill Hansen in Arkansas.

23. Stoper, *Student Nonviolent Coordinating Committee*, 84. King, *Freedom Song*, 145–46. Dick Gregory introduced Moses at a Berkeley teach-in in 1965 as "a man who to me and to many people, will stand up among the greatest human beings who have ever walked the face of the earth" (Jack Newfield, *A Prophetic Minority* [New York: New American Library, 1966], 74).

24. See Elizabeth Sutherland, ed., *Letters from Mississippi* (New York: McGraw-Hill, 1965), 15. Anne Moody, *Coming of Age in Mississippi* (New York: Laurel, 1968), 252.

25. King, *Freedom Song*, 146.

26. Interview with John Lewis, in Stoper, *Student Nonviolent Coordinating Committee*, 240.

27. Steven V. Roberts, "Will Tom Hayden Overcome?" *Esquire* 70 (December 1968), 208, 177. Andrew Kopkind, "Looking Backward: The Sixties and the Move-

ment," *Ramparts* (February 1973), 29. Kopkind added, parenthetically, "People from SNCC tell me that they felt the same vibratory relationship with Bob Moses."

28. Tom Hayden, "A Letter to the New (Young) Left," in Cohen and Hale, *The New Student Left*, 4, 8–9. Miller, *Democracy Is in the Streets*, 406n19.

29. C. Wright Mills, *Listen, Yankee: The Revolution in Cuba* (New York: Ballantine, 1960), 117, 122, 123.

30. Not coincidentally, both Moses and Hayden soon retreated from the organizational limelight. Hayden submerged himself in Newark, while Moses resigned from SNCC altogether, participated in a few antiwar speeches and marches, and then left to teach in Tanzania.

31. Richard Rothstein, "A Short History of ERAP," p. 3, SDS Microfilm, Series 2B, No. 21. "The notion of 'nonleadership' and the fear of manipulation," Jack Newfield reported, "are definitive characteristics of the New Left" (*Prophetic Minority*, 121).

32. Richard Rothstein, "A Short History of ERAP," p. 2, SDS Microfilm, Series 2B, No. 21.

33. Todd Gitlin, *The Sixties: Years of Hope, Days of Rage* (New York: Bantam, 1987), 149.

34. Hayden's fevered attempt to deny his leadership role was brought into comical relief when he opted to debate while sitting in the audience rather than appear on the stage with his opponent. This brought the delicious retort from his opponent, future congressman Barney Frank: "You're such a grass root, Tom, that I don't know whether to debate you or water you" (Roberts, "Will Hayden Overcome?" 179; the opponent is identified as Frank in David Bromwich, "A Passion for Politics," *Dissent* [Fall 1994], 555). Steven Roberts also quotes a participant at the 1967 conference in Bratislava complaining that "Tom [Hayden] ran the conference without seeming to" (Roberts, "Will Hayden Overcome?" 207). Hayden's role at Columbia University in 1968 earned him the designation "a maestro of participatory democracy" (quoted in Miller, *Democracy Is in the Streets*, 291). Also see Newfield, *Prophetic Minority*, 141; and Kirkpatrick Sale, *SDS* (New York: Random House, 1973), 158–59.

35. Gitlin, *The Sixties*, 149. The same point was brilliantly made by Jo Freeman in "The Tyranny of Structurelessness." Her analysis was developed in the specific context of the women's liberation movement in the late 1960s and early 1970s, but it applies to virtually all the egalitarian organizations of the New Left and is worth quoting at length. "Structurelessness," Freeman suggested, "becomes a way of masking power. . . . When informal elites are combined with a myth of structurelessness, there can be no attempt to put limits on the use of power. It becomes capricious. . . . If the movement continues to deliberately not select who shall exercise power, it does not thereby abolish power. All it does is abdicate the right to demand that those who do exercise power and influence be responsible for it." The essay is reprinted in Jo Freeman, ed., *Social Movements of the Sixties and Seventies* (New York: Longman, 1983), 202–14 (quotations on 203, 207, 212) but was originally published in the *Berkeley Journal of Sociology* (1973).

36. "Paul Booth — Outgoing Secretary — June 1966," *New Left Notes*, August 24, 1966, p. 7. Also see Miller, *Democracy Is in the Streets*, 254.

37. Aldon D. Morris, *The Origins of the Civil Rights Movement: Black Communities Organizing for Change* (New York: Free Press, 1984), 231.

38. Carson, *In Struggle*, 169–70. King, *Freedom Song*, 488–89. Stoper, *Student Nonviolent Coordinating Committee*, 79–80. Both King (488) and Stoper (80) use the term "purge" to describe what occurred.

39. Within the New Left there were always dissident voices who warned that bureaucratic structures and procedures could be beneficial. Perhaps the most persistent and astute critic of the extreme antistructure sentiment prevalent in SDS was Steve Max, who warned against confusing democracy with lack of structure: "To destroy formal structures in society is unfortunately no small task, but to do so in one's own organization is not only possible, but easy" (Max, "The 1965 SDS Convention: From Port Huron to Maplehurst," quoted in Miller, *Democracy Is in the Streets*, 242). Paul Booth, too, cautioned that "a test of the strength of an institution is its ability to pass on accumulated experience. Only an institution with the paraphernalia of structure, tradition, administrative procedures . . . will be successful" (Booth, "National Secretary's Report, 12–65," quoted in Breines, *Community and Organization*, 84; also in Miller, *Democracy Is in the Streets*, 255–56). More than a few probably felt, as Helen Garvy expressed it in the spring of 1965, "caught . . . between a hate of bureaucracy and feeling that some of it enables more of what I want" (Helen Garvy to Dick Magidoff, [1965], SDS Microfilm, Series 2A, No. 14).

40. Miller, *Democracy Is in the Streets*, 244. Sale, *SDS*, 221.

41. Paul Booth to Mike Davis [Nov–Dec?, 1965], SDS Microfilm, Series 3, No. 1, quoted in Miller, *Democracy Is in the Streets*, 253–54.

42. Sale, *SDS*, 225, 704. This despite the fact that even under Booth's more structured regime, the entire staff in the National Office lived in the same large apartment and received identical wages.

43. C. Clark Kissinger, "Notes on Structure," p. 2, SDS Microfilm, Series 4B, No. 198.

44. Jonathan Eisen, "Heads You Win, Tails We Lose: A Report on the SDS Convention," in Cohen and Hale, *The New Student Left*, 311. Todd Gitlin, "Notes on the Pathology of the N.C.," *New Left Notes*, February 4, 1966, p. 4. Also see Paul Booth's and Bob Ross's recollections in Miller, *Democracy Is in the Streets*, 257.

45. Don McKelvey, "Intellectual Elitism and the Failure of Teaching," *New Left Notes*, August 12, 1966, p. 1. Donald McKelvey, "Some Notes on Participatory Democracy," *New Left Notes*, May 6, 1966, p. 8. "Representative democracy," McKelvey also insisted, "depends too greatly on charisma."

46. Todd Gitlin, "Notes on the Pathology of the N.C.," *New Left Notes*, February 4, 1966, p. 4. Steve Max, "Reply to Gitlin," *New Left Notes*, February 18, 1966, p. 2.

47. Clark Kissinger, "Proposed Constitutional Amendments," *New Left Notes*, July 15 and 22, 1966, p. 1.

48. C. George Benello, "Some Key Issues in Participatory Democracy" [December 1965], SDS Microfilm, Series 2A, No. 130. Henry W. Haslach, Jr., "Thoughts on Leadership," *New Left Notes*, June 26, 1967, pp. 5, 8. Tom Condit, "Propose[d] Constitutional Amendments," *New Left Notes*, August 5, 1966, p. 4. Also see Rothstein, "Representative Democracy in SDS," 12, 16.

49. Rothstein, "Representative Democracy in SDS," 15. By 1967, according to Rothstein, "random members who showed up outvoted chapter delegates, making it possible for non–chapter members to relate to SDS only at the top . . . while destroying the chapter as the essential constitutive unit of the organization."

50. For two of many testimonies to the degeneration of National Council meetings, see Dick Flacks, "Whatever Became of the New Left?" *New Left Notes*, August 12, 1966, p. 1; and Robert Pardum, "The Political Function of the NC," *New Left Notes*, December 11, 1967, p. 1.

51. Rothstein, "Representative Democracy in SDS," 10.

52. Ibid., 12. Also see Sale, *SDS*, 92.

53. Rothstein, "Representative Democracy in SDS," 15.

54. Sale, *SDS*, 365–66. "Constitutional Amendments," *New Left Notes*, July 10, 1967, p. 6. Also see Rothstein, "Representative Democracy in SDS," 13–14.

55. Sale, *SDS*, 366. Rothstein, "Representative Democracy in SDS," 14. Miller, *Democracy Is in the Streets*, 258.

56. Mike Spiegel, "National Secretary's Report: On Organizational Responsibility and Political Maturity," *New Left Notes*, December 4, 1967, p. 3. Sale, *SDS*, 392. Also see Mike Spiegel, "National Secretary's Report: Success and Failures of the NC," *New Left Notes*, January 8, 1968, p. 1.

57. Sale, *SDS*, 392. Carl Davidson, "National Vice-President's Report — Has SDS Gone to Pot," *New Left Notes*, February 3, 1967, p. 4. Cf. Tom Hayden in 1964: "We should take note of the manipulative approach as one which many of our comrades use and advocate. . . . This is where Malcolm X and Saul Alinsky fall together, in their common theory that the masses are needed primarily as the shock troops — while our notion is that they should be leaders. Their formulas lead directly to the justification of a hierarchical organizational setup" (Memo: to all the guys on ERAP, From Tom [Hayden], p. 4, SDS Microfilm, Series 2B, No. 1).

58. Sale, *SDS*, 392, 395.

59. Greg Calvert, "Beyond the Beloved Community: A Response to Pat and Ken," National Secretary's Report, *New Left Notes*, November 25, 1966, pp. 1, 3, 8. Calvert's response was to "A Statement of Values," by Pat Hansen and Ken McEldowney, in *New Left Notes*, November 4, 1966, pp. 5, 8.

60. Greg Calvert, "Participatory Democracy, Collective Leadership and Political Responsibility," *New Left Notes*, December 18, 1967, pp. 1, 7. SNCC had arrived at the same conclusion roughly two years before that one could not "make the new world and live in it, too" (Stoper, *Student Nonviolent Coordinating Committee*, 79).

61. Calvert, "Participatory Democracy," 7.

62. After SDS succumbed to the Marxist-Leninist Progressive Labor party and the violent rage of the Weathermen, Calvert recanted on the question of participatory democracy.

63. C. Clark Kissinger, "On Convention Document," a National Council Working Paper, printed in *New Left Notes*, June 10, 1966, p. 2.

64. Richard Rothstein to Rennie Davis, March 15, 1965, SDS Microfilm, Series 2B, No. 35.

65. See, for example, S.P.A.C., "Chester, PA.: Community Organization in the

Other America," December 1963, p. 4, SDS Microfilm, Series 2B, No. 25; Memo: to all the guys on ERAP, From: Tom [Hayden], p. 6, SDS Microfilm, Series 2B, No. 1; and George Graham to Richard Rothstein, [1965], SDS Microfilm, Series 2B, No. 35. Particularly troubling are Jeremy Brecher to Rennie Davis, *ERAP Newsletter*, November 6, 1964, SDS Microfilm Series 2B, No. 24, and the description of the New Haven freedom school in *ERAP Newsletter*, June 30, 1965, p. 4, SDS Microfilm, Series 2B, No. 24.

66. See "A Movement of the American Poor" [c. summer 1965], SDS Microfilm, Series 2B, No. 26; To: ERAP staff and friends, From: Cleveland Project, Re: Summer Institute, May 5, 1965, p. 3, SDS Microfilm, Series 2B, No. 18; "Training Institute of the Economic Research and Action Project, June 6–11, 1964," SDS Microfilm, Series 2B, No. 17; and "The West Oakland Community Project of SDS," SDS Microfilm, Series 2B, No. 30.

67. Staughton Lynd, quoted in Breines, *Community and Organization*, 63.

68. On this fallacy see Isaiah Berlin, *The Crooked Timber of Humanity* (New York: Vintage, 1992), especially chapter 1 ("The Pursuit of the Ideal").

69. Sale, *SDS*, 451, 572.

70. It is for this reason that Gitlin is right to say that "in [SDS'] beginning as a mass organization was its end" (*The Whole World Is Watching*, 31).

71. The figure is taken from Sale, *SDS*, 664.

72. Irving Howe complained that SDSers contrasted participatory democracy and representative democracy "as if somehow the two were contraries" (Gitlin, *The Sixties*, 172).

73. For sober second thoughts, see Gitlin, *The Sixties*, 149; Staughton Lynd, quoted in Breines, *Community and Organization*, 64; and Paul Booth, quoted in Miller, *Democracy Is in the Streets*, 255.

74. Michels, *Political Parties*, 335.

CHAPTER 7. Radical Feminism

1. Lewis Mumford, *The Story of Utopias* (1922; reprint ed., New York: Viking Press, 1962), 50.

2. Andrea Dworkin, "A Battered Wife Survives" (1978), in *Letters from a War Zone: Writings, 1976–1989* (New York: Dutton, 1988), 104.

3. See Stephen Macedo, ed., *Reassessing the Sixties: Debating the Political and Cultural Legacy* (New York: Norton, 1997), especially the chapters by Harvey C. Mansfield, Jeremy Rabkin, and Martha Nussbaum.

4. See Blanche Glassman Hersh, *The Slavery of Sex: Feminist-Abolitionists in America* (Urbana: University of Illinois Press, 1978).

5. Rosabeth Moss Kanter, *Commitment and Community: Communes and Utopias in Sociological Perspective* (Cambridge, Mass.: Harvard University Press, 1972), especially 86–91. Carl J. Guarneri, *The Utopian Alternative: Fourierism in Nineteenth-Century America* (Ithaca, N.Y.: Cornell University Press), especially 197–211, 353–63; "isolated household" quotation on 199. John Humphrey Noyes, *History of*

American Socialisms (Philadelphia: Lippincott, 1870). John L. Thomas, "Antislavery and Utopia," in Martin Duberman, ed., *The Antislavery Vanguard: New Essays on the Abolitionists* (Princeton, N.J.: Princeton University Press, 1965), 257. Robert F. Fogarty, *All Things New: American Communes and Utopian Movements, 1860–1914* (Chicago: University of Chicago Press, 1990), 106, 199, 215; also see 66–72 for a description of the Women's Commonwealth, or the Sanctified Sisters of Belton, which Fogarty characterizes as "the first feminist collective in the United States" (66).

6. Nancy Cott, *The Grounding of Modern Feminism* (New Haven, Conn.: Yale University Press, 1987), 3, 13–15.

7. Ibid., 15.

8. Christopher Lasch, *The New Radicalism in America, 1889–1863: The Intellectual as a Social Type* (New York: Vintage, 1965), 90.

9. Cott, *Grounding of Modern Feminism*, 15, 35. Ludwig Von Mises, *Socialism: An Economic and Sociological Analysis* (1922; reprint ed., Indianapolis: Liberty Classics, 1981), 74–92. Lasch, *New Radicalism in America*, 91.

10. Cott, *Grounding of Modern Feminism*, 35.

11. June Sochen, ed., *The New Feminism in Twentieth-Century America* (Lexington, Mass.: Heath, 1971), viii–ix, 33–36, 45–46. Lasch, *New Radicalism in America*, 91.

12. At the same time, for most people, women included, the term "feminism" seemed to have undesirable radical connotations. NOW's founding statement in 1967, for instance, notes, "Too many women have been restrained by the fear of being called 'feminist'" (Aileen S. Kraditor, ed., *Up from the Pedestal: Selected Writings in the History of American Feminism* [Chicago: Quadrangle, 1968], 366; also see Sara M. Evans, *Born for Liberty: A History of Women in America* [New York: Free Press, 1989], 277).

13. Alice Echols, *Daring to Be Bad: Radical Feminism in America, 1967–1975* (Minneapolis: University of Minnesota Press, 1989), 14–15, 54, 314n2; quotations on 54. Echols adds that "eventually some [radical women] used feminism and radical feminism interchangeably because they believed that feminism was by definition radical" (315n21). Also see Barbara Ryan, *Feminism and the Women's Movement: Dynamics of Change in Social Movement Ideology and Activism* (New York: Routledge, 1992), 63; and Linda J. Nicholson, *Gender and History: The Limits of Social Theory in the Age of the Family* (New York: Columbia University Press, 1986), 26.

14. Alice Echols, "Nothing Distant About It: Women's Liberation and Sixties Radicalism," in David Farber, ed., *The Sixties: From Memory to History* (Chapel Hill: University of North Carolina Press, 1994), 163. Echols, *Daring to Be Bad*, 28–29. Also see Sara Evans, *Personal Politics: The Roots of Women's Liberation in the Civil Rights Movement and the New Left* (New York: Knopf, 1979), 104–5; James Miller, *"Democracy Is in the Streets": From Port Huron to the Siege of Chicago* (New York: Touchstone, 1987), 87; and Todd Gitlin, *The Sixties: Years of Hope, Days of Rage* (New York: Bantam, 1987), 344, 362–76.

15. Ellen Willis, "Radical Feminism and Feminist Radicalism" (1984), in Willis, *No More Nice Girls: Countercultural Essays* (Hanover, N.H.: Wesleyan University Press, 1992), 120.

16. National Organization for Women, Statement of Purpose (1966), in Kraditor, *Up from the Pedestal*, 363; also 368. Evans, *Born for Liberty*, 276–77. Echols, "Nothing Distant About It," 156–57.

17. On the events at Columbia, see Terry H. Anderson, *The Movement and the Sixties: Protest in America from Greensboro to Wounded Knee* (New York: Oxford University Press, 1995), 194–200.

18. Ti-Grace Atkinson, "Resignation from N.O.W.," in Atkinson, *Amazon Odyssey* (New York: Links Books, 1974), 9–11. Also see Echols, *Daring to Be Bad*, 168–69.

19. Ti-Grace Atkinson, "Movement Politics and Other Sleights of Hand," in *Amazon Odyssey*, 98. On the New Left's "prefigurative" politics, see Wini Breines, *Community and Organization in the New Left, 1962–1968: The Great Refusal*, 2d ed. (New Brunswick, N.J.: Rutgers University Press, 1989).

20. Echols, *Daring to be Bad*, 175–76. One former member recalled that The Feminists "made the lot system into a religion, lotting each other to death. The principle of equality was distorted into an anti-individualist mania" (Evans, *Personal Politics*, 223).

21. Echols, *Daring to Be Bad*, 176–77.

22. Ibid., 170–71, 177–78.

23. Ibid., 179. The nation's first women's liberation group, the Chicago-based West Side group, also toyed with the idea of a uniform, primarily as a way of fostering egalitarian solidarity and as "a public way to disassociate ourselves from the 'women as consumer and clothes-horse image.'" The uniform would be "un-cooptable by the fashion industry." Those who worried that a uniform would erode individuality were dismissed as "dupes of consumerism" (ibid., 68).

24. Ibid., 179.

25. Ibid., 181. Atkinson's "trashing," to use the language of the movement, led her to quip: "Sisterhood is powerful: it kills sisters" (quoted in Ryan, *Feminism and the Women's Movement*, 62).

26. Echols, *Daring to Be Bad*, 182–83.

27. Ibid., 209–10; also see 89, 150–51, 191–95, 198, 204–8. Also see Evans, *Personal Politics*, 223; Joan Cassell, *A Group Called Women: Sisterhood and Symbolism in the Feminist Movement* (1977; reprint ed., Prospect Heights, Ill.: Waveland Press, 1989), especially 128–33; and Rita Mae Brown, "The Furies Collective," in Penny A. Weiss and Marilyn Friedman, eds., *Feminism and Community* (Philadelphia: Temple University Press, 1995), 128–31. Particularly revealing of the pathology of radical egalitarianism is Robin Morgan's recollection of her time with *Rat* after the underground paper had been "liberated" by female staffers. Morgan remembers that when "the Rat collective decided it was elitist for any member to sign her name to her work, I dutifully dropped my byline. . . . When the collective, a few months later, criticized me for writing in a style apparently still identifiable to our readers ('You write too well' was the flattering accusation), I even tried to worsen my writing: I spelled America with three k's instead of one, as I had done previously. . . . But this still was insufficient: it was suggested that I not write for the paper at all — but not quit, either (that would be a 'cop-out'). I must stay and work on proofreading, layout, and distribution — but not write. Appallingly enough, I even did that — wearing a fixed

Maoist smile to cover my indignation — for about a month. Then something cracked open inside me, and it was over" (Robin Morgan, *The Word of a Woman: Feminist Dispatches, 1968–1992* [New York: Norton, 1992], 55–56). Sober second thoughts on the leaderless ideal can be found in Joreen [Jo Freeman], "The Tyranny of Structurelessness," in Anne Koedt, Ellen Levine, and Anita Rapone, eds., *Radical Feminism* (New York: Quadrangle, 1973), 285–99; Robin Morgan, *Going Too Far: The Personal Chronicle of a Feminist* (New York: Random House, 1977); Willis, *No More Nice Girls*, 140; and Carol Hanisch, "The Liberal Takeover of Women's Liberation," in Redstockings of the Women's Liberation Movement, ed., *Feminist Revolution: An Abridged Edition with Additional Writings* (New York: Random House, 1978), especially 164–65.

28. Echols, *Daring to Be Bad*, 198; also see 100–101, 152; and Evans, *Personal Politics*, 225. Particularly good on the schismatic tendencies of radical feminism is Ryan, *Feminism and the Women's Movement*, chapter 4 ("Ideological Purity: Divisions, Splits, and Trashing").

29. Mearhof and Kearon, quoted in Echols, *Daring to be Bad*, 184; also see 165.

30. Evans, *Personal Politics*, 223.

31. New York Radical Women, formed by Shulamith Firestone and Pam Allen in the fall of 1967, was the first women's liberation group in New York City. Among its members were Kathie Sarachild, Carol Hanisch, Kate Millett, Irene Peslikis, Ros Baxandall, Ellen Willis, Robin Morgan, and Patricia Mainardi. The group dissolved in the winter of 1969 (Echols, *Daring to Be Bad*, 388, 383, 318n109).

32. Ibid., 83–84; also see Evans, *Personal Politics*, 214; and Kathie Sarachild, "Consciousness-Raising: A Radical Weapon," in Redstockings, *Feminist Revolution*, 145. The quotation is from a 1968 handout by "The New York Consciousness Awakening Women's Liberation Group." The handout is titled "Who We Are: Descriptions of Women's Liberation Groups."

33. Kathie Sarachild, "A Program for Feminist Consciousness-Raising" (November 1968), in Redstockings, *Feminist Revolution*, 202; this was previously published in Shulamith Firestone and Anne Koedt, eds., *Notes from the Second Year: Women's Liberation* (New York: New York Radical Feminists, 1970), 78–80. An editorial preface to "Program" in *Notes from the Second Year* credited Sarachild with being "the originator of the concept of 'consciousness-raising'" (78).

34. Sarachild, "Consciousness-Raising: A Radical Weapon," 145.

35. Sarachild, "A Program for Feminist Consciousness-Raising," 203. Also see Irene Peslikis, "Resistance to Consciousness," in Firestone and Koedt, *Notes from the Second Year*, 81; also reprinted in Robin Morgan, ed., *Sisterhood Is Powerful: An Anthology of Writings from the Women's Liberation Movement* (New York: Random House, 1970), 337–39.

36. Echols, *Daring to Be Bad*, 88, 151.

37. Leaflet written by Kathie Amatniek (Sarachild) for NYRW, January 15, 1968, excerpted in Redstockings, *Feminist Revolution*, 154.

38. Kathie Sarachild, "Psychological Terrorism," in Redstockings, *Feminist Revolution*, 59–60. Cf. "Consciousness-Raising: A Radical Weapon," in which Sarachild writes that "what really counts in consciousness-raising are not methods, but results"

(147). Mao's influence on Sarachild is pointed out in Echols, *Daring to Be Bad*, 85; also see Sarachild, "Consciousness-Raising: A Radical Weapon," 146; and Sarachild's preface to *Feminist Revolution*, 11.

39. Echols, *Daring to Be Bad*, 90.

40. Sarachild, "Consciousness-Raising: A Radical Weapon," 145. Also see Anne Forer, "Thoughts on Consciousness-Raising," in Redstockings, *Feminist Revolution*, 151.

41. Pamela Allen, "Free Space," in Anne Koedt and Shulamith Firestone, eds., *Notes from the Third Year: Women's Liberation* (New York: New York Radical Feminists, 1971), 94. Also reprinted in Koedt et al., *Radical Feminism*, 271–79.

42. Hanisch, quoted in Echols, *Daring to Be Bad*, 88. Also see Carol Hanisch, "The Liberal Takeover of Women's Liberation," in Redstockings, *Feminist Revolution*, 166.

43. The "left-liberalism error," in contrast, was the bookish study group that does not really investigate things but instead reaches "pre-ordained conclusions" and is characterized by dogmatism rather than the radical commitment to "investigation and discovery" that characterizes the consciousness-raising group (Sarachild, "Consciousness-Raising: A Radical Weapon," 150).

44. Irene Peslikis, quoted in Echols, *Daring to Be Bad*, 87; emphasis added.

45. C.f. the misleading account in ibid., 88.

46. Allen, "Free Space," in Koedt and Firestone, *Notes from the Third Year*, 94–95; emphasis added.

47. Ibid., 95, 98; second emphasis added.

48. On Forer's role in initiating consciousness-raising sessions within NYRW, see Echols, *Daring to Be Bad*, 83; and Sarachild, "Consciousness-Raising: A Radical Weapon," 144.

49. Forer, "Thoughts on Consciousness-Raising," 151; emphasis added. Cf. the editorial by Shulamith Firestone and Anne Koedt in *Notes from the Second Year* in which they suggested that "one of the most exciting things to come out of the women's movement so far is a new daring, a willingness — eagerness — to tear down old structures and assumptions and let *real* thought and feeling flow" (2; emphasis added). On the use of the vocabulary of false consciousness, see also Meredith Tax, "Woman and Her Mind: The Story of Everyday Life," and Jennifer Gardner, "False Consciousness," in Firestone and Koedt, *Notes from the Second Year*, 10–16, 82–83.

50. The Redstockings were founded by Shulamith Firestone and Ellen Willis in February 1969, immediately after the demise of NYRW. Among the NYRW members who joined the Redstockings (in addition to Firestone and Willis) were Sarachild, Irene Peslikis, and Patricia Mainardi. The group disbanded in the autumn of 1970 (Echols, *Daring to Be Bad*, 388), although a group of former Redstockings, including Sarachild, reconstituted the group in the mid-1970s.

51. "Redstockings Manifesto," July 7, 1969, in Firestone and Koedt, *Notes from the Second Year*, 112–13; the manifesto is reprinted in Alexander Bloom and Wini Breines, eds., *"Takin' it to the streets": A Sixties Reader* (New York: Oxford University Press, 1995), 485–87.

52. Sarachild, "A Program for Feminist Consciousness-Raising," 202; emphasis added. Also see Echols, *Daring to Be Bad*, 83.

53. Sarachild, "A Program for Feminist Consciousness-Raising," 202. Cf. the NYRW's statement of principles: "We define the best interests of women as the best interests of the poorest, most insulted, most despised, most abused woman on earth. . . . She is Everywoman: ugly, dumb (dumb broad, dumb cunt), bitch, nag, hag, whore, fucking and breeding machine, mother of us all. Until Everywoman is free, no woman will be free. When her beauty and knowledge is revealed and seen, the new day will be at hand" (Bloom and Breines, *Takin' it to the streets*, 485).

54. "Redstockings Manifesto," 113. New York Radical Women, "Principles," in Morgan, *Sisterhood Is Powerful*, 520.

55. As Ann Snitow later remembered: "The dream was that underneath our differences, our oppression unified us in a very fusing way. Women's experience had an interior coherence — both political and historical. There was a great desire to find in those c-r questions that, different as we all were, we were not" (Echols, *Daring to Be Bad*, 90; also see "Congress to Unite Women: Report from the New York City Meeting of November 21, 22, 23, 1969," in Koedt et al., *Radical Feminism*, 309–10; and Sarachild, "Consciousness-Raising: A Radical Weapon," 147).

56. Forer, "Thoughts on Consciousness-Raising," 151. In the influential paper, "The Woman Identified Woman" (1970), the Radicalesbians wrote: "Together we must find, reinforce, and validate our *authentic* selves." Only then will "we feel a realness, feel at last we are coinciding with ourselves. With that real self, with that consciousness, we begin a revolution to end the imposition of all coercive identifications" (*Notes from the Third Year*, 84; emphasis added; also reprinted in Koedt et al., *Radical Feminism*, 240–45; and Bloom and Breines, *Takin' it to the streets*, 514–20).

57. Bernard Yack, *The Longing for Total Revolution: Philosophic Sources of Social Discontent from Rousseau to Marx and Nietzsche* (Princeton, N.J.: Princeton University Press, 1986). Yack's definition of "total revolution" is "a revolution in what is perceived as the definitive sub-political sphere of social interaction. . . . All who long for total revolution recognize that political institutions are secondary obstacles to human satisfaction" (10). Also relevant is Marshall Berman, *The Politics of Authenticity: Radical Individualism and the Emergence of Modern Society* (New York: Atheneum, 1972).

58. Echols, "Nothing Distant About It," 162. Atkinson, *Amazon Odyssey*, 119. Also see Yack, *Longing for Total Revolution*, especially 365–69.

59. The use of the term "brainwashed" to describe women was omnipresent in the early women's liberation movement. See, for example, the leaflet written by Kathie Amatniek (Sarachild), January 15, 1968 (Redstockings, *Feminist Revolution*, 154); Point 6 in "The Ten Points" from the August 1968 protest against the Miss America pageant (Bloom and Breines, *Takin' it to the streets*, 483); Pat Mainardi, "The Politics of Housework," in Firestone and Koedt, *Notes from the Second Year*, 28; and the statement by a group called "The New Women" (quoted in Echols, *Daring to Be Bad*, 98). Because the brainwashing line seemed at times to lead to blaming the victim — if only women would just perceive the situation correctly their oppression

would disappear — there developed a "pro-woman line," usually associated with the Redstockings, that "women's submission is not the result of brainwashing, stupidity, or mental illness but of continual, daily pressure from men. We do not need to change ourselves, but to change men" ("Redstockings Manifesto," 113). But the primary division within radical feminism was not whether women were "messed up" or "messed over," as Hanisch put it, but rather whether it was capitalism or patriarchy that was responsible for messing up *and* messing over women (see Echols, *Daring to Be Bad*, 92, 104). So-called politicos such as Marilyn Webb took the New Left line that "our minds have been permanently drugged [by] . . . the Capitalist system," but most radical feminists followed Shulamith Firestone in insisting that "capitalism and all those other systems of exploitation" began at home with the oppression of women (ibid., 116). Or, as the Redstockings Manifesto expressed it, "all other forms of exploitation and oppression (racism, capitalism, imperialism, etc.) are extensions of male supremacy" ("Redstockings Manifesto," 113).

60. Echols, *Daring to Be Bad*, 161, 97–98; also see 95–96. Robin Morgan, a central figure in the bridal fair protest, later regretted the action as a "self-indulgent insult to the very women we claimed we wanted to reach" (Morgan, *Going Too Far*, 74). On Cell 16, see Echols, *Daring to Be Bad*, 158–66.

61. Echols, *Daring to Be Bad*, 281; Echols, "Nothing Distant About It," 165.

62. Morgan, "The Wretched of the Hearth" (1969), in Morgan, *Word of a Woman*, 36.

63. Ryan, *Feminism and the Women's Movement*, 56, 69. Myra Marx Ferree and Beth B. Hess, *Controversy and Coalition: The New Feminist Movement* (Boston: Twayne, 1985), 62. Echols, *Daring to Be Bad*, 198, 387–89. Of the almost dozen groups studied by Echols, only the Chicago Women's Liberation Union outlasted Nixon. Established in 1969, it lasted until 1977.

64. Ryan, *Feminism and the Women's Movement*, 67, 56. Nancy Whittier, *Feminist Generations: The Persistence of the Radical Women's Movement* (Philadelphia: Temple University Press, 1995). Myra Marx Ferree and Patricia Yancey Martin, eds., *Feminist Organizations: Harvest of the New Women's Movement* (Philadelphia: Temple University Press, 1995).

65. Echols, *Daring to Be Bad*, 199.

66. Martial arts were an important part of the early radical feminist movement, from the emphasis on karate in Cell 16 (Echols, *Daring to Be Bad*, 158, 160) to a host of other radical feminist organizations across the country specializing in martial arts (e.g., see Whittier, *Feminist Generations*, 39, 48, 231–32). The importance MacKinnon continues to attach to martial arts is evident in a 1981 speech she delivered at Stanford University in which she closed by recommending that women work "to make fear unnecessary" through "real training in self-defense." She explained that "martial arts is not just physical preparation for a one-time shot or quick fix or a bag of tricks. It is a spiritual, integrated way of relating to one's body as one's own, in which one acts and lives and embodies oneself in the world. Not something that exists only for carrying your head about or to be looked at by other people. Self-defense, if it's done right, can begin to give us back a sense that we have a self worth

defending" (Catharine A. MacKinnon, *Feminism Unmodified: Discourses on Life and Law* [Cambridge, Mass.: Harvard University Press, 1987], 83–84).

67. Fred Strebeigh, "Defining Law on the Feminist Frontier," *New York Times Magazine*, October 4, 1991, p. 31. Entry on Catharine A. MacKinnon in *Current Biography Yearbook, 1994* (New York: H. W. Wilson, 1994), 364.

68. MacKinnon, "Liberalism and the Death of Feminism," in Dorchen Leidholdt and Janice G. Raymond, eds., *The Sexual Liberals and the Attack on Feminism* (New York: Pergamon Press, 1990), 3. Also see Echols, *Daring to Be Bad*, 248. MacKinnon singles out in particular Robin Morgan, then a member of WITCH and formerly of NYRW. Morgan's contribution to the inaugural issue of the "liberated" *Rat* was "Goodbye to All That," a highly influential essay that was widely reprinted in subsequent years (and featured the debut of the word "herstory"). Many of MacKinnon's ideas closely echo the ideas expressed in Morgan's essay. Strikingly similar, for instance, are Morgan's claims that convicted mass murderer "[Charles] Manson is only the logical extreme of the normal American male's fantasy," that men must be "divest[ed] of . . . cock privilege," that "the so-called Sexual Revolution . . . has functioned toward women's freedom as did the Reconstruction toward former slaves — reinstituting oppression by another name," and that "women were the first property when the Primary Contradiction occurred: when one-half of the human species decided to subjugate the other half." Even more similar is Morgan's vision of "a genderless society. . . . Beyond what is male or female. Beyond standards we all adhere to now without daring to examine them as male-created, male dominated, male-fucked-up, and in male self-interest" (Morgan, *Word of a Woman*, 51, 59, 68, 61, 63, 65). Also strikingly similar to MacKinnon, not only in argument but also in language and cadence, is another of Morgan's influential early essays, "Theory and Practice: Pornography and Rape" (1974). In it, Morgan claimed that "rape is the perfected act of male sexuality in a patriarchal culture," and that "rape exists any time sexual intercourse occurs when it has not been initiated by the woman, out of her own genuine affection and desire." The essay's most memorable line — "Pornography is the theory, and rape the practice" — became *the* slogan for the feminist antipornography movement (82, 84, 88).

69. The first principle enunciated by the New York Radical Women was, "We take the woman's side in everything" (New York Radical Women, "Principles," in Morgan, *Sisterhood Is Powerful*, 520; also see Redstockings, *Feminist Revolution*, 205).

70. Catharine MacKinnon, "Liberalism and the Death of Feminism," 4–6. MacKinnon's frequent use of vulgar language — particularly the word "fuck" — also bears the strong imprint of the early radical feminist movement. As Maren Carden wrote in 1974, "The use of obscene or scatological terms common in parts of the movement can, itself, symbolize the escape from men's dominance: a man cannot use such language to embarrass and insult a woman if she replies in the same vein. More commonly, however, this language which seems so shocking to the outsider is adopted simply because the feminist belongs to the larger radical subculture where it is a convenient, common and group-identifying means of expression" (Maren Lockwood Carden, *The New Feminist Movement* [New York: Russell Sage, 1974], 51).

71. MacKinnon has refused to give interviews on her personal life because she finds they are "trivialising, intrusive, [and] largely irrelevant" (Catharine MacKinnon, "Weekend Letter: So, Sense or Sophistry," *The Guardian*, June 10, 1994, p. T18). It seems more than a little ironic that an outspoken critic of the right to privacy (see Catharine A. MacKinnon, *Toward a Feminist Theory of the State* [Cambridge, Mass.: Harvard University Press, 1989], 168, 184–94; and MacKinnon, "Liberalism and the Death of Feminism," 7) so jealously guards her own privacy and insists on the irrelevance of her personal life to her public persona. But irony, even MacKinnon's defenders will concede, is not her strong suit. How else to explain MacKinnon's lament that censorship and silencing today occur "by the refusal of publishers and editors to publish, or publish well, uncompromised expressions of dissent that make them uncomfortable by challenging the distribution of power, including sexual power" (*Only Words* [Cambridge, Mass.: Harvard University Press, 1993], 77)? This from an author whose last three blistering attacks on the distibution of sexual power have been published by Harvard University Press, one of the most prestigious presses in the English-speaking world.

72. MacKinnon, *Toward a Feminist Theory of the State*, xv; also see x, xiv.

73. Ibid., 116–17; emphasis added. She also writes that "in male law, public oppression masquerades as private freedom and coercion is guised as consent" (169), and describes "force that is not seen as force because it is inflicted on women and called sex" (208).

74. Ibid., 186. Similarly, MacKinnon writes that "sexual harassment looks a great deal like ordinary heterosexual initiation under conditions of gender inequality. Few women are in a position to refuse unwanted sexual initiatives" (112), and "it is difficult to discern sexual freedom against a background, a standard, of sexual coercion" (203).

75. MacKinnon, *Feminism Unmodified*, 54. As Echols points out, this passage bears a striking resemblance to the thought of The Feminists. See Echols, *Daring to Be Bad*, 363n18; also Alice Echols, "Sex and the Single-Minded: The Dworkinization of Catharine MacKinnon," *Village Voice Literary Supplement* (March 1994), 13–14.

76. MacKinnon, *Toward a Feminist Theory of the State*, 51. MacKinnon, *Feminism Unmodified*, 39.

77. Cf. the formulation of Meredith Tax: "We have to face the fact that pieces have been cut out of us to make us fit into society. . . . We didn't get this way by heredity or by accident. We have been *molded* into these deformed postures, *pushed* into these service jobs, *made* to apologize for existing, *taught* to be unable to do anything requiring any strength at all, like opening doors or bottles. We have been told to be stupid, to be silly" (Tax, "Woman and Her Mind," *Notes from the Second Year*, 11; emphasis added; this passage, except for the first sentence, is quoted in MacKinnon, *Toward a Feminist Theory of the State*, 90).

78. See MacKinnon's critique of the "intuitionist approach" of the California Redstockings in MacKinnon, *Toward a Feminist Theory of the State*, 52.

79. MacKinnon, *Feminism Unmodified*, 54.

80. Ibid., 52. MacKinnon, *Toward a Feminist Theory of the State*, 204. Cf. the first line of *The Dialectic of Sex*, in which Firestone writes that "sex-class is so deep as to be invisible" (1). MacKinnon's early writings from the 1970s are, like Firestone's

seminal book, an attempt to marry Marxist method with feminism. In *Toward a Feminist Theory of the State*, MacKinnon is critical of Firestone for explaining male dominance in terms of biology. Where Firestone (borrowing from Simone de Beauvoir) argues that women's "original and continued oppression" is due to the "inherently unequal power distribution" that results from "women's reproductive biology," MacKinnon counters that this makes a "woman's body . . . the root of her oppression rather than a rationalization or locale for it." MacKinnon dismisses such "anatomy is destiny" explanations because they miss the way that "society enforces a meaning of women's biology." In such explanations, she reasons, "social power is not explained, it is only restated" (*Toward a Feminist Theory of the State*, 54–56). But in fact while MacKinnon repeatedly claims to be "attempting to *explain* [the] reality [of male dominance]" (*Feminism Unmodified*, 53), she offers no explanation of its historical ubiquity that is anywhere near as compelling as the biological one offered by Firestone and de Beauvoir. MacKinnon's explanation is much cruder: "On the first day," she tells us, "dominance was achieved, probably by force" (quoted in Brian Appleyard, "Thinkers of the Nineties," *The Independent*, December 18, 1995, p. 13). It is MacKinnon who restates (as well as misstates) rather than explains the original problem.

81. MacKinnon, *Toward a Feminist Theory of the State*, 89, 84–85, 87.

82. Ibid., 104.

83. Ibid., 114–16, 119.

84. Ibid., 116.

85. The law was originally struck down by a (female) federal judge, and her ruling was affirmed in 1985 by the United States Court of Appeals for the Seventh Circuit. The next year the U.S. Supreme Court summarily affirmed the ruling.

86. Nadine Strossen, *Defending Pornography: Free Speech, Sex, and the Fight for Women's Rights* (New York: Scribner, 1995), 229.

87. This is a point feminists have increasingly made in countering MacKinnon. Carole Vance, for instance, points out that "it's a little foolish to be handing this [power] over to a state, which is usually not feminist-controlled" (Janine Fuller and Stuart Blackley, *Restricted Entry: Censorship on Trial* [Vancouver, Can.: Press Gang Publishers, 1996], 39).

88. Strossen, *Defending Pornography*, 231, 237. MacKinnon dismisses this as "disinformation" since Canadian customs officials had seized this sort of material before *Butler* ("The First Amendment Under Fire from the Left: A Conversation with Floyd Abrams and Catharine A. MacKinnon," in Adele M. Stan, ed., *Debating Sexual Correctness: Pornography, Sexual Harassment, Date Rape, and the Politics of Sexual Equality* [New York: Delta, 1995], 116). Although it is true that *Butler* did not have much effect on the behavior of customs officials, it certainly did shape judicial opinions in the lower courts. In the first post-*Butler* case, *Glad Day v. Canada*, which involved explicit gay literature, comic books, and soft-porn magazines that had been seized before *Butler*, Judge Frank Hayes "liberally paraphrased the language and conceptual framework of *Butler*" to justify the censorship of this material. A subsequent case, *R. v. Scythes*, relied upon *Butler* to uphold the police seizure of a lesbian sex magazine, *Bad Attitude*, which the (male) judge argued violated women's equality because it portrayed "enjoyable sex after subordination by bondage and physical abuse at the hands

of a total stranger." See Fuller and Blackley, *Restricted Entry*, 44–46. Moreover, MacKinnon's own writings make clear that she would accept the Canadian judge's ruling that sexual orientation is irrelevant. Lesbian sadomasochism, in MacKinnon's view, does not challenge "the paradigm of male dominance" but in fact reenacts its hegemony. "Sexuality," she explains, "is so gender marked that it carries dominance and submission with it, whatever the gender of it participants" (*Toward a Feminist Theory of the State*, 142).

89. Some sympathetic reviewers of *Only Words* have attempted to characterize MacKinnon's position as "we need to balance First Amendment concerns for free speech with Fourteenth Amendment protection of equality" (*Publishers Weekly*, August 2, 1993, pp. 69–70). At times, to be sure, MacKinnon does speak the language of "balance between two cherished constitutional goals" (*Only Words*, 73), but her argument ultimately leaves little or no room for compromises and trade-offs between competing values. For MacKinnon, equality is not something to be balanced against competing goods, because a society that lacks substantive equality is necessarily an unjustifiable system of domination. For MacKinnon, as Brian Appleyard points out, "equality cannot be diluted in the name of freedom because equality is the only freedom" (*The Independent*, December 18, 1995, p. 13; also see David McCabe's review in *Commonweal*, February 11, 1994, pp. 22–23). Equality is the trump card without which freedom or any other good is meaningless.

90. MacKinnon, *Only Words*, 72–73, 78. In *Toward a Feminist Theory of the State*, MacKinnon develops the same point, although without the reference to corporations: "In a society of gender inequality, the speech of the powerful impresses its view upon the world, concealing the truth of powerlessness under a despairing acquiescence that provides the appearance of consent and makes protest inaudible as well as rare" (205). The "liberal assumptions" that underpin the First Amendment, she flatly declares, "do not apply to the situation of women" (204). Also see *Feminism Unmodified*, 204.

91. The same point was made in an op-ed column by history professor Ruth Rosen, who suggested that "MacKinnon's effort to pit free speech against women's equality creates a bogus choice. Chipping away at the First Amendment is rarely a good idea, and especially dangerous for groups committed to radical social change. Censorship, as history teaches, is more likely to be used to silence leftists and feminists than pornographers" (*Los Angeles Times*, February 9, 1994, p. B:7). Also see the comments by Abrams in "The First Amendment Under Fire from the Left," 112, 119.

92. MacKinnon, *Only Words*, 86. MacKinnon argues that "when [the state] is most ruthlessly neutral, it is most male" (*Toward the Feminist Theory of the State*, 248). Also see *Feminism Unmodified*, 33.

93. MacKinnon's ideas here as elsewhere closely resemble those expressed by Herbert Marcuse in his essay "Repressive Tolerance" (in Robert P. Wolff, Barrington Moore, Jr., and Herbert Marcuse, *A Critique of Pure Tolerance* [Boston: Beacon Press, 1965], 81–123). According to Marcuse, "Law and order are always and everywhere the law and order which protect the established hierarchy" (116). What Marcuse calls "indiscriminate tolerance" (88) or "spurious neutrality" merely "serves to reproduce acceptance of the dominion of the victors in the consciousness of man"

(113). Thus the realization of a genuine "liberating tolerance" requires "intolerance toward prevailing policies, attitudes, opinions" (81); it requires "intolerance against movements from the Right and toleration of movements from the Left" (109).

94. MacKinnon, *Toward a Feminist Theory of the State*, 247.

95. Related to this is MacKinnon's lack of concern about allowing the government to determine what is and is not pornography. For MacKinnon, the distinction is self-evidently obvious (so much for social construction), but a glowing promotional blurb by Patricia Williams on the back of MacKinnon's *Only Words* dramatically if inadvertently serves to remind us of just how contested the concept of pornography remains. In the blurb Williams insists that "because [MacKinnon's] brilliant writing is largely unread [*sic*], she has become an ideological easy mark, the object of a peculiar intellectual *pornography*." A further reminder is evident in Roger Scruton's hostile review, which criticizes *Only Words* as itself pornographic. "Miss MacKinnon's diatribe," Scruton writes, "is a vivid instance of what she condemns, a dirtying of life and love that deploys all the dehumanizing tricks of the pornographer, blocking out the soul with the hate-filled image of the body. I fully agree with her that pornography should be banned; and there is no better candidate for the bonfire than this book" (*National Review*, November 1, 1993, p. 61).

96. Nor does MacKinnon deem it relevant that in societies where pornography is freely available, such as Japan and Denmark, rape is less common than in societies where its availability is relatively restricted. Or, more precisely, she explains away these inconvenient facts. She counters that "once pornography is legitimized throughout society, you get an explosion in sexual abuse, but women don't report it anymore because they know that nothing will be done about it" ("The First Amendment Under Fire from the Left," 117). MacKinnon protects her own biases by making her theory nonfalsifiable: the theory is confirmed whether rape rates go up or down. Similarly, when asked to consider the possibility that women might exercise power, MacKinnon assures her listeners that "female power . . . is a contradiction in terms." When she herself is in an authoritative position, as when she is lecturing to an audience, this is not female power, she insists, but rather "an exercise of male power. It's hierarchical, it's dominant, it's authoritative. You're listening, I'm talking; I'm active, you're passive. I'm expressing myself; you're taking notes. Women are supposed to be seen and not heard" ("Desire and Power" [1983], in *Feminism Unmodified*, 53, 52). Any and every occurrence can be made to fit MacKinnon's impregnable thesis.

97. MacKinnon, *Only Words*, 33, 30. MacKinnon had been pressing this view for at least ten years before the publication of *Only Words*. In a 1982 lecture at Stanford University, published as "Linda's Life and Andrea's Work," MacKinnon stated that the "*viewing* [of a pornographic picture] is an *act*, an act of male supremacy" (MacKinnon, *Feminism Unmodified*, 130).

98. The evidence on this score, most dispassionate observers would agree, is mixed, which is hardly surprising in view of the difficulties of extrapolating to real life from laboratory experiments and of sorting out vexing problems of causation. But MacKinnon will brook no doubters. "Researchers and clinicians documented what women know from life: that pornography increases attitudes and behaviors of aggression and other discrimination, principally by men against women. The relation-

ship is causal. It is better than the smoking/cancer correlation and at least as good as the data on drinking and driving. . . . *There are no contradictions in this evidence*" (*Feminism Unmodified*, 202; emphasis added). Questioned about the studies that dispute the link between violence and porn, MacKinnon scoffs: "There are lots of lies . . . a bunch of very highly educated people making very slimy, very closely worded statements in order to give the impression that pornography is harmless" (Dan Cryer, "Talking with Catharine MacKinnon," *Newsday*, September 26, 1993, p. 36).

99. MacKinnon, *Feminism Unmodified*, 148. MacKinnon's critique of pornography as "a form of forced sex [and] . . . an institution of gender inequality" echoes the broadside of Cell 16's Roxanne Dunbar, who as early as 1969 articulated a radical feminist critique of pornography, which, she said, "expresses a masculine ideology of male power over females." For Dunbar, like MacKinnon, pornography doesn't just lead to violence against women but *is* violence against women, just as lynching is violence against blacks. See Echols, *Daring to Be Bad*, 165; also see 361–62n7, 288–91.

100. For a critique of this "PC Logic," see John M. Ellis, *Literature Lost: Social Agendas and the Corruption of the Humanities* (New Haven, Conn.: Yale University Press, 1987), chapter 7.

101. MacKinnon, *Toward a Feminist Theory of the State*, 206.

102. Strossen, *Defending Pornography*, 147. Similar concerns are expressed by Helena Kennedy in her review of *Only Words* for the London *Observer*. Kennedy notes it is "dangerous to collapse the distinction between fantasy and deed, thought and behavior. It invites the law to play a role which is abhorrent and fraught with risk for civil liberties" (Helena Kennedy, "How Can She Guess When Yes Means No," *The Observer*, June 19, 1994, p. 20). Similarly, Natasha Walter warns against MacKinnon's "totalitarian" tendency and cautions that "it is abuse, not dreams or desires, that we should try to control" (*The Independent*, June 11, 1994, p. 26). The "totalitarian" charge is also made by Jonathan Yardley, "Sticks and Stones," *Washington Post*, September 19, 1993; Kyle A. Pasewark in *The Christian Century*, November 17–24, 1993, p. 1164; Brian Appleyard in *The Independent*, December 18, 1995; and Charlotte Allen, "Penthouse Pest: Why Porn Crusader Catharine MacKinnon Is Right," *Washington Post*, November 28, 1993, p. C1.

103. MacKinnon, "Liberalism and the Death of Feminism," 11–12. Strebeigh, "Defining Law on the Feminist Frontier," 56. MacKinnon, *Feminism Unmodified*, 205; also see 145. In a recent interview, MacKinnon characterizes the civil libertarians and feminists who have criticized her as "brainwashed" pawns of the pornography industry. Arguments about the danger of a "slippery slope" toward censorship are never genuine. "When you have arguments with people about the First Amendment," MacKinnon explains, "you really are talking about what they can masturbate to." Her feminist opponents are not worth talking to because they are, wittingly or unwittingly, doing the bidding of the porn industry. "There are always oppressed people who side with the oppressor," MacKinnon opines. "Pornographers need women to oppose us because we are opposing them in the name of women. . . . If women always acted in their own interests, we would have been free and equal centuries ago" (Cryer, "Talking with Catharine MacKinnon," 36). In the same vein, MacKinnon dismisses efforts to get her to debate "First Amendment feminists" as

"the pimps' current strategy for legitimizing a slave trade in women" (Nat Hentoff, "Catharine MacKinnon v. the First Amendment," *Washington Post*, November 27, 1993, p. A27).

104. Maureen Mullarkey, "Hard Cop, Soft Cop," *The Nation*, May 30, 1987, pp. 720–26. Wendy Brown, "Consciousness Razing," *The Nation*, January 8/15, 1990, pp. 61–64. Carlin Romano, "Between the Motion and the Act," *The Nation*, November 15, 1993, pp. 563–70. Particularly controversial was Romano's tasteless review of *Only Words*, which begins by imagining the rape of MacKinnon as a way of testing her thesis that there is no difference between "doing it" and "saying it." In Romano's complex hypothetical situation, he imagines rather than commits rape, but another critic decides to test MacKinnon's thesis by actually raping her. The next morning, both Romano and the other critic are arrested and taken to jail for raping MacKinnon. Romano's point is that if one accepts MacKinnon's logic, both critics are equally culpable of rape, a conclusion few people would presumably be willing to accept. MacKinnon was outraged by Romano's real-life review and charged Romano with "public rape." Romano, she insisted, should be "held accountable for what he did," adding ominously that "there a lot of people out there and a lot of ways that can be done" (David Mehegan, "War of Words Erupts over 'Rape' Review," *Boston Globe*, January 6, 1994, p. 45). MacKinnon's long-term fiancé, Jeffrey Masson, added fuel to the fire by chivalrously writing Romano a letter in which he promised: "If there is ever anything I can do to hurt your career, I will do it." When Romano expressed concerns about such threats, MacKinnon dismissed such worries, explaining that Masson "has never hit anyone in his entire life." Evidently, Masson's threats, as *Washington Post* staff writer David Streitfeld could not resist pointing out, were "only words" (David Streitfeld, "Rape by the Written Word? Book Review Sparks Pornography Debate," *Washington Post*, January 4 1994, p. C1).

105. Brown, "Consciousness Razing," 61–62. For Brown, MacKinnon is engaged with "relics of radical feminism's early years" (61), constructing an "argument [that] takes place in a now largely uninhabited corner" (62). Brown also comments on "the obsolete milieu of MacKinnon's arguments" (62) and dismisses it as "a new book of mostly old writings" (64).

106. Positive reviews of *Feminism Unmodified* include Alison Jaggar's review in the *New York Times Book Review*, May 3, 1987, pp. 3, 51, and Carole Pateman, "Sex and Power," *Ethics* 100 (January 1990), 398–407. *Toward a Feminist Theory of the State* is given a glowing back-cover blurb by Gloria Steinem. Patricia Williams provides the same for *Only Words*. This is not to say that some of these women are not also critical of MacKinnon. Jaggar and particularly Pateman make a number of telling criticisms of MacKinnon in their generally appreciative reviews.

107. According to the sales department of Harvard University Press, MacKinnon's three Harvard books (*Feminism Unmodified, Only Words*, and *Toward a Feminist Theory of the State*) have together sold about ninety-thousand copies. In the *Social Sciences Citation Index*, her citations began to rise steadily in the mid-1980s, passing the one hundred mark in 1987 and the two hundred mark in 1989. Between 1991 and 1995 she has averaged around three hundred citations a year, with no signs of decline. Of the six course syllabi on "Feminist Theory" included in *Liberal Learning and*

the Women's Studies Major (*National Women's Studies Association*, 1991), three included works by MacKinnon (Appendix C). Among the feminist anthologies that include MacKinnon's work are Sandra G. Harding, ed., *Feminism and Methodology: Social Science Issues* (Bloomington: Indiana University Press, 1987); Catherin Itzin, ed., *Pornography: Women, Violence, and Civil Liberties* (New York: Oxford University Press, 1993); Patricia Smith, ed., *Feminist Jurisprudence* (New York: Oxford University Press, 1993); and Anne C. Herrmann and Abigail Stewart, eds., *Theorizing Feminism: Parallel Trends in the Humanities and Social Sciences* (Boulder, Colo.: Westview Press, 1994).

108. MacKinnon's arguments in *Toward a Feminist Theory of the State* are relied upon, for example, in Mari Matsuda, Charles Lawrence III, Richard Delgado, and Kimberle Williams Crenshaw, eds., *Words That Wound: Critical Race Theory, Assaultive Speech, and the First Amendment* (Boulder, Colo.: Westview Press, 1993), especially 62, 79. Both Matsuda and Lawrence provide enthusiastic back-cover blurbs for *Only Words.*

109. This is not to say that most women's study programs espouse radical feminist values; that is a judgment that would require systematic empirical studies of the sort we do not have. Nor, I must emphasize at the outset, should what follows be construed as a criticism of the extremely valuable work that has been done over the past thirty years studying women and gender. To highlight the illiberal side of some women's studies programs, as I do in this section, is to make no judgment about the importance of scholarship on women, the best of which has generally been done by people working with appointments in conventional academic departments.

110. Carden, *New Feminist Movement*, 198n19. The first course in the women's studies program at Yale University was created by Catharine MacKinnon (Strebeigh, "Defining Law on the Feminist Frontier," 31).

111. Daphne Patai and Noretta Koertge, *Professing Feminism: Cautionary Tales from the Strange World of Women's Studies* (New York: Basic Books, 1994), 1–2. Christina Hoff Sommers, *Who Stole Feminism? How Women Have Betrayed Women* (New York: Simon and Schuster, 1994), 113.

112. Patai and Koertge, *Professing Feminism*, 12, 20, 24, 32–38, 192.

113. See Mary Douglas, "The Problem of Evil," in Douglas, *Natural Symbols: Explorations in Cosmology* (New York: Pantheon, 1982); and Mary Douglas, "Cultural Bias," in Douglas, *In the Active Voice* (London: Routledge, 1982). Although Patai and Koertge do not cite Douglas's work, they do draw attention to the strong parallels between women's studies programs and religious sects as well as utopian communes. See Patai and Koertge, *Professing Feminism*, 186–93.

114. Patai and Koertge, *Professing Feminism*, 5; also see 191–92, 196.

115. See ibid., especially 45–47. Patai and Koertge relate that among the women they interviewed the most frequent response when asked to explain the problems within women's studies was "to blame patriarchy" (45). Particularly worth quoting is the women's studies professor who explained why patriarchy was to blame for the competitiveness within and between oppressed groups and their programs: "If there were no patriarchy, there would be no oppression. If there were no oppression, there

would be no need for affirmative action. If there were no affirmative action, we wouldn't be here acting like pigs trying to shoulder each other away from the trough!" (Patai and Koertge, *Professing Feminism*, 75–76).

116. Patai and Koertge, *Professing Feminism*, 195. It is impossible to say precisely how widespread is the separatism and ideological policing that Patai and Koertge describe (for at least one reviewer's belief that the problems documented by Patai and Koertge are "systemic" and accurately "mirror what many of us who are actively involved in women's studies have experienced," see Joan Mandle's review in *Gender and Society* 9 [August 1995], 524–25). It is possible, though, to put forth a cultural hypothesis based on Patai and Koertge's findings: the less integrated the women's studies program is into the rest of the university, the more the pathologies that Patai and Koertge describe (ideological policing, intolerance, dogmatism, politicization) will flourish. That is, the more closely a women's studies program resembles an egalitarian collective with well-defined boundaries, the more likely that program is to exhibit illiberal features that compromise open intellectual inquiry.

117. Patai and Koertge, *Professing Feminism*, 195–96; also see 189–90. Cf. the tale told by Heather Hart, who, while a student at Brandeis University, suffered near-ostracism from her fellow feminists for refusing to give up lipstick. "They condemned me from the get-go. . . . They were quick to dismiss me as a boy-toy just because I like the concept of decoration. . . . I was different and, therefore, a threat to the neat, closed, secret, homogenous community" (Sommers, *Who Stole Feminism?*, 111). Also see Patai and Koertge, *Professing Feminism*, 196.

118. This definition of feminist pedagogy is from the women's studies program at Penn State University. See Patai and Koertge, *Professing Feminism*, 180.

119. Ibid., 88; also see 112.

120. Karen Lehrman, "Off Course," *Mother Jones* 18 (September/October 1993), 48.

121. Sommers, *Who Stole Feminism?*, 88, 107.

122. Johnella Butler et al., *Liberal Learning and the Women's Studies Major* (Washington, D.C.: Association of American Colleges, 1991), Appendix B, cited in Sommers, *Who Stole Feminism?*, 88–89.

123. The Penn State women's studies program describes feminist pedagogy as emphasizing "the importance of using techniques which recognize and validate students' life experiences as legitimate data" (Patai and Koertge, *Professing Feminism*, 180).

124. Echols, *Daring to Be Bad*, 87.

125. One of Karen Lehrman's chief criticisms of the women's studies classes that she visited was that "self-revelation" and "group therapy," and "consciousness-raising psychobabble" too often substituted for the hard work of "building [women's] intellects" ("Off Course," 46, 48, 49).

126. Rosanna Hertz and Susan Reverby, "Wellesley College: Counting the Meanings," in Caryn McTighe Musil, ed., *The Courage to Question: Women's Studies and Student Learning* (Washington, D.C.: Association of American Colleges and National Women's Studies Association, 1992), 121.

127. Patai and Koertge, *Professing Feminism*, 174.

128. Quoted in ibid., 94. See, for example, bell hooks, *Killing Rage: Ending Racism* (New York: Holt, 1995).

129. Margo Culley et al., *Gendered Subjects: The Dynamics of Feminist Teaching* (1985), 19, quoted in Sommers, *Who Stole Feminism?*, 87.

130. Patai and Koertge, *Professing Feminism*, 97.

131. So Ann Ferguson writes that "the goal of feminist teaching is not only to raise consciousness about . . . [the] male domination system but also to create women and men who are agents of social change" ("Feminist Teaching: A Practice Developed in Undergraduate Courses," *Radical Teacher* [April 1982], 28, as quoted in Sommers, *Who Stole Feminism?*, 52).

132. So, for instance, Marilyn Schuster and Susan R. Van Dyne write, "The number of female professors who still see no inequity or omissions in the male-defined curriculum . . . serves to underscore dramatically how thoroughly women students may be deceived in believing these values are congruent with their interests" (*Women's Place in the Academy* [1985], quoted in Sommers, *Who Stole Feminism?*, 96).

133. So, for instance, Rosemary Dempsey, a vice president of NOW, dismisses Lehrman's critique in *Mother Jones* as part of "a backlash against women's studies" (*Mother Jones* 18 [November/December 1993], 8), and Suzanna Walters of Georgetown University dismisses Naomi Wolf's *Fire with Fire* (1993) as "trash and backlash and everything nasty (including homophobic and racist)" (Sommers, *Who Stole Feminism?*, 245; also see 93, 119, 52). See also Susan Faludi, *Backlash: The Undeclared War Against American Women* (New York: Crown, 1991).

134. Sommers, *Who Stole Feminism?*, 89, 92–95, 102.

135. Daphne Patai, "What's Wrong with Women's Studies," *Academe* 81 (July/August 1995), 30. Also see Lehrman, "Off Course," 68; and Sommers, *Who Stole Feminism?*, 51.

136. Sommers, *Who Stole Feminism?*, 51. Patai and Koertge, *Professing Feminism*, 4.

137. Patai and Koertge, *Professing Feminism*, 4, 33.

138. This is precisely Susan Faludi's response, for example, to Lehrman's critique in *Mother Jones*: "Lehrman seems to want to indict women's studies for the mortal sin of harboring a political perspective. . . . Like other academic disciplines are devoid of political content?" ("Faludi Lashes Back," *Mother Jones* 18 [November/December 1993], 4). But as Patai points out, "The facile retort that 'education is always political' is a disingenuous response. Intended to shut down discussion, it tries to ward off the important questions. Political in what way? With what aims? Leading to what results? At what costs? Bearing what relationship to other historical efforts to use education for purposes of indoctrination?" (Patai, "What's Wrong with Women's Studies," 35).

139. Laurie Finke et al., "Lewis and Clark College: A Single Curriculum," in Musil, *Courage to Question*, 48. Also see Sommers, *Who Stole Feminism?*, 95; and Patai and Koertge, *Professing Feminism*, 97.

140. The women's studies program at Lewis and Clark College, for example, identified "understanding the social construction of knowledge" as a basic "learning skill" that all students should acquire in a gender studies course. "Students ought

to "move . . . to a meta-analysis of how knowledge is socially constructed and not simply 'there' to be discovered" (Musil, *Courage to Question*, 53). Also see Patai and Koertge, *Professing Feminism*, 174–75; and Sommers, *Who Stole Feminism?*, 50.

141. Sommers, *Who Stole Feminism?*, 74; also see chapters 3 and 4, as well as Patai and Koertge, *Professing Feminism*, 106.

142. Alison Jaggar, "Teaching Sedition: Some Dilemmas of Feminist Pedagogy," *Report from the Center for Philosophy and Public Policy* (Fall 1984), 6–9; emphasis added. Jaggar goes one step further to argue that "philosophy itself is intrinsically subversive to a hierarchical, authoritarian, and male dominant society."

143. For a thoughtful early critique of radical feminism along these lines, see Benjamin R. Barber, *Liberating Feminism* (New York: Delta, 1975), chapter 2.

144. Sommers, *Who Stole Feminism?*, 99.

145. Patai and Koertge report that many of the disillusioned women's studies teachers they talked to "attributed a large share of the blame for creating an inhospitable atmosphere to militant feminist students, and each described how such students tried in various ways to impede open class discussion of ideas that did not conform to these students' politics" (*Professing Feminism*, 13).

146. Patai and Koertge, *Professing Feminism* 18, 22, 59, 145; also see 25–26. Also see Lehrman, "Off Course," 64; and Musil, *Courage to Question*, 165.

147. Feminist critics of *Professing Feminism* have zeroed in on the fact that Patai and Koertge rely on the personal testimony of a small, unrepresentative group of thirty women rather than systematic statistical data about women's studies programs across the country (see Louise Antony, "Feminists Under Fire," *Times Literary Supplement*, October 20, 1995, p. 25). This is more than a little ironic in view of the widespread emphasis within feminism on the "authority of experience" and the need to listen to women's stories and voices. One has reason to doubt whether the same methodological criticisms would have been heard had the women's voices told tales of sexual harassment, male violence, or patriarchal oppression. The irony aside, if we wish to know how widespread are the problems of politicization that Patai and Koertge (and Sommers and Lehrman and Elizabeth Fox-Genovese, among others) identify, we do need, as Patai freely acknowledges, "a comprehensive empirical analysis of women's studies programs" ("What's Wrong with Women's Studies," 33; also see 34). But we are unlikely to get such an objective study by obscuring the difference between knowledge and politics, or denying that objectivity is any way meaningful or desirable.

148. Musil, *Courage to Question*, 120–21, 128n17.

149. See Sommers, *Who Stole Feminism?*, 96–98. Lehrman, "Off Course," 51.

150. Cf. Lehrman's observation that discussions in women's studies classes tend to "alternate between the personal and the political, with mere pit stops at the academic" ("Off Course," 90).

151. See Alison M. Jaggar, *Feminist Politics and Human Nature* (Totowa, N.J.: Rowman and Allanheld, 1983), 145, 254–55.

152. Firestone, *Dialectic of Sex*, 206. Also see Robin Morgan's "The Wretched of the Hearth," in which she suggests that "marriage as a bourgeois institution is

beginning to fade slowly but surely" and that people are thinking "more in terms of the communal family, where children are raised by men as well as by women, and by more than one pair" (46–47).

153. MacKinnon, "Liberalism and the Death of Feminism," 7. MacKinnon, *Toward a Feminist Theory of the State*, 168. For MacKinnon, "the personal is *the* political" (ibid., 95; emphasis added).

154. Dworkin, *Letters from a War Zone*, 104; Dworkin's words are quoted approvingly by MacKinnon in *Feminism Unmodified*, 196.

155. This rhetorical question is taken from Ann Hulbert's review essay, "Home Repairs," *New Republic*, August 16, 1993, pp. 26–32. Among the books Hulbert reviews is Stephanie Coontz, *The Way We Never Were: American Families and the Nostalgia Trap*. Hulbert writes: "Coontz implicitly hopes for . . . a flood of civic equality and community that would all but drown [the] private world. In the vision of seamless interpenetration between the personal and the social that underlies her history, any real interest in the private power and importance of marriage and childbearing tends to fade away. It all but disappears . . . in the more doctrinaire feminist history, with its emphasis on women as mere victims, and of motherhood as mere subjugation. Who needs privacy if it is synonymous with oppression?" (30).

156. Susan Moller Okin, *Justice, Gender, and the Family* (New York: Basic Books, 1989), 125, 127–28. Also see Carole Pateman, "Feminist Critiques of the Public/Private Dichotomy," in Pateman, *The Disorder of Women: Democracy, Feminism and Political Theory* (Stanford, Calif.: Stanford University Press, 1989), especially 133–34. Although Okin adopts a less literal interpretation of "the personal is political" than radical feminists such as MacKinnon, she attaches the same central importance to the slogan. For Okin, "'The personal is political' is the central message of feminist critiques of the public/domestic dichotomy [and] the core idea of most contemporary feminism" (*Justice*, 124; also 111).

157. Okin's universalistic liberalism is abundantly clear in her recent critique of "difference" feminism, "Gender Inequality and Cultural Differences," *Political Theory* 22 (February 1994), 5–24, as well as in her devastating response to Jane Flax's postmodern reply to Okin's article. For the Okin-Flax exchange see *Political Theory* 23 (August 1995), 500–516.

158. Susan Moller Okin, "Humanist Liberalism," in Nancy Rosenblum, ed., *Liberalism and the Moral Life* (Cambridge, Mass.: Harvard University Press, 1989), 40. Okin, *Justice*, 61. Okin goes much too far, however, in suggesting that "virtually all" feminists acknowledge feminism's debts to liberalism.

159. Okin, *Justice*, 16. On these rival visions of equality, see the illuminating discussion in Thomas Sowell, *A Conflict of Visions: Ideological Origins of Political Struggles* (New York: Quill, 1987), chapter 6.

160. Okin, "Humanist Liberalism," 41. Okin, *Justice*, 171, 105.

161. As Okin recognizes, liberal theorists have not neglected the impact of disparities on equal opportunities *among* families. What they have neglected is disparities *within* the family (*Justice*, 16). It is refreshing to find a feminist who recognizes the similarity between feminist challenges to liberalism and earlier leftist challenges to liberalism: "In certain respects," Okin acknowledges, "the challenges of feminists

who endorse the fundamental aims of liberalism are parallel to some of the challenges that liberals with leftist sympathies present to more traditional versions of liberalism. Just as the left disputes the liberal definition of politics that has drawn a firm line between state and society and claims that 'the economic is political,' so feminists challenge the traditional liberal dichotomy between public and private that divides the personal and domestic from the rest of life" ("Humanist Liberalism," 41). Also see Nicholson, *Gender and History*, 24.

162. Okin, *Justice*, 116, 17, 22; also see 135, 4. Cf. Robin Morgan's question "Where else do we first learn the dynamics of domination but in the family, in which the woman is treated as a distinct inferior?" ("Wretched of the Hearth," 46).

163. Okin's effort to take male liberal theorists seriously was not exactly appreciated in some feminist quarters. In a review in *Dissent*, Ann Snitow complained that because Okin is "talking to the brothers," her efforts are "inevitably limited by [her] project of bringing light to the heathen. . . . She can't debate feminism at its own current cutting edge; that would leave the brothers behind." Okin, in Snitow's view, "shares [the brothers'] questions, categories, and worries [and thus] their sexism poisons the well from which they both must drink" ("Talking to the Brothers," *Dissent* 38 [Winter 1991], 125, 123). Also see the review by Virginia Held in *Political Theory* 19 (May 1991), 299–303.

164. Okin, *Justice*, 171.

165. See Stephen Macedo, "Review Essay: Justice, Sex, and Doing the Dishes," *Polity* 24 (Spring 1992), 524; and Joshua Cohen, "Okin on Justice, Gender, and Family," *Canadian Journal of Philosophy* 22 (June 1992), 264–65, 277. These are the two most incisive reviews of Okin's book that I have come across.

166. Okin, *Justice*, 116, 105.

167. Okin, "Humanist Liberalism," 53; also see Okin, *Justice*, 172.

168. Okin, *Justice*, 126.

169. If by "vulnerable" Okin meant purely physical harm — battered wives and the like (e.g., *Justice*, 129) — her case would be considerably stronger. But as her chapter entitled "Vulnerability by Marriage" makes clear, her conception of vulnerability is far broader than this.

170. Okin and I are in full agreement on the desirability of the former regulation and the undesirability of the latter.

171. Okin, *Justice*, 111; also see 130–31.

172. Ibid., 179, 183.

173. I describe Okin's vision of a genderless future as utopian not only because I think it is unlikely ever to be approximated (among other things it ignores biological differences altogether), but also because of the way Okin invests this imagined future with redemptive promise. Okin envisions "the moral possibilities of a transformed family — a place where reason and emotion are equally called for, where all people care for others on a day-to-day basis and, through doing so, can learn to reconcile their own ambitions and desires with those of others and to see things from the points of view of others who may differ from themselves in important respects" (*Justice*, 119).

174. Ibid., 171. Of "no little concern" to whom, one wonders? To the theorist? To busybody neighbors? To the state?

175. Ibid., 117, 171–72, 174–75; also see 180. At times Okin seems tempted to follow MacKinnon's lead and question whether women have really consented. In criticizing Michael Walzer, for instance, Okin notes that "when meanings *appear* to be shared, they are often the outcome of the domination of some groups over others, the latter being silenced or rendered 'incoherent' by the more powerful" (112). And at another point, Okin again sounds a MacKinnon-like theme: "Women . . . are often handicapped by being deprived of any authority in their speech. . . . 'Authority currently is conceptualized so that female voices are excluded from it'" (132).

176. Ibid., 113. Elsewhere, Okin writes that "the institution in which we are primarily socialized is pervaded by domination" (119).

177. Isaiah Berlin's warning is relevant here: "Nothing is gained by a confusion of terms. To avoid glaring inequality or widespread misery I am ready to sacrifice some, or all, of my freedom. . . . But a sacrifice is not an increase in what is being sacrificed, namely freedom, however great the moral need or the compensation for it. Everything is what it is: liberty is liberty, not equality or fairness or justice or culture, or human happiness or a quiet conscience" ("Two Concepts of Liberty," in Berlin, *Four Essays on Liberty* [New York: Oxford University Press, 1969], 125).

CHAPTER 8. Earth First! and the Misanthropy of Radical Egalitarianism

1. Richard Hofstadter, *The Age of Reform* (New York: Vintage, 1955), 19.

2. Steven Lukes, *The Curious Enlightenment of Professor Caritat: A Comedy of Ideas* (London: Verso, 1995), 257.

3. Terry H. Anderson, "The New American Revolution: The Movement and Business," in David Farber, ed., *The Sixties: From Memory to History* (Chapel Hill: University of North Carolina Press, 1994), 184. Kirkpatrick Sale, *The Green Revolution: The American Environmental Movement, 1962–1992* (New York: Hill and Wang, 1993), 24.

4. Sale, *Green Revolution*, 25.

5. Anderson, "The New American Revolution," 184. Also see Terry H. Anderson, *The Movement and the Sixties* (New York: Oxford University Press, 1995), 348–49.

6. Riley E. Dunlap, "Trends in Public Opinion Toward Environmental Issues, 1965–1990," in Riley E. Dunlap and Angela G. Mertig, eds., *American Environmentalism: The U.S. Environmental Movement, 1970–1990* (Philadelphia: Taylor and Francis, 1992), 89–116, especially 92.

7. Sale, *Green Revolution*, 23. Christopher J. Bosso, "After the Movement: Environmental Activism in the 1990s," in Norman J. Vig and Michael E. Kraft, eds., *Environmental Policy in the 1990s*, 2d ed. (Washington, D.C.: Congressional Quarterly, 1994), 36.

8. Sale, *Green Revolution*, 32–33. Bosso, "Environmental Activism in the 1990s," 37. Samuel P. Hayes, *Beauty, Health, and Permanence: Environmental Politics in the United States, 1955–1985* (Cambridge: Cambridge University Press, 1987), 215.

9. Appendix 1 in Vig and Kraft, *Environmental Policy in the 1990s*.

10. Bosso, "Environmental Activism in the 1990s," 35.

11. Martha F. Lee, *Earth First! Environmental Apocalypse* (Syracuse, N.Y.: Syracuse University Press, 1995), 28.

12. Rik Scarce, *Eco-Warriors: Understanding the Radical Environmental Movement* (Chicago: Noble Press, 1990), 62. The other founding members were Bart Koehler, who like Foreman worked for the Wilderness Society, Ron Kezar, a longtime member of the Sierra Club, and Howie Wolke, who had been the Wyoming representative with Friends of the Earth. Only Mike Roselle, an ex-Yippie and veteran of the anti–Vietnam War movement, had no experience working with mainstream environmental groups. See Scarce, *Eco-Warriors*, 58–61; and Lee, *Earth First! Journal*, 31.

13. The abolitionist comparison is worked fruitfully in the epilogue of Roderick Frazier Nash, *The Rights of Nature: A History of Environmental Ethics* (Madison: University of Wisconsin Press, 1989), 199–213. The abolitionist parallel is also pursued in Lester Rhodes, "Radical Environmentalism: Carrying on a Venerable Tradition," *Earth First! Journal*, February 2, 1990, p. 31. Also atop the *Earth First! Journal* was a clenched-fist logo reminiscent of that popularized by the New Left during the 1960s. The artist responsible for the logo was former 1960s activist Mike Roselle. See Nash, *Rights of Nature*, 192; Scarce, *Eco-Warriors*, 61; and Christopher Manes, *Green Rage: Radical Environmentalism and the Unmaking of Civilization* (Boston: Little, Brown, 1990), 69–70.

14. David Brower, Foreword, to Scarce, *Eco-Warriors*, xii. Also see Scarce, *Eco-Warriors*, 246, 251. The misanthropy charge can be found in many places. See, for example, Murray Bookchin, "Social Ecology Versus 'Deep Ecology': A Challenge for the Ecology Movement," *Green Perspectives: Newsletter of the Green Program Project* (Summer 1987), 1–23; and Robert James Bidinotto, "Environmentalism: Freedom's Foe for the '90s," *The Freedman* 40 (November 1990), 409–20.

15. Judi Bari, "Timber Wars," *Earth Island Journal* 5 (Summer 1990), 30. Brian Tokar, "Social Ecology, Deep Ecology, and the Future of Green Political Thought," *Ecologist* 18 (January/February 1988), 138.

16. Tree-spiking became particularly infamous after a 1987 incident in which a California lumber mill worker was severely injured when his saw struck an eleven-inch spike. Contrary to public impressions, the evidence suggests that Earth First! had nothing to do with this particular spiking, and perhaps also that poorly maintained machinery was at fault. Still the incident showed the harm to humans that tree-spiking could cause, and thus sparked a heated debate within Earth First! about its merits. Some insisted that "in a biocentric context, arguments against spiking based on injury to humans can never be persuasive" (California Foremanista, Letters to the Editors, *Earth First! Journal*, December 21, 1990, p. 5; also see Nash, *Rights of Nature*, 194), while others reacted, following the example of Northern California and Oregon Earth First! groups, by renouncing tree-spiking. The tactic continues to be extensively debated in the *Earth First! Journal*. See Judi Bari, "The Secret History of Tree Spiking," *Earth First! Journal*, December 21, 1994, pp. 11, 15; and Judi Bari, "Spiking: It Just Doesn't Work," Mike Roselle, "Spike a Tree for Me," Captain Paul Watson, "In Defense of Tree Spiking," and Pileated Woodpecker, "To Spike or Not

to Spike? That Is *Not* the Question," in *Earth First! Journal*, February 2, 1995, pp. 8–11.

17. Scarce, *Eco-Warriors*, 74.

18. Ibid., 91–93. The controversial Miss Ann Thropy columns are "Population and AIDS," *Earth First! Journal*, May 1, 1987, p. 32; and "Miss Ann Thropy Responds to 'Alien-Nation,'" *Earth First! Journal*, December 22, 1987, p. 17. Foreman later apologized for his remarks, calling them "horribly insensitive and superficial" (Stephen Talbot, "Earth First! What Next?" *Mother Jones* 15 [November/December 1990], 80; also see Foreman, "Second Thoughts of an Eco-Warrior," in Murray Bookchin and Dave Foreman, *Defending the Earth: A Dialogue Between Murray Bookchin and Dave Foreman* [Boston: South End Press, 1991], 107–12). Earth First!ers have commonly likened humans to a "cancer" on the earth. See, for example, "Continuing the Children Debate," *Earth First! Journal*, June 21, 1990, p. 29; Whaley Mander, "Quest for the Human Niche," *Earth First! Journal*, August 1, 1994, p. 2; and Trip Gabriel, "If a Tree Falls in the Forest, They Hear It," *New York Times Magazine*, November 4, 1990, p. 64. Also see the review of Bill McKibben's *The End of Nature* by David Graber, a research biologist with the National Park Service. Graber not only identifies human beings as a cancer and plague on the planet, but concludes that "until such time as Homo sapiens should decide to rejoin nature, some of us can only hope for the right virus to come along" (Graber, "Mother Nature as a Hothouse Flower," *Los Angeles Times*, October 22, 1989, book review section, p. 9; also cited in Virginia Postrel, "The Green Road to Serfdom," *Reason* 21 [April 1990], 28).

19. A number of Earth First!ers have unapologetically embraced the misanthrope label. See, for instance, Christopher Manes, "Why I Am a Misanthrope," *Earth First! Journal*, December 21, 1990, p. 29; and Sarah E. Bearup-Neal, "Trees: A Misanthropic View," *Earth First! Journal*, November 1, 1990, p. 30, who is not shy about telling us, "I am fonder of trees than I am of people." Earth First!'s literary inspiration, Edward Abbey, is well known for his opinion that he would rather kill a man than a snake, a sentiment that is echoed in different ways by many Earth First!ers. See Nash, *Rights of Nature*, 153; as well as Buffalo Dreamin' in Topeka, Letters to the Editors, *Earth First! Journal*, December 21, 1990, p. 6. Also see Captain Paul Watson, "In Defense of Tree Spiking," *Earth First! Journal*, September 22, 1990, p. 9; and Michael Parfit, "Earth First!ers Wield a Mean Monkey Wrench," *Smithsonian* 21 (April 1990), 198.

20. See Devil's Avocado, Letters to the Editors, *Earth First! Journal*, December 21, 1994, p. 31; Wraith Walker, "Kamikaze Last!" *Earth First! Journal*, March 21, 1993, p. 11; and Whaley Mander, "Quest for the Human Niche," *Earth First! Journal*, August 1, 1994, p. 2. Also see Parfit, "Earth First!ers Wield a Mean Monkey Wrench," 198; and Dave Foreman, quoted in Bidinotto, "Environmentalism: Freedom's Foe," 414.

21. See Daniel Metz, "Dissecting the Voluntary Human Extinction Movement," typescript, Willamette University, 1995. The sample of Earth First!ers is a subset of a larger survey of the Voluntary Human Extinction Movement (VHEMT). The survey went out to all VHEMT members, and the response rate was just under 60 percent. VHEMT members were asked to indicate whether in the last five years

they had given money or time to Earth First! or considered themselves a member of that group. Of the 219 VHEMT respondents, 79 (or 36 percent) indicated that they had. It is possible, of course, that this relatively small sample of Earth First!ers is unrepresentative in some ways, but it seems unlikely that it overstates the egalitarianism of Earth First! One would expect a priori that it would not be the more egalitarian but the more antisocial Earth First!ers who would be most likely to belong to an organization that has as its stated objective the voluntary extinction of the human race. There is, moreover, a striking congruence between the attitudes expressed in the survey and the opinions commonly voiced in the *Earth First! Journal*.

22. This item was adapted from statements made by the self-described "social ecologists" Murray Bookchin and Brian Tokar. Bookchin writes: "We are talking about uprooting *all* forms of hierarchy and domination, in all spheres of social life" (*Defending the Earth*, 57–58), and Tokar insists that we must "seek an end to all relationships of domination" (Brian Tokar, *The Green Alternative: Creating an Ecological Future*, 2d ed. [San Pedro, Calif.: R. & E. Miles, 1992], 5).

23. A survey Fred Thompson and I conducted of Audubon Society and Sierra Club members in Oregon found, for instance, that only about four in ten respondents agreed to the "fairness revolution" item and only about half endorsed the "peaceful place" statement. The level of support for these items was even lower among our sample of the general public in Yamhill County and Oregon's capital city, Salem. Only about one-third of Salem-Yamhill residents assented to the "fairness revolution" item, and the same proportion agreed to the "peaceful place" statement. See Richard J. Ellis and Fred Thompson, "The Culture Wars by Other Means: Environmental Attitudes and Cultural Biases in the Northwest," Table 16, paper delivered at the Annual Meeting of the Western Political Science Association, San Francisco, March 14–16, 1996. The "fairness revolution" item has also been used in phone surveys of New Mexico residents and U.S. residents conducted by Hank Jenkins-Smith of the University of New Mexico. In both the New Mexico and the U.S. survey, approximately 40 percent endorsed the statement. See "Frequency Report: USA and NM Samples Combined, October 1994," Probabilistic Risk Assessment Project, UNM Institute for Public Policy, p. 3.

24. The Earth Island results are reported in Ellis and Thompson, "Culture Wars by Other Means." The statement "We should seek to eliminate all forms of inequality, hierarchy and domination" was not included in the Earth Island survey. The Earth First! mean for this question was 5.4.

25. A "very strong" egalitarian ($n = 45$) was operationalized as someone who averaged a score of greater than 6 across the five egalitarian items, each of which was arrayed on a seven-point scale running from strongly disagree ($+1$) to strongly agree ($+7$), with $+4$ as the neutral midpoint. "Strong" egalitarians ($n = 60$) were those who averaged more than 5 but less than or equal to 6; "moderate" egalitarians ($n = 53$) were those who scored greater than 4 but less than or equal to 5; and "weak" egalitarians ($n = 50$) were those who scored less than or equal to 4.

26. Bill Weinberg, "Social Ecology and Deep Ecology Meet," *Earth First! Journal*, February 2, 1990, p. 10. Also see David Levine, "Foreword: Turning Debate into Dialogue," in Bookchin and Foreman, *Defending the Earth*, 1.

27. John Young, *Sustaining the Earth* (Cambridge, Mass.: Harvard University Press, 1990), 129, 131; Bookchin and Foreman, *Defending the Earth*, 8–11. Also see Bookchin, "Social Ecology Versus 'Deep Ecology,'" and Murray Bookchin, "Crisis in the Ecology Movement," *Z Magazine* 1 (July–August 1988), 121–23.

28. Bookchin and Foreman, *Defending the Earth*, 11. Christopher Manes, "Why I Am a Misanthrope," *Earth First! Journal*, December 21, 1990, p. 29. Manes, *Green Rage*, 160; also see 135.

29. The same point is made by Michael Young in *Sustaining the Earth*, 131–32. Much of this common ground becomes abundantly clear in *Defending the Earth*, the much-publicized dialogue between Foreman and Bookchin.

30. Nash, *Rights of Nature*, 11–12 and passim. Also see Lester Rhodes, "Radical Environmentalism: Carrying on a Venerable Tradition," *Earth First! Journal*, February 2, 1990, p. 31; and George Wuerthner, "Tree Spiking and Moral Maturity," *Earth First! Journal*, August 1, 1985, p. 20.

31. See Aaron Wildavsky, *The Rise of Radical Egalitarianism* (Washington, D.C.: American University Press, 1991).

32. Manes, *Green Rage*, 166. Also see Randall Restless, "Wild Rockies EF! Demands Equal Rights for All Species," *Earth First! Journal*, March 21, 1989, p. 5; Pine Marten, Letters to the Editors, *Earth First! Journal*, February 2, 1995, p. 3; and "More Roads = More People," *Earth First! Journal*, November 1, 1993, p. 20. Also see Edward Abbey's remark: "I'm here today in support of the E.R.A. I mean Equal Rocks Amendment, or equal rights for rocks, and for trees and grass and clouds and flowing streams and bull elk and grizzly and women" (Susan Zakin, *Coyotes and Town Dogs: Earth First! and the Environmental Movement* [New York: Penguin Books, 1993], 216–17).

33. Mike Roselle, "Deep Ecology and the New Civil Rights Movement," *Earth First! Journal*, May 1, 1988, p. 23. Cf. Darryl Cherney: "We believe the Earth deserves civil rights the same as people do" ("Freedom Riders Needed to Save the Forest," *Earth First! Journal*, May 1, 1990, p. 1).

34. Nash, *Rights of Nature*, 152–53. Also see Darryl Cherney, "Freedom Riders Needed to Save the Forest," *Earth First! Journal*, May 1, 1990, p. 1.

35. "Excerpts of EF!'s Statement at Martin Luther King Day Protest," *Earth First! Journal*, March 21, 1989, p. 5. Also see Nash, *Rights of Nature*, 11; and Devil's Avocado, Letters to the Editors, *Earth First! Journal*, December 21, 1994, p. 31.

36. Indeed, as Roderick Nash emphasizes, from the outset Earth First! invoked the memory and emulated the tactics of the civil rights movement. In the first issues of the *Earth First! Journal*, for example, Dave Foreman held up as exemplary "the courage of the civil rights workers who went to jail" for their beliefs (Nash, *Rights of Nature*, 190). And Foreman's call "to put a monkeywrench into the gears of the machinery destroying natural diversity" (193) directly echoed Mario Savio's call to throw one's body on the gears of the machinery.

37. Judi Bari writes: "I came of age during the Vietnam era, and I've known for a long time that the system is enforced by violence" (Bari, "Our Community Is Under Siege," *Earth Island Journal* 6 [Summer 1991], 49). On Bari's background, see Scarce, *Eco-Warriors*, 80–83. Also see Talbot, "Earth First! What Next?"

38. "Redwood Summer Lives!" *Earth First! Extra*, 1. Karen Pickett, "Redwood Summer," *Earth Island Journal* 5 (Summer 1990), 29. Also see Darryl Cherney, "Freedom Riders Needed to Save the Forest," *Earth First! Journal*, May 1, 1990, p. 1.

39. Bill Weinberg, "Social Ecology and Deep Ecology Meet," *Earth First! Journal*, February 2, 1990, p. 10. Lone Wolf Circles, Letters to the Editors, *Earth First! Journal*, December 21, 1990, p. 6. Stephanie Mills, book review of Judith Plant, ed., *Healing the Wounds*, in *Earth First! Journal*, February 2, 1990, p. 33. *Journal* Staff (Tim Ballard, Jacob Bear, Lara Mattson, and Don Smith), "Earth First! and Social Justice," *Earth First! Journal*, December 21, 1992, p. 2. Also see Gene Lawhorn, "Why Earth First! Should Renounce Tree Spiking," *Earth First! Journal*, September 22, 1990, p. 9; Anne Herbert, "Death of the World," *Earth First! Journal*, March 21, 1995, p. 23; Don Smith, "Direct Action, Social Movements and Deep Ecology," *Earth First! Journal*, December 21, 1992, p. 14; She Bear, Letters to the Editors, *Earth First! Journal*, September 22, 1992, p. 35; and "Earth First! Is Different," *Earth First! Primer*, 2. This is also a central tenet of ecofeminism, which has become increasingly strong within Earth First! See, for example, the articles on ecofeminism by Peggy Sue McRae, Anne Petermann, Judi Bari, and especially Cecilia Ostrow, all in *Earth First! Journal*, February 2, 1993, pp. 17–20, 24. But even in the early 1980s an Earth First! bumper sticker denounced Coors for being "anti-earth," "anti-women," and "anti-labor" (Zakin, *Coyotes and Town Dogs*, 208).

40. The precise wording was, "We can only save the planet by radically transforming our social lives with each other." Slightly over three fourths of Earth First!ers agreed, while only 12 percent disagreed. The Earth First! mean score was 5.6, compared with 5.4 for Earth Island.

41. Louis Head, Letters to the Editors, *Earth First! Journal*, September 22 1994, p. 28. Also see Don Smith, "Direct Action, Social Movements and Deep Ecology," *Earth First! Journal*, December 21, 1992, p. 14; Orin Langelle, "Defining Practice from the Field: Revolutionary Ecology," *Alarm: A Voice of Revolutionary Ecology* (Summer Solstice 1993), 4; and Pileated Woodpecker, "To Spike or Not to Spike: That Is *Not* the Question," *Earth First! Journal*, February 2, 1995, p. 11. Cf. Anna Bramwell's remark that "the real target [of today's Green parties] is a change of human power structures rather than saving the planet" (*The Fading of the Greens: The Decline of Environmental Politics in the West* [New Haven, Conn.: Yale University Press, 1994], 74). Bramwell would have been right if she had said instead that "the target of radical environmentalists is not only saving the planet but *also* changing human power structures."

42. Dave Foreman broke with Earth First! at the end of 1990, lamenting that the Earth First! movement had been transformed "into an environmental reincarnation of the New Left" (Dave Foreman and Nancy Morton, "'Good Luck Darlin'. It's Been Great," *Earth First! Journal*, September 22, 1990, p. 5; also see the parting comments of the journal staffers, Kris Sommerville, Nancy Zierenberg, and John Davis, in the same issue). While Earth First! had become more radically egalitarian, Foreman had also become substantially less radical, less utopian, and more comfortable with the sort of reformist stance that he had earlier scorned. See Zakin, *Coyotes and Town Dogs*.

43. Terry Morse, Letters to the Editors, *Earth First! Journal*, November 1, 1990, p. 4. Morse himself confuses the issue further by adding that "while preservation of big wilderness and biodiversity" should be our focus, "it is important to realize that their loss is a symptom of a dysfunctional socio-economic system." For the long term, therefore, "changing the system must be our goal (subverting the dominant paradigm)."

44. Van Howell, "Earth Day, Earth First!, and the Ecology Movement," *Earth First! Journal*, March 20, 1990, p. 5. Also see Bill Devall, *Simple in Means, Rich in Ends: Practicing Deep Ecology* (Layton, Utah: Gibbs Smith, 1988), 19, 200; and Lone Wolf Circles, Letters to the Editors, *Earth First! Journal*, December 21, 1990, p. 6.

45. Garth Allen, "*Alarm* Letter Writing Policy," *Alarm: A Voice of Revolutionary Ecology* (Summer Solstice 1993), 3.

46. Rik Scarce reaches the same conclusion that an emphasis on wilderness "while excluding all else . . . ignores the political reality of Earth First!'s message, namely, that the entire social system must change before there can be assurance of permanent wilderness protection" (*Eco-Warriors*, 89).

47. Judi Bari, "Expand Earth First! Journal," *Earth First! Journal*, September 22, 1990, p. 5. Also see the report from the *Earth First! Journal's* Advisory Committee suggesting that "many people [within Earth First!] feel that the wilderness can't be saved without taking a look at the bigger picture, the government and corporate world of greed, to see what's at the root of the problem and what we can do about it" ("A Report from the Journal Advisory Committee," *Earth First! Journal*, September 22, 1990, p. 4). Bill Devall agreed that "we know that preservation of wilderness and native biodiversity have little chance of success in political arenas unless activists address the issues of imperialism, militarism, and poverty and debt in the Third World" (Bill Devall, "'Maybe the Movement Is Leaving Me,'" *Earth First! Journal*, September 22, 1990, p. 6)

48. This statement can be found on the second page of every *Journal* issue, up until 1992, when it was dropped. The same statement can be found in every issue of *Alarm*, which is a voice for Earth First! groups in the northeast. The only difference is that *Alarm* says it "does not accept the authority of the hierarchal *and patriarchal* state."

49. Quoted in Bill Weinberg, "Social Ecology and Deep Ecology Meet," *Earth First! Journal*, February 2, 1990, p. 10.

50. Karen Wood, "Seeing Through the Hatemongers," *Earth First! Journal*, September 22, 1994, p. 30. Similarly, the *Earth First! Primer* explains, "Earth First! is a movement not an organization. Our structure is non-hierarchical. We have no highly-paid 'professional staff' or formal leadership" ("Earth First! Is Different," *Earth First! Primer*, 2; also "Why Earth First!" *Earth First! Primer*, 1; and John Davis, "On the Triune Nature of Earth First!" *Earth First! Journal*, May 1, 1990, pp. 2, 3, 5). Earth First!ers also frequently liken themselves to a tribe—"a tribe without chiefs," the *Earth First! Primer* hastens to add ("Forming an Earth First! Group," *Earth First! Primer*, 4). Also see the letter writer who describes Earth First! as "a movement with no leaders" and as "one big tribe made of lots of small autonomous clans" (G. T., Letters to the Editors, *Earth First! Journal*, February 2, 1991, p. 27).

51. "To avoid co-option, we feel it is necessary to avoid the corporate organizational structure so readily embraced by many environmental groups" ("Earth First! Is Different," *Earth First! Primer*, 2). Also see Slugthang, "Crossover Dreams," *Earth First! Journal*, September 22, 1994, p. 2.

52. According to the *Earth First! Primer*, "The journal is put out by a nonhierarchical, rotating collective, and any earnest Earth First! activist can work a stint on its production" ("Forming a Group . . . ," *Earth First! Primer*, 6). Also see Nancy Zierenberg, "How the Journal Works," *Earth First! Journal*, May 1, 1990, p. 2.

53. Phil Knight, "RRR Rocks and Rolls in Montana," *Earth First! Journal*, August 1, 1990, p. 19.

54. "The circle visually demonstrates our equality," explains Mary Beth Nearing. "No one person is leading; rather we all create proposals and enact solutions together. . . . The circle demonstrates our unity, group strength and equality to onlookers" (Nearing, "Steps to a Consensus Decision," *Earth First! Journal*, February 2, 1990, p. 24).

55. Dennis Fritzinger, "The RRR EF! Journal Meeting — A Watershed," *Earth First! Journal*, August 1, 1990, pp. 2, 4. "We don't want to formalize the leadership," Foreman explained in 1986. "We try to operate with a consensus process, recognizing that consensus can work only with trust" (Kirkpatrick Sale, "The Forest for the Trees," *Mother Jones* 11 [November 1986], 58). Writing about the consensus process, Earth First!er Mary Beth Nearing explains: "Failures are the fault of the group or the facilitator, not the process itself. . . . Consensus works best for people who truly believe in the superior intelligence of the 'group mind'" ("Steps to a Consensus Decision," *Earth First! Journal*, February 2, 1990, p. 24).

56. Our elections, says Judi Bari, "are just a facade to maintain corporate control" (Bari, "Monkeywrenching," *Earth First! Journal*, February 2, 1994, p. 8). Also see Anne Peterman, "If Voting Could Change Things They'd Make It Illegal," *Alarm: A Voice of Northeast Earth First!* (Autumnal Equinox 1992), 10. On radical environmentalists' disdain for representative democracy, see Martin Lewis, *Green Delusions: An Environmental Critique of Radical Environmentalism* (Durham, N.C.: Duke University Press, 1992); and Joel Schwartz, "The Rights of Nature and the Death of God," *The Public Interest* (Fall 1989), 3–14, especially 9.

57. Dennis Fritzinger, "The RRR EF! Journal Meeting — A Watershed," *Earth First! Journal*, August 1, 1990, pp. 2, 4.

58. "Organizational Model for the Earth Island Institute," in Earth Island Institute 1993 Annual Report (p. 7), which is included as an insert in *Earth Island Journal* 9 (Fall 1994).

59. *Native Forest News* (1st Quarter 1995), 12. The statement of NFN philosophy continues, "Furthermore, NFN is non-discriminatory on grounds of race, gender, culture, class or species." Also see "The Autonomous Collective Process," ibid., 11–12; as well as "What Is the Native Forest Network," *Native Forest News* Special Edition (Winter 1993/94), 2, included as insert in *Earth First! Journal*, December 21, 1993.

60. Karen Wood, quoted in Dennis Fritzinger, "The RRR EF! Journal Meeting — A Watershed," *Earth First! Journal*, August 1, 1990, p. 2.

61. Jason Halbert, "Urban Mayhem," *Earth First! Journal*, February 2, 1995, p. 15.

62. See Captain Paul Watson, Letters to the Editors, *Earth First! Journal*, September 22, 1990, p. 11. John Davis, "On the Triune Nature of Earth First!," *Earth First! Journal*, May 1, 1990, p. 5. Parfit, "Earth First!ers Wield a Mean Monkey Wrench," 186.

63. Scarce, *Eco-Warriors*, 107–8. The Sea Shepherds struck Scarce as "a group of people who worked with a profound sense of purpose but with minimal control and direction" (107). In recent years, however, there have been signs of tremendous friction between the egalitarian expectations of those attracted to the Sea Shepherds and the demands of the charismatic and increasingly authoritarian "Captain" Paul Watson. In a recent letter to the *Earth First! Journal*, Watson acknowledged there had been complaints but dismissed them as coming from "the politically correct consensus crowd." The Sea Shepherd society, he insisted, "is NOT politically correct nor do we operate by consensus. To quote Captain James T. Kirk, 'When this ship becomes a democracy, you'll be the first to know.' . . . They are all free agents when they are not at sea under my direct command. At sea, they are mine" (Letters to the Editors, *Earth First! Journal*, March 21, 1993, p. 23).

64. "Why Earth First!," *Earth First! Primer*, 1. Also see John Davis, "On the Triune Nature of Earth First!," *Earth First! Journal*, May 1, 1990, p. 3.

65. Anonymous, Letters to the Editors, *Earth First! Journal*, August 1, 1994, p. 30; emphasis added. Also see Jessie Friedlander, Letters to the Editors, *Earth First! Journal*, February 2, 1994, p. 32.

66. "Forming an Earth First! Group," *Earth First! Primer*, 4. Monkeywrenching, Foreman writes in *Ecodefense: A Field Guide to Monkeywrenching*, gives people "a rush of excitement, a sense of accomplishment, and *unparalleled camaraderie*" (Allan Pell Crawford, "Planet Stricken," *Vogue* 179 [September 1989], 715, emphasis added). On the powerful group bonding among the Sea Shepherds, see Scarce, *Eco-Warriors*, especially 109.

67. John Green, "The Facade of Civilization," *Earth First! Journal*, February 2, 1994, p. 2.

68. Not that radical environmentalists have not had their own love affair of sorts with Cuba. The *Earth Island Journal* has printed several articles in recent years characterizing Cuba as a virtual ecotopia. See, for example, Robert Benson, "Ecotopia Found," *Earth Island Journal* 7 (Fall 1992), 16; Karen Wald, "Cuba Goes Green," *Earth Island Journal* 6 (Winter 1991), 26–27; Karen Lee Wald, "Cuba Halts Nuclear Plant," *Earth Island Journal* 7 (Fall 1992), 10; and "Cuba Pioneers the Post-Petroleum Century," *Earth Island Journal* 7 (Fall 1992), 16. Also see Lewis, *Green Delusions*, 201, 206.

69. Some radical environmentalists also hope that we will learn the egalitarian virtues from those in the natural world that humans have oppressed and brutalized. They frequently enjoin each other "to think like a mountain" (Foreman, quoted in Zakin, *Coyotes and Town Dogs*, 198) or "to think like a river" (Donald Worster, *Rivers of Empire: Water, Aridity, and the Growth of the American West* [New York: Pantheon, 1985], 331). Earth First!er Erik Ryberg urges us to learn how to live by watching "a fish like the chinook salmon, who like no other creature understands *struggle* and

understands *home*," and understands the need not to compromise (Ryberg, "A Lot of Bad News from Idaho: Salvage Sales Spread Like Wildfire," *Earth First! Journal*, February 2, 1995, p. 5; Erik Ryberg, "Chinook Salmon Nearly Gone From Idaho," *Earth First! Journal*, March 21, 1995, p. 1. Also see Dolores La Chapelle, "Ritual Is Essential," in Bill Devall and George Sessions, *Deep Ecology: Living as If Nature Mattered* [Salt Lake City, Utah: Peregrine Smith, 1985], 248–49.). Another Earth First!er points to "the sociable Weaverbird of South Africa, [which] build communal nests for their colonies . . . [as] a fitting model for our endeavors." Termites, he adds, "might also provide a model for humans [since they] build their mound like an aboriginal offering to the living community of the Earth" (Peter Bralver, "Renegade Rangers," *Earth First! Journal*, November 1, 1989, p. 23). Also see John Daniel, "Toward Wild Heartlands," *Audubon* 96 (September/October 1994), 47. Daniel is poetry editor of *Wilderness* magazine.

70. Manes, *Green Rage*, 73. Cedar, "EF! Beats Up on Jim Bob Moffett . . . ," *Earth First! Journal*, March 21, 1995, p. 9. Also see Mira Goldberg, "Toward Stronger Alliances: A Response to 'Rethinking Environmental-First Nations Relationships,'" *Earth First! Journal*, February 2, 1995, p. 3.

71. Some misgivings about the "Indians as the first ecologists hypothesis" are expressed by John Davis in his review of Kirkpatrick Sale's *The Conquest of Paradise: Christopher Columbus and the Columbian Legacy* (New York: Knopf, 1990) in *Earth First! Journal*, December 21, 1990, p. 33. But Davis, who was essentially driven out as editor of *Earth First! Journal* at about this time, was atypical in this and other respects. On Davis, see Zakin, *Coyotes and Town Dogs*, especially 350.

72. "The 1995 Earth First! Activist Conference," *Earth First! Journal*, December 21, 1994, p. 26. Lone Wolf Circles, "The Native: Of the Earth, With/in the Earth," *Earth First! Journal*, September 22, 1993, pp. 3, 28. Also see Daniel Dancer, Letters to the Editors, *Earth First! Journal*, November 1, 1990, p. 5; Michael Lewis, "Bering Sea—An Ecosystem Run Amok," *Earth First! Journal*, February 2, 1991, p. 14; and Orin Langelle, "Indigenous Abenaki and Earth First! Form Northeast Alliance," *Alarm: A Voice of Northeast Earth First!* (Autumnal Equinox 1992), 9. A devastating critique of this romantic view of indigenous peoples as uniformly nature-loving is delivered in Martin Lewis's *Green Delusions*, especially chapter 2, "Primal Purity and Natural Balance." Also see Wallace Kaufman, *No Turning Back: Dismantling the Fantasies of Environmental Thinking* (New York: Basic Books, 1994), chapter 5.

73. Abbey Edwards, "Do you know where your local Native Americans are?" *Alarm: A Voice of Northeast Earth First!* (Autumnal Equinox 1992), 6.

74. Zakin, *Coyotes and Town Dogs*, 398; also 399, 60–62, 194, 230. Also see Manes, *Green Rage*, 123, 172–73, 237–40; Christopher Manes, "Why I Am a Misanthrope," *Earth First! Journal*, December 21, 1990, p. 29; Andrea Caruso and Kevin Russell, "Journey to Borneo and the Resistance of the Penan," *Earth First! Journal*, August 1, 1992, p. 14; Richard DeNeale, "Letters to the Editors," *Earth First! Journal*, August 1, 1992, p. 33; "Sacred Lands, Native Claims," *Earth First! Journal*, May 1, 1992, p. 21; Chris Roth, "Book Review: In the Absence of the Sacred," *Earth First! Journal*, November 2, 1992, p. 32; George French, "Settlement with Nature," *Earth First!*

Journal, May 1, 1992, p. 29; Devall and Sessions, *Deep Ecology,* 96–98; and Worster, *Rivers of Empire,* 331.

75. The pages of the *Earth First! Journal* are generously laden with sympathetic portraits of the resistance efforts of indigenous peoples in North America (see, for example, "Big Mountain: Resistance at Ticc-Yaa'toh" *Earth First! Journal,* September 22, 1993, p. 15; and Karen Pickett, "On Top of Mt. Graham," *Earth First! Journal,* August 1, 1993, p. 8) and occasionally even the world (see, for example, "Penan Blockade Smashed," *Earth First! Journal,* November 1, 1993, p. 16). Also see Orin Langelle, "Indigenous Abenaki and Earth First! form Northeast Alliance," *Alarm: A Voice of Northeast Earth First!* (Autumnal Equinox 1992), 8–9. Such accounts are if anything even more plentiful in the *Earth Island Journal.*

76. Indigenous people, according to Winona La Duke, are "people of the land," and there can be "no reconciliation between industrial society and people of the land." Those within industrial society necessarily look only to reform society rather "to change or to challenge the structural basis of the problem [that] is inherent in industrial society." Only indigenous peoples, who are necessarily enemies of that system, can show us how to revolutionize the way we live by teaching us "to live in a society that is not based on conquest, but on survival" (La Duke "The Trouble with Wasichu," *Earth Island Journal* 6 [Winter 1991], 42). Cf. the remarks of the Indian feminist and physicist Vandana Shiva, who writes that "while Third World women have privileged access to survival expertise, their knowledge is inclusive, not exclusive. [Their] ecological categories . . . can become the categories of liberation for all, men as well as for women . . . and for the human as well as the non-human elements of the Earth" ("Indigenous Love," *Earth Island Journal* 8 [Winter 1993], 33).

77. Lone Wolf Circles, "The Native: Of the Earth, With/in the Earth," *Earth First! Journal,* September 22, 1993, p. 3. "Ecocide as Genocide," *Earth First! Journal,* August 1, 1993, p. 3, of insert entitled "Stop Destroying Native Lands." In the real world, of course, indigenous rights can and often do conflict with environmental concerns. This conflict was forcefully brought out by Canadian David Orton, who pointedly reminded his fellow Earth First!ers that "past relationships to wildlife by indigenous peoples in the Americas and elsewhere were not always benign and based on mutual respect." Orton insisted that "the ecological shortcomings of contemporary indigenous world views need to be discussed frankly and fairly," although he quickly added that of course "our main preoccupation must remain with the sicknesses of contemporary industrial society" (Orton "Rethinking Environmental-First Nations Relationships," *Earth First! Journal,* December 21, 1994, p. 3). Orton's argument was quickly met with a stinging rejoinder from Mira Goldberg, who chastised Orton for daring to criticize the natives. Whatever problems indigenous peoples might have (which she attributed to "native collaborators"), it was not the place of nonindigenous people "to take leadership in criticizing the collaborators or otherwise determining the progress of native liberation." That task must be left to indigenous peoples. Our task, she explained, is to support indigenous peoples whatever their alleged failures "to live up to our own 'environmentally pure' standards." This support was necessary because "corporate destruction of the land is intertwined with genocide of native peoples and colonial occupation of native lands. [Therefore] to

destroy capitalism, we must support indigenous liberation" (Goldberg, "Toward Stronger Alliances: A Response to 'Rethinking Environmental-First Nations Relationships,'" *Earth First! Journal*, February 2, 1995, p. 3). A more measured but not dissimilar response to Orton is offered by Brian Tokar, "Respecting Native Struggles," *Earth First! Journal*, February 2, 1995, p. 26.

78. Devall and Sessions, *Deep Ecology*, 97. Devall has been a prominent contributor to the *Earth First! Journal*. See, for example, "Deep Ecology and Its Critics," *Earth First! Journal*, December 22, 1987, p. 18; and "'Maybe the Movement Is Leaving Me,'" *Earth First! Journal*, September 22, 1990, p. 6.

79. Tim Haugen, "The Wild Ranch Manifesto," *Earth First! Journal*, December 21, 1993, p. 4. Cf. the leisurely ecotopia described in Ernest Callenbach's *Ecotopia* (New York: Bantam, 1977). According to Jerry Mander, the Iroquois and other Indian tribes were the model on which Marx and Engels based their vision of "a successful classless, egalitarian, non-coercive society" (Mander, "Our Founding Mothers and Fathers, the Iroquois," *Earth Island Journal* 6 [Fall 1991], 31).

80. Dolores La Chapelle, "Fragments of Earth Wisdom: The Norwegian Roots of Deep Ecology," *Earth First! Journal*, February 2, 1990, p. 29. Also see Dolores La Chapelle, "Ritual Is Essential," in Devall and Sessions, *Deep Ecology*, 247–50; as well as Dolores La Chapelle, *Earth Wisdom* (Los Angeles: Guild of Tutors Press, 1978). La Chapelle's "Fragments of Earth Wisdom" appear frequently in the *Earth First! Journal*. See, for example, Dolores La Chapelle, "Living 'Earth Day' Every Day," *Earth First! Journal*, March 20, 1990, p. 31.

81. Wm. H. Kotke, *The Final Empire: The Collapse of Civilization and the Seed of the Future* (Portland, Ore.: Arrow Point Press, 1993), 248, 252, 253, 256. Kotke's book is reviewed glowingly by Wolf Hardin in *Earth First! Journal*, March 21, 1995, p. 33; and is recommended to Earth First! readers in *Earth First! Journal*, August 1, 1994, p. 21.

82. Bookchin and Foreman, *Defending the Earth*, 57. Murray Bookchin, *The Ecology of Freedom: The Emergence and Dissolution of Hierarchy*, rev. ed. (Montreal: Black Rose Books, 1991), 45. Also see Tokar, "Social Ecology, Deep Ecology," 136, 139; and Tokar, *Green Alternative*, 9, 139–40.

83. Carolyn Merchant, *Ecological Revolutions: Nature, Gender, and Science in New England* (Chapel Hill: University of North Carolina Press, 1989), 20, 24–25. Also see Lewis, *Green Delusions*, 45–46.

84. Kirkpatrick Sale, "The Columbian Legacy: We'd Better Start Preparing Now," *Earth First! Journal*, February 2, 1990. p. 25. Also see Sale, *Conquest of Paradise*; as well as Annie L. Booth and Harvey M. Jacobs, "Ties That Bind: Native American Beliefs as a Foundation for Ecological Consciousness," *Environmental Ethics* 12 (Spring 1990), 27–43.

85. An example of this undifferentiated view of indigenous peoples is Kimla McDonald and Christopher McLeod's claim that "around the globe, indigenous peoples sing the same songs. They sing of sacred land. . . . [They] sing also of loss, strife and grief" ("Songs of Land, Songs of Loss," *Earth Island Journal* 6 [Summer 1991], 12).

86. Manes, *Green Rage*, 123. Gar Smith, "A New Beginning," *Earth Island Journal* 8 (Winter 1993), inside front cover.

87. Ceal Smith, "Can Sea Turtles and Seri Indians Coexist?" *Earth Island Journal* 6 (Winter 1991), 19. Also see Joe Lamb, "Our Land, Our Life, Our Blood," *Earth Island Journal* 6 (Fall 1991), 12; Bill Weinberg, "Grandfather Corn and the Three Sisters," *Earth Island Journal* 9 (Summer 1994), 34–35; and even the Prince of Wales, "Homage to the Peoples of the Forests," *Earth Island Journal* 5 (Summer 1990), 48.

88. Joe Lamb, "Our Land, Our Life, Our Blood," *Earth Island Journal* 6 (Fall 1991), 12. Also see Gar Smith, "The Elder Brothers' Warning," *Earth Island Journal* 8 (Winter 1993), 31; and Winona La Duke, "The Trouble with Wasichu," *Earth Island Journal* 6 (Winter 1991), 42.

89. See Eric Zencey, "Apocalypse and Ecology," *North American Review* 273 (June 1988), 54.

90. Jerry Mander, "Our Founding Mothers and Fathers, the Iroquois," *Earth Island Journal* 6 (Fall 1991), 30. Also see Tokar, *Green Alternative*, 13; Kotke, *Final Empire*, 255–56; and "The Autonomous Collective Process," *Native Forest News* (1st Quarter 1995) 11–12. None of these authors make any mention, of course, as Lewis points out, of "a highly successful campaign of ethnocide [the Iroquois waged] against their competitors in the fur trade, the Hurons," or the fact that the Iroquois "raised the torture of war captives . . . to an art. Victims were taunted while being slowly burned alive and having their flesh gouged from their bodies" (*Green Delusions*, 92).

91. Cf. Charles T. Rubin: "Their misanthropy, if that is the right term, is that of the social reformer, not of the hermit" (*The Green Crusade: Rethinking the Roots of Environmentalism* [New York: Free Press, 1994], 249).

92. Kelpie Wilson, "Enough Already," *Earth First! Journal*, June 21, 1993, p. 23.

93. Scarce, *Eco-Warriors*, 89. One letter writer to Earth First! spoke of "vomit-inducing commercialisation" (Dylan Biezanek, Letters to the Editors, *Earth First! Journal*, November 1, 1990, p. 5).

94. Howie Wolke, "Thoughtful Radicalism," *Earth First! Journal*, December 21, 1989, p. 29. On Foreman's criticisms, see Scarce, *Eco-Warriors*, 89.

95. See A Dangerous Woman, Letters to the Editors, *Earth First! Journal*, February 2, 1990, p. 3, who speaks of being "disgusted with consumerism."

96. See, for example, "Simple in Means, Rich in Ends," an interview with Arne Naess by Stephen Bodian, in Michael E. Zimmerman, ed., *Environmental Philosophy: From Animal Rights to Radical Ecology* (Englewood Cliffs, N.J.: Prentice-Hall, 1993), 182–92; Devall, *Simple in Means*; Duane Elgin, *Voluntary Simplicity: Toward a Way of Life That Is Outwardly Simple, Inwardly Rich* (New York: Morrow, 1981); and Lester Milbrath, "Redefining the Good Life in a Sustainable Society," *Environmental Values* 2 (Autumn 1993), 261–69.

97. Elgin, *Voluntary Simplicity*, quoted in Guy Claxton, "Involuntary Simplicity: Changing Dysfunctional Habits of Consumption," *Environmental Values* 3 (Summer 1994), 72.

98. See Paul E. Corcoran, "The Bourgeois and Other Villains," *Journal of the History of Ideas* 38 (July–September 1977), 477–85.

99. Roadblock, "Through the Hinterlands," *Alarm: A Voice of Northeast Earth First!* (Autumnal Equinox 1992), 17.

100. Anne Petermann, "The Marketplace or Yuppie Hell," *Alarm* (Autumnal Equinox 1992), 20.

101. Feral Sage, "Holding Back Babylon," *Earth First! Journal*, June 21, 1993, p. 8. Also see Mick Womersley, "Ghost Dancers," *Earth First! Journal*, March 21, 1993, p. 4; Susan Meeker-Lowry, Letters to the Editors, *Earth First! Journal*, December 21, 1992, p. 3; and Dave Foreman, "We Aren't a Debating Society," *Earth First! Journal*, December 21, 1992, pp. 8, 13 (a speech originally given in 1987 at Grand Canyon Round River Rendezvous); as well as Jeremy Rifkin, *Biosphere Politics: A New Consciousness for a New Century* (New York: Crown, 1991), especially chapter 23; and "Brower Addresses Global Forum," *Earth Island Journal* 7 (Summer 1992), 16.

102. Michael Lewis, "Technology and the Tools of Ecodefense," *Earth First! Journal*, November 1, 1990, p. 36. Another Earth First!er speaks of people being "chained to internal combustion engines and a job in a concrete tower with no windows" (Karen Pickett, "Redwood Summer," *Earth First! Journal*, November 1, 1990, p. 8).

103. Tim Haugen, "The Wild Ranch Manifesto," *Earth First! Journal*, December 21, 1993, p. 4. Also see Flammulated Owl, "We're All Out on a Limb," *Earth First! Journal*, August 1, 1994, p. 20, which refers to the "wage-slave yoke of daily drudgery," as well as Michael Lewis, "Technology and the Tools of Ecodefense," *Earth First! Journal*, November 1, 1990, p. 36, which speaks of the "wage-slave relationship" (36); and Asante Riverwind, "Blue Mountains: Next Silent Salvage Victim," *Earth First! Journal*, February 2, 1993, who speaks dismissively of "wage slave serfs" (10).

104. Tim Haugen, "The Wild Ranch Manifesto," *Earth First! Journal*, December 21, 1993, p. 4.

105. Earth First! is hardly alone among radical environmentalists in this respect. See, for example, Gar Smith, "Pull the Plug?" *Earth Island Journal* 6 (Summer 1991), 20; and Young, *Sustaining the Earth*, 197.

106. John Potter, Letters to the Editors, *Earth First! Journal*, December 21, 1989, p. 4. Also see Pete Jones, "10 Things Real Environmentalists Already do to Save the Earth (and Have for 20 years)," *Earth First! Journal*, December 21, 1990, p. 32, which urges readers to "destroy the TV" as a way to "fight the conspiracy of consumerism through thought control."

107. John Green, "The Facade of 'Civilization,'" *Earth First! Journal*, February 2, 1994, p. 2.

108. Flammulated Owl says "the majority of humans have behaved like the domesticated genetically inbred critters they eat — an easily manipulated herd" ("We're All Out on a Limb," *Earth First! Journal*, August 1, 1994, p. 20).

109. Devall, quoted in Manes, *Green Rage*, 231. Also see Bill Devall, "An Open Letter to EF!ers," *Earth First! Journal*, December 21, 1990, p. 30.

110. "Jack Pine," Letters to the Editors, *Earth First! Journal*, February 2, 1995, p. 30. Pete Jones, "10 Things Real Environmentalists Already Do to Save the Earth," *Earth First! Journal*, December 21, 1990, p. 32. Tim Haugen, "The Wild Ranch Manifesto," *Earth First! Journal*, December 21, 1993, p. 4. Also see Manes, *Green Rage*, 139, 220–21; and Daniel Press, *Democratic Dilemmas in the Age of Ecology: Trees and Toxics in the American West* (Durham, N.C.: Duke University Press, 1994), 88.

111. Claxton, "Involuntary Simplicity," 73. Earth First!ers often describe consumerism and materialism as an addiction; see, for example, Kelpie Wilson, "Direct Action for Appropriate Technology," *Earth First! Journal*, May 1, 1991, p. 40; and Mick Womersley, "Ghost Dancers," *Earth First! Journal*, March 21, 1993, p. 4.

112. In *Environmentalists: Vanguard for a New Society* (Albany: State University of New York Press, 1984), Lester Milbrath distinguishes between the ecological "vanguard," who adhere to the New Ecological Paradigm (NEP), and the benighted "rearguard," who cling to the "Dominant Social Paradigm" (DSP).

113. Editorial preface to George Wuerthner's "Wildlands Economy," *Earth First! Journal*, December 21, 1992, p. 31; emphasis added.

114. Timothy Bechtold, "Destroying False Idols," *Earth First! Journal*, May 1, 1991, p. 11.

115. Louis Head, Letters to the Editors, *Earth First! Journal*, September 22, 1994, p. 28.

116. Marion H., Letters to the Editors, *Earth First! Journal*, March 21, 1995, p. 31. "The 1995 Earth First! Activist Conference," *Earth First! Journal*, December 21, 1994, p. 26.

117. Robert Streeter, "Continuing the Children Debate," *Earth First! Journal*, June 21, 1990, p. 29.

118. Book reviews, *Earth First! Journal*, August 1, 1990, p. 32.

119. Maria Quintana, "EF! Scuttles Blockbuster!" *Earth First! Journal*, February 2, 1992, p. 29.

120. Mark Davis, "If It's So Bad, Why Isn't Everybody Worried?" *Earth First! Journal*, December 21, 1992, p. 16.

121. Maria Quintana, "EF! Scuttles Blockbuster!," *Earth First! Journal*, February 2, 1992, p. 29.

122. Philip Goff, Letters to the Editors, *Earth First! Journal*, March 21, 1995, p. 31.

123. Nina Alvarez, Letters to the Editors, *Earth First! Journal*, May 1, 1991, p. 3. Also see Roadblock, "Support Mark Davis and Peg Millett," *Alarm: A Voice of Northeast Earth First!* (Autumnal Equinox 1992), which describes America as "a brain dead society" (19).

124. Susan Meeker-Lowry, Letters to the Editors, *Earth First! Journal*, December 21, 1992, p. 3.

125. Kelpie Wilson, "Enough Already!" *Earth First! Journal*, June 21, 1993, p. 23.

126. Pete and D'eby, "Letter from the Brazilian Rainforest: A Plea for Its Defense," *Earth First! Journal*, August 1, 1992, p. 15. Also see Michael Lewis, "Reflections on Oily Waters," *Earth First! Journals*, May 1, 1991, p. 17.

127. Michelle Stewart, "Op-Ed: We May Not Have Leaders . . . ," *Earth First! Journal*, December 21, 1993, p. 3.

128. Worster, *Rivers of Empire*, 57–58. Worster is summarizing Horkheimer's analysis, but he is also clearly endorsing that analysis and insisting on its relevance for the contemporary period.

129. *Earth First! Primer*, 4.

130. Lone Wolf Circles, "Pagan Gatherings," *Earth First! Journal*, March 21,

1993, p. 30. Also see Darryl Cherney, quoted in Parfit, "Earth First!ers Wield a Mean Monkey Wrench," 198; and John Seed and Dave Foreman, quoted in Manes, *Green Rage*, 117, 226.

131. Joanie Berde, "Red Mountain Protesters Tried," *Earth First! Journal*, February 2, 1994, p. 18. Also see Theodore Roszak, *The Voice of the Earth* (New York: Simon and Schuster, 1992), as well as Wayland Drew, quoted in Manes, *Green Rage*, 220.

132. Chad Hanson, "Sierra Club Management: Shaming Muir's Memory," *Earth First! Journal*, March 21, 1995, p. 26.

133. See the penetrating discussion in Schwartz, "The Rights of Nature and the Death of God."

134. Captain Paul Watson, "In Defense of Tree Spiking," *Earth First! Journal*, February 2, 1995, p. 10.

135. Cf. Richard Hofstadter, *The Paranoid Style in American Politics and Other Essays* (New York: Vintage, 1967), 39. Also see Dave Foreman, "The Perils of Illegality," *Earth First! Journal*, November 1, 1989, p. 25.

136. Dave Foreman, quoted in Zakin, *Coyotes and Town Dogs*, 298. Mark Davis, "An Open Letter to Susan Zakin," *Earth First! Journal*, December 21, 1993, p. 14. Manes, *Green Rage*, 234. Kirkpatrick Sale, "The Columbian Legacy: We'd Better Start Preparing Now," *Earth First! Journal*, February 2, 1990, p. 25. Anonymous flyer posted at Redwood Summer, reprinted in *Earth First! Journal*, May 1, 1991, p. 8. David Orton, "Rethinking Environmental-First Nations Relationships," *Earth First! Journal*, December 21, 1994, p. 28.

137. Christi Stevens, "What Goes Up Must Come Down," *Earth First! Journal*, May 1, 1991, p. 27. "Against Bio-Technology! (Part II)," *Alarm* (Summer Solstice 1993), 8. Todd Shuman, "Misanthropy or No—Where Does It Go?," *Earth First! Journal*, May 1, 1991, p. 9.

138. Lone Wolf Circles, Letters to the Editors, *Earth First! Journal*, February 2, 1990, p. 3. Each "Dear Nedd Ludd" column, a regular feature of the *Earth First! Journal*, is prefaced with a reference to "the forces of industrial totalitarianism." Mike Lewis, "Response to Violence," *Earth First! Journal*, June 21, 1990, p. 6.

139. Mike Roselle, quoted in Scarce, *Eco-Warriors*, 94. Mike Lewis, "Response to Violence," *Earth First! Journal*, June 21, 1990, p. 6. John Green, "The Facade of Civilization," *Earth First! Journal*, February 2, 1994, p. 2.

140. Mike Lewis, "Response to Violence," *Earth First! Journal*, June 21, 1990, p. 6. Also see Judi Bari, "'Our Community Is Under Siege,'" *Earth Island Journal* 6 (Summer 1991), 49. Bari's theory is that "the Wise Use Movement directed the set-up for the bombing with the FBI helping to cover it up" (Anne Petermann, "Earth First! Meets Wise Use Guru," *Alarm* [Summer Solstice 1993], 24).

141. Anonymous, Letters to the Editors, *Earth First! Journal*, August 1, 1994, p. 30.

142. John Davis, "Ramblings," *Earth First! Journal*, June 21, 1990, p. 2. Denigration of American democracy suffuses the radical environmental movement. David Brower, for instance, dismisses America as "ostensibly a democracy," and suggests that "we in the United States should watch the former Soviet Union very closely, and if the republics can make democracy work, we should try it" ("Fiddling While the

Earth Burns," *Earth Island Journal* 7 [Summer 1992], 2). Similarly, Donald Worster writes of the "so-called democracies" of the West (Worster, *Rivers of Empire*, 53); and Murray Bookchin also insists on placing the term "democracies" in quotation marks when describing "our" political systems (*Remaking Society* [1989], quoted in Lewis, *Green Delusions*, 83). Also see Lewis, *Green Delusions*, 40, 153–54.

143. "Forming an Earth First! Group," *Earth First! Primer*, 4. Chad Hanson, "Sierra Club Reform: Restoring Muir's Legacy," *Earth First! Journal*, September 22 1994, p. 1. Paul Watson, quoted in Scarce, *Eco-Warriors*, 102. Jeffrey St. Clair, "Losing It at the Courthouse," *Earth First! Journal*, February 2, 1995, p. 25. Jeffrey St. Clair, "Cashing Out: Corporate Environmentalism in the Age of Newt," *Earth First! Journal*, March 21, 1995, p. 27.

144. Hofstadter, *Age of Reform*, 19.

CHAPTER 9. Apocalypse and Authoritarianism
in the Radical Environmental Movement

1. Raymond Aron, *The Opium of the Intellectuals* (New York: Norton, 1962), 324.

2. E. E. Schattschneider, *Two Hundred Million Americans in Search of a Government* (New York: Holt, Rinehart, and Winston, 1969), 53.

3. Richard Hofstadter, *The Paranoid Style in American Politics and Other Essays* (New York: Vintage, 1967), 3–40.

4. See ibid., 29.

5. For one social scientist's heroic effort to wrestle with the scientific data, see Aaron Wildavsky, *But Is It True? A Citizen's Guide to Environmental Health and Safety Issues* (Cambridge, Mass.: Harvard University Press, 1995).

6. Hofstadter, *Paranoid Style*, 29.

7. The literature here is vast. For a start, see Karl Dake and Aaron Wildavsky, "Theories of Risk Perception: Who Fears What and Why?" *Daedalus* 119 (Spring 1990), 41–60; and Karl Dake, "Orienting Dispositions in the Perception of Risk: An Analysis of Contemporary Worldviews and Cultural Biases," *Journal of Cross-Cultural Psychology* 22 (1991), 61–82.

8. Mary Douglas and Aaron Wildavsky, *Risk and Culture* (Berkeley: University of California Press, 1982). Also see Mary Douglas, *Risk Acceptability in the Social Sciences* (New York: Russell Sage, 1985); Hank C. Jenkins-Smith and Walter Smith, "Ideology, Culture, and Risk Perception," in Dennis Coyle and Richard J. Ellis, eds., *Politics, Policy, and Culture* (Boulder, Colo.: Westview Press, 1994), 17–32; and Steve Rayner, "Cultural Theory and Risk Analysis," in Sheldon Krimsky and Dominic Golding, eds., *Social Theories of Risk* (Westport, Conn.: Praeger, 1992), 83–115.

9. John McCormick, *Reclaiming Paradise: The Global Environmental Movement* (Bloomington: Indiana University Press, 1989), 69–80.

10. William Ophuls, "Locke's Paradigm Lost: The Environmental Crisis and the Collapse of Laissez-Faire Politics," *Beyond Growth: Essays on Alternative Futures*, Yale University School of Forestry and Environmental Studies Bulletin No. 88 (New

Haven, Conn.: Yale University School of Forestry and Environmental Studies, 1975), 171.

11. William Ophuls, *Ecology and the Politics of Scarcity: Prologue to a Political Theory of the Steady State* (San Francisco: Freeman, 1977), 2.

12. Ophuls, "Locke's Paradigm Lost," 159, 160.

13. Ibid., 164–65; also 168. Also see Ophuls, *Ecology and the Politics of Scarcity*, 162–63.

14. Ophuls, "Locke's Paradigm Lost," 169; also see Ophuls, *Ecology and the Politics of Scarcity*, 156.

15. Ophuls, "Locke's Paradigm Lost," 156–57. Ophuls, *Ecology and the Politics of Scarcity*, 152; emphasis added.

16. Ophuls, "Locke's Paradigm Lost," 163; emphasis added.

17. Ibid., 171.

18. See Gregg Easterbrook, "The Dirt on Communism," *New Republic*, February 20, 1995, pp. 41–45.

19. Ophuls, "Locke's Paradigm Lost," 170, 172.

20. See David W. Orr and Stuart Hill, "Leviathan, the Open Society, and the Crisis of Ecology," *Western Political Quarterly* 31 (December 1978), 457–69; Susan M. Leeson, "Philosophical Implications of the Ecological Crisis: The Authoritarian Challenge to Liberalism," *Polity* 11 (1978), 303–18; Robert D. Holsworth, "Recycling Hobbes: The Limits to Political Ecology," *Massachusetts Review* 20 (1979), 9–40; Richard J. Barnet, *The Lean Years: Politics in the Age of Scarcity* (New York: Simon and Schuster, 1980), especially 296–98. Other commentaries on Ophuls include Robert W. Hoffert, "The Scarcity of Politics: Ophuls and Western Political Thought," *Environmental Ethics* 8 (Spring 1986), 5–32; and K. J. Walker, "The Environmental Crisis: A Critique of Neo-Hobbesian Responses," *Polity* 21 (Fall 1988), 67–82.

21. See William Ophuls and A. Stephen Boyan, Jr., *Ecology and the Politics of Scarcity Revisited* (New York: Freeman, 1992).

22. Robyn Eckersley, *Environmentalism and Political Theory: Toward an Ecocentric Approach* (Albany: State University of New York Press, 1992), 17.

23. Indeed, Ophuls himself shares these egalitarian and antiauthoritarian premises. Ophuls rejects market devices for dealing with environmental problems on the grounds that they would increase inequality of purchasing power, since lower-income groups would be hit hardest by such schemes (Ophuls, "Locke's Paradigm Lost," 148–49). Ophuls also urges us to switch to "a much more communitarian ethic" (169) and indicates his preference for small-scale, face-to-face democracy along the lines of the Greek city-state or Jeffersonian agrarianism (William Ophuls, "Leviathan or Oblivion?" in Herman E. Daly, ed., *Toward a Steady State Economy* [San Francisco: Freeman, 1973], 226). Similarly, Robert L. Heilbroner, who, like Ophuls, argued that survival required a centralized, authoritarian state, also harbored egalitarian commitments. Heilbroner hoped that an authoritarian state might be only a transitional stage toward an egalitarian, steady-state future characterized by "a diminution of scale, a reduction in the size of the human community from the

dangerous level of immense nation-states toward the 'polis' that defined the appropriate reach of political power for the ancient Greeks" (*An Inquiry into the Human Prospect* [New York: Norton, 1974], 135).

24. Christopher Manes, *Green Rage: Radical Environmentalism and the Unmaking of Civilization* (Boston: Little, Brown, 1990), 183, 178, 234, 135, 234.

25. Ibid., 232. Trip Gabriel, "If a Tree Falls in the Forest, They Hear It," *New York Times Magazine*, November 4, 1990, p. 64. Brian Tokar, "Social Ecology, Deep Ecology, and the Future of Green Political Thought," *Ecologist* 18 (January/February 1988), 138. Cf. Howie Wolke: "When [industrial society] finally, mercifully, chokes on its own dung pile, [thoughtful radicalism will have made sure that] there'll at least be *some* wilderness remaining as a seedbed for planet-wide recovery" (Manes, *Green Rage*, 187).

26. Traci and Dennis, Letters to the Editors, *Earth First! Journal*, May 1, 1994, p. 30. Also see, for example, "Option 9: The Final Solution," *Earth First! Journal*, August 1, 1993, p. 17; Christi Stevens, "What Goes Up Must Come Down," *Earth First! Journal*, May 1, 1991, p. 27; Mark Davis, "If It's So Bad, Why Isn't Everybody Worried?" *Earth First! Journal*, December 21, 1992, p. 12; Mic Womersley, "Speciesism, Nazis, and the New Resistance," *Earth First! Journal*, June 21, 1993, p. 11; and Mike Roselle, "Traditional Family Values, Anyone?" *Earth First! Journal*, September 22, 1992, p. 2.

27. Judi Bari, quoted in Rik Scarce, *Eco-Warriors: Understanding the Radical Environmental Movement* (Chicago: Noble Press, 1990), 266–67. Also see Judi Bari, "Our Community Is Under Siege," *Earth Island Journal* 6 (Summer 1991), 50.

28. Manes, *Green Rage*, 168. Also see Jonathan Paul, "The Grand Jury Dilemma," *Earth First! Journal*, August 1, 1994, p. 11.

29. Tokar wrote, "Our present civilization is clearly headed for collapse, and is currently poised to carry the rest of the earth down with it" (Tokar, "Social Ecology, Deep Ecology," 138–39).

30. Ibid., 132, 139.

31. Gar Smith, "Save the Tuna!" *Earth Island Journal* 9 (Fall 1994), 19. "The Chlorine Cover-Up: An Interview with Adam Trombly," *Earth Island Journal* 7 (Fall 1992), 26. "America the Poisoned: The Legacy of Lead," *Earth Island Journal* 7 (Fall 1992), 13. Donella Meadows, quoted in Gar Smith, "Beyond the Limits," *Earth Island Journal* 7 (Fall 1992), 13. Also see "Vanishing Forests, Disappearing Clouds," *Earth Island Journal* 7 (Fall 1992), 27; "Are We Running Out of Oxygen?" *Earth Island Journal* 7 (Fall 1992), 27; "What's Happening to the World's Weather?" *Earth Island Journal* 6 (Summer 1991), 38; "Health Risks and Global Warming," *Earth Island Journal* 6 (Summer 1991), 40; and "Comparing Notes," *Earth Island Journal* 6 (Summer 1991), 40.

32. Richard J. Ellis and Fred Thompson, "The Culture Wars by Other Means: Environmental Attitudes and Cultural Biases in the Northwest," Tables 13 and 14, paper delivered at the Annual Meeting of the Western Political Science Association, San Francisco, March 14–16, 1996. The statement "Our present civilization is headed for collapse, and is poised to carry the rest of the world down with it," which was asked of Earth First!ers, was not asked of Earth Island members.

33. Jimmy Langman, "Restoration a Priority at Global Forum," *Earth Island Journal* 7 (Summer 1992), 36.

34. "The Global CPR Magazine," supplement in *Earth Island Journal* 9 (Summer 1994).

35. David Ross Brower with Steve Chapple, from the book *Let the Mountains Talk, Let the Rivers Run*, in *Earth Island Journal* 10 (Spring 1995), 19.

36. Hofstadter, *Paranoid Style*, 30.

37. Quoted in Daniel A. Coleman, *EcoPolitics: Building a Green Society* (New Brunswick, N.J.: Rutgers University Press, 1994), 201. Also see "RAN warns of 'Bio Meltdown,'" *Earth Island Journal* 7 (Summer 1992), 31.

38. Coleman, *EcoPolitics*, 201.

39. Manes, *Green Rage*, xi; also 170–71. Jacob Bear, "Southern California's Sage Scrub Wilderness," *Earth First! Journal*, December 21, 1992, p. 24. Tom Ehresman, Letters to the Editors, *Earth First! Journal*, February 2, 1994, p. 31. Leslie Sellgrin, quoted in Scarce, *Eco-Warriors*, 80. Alan Pell Crawford, "Planet Stricken," *Vogue* 179 (September 1989), 712. "The 1995 Earth First! Activist Conference," *Earth First! Journal*, December 21, 1994, p. 26. Also see Mouse That Roars, Letters to the Editors, *Earth First! Journal*, June 21, 1993, p. 32.

40. See James Rule, "The Conundrum of Green Consciousness," *Dissent* 41 (Summer 1994), 402.

41. Caldicott, quoted in Theodore Roszak, "Green Guilt and Ecological Overload," *New York Times*, June 9, 1992. Also see Michael de Liuda, "Unplug," *Alarm: A Voice of Northeast Earth First!* (Winter Solstice 1992), 12.

42. Allan Hunt Badiner, Letters to the Editors, *Earth First! Journal*, August 1, 1993, p. 32. Also see Mamoo the Wise, Letters to the Editors, *Earth First! Journal*, February 2, 1992, p. 24; and George Wuerthner, "The Emperor Has No Clothes," *Earth First! Journal*, May 1, 1992, p. 14.

43. Chellis Glendinning, "Notes Toward a Neo-Luddite Manifesto," *Utne Reader* (March/April 1990), 52. Robert Streeter, "Wilderness and Photography: The Killing Films," *Earth First! Journal*, March 20, 1990, p. 30. "Clean Colors," *Earth Island Journal* 10 (Spring 1995), 5. Slugthang, Letters to the Editors, *Earth First! Journal*, May 1, 1994, p. 3. Also see "50 Difficult Things You Can Do to Save the Earth," *Earth Island Journal* 6 (Winter 1991), 12.

44. Linda Palter, Letters to the Editors, *Earth First! Journal*, June 21, 1993, p. 32. Also see Robin Carlson, Letters to the Editors, *Earth First! Journal*, November 1, 1993, p. 33; and Jean Welch, Letters to the Editors, *Earth First! Journal*, March 21, 1993, p. 25.

45. See, for example, Linda Palter, Letters to the Editors, *Earth First! Journal*, June 21, 1993, p. 32.

46. The radical environmentalist dilemma, as Robert Streeter frames it, is "how best to remain organic and effective" (Streeter, "Wilderness and Photography: The Killing Films," *Earth First! Journal*, March 20, 1990, p. 30). And Dave Foreman asks: "How do you change society when you are apart from it?" ("The Perils of Illegality," *Earth First! Journal*, November 1, 1989, p. 25).

47. Hofstadter, *Paranoid Style*, 30. Also see Booth Fowler, *The Dance with Com-*

munity: The Contemporary Debate in American Political Thought (Lawrence: University Press of Kansas, 1991), especially 107; as well as Stephen D. O'Leary, *Arguing the Apocalypse: A Theory of Millennial Rhetoric* (New York: Oxford University Press, 1994).

48. See Eckersley, *Environmentalism and Political Theory*, especially 13–17.

49. Ibid., 13.

50. Ophuls, "Locke's Paradigm Lost," 169.

51. R. A. Falk, *The Endangered Planet* (1972), as summarized in Timothy O'Riordan, *Environmentalism*, 2d ed. (London: Pion, 1981), 301.

52. Tokar, *Green Alternatives*, 140.

53. Donald Worster, *Rivers of Empire: Water, Aridity, and the Growth of the American West* (New York: Pantheon, 1985), 330.

54. Tom Burke, "The Next Ten Years," *Not Man Apart* 9 (September 1979), 16, as quoted in Douglas and Wildavsky, *Risk and Culture*, 135. Also see Stephen Cotgrove, *Catastrophe or Cornucopia: The Environment, Politics and the Future* (Chichester, Eng.: John Wiley, 1982), especially 5–6. See Sacvan Bercovitch, who argues that the American jeremiad is characterized by "affliction *and* promise." It "both laments an apostasy and heralds a restoration." "Thundering denunciations of a backsliding people" are joined to "the promise of the millennium." "Cries of declension and doom" are accompanied by promises of "a second paradise, a Canaan abounding in blessings beyond anything they had had or imagined" (*The American Jeremiad* [Madison: University of Wisconsin Press, 1978], 209, 31, 6, 8, xiv, 31). For a critical discussion of Bercovitch's ideas and a brief analysis of their relevance to the radical environmental movement, see Richard J. Ellis, *American Political Cultures* (New York: Oxford University Press, 1993), 170–74.

55. Richard Register, "Rebuilding Our Cities," *Earth Island Journal* 5 (Summer 1990), 45.

56. Edward Abbey, "A Response to Schmookler on Anarchy," *Earth First! Journal*, August 1, 1986, p. 22, quoted in Manes, *Green Rage*, 241. On Dave Foreman's early hopes that Earth First! would help build "a new society," see Susan Zakin, *Coyotes and Town Dogs: Earth First! and the Environmental Movement* (New York: Penguin Books, 1993), especially 194, 230, 281.

57. Earth Island Institute, 1993 Annual Report, p. 16; available as insert in *Earth Island Journal* 9 (Fall 1994); also see p. 5; David Brower, "Embracing the Green Circle," *Earth Island Journal* (Summer 1990), 47. In the foreword to *Progress as If Survival Mattered* (San Francisco: Friends of the Earth, 1977), Brower, who was then president of Friends of the Earth, wrote hopefully that "our anxiously acquisitive consumer society will give way to a more serenely thrifty conserver society. . . . Restless mobility will diminish; people will put down roots and recapture a sense of community. Full employment will be the norm in a sustainable, skill-intensive economy" (7). Also see Brower, circa 1970, as quoted in Douglas and Wildavsky, *Risk and Culture*, 136.

58. Coleman, *EcoPolitics*, 204–5.

59. Tokar, "Social Ecology, Deep Ecology," 139. Murray Bookchin, *The Ecology of Freedom: The Emergence and Dissolution of Hierarchy*, rev. ed. (Montreal: Black Rose Books, 1991), 318.

60. Fritjof Capra, for example, writes that "the nineties are going to be the decade of the environment — not because we say so but because of events almost beyond our control. . . . We are at the beginning of a fundamental change of world-view in science and in society. . . . Value systems emphasizing quantity, expansion, competition, and domination will give way to greater emphasis on quality, conservation, cooperation and partnership" ("Rebuilding Our Thinking," *Earth Island Journal*, 5 [Summer 1990], 46). Also relevant is Lester W. Milbrath, *Environmentalists: Vanguard for a New Society* (Albany: State University of New York Press, 1984), and empirical research investigating the so-called New Environmental Paradigm, as, for example, in Riley Dunlap and Kent D. Van Liere, "The 'New Environmental Paradigm,'" *Journal of Environmental Education* 9 (Summer 1978), 10–19.

61. Wm. H. Kotke, *The Final Empire: The Collapse of Civilization and the Seed of the Future* (Portland, Ore.: Arrow Point Press, 1993). All quotations are from Wolf Hardin's review in *Earth First! Journal*, March 21, 1995, p. 33.

62. Coleman, *EcoPolitics*, 202; also 204–5. Kirkpatrick Sale, *Dwellers in the Land: The Bioregional Vision* (San Francisco: Sierra Club Books, 1985), 176–77. Also see Robert C. Paehlke, *Environmentalism and the Future of Progressive Politics* (New Haven, Conn.: Yale University Press, 1989); and especially the relevant empirical findings in Daniel Press, *Democratic Dilemmas in the Age of Ecology: Trees and Toxics in the American West* (Durham, N.C.: Duke University Press, 1994). Sale's bioregional vision is troubling for other reasons, however. For while he hopes that his bioregional principles of decentralization and cooperation would "impel its polity in the direction of libertarian, noncoercive, open, and more-or-less democratic governance," he concedes that this need not be the case. Bioregions, he admits rather cavalierly, may not "heed the values of democracy, equality, liberty, freedom, justice, and the like" (Sale, *Dwellers*, 108). That is scant comfort for those who may be systematically oppressed or excluded within a bioregion. The same unresolved problem of what happens when local communities adopt illiberal or oppressive political arrangements also haunts Sale's earlier decentralist manifesto, *Human Scale* (New York: Coward-McCann, 1980).

63. Laura Westra, "The Ethics of Environmental Holism and the Democratic State: Are They in Conflict?" *Environmental Values* 2 (Summer 1993), 125–36; quotations on 128–29. At the conclusion of her paper, Westra blithely disenfranchises those deemed environmentally uneducated or unconcerned. "All *educated* and *aware* cosmic citizens," she writes, "ought to have a voice in environmental questions that will affect them, no matter what their other citizenship, race, or political ideology" (135; emphasis added). Who, one wonders, will make the judgment about who are the "educated and aware" cosmic citizens? What will count as "aware" or "educated"?

64. Ibid., 130, 129.

65. Ibid., 131, 135. Our confidence in this being a sharply limited power is further eroded when Westra also proposes that we might establish an international supervisory organization "endowed with a large grant to attempt to redress serious problems, such as (a) ecosabotage, (b) racism and (c) sexism."

66. See James D. Thompson and Arthur Tuden, "Strategies, Structures, and Processes of Organizational Decisions," in James D. Thompson, ed., *Comparative Studies in Administration* (Pittsburgh, Pa.: University of Pittsburgh Press, 1959).

67. William R. Catton, Jr., *Overshoot: The Ecological Basis of Revolutionary Change* (Urbana: University of Illinois Press, 1980), 170, 236–37.

68. Paul R. Ehrlich and Anne H. Ehrlich, *The Population Explosion* (New York: Touchstone, 1990), 189. Also see Martin Lewis, *Green Delusions: An Environmental Critique of Radical Evironmentalism* (Durham, N.C.: Duke University Press, 1992), 200. Lewis's demonstration of the pseudoscientific absurdity of the Ehrlichs' widely used formula (Environmental Impact = Population × Affluence × Technological Level) should be required reading (199–200, 237–41).

69. Zorro, Letters to the Editors, *Earth First! Journal*, August 1, 1990, p. 5.

70. Kelly Eastwood, "Dear Journal," *Earth Island Journal* 6 (Summer 1991), 2.

71. The Hermit of Fire Mountain, Letters to the Editors, *Earth First! Journal*, February 2, 1992, p. 25. Also see Scarce, *Eco-Warriors*, 263.

72. Jamie Sayen, "Obligatory Skepticism: The Environmental Movement's Internal Enemy," *Earth Island Journal* 10 (Spring 1995), 31.

73. Yellow Grass Dog, Letters to the Editors, *Earth First! Journal*, March 21, 1993, p. 25. Also see Edward Abbey, quoted in Manes, *Green Rage*, 175.

74. Foreman, *Ecodefense: A Field Guide to Monkey-wrenching*, quoted in Roderick Frazier Nash, *The Rights of Nature: A History of Environmental Ethics* (Madison: University of Wisconsin Press, 1989), 193; emphasis added.

75. Karen Pickett, "On Top of Mt. Graham," *Earth First! Journal*, August 1, 1993, p. 8. Also see Rod Coronado, "'Spread Your Love Through Action,'" *Earth First! Journal*, March 21, 1995, p. 8; and Bill Devall, quoted in Manes, *Green Rage*, 176.

76. Buck Young, "Letters to the Editors," *Earth First! Journal*, February, 2, 1992, p. 3.

77. The "non-apocalyptic" were those who scored less than or equal to 4 (the midpoint) on a seven-point scale ($n = 28$). The strongly apocalyptic scored seven ($n = 65$). A "high" score on the illiberalism index was operationalized as a mean score of six or higher; a "low" score on the illiberalism index was operationalized as a mean score of less than or equal to 4.

78. Using somewhat different questions, a strong relationship between apocalyptic views and a willingness to endorse illiberal statements was also found in our survey of the memberships of the Earth Island Institute, the Sierra Club, and the Audubon Society. The correlation between apocalyptic views (measured by the "Oceans are dying" item plus two new items, "Unrelenting exploitation of nature has driven us to the brink of ecological collapse" and "If things continue on their present course, we will soon experience a major ecological catastrophe") and illiberalism (measured by the same three items as in the Metz survey plus one additional statement, "Environmental protection may be a just course for society even if that course is taken undemocratically") was .39.

79. Hofstadter, *Paranoid Style*, 31, 29.

80. Paul Watson, quoted in Michael Parfit, "Earth First!ers Wield a Mean Monkey Wrench," *Smithsonian* 21 (April 1990), 186. Scarce, *Eco-Warriors*. Robert Hunter, *Warriors of the Rainbow: A Chronicle of the Greenpeace Movement* (New York: Holt, Rinehart and Winston, 1979). David B. Morris, *Earth Warrior: Overboard with Paul Watson and the Sea Shepherd Conservation Society* (Golden, Colo.: Fulcrum Publishing,

1995). Rod Coronado, "'Spread Your Love Through Action,'" *Earth First! Journal*, March 21, 1995, p. 8. Dave Foreman, quoted in Zakin, *Coyotes and Town Dogs*, 399; and in Nash, *Rights of Nature*, 193. Jessie Friedlander, Letters to the Editors, *Earth First! Journal*, February 2, 1994, p. 32. "1995 Earth First! Activist Conference," *Earth First! Journal*, December 21, 1994, p. 26. Also see Crawford, "Planet Stricken," 713; Dave Foreman, "We're Not a Debating Society," *Earth First! Journal*, December 21, 1992, p. 8; and Beverly Cherner, "Rising to the Challenge," *Earth First! Journal*, November 1, 1993, p. 2.

81. Mike Roselle, "Forrest Grump," *Earth First! Journal*, December 21, 1994, p. 23. Dear Nedd Ludd, "S.P.I.K.E. Nails Sugarloaf," *Earth First! Journal*, November 2, 1992, p. 31.

82. For a taste of the intensity of the radical environmental hostility to mainstream or reformist environmentalism, particularly the Sierra Club, see Asante Riverwind, Letters to the Editors, *Earth First! Journal*, February 2, 1994, p. 3; Erik Ryberg, "Chinook Salmon Nearly Gone from Idaho," *Earth First! Journal*, March 21, 1995, p. 14; Chad Hanson, "Sierra Club Management: Shaming Muir's Memory," *Earth First! Journal*, March 21, 1995, p. 26; Jeffrey St. Clair, "Cashing Out: Corporate Environmentalism in the Age of Newt," *Earth First! Journal*, March 21, 1995, pp. 3, 27; Jeffrey St. Clair, "Losing It at the Courthouse," *Earth First! Journal*, February 2, 1995, p. 25; and Paul Watson, quoted in Scarce, *Eco-Warriors*, 102.

83. Dave Foreman, "The Perils of Illegality," *Earth First! Journal*, November 1, 1989, p. 25.

84. Weirdwolf, Letters to the Editors, *Earth First! Journal*, December 21, 1993, p. 3.

85. Dave Foreman, "The Perils of Illegality," *Earth First! Journal*, November 1, 1989, p. 25. Toward the end of 1990, Foreman told a reporter that Earth First! was "not my tribe anymore. These days, I'm more comfortable at a Sierra Club or Nature Conservancy gathering than I am at an Earth First! rendezvous" (Stephen Talbot, "Earth First! What Next?" *Mother Jones* 15 [November/December 1990], 80). In 1995 Foreman was actually elected to the Sierra Club Board of Directors.

86. On the paranoia that wracked Earth First! in the wake of the 1990 schism and genuine FBI infiltration and harassment, see Leslie Helmstreet, "Some Thoughts on Paranoia," *Earth First! Journal*, September 22, 1994, p. 3; and Judi Bari, "Our Community Is Under Siege," *Earth Island Journal* 6 (Summer 1991), 50. Also see Randy Ghent, "Thoughts on Debate and Censorship," *Earth First! Journal*, February 2, 1993, p. 16; The Vegan Treeman, Letters to the Editors, *Earth First! Journal*, December 21, 1994, p. 30; and "FBI Alert!" *Earth First! Journal*, November 1, 1993, p. 9.

87. See, for example, "The 1995 Earth First! Activist Conference," *Earth First! Journal*, December 21, 1994, p. 26; and Lone Wolf Circles, "The Native: Of the Earth, With/in the Earth," *Earth First! Journal*, September 22, 1993, p. 28.

88. Mark Davis, "An Open Letter to Susan Zakin," *Earth First! Journal*, December 21, 1993, p. 14. Jeffrey St. Clair, "Losing It at the Courthouse," *Earth First! Journal*, February 2, 1995, p. 25. Also see Randall Restless, "Keep the Wild Rockies Wild!!!" *Earth First! Journal*, September 22, 1993, p. 9.

89. Radical environmentalists tend to be much more concerned with corporations running the world. See, for example, Asante Riverwind, "Freddies, You're Fired!" *Earth First! Journal*, February 2, 1993, p. 9; Mark Sigel, "Plugging the Ozone Hole with Media Misinformation," *Earth First! Journal*, November 1, 1993, p. 26. Also see Gar Smith, "Changing Climate, Changing Priorities," *Earth Island Journal* 10 (Spring 1995), 25; and Fran Edinger, Letters to the Editors, *Earth Island Journal* 9 (Fall 1994), 2. On the rhetorical and historical connection between radical ecology and reactionary politics, see Anna Bramwell, *Ecology in the 20th Century: A History* (New Haven, Conn.: Yale University Press, 1989). Also see Lewis, *Green Delusions*, 37–40.

90. Norman Cohn, *The Pursuit of the Millennium: Revolutionary Messianism in Medieval and Reformation Europe and Its Bearing on Modern Totalitarian Movements* (New York: Harper Torchbooks, 1961), 309–10; quoted in Hofstadter, *Paranoid Style*, 38.

CONCLUSION

1. Michael Kazin, "Review Article: The Agony and Romance of the American Left," *American Historical Review* 100 (December 1995), 1511.

2. Daniel Bell, *Marxian Socialism in the United States* (Princeton, N.J.: Princeton University Press, 1967), 5. Also see Warren Susman, *Culture as History: The Transformation of American Society in the Twentieth Century* (New York: Pantheon, 1984), especially 75–97.

3. Edward Bellamy, quoted in John Thomas, *Alternative America: Henry George, Edward Bellamy, Henry Demarest Lloyd and the Adversary Tradition* (Cambridge, Mass.: Harvard University Press, 1983), 91.

4. Thomas, *Alternative America*, 181, 115.

5. Daniel Aaron, *Writers on the Left* (New York: Avon, 1965), 26. Tom Hayden, "Proposed Book of Essays," SDS Microfilm, Series 1, No. 11, Wisconsin State Historical Society, Madison. Thomas Hayden, "A Letter to the New (Young) Left," in Mitchell Cohen and Dennis Hale, eds., *The New Student Left: An Anthology*, rev. and exp. ed. (Boston: Beacon Press, 1967), 6. "Redstockings Manifesto," in Shulamith Firestone and Anne Koedt, eds., *Notes from the Second Year: Women's Liberation* (New York: New York Radical Feminists, 1970), 113. Cornel West, "The New Cultural Politics of Difference," in Simon During, ed., *The Cultural Studies Reader* (London: Routledge, 1993), 213.

6. Randolph Bourne, "War and the Intellectuals," in Olaf Hansen, ed., *Randolph Bourne: The Radical Will, Selected Writings, 1911–1918* (Berkeley: University of California Press, 1992), 309.

7. Tom Hayden, "Liberal Analysis and Federal Power," p. 1, SDS Microfilm, Series 4B, No. 152. Henry George, quoted in Thomas, *Alternative America*, 70.

8. Judith Shklar, "The Liberalism of Fear," in Nancy L. Rosenblum, ed., *Liberalism and the Moral Life* (Cambridge, Mass.: Harvard University Press, 1989), 24.

9. Thomas, *Alternative America*, 145.

10. See Jean Bethke Elshtain's incisive review of Hillary Clinton's book, *It Takes a Village*, in the *New Republic*, March 4, 1996, pp. 33–38. "A home," Elshtain reminds us, "is not a polity, and a polity is not a home" (38).

11. Edward N. Luttwak, "From Homer to the Unabomber: Declinists Across the Ages," *Foreign Affairs* 76 (January/February 1997), 155. Thanks to Fred Woodward for bringing this passage to my attention. Also see Arthur Herman, *The Idea of Decline in Western History* (New York: Free Press, 1997), 39.

12. Stephen Holmes, *Passions and Constraint: On the Theory of Liberal Democracy* (Chicago: University of Chicago Press, 1995), 48. Also see Stephen Holmes, *The Anatomy of Antiliberalism* (Cambridge, Mass.: Harvard University Press, 1993), 254.

13. James M. McPherson, *Battle Cry of Freedom: The Civil War Era* (New York: Oxford University Press, 1988), 204.

14. Holmes, *Passions and Constraint*, chapter 2.

15. Todd Gitlin, *The Sixties: Years of Hope, Days of Rage* (New York: Bantam, 1987), 415.

16. Tom Hayden, *Reunion: A Memoir* (New York: Random House, 1988), 324.

17. Leon Fink, "The New Labor History and the Powers of Historical Pessimism: Consensus, Hegemony, and the Case of the Knights of Labor," *Journal of American History* 75 (June 1988), especially 128–29.

18. In *The Age of Reform* (New York: Vintage, 1955), Richard Hofstadter confronted the same issue, conceding that "most of the failings in the liberal tradition that have attracted my interests are also failings of American political culture in general, and . . . they are usually shared by American conservatives" (15).

19. Thomas, *Alternative America*, 333; also 198.

20. See Seymour Martin Lipset, *American Exceptionalism: A Double-Edged Sword* (New York: Norton, 1996), especially 63, 176; and Samuel P. Huntington, *American Politics: The Promise of Disharmony* (Cambridge, Mass.: Harvard University Press, 1981).

21. Stephen Foster, *Their Solitary Way: The Puritan Social Ethic in the First Century of Settlement in New England* (New Haven, Conn.: Yale University Press, 1971), 165. Also see Michael Walzer, *The Revolution of the Saints* (Cambridge, Mass.: Harvard University Press, 1965).

22. On the abolitionists, see Robert H. Abzug, *Cosmos Crumbling: American Reform and the Religious Imagination* (New York: Oxford University Press, 1994); on late-nineteenth-century reformers, see Thomas, *Alternative America*.

23. Seymour Martin Lipset, "Why No Socialism in the United States," in Seweryn Bialer, ed., *Radicalism in the Contemporary Age* (Boulder, Colo.: Westview Press, 1977), 125; also see Lipset, *American Exceptionalism*, 65–67.

24. Lipset, "Why No Socialism in the United States," 125.

25. Paul Berman, *A Tale of Two Utopias: The Political Journey of the Generation of 1968* (New York: Norton, 1996), 38, 63.

26. Huntington, *American Politics*, 154. This paragraph and the following one have been adapted from Richard J. Ellis, *American Political Cultures* (New York: Oxford University Press, 1993), 26.

27. Mary Douglas, *Natural Symbols: Explorations in Cosmology* (New York: Pantheon, 1982), 119.

28. Douglas, *Natural Symbols*, 125. Also see Mary Douglas, *How Institutions Think* (Syracuse, N.Y.: Syracuse University Press, 1986), 38–41; Mary Douglas, *Purity and Danger: An Analysis of the Concepts of Pollution and Taboo* (London: Routledge and Kegan Paul, 1966); and Mary Douglas and Aaron Wildavsky, *Risk and Culture: An Essay on the Selection of Technological and Environmental Dangers* (Berkeley: University of California Press, 1982).

29. On "radical liberalism," see Ira Katznelson, *Liberalism's Crooked Circle: Letters to Adam Michnik* (Princeton, N.J.: Princeton University Press, 1996), 10. On "egalitarian liberalism," see Kerry Whiteside, "Backing into Liberalism: Skepticism and Equality in the Works of Judith Shklar," paper delivered at the Annual Meeting of the American Political Science Association, San Francisco, August 1996. Also see Amy Guttman, "How Limited Is Liberal Government?" in Bernard Yack, ed., *Liberalism Without Illusions: Essays on Liberal Theory and the Political Vision of Judith N. Shklar* (Chicago: University of Chicago Press, 1996), 64–81; Holmes, *Passions and Constraint*, chapter 8; and Stephen Darwell, ed., *Equal Freedom: Selected Tanner Lectures on Human Values* (Ann Arbor: University of Michigan Press, 1995).

30. Benjamin R. Barber, "An Epitaph for Marxism," *Society* 33 (November/ December 1995), 25. Cf. *Strong Democracy: Participatory Politics for a New Age* (Berkeley: University of California Press, 1984), where Barber has much less time for liberalism, arguing that "liberalism serves democracy badly if at all" (xiv).

31. The proposition that "limited government is, or can be, more powerful than unlimited government" is advanced by Stephen Holmes, who explores the ways in which liberal, constitutional restraints can actually increase the state's capacity "to focus on specific problems and mobilize collective resources for common purposes" (*Passions and Constraint*, xi). Also relevant is Jessica Korn's recent reminder that the American system of separation of powers was designed not only to protect liberty but also to promote effective governance through "foster[ing] institutional adaptation and reversibility, promot[ing] the enactment of substantive laws that rest on broad-based consensus, and protect[ing] the capacity for energetic exercise of executive power" (*The Power of Separation: American Constitutionalism and the Myth of the Legislative Veto* [Princeton, N.J.: Princeton University Press, 1996], 26).

32. See Holmes, *Passions and Constraint*, chapter 8, especially 240–41.

33. Katznelson, *Liberalism's Crooked Circle*, 17.

34. Indispensable not only for the affluence they generate but also because private ownership of realty and the means of production are, as Judith Shklar points out, "an indispensable and excellent way of limiting the long arm of government and of dividing social power, as well as of securing the independence of individuals" ("Liberalism of Fear," 31).

35. Barber, "An Epitaph for Marxism," 25–26.

36. Leszek Kolakowski, "In Praise of Inconsistency," in Kolakowski, *Toward a Marxist Humanism: Essays on the Left Today* (New York: Grove Press, 1969), 217.

INDEX

Aaron, Daniel, 102, 108, 317n118, 320n143
Abbey, Edward, 261–62, 382n19, 384n32
Abolitionists
  anti-authority views of, 18–21, 23, 25–26,
    42–43
  on capital punishment, 28, 30, 41
  on capitalism, 22–24, 293nn21,22
  charismatic leaders sought by, 6–7, 27–29,
    40, 43, 274–75
  and civil liberties, 17–18, 28, 35
  and the Civil War, 25–32, 294n40, 296n60
  compromise rejected by, 18, 25–26, 29
  and democracy, 25, 29–30, 43
  despotic power desired by, 28–29, 295n48
  egalitarianism of, 19–25
  General Benjamin Butler as viewed by, 6,
    28
  General John C. Fremont as viewed by, 27
  on human nature, 23
  hypocrisy put first by, 18, 41–42
  illiberalism of, 6–7, 18–19, 25–43
  John Brown as viewed by, 7, 36–40, 278
  and liberalism, 7, 17–18, 40–42
  Lincoln as viewed by, 26–29, 41,
    295nn48,49
  and Lovejoy murder, 32–34
  Manichaeanism of, 7, 18, 26, 30–31, 34–
    36, 38–39, 42
  at the margins of society, 18, 21–25, 31–
    32, 39
  on marriage and gender roles, 19–20, 41,
    193
  the New Left, compared with, 150
  pacifism of, 18, 21, 25, 30–35, 40
  on political parties, 18, 25, 281
  and purity, 25–26, 31–32, 41,
    298nn99,100
  radical environmentalists, compared with,
    230, 381n13
  and "righteous violence," 7, 26, 30–40,
    296n60, 297nn72,83
  romanticized view of "African race,"
    344n16

  on selflessness, 39, 278, 298nn95,99,100
  on the "slave power," 7, 34–35, 293n22
  and "status anxiety" hypothesis, 4
  and utopian communities, 23–24
  utopianism of, 19, 42–43
  violence visited upon, 17–18, 32–33, 272
Affirmative action, x, 374n115
African Americans
  romanticized by abolitionists, 344n16
  romanticized by New Left, 150–53,
    345nn23,24
ADA (Americans for Democratic Action),
  118
Adorno, Theodore, 312n64
Against Our Will: Men, Women, and Rape
  (Brownmiller), 207
Albertson, Ralph, 62
Alcott, Bronson, 24, 37
Alien and Sedition Acts, x, 281
Alinsky, Saul, 359
Allen, Pam, 202–3, 207–8, 363n31
Altruria Colony, 62, 67–68, 306n108
American Anti-Slavery Society, 24, 32,
  295n49
American Peace Society, 36
Americans for Democratic Action (ADA),
  118, 330n68
America's Coming-of-Age (Brooks), 83, 85
Anderson, Sherwood, 87, 90, 105
Anderson, Terry, 229
Andrew, John, 27
Anti-intellectualism, 1, 9, 276–77, 342n163
Anti-Semitism, x, 1–2, 4
Apocalypticism
  and the American jeremiad, 400n54
  anti-democratic and illiberal consequences
    of, 12–13, 253–57, 264–70, 273–74,
    402n78
  in Caesar's Column (Donnelly), 56–61, 273
  of the Coming Nation, 304n67
  measured, 267, 402n77
  and millennialism, 260–64, 273
  and the paranoid style, 252–53

Apocalypticism (*continued*)
in the radical environmental movement,
12–13, 252–70, 273, 398nn25,29,
402n78
and the radical right, 252
Appleyard, Brian, 370n89
Aptheker, Herbert, 162
Aron, Raymond, 170, 252, 269–70
Aspiz, Harold, 79
Atkinson, Ti-Grace, 196–99, 205, 362n25
Audubon Society, 229, 383n23, 402n78
Authoritarianism
and apocalypticism, 254–57, 264–67
in Cuba, 165–69
and egalitarianism, 7, 52, 197, 274–75,
357n35
egalitarians overlook, 8, 10, 165–69, 273
Hayden on, 321n153
in *Looking Backward* (Bellamy), 46–53
in Marxism, 302n42
and Michels' "iron law of oligarchy," 175–
76, 189–90
in radical environmental movement, 254–
57, 264–67, 388n63, 397n23,
401nn62,63,65
in radical feminist groups, 197–99,
362n27
in SDS, 174–75, 177, 180–90
and the "two souls of socialism," 51
in utopian colonies, 7–8, 66, 71–72,
306n99

Babbitt, Irving, 74
Baez, Joan, 342n163
Ballou, Adin, 23
Barber, Benjamin, 14, 44, 73, 284, 286,
377n143, 406n30
Bari, Judi, 234, 236, 250, 257, 384n37,
387n56, 395n140
Barnet, Richard, 256
Barres, Maurice, 314n85
Bartlett, Irving, 28
Basu, Sammy, 343n4
Bateson, Nick, 322n9
Baxandall, Ros, 363n31
Beard, Charles, 92, 300n7
Bell, Daniel, 118, 271
Bellamy, Edward, 72, 275, 277, 281, 305n82
abolition of the family favored by, 51
authoritarianism of, 7, 50, 53, 302n34
egalitarianism of, 46–47, 50–51, 302n33
influence of, 300n7
on human nature, 53–55
Marx contrasted with, 46, 301n23, 302n42

utopian colonies disapproved of by, 63
*See also Looking Backward; Equality; Religion
of Solidarity*
"Beloved community," 92–95, 187, 193,
314n83, 315n77
Bender, Thomas, 309n32, 316n108
Bennett, William, ix–x
Benson, George, 24
Bercovitch, Sacvan, 311n64, 400n54
Berlin, Isaiah, xii, 50, 299n4, 344n15,
380n177
Berman, Paul, 282
Bernstein, David, 347n37
Black Panthers, 207
Black Power, 3
Blake, Casey, 87, 93, 312n64
Bloom, Allan, ix
Boas, Franz, 92
Bookchin, Murray, 233, 241, 262, 383n22,
395n142
Boone, Daniel, 233
Booth, Paul, 125, 133, 180–82, 325n36,
330n69, 334n99, 335n109, 358n39,42
Borus, Daniel, 47
Boston Clique, 21, 41, 293n18
Bourne, Randolph, 150, 281
on the "beloved community," 92–95,
314n83, 315n77
on the city, 93–94, 314n84
contrasted with Mike Gold, 8–9, 107
despair of, 99–100, 315n97
and Dewey, 92, 96–97, 313n77, 315n94
in Europe, 93–94
French gemeinschaft praised by, 93, 95
German efficiency admired by, 94–95
on Greenwich Village feminism, 194
on Jules Romaines, 93, 313n82
liberals scored by, 96–97
on mass culture, 92, 313n76
on Maurice Barres, 314n85
and multiculturalism, 314n90
"negative rights" criticized by, 92
on pluralism's virtues, 98–99
pragmatism's influence on, 92, 315nn77,94
as radical critic, 8–9, 13, 95–96
radical skepticism of, 99, 276
and the *Seven Arts*, 8, 83, 92
socialist preferences of, 93
Whitman's influence on, 80, 92, 93,
313nn75,82, 314n84
on World War I, 8–9, 96–99, 315n103
and *Youth and Life*, 95
Bramwell, Anna, 385n41
Bread and Roses, 206–7

Brecher, Jeremy, 334n101
Brecht, Bertolt, 138–39
Brock, Peter, 30
Brooks, Van Wyck, 8, 80, 88–89, 315n103
  America's Coming of Age, 83–85
  charismatic genius sought by, 83–84,
    86–87, 275
  despair of, 86, 100, 102
  egalitarianism of, 311n51
  elitism of, 86–87, 92
  on mass culture, 83–85, 106–7
  and the *New Masses*, 103
  and the *Seven Arts*, 83–87, 309n33,
    311n56
  on Whitman, 83–85
  and William Morris, 85–86
Brotherhood of the Cooperative
  Commonwealth (BCC), 63–64
Brower, David, 230, 259, 262, 395n142,
  400n47
Brown, Connie, 131
Brown, John, 7, 19, 29, 36–40, 42, 278,
  297n83, 298nn95,99,100. *See also*
  Abolitionists
Brown, Rita Mae, 199
Brown, Wendy, 213–14
Brownmiller, Susan, 207
Buffman, Arnold, 24
Burlage, Dorothy, 133
Burlage, Robb, 133, 348n44
Burley Colony, 62, 67
Butler, Benjamin, 6, 28, 42
Butler v. Queen, 210–11, 369n88

Caesar's Column (Donnelly), 7, 55–62,
  300n9, 303n59, 304n66
Caldicott, Helen, 259
Calvert, Greg, 139, 186–89, 325n35,
  355n15, 359n62
Calverton, V. F., 108–9, 306n108, 317n120,
  320n143
Camus, Albert, 120, 138, 143, 171, 323n18
Capital punishment, 28, 30, 41
Capra, Fritjof, 401n60
Carlyle, Thomas, 308n11
Carson, Clayborne, 180–81, 345n23
Carter, Jimmy, ix
Casson, Herbert, 68
Castro, Fidel, 164–65, 168–69, 179,
  327n55, 338n129
Cathedral Action Forest Group, 237
Catton, William, 265–66
Cell 16, 205–6, 366n66, 372n99
Chabot, Joe, 154

Chaplin, Charlie, 87
Charismatic leadership
  abolitionists' desire for, 6–7, 27–29, 40,
    43
  of Bob Moses, 178–80, 356nn23,27,
    357n30
  Brooks' search for, 86–87
  egalitarian need for, 107, 177–80, 274–75
  in feminist groups, 198
  of Hayden, 138, 178–80, 184, 357nn30,34
  Oppenheim's search for, 81, 310n35
  in the New Left, 168, 177–80,
    356nn20,22,23,27
  of Paul Watson, 388n63
  in utopian colonies, 66, 71–72
  Waldo Frank's search for, 87–88
  Whitman's search for, 75–76, 79
Che Guevara, 179
Cheney, Lynne, ix
Cherny, Darryl, 250, 384n33
Chicago 8, 115
Chicago Women's Liberation Union,
  366n63
Child, Lydia Maria, 20, 22, 31, 33
China, 10, 141, 278, 327n55
Christian Commonwealth Colony, 62, 67
Civil Rights Act, 129, 195–96, 228, 330n73
Civil War, 6, 19, 25–32, 77–78, 277–78,
  281, 294n40
Clark, Elizabeth, 41
Clayton, Bruce, 95, 313n75
Clean Air Act, 229
Clean Water Act, 229, 254
Cleveland, Bradley, 140
Clinton, Bill, 287n7
Clinton, Hillary, 287n7, 404n10
Club of Rome, 259
Cohen, Jean, 10
Cohn, Norman, 269
Coleman, Daniel, 259, 262, 264
Collins, John A., 23–24
Colorado, University of, 219
Columbia University, 19, 92, 96, 121–22,
  136, 169, 357n34
Coming Nation, 63, 65, 67–68
Communism, 91, 100–110, 117, 143,
  319n133, 320n146
Communist Manifesto (Marx and Engels), 148
Communist Party, 103–4, 108, 199, 317n120
Compromise
  abolitionists reject, 18, 25–26, 29
  environmentalists reject, 230
Confiscation Act, 27
Congress, U.S., 17, 118, 125, 250

Conkin, Paul, 70, 306n106
Connor, Bull, 158
"Consciousness-raising," 199–204, 206,
  209–10, 216–18, 363n38, 364n43
Consensus decision-making
  in Earth First!, 236–37, 387n55
  and egalitarianism, 132–33
  in primitive societies, 241
  in radical environmental groups, 237,
    388n63
  in SDS, 132, 134, 145, 176–77, 182, 184,
    333n97
  in SNCC, 176–78
Coser, Lewis, 1, 306n100
Cott, Nancy, 194
Cousteau Society, 229
Cowley, Malcolm, 109, 312n66
Cram, Ralph Adams, 74
Critical Mass rides, 237
Cuba
  environmentalists' attitude toward, 388n68
  New Left's romance with, 10, 141, 162,
    164–70, 179, 239, 327n55, 338n129,
    342n163, 351n76, 352nn93,102
Cultural Revolution, Chinese, 278
"Culture wars," ix

Daily Worker, 109
Das Kapital (Marx), 300n7
Davidson, Carl, 186
Davis, Jefferson, 26, 28, 30
Davis, John, 246, 389n71
Davis, Mark, 246
Davis, Rennie, 159, 161, 175, 332n80,
  334n97, 346n33, 347n36, 348n43, 349n47
Dawn in Russia (Frank), 91
De Beauvoir, Simone, 369n80
Debs, Eugene, 63–64, 305n89
Declaration of Independence, x, 37
Delay, Tom, 288n7
Dell, Floyd, 107–8, 194
Dellinger, Dave, 165–69, 351n76
Deming, Barbara, 170
Democratic party, 74, 121, 128, 144, 329n66
Democratic Vistas (Whitman), 75–79, 308n11,
  309n27, 311n49
Dempsey, Rosemary, 376n133
Devall, William, 240, 386n47
Dewey, John, 86, 92, 96–97, 109, 300n7,
  315n94, 319n143
Dialectic of Sex (Firestone), 205, 207, 368n80
Dogmatism
  Bourne on war and, 96
  Cornel West rejects, 276

feminists reject, 204, 276
  Hayden rejects, 119–20, 173, 276, 324n24
  the Masses reject, 103
  of Mike Gold, 103, 276
Dohrn, Bernardine, 188
Dominican Republic, 120, 142
Donald, David, 4
Donnelly, Ignatius, 273
  Bellamy contrasted with, 56, 60
  on capitalism, 56–57
  on the 1896 election, 59
  on human nature, 56–57
  and the Omaha Platform of 1892, 56, 59
  political career of, 55–56
  utopianism of, 60–61
  See also Caesar's Column
Dos Passos, John, 109, 306n108, 320n143
Douglas, Mary, 5, 115, 172, 215, 253, 283,
  290n18, 374n113
Draper, Hal, 52
Dreiser, Theodore, 109, 320n143
D'Souza, Dinesh, ix–x, 3
Du Bois, W. E. B., 297n83, 298nn99,100
Dukakis, Michael, ix
Dunbar, Roxanne, 207, 372n99
Dwight, Timothy, 74
Dworkin, Andrea, 193, 210–11, 223, 277

Earth Day, 229
Earth First!, 6, 262, 403n86
  apocalypticism of, 12–13, 257–60, 266–
    67
  compromise rejected by, 230, 245–46
  connection between ecological and social
    transformation perceived by, 234–36,
    238, 385n41, 386nn43,46,47
  consumerism scored by, 242–47, 393n106,
    394n111
  Dave Foreman's break with, 268–69,
    385n42, 403n85
  and deep ecology, 232–34
  and the dilemma of radical egalitarian
    politics, 260, 399n46
  Earth Island Institute compared with, 232,
    237, 241, 258–59, 385n40, 398n32
  ecofeminism in, 385n39
  egalitarianism of, 12, 231–38, 382n21
  elections rejected by, 237, 387n56
  elitism of, 243, 245
  founding of, 230, 381n12
  group solidarity in, 238, 387n54
  hostility to mainstream environmental
    groups, 250–51, 268, 403n82
  illiberalism of, 11, 13, 245–51, 266–69

indigenous peoples, romanticized by, 238–42, 389nn71,72, 390nn75,77
leadership in, 236–37, 386n50, 387nn54,55
millennialism of, 13, 263–64
misanthropy of, 230–31, 238–39, 242, 381n14, 382nn18,19, 392n91
and "monkey-wrenching," 230–31, 381n6, 384n36, 388n66
New Left's influence on, 234, 381nn12,13, 384nn36,37
organizational structure of, 236–37, 386n50, 387nn51,54,55, 388n63
and Redwood Summer campaign, 234
and tree-spiking, 230, 381n16
and vanguardism, 245–48
Western civilization repudiated by, 248–51
Earth First! Journal, 236–37, 381n13
Earth Island Institute, 232, 237, 241, 258, 266, 402n78
Earth Island Journal, 241, 258–59, 388n68
Earthwatch, 229
Eastman, Max, 5, 52–53, 80, 108, 194, 309n30, 317n116
Echols, Alice, 194–95, 197, 201, 205, 361n13, 366n63
Eckersley, Robyn, 256
Economic Research and Action Project (ERAP), 128, 131, 138, 140–41, 143, 146, 200, 327n54, 338n136, 339n137, 347n36
accomplishments of, 159–60
Bayard Rustin's support of, 332n84
demise of, 155–62, 174, 347n37, 350n6
difficulties of organizing the poor encountered by, 154–56, 158–62
and the egalitarian dilemma, 124–26, 129, 132–33, 149
egalitarian structure of, 132, 145, 179–80, 333nn94,97, 334n98, 354n7
group cohesion within, 125, 132–33, 329n64, 334n98
on liberalism and liberals, 126, 129, 327n51, 332n80, 339n139
leadership within, 179–80, 335n109, 354n7
origins of, 124–25, 148–49, 153–55, 343n6
radical potential of the poor seen by, 153–57, 343n7, 346n32,33, 347n34, 349n51, 350n69
SNCC's influence on, 141, 153–54, 158, 326n48, 349n47
variations by project within, 159, 327n51

Edwards, A. S., 68
Egalitarianism
of Bellamy, 46–47, 50–51, 302n33
of Brooks, 311n51
defined, 5, 290n18
and equality, 5, 52–53
human nature as viewed in, 53–55, 73, 273, 279
liberal, 284–86
and liberalism, 13, 53, 284–86, 406n29
measured, 383nn23,24,25
negative, 52–53
and privacy, 277–78
radical egalitarianism distinguished from, 5–6
of Walt Whitman, 74–75, 307n10
See also Radical egalitarianism
Egleson, Nick, 125
Ehrenreich, Barbara, 206
Ehrlich, Paul, 266, 402n68
Eliot, T. S., 105
Emancipation Proclamation, 295n49
Emerson, Ralph Waldo, 37, 39, 298n95, 298n100
Endangered Species Act, 229
Engels, Friedrich, 148, 150, 171
Enlightenment, 118, 249
Environmentalism, Harvey Mansfield on, ix.
See also Earth First!; Radical environmentalists
Environmentalists for Full Employment, 229
Environmental Policy Institute, 229
Environmental Protection Agency (EPA), 230, 254, 288n7
Ephron, Nora, 199
Equal Employment Opportunity Commission (EEOC), 196
Equality
in conflict with liberty, 11, 227, 277, 284–85, 370n89, 380n177
in conflict with privacy, 224–25, 227, 277–78
and egalitarianism, 5, 52–53
and liberalism, x–xi, 223–24, 284–86
rival visions of, 223–24, 291n20, 378n159
Equality (Bellamy), 49, 51, 63
Equality colony, 62, 64, 67
Equal Rights Amendment (ERA), 205
ERAP. *See* Economic Research and Action Project
Erkkila, Betsy, 74–75, 307n10

Fabianism, 85–86
Falk, R. A., 261

False consciousness, 55
and the New Left, 188
and radical egalitarianism, 55, 275–76
and radical environmentalism, 11, 244–45
and radical feminism, 11–12, 199–206,
208–10, 218, 364n49, 365nn56,59,
376n132, 380n175
Faludi, Susan, 376n138
Family, the
abolitionists on, 20, 41, 193
Andrea Dworkin on, 223
Bellamy on, 51
capitalism as cause of breakdown of, 285
Firestone assails, 220
NOW and, 196
Okin on, 223–27, 378n161, 379n172
radical environmentalists on, 266
relationships with, in SDS, 124, 134,
326n44, 336n114
Robin Morgan looks to emergence of
communal, 377n152
in utopian communities, 193
Fanon, Frantz, 138, 141, 341n150
Fatalism, 290n18
egalitarian belief in human plasticity as
antidote to, 53
of Hayden, 136
of literary radicals after World War I, 99–
100
of Marcuse, 337n126
of the poor, 154, 158–59, 160–61
radical environmentalists reject, 260
totalistic systems of thought produce, 209
FBI, 250–51, 395n140, 403n86
Federalist, The, 74
Federalist party, 281
Fellowship Farm, 66
*Female Liberation as the Basis for Social
Revolution* (Dunbar), 207
Feminism, ix
and abolitionism, 193
liberalism's relationship to, 11, 223,
378n158
of NOW, 195–97, 206–7, 228, 361n12,
376n133
origins of term, 193–94, 361nn12,13
"the personal is political" in, 11–12, 194–
95, 200, 202–4, 222–23, 227,
378n153,156
privacy and, 12, 222–25, 227, 378n155
radical feminism distinguished from, 194,
361nn12,13
See also Radical feminism

Feminist Anti-Censorship Task Force
(FACT), 212–13
Feminists, 195, 197–99, 206, 362n20
Ferguson, Ann, 376n131
Fink, Leon, 280
Firestone, Shulamith, 194, 364n49, 365n59
child-care centers rejected by, 205
and *Dialectic of Sex*, 205, 207, 368n80
family rejected by, 222
MacKinnon compared with, 368n80
and New York Radical Feminists, 206
and New York Radical Women, 204,
363n31
and Redstockings, 204, 364n50
First Amendment, 119, 211–12, 214, 266,
370nn90,91, 372n103
Fitzhugh, George, 74
Flacks, Richard, 134, 147, 160, 325n37,
339n137
Fogarty, Robert, 62, 360n5
Foreman, Dave, 235, 266, 381n12
apocalypticism of, 257
apologizes for insensitive remarks, 382n18
civil rights workers lauded by, 384n36
on the dilemma of radical politics, 399n46
Earth First! founded by, 230
on indigenous peoples, 239–40
leaves Earth First!, 268–69, 385n42,
403n85
leaves the Wilderness Society, 230
Manichaeanism of Earth First! criticized
by, 268–69
on monkey-wrenching, 231
on organization of Earth First! 236,
387n55
political compromise rejected by, 230
right-wing background of, 231
Forer, Anne, 203, 364n48
Forman, James, 176, 180
Foster, Abigail Kelly. *See* Kelly, Abigail
Foster, Stephen, 20–21, 25–26, 193, 281–82
France, Anatole, 5
France, 8, 74, 93, 95, 283
Frank, Barney, 357n34
Frank, Waldo, 93, 312n62
Brooks compared with, 87, 89
on capitalism, 309n39, 312n71
on Lincoln, 87
Mike Gold compared with, 102, 106–7
and the *New Masses*, 103
popular culture scored by, 88–89
post-war despair of, 100, 102
prophetic leadership sought by, 87–88

representative democracy scored by, 90–91

romanticizes the excluded, 8, 89–90, 150, 272, 312n71

and the *Seven Arts*, 83, 309nn32,33,39, 311n56

Soviet Union praised by, 91–92

and Whitman, 87, 309n32, 311n58, 312n66

Fredrickson, George, 26, 344n16

Freedom Rides, 118, 345nn23,24

Freedom Summer, 234

Freeman, Jo, 357n35

Freeman, Joseph, 102–3, 107–9, 320n143

Free Soil party, 41, 74

"Free Space" (Allen), 208

Free Speech Movement, 110, 119, 140

Fremont, John C., 27, 29

Friedan, Betty, 196, 213–14, 217

Friedman, Lawrence, 19, 21–22, 24, 31, 33–34, 40

Friends of the Earth, 381n12, 400n57

Fromm, Eric, 303n49

Fruchter, Norm, 152, 328n59

Fugitive Slave Law, 34, 297n72

Furies, The, 206

Furness, William, 31

Gag Rule, 17, 272

Gans, Herbert, 130

Garrison, William Lloyd, 4, 6, 30, 32, 147, 278
  anti-authority views of, 19
  and the Boston Clique, 22
  the Civil War supported by, 26, 294n37
  competitive individualism scored by, 22
  on Elijah Lovejoy, 33
  and John Brown, 37–39
  on Lincoln, 27, 295n49
  pacifism of, 21, 33, 35–37, 39
  and utopian colonies, 23–24
  righteous violence supported by, 31, 36, 38
  See also Abolitionists

Garrisonians. *See* Abolitionists

Garvy, Helen, 332n83, 358n39

George, Henry, 275, 305n82

Georgetown Univerity, 376n133

Germany, 8, 74, 86, 94–95

Ghandi, 141, 323n18

Gilligan, Carol, 208

Gingrich, Newt, 285

Gitlin, Todd
  as analyst of New Left, 146, 180, 279,

288n7, 329n64, 331n75, 332n85, 335nn110,112,113, 348n40, 349n49, 351n75, 356n20, 360n70
  on Cuba, 168–69
  on purity, 115
  on the radical potential of the poor, 153, 155–56, 348n40
  as SDS activist, 125, 133, 134, 140, 184, 325n36, 329n64, 333n88, 335nn112,113
  on SDS organization and leadership, 180, 182–83, 335n110

Glad Day v. Canada, 369n88

Global CPR Service, 259

Goethe, 86–87

Gold, Mike, 316n108
  on art and politics, 102–5, 318n125
  and the Communist party, 102–4, 108, 317n120, 319n133
  confidence in future of, 101–2, 316nn110,111
  contrasted to Bourne, 9
  dogmatism of, 103, 276
  and the *New Masses*, 102–3, 106, 108–9
  popular U.S. culture scored by, 8, 106–9
  on proletarian art, 103–6
  Soviet Union idealized by, 104, 107–9, 317n121
  Thornton Wilder attacked by, 105
  Whitman's influence on, 101, 104–6, 108, 316n109

Goldberg, Mira, 390n77

Goldwater, Barry, 2–3, 231

Goodell, William, 21

Gordon, Linda, 206

Gorman, Paul, 318n131

Graber, David, 382n18

Great Depression, 107, 109

Great Society, 285, 304n60

Green, John, 244

Greenpeace, 229, 237, 250–51

Greenstone, J. David, 292n6

Greenwich Village, 80, 194

Gregory, Dick, 356n23

Grimké, Angelina, 20, 21, 32

Grimké, Sarah, 30, 32

Haber, Alan, 116–17, 154, 322nn8,9, 323n12, 324n21, 325n36, 327n54, 338n136, 339n137, 349n51, 353n111

Hamann, Johann Georg, 74

Hanisch, Carol, 202, 363n31

Hansen, Bill, 356n22

Hardin, Wolf, 263
Harpers Ferry. *See* Brown, John
Harriman, Job, 68–69, 306n106
Hartz, Louis, 86
Harvard University, 140, 368n71
Haskell, Burnette, 66
Haugen, Tim, 240, 244
Hayden, Casey, 152, 158, 176, 180, 322n4,
    335n112, 350n59
Hayden, Tom, 4, 6, 131, 281–82, 325n36
    on America as totalitarian state, 135–36,
        336n115
    American society, attitude toward, 111,
        118, 134–35, 321n150, 329n65
    anti-intellectualism of, 277, 342n163
    and Bayard Rustin, 130, 332n84
    and C. Wright Mills, 119, 147, 171,
        323n19
    as charismatic leader, 138, 178–80, 184,
        357nn30,34
    co-optation feared by, 130, 326n47
    on counter-institutions, 123, 127, 151,
        326n38, 329n63
    defeatism of, 136
    dogmatism rejected by, 103, 119–20, 173,
        276, 324n24
    and ERAP, 124–26, 128, 153–56, 160–61,
        172, 351n8
    family's relationship with, 134, 326n44,
        336n114
    on guerrilla warfare, 143–44, 169,
        341n154
    on human nature, 336n120
    illiberal trajectory of, 116, 120, 135–40,
        142–46, 276–77
    influence of, 117, 320n149, 325n35
    on leadership, 172, 176, 178–79, 355n11,
        359n57
    on liberalism and liberals, 118–20, 126–
        28, 323nn16,18, 326nn45,47, 328n60
    and Marcuse, 135–36, 337nn124,126
    on Marxism, 119, 147, 171
    on the Newark riots, 143–44,
        341nn156,157,158
    the oppressed idealized by, 126–27, 151,
        153, 155–57, 160–64, 272, 348n43,
        351nn71,72
    and the *Port Huron Statement*, 116, 123–
        24, 137, 145, 321nn150,153, 324n24,
        336n115, 342n163
    on revolution, 119, 137–40, 142–43,
        326n48, 338n136, 339n137, 341n156
    and SNCC, 117, 127, 139–40, 142, 151,
        153, 326n48

on the tension between reform and purity,
    123–25, 326nn39,47
university criticized by, 110–11, 119–20
at the University of Michigan, 110–11,
    116–19
on the Vietnamese, 162–64, 351nn71,72
on violence, 115–16, 135–40, 143–45,
    321n150, 340nn144,157,158,159
and the Weathermen, 115
Hayes, Frank, 369n88
Hayes, Randall, 259
Haywood, Bill, 87
Hegel, 76, 94
Heilbroner, Robert L., 397n23
Hersh, Blanche, 19–20
Hertzka, Theodor, 62
Herzen, Alexander, 299n4
Hicks, Granville, 108
Higgins, James, 168
Hill, Stuart, 256
Himmelfarb, Gertrude, ix
Hine, Robert, 68, 306n106
Hispanics, 8, 90, 272
Hitler, Adolf, 108, 268
Hoffman, Christian B., 63
Hofstadter, Richard, 6, 228, 251, 405n18
    and the *Age of Reform*, 1–4, 45–46, 287n6,
        288n10, 289n2, 300nn8,9
    on apocalypticism, 259–60, 267–68
    Looking Backward slighted by, 45–46,
        300n9
    on the paranoid style, 1–2, 4, 252–53,
        290n16
    on the radical right, 1–4
    and status anxiety, 2, 4, 290n16
    Tom Hayden on, 118
Hollywood, 233
Holmes, Stephen, 278, 406n31
Holsworth, Roger, 256
Home Colony, 62, 67
Homosexuality, x, 369n88
Hopedale Community, 23, 24, 40
Horkheimer, Max, 394n128
Howe, Irving, 1, 135, 342n163, 360n72
Howell, William Dean, 62
Human nature
    abolitionists on, 23
    Bellamy on, 53–55
    and egalitarianism, 53–55, 73, 273, 279
    Donnelly on, 56–57
    Hayden on, 336n120
    Job Harriman on, 69–70
Huron Indians, 392n9
Hypocrisy, 18, 41–42

Icaria, 68
Illiberalism
of abolitionists, 6–7, 18–19, 25–43
and apocalyticism, 12–13, 253–57, 264–
70, 273–74, 402n78
defined, xi
of Earth First!, 11, 13, 245–51, 266–69
Hofstadter's analysis of, 1–4
of *Looking Backward*, 7, 45–55
measured, 267, 402n77
of the New Left, 9–10, 122, 135, 144–45,
150, 171–73, 187–89, 279–83
psychological analysis unable to account
for, 4, 144–45, 171–72, 188, 253,
290nn16,18, 353nn109,110
of radical egalitarianism, 4–14, 42–43, 45,
52–53, 73–74, 145–46, 149–50, 171–
73, 188–90, 199, 269–86, 375n116
and radical environmentalism, 245–51,
253–54, 256–57, 264–70, 402n78
and radical feminism, 199, 208, 213, 226,
375n116
of the right, x, 1–2, 74, 252, 281, 287n7
of slaveholders, 17
and utopianism, 7–8, 42–43, 45, 273–74,
303n45
See also Apocalypticism; Authoritarianism;
Manichaeanism; Righteous violence;
Tolerance
Indigenous peoples
Earth First! idealizes, 238–42,
389nn71,72, 390n75, 391n77
radical environmentalists idealize, 238–42,
272, 389nn71,72, 390nn75,76,77,
391nn79,85, 392n90
Industrial Workers of the World (IWW),
291n24, 300n7
International Bureau of Revolutionary
Literature, 317n120
International Workingmen's Association, 66
"Iron law of oligarchy," 175
Iroquois Indians, 241–42, 391n79, 392n90

Jacksonians, 76
Jacobs, Lewis, 318n131
Jaggar, Alison, 213, 219–20, 373n106,
377n142
James, William, 86, 111
Jazz, 88, 107
Jefferson, Thomas, 118, 323n18
Jeffrey, Sharon, 125, 132, 326n44, 335n112,
339n137
Jenkins-Smith, Hank, 383n23
Jesus Christ, 178

John Birch Society, 2–3
Johnson, Lyndon Baines, 121, 128–30, 167,
281, 288n7
Johnson, Steve, 326n46
Josephson, Matthew, 312n66
Judaism, 282
Julian, George, 31

Kann, Mark E., 4
Katznelson, Ira, 285
Kaufman, Arnold, 333n87
Kaweah Colony, 62–63, 66–68
Kayapo Indians, 240
Kazin, Michael, 271
Kearon, Pam, 197–98
Kelly, Abigail, 21, 193
Keniston, Kenneth, 353n109
Kennedy, Helena, 372n102
Kennedy, John F., 120, 331n74
Kennedy, Robert, 120, 139
Keynes, John Maynard, 320n146
Kezar, Ron, 381n12
Khmer Rouge, 278
King, Martin Luther, Jr., 121, 128, 139, 141,
228
King, Mary, 178, 180
Kissinger, C. Clark, 177, 183
Koedt, Anne, 197, 206, 364n49
Koehler, Bart, 381n12
Koertge, Noretta, 215–17, 287n4,
374nn115,116, 377n147
Kolakowski, Leszek, 44–45, 286, 303n45
Kopkind, Andrew, 178, 356n27
Korn, Jessica, 406n31
Kotke, Wm. H., 240, 263–64
Ku Klux Klan, 158

"Labor metaphysic," 147–48, 156
La Chapelle, Dolores, 240
La Duke, Winona, 390n76
Langer, Elinor, 199
Lasch, Christopher, 287n6
Lawrence, D. H., 89
Leadership. *See* Authoritarianism;
Charismatic leadership; Participatory
democracy
League for Industrial Democracy (LID),
116–17, 124, 322n8
Lears, Jackson, 287n6
Leggett, William, 74
Lehrman, Karen, 216, 375n125,
376nn133,138, 377n150
Lenin, 105
Leninism, 162, 175, 186–90

Levine, Lawrence, ix
Lewis, John, 141, 178, 340n145
Lewis, Martin, 392n90, 402n68
Lewis and Clark College, 376n140
Liberalism
  and abolitionism, 7, 17–18, 40–42
  Barber on, 406n30
  and conservatism, 288n11, 405n18
  defined, xi, 284–85
  and democracy, 285, 406nn30,31
  and equality, x–xi, 223–24, 284–86
  and egalitarianism, 53, 284–86, 406n29
  feminism indebted to, 11, 223, 378n158
  Hayden on, 118–20, 126–28, 323nn16,18,
    326nn45,47, 328n60
  Hofstadter on, 288n11, 405n18
  and the New Left, 117–22, 124–30, 145,
    322n9, 323nn10,11,12, 327n51,
    330nn68,69,72,73, 331n74, 332n80
  of Okin, 223–25, 378nn157,161
  radical feminism critical of, 11–12, 194,
    196, 222–23, 227, 370n90
  radicalism distinguished from, 118–19,
    323nn9,12
  Shklar on, xi–xii, 11–12, 40–42, 99, 277,
    406n34
"Liberalism of fear," xi, 40–42, 99
Liberation, 165–66, 168
Liberator (1830s–1860s), 27, 30, 34–35, 38,
  39, 230, 294n48
Liberator (1920s), 101–2, 104, 106, 108,
  319n133
Liberty party, 21, 41
Lichter, S. Robert, 171, 324n34, 353n110
Lincoln, Abraham, 281, 311n59
  abolitionists' attitude toward, 26–29, 41,
    29n5n48,49
  on John Brown, 38
  on slavery, 28, 295n47
  Waldo Frank on, 87
Lincoln Memorial, 23
Lipow, Arthur, 50, 52–53, 55, 302nn33,34,42
Lippmann, Walter, 310n40
Lipset, Seymour Martin, 118
Listen, Yankee (Mills), 164
Literature and Revolution (Trotsky), 104
Littlefield, George, 66
Llano Colony, 68–70, 305n96
Lloyd, Henry Demarest, 52, 64–67, 278
London, Jack, 319n136
London Peace Society, 30
Looking Backward, 72
  artificiality banished in, 51, 277

as authoritarian utopia, 7, 46–55, 302n34
Caesar's Column contrasted with, 56
the economy in, 48, 301n21
equality in, 46–47, 51
Hofstadter slights, 45–46, 300n9
on hierarchy, 51
human nature in, 54–55
influence of, 45–46, 62–63, 300nn7,9,
  304n78
News from Nowhere (Morris) contrasted
  with, 300n16
plot of, 46
politics parties absent in, 47
solidarity in, 47–50, 52
and the Religion of Solidarity, 301n29
the state in, 47–50, 54–55, 301n21
See also Bellamy, Edward
Los Angeles Times, 306n106
Lovejoy, Elijah, 17, 32–33
Lynd, Staughton, 126, 130, 142–43, 153,
  162–63, 332n85, 335n112, 337n125,
  340n150

McCarthyism, x, 2
McCormack, Thelma, 212
McDonald, Kimla, 391n85
McEldowney, Carol, 177
McEldowney, Ken, 329n64
McKay, Claude, 102
McKelvey, Donald, 183, 338n129
MacKinnon, Catharine, 6, 11
  and Butler v. the Queen, 210–11, 368n88
  on consciousness-raising, 209–10
  on coercion disguised as consent, 207–8,
    368nn73,74, 370n90
  distinction between words and deeds
    denied by, 212, 372n102, 373n104
  on false consciousness of women, 208–10
  feminists attacked by, 212–13, 372n103
  feminists criticize, 213–14, 369n87,
    370n91, 373nn105,106
  and the First Amendment, 211–12,
    370nn89,91, 372n103
  influence of, 213–14, 373nn106,107,
    374n108
  Marcuse compared with, 370n93
  and martial arts, 207, 366nn66,67
  on neutrality as the male perspective, 211,
    370n92
  on objectivity as a male social
    construction, 214
  Okin compared with, 222–23, 378n156,
    380n175

on pornography, 207, 210–12,
369nn85,88, 370n91,
371nn95,96,97,98, 372nn99,103
privacy right criticized by, 222–23,
368n71
on rape, 212, 373n104
on sexual desire as a social construction,
207–8, 210
on sexual harassment, 368n74
Shulamith Firestone criticized by, 368n80
and the women's movement of the 1960s
and early 1970s, 207–8, 213, 366n66,
367nn,68,69,70, 368nn75,77,78,
368n80, 372n99, 373n105
and women's studies, 214, 373n107,
374n110
McLeod, Christopher, 391n85
McPherson, James, 25–26
Mademoiselle, 117
Madison Square Garden, 206
Mailer, Norman, 331n76
Mainardi, Patricia, 199, 207, 363n31, 364n50
Maistre, Joseph de, 74
Malcolm X, 120, 359n57
Mander, Jerry, 241–42, 391n79
Manes, Christopher, 231, 246, 257, 259
Manichaeanism, 304n67
of abolitionists, 7, 18, 26, 30–31, 34–36,
38–39, 42
of *Caesar's Column*, 59
of conservative activists today, 287n7
of Earth First! criticized by Dave
Foreman, 268–69
illiberalism defined in terms of, xi
of New Left, 4, 9, 120, 123, 132–37, 145–
46, 170–71, 281–83, 342n65
of Populists, 1
Shklar on, 42
of radical egalitarianism, 271–72, 281–84,
286
of radical environmentalism, 245–51,
260–64, 267–69
of radical feminism, 201, 215–16
Mansfield, Harvey, ix, 10
Mao, 143, 179, 327n55, 364n38
Maoist, 144, 363n27
Marcuse, Herbert, 312n64
Earth First!'s views compared to those of,
245
influence of, on Hayden, 135–36
MacKinnon's views compared to, 370n93
and the New Left, 120, 135, 137,
337nn124,126, 349n45

on the New Left's murder, 279
on repressive tolerance, 120, 370n93
on violence, 137, 337n126
Margalit, Avishai, 288n14
Marine Protection Act, 229
Marriage, 378n155
abolitionists on, 190–20, 41, 193
feminists on, 197–98
gay, 226
and NOW, 196
Okin on, 226, 379n169
Robin Morgan predicts demise of,
377n152
utopian communities forbid, 193
WITCH on, 205–6
Martial arts, 207, 366nn66,67
Marx, Karl, 13–14, 21
compared with Bellamy, 46, 52, 300n7,
301n23, 302n4
Hayden on, 119
on Henry George, 275
and Max Eastman, 80
and Mike Gold, 105
on the lumpenproletariat, 148
and the New Left, 119, 148, 150, 171–72
on the peasantry, 148
on the proletariat, 204, 209
and radical environmentalists, 240, 243,
391n79
and radical feminists, 204–5, 209
romanticizes the poor, 150, 333n17
and Waldo Frank, 100
Whitman as an Americanized, 307n10
Marxism, 64, 100, 275, 301n23
and Mike Gold, 101
and MacKinnon, 368n80
and the New Left, 110, 112, 120, 143,
147–48, 156, 171
and "false consciousness," 200, 203–6, 209
and radical feminism, 203–6, 209
Massachusetts, University of, 217
Massachusetts Anti-Slavery Society, 33
Masses, 98, 101, 103, 107, 194, 317n116
Mass media, 88, 198, 220–21, 244–45,
393n106
Masson, Jeffrey, 373n104
Maurras, Charles, 74
Max, Steve, 125, 133, 183, 329n64, 353n111,
358n39
May, Samuel J., 20, 30, 32
Meese, Ed, 213
Mehrhof, Karen, 198
Memphis, University of, 220

Merchant, Carolyn, 241
Metz, Dan, 231
Michels, Robert, 175–76, 189–90, 354n6, 355n9
Michigan, University of, 110–11, 115, 116, 119, 154, 195, 320n149, 333n87
Michigan Daily, 117
Mill, John Stuart, x, 75, 323n18
Milbrath, Lester, 394n112
Miller, James, 116, 144, 181, 326n39, 335n112, 339n137, 340n143, 351n72
Millett, Kate, 207–8, 213, 363n31
Mills, C. Wright, 5, 119, 147, 164, 171, 179, 324n19, 355n9
Mills, Stephanie, 235
Minkoff, Nathaniel, 322n8
Minnesota, University of, 214, 220
Miss America Pageant, 207
Mississippi Freedom Democratic party, 121, 127–28, 142
Mitchell, Seward, 30
Mondale, Walter, ix
Moody, Kim, 353n111
Moore, Barrington, 140
Moral Majority, x
Morgan, J. P., 23
Morgan, Robin, 205, 207, 362n27, 363n31, 366n60, 367n68, 377n152
Morris, William, 85–86, 300n16
Morse, John T., Jr., 298n83
Morse, Terry, 235, 386n43
Moses, 87, 178
Moses, Bob, 141
    Camus' influence on, 138
    as a charismatic leader in SNCC, 178–80, 356nn23,27, 357n30
    on leadership, 176
    on the poor, 152
Mother Jones, 216, 376nn133,138
Multiculturalism, 9, 14
Mumford, Lewis, 193

Nash, Roderick, 234, 384n36
Nation, 213
National Anti-Slavery Standard, 35
National Conference on Women and the Law, 213
National Environmental Policy Act, 229
Nationalist Movement, 300n9
National Liberation Front, 352n83
National Organization for Women (NOW), 195–97, 206–7, 228, 361n12, 376n133
National Student Association (NSA), 117

National Women's Studies Association (NWSA), 215, 218
Native Americans, 8, 89, 92, 239, 272
Native Forest Network, 237, 387n59
Nativism, x, 1, 2, 4
Nature Conservancy, 403n85
Nazism, 144
Nearing, Mary Beth, 387nn43,55
Negative Population Growth, 229
Nelson, Gaylord, 229
Nepal, 250
New Deal, 277, 300n8
New England Anti-Slavery Society, 30
Newfield, Jack, 111, 151, 304n60, 340n142, 357n31
New Left
    abolitionists compared with, 150
    African Americans romanticized by, 150–53, 345n24
    alienation from middle-class American life of, 111–12, 321n151
    charismatic leadership in, 168, 177–80, 356nn20,22,23, 357n27
    conservatives blame, for breakdown of communities, 285
    Cuba idealized by, 10, 141, 162, 164–70, 179, 239, 327n55, 338n129, 342n163, 351n76, 352nn93,102
    Earth First! influenced by, 234, 381nn12,13, 384nn36,37
    and environmentalism, 10–11, 12, 228–29
    and false consciousness, 188
    and feminism, 10–11, 193–96
    Manichaeanism of, 4, 9, 120, 123, 132–37, 145–46, 170–71, 281–83, 342n65
    Marcuse and, 120, 135, 137, 279, 337nn124,126, 349n45
    Marx and, 119, 148, 150, 171–72
    Marxism and, 110, 112, 120, 143, 147–48, 156, 171
    nonviolence in, 116, 141
    Old Left compared to, 110, 112, 156, 171, 176, 272–73
    and participatory democracy, 10, 122, 132–33, 176, 180–89, 331n75, 333n87, 357n34, 359n62, 360n72
    and Protestantism, 282–83
    purity and, 123–27, 130, 137, 145, 149–50, 172, 325n37, 326nn39,47, 329n64
    right wing activists compared to, 287n7
    and the Third World, 10, 162–70, 173, 179, 273, 351n75, 352nn83,102

in United States compared to New Left elsewhere, 282–83

and the universities, 9, 110–11, 119–20, 140, 324n23

Vietnamese idealized by, 10, 170, 239, 348n43, 351n75, 352n83

See also ERAP; Hayden, Tom; SDS

New Masses, 100, 102–4, 106–9, 318n131, 320n143

New Mexico, University of, 383n23

New Republic, 86, 94, 319n143

News from Nowhere (Morris), 300n16

Newton, Huey, 173

New York Radical Feminists, 202, 206, 207

New York Radical Women, 200, 203–4, 206, 363n31, 364n50, 365n53, 367nn68,69

Niebuhr, Reinhold, 118

Nietzsche, Friedrich, 94

Nixon, Richard, 206, 288n7, 366n63

Non-Partisan League, 90

Nonresistance/nonviolence. *See* Pacifism

NOW. *See* National Organization for Women

Oates, Stephen, 37

Oglesby, Carl, 170

Okin, Susan, 378n158, 379nn169,174,176
on the family, 224–27, 379n173
feminist criticism of, 379n163
on gender, 224–25, 227
illiberalism of, 225–27
liberalism of, 223–25, 378n161
MacKinnon compared with, 222–23, 378n156, 380n175
reforms proposed by, 226
utopian vision of, 226, 379n173

Oklahoma City bombing, x, 252

Old Left
counterculture sought by young, 320n148
New Left compared to, 110, 112, 156, 171, 176, 272–73
Soviet communism and, 273

Omaha Platform of 1892, 56, 59

Operation Rescue, 279

Ophuls, William, 254–56, 260, 265, 397n23

Oppenheim, James, 89, 92
common people condescended to by, 81–82, 310n40
on materialism and capitalism, 81–82, 321n153
prophetic leadership sought by, 81, 310n35
Russian Revolution romanticized by, 82–83

as *Seven Arts* editor, 80
on Whitman, 80–81, 310n36

Oppressed, the
Garrison on, 147
middle class guilt and, 149, 344n10
the New Left identifies with, 9, 126–27, 148–73, 272, 348nn40,43, 349n51, 350n69, 351nn71,72
Orwell on, 147
radical egalitarians identify with, 8–10, 147, 149–50, 272–73, 344n11, 344nn15,16,17, 348n40
radical environmentalists identify with, 238–42, 249–50, 272, 389nn71,72, 390nn75,76,77, 391nn79,85, 392n90
See also African Americans; Cuba; ERAP; Indigenous peoples; Third World

Orr, David, 256

Orton, David, 390n77

Orwell, George, x, xii, 147, 344n10

Orwellianism, 48

Our America (Frank), 100

Owen, Robert, 24

Pacifism
of abolitionists, 21, 25, 30–35, 40
of Garrison, 21, 33, 35–37, 39
in the New Left, 116, 141
of SNCC, 138, 141
of Staughton Lynd, 142, 340n150

Pardum, Robert, 182

Parker, Theodore, 37

Participatory democracy, 333n87
accountability undermined by, 184–89
and ERAP, 132–33, 176, 188
Gitlin on, 331n75
Greg Calvert on, 187, 359n62
Hayden and, 357n34
Irving Howe on, 360n72
limitations of, 132–33, 180–83, 189, 274
Mark Rudd on, 122
as New Left's defining idea, 176
in radical feminist groups, 196–99
in SDS, 10, 176, 180–82

Patai, Daphne, 215–17, 287n4, 374n115, 375n116, 376n138, 377n145

Pateman, Carole, 213, 373n106

Peace Corps, 239–40

Pells, Richard, 109

Pelton, G. E., 64

Pennsylvania State University, 220

Pentagon, 228

Perry, Lewis, 21, 39

Peslikis, Irene, 208, 363n31, 364n50
Phillips, Wendell, 6, 281, 295n49
    on the Boston Clique, 293n18
    on capitalism, 22, 293n21
    charismatic leader sought by, 28, 275
    civil libertarian concerns of, 17–18, 28
    on the Civil War, 26, 294n40
    despotic power sought by, 28–29
    Elijah Lovejoy lauded by, 33
    General Benjamin Butler praised by, 28
    General John Fremont lauded by, 29
    John Brown eulogized by, 29, 42
    Lincoln criticized by, 29, 40–41
    on need for oppositional stance, 31–32
    postwar reconstruction envisioned by,
        29–30
Pickett, George, 70, 72
Pickett, Karen, 266
Pillsbury, Parker, 21, 25–26
Political correctness, 3, 11, 335n109, 388n63
    in radical feminism, 198, 202, 218, 221–22,
        377n145
Political Education Project (PEP), 125
Political parties
    abolitionists reject, 18, 25, 281
    absent in Looking Backward, 47
"Politics of Housework, The" (Mainardi),
    207
Populist movement
    Donnelly and, 56
    Hofstadter's analysis of, 1–2, 4, 46, 287n6
    Looking Backward's influence on, 45, 300n7
Pornography, 3
    MacKinnon on, 207, 210–12, 369nn85,88,
        370n91, 371nn95,96,97,98,
        372nn99,103
    Robin Morgan on, 367n68
Port Huron Statement, 116, 120, 123–24, 134,
    137, 144–46, 152, 195, 320n149,
    321nn150,153, 324n24, 326n44,
    336n115, 342n163
Potamkin, Harry Alan, 318n131
Potter, John, 24
Potter, Paul, 125, 164, 325n36, 330n68,
    352n83
Pragmatism, 92, 120, 313n77, 315n94
Privacy
    egalitarianism and, 277–78
    equality in tension with, 224–25, 227,
        277–78
    feminism and, 12, 222–25, 227, 378n155
    Hayden on, 119
    MacKinnon on, 222–23, 368n71
    Okin on, 223–25

Private property, 212
    abolitionists on, 21
    Dave Dellinger on, 165
    John A. Collins on, 24
    Julius Wayland on, 65, 305n94
    and liberal democracy, 285, 406n34
    in Looking Backward, 46, 302n42
    Marx on, 302n42
    in Ruskin colony, 67
Progressive labor, 189
Progressivism
    and feminism, 193–94
    Hofstadter's analysis of, 1–2, 4, 45–46,
        287n6
Prophetic Minority, A (Newfield), 151
Protestantism, 20, 281–83
Puritanism, 85, 283, 292n6
Purity
    abolitionists' concern with, 18, 25–26,
        31–32, 41, 298nn99,100
    and the egalitarian dilemma, 18, 123–27,
        145, 149–50, 260, 271–73, 280, 286,
        325n37, 326nn39,47, 329n64, 399n46
    and the New Left, 123–27, 130, 137, 145,
        149–50, 172, 325n37, 326nn39,47,
        329n64
    and radical environmentalism, 260,
        399n46
    reform in tension with, 18, 25, 123–27,
        145, 260, 271–73, 280, 286, 292n6,
        325n37, 326nn39,47, 329n64, 399n46
    and violence, 39–40

Quakers, 142

R. v. Scythes, 369n88
Racism, 342n165
    environmental, 232
    Gitlin on absence of, in Cuba, 168–69
    Hayden on, 118
Radical Education Project (REP), 186
Radical egalitarianism
    of abolitionists, 19–25
    as an astringent for the establishment, 13
    and authoritarianism, 7–8, 10, 52, 165–
        69, 197, 273–75, 357n35
    and charismatic leadership, 107, 177–80,
        274–75
    and consensus decision-making, 132–33
    defined, 5–6
    of Earth First!, 12, 231–38, 382n21
    of ERAP, 132, 145, 179–80, 333nn97,98,
        354n7
    and false consciousness, 55, 275–76

and false friends, 272, 332n82
illiberalism of, 4–14, 42–43, 45, 52–53,
  73–74, 132–33, 145–46, 149–50,
  171–73, 188–90, 199, 269–86,
  375n116
and Manichaeanism, 271–72, 281–84, 286
oppositional politics of, 5–6, 271–72
and the oppressed, 8–10, 147, 149–50,
  272–73, 344nn11,15,16,17
purity and the dilemma of, 18, 123–27,
  145, 149–50, 260, 271–73, 280, 286,
  325n37, 326nn38,39,47, 329n64,
  399n46
and righteous violence, 278–79
and sectarianism, 272, 280
on selfishness, 277–79
and tolerance, 13–14, 269–70
and totalitarianism, 7, 52, 55
in utopian colonies, 23–25, 63–64, 67–68,
  70
and utopianism, 13, 44–45, 53–55, 270,
  273–74, 276
and violence, 9, 136, 145–46, 278–80
of women's studies programs, 215–16
See also Egalitarianism
Radical environmentalists. See also Earth
  First!
  abolitionists compared with, 230, 381n13
  American democracy denigrated by, 250,
    395n142
  apocalypticism of, 12–13, 252–70, 273,
    398nn25,29, 402n78
  authoritarianism of, 254–57, 264–67,
    388n63, 397n23, 401nn62,63,65
  compromise rejected by, 230, 245–46
  and consensus decision-making, 237,
    388n63
  on Cuba, 388n68
  on false consciousness, 11, 244–45
  on the family, 266
  fatalism rejected by, 260
  illiberalism of, 245–51, 253–54, 256–57,
    264–70, 402n78
  indigenous peoples, romanticized by, 238–
    42, 272, 389nn71,72, 390nn75,76,77,
    391nn79,85, 392n90
  on mainstream environmental groups,
    250–51, 268, 403n82
  Manichaneanism of, 245–51, 260–64,
    267–69
  and Marx, 240, 243, 391n79
  and the New Left, 9–12, 228–29, 234
  population explosion feared by, 254, 257,
    265–66

and purity, 260, 399n46
radical right rhetoric compared with that
  of, 252, 269
and righteous violence, 239, 381n16
and the Third World, 249–50, 386n47,
  390n76
utopianism of, 260–64, 400n57
Radicalesbians, 365n56
Radical feminism
  on capitalism, 195, 365n59
  charges of backlash within, 376n133
  and condescension toward women, 205–6,
    366n60
  and "consciousness-raising," 199–204,
    206, 209–10, 216–18, 363n38, 364n43,
    365n50
  on consumerism, 362n23
  co-optation feared by, 205, 362n23
  and dogmatism, 204, 276
  false consciousness and, 11–12, 199–206,
    208–10, 218, 364n49, 365nn56,59,
    376n132, 380n175
  on the family, 220, 223, 377n152
  feminism distinguished from, 194, 361n13
  and group solidarity, 197–99, 362n23
  illiberalism of, 199, 208, 213, 226, 375n116
  leaderless ideal of, 196–99, 362n27
  liberal feminism and, 11, 194, 196, 222–23
  and liberalism, 11–12, 194, 196, 222–23,
    227, 370n90
  Manichaeanism of, 201, 215–16
  on marriage, 197–98, 205–6, 377n152,
    378n155
  and martial arts, 207, 366nn66,67
  and Marxism, 203–6, 209, 368n80
  and the New Left, 10–11, 193–96, 204
  and participatory democracy, 195–96
  and political correctness, 198, 202, 218,
    221–22, 377n145
  and pornography, 367n68
  and the "pro-woman line," 365n60
  Robin Morgan on, 362n27, 366nn60,68
  schismatic tendencies of, 197–99, 363n28
  See also Feminism; MacKinnon, Catharine;
    Okin, Susan; Women's studies
    programs
Radical right
  apocalypticism of, 252, 269
  Hofstadter on, 1–2
  illiberalism of, x, 1–2
  New Left on, 128, 130
  radical environmentalists' rhetoric
    compared with that of, 252, 269
Radosh, Ronald, 352n102

Rahv, Philip, 318n126
Rainforest Action Network, 259
Rape, 212, 373n104
Rat, 207, 362n27, 367n68
Rauh, Joseph, 128
Reconstruction, 30, 367n68
Red scare, x
Redstockings, 204, 207, 276, 364n50, 365n59
Redwood Summer, 234
Reed, John, 80
Register, Richard, 261
Religion of Solidarity (Bellamy), 49, 301n29
Representative democracy
  compared with participatory democracy,
    360n72
  Hayden on, 327n54
  Irving Howe on, 360n72
  Richard Rothstein on, 184
  mundane virtues of, 189–90
Republican party, 196, 285
Resek, Carl, 98
"Resistance to Consciousness" (Peslikis), 208
Resource Conservation and Recovery Act,
  229
Revolution, American, 38
Revolution, French, 5, 278
Revolution, Russian, 82–83
Revolutionary Youth Movement, 189
Reynolds, David, 78
Rich, Adrienne, 213
Richard, Henry, 30
Richmond Enquirer, 38
Righteous violence
  abolitionists support, 7, 26, 30–40,
    296n60, 297nn72,83
  in *Caesar's Column*, 58–59
  Garrison supports, 31, 36, 38
  of John Brown, 19, 36–40, 278–79
  Marcuse embraces, 137, 337nn126,128
  and the New Left, 137–44, 338n129
  and radical egalitarianism, 278–79
  and radical environmentalism, 239, 381n16
Roberts, Steven, 178
Robert's Rules of Order, 175, 183
Robinson, James Harvey, 92
Romaines, Jules, 93, 313n82
Romano, Carlin, 373n104
Roosevelt, Theodore, 281
Roselle, Mike, 234, 241, 268, 381nn12,13
Rosen, Ruth, 370n91
Rosenblum, Nancy, 302n32, 308n23
Ross, Bob, 125, 178
Ross, E. A., 313n75
Rothman, Stanley, 171, 324n34, 351n110

Rothstein, Richard, 161, 180, 184, 186,
  355n9, 359n49
Rousseau, Jean-Jacques, 205, 255
Royce, Josiah, 313n77
Rubin, Charles T., 392n91
Rudd, Mark, 122, 342n163
Ruskin Colony, 62, 64, 67–68
Russia, 8, 82–83, 92, 100–101, 103–4, 107–
  10, 150, 319nn133,143, 344n15
Rustin, Bayard, 128, 130, 332n84
Rutgers University, 216, 219–20
Ryberg, Erik, 388n69

Safe Drinking Water Act, 229
Sale, Kirkpatrick, 121, 133, 139, 159, 185,
  241, 264, 325nn35,36, 329n63, 338n136,
  401n62
Sanborn, Franklin, 37
Sanctified Sisters of Belton, 360n5
Sarachild, Kathie, 200–204, 363nn31,38,
  364n50
Saturday Evening Post, 106
Savio, Mario, 110–11, 320n149, 384n36
Sayen, Jamie, 266
Scarce, Rik, 237, 257, 386n46, 388n63
Schattschneider, E. E., 252
Schiller, Friedrich, 205
Schlegel, Friedrich von, 278
Schmitt, Carl, 74
Schumpeter, Joseph, 285
Schuster, Marilyn, 376n132
Schwinn, Jerry, 323n12
Scruton, Roger, 371n95
SDS. *See* Students for a Democratic Society
Sea Shepherds, 237, 388n63
Sectarianism, 125, 272, 280, 334n99
Selfishness
  abolished in *Looking Backward*, 48, 54
  abolitionists condemn, 22–23, 293n22
  capitalism as cause of, 54, 67
  radical egalitarians see as illegitimate,
    277–79
Selflessness
  John Brown hailed for his, 39–40, 278,
    298nn95,99,100
  leads to cruelty, 278–79
  in *Looking Backward*, 48, 54
Sessions, George, 240
Seven Arts, The, 8, 80–99, 309n33
  Greenwich Village radicalism represented
    in, 80
  Mike Gold criticizes, 101
  Whitman's influence on, 80, 92–93,
    309n32, 313n75, 314n84

See also Bourne, Randolph; Brooks, Van
  Wyck; Frank, Waldo; Oppenheim,
  James
Seward, William Henry, 38, 281
Sexual harassment, 368n74
Sexuality
  MacKinnon on, 207–13, 370n88
  Robin Morgan on, 367n68
  social construction of, 219
Sexual Politics (Millett), 207–8
Shakespeare, 104
Shero, Jeffrey, 122, 130, 181, 336n114
Sherrod, Charles, 356n22
Shiva, Vandana, 390n76
Shklar, Judith, 17
  on the boundary between the personal and
    the political, 11–12, 277
  and the liberalism of fear, xi–xii, 40–42,
    99
  on liberalism's overriding aim, xi
  on Manichaneanism, 42
  on negative egalitarianism, 52–53
  on private property, 406n34
"Shooting Niagara and After?" (Carlyle),
  308n11
Sierra Club, 229, 250–51, 381n12, 383n23,
  402n78, 403nn82,85
Sinclair, Upton, 108, 317n120, 318n125,
  319n133
Single-Tax Colony, 62
Sisterhood Is Powerful (Morgan), 207
Skepticism, xii, 40–42, 96–97, 204, 227, 276
Slaveholders
  abolitionists demonize, 30, 34–36, 39
  Garrison affirms humanity of, 35–36
  illiberalism of, 17
  wage slavery condemned by, 21, 23
Slavery
  Lincoln on, 28, 295n47
  Whitman on, 74–75
  See also Abolitionists
Smith, Gar, 241
Smith, Gerrit, 21, 22, 27
Smith College, 207
SNCC. *See* Student Nonviolent
  Coordinating Committee
SNCC: The New Abolitionists (Zinn), 127, 151
Snitow, Ann, 202, 365n55, 379n163
Social constructionism, 211, 214, 219,
  376nn140,141
Social Democracy of America (SDA), 63,
  305n89
Socialism, 46
  Bourne on, 93, 97

and early feminism, 194
  Eastman on, 52
  "the two souls of," 52
Socialist party, 69, 291n24, 318n125
Soviet Union, 8, 49, 140, 166, 250, 273,
  319n143, 395n142
Spann, Edward, 62
Spence, Larry D., 321n151
Spencerians, 50
Spiegel, Mike, 186
Spring, Marcus, 24
Stalin, 91, 105, 108
Stalinism, 8, 91, 108, 273, 319n133
Standard Oil, 251
Stanford University, 223, 345n23, 366n66,
  371n97
Stearns, Charles, 35, 36, 278
Stearns, George Luther, 37
Steffens, Lincoln, 109, 320n143
Steinem, Gloria, 213
Stembridge, Jane, 152
Sterling, Philip, 318n131
Stieglitz, Alfred, 87
Stoper, Emily, 178
Stop the Draft Week, 228
Streeter, Robert, 246, 399n46
Streitfeld, David, 373n104
Strossen, Nadine, 214
Student League for Industrial Democracy
  (SLID), 119
Student Nonviolent Coordinating
  Committee (SNCC), 121, 128, 130, 200,
  202, 330n72, 340n149, 342n163, 345n23
  black power replaces integration in, 174,
    345n24
  on Communists, 332n84
  ERAP contrasted with, 157–58
  Hayden on, 117, 127, 139–40, 142, 151,
    153, 326n48, 328n59
  Howard Zinn on, 127, 151
  leadership in, 176–78, 180–81
  as model for SDS and New Left, 128,
    141–42, 150–54, 158, 326n48,
    328n59, 336n116, 340n143, 349n47,
    359n60
  Moses as charismatic leader of, 138, 178–
    80, 356nn23,27, 357n30
  nonviolence repudiated by, 138, 141
  organizational structure of, 176–78, 180–
    81
Students for a Democratic Society (SDS), 112
  authoritarianism in, 174–75, 177, 180–90
  consensus decision-making in, 132, 134,
    145, 176–77, 182, 184, 333n97

Students for a Democratic Society (SDS),
    (*continued*)
    co-optation feared by, 127–31, 136, 145,
        162, 326n47, 330n68, 330nn73,74,
        333nn86,88
    counter-institutions sought by, 123, 126–
        27, 129, 132, 138, 141–43, 151–53,
        327n55, 328n59, 340n148
    and the desire to disengage from society,
        9, 125–27
    ERAP established by, 124–25
    on guerrilla warfare, 141, 143–44, 165,
        169, 341n154
    labor metaphysics rejected by, 147–48
    leadership in, 10, 174–90, 358n39
    Leninism in, 162, 175, 186–90
    liberals and, 116–20, 124–27, 322n10,
        323nn12,18, 326nn45,47, 330n68,
        332n80
    Manichaeanism of, 9, 120, 123, 132–37,
        145–46, 170–71, 282–83, 342n65
    the oppressed romanticized by, 149–64,
        168–73
    organizational structure of, 10, 174–90,
        334n101, 358n42, 359n49
    origins of, 116–18
    participatory democracy in, 10, 122, 176,
        180–82, 331n75, 357n34
    and the "Rethinking Conference" of 1965,
        162, 174, 181–82
    Robert's Rules of Order in, 175, 183
    sectarianism in, 125, 280, 334n99
    SNCC as model for, 128, 141–42, 150–
        54, 158, 326n48, 328n59, 336n116,
        340n143, 349n47, 359n60
    usual explanations of the degeneration of,
        120–23, 279–80
    and the Vietnam war, 121–22, 128–30,
        140, 159, 174, 330n69
    violence embraced by, 9, 135–46
    See also ERAP; Hayden, Tom; New Left
Suffragism, 194
Sumner, Charles, 296n60
Sumner, William Graham, 281
Supreme Court (American), 210, 250–51,
    369n85
Supreme Court (Canadian), 210
Swarthmore College, 126, 141, 154

Tappan, Lewis, 22
Tax, Meredith, 206, 208, 368n77
Tet Offensive, 139
Third World
    Hayden identifies with, 162–64, 351n72

    the New Left identifies with, 10, 162–70,
        173, 179, 273, 351n75, 352nn83,102
    and radical environmentalists, 249–50,
        386n47, 390n76
Thomas, John, 22, 24, 63, 281
Thompson, Fred, 383n23
Thoreau, Henry David, 39–40, 123,
    298n99
Tokar, Brian, 258, 261–62, 383n22,
    398n29
Tolerance
    and liberalism, xi, 284
    Marcuse on, 370n93
    and radical egalitarianism, 13–14
    radical groups' stake in, 269–70
Topolombampo Colony, 63
Totalitarianism
    Dave Dellinger on, 167
    Eastman on, 52
    and egalitarianism, 7, 52, 55
    Hayden on, 135, 321n53, 336n115
    Looking Backward foreshadows, 46, 48, 55
    and MacKinnon, 212, 372n102
    Marcuse on, 135, 337n124
    and SDS, 136, 337n125
"Total revolution," 139, 205, 365n57
Toxic Substances Control Act, 229
Traubel, Horace, 104
Traveler from Altruria, A (Howell), 62
Trotsky, 103, 104–5
Twain, Mark, 44

"Unanimistes," 93, 313n82
United Automobile Workers, 116, 332n80,
    343n6
Universities
    anti-capitalist sentiment in, 285
    Hayden scores, 110–11, 119–20
    the New Left on, 9, 110–11, 119–20, 140,
        324n23
Urban ecology, 261
Utne Reader, 259
Utopian colonies
    in antebellum period, 23–25
    authoritarian leaders in, 7–8, 66, 71–72,
        306n99
    Bellamy's influence on, 45, 62–63,
        300nn7,9, 304n78
    and conflict, 67–72, 306n100
    egalitarianism of, 23–25, 63–64, 67–68,
        70
    and Eugene Debs, 63–64, 305n89
    family and marriage in, 193
    and Henry George, 305n82

in late nineteenth century, 7–8, 62–72,
304n76, 305n96, 306n108
parallels drawn with women's studies
programs, 374n113
Utopianism
of abolitionists, 19, 42–43
and the American jeremiad, 400n54
Bourne criticizes liberals for their, 97
of the egalitarian left, 13, 44–45, 53–55,
270, 273–74, 276
of Ignatius Donnelly, 60–61
and illiberalism, 7–8, 42–43, 273–74,
303n45
Isaiah Berlin rejects, xii
of Marx, 302n42
and perfectionist view of human nature, 7,
53–55, 273, 276
of radical environmentalism, 260–64,
400n57
of Susan Okin, 226, 379n173
See also Bellamy, Edward; *Looking
Backward*; Utopian colonies

Van Dyne, Susan R., 376n132
Value conflicts, xii, 227, 284–86
Vance, Carole, 369n87
Vietnam, 142, 342n163
Hayden and Lynd idealize people of, 143,
162–64, 351n72
New Left idealizes people of, 10, 170, 239,
348n43, 351n75, 352n83
Vietnam War, 207, 381n12
causes growth of SDS, 122, 130, 174
poor's support for, 162
protests against the, 159, 228
and SDS's disenchantment with liberalism,
128–30
SDS's radicalization preceded escalation
of, 128, 140
Violence
in *Caesar's Column*, 56–60
and Earth First!, 239, 381n16
glorification of, as part of definition of
illiberalism, xi
Hayden and, 115–16, 135–45, 340n144,
341nn157,159
Judi Bari on, of the system, 384n37
at Llano colony, 72
Marcuse on, 137, 337nn126,128
and radical egalitarianism, 9, 136, 145–46,
278–80
and SDS, 9, 115–16, 121, 135–46,
338n129
of slavery, 26, 41

of the Weathermen, 115, 144, 189, 281
See also Abolitionists; Pacifism; Righteous
violence; War
Voluntary Human Extinction Movement,
232, 267, 382n21

Wald, Alan, 316n108, 317n118
Walker, Amasa, 30
Walter, Natasha, 372n102
Walters, Ronald, 19, 20, 21–22, 23
Walters, Suzanna, 376n133
Walzer, Michael, 73, 174, 294n32, 380n175
War
abolitionists on, 26–27, 30–32, 294n40,
296n60
Bourne on, 8–9, 96–99, 315nn97,103
romantic glorification of, 308n23
Whitman on, 77–78, 277–78
War on Poverty, 129
Washington, D.C., 65, 206, 228, 230, 234
Washington, George, 38
Watson, Paul, 237, 248, 388n63
Watts, 120, 140, 251
Wayland, Julius, 62–63, 65, 67–68, 304n67,
305n94
Weathermen, 3, 11, 115, 120, 144, 146, 189,
281
Webb, Lee, 125, 333n97
Webb, Marilyn, 365n59
Weber, Max, 17
Weberian bureaucracy, 189
Weinberg, Bill, 234
Weinberg, Jack, 335n112
Weissman, Steve, 186
Weld, Angelina Grimké. *See* Grimké,
Angelina
Weld, Theodore, 20–21, 23–24
Welfare state, xii, 284–85
Wellesley, 217, 221–22
Wells, H. G., 310n40
West, Cornel, 276
Westra, Laura, 264–65, 401nn63,65
Whipple, Charles, 30
White Citizens Councils, 158
Whitman, Walt
as an Americanized Marx, 307n10
on art as a political tool, 104
Brooks on, 83–85
and Carlyle, 308n11
charismatic prophet sought by, 75–76, 79,
275
on the Civil War, 77–78, 277–78
and the common people, 8, 74–79,
308nn11,16, 309n27,29, 312n66

Whitman, Walt (*continued*)
  egalitarianism of, 74–75, 307n10
  and eugenics, 79
  on individuality and unity, 75–76
  influence of, on the artists at the *Seven
    Arts*, 80, 92–93, 309n32, 313nn75,82,
    314n84
  influence of, on Max Eastman, 80, 309n30
  influence of, on Mike Gold, 101, 104,
    105–6, 108, 316n109
  influence of Hegel on, 76
  on materialism, 77–78, 85, 308n11, 311n49
  Oppenheim on, 80–81, 310n35
  as radical Democrat, 74, 77
Whittier, John Greenleaf, 32
Wildavsky, Aaron, 253
Wilde, Oscar, 174
Wilder, Thornton, 105
Wilderness Society, 230, 381n12
Will, George, ix
Williams, Jim, 125
Williams, Patricia, 213, 371n95
Willis, Ellen, 214, 363n31, 364n50
Wilson, Edmund, 109, 306n108
Wilson, Woodrow, 81, 281
Wise Use Movement, 250, 395n40
WITCH (Women's International
  Conspiracy from Hell), 205–6, 367n68
Wittman, Carl, 125, 153–54, 347n37
Wolf, Naomi, 376n133
Wolf, Robert, 316n108
Wolke, Howie, 243, 381n12, 398n25
"Woman and Her Mind: The Story of
  Everday Life" (Tax), 208
Women's Commonwealth, 360n5
Women's Liberation Group, 206
Women's studies programs, 374nn109,113,
  375n116

  anti-authority ethos of, 215–16, 221,
    377n142
  conflict within, 215, 217–18, 221
  consciousness-raising in, 216–18, 375n125
  criticism feared by those in, 221, 287n4
  egalitarianism of, 215–16
  knowledge is political in, 218–19, 222,
    376n138
  and MacKinnon, 214, 373n107, 374n110
  Manichaeanism in, 215–16
  origins of, 214–15
  patriarchy blamed in, 216, 218, 220,
    374n115
  pedagogy in, 216–20, 375nn118,123,
    376nn131,132,140, 377n150
  political correctness in, 216, 218, 221–22,
    375n117, 377n145
  politicized education in, 218–22,
    376n138, 377n147
  separatism in, 214–15
  social constructionism in, 214, 219,
    376n140
  See also Radical feminism
Wood, Karen, 236
World War I, 8, 45, 82, 94, 96–97, 100, 272,
  318n131
Worldwatch Institute, 229
Worster, Donald, 247, 261, 395n142
Wretched of the Earth, The (Fanon), 138
Wright, Henry, 21, 27, 32, 34–35, 38, 39

Yack, Bernard, 139, 205, 365n57
Yale University, 142, 207, 374n110
Young American critics, 8, 83, 150
Youth and Life (Bourne), 95

Zero Population Growth, 229
Zinn, Howard, 127, 151